AF673577

MARKETING MANAGEMENT

ARUN KUMAR
RACHANA SHARMA

Published by

ATLANTIC

PUBLISHERS & DISTRIBUTORS (P) LTD

7/22, Ansari Road, Darya Ganj, New Delhi-110002
Phones : +91-11-40775252, 40775214, 23273880, 23275880
Fax : +91-11-23285873
Web : www.atlanticbooks.com
E-mail : orders@atlanticbooks.com

Branch Office: Chennai
Phones : +91-44-48531784, 28291383
E-mail : chennai@atlanticbooks.com

Printed & bound in India by Atlantic Print Services

PREFACE

Marketing Management is the most important part of industrial management. Though the quality and comparable price of a product is the most solid basis for success, it has been found that without a proper sales management even the best product does not get proper circulation. On the other hand, many not so good products are widely sold simply on the basis of an efficient sales management. Therefore, it is useful to present a concise, lucid and systematic textbook on the subject.

This book, as the title suggests, covers all the topics prescribed by various Universities and Management Institutions on Marketing Management and Sales Management. With data gathered from latest publications on the subject, material drawn from standard textbooks, narration in simple language, analytic presentation using central, side and running headings, examples drawn from Indian context and actual examination questions at the end of each chapter, this book has been designed as an ideal textbook for the student and a reference work for the teacher of the subject.

However, suggestions for improvement are invited from the indulgent readers for future improvement of the book.

ARUN KUMAR
RACHANA SHARMA

CONTENTS

1

Market and Marketing

The word 'market' is a derivative of the Latin word *Marcatus* meaning merchandise, ware, traffic, trade or a place where business is conducted. Broadly speaking, for a layman and an educated person the idea of a market is not different from that of a businessman's. If at all there is any difference that may be of degree.

Definition of Market

1. *G.F. Pyle*: "Market includes both place and region in which buyers and sellers are in free competition with one another."[1]

2. *Cornot*: "By marketing is meant not any particular place in which things are bought and sold, but the whole of any region in which the buyers and sellers are in such free intercourse with one another that the price of the same goods tends to equality easily and quickly."[2]

3. *Chapman*: "The term market refers not to a place but to a commodity or commodities and buyers and sellers who are in direct competition with one another."[3]

4. *Clark and Clark*: "A market is a centre about which or an area in which the forces leading to exchange or title to a particular product operates and towards which the actual goods tend to travel."[4]

5. *H.E. Mitchell*: "Market, for most commodities, may be thought of not as a geographical meeting place but as getting together of

---

1. Pyle, G.F., *Principles of Marketing*, 1936, pp. 24-25.
2. Cornot, *Principles of Economics*, p. 10.
3. Chapman, *Economics*.
4. Clark and Clark, *Principles of Marketing*, 1947, p. 7.

buyers and sellers in person, by mail, telephone, telegraph or any other means of communication."[1]

6. *Duddy and Reizan*: "An economic market is said to exist wherever and whenever the buyers and sellers of goods and services meet in search of opportunities for the adjustment of their mutual interest and transact business in an atmosphere of free and open competition."[2]

7. *Tousley, Rayburn and Clark:* "A centre about which, or an area in which, the force, leading to exchanges of title to a particular product operate, and toward which and from which goods tend to travel."[3]

This implies that a market has a physical location and potential customers (buyers) and consumers (users).

Elements of Market

On the basis of the above definitions it may be said that the term "market" may mean and include the following elements:

(1) Place: It means place as an open space (in the village) or a large building (public or private) where actual buying and selling takes place.

(2) 'An assembly' or 'a meeting together of people: This is for their purchases and sale of goods at a stated time and place. Such are the periodical markets of village fairs frequently held in India and other developing countries where both buyers and sellers come together and conduct their transactions.

(3) 'An area of operation' or the geographical or economic extent: This is for the commercial demand for commodities. The market may extend to a locality, village, town or a country according to the demand of a commodity.

(4) Any organisation by which the exchange of goods is effected: It may be an association of private individuals drawn together by common interest or an organised institution governed by written rules or by conventions or by State regulations, *e.g.*, Bombay Stock Exchange, Calcutta Phatka Market and Wheat Market of Hapur (regulated Market), or Cotton Market of Bombay.

---

1. Mitchell, HE., *The Textile Industries in Economic Analysis*, pp. 26-21.
2. Duddy and Reizan, Marketing. *An Institutional Approach*, 1953.
3. Tousley, Rayburn D., Eugene Clark and Fred E. Clark, *Principles of Marketing*, New York, 1962, p. 10.

(5) The act of buying and selling: It represents an economic function in the satisfaction of human wants and is, therefore, performed in an atmosphere of free and open competition, such as the *perfect markets.*

(6) 'The phase or course of commercial commodity': It effects exchange of commodity. It represents opportunity for buying and selling and serves as an index for the conduct of business, *e.g.*, the market may be bright or dull as in the case of agricultural commodities or securities and bullion.

(7) All the inhabitants of a country: For example, the Indian Market. It refers to the total population of India and its purchasing power in the aggregate. An aggregate may compose of prospective buyer/buyers and seller/sellers that brings to focus the conditions and forces which determine prices.

Thus, Market is the place or area in which buyers and sellers function; the aggregate of factors or conditions within which buyers and sellers make decisions that result in the transfer of goods and services; and the aggregate of demand of the potential buyers of a commodity or service.

Classification of Market

Markets may be classified according to area such as local, regional, national and international, according to the type of business undertaken such as wholesale and retail and according to period such as long-term and short-term. Following is the division of markets according to nature:

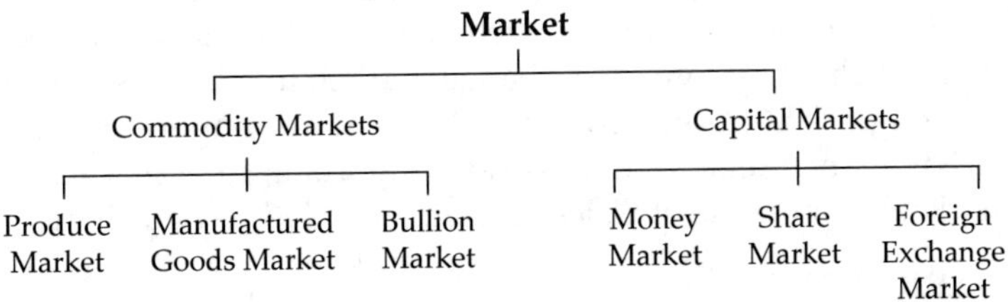

1. Commodity Market: It relates to the purchase and sale of goods. Goods may be consumer's goods and producer's goods. Consumer's goods are those which are required for consumption by consumers. Producer's goods are those which are required by manufacturers for producing more goods. Commodity markets can be divided as follows:

(*i*) *Produce Market*: It deals in agricultural products such as wheat, rice, cotton, maize, etc. These are either required for producing further goods or for consumption. Some examples of produce exchange markets are Cotton Exchange of Bombay and Liverpool and Jute Exchange of Calcutta.

(*ii*) *Manufactured Goods Market*: It is the market where manufactured and semi-manufactured goods are purchased and sold. Some examples of such markets are Leather Exchange of Kanpur, Sugar Exchange of Liverpool, Gunny Trade Exchange of Calcutta.

(*iii*) *Bullion Market*: It deals in the trade of precious metals like gold, silver, precious stones, etc. It is sensitive and influenced by important happenings in any part of world. Some important markets in India are Bullion markets of Bombay, Calcutta, Kanpur and Delhi.

2. Capital Markets: These are classified as follows:

(*i*) *Money Market*: It includes those institutions which provide short-term funds to the business. Lenders, borrowers and middlemen are the important constituents of money markets.

(*ii*) *Share Market*: It is the organised market for purchase and sale of stocks, shares and debentures. Joint stock companies get their shares and debentures registered in these exchanges and investors trade in these securities. Stock Exchanges are important centres of channelising investments. Some of the important Stock Exchanges in India are the exchange at Bombay, Calcutta, Madras, Delhi and Ludhiana.

(*iii*) *Foreign Exchange Market*: It trades in foreign currencies and purchase and sale of foreign exchange. The international trade is greatly helped by foreign exchange market. It helps in settlement of foreign debts. New York and London are important foreign exchange markets in the world. Important foreign exchange markets in India are at Calcutta, Bombay, Madras and Delhi.

MARKETING

According to Philip Kotler, "Any interpersonal or inter-organisational relationship involving an exchange (a transaction) is marketing. Thus, the essence of marketing is a transaction. Consequently, marketing occurs any time one social unit strives to exchange something of value with another social unit. Marketing consists of all the activities designed to facilitate that exchange.... Within this societal perspective, then (1) the marketers, (2) what they are marketing and (3) their potential markets all assume new and far broader dimensions."[1] Thus, in addition to business firms, the category of marketers might include such diverse social units as: (1) a political party trying to market its candidate to the public, (2) the director of an art museum providing new exhibits to generate greater attendance and financial support, (3) a labour union that markets its ideas or terms to its members and the company management, and (4) a Professor who is trying to make his/her course interesting and meaningful to the students.

Under "what is being marketed" are normally included the products and services, the ideas such as reducing air pollution, stopping smoking, or contributing to the charitable fund raising, etc.

Under "potential market" (or target markets) are included more than the consumers of products, services, ideas, etc. A business firm's market may include government regulatory agencies, environmentalists, and local tax assessors.

What is Marketing?

Marketing has been described differently and in different ways. According to some it is a business activity; while according to others it is a group of related business activities; a trade phenomenon; a frame of mind; a coordinate, integrative function in policy making, a sense of business purpose; an economic process; a structure of institutions; the process of exchanging or transferring ownership of products; a process of concentration, equalisation, and dispersion; the creation of time, place and possession utilities; a process of demand and supply adjustment; and as many other things.[2]

Definition of Marketing

1. *William J., Stanton*: "Marketing is the creation and delivery of a standard of living; it is finding out what consumers want, then planning and developing a product or service that will satisfy those wants; and then determining the best way to price, promote, and distribute that product or service....Stated more formally,

---

1. Kotler, Philip, "A Generic Concept of Marketing", in *Journal of Marketing*, April 1972, pp. 49-52.
2. Marketing Staff of the Ohio State University "A Statement of Marketing Philosophy", *Journal of Marketing*, January 1955, p. 43.

marketing is a total system of business activities designed to plan, price, promote, and distribute want-satisfying goods and services to the benefit of the present and potential customers."[1]

This definition brings forth following characteristics of marketing:

(*i*) It is a total system of business activities which are undertaken with a view to satisfy customers' wants, *i.e.*, the business action should be market or consumer-oriented;

(*ii*) It is an integrated process—not one activity but a sum of several activities taken together, and hence, it is the result of interaction of many activities;

(*iii*) Marketing programme starts from recognising the consumer needs, through producing goods/services to satisfying them;

(*iv*) Marketing must maximise profitable sales over the *long run.*

2. *Cundiff, Still and Govoni*: "Marketing is the managerial process by which products are matched with markets and through which the consumers are enabled to use or enjoy the product."[2]

The above definition brings out following facts:

(*i*) *Marketing and producting activities are interlocked, i.e.,* only those products should be produced that can be marketed. This matching of products with markets can be or is usually done by the marketing management by making decision in such areas (known as marketing controllables).

(*ii*) Ownership transfers occur repeatedly as physical products flow from producers to consumers. This transfer takes place three times (from manufacturer to wholesaler, from wholesaler to retailer, and from retailer to consumer).

(*iii*) Services and transfers bring the consumer the right to enjoy these.

(*iv*) Consumers/users are the "targets" of marketing activities—the whole movement of products from producers to consumers anticipates a final buying action by the users, and the whole distribution of services anticipates consumption on the part of these buyers. Thus, there can be no marketing unless ownership transfers or consumption are affected.

1. Stanton, William J., *Fundamentals of Marketing*, 1983, p. 4.
2. Cundiff, Edward, W., Richard, R. Still and Norman, A.P. Govoni, *Fundamentals of Modern Marketing*, 1980, p. 6.

3. *The American Marketing Association (AMA)*: Marketing is "the performance of business activities that direct the flow of goods and services from producer to consumer or user."[1]

This definition 'includes a wide range of activities, such as (*i*) the activities that begin before the production process (namely research on design, styling and demand for the product); (*ii*) pricing; (*iii*) marketing of services (tangible products that are usually consumed immediately—such as entertainment, lodging or transportation); (*iv*) marketing of money, financial services and insurance; (*v*) advertising, provision of sales tools and promotion aids to the dealers; personal selling by dealer personnel; and (*vi*) provision of post-purchase services to ensure consumer services. Thus, marketing includes all activities that move goods and services from producer to consumer.

4. *B.M. Enis*: Marketing is "a fundamental human activity, which encompasses exchange activities conducted by individuals and organisations for the purpose of satisfying human wants."[2]

According to this definition, (*a*) anything that has a value to any individual or organisation is a product and as such is eligible for exchange; (*b*) marketing is not synonymous with such activities as love, worship, learning, eating and sleeping—but there are often marketing aspects of loving, religion, education and obtaining food and shelter. Conversely, such activities frequently occur in conjunction with exchange activities; and (*e*) marketing is an activity which can be engaged in by all people, *i.e.*, it has both micro and macro dimensions.

5. *M. M. Bell*: He has defined marketing both in a broader as well as a narrower sense.[3]

(*i*) *The broader or 'macro-marketing' point of view*: Marketing is related to the national economy and other aspects of the total social and cultural complex. It is a complex system of organisations and processes by which a nation's resources are distributed to the people to satisfy their wants. It can be likened to the panoramic view an aviator has of a large geographical area—where the pilot sees the big picture.

---

1. Committee on Definitions (Chairman: Ralph S. Alexander, *Marketing Definitions: A Glossary of Marketing Terms*, AMA, Chicago, 1960, p. 15.
2. Enis, Ben, M., *Marketing Principles. The Management Process*, 1974, p. 21.
3. Bell, Martin, M., *Marketing: Concepts and Strategy*, 1979, p. 4.

(*ii*) *The narrower sense, or micro-marketing*: Marketing is the process of managing an individual business firm in such a way as to satisfy its particular customers. It involves many specialised tasks, such as product development, advertising and pricing but it is the relationship of these activities to the Company's total efforts. It also involves the management of every aspect of a business with the ultimate consumer in mind. It can be likened to a close-up perspective of a scientist who inspects a small object through a microscope.

6. *Philip Kotler*: "Marketing is the set of human activities directed at facilitating and consummating exchanges....Three elements must be present to define a marketing situation: (*i*) two or more parties who are potentially interested in exchange, (*ii*) each possessing things of value of the other; and (*iii*) each capable of communication and delivery."[1]

In the revised edition, Kotler states, "Marketing means working with *markets,* which in turn means attempting to actualise potential exchanges for the purpose of satisfying human wants and needs...marketing is human activity directed at satisfying needs and wants through exchange process.[2]

7. *Peter F. Drucker*: "Marketing is not a function of business, but a view of the entire business seen as the economic organ to provide goods and services. This is the marketing view of business. Everything the business does in that respect is marketing. Marketing is not only much broader than selling, it is not specialised activity at all. It encompasses the whole business concern, and responsibility for marketing must, therefore, permeate all areas of the enterprise."[3]

He further says, "Marketing is the only distinguishing and unique function of business. If we want to know what a business is we have to start with its purpose. And its purpose must be outside the business itself. In fact, it must lie in society since a business enterprise is an organ of society. There is only one valid definition of business purpose: to create a customer."[4]

---

1. Kotler, Philips, *Marketing Management, Analysis Planning and Control*, pp, 11-12.
2. *Ibid.*, 1976 Ed., pp. 5 and 7.
3. Drucker, P.F., *The Practice of Management*, 1954, pp. 38-39.
4. *Ibid.*, p. 37.

Marketing according to him is then, *"A process which converts a source, distinct knowledge into a contribution of economic value in the market place. The purpose of the business is to create a customer.*[1]

8. *Converse, Hugey and Mitchell*: "Marketing includes all activities involved in the creation of place, time and possession utilities. *Place utility* is created when goods and services are available at the places they are needed; *time utility* when they are needed; and *possession utility* when they are transferred to those who need them."[2]

9. *Duddy and Reizan*: "Marketing is the economic process by which goods and services are exchanged and their values determined in terms of money prices."[3]

10. *H.L. Hansen*: "Marketing is the process of discovering and translating consumer needs and wants into product and service specifications, creating demand for these products and services and then in turn expanding this demand."[4]

11. *Cundiff and Still*: "Marketing is the business process by which products are matched with markets and through which transfers of ownership are effected."[5]

12. *Leslie Rodger*: "Marketing is the primary management function which organises and directs the aggregate of business activities involved in converting customer purchasing power into effective demand for a specific product or service and in moving the product or service to the final consumer or user so as to achieve the company-set profit or other objectives."[6]

13. *Institute of Marketing, U.K.*: "Marketing is the management function which organises and directs all those business activities involved in assessing and converting customer purchasing power into effective demand for a specific product or service and in moving the product or service to the final consumer or user so as to achieve the profit target or other objectives set by a company."[7]

---

1. *Ibid.*, p. 39.
2. Converse, Hugey and Mitchell, *Elements of Marketing*, p. 1.
3. Duddy and Reizan, *Marketing: An Institutional Approach*, p. 6.
4. Hansen, H.L., *Marketing: Text Techniques and Cases*, 1971, p. 4.
5. Cundiff, E.W., and Still, R.S. *Basic Marketing*, 1972, p. 2.
6. Rodger, Leslie, *Marketing in a Competitive Economy*. 1965.
7. Institute of Marketing, UK., "Council Codifies *A New Definition of Marketing*". Marketing, October, 1966, Vol. 35, No. 10, p. 1285.

14. *Paul Mazur*: "Marketing is the delivery of a standard of living to society."[1]

15. *N.C. Nair*: "Marketing is a creation and delivery of a standard of living to society."[2]

16. *T.A.A. Latif*: "Marketing is not a high pressure selling, nor is it fancy advertising. The philosophy of marketing is the philosophy of consumer service. It is the chain of process backed by creative thinking that spreads from the concept of the product through strengthening the 'want' for the product when it is consumed or used."[3]

17. *Backman and Davidson*: "Marketing is the performance of all activities necessary for ascertaining the needs and wants of markets, planning product availability, effecting transfers in ownership of products, providing for their physical distribution and facilitating the entire marketing process. It is a sphere within which price-making forces operate and in which exchanges of title tend to be accompanied by the actual movement of the goods affected."[4]

18. *R. Buskirk*: "Marketing is an integrated system of action that creates value in goods through the creation of form, place, time and ownership utilities."[5]

19. *Keegan*: "Marketing is the process of focusing the resources and objectives of an organisation on environmental opportunities and needs...It is a concept, a business process, and a set of activities, as given below:[6]

(*a*) *Marketing Concept:*

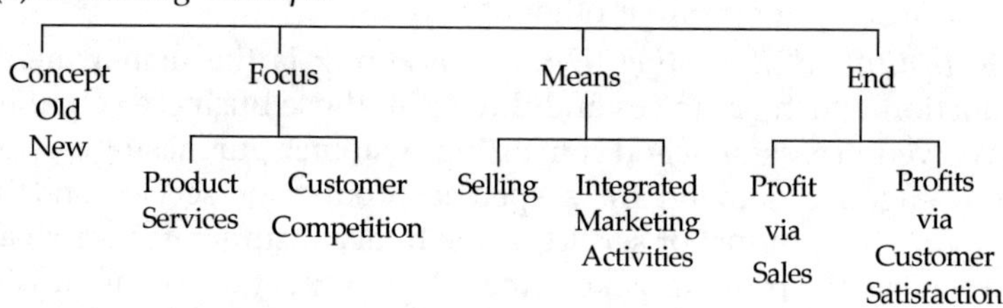

1. Mazur, Paul, "Dost Distribution Cost Enough, Fortune", November, 1947, p. 138.
2. N.C. Nair, Malcolm, his speech, "Progress in Distribution. An Appraisal. After Thirty Years", Thirteenth Annual Boston Conference on Distribution, 1958—Quoted by Hansen, H.L. *Marketing: Text Cases and Readings*, 1961, p. 1.
3. Latif, T.A.A., *The Practice of Marketing*, S. Chand & Co. Ltd., New Delhi, 1976, p. 6.
4. Backman and Davidson, *Marketing*, p. 4.
5. Buskirk, Richard, *Principles of Marketing*, p. 5.
6. Keegan, *Multinational National Marketing*, 1982.

(*b*) *Marketing Activities*:

1. Product Decisions.
2. Pricing Decisions.
3. Distribution Decisions.
4. Communication Decisions.
5. Service.
6. Research.

(*c*) *Marketing Management Process:*

Marketing is the process of focusing the resources and objectives of an organisation upon opportunities in the environment.

Broadening Controversy about the Definition of Marketing

Kotler and Levy assert: "The Principles of good marketing in the traditional product areas can be transferred to the marketing of services, persons and ideas....Whether marketing is viewed in the old sense of pushing products or in the new sense of customer satisfaction engineering it is almost always viewed and discussed as business activity." They further conferred that "marketing is a pervasive social activity that goes considerably beyond the selling of tooth paste, soap, and steel...".

They define marketing as "that function of the organisation that can keep in constant touch with the organisation's consumers, read their needs, develop products that meet these needs and build a programme of communication to express the organisation's purposes. The choice of facing those who manage non-business organisations is not whether to market or not to market, for no organisation can afford to avoid marketing. The choice is whether to do it well or poorly...".[1]

In a critique to this, Luck argues that "if a definition were framed to meet the author's contentions, marketing no longer would be bounded in terms of either institution or the ultimate purpose of its activities. If a task is performed, any whereby any body, that has some resemblance to a task performed in marketing, that would be marketing...marketers' image may be pleasurably inflated by claiming that political campaigns are just another part of marketing, but what progress is to be gained by

---

1. Kotler, P. and Sidney, J. Levy, "Broadening the Concept of Marketing," *Journal of Marketing*, January 1967, pp. 10-15.

by such reasoning?...attenuate marketing's definition to make it more universal, it will wholly lose its identity". He contends that "a manageable intelligible and logical definition of marketing can be fashioned when its scope is bounded within those processes or activities whose ultimate result is market transaction.[1]

Marketing, Selling, Merchandising and Distribution

Marketing is a comprehensive term. *Merchandising* may be defined as "product planning". It includes internal planning needed to get the right product or service to the market at the right time, at the right place, and in proper colours, quantities, and sizes. *Selling* is one method of promotion, and promotion is only a part of the total marketing programme. *Distribution* is the market coverage, *i.e.,* the retailing and wholesaling structure—the channels used to get the product to the market.

Distinction between marketing and selling Levitt has brought out as follows:

"The difference between marketing and selling is more than semantic. 'Selling' focuses on the needs of the seller, 'marketing' on the needs of the buyer. 'Selling' is pre-occupied with the seller's need to convert his product into cash; 'marketing' with the idea of satisfying the needs of the customer by means of the product and the whole cluster of things associated with creating, delivering, and finally consuming it."[2]

Objectives of Marketing

The object of marketing, as of all productive activities, is to satisfy human wants.[3] According to Barker and Anshen, "The end of all the marketing activities is the satisfaction of human wants."[4] The earning of profit is the incentive which induces businessmen to attempt to satisfy wants. A business may lose money for a time and continue to operate, unless profits eventually appear that business must cease to exist. This principle guides the operations of every phase of marketing. The performance of a service which

---

1. Luck, David, J., "Broadening the Concept of Marketing — Too Far," *Journal of Marketing*, July 1969, pp. 53-57.
2. Levitt, Theodore, "Marketing Myopia", *Harvard Business Review*, July-August 1960, p. 50.
3. Converse, Hugey and Mitchell, *The Elements of Marketing*, 5th Edition, p. 2.
4. Barker and Anshen, *Modern Marketing*, p. 6.

assists marketing activities, the handling of merchandise, the incurring of risk, merchandise flow direction, provision of storage space, etc., all these are carried on in the hope of earning profit.

However, in the long range view, the object of marketing is more than the securing of profit. It is the successful distribution of the products of land, or its mineral wealth, and the products of factories. It is the raising of the standard of living by increasing the flow of goods and services to consumers. It is the ultimate satisfaction of human wants. According to Hepner, the studying of marketing aims at:[1]

(*i*) developing an intelligent appreciation of modern marketing practices and the influences in marketing situation;

(*ii*) developing a broader framework for thinking about marketing;

(*iii*) providing guiding policies regarding marketing procedures and their implementations;

(*iv*) intensifying one's feeling of participation in marketing;

(*v*) creating an open-minded, hopeful attitude towards the efforts of those scholars in marketing who are trying to develop it into a science;

(*vi*) indicating the sources from which further information can be obtained concerning marketing problems or situations;

(*vii*) supplying the factual background and analytical judgement necessary for dealing with marketing problems; and

(*viii*) helping oneself to decide whether his career shall be marketing.

NATURE OF MARKETING

Often a controversy has been raised on the issue whether marketing is a science or an art. "Science" is a word applied to multitude of varying activities carried on by man in his effort to understand his environment. Marketing cannot be regarded as a science, because it does not conform to the basic characteristics of a science. Further, the field of marketing has been slow to develop a unique body of theory. It is, therefore, not a science but rather an *art* or a *practice* and as such much more closely

1. H.W. Hepner, *Modern Marketing: Dynamics and Management*, 1955, pp. 12-15.

resembles engineering, medicine, and architecture than it does physics, chemistry or biology.[1]

FUNCTIONS OF MARKETING

A marketing function is, "an act or operation or service by which original product and the final consumer are linked together." Sometimes it is not possible to divide the marketing process into few functions. There is no unanimity regarding a classification of marketing functions. F.W. Rayn lists 120 functional elements grouped into 16 categories. Other writers suggest as few as eight to as many as twenty or thirty such functions. Various functions of marketing can be lumped into the following three major heads:

1. Merchandising Functions,
2. Physical Distribution Functions, and
3. Facilitating Functions.

1. Merchandising Functions

(*i*) *Buying*: Buying is the first step in the process of marketing. A manufacturer has to buy raw materials for production. A wholesaler has to buy goods to sell them to the retailer. A retailer has to buy goods to be sold to the consumer. Buying involves transfer of ownership of goods.

(*ii*) *Assembling*: Assembling means creation and maintenance of the stock of goods, purchased from different sources. These are sometimes collected and assembled at one place by middlemen. As two distinct processes both buying and assembling involve related elements such as kind, quality, price, date of delivery and other terms and conditions. All these require specialised knowledge on the part of the buyers.

(*iii*) *Selling*: Selling is important from the point of view of the seller as well as the consumer. Only through the sale of goods,

1. For this controversy, refer to Bertels, Robert "Can Marketing Be a Science", *Journal of Marketing,* Vol XV, No. 3, January 1951; Converse, P.D., The Development of a Science of Marketing", *Journal of Marketing,* Vol X, No. 1, July 1945; Brawn, Lyndon O." "Toward a Profession of Marketing" *Journal of Marketing,* Vol. XIII, No. 1, July 1948, Cox, R and W. Aldersan (Eds.) *Theory in Marketing,* Richard, D. Irwin, Chicago, 1950; Vaile, Rolan, S., "Toward a Theory of Marketing", *Journal of Marketing,* Vol. XIII, No. 4, April 1949, and Hutichinson, Kenneth D. "Marketing As a Science; An appraisal". *Journal of Marketing,* Vol. XVI, January 1952.

the profit-making object of a business concern is achieved. After Industrial Revolution and increasing use of machinery, mass-production has become possible which in its turn requires mass selling complicated by the presence of legal restraints. It involves creation of demand market research, selection of channel for distribution, etc.

2. Physical Distribution Functions

These relate to the process of transporting the goods from the place of seller to the place of buyer. These include two main functions: (*i*) Transportation, and (*ii*) Storage and Warehousing.

(*i*) *Transportation*: A good system of transportation increases the value of goods by the creation of place utility. The quick development of transportation and communication and the opening of new markets has resulted extension of markets, regular supply, lower price and improved services to the consumers.

(*ii*) *Storage and Warehousing*: Storage becomes necessary, when production is seasonal but consumption is perennial or when production is continuous but consumption is seasonal. Storage involves holding and preserving goods between the time of their production and the time of their consumption. Storage tends to adjust the supply to demand of the product and holds the price line. It is a function of equalisation. It creates time and place utilities.

Facilitating Functions

These make the marketing process easy. These include financing, riskbearing, standardization, pricing, advertising and sales promotion and market information, etc.

(*i*) *Financing*: Without the availability of adequate and cheap finance, it is very difficult to carry on marketing activities smoothly. Commercial Banks, Cooperative Credit Societies and Government Agencies arrange for short term finance, medium term finance and long term finances. Trade credit is also one of the important sources of finance.

(*ii*) *Standardization*: Standardization is an ethical basis of marketing. A standard is a measure generally recognised as a model for comparison. Standards are determined on the basis of colour, weight, quality and other factors of a product. Standardization facilitates purchase and sale of goods. Goods are purchased by brand name.

(*iii*) *Market Information*: Decisions on marketing are based on information regarding market conditions. Marketing research has now become an independent branch of marketing.

(*iv*) *Risk-bearing*: Marketing of goods involves innumerable risks due to theft, deterioration, accidents, etc. The most important factor responsible for the risk is fluctuation in prices. The other factors may be change in fashion, increased competition, change in habits of the consumers, natural calamities, etc.

Businessmen have to foresee the business risks and take concrete steps to avoid them by insurance and hedging. Still unavoidable risks have to be borne by the businessmen.

(*v*) *Pricing*: Pricing is an important function closely related to selling. Pricing policy of the concern directly affects the profit element and its successful functioning. Several factors are to be borne in mind in determining the price policy such as cost of the product, competitors' prices, marketing policies, government policy or customary or convenient prices, etc.

IMPORTANCE OF MARKETING

According to Philip Kotler, "Marketing is analysing, organising, planning and controlling of the firm's customer-impinging resources, policies, activities, with a view to satisfying the needs and wants of chosen customer groups at a profit." William J. Stanton mentions that "Marketing is a total system of interacting business activities designed to plan, price promote and distribute wants-satisfying products and services to present and potential customers." Without marketing, the president cannot plan, the production manager cannot manage, the purchasing agent cannot purchase, the chief financial officer cannot budget and the engineer and designer cannot design. A writer has aptly remarked that "Nothing happens in our economy until somebody sells something." Following is the importance of marketing.

1. Importance to Society

(*i*) *Delivery of Standard of living*: Paul Mazur has said, "Marketing is the delivery of standard of living of Society." Marketing creates and increases demand of the new and existing products and thus raises the standard of living of the people.

(*ii*) *Provision of Employment*: According to an estimate 40 per cent of the labour force in developed economies like U.S.A., Japan,

Germany, etc. is engaged in different marketing processes such as marketing research work, wholesale and retail business, transport, communications, storing and warehousing, publicity work, etc. In underdeveloped economies like India there is a much scope for increasing opportunities for employment by developing marketing processes.

(*iii*) *Decrease of Distribution Cost*: Marketing aims at reducing the cost of distribution as far as possible so that the commodities might be within the reach of maximum number of consumers. It increases the level of consumption in society. In spite of decrease in distribution cost, prices of goods do not register a lower trend. It increases the profits of the producer which filter down to the shareholders and debenture holders. A part of the profit may also be utilised for further research. Thus, the society is benefited in the long run.

(*iv*) *Increase in National Income*: *A* marketing system is associated with creation of increased demand for goods and services. A period of depression and low prices is very harmful to the economy, as many small units stop production leading to widespread discovering of new markets, reducing cost of distribution, marketing it customer-oriented, diversifying and improving the product and suggesting alternative uses. A sound marketing system can give protection against business slump.

2. Importance to the Firm

As is evident from the following words of Peter F. Drueker, "Marketing is the distinguishing, the unique function of the business." The importance of marketing to a business firm may be summarised under following heads:

(*i*) *Help in Business Planning and Decision-making*: Marketing is helpful in business planning and taking various decisions regarding business. In today's economy, production is planned according to the sales forecasts and not according to the production capacity of the firm. A firm produces what it can sell or as much quantity as it can sell and not what and how much it can produce. Thus, marketing decisions affect the business decisions. Activities such as planning, production, purchase, finance or design revolve around the marketing decisions.

(*ii*) *Help in Increasing Profits*: Marketing helps in increasing the business profits by reducing the selling cost on the one hand and by increasing the demand of the product through advertising and sales promotion activities on the other.

(iii) Help in Communication between Firm and Society: Marketing provides information to the firm regarding consumer's behaviour changes from time to time and of the competitors' production and price policies. It helps a firm in framing its own policies and making necessary adjustments.

3. Importance in Underdeveloped Economy

Marketing in underdeveloped economies is still in its infancy. Industrialisation and organisation go hand in hand with application of modern refinements in the field of marketing. An effective marketing system alone can bring the fruits of production to the people.

4. Importance in Developing Economy

Marketing is the most important "multiplier" and an effective engine of development. It mobilises latent economic energy and creates small business. It develops standard for product and sendees as well as conduct, integrity and reliability. Economic integration is made possible through proper distribution of products. Thus, the concept of marketing in developing economies has to go a long way to catch up with the requirements of rapid industrial growth.

5. Importance in Developing Economy

Rich economies or the economies of abundance connote a certain degree of development in marketing. In such countries the volume of production is generally more than the demand. In order to maintain the level of production it is absolutely necessary that the produced amount is disposed of readily in the country itself or abroad on the basis of non-price completion. This is possible only by a very sound and advanced marketing system.

6. Distinction between a Seller's and Buyer's Market

A Seller's market is one in which the demand for goods and services exceeds the supply. In such a situation there is tendency of growing monopolies. A buyer's market is one in which the supply of goods exceeds the demand. Every firm is eager to sell its goods but only that firm succeeds which adopts the scientific ways of marketing of goods much as adopting the designs and quantity of goods in accordance with the changing tastes and likings of the common consumers. Thus, there is importance of marketing in both a sellers and buyers market.

To conclude, marketing is a potential force that commands high significance. An increase in efficiency of marketing results in a lower cost of distribution. Low prices are a boon to the entire population. Marketing brings new varieties of useful and quality goods to consumers, thus helping to improve the standard of living. It provides wide employment opportunities. It has converted yesterday's luxuries into today's necessaries. It converts latent demand into effective demand.

Distinction between Marketing and Selling

In marketing, the main emphasis is laid on the selling aspect of the marketing activities because sale is the very basis of success of all business activities. Selling is a process whereby goods and services finally flow to the customers who need them. The firm performs its functions of creating a customer and meeting his needs and requirements. The function of selling includes the sales planning, marketing sales forecast, doing market research, familiarising the customer with the product advertising and arranging the display of goods, and making the goods available to them. In the words of Edward G. Koch, "The difference between selling and marketing is more than a semantic exercise. Selling focuses on the needs of the seller, marketing on the needs of purchaser. Selling means moving products while marketing means obtaining customer." Following are the distinctions between these activities.

1. Distinction in Scope: The scope of 'marketing' is much wider than that of 'selling'. Marketing includes all activities starting with the idea of producing a product to satisfy the needs of the customers and ending with the satisfaction of customer even after the product is sold. Thus, it involves planning, producing, selling and serving the customers. Changes in product-line, quality, shape and design, price channels of distribution, etc. are made on the basis of information picked up from the market through constant and systematic research. On the other hand, selling refers to functions and activities undertaken to secure the sale of distribution of the quality and design of the products, already manufactured by the firm, among customers. It involves efforts to sell what has already been produced without taking the trouble of adapting production to consumer needs and preferences.

2. Distinction in the Object of Profit Earning: The object of marketing is to earn profits through satisfaction of customers while selling concentrates on sale volume and makes efforts to earn profits by selling the more quantity of products. Thus, profitability of a marketing is oriented by customers and their satisfaction while the profitability of a selling-oriented firm is concerned with the sale volume.

3. Distinction in Relation: As marketing is related to customer satisfaction it includes pre-production and post-sale activities. Selling is concerned only with the physical transfer of goods from one person to another and includes activities relating to transfer of goods.

4. Distinction in Orientation: As marketing is consumer-oriented more attention is paid to consumer's needs. Selling is basically production-oriented and concentrates much on production and distribution of goods.

5. Distinction in Solution of Problems: While problems of marketing are the main concern of the producers or businessmen, selling problems are solved by other channels of distribution like retailer, wholesaler, etc.

CONCEPT OF MARKETING AT DIFFERENT STAGES OF ECONOMIC DEVELOPMENT

Economic life evolves through different stages of economic development. For convenience, economic history can be divided into eight stages. Depending on the character of the economy the concept of marketing in each stage is different according to the following stages of economic development.

1. Economic Self-Sufficiency: In the earliest stage of economic development there were small family units carrying out all the work to satisfy all their wants for food, clothing and shelter. There was no exchange at all. It was a stage of self-sufficiency devoid of a concept of marketing.

2. Primitive Communism: In primitive communism the land was owned in common and the frutis of the labour were shared in common. The Eskimo hunter had no personal right to his catch; it had to be divided among the inhabitants of the whole village.

The tools and provisions were the common property of all. There was no need of exchange in this type of society which removed the basis for marketing.

3. Simple Barter: Soon the realisation that some people are able to turn out certain goods quickly than others led to economic specialisation. Gradually not only individuals and families but the whole tribes and communities turned to specialisation for its beneficial effects on human productivity. The family or tribe engaged in a particular trade entered into bartering relationship with others for the goods it did not produce. Those who were in possession of surpluses bartered their goods which they did not produce themselves. It involved some search and negotiations. Thus, personal selling practices originated during barter.

4. Local Markets: Barter system encouraged the emergence of local markets which were at first temporary affairs such as trade fairs taking place only on certain days of the week or at times of festivals. But soon, they took on more permanent shape with stalls, shops and bazaars. These local markets led to specialisation of certain persons in marketing as opposed to production. The appearance of specialisation in selling expanded the concept of marketing which was the process of exchange of economic goods and the set of specialised institutions that facilitated the exchange.

5. Money Economy: Simple barter system was wrought with certain difficulties such as the common measure of value, double coincidence, difficulties of storage and carrying goods from place to place in search of parties, etc. The solution came through the development of a common medium of exchange that took various forms such as fish, hooks, shells, pearls, beads, sheep, cows, slaves, etc. But ultimately they were given up in favour of metallic coins which quickened the pace of trade and provided an even more durable base for the operation of local markets.

6. Early Capitalism: There were persons who were successful at accumulation by dint of their talent or force. They began to exchange goods and services that they had in surplus for the labour of other men. Thus, arose a property class and a labour class. The early capitalists organised workers into productive units and sought markets to trade their output. There was no brand, grading, packaging or advertising at that time. A merchant class facilitated the distribution of goods in large towns. Peddlers and hawkers carried goods from door to door. Early capitalism operated in an economy of scarcity. There was no serious effort to study the needs of consumers. The concept of marketing under early capitalism was that of the business activities specially involved in searching for customers or markets and moving goods from producer to consumers for the purpose of the seller's gain.

7. Mass Production: The Industrial revolution, invention of machines, improvement in means of transportation and communication, growth of industrial towns, etc. pushed the growth of large scale enterprises. A profession of management developed to organise men, machines, material and money to maximise the profitable return on the invested resources. The producers sought means of increasing the stability of demand for their products. Out of this search originated various modern marketing practices such as branding and packaging, advertising, agency system, sale promotion, etc. These marketing activities became increasingly popular. Thus, in an economy of mass production, marketing became the name for a whole variety of business activities undertaken by sellers to improve and stimulate the new flow of goods and services from producers to consumers.

8. Affluent Society: In highly developed economies producers and sellers of goods and services probed deep into the question of what people want rather than what they need and adjusted their productive capacity and productions to meet these interpreted wants. Emphasis was laid on marketing research before decisions on product and product lines were made. Salesmen were increasingly used to provide feedback on evolving customer wants. Advertising was used to inform buyers of new goods designed to meet new wants in the market place. Various marketing tools were used to give consumer-oriented decision to their business.

Thus, the concept of marketing became increasingly that of interpreting consumer desires and creating the goods that will satisfy their desires. The affluent society was composed of huge orgnisations not only business organisations but also military, government and social and political organisations completing for recognition and acceptance in the public mind.

ALTERNATIVE CONCEPTS OF MARKETING

Following concepts have been developed so far by the different authorities of management on marketing.

1. Distribution of Goods and Services: This is the traditional concept of marketing as an economic activity that facilitates the flow of goods and services from producer to consumer, F.E. Clark has defined the marketing as consisting 'of those efforts which affect transfers in ownership of goods and care for their physical distribution.' Another definition under this category is that of American Marketing Association that says, "Marketing is the performance of business activities that direct the flow of goods and services from producer to consumer or user." Thus, marketing includes all activities relating to transfer of ownership in goods and services to the actual consumer, from their point of origin. It has no concern with the production activities. It begins when production process is complete.

This concept represents a narrow view of marketing that insists much on the flow of goods and services and leaves the other important managerial aspects of marketing untouched.

2. Delivery of Standard of Living: This concept was originated by Paul Mazur, According to him "Marketing is the delivery of standard of living to society." Professor McNair made an important amendment in this definition. He added "Marketing is the creation and delivery of a standard of living to the society." Thus, marketing includes all those activities that create and give a better standard of living to the society. It may be said to be a consumer-oriented concept and is nearer to the modern concept of marketing. Producer tries to know the customer's needs plans his production accordingly and directs the flow of goods and services to them. He tries to lower down the cost of production by making necessary changes in channels of distribution and taking up of sales promotion activities. Thus, customers get quality goods at cheaper rates and better standard of living is delivered to the society.

3. Creation of Utility: Richard Bushirk has defined marketing as an activity that creates form, place, time, and ownership utility. According to him, "Marketing is an integrated system of action that creates value in goods through the creation of form, place, time and ownership utility." This means: (*i*) Product planning and development activities create form utility, (*ii*) Flow of goods through different distribution channels from producer to consumer from the place of abundance to the place or where they are needed creates place utility, (*iii*) After production goods are stored by the manufacturer, wholesalers or retailers till such time, the demand of the product is created and such goods are made available to customer at the time when they are needed or demanded, thus creating time utility for them, (*iv*) Goods may be lying in a reliable state with the producer or the manufacturer or their agents while some other persons need them. In such cases, possession utility is created by the transfer of possession of goods to the person who needs it. Marketing, therefore, consists in moving goods from the manufacturers, in a form in which it is required at a time when they are required, to the place where they are to be used and for those who are to use them for various purpose.

4. Generation of Revenue: This concept maintains that the main object of any business firm should be to generate revenue of income by selling the products. The product should be sold out at a price which allows reasonable expenses. Marketing should stress on increasing the profits of the firm by reducing various production and selling cost and not by increasing the selling price. Richard Bushirk has explained that concept as "It is marketing responsibility to generate revenue at a cost which will allow a reasonable profit to be realised from operations. Thus, marketing consists of all activities which are performed with a view to allow the firm to earn a reasonable profit.

5. Social System: Just like social system, marketing is not only one activity, but a sum of several business activities and, rather interaction of many activities. In the words of William J. Stanton, 'Marketing is a total system of interacting business activities designed to plan, price, promote and distribute customers.' Thus, under this concept the entire system of business action is market-oriented or customer-oriented.

6. Customer's Satisfaction-Modern Concept: The modern concept of marketing emphasises the complete satisfaction of customers' needs. This is also known as Marketing Concept. It integrates maketing function with the other functions of the management with this realisation that business is basically a marketing organisation. It is based on two fundamental concepts: (*i*) that the company policies and operations should be customer-oriented, and (*ii*) that the goal of the firm should be profitable sales. According to Peter F. Drucker, "The purpose of a business is to create a customer." Creation of customer means the identification of consumer needs and organising the business to meet these needs. A firm makes sincere efforts to find out the needs of the members of the community and tries to provide the maximum measure of satisfaction to them. Thus, everything a firm does is marketing. However, it is convenient to separate marketing as a distinct activity. The marketing thus includes:

(*i*) Identification and assessment of markets.

(*ii*) Formulation of marketing policy to cater to the target market.

(*iii*) The planning and operation of the marketing organisation to achieve the desired level of sales and to deal with customers.

(*iv*) Organisation and conduct of sales promotion through salesmanship, advertising and other media.

(*v*) Costing and budgeting of marketing efforts.

(*vi*) Review of the marketing efforts and to assess whether the desired level of consumer satisfaction is being achieved or not.

APPROACHES TO THE STUDY OF MARKETING

The approach to the subject of marketing has passed through several stages before reaching the present-day management orientation. In the first two decades of the present century, there were many generalisations about the system of exchange. Functions performed in the system were identified and described. Institutions performing within the system were analysed. Flows of commodities through the system were traced. Functional, institutional or commodity-oriented, the approach was descriptive. The major emphasis in early marketing literature was on farm products and on means by which these products reached consumers through a marketing mechanisms. The farm products were gathered or "concentrated" from widely scattered small producers, then "equalised" in storage locations to be available as the demand prompted a "dispersion" through wholesale and retail intermediaries to the consumer.

But now, following approaches are used to understand and direct marketing activities:

1. The Commodity Approach;
2. The Institutional Approach;
3. The Functional Approach;
4. The Conceptual Approach;

5. The Managerial Approach;
6. The Eclectic Approach;
7. The Systems Approach; and
8. Inter-disciplinary Approach.

1. The Commodity Approach: It emphasises the individual commodities or goods and the market effort needed to get them from the source of their production/supply to their place of consumption or the ultimate consumers. For example, while studying the marketing of a commodity, one will examine the source and conditions of supply, the nature and volume of demand for it, the purpose for which it is required, the various agencies/ marketing institutions involved in marketing, processing and the channels that may be used for transportation of the commodity to the wholesalers and retailers and from there to the ultimate consumer; along with the activities of storage, standardisation, grading, packaging, branding and financing.

The commodity approach discovers the basic principles, strategies and techniques that underlie the marketing of most goods and services. Its framework for the analysis of marketing provides for detailed descriptions of the system used in marketing of each item.

Its *advantage* is that both the flow of a product and the institutions handling it are studied in detail. It is concrete since all work relates to a specific product, the goal being to establish an ideal marketing system for each commodity. However, its main *disadvantage* is that it is a time consuming process which often results in much duplication of effort. Further, the totally marketing effort for a whole class of commodities is nearly the same.

Therefore, the modern marketers insist on the study of *product classes,* such as automobiles, cameras, appliances, furniture, etc. rather than individual commodities—for the marketing process of the former, certain vital differences in the activities are needed to move these products to consumers. This type of approach is valuable in solving highly specialised marketing problems.[1]

2. The Institutional Approach: It is used in studying the marketing of goods/services, through a detailed analysis of the specific activities, such as research, product development, pricing,

---

1. Schwartz, David, J : *Marketing Today: A Basic Approach,* 1973, p. 17.

advertising, personal selling and physical distribution, involved in the marketing process. It describes and analyses how various marketing institutions operate in performing marketing functions. It centres on middlemen and describes the activities of such marketing institutions as are engaged in the overall marketing process. In the *retail area,* its principles pertain to institutions such as department stores, chain stores, independent stores, supermarkets, discount houses and door-to-door merchants. In the wholesale area, it is concerned with the activities of services of wholesalers, brokers, wholesale receivers, auctioneers, etc. In the process of moving goods from producers to consumers a large number of persons take part who are known as producers, manufacturers, wholesalers and retailers middlemen and facilitating institutions which aid in the performance of business functions but do not take title to goods or negotiate purchase or sale. Pack animal, bullock-cart, human porters, trucks, bus, airline, steamship, and rail-road companies do the actual physical work of transporting merchandise from the producers to the consumers. Banks and other financial institutions assist in financing marketing operations, while warehouses provide facilities for storage. Other facilitating institutions include commodity and livestock exchanges, *marketing consultants, freight forwarders, advertising agencies,* insurance companies, licensed graders and inspectors, furniture markets, and credit institutions.

In Institutional Approach though a detailed understanding of how each institution operates is helpful, treating all institutions as a special case obscures the interactions between them. This makes a total systems view of the marketing process more difficult.[1]

3. The Functional Approach: It is a cross between the commodity and the institutional approaches. In it, marketing process is studied both, according to the products and the institutions involved in their movement. Marketing is viewed from the standpoint of marketing function: *Exchange functions* (buying, selling), *Physical distribution functions* (transportation, storage), *auxiliary functions* (standardisation, grading, financing, assumption of risk, transmission of marketing information) which involve inter-actions between marketing institutions; and marketing processing (equalising supply and demand, concentrating resources and dispersion).

1. Mellot, Douglas W, *Marketing: Principles and Practices,* 1978, p. 11.

In the initial stages, the functional orientation became the basis for the description of activities performed within the marketing mechanism. *Buying and selling* were two major functions each of equal importance. Supporting these primary marketing functions were functions of physical supply, which had to do with *transportation and storage* and additional facilitating functions related to *financing, standardisation* and *risk bearing.* Later on *market information* was added as a facilitating function due to the increased attention to the marketing of manufactured goods and a growing appreciation of marketing research. Other functions were also added from time to time by different observers.

The main limitation of functional approach is that it lays too much emphasis on the various marketing functions instead of knowing how they are applied to the specific business operations. To quote Philips and Duncan, "The nature of marketing is such that it can be best understood if all these three approaches are used in covering various aspects of the subject."[1]

4. Conceptual Approach: In this approach, marketing is studied through theoretical analysis of marketing institutions, functions and policies. For finding solutions to marketing problems, hypothetical models of consumer behaviour are devised and attempts are made to predict the reactions of consumers to various marketing situations. Marketing is improved through research and innovation.

5. The Managerial Approach: This approach combines certain features of the first three approaches and seeks to relate them from the decision-making viewpoint. The areas of marketing decision are: the marekting organisation, the product, distribution policies, and physical distribution, pricing, advertising, and personal selling. In this latest approach marketing is studied from the marketing management's point of view. After analysing uncontrollable factors in marketing like the marketing environment an attempt is made to find out how marketing decisions are and should be made.

This approach is based on the new concept, where marketing is considered in terms of how decision-makers handle specific problems and situations. It emphasises evaluating current marketing practices and developing qualitative and quantitative

1. Phillip Charles E. and Duncan Delbert, J., *Marketing: Principles and Methods,* 1968, p. 7.

techniques and strategies, ranging from decision theory and simulation to statistical analysis and empirical investigations to ensure that those decisions are rational. Managerial approach is extensively used by marketing executives.

6. Eclectic Approach: As the name implies, it comprises in drawing from the best of all available approaches. It is used to present marketing in the total context of its social, economic and cultural significance. It poses questions like the following and obtains answers to study marketing in true perspective: How does the marketing system work? What functions are performed and which agencies and institutions are engaged in it? How can marketing system be further improved to get higher levels of economic activity? How can marketing system be made more effective? What should be the role of the government in regulating marketing activities? Should the consumers be protected? What are the responsibilities of marketers towards the society, the consumer and others? How can marketing help in meeting ecological problems and conserving natural resources? What career opportunities are available in marketing? etc.

7. The Systems Approach: It provides the best method for marketing study. It lays emphasis on the inputs to the system and the outputs produced. It aims at designing the achievement of the objectives or goals according to a plan which provides for the processing of inputs and the discharge of appropriate outputs. It helps in determination of marketing and company goals and the developing of marketing programmes and total marketing mix.

8. Inter-disciplinary Approach: In recent years, a more scientific approach has been devised to the study and practice of marketing. It is better known as *Inter-disciplinary Approach.* As Lazer defines it, "By definition the Interdisciplinary approach to marketing refers to the use of all disciplines: social, physical, quantitative and business to develop marketing insights, concepts and theories and illuminate, investigate and solve marketing problems. It includes the application and integration of pertinent material to advance marketing. It refers to the blending and cross fertilisation of various disciplines and their solidification in marketing thought. Through this integration more widely acceptable and useful marketing concepts and generalisation are evolving."[1]

---

1. Lazer, William, "The Interdiscipline Approach to Marketing" *A Marketing Overview : Application of Science in Marketing Management*. Edited by Frank M. Bass, Charles, W. King and Edgar, A. Posessemier, 1968, p. 3.

Many new concepts on perception attitude, opinion, leadership communication, and consumer behaviour have been developed with the application of behavioural sciences which are of vital importance to the marketers. The field of statistics, mathematics, and electronics have developed many new analytical tools which are being increasingly applied to identify and solve marketing problems; and research results have provided tool for executive decision-making.

QUESTIONS FOR EXERCISE

1. "The Marketing Concept says, find wants and fill them rather than create products and sell them." Discuss.
2. "Marketing begins with customer and ends with customer." Discuss.
3. "Marketing is the performance of business activities that direct the flow of goods and services from producer to consumer or users." Explain.
4. Discuss clearly the old and New Concept of Marketing, how do they differ from each other?
5. What to you understand by Product or Consumer-oriented Concepts of Marketing? Discuss.
6. Define 'Marketing' and discuss its importance in modern world?
7. Explain the main Functions of Marketing.
8. How would you determine the value of marketing to the society? Explain the role of government in ensuring effectiveness of marketing mechanism.
9. "Marketing is an indispensable aid for smooth functioning of the present-day industrial structure." Discuss this statement fully.
10. Discuss the significance of marketing in the context of Indian Economy.
11. Distinguish between 'Marketing and Selling'.
12. Is there any difference between marketing management and sales management? If yes, then discuss how do they differ from each other on the basis of scope and functions?
13. Trace briefly the concept of marketing and marketing management at different stages of economic development?

14. Explain and illustrate the different approaches of marketing system.
15. "Three basic approaches are used customarily in describing and explaining the marketing system: the commodity, the institutional and the functional." Explain briefly these approaches.
16. "Marketing has been defined as creation of time, place and possession utilities." Explain the idea involved in this definition.
17. "Marketing is the performance of business activities that direct the flow of goods and services from producer to consumer or user." Discuss.
18. "Just as Marketing does not begin at the end of production line, it does not end with the final sale." Explain this statement.
19. A businessman has said, "We have to produce that commodity which is liked by people, not which we can sell." Give your views.
20. "Consumer is the King." Comment on the statement in the light of Marketing Concept.

2

Modern Concept of Marketing

Marketing concept is "a way of thinking", or "a management philosophy" about an organisation's total marketing activities. When the philosophy is adopted, it affects not only marketing activities but also all the organisation's activities—including planning of action, control, objectives, follow-through, etc.; finance and other activities which are geared toward satisfying customers' needs, wants and desires.

Definition of Marketing Concept

1. ***Theodore Levitt*****:** "Management must think itself not as producing products but as providing customer creating value satisfactions. It must put this idea into every nook and cranny of the organisation. It has to do this continuously and with the kind of flair that excites and stimulates the people in it. Otherwise, the company will be merely a series of pigeon-holed parts, with no consolidation sense of purpose or direction. In short, the organisation must learn to think of itself not as producing goods or services but as buying customers, as doing the things that will make people want to do business with it."[1]

2. ***J.B Kitterick*****:** "Marketing concept introduces the marketing men at the beginning rather than at the end of the production cycle and would integrate marketing into each phase of business. Thus, marketing through its studies and research will establish for engineers, the designers and the manufacturing men what the customer wants in a given product, what price he is willing

1. Levitt, Theodore, "Marketing Myopia", *Harward Business Review*, July-August, 1960, p. 56.

to pay and where and when it will be wanted. Marketing would have authority in product planning, production scheduling and inventory control as well as in sales, distribution and serving the product."[1]

3. *Martin L. Bell*: Marketing concept means "developing a strategy to get the product in front of customers so they have the opportunity to buy it...determining scientifically what products or services to make and how best to market them to meet consumer needs."[2] Planning, developing strategy systematically and scientifically selecting among available alternatives, and controlling the operation in order to provide customer satisfaction are relatively new implications in the marketing concept.

4. *William J. Stanton*: "In its fullest sense the market concept is a philosophy of business which states that the customers want satisfaction is the economic and social justification of a company's existence. Consequently all company activities in production, engineering and finance as well as in marketing must be devoted to first, determining what the customer's wants are and then, satisfying these wants still making a reasonable profit."

5. *Arther P. Felton*: "The marketing concept is a philosophy applied to the operation of a business as which customer and consumer needs will be uppermost in importance. These needs will govern the separate planning of each function of the business, as well as the overall plan aimed at achieving its predetermined profit objective."

6. *Philip Kotler*: "The market concept is customer-orientation backed by integrated marketing aimed at generating customer satisfaction as the key to satisfy organisational goals."

Constituents of Modern Marketing Concept

1. Adoption of a predominantly market or customer-orientation.
2. A coordinated set of activities that allows the organisation to achieve the goals.
3. Result-oriented marketing:

---

1. General Electric Company, *Annual Report for* 1952.
2. Bell, Martin L., *Marketing Concepts and Strategy*, 1979, p. 8.

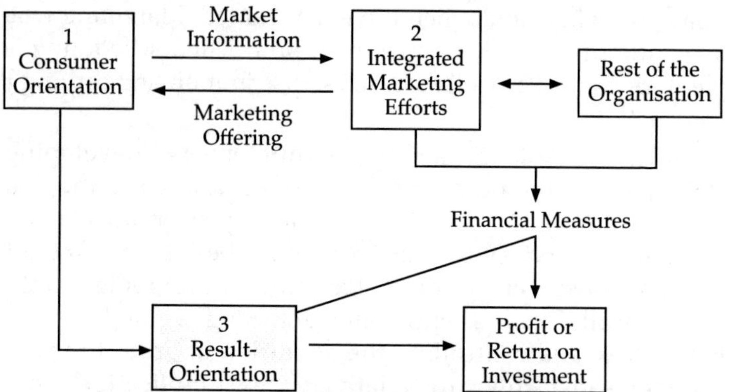

Fig. 2.1: Dynamics of Modern Marketing Concept

1. Market Orientation: It is the principal element in the modern concept of marketing. It lays emphasis on using market research to keep abreast of market trends and developments and on doing research and development work. The company wedded to this principle, makes every effort to supply the right product/service at the right time and in the right way. Marketing thus, originates with the recognition that a need exists. It terminates with the satisfaction of that need by the delivery of a usable product, at the right place and at an acceptable price. Marketing starts with the determination of consumer wants and ends with the satisfaction of these wants. A cousumer-oriented firm recognises the need to monitor the post-purchase behaviour of its customers by determining who purchased the product, whether the product was satisfactory, and what changes in the firm's market offering would make its products more successful.

2. Integration of Management Function: Modern marketing concept integrates and coordinates the diverse functions of marketing—*viz.*, such activities as product development, physical distribution, control, forecasting, pricing, advertising, selling and marketing research. Integration is a must to carry on these activities successfully. 'These activities must also be coordinated with other functional areas of a business like finance, personnel, administration, research, advertising and other departments. It means the formulation of a set of company goals to which individual goals are subordinated. The company exists to achieve something as a company rather than as a collection of uncoordinated individual departments. For example, achieving a certain percentage of profit on a certain investment may be the company goal. In working towards the achievement of this goal the finance department decides how much and from which source the needed capital is to be raised. The personnel department lays down the personnel policies for all departments on personnel matters. Research and development department takes up only one project at a time. The production department knows that obtaining low manufacturing costs is not enough, quality improvement is also needed. The marketing department places less emphasis on "high sales volume" and more on "making profitable sales". The advertising department launches a campaign for a new product only when the production department has adequate stock. Thus, an integration and coordination of different functions becomes necessary.

3. Result-Oriented Marketing: The modern marketing concept believes that marketing must be result-oriented. According to the traditional concept the measure of marketing success was an increase in sales volume. Under new concept, sales are made more profitable by dropping unprofitable products, territories or customers; or devising better methods of marketing and closely matching these to the profit potential of a particular market.

Thus, the modern concept of marketing is constituted of three basic ingredients: customer orientation, integrated effort, and result direction. It assumes that "the purpose of the business is to create a satisfied customer and that profit is not a meaningful objective by itself but rather the reward for delivering customer satisfaction. It recognises that marketing is more than selling, it is the total business seen from the customers' viewpoint. It brings customer's needs into all areas of business decision-making as the major criterion of business action and effectiveness. It is based on a realisation that short-term sales volume objectives are most easily achieved when all other elements of the marketing mix have been integrated within a longer term view of business purpose.[1] In Ansoffs phraseology, "the marketing concept takes the firm from lagged response to anticipatory or self-triggered responses to environmental change".[2]

1. Webster, Fredrick, E., *Marketing for Managers*, 1974, pp. 10-11.
2. Ansoff H. Igor, "Toward a Strategy Theory of the Firm," in Ansoff H.I. (Ed.) *Business Strategy*, Penguin Books, 1971, p. 21.

Planning, developing strategy, systematically and scientifically selecting among available alternatives, and controlling the operation in order to provide customer satisfaction is also an important and essential element of marketing concept.

FACTORS FOR EFFECTIVE CUSTOMER ORIENTATION

1. The basic needs of customers, it can satisfy.

2. Market segments, it can serve better, taking into account its limited resources.

3. Colour, size and design of the product, it can choose to satisfy the specific needs of specific customers and introduce it in the market through product differentiation.

Consumer research should be carried on to study the new and changing needs of the consumers so that the firm may cope with them.

2. Integrated Marketing: Many companies agree with Drucker that "the purpose of the company is to create a customer" but most of them fail to take the necessary organisational steps to implement the marketing concept. Integrated marketing means the following:

(*i*) The various departments in the company must recognise that the action they take, and not just the actions of the sales and marketing people, may have a profound effect on the company's ability to create and retain customers. Though the central logic of the business firm is profit, but some means must be developed to coordinate the impacts of the departments of the firm on the customer.

(*ii*) Integrated marketing also means that within the marketing function proper there is intelligent adaptation and coordination of the four P's of produce, price, place, and promotion to build strong exchange relationships with customers. To achieve this type of integration many companies have created product managers and market managers. Thus, the marketing-oriented company is one which has developed effective machanisms for coordinating the various customer-impinging forces. It is reflected in satisfied and loyal company customers.

3. Customer Satisfaction: Every firm should strive to maximise customer satisfaction. Happiness is best achieved by rendering substantial forms of assistance to others rather than by direct pursuit. The aim of the marketing concept is more to help them to please following slogans of the employees of Marshall Field and Company, may be remembered in this connection:

(*i*) Customer is always right if she thinks she is right.

(*ii*) We are more interested in pleasing a customer than in marketing sale.

(*iii*) Every sale of merchandise or service includes the obligation to accept the article for credit refund, exchange for adjustment promptly and courteously to the customer's satisfaction.

(*iv*) We strive to give completely satisfactory service to every customer.

Thus, modern marketing starts and ends with the consumer.

DIFFERENCE BETWEEN OLD AND NEW (MODERN) CONCEPT OF MARKETING

1. Orientation: The old concept is production-oriented because it emphasises on production. The new concept insists on consumers' need satisfaction and therefore it is consumer-oriented.

2. Targets: In the old concept, the main target of the firm was to earn profits through more and more production and higher sales volume. In modern concept of marketing, the target of the firm is to earn more profits through customer satisfaction.

3. Scope of Marketing: In the old concepts production and sales were the main activities included in the marketing function. Pre-production and post sales problems were out of its scope. Under new concept the scope of marketing has been widened to include the pre-production and after sales problems too.

4. Inter-departmental Integration: Under the old concept, different departments of the firm were independent and had no integration with the marketing department. They were mainly concerned with the production and not with the sales. In the new concept of marketing the activities of each department are directed by the marketing department and the various departments are better integrated with the marketing department.

5. Consumer Welfare: There was no place of consumer welfare under old concept of marketing. The new concept is fully dedicated to the consumer welfare. The main responsibility of marketing is to raise the standard of living of the society through consumer welfare and consumer satisfaction.

FACTORS RESPONSIBLE FOR THE GROWTH OF MODERN CONCEPT OF MARKETING

According to Cundiff and Still, ''Marketing is the business process by which products are matched with the markets and through which transfers of ownership are effected.'' There have been a number of factors responsible for the development of this modern concept of marketing such as the recognition of the supremacy of consumer in the overall system of production and distribution, the diversity in their demands, tastes and preferences, increases in their knowledge and experience, the widening of product markets and severe competition among the manufacturers. Now, the marketing concept emphasises that the production activity should be directed by the requirements of the people of the country and should not be aimed at fultilling the wants of a small fraction of the total population. Following factors are responsible for the adoption of the modern marketing concept:

1. Population Growth: Increase in population has brought not only an increase in demand for more products and services but has also created a variety in tastes and preferences. The different types of demands of teeming millions are to be met by the marketing executives of today.

2. Growing Number of Household: The growing number of household has created more demand for goods. The 'small family' concept has thrown new challenges before marketing men.

3. Growth in Disposable Income: With an increase in personal income, employment and education, the growth in disposable personal income has also necessitated the manufacture of new styles of goods and services. People want to spend more and to procure more comforts, more satisfaction and more variety in consumption. This has given a new momentum to the development of new marketing ideas, strategies and techniques.

4. New Attitude Towards Life: Today, the propensity to save has changed into the propensity to spend. People are after rew styles, new fashions and newer things. They want more and more fancy goods. This change has widened the product market and has developed new ideas in marketing concepts.

5. Technological Changes: Science is making progress by leaps and bounds. Hence, technological changes have created the demand for more sophisticated goods and services and changes in marketing techniques have also been necessitated.

6. Growth of Mass Communication Media: During the last two decades, radio receiving sets, transistors and television sets have been very popular with the masses. This has enlightened the minds of public and broadened mental outlook. The continuous advertisement of goods makes the people informed and creates more demand. The growth of these media has brought social awakening in the minds of consumers. The concept of the supremacy of customer has given momentum to the modern concept of marketing.

7. Growth of Marketing Channels: In old times, the distribution network was very simple. The manufacturer had direct contact with the customers. But now-a-days, a wide network of middlemen exists while it has created many problems related to management of marketing channels or distribution outlets. Hence, a new philosophy of a marketing has emerged.

FEATURES OF MODERN CONCEPT OF MARKETING

1. Customer Orientation: The essence of modern marketing concept is that "the firm must take its marching orders from the market and it must produce what the market needs." All elements of business should be geared towards the customer satisfaction. Corporate plans, programmes and operations must be focused around customer needs and desires. According to Philip Kotler, "Customer is at the top of organisation chart in this concept of marketings."

2. Systems Approach: Modern marketing concept adopts a unified view of the study of marketing. Marketing activities must be properly integrated and co-ordinated to accomplish a set of objectives.

3. Dual Objectives: Modern marketing concept advocates serving the consumers and maximising profits at the same time. These objectives, though conflicting, can be reconciled. Guaranteed route to profits is through customer satisfaction. Profit is a by-product of supplying what the customer wants.

4. Marketing Information System: Modern marketing concept emphasizes the role of information as the key to both customer satisfaction and profitability. Customer demand can never be satisfied without integrated marketing programmes based upon adequate and accurate information about customer, customer needs and competition. Information is a vital resource in planning-action-control process of management.

5. A Social Approach: Modern marketing concept is a social approach in its nature. Environmental trends like public welfare, concern for better living, etc., indicate that organisations would have to adopt socially responsible marketing policies and plans in order to assure social welfare in addition to customer welfare.

ADVANTAGES OF MODERN MARKETING CONCEPT

1. Long-term Success: Long-term success is assured to an enterprise if it recognises that needs of the market are paramount.

2. Capitalise Opportunities: It enables the firm to move quickly to capitalise on market opportunities; marketing risks can be reduced by knowing and understanding the market.

3. Customer Orientation: Customer needs, wants and desires receive top consideration in all business activities.

4. Product Planning and Development: Greater attention is paid to the product planning and development so that merchandising can become more effective.

5. Supply as Per Thousand: Demand side of the equation of exchange is honoured more and supply is adjusted to changing demand. Hence, more emphasis is given to research and innovation.

6. Integrated Approach: Marketing system based on this concept assures integrated view of business operations and indicates interdependence of different departments of a business organisation.

7. Social Benefits: Interests of the enterprise and society can be harmonised as profit through service is emphasised.

8. Research and Information: Marketing information and research is now an integral part of marketing process and it is a managerial tool in decisionmaking in the field of marketing.

9. Market-oriented: The customer-oriented concept of marketing has an appreciable effect on the business organisation. The management of company becomes market-oriented and its marketing activity becomes cornerstone of all activities. The organisation of the entire enterprise becomes market-oriented.

10. Effective Utilisation of Resources: It ensures effective utilisation of resources—physical as well as human. It develops consumerism which is a challenge to the management of organisation. Under a market-minded firm, management has the responsibility to create value-satisfying goods and services that consumers will want to buy.

MARKETING IN DEVELOPING ECONOMICS

According to Leon V. Hirach, "Distribution is *terra incognita* in the underdeveloped two-third of the world."

In the word of Peter F. Drucker, "In the underdeveloped countries as a group, marketing has traditionally been the forgotten area of economic thinking."

Causes of Inattention

Following are the reasons why marketing has not been given much and due attention in developing countries:

1. Agriculture Economy: One of the main characteristics of a developing economy is its excessive dependence on agriculture. Not only there is overpopulation in agriculture but the productivity is also very low. This leads to low income and low standard of living of the people. Individuals in these countries spend mostly all their incomes on necessities and greater income would only mean more spending. In view of the low income of the people, their excessive dependence on agriculture and less developed industrial sector, larger markets are not readily available within the country.

2. Excess Demand: In a developing economy there is always the presence of excess demand for many products. Almost very product is sold with little or no effort so long as there is need for it. There is relatively little need for promotional activities. Advertising is generally more informative rather than persuasive. The perennial scarcity economy and the resulting "Seller's Market" lead the management to concentrate more on products rather than on marketing. As the demand for many products exceeds their supply, the need to improve the existing marketing techniques, methods and practices is not felt by the management.

3. Lack of Professional Approach: Many of the developing nations are still in the process of industrialisation. Their management has not yet been professionalised. Their business still remains with a trading community whose practices are not always considered to be in tune with the needs and interests of the society.

4. Prejudice against Middlemen: There is a universal prejudice against the middlemen and traders who are engaged in marketing goods and services. This partly explains why low valuation is placed on the functions of marketing in many of the developing countries.

Importance of Marketing

According to Peter F. Drucker, the neglect of marketing is one of main factors which keeps an economy underdeveloped. He strongly argues that "Marketing might by itself go far towards changing the entire economic tone of the existing system without any change in methods of production, distribution of population or of income." A similar view is expressed by W.J. Emlen: "Production may be the door to economic growth of the underdeveloped countries but marketing is the key that turns the lock."

While many reasons are given for the neglect of marketing in developing countries, it is strongly argued that the application of the marketing concept is of greater value to a country with a developing economy than to a matured industrialised nation. Based on his study of Egyptian economy, Boyd, for instance, argues that marketing concept must be adopted if Egypt's efforts at rapid industrialisation are to succeed. He said, "Marketing is presently viewed with disdain; firms sell protected markets with little local competition, there is no concept of demand creation through the manipulation of the various elements of the marketing mix; little attention is paid to the wants and needs of consumers; and advertising is regarded with hostility."

It is now strongly held that the process of economic growth is one of increasing the size of the market. Narrowness of market, a general characteristic of developing economy, is in fact an impediment to economic growth. Mass production becomes possible only at a certain level of output for which larger markets are highly essential. The enlarged market not only reduces costs and avoids wastage but also facilitates the growth of communication, transport and other services.

Marketing cannot itself create purchasing power. But by converting the latent demand into effective-demand and by challenging all the purchasing power in the desired direction it promotes a high legal of economic activity. Thus, marketing has played a key role in bringing about economic and social changes in the developing countries. It contributes to higher living standards, promotes the development of entrepreneurs and makes the distribution system more productive and purposeful. As Kindelberger rightly puts it, in a developing economy, "even though the growth process is led by efficiency in production, however, the requirements of distribution are inescapable."

MARKETING IN INDIA

Developing Economy

Like other developing countries, marketing in India has been a neglected aspect of the economy. The reasons for the neglect of marketing in other developing countries are equally applicable to India.

Objective of Planning

India today, is undergoing a profound process of economic change and development According to the Government resolution of March 1950. Planning in India was intended: "To promote a rapid rise in the standard of living of the people by efficient exploitation of the resources of the country, increasing production and offering opportunities to all for employment in the service of community." Thus, the objective of economic planning in India primarily rests on the desire to improve the standards of living of her relative economic status in the world. In other words, the aim is to raise the national real income by efficient exploitation of the resources, increased production and accelerated tempo of economic activity in the country.

Three Five Year Plans

India has already completed three-five year plans. The First Plan concentrated on many projects and schemes and undertook to attain a modest average per capita income of 1.4 per cent. The Second Plan led to a clear and more comprehensive long-term approach to the problem of economic and industrial development. It aimed at a sizable increase of 20 per cent in national income, rapid industrialisation with particular emphasis on basic and heavy industries, a large expansion of employment opportunities, and finally at a reduction of inequalities of income and wealth and a more even distribution of powers. Tins was followed by the Third Plan which had more of less the same objective as of the Second Five-Year Plan, with additional emphasis on self-sufficiency. Fourth, Fifth and Sixth Plans have also strived to bring self-sufficiency and improve the standard of living of the masses. The market mechanism is to be improved, streamlined and rationalised in this context.

Industrial Revolution

Despite various adverse developments, during the last thirty years of planning India has made considerable progress in many directions. The beginning of industrial revolution has already been made. There is no doubt that the various developmental efforts undertaken through planning have introduced growth and dynamism into the economy.

Substantial progress has been made in a number of sectors. The rate of growth of key industrial sectors including machinery and metals has been more than 15 per cent per annum. Public Sector investment for industry and mining increased from ₹ 35 and ₹ 1,250 crore in the Third Plan. It is expected that this investment will go up to ₹ 55,000 crore by the end of the Seventh Plan. In the Private Sector, investment in industries increased from ₹ 233 crore in the First Plan to ₹ 1,050 crore in the Third Plan and will go up to ₹ 90,400 crore in the Seventh Plan. Import of many items including machine tools, sugar machinery, textile machinery, commercial vehicles and petroleum has been substantially reduced.

Thus, the role and functions of marketing in India have undergone a tremendous change in recent years. It is being rapidly transformed from an art based on mere experience into a profession based on a systematised body of knowledge. The blending and cross fertilisation of different disciplines have increased the value of marketing as a respectable field of study.

New Marketing Concept

The emergence of the new "Marketing Concept" has revolutionised the thinking of Indian executives towards marketing. Marketing is now viewed in a broad context composed of several other elements besides selling. Marketing means creation of customers and satisfaction of human needs of the society. Enlarged view of marketing has brought about several changes and broadened the responsibilities of the modern marketing manager who, in addition to discharging his traditional responsibilities, has to become more creative, knowledgeable and receptive to new ideas and development. It is gratifying to note a visible change in the attitudes and thinking of modern marketing executives in the corporate sector.

FUTURE OF THE MARKETING CONCEPT

The "consumer-orientation" concept has been severely criticised by many on the grounds that it has been "bankrupt" or has at least "faltered"—because the need for consumer protection from usurious high interests, deceptive packing, false and untrustworthy advertising, and other fraudulent promotional practices—is a clear proof of this. Further, air, water and land pollution provide another evidence of the failure of the concept. But the indications are that consumers, as hitherto, will be given due attention in future also and the balance between profit attainment and consumer satisfaction might swing more towards serving the consumer. This will involve greater marketing costs and high pay offs from questionable selling tactics will no longer exist. Martin Bell hopes that, "The marketing concept will go into a second formulation in which genuine consumer concern will replace customer orientation. Profit will no longer be the principle operational goal, nor will it be the sole criterion of effective marketing performance. Profit will be the reward for the skilful delivery of satisfaction....The need for integrated effort and the use of scientific methods of planning and problem solving will be even greater. The marketing concept very likely will be the way of business life for many years to come.[1]

Conditions of Implementation of the Marketing Concept

1. Favourable Management's Support: Regarding the management's support, an executive of the Chase Manhattan Bank (USA) has stated: "Marketing begins with top management. Only top management can provide the climate, the discipline and the

1. Bell, M.L., and C.W. Emory, "Faltering Marketing Concept", *Journal of Marketing*, October 1971, pp. 37-42.

leadership required for a successful marketing programme. Top management must know the customers and the prospects; it must set its objectives, establish the policies, develop the plans and create the organisation."[1] A favourable marketing climate should be created throughout the organisation. Written company policies will contribute to a general understanding and acceptable basic goals. Internal education programmes for company personnel will increase communication between management groups and the workforce. The area of the company should be studied to determine whether the work being done there takes into account customer needs.

2. Establishment of Information System: It consists in obtaining information about customers' needs and to use that information internally to create satisfying products.

3. Reorganisation of the Firm: In order to satisfy customer's objectives as well as its own, a firm must coordinate all activities.

4. Understanding of the Usefulness in Strategic Planning: Focus should be put on the benefits delivered by a product rather than its physical characteristics. Raymond Corey says that "A product is what it does", *i.e.*, when a housewife buys some food product, she buys not only nutrition but also convenience, affection, creativity and social approval. This is known as the generic product concept."

5. Adoption of a "Product Mix": In order to make a marketing programme successful, a company has to adopt a "marketing mix" suited to its customer's wants, competition, social and legal controls and other environmental factors/forces.

6. Definition of Marketing Responsibilities: Marketing research should underline almost every action taken by the firm. All proposals should be analysed in terms of their ultimate benefit to both the company and consumer. Research should also be used to determine how well new products are doing and how market-oriented each of the firm's activities is.

The pillars of the marketing concept are generic product definition, customer orientation, market information, market segmentation, integrated marketing, and long-term viewpoint.

---

1. "The Marketing Executive Industry: The New Crown Prince," *New Front*, August 1963, p. 30.

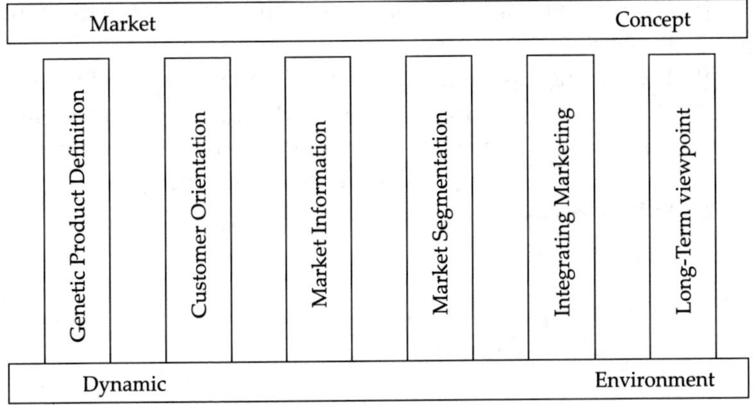

Fig. 2.2: Pillars of Marketing Concept (Frederick E., Webster, J.)

USE OF MARKETING CONCEPT

Marketing concept is now used more by consumer goods companies rather than by industrial goods firms, because consumer goods are needed by the people and the companies realise immediate gains by adopting consumer orientation. The concept is being adopted more by large companies than by the small ones, because large companies have more goods to sell.

QUESTIONS FOR EXERCISE

1. Explain the difference between Old and New Concept of Marketing.
2. Explain the factors responsible for the Growth of Modern Concept of Marketing.
3. Discuss main features and benefits of Modern Concept of Marketing.
4. Explain with special reference to Indian Economies why marketing has not been recognised so far in development economies.
5. Someone said, "Marketing begins with consumer and end's with consumer." Discuss.
6. A businessman recently said, "We are to produce what the people want, not what we can sell." Explain.
7. "Marketing should aim at meeting a given customer need rather than selling a given product." Comment.

8. "Consumer is king." Comment on the statement in the light of marketing concept.
9. Is consumer sovereignty a fact or fiction? Why so? Discuss.
10. Discuss in detail the meaning and importance of Modern Marketing Concept. In your opinion to what extent this concept can be applicable in India? Suggest your answer with reasons.

3

Marketing Organisation

An 'organisation' is the mechanism through which a managerial philosophy is translated into action. As philosophy changes, organisational goals are modified and basic changes made in the organisation itself. The Marketing Organisation establishes the authority relationships among marketing personnel and specialists who are responsible for making certain decisions and performing certain activities. 'File Marketing Organisation provides the vehicle for marketing decisions on products, marketing channels, physical distribution, promotion, and prices. It is the vehicle through which these decisions are implemented. In the words of Peter Drucker, "Organisation is not an end in itself, but means to the end of business results. Organisation structure is an indispensable means and a wrong structure will seriously impair business performance and may even destroy it. The structure must be so designed as to make it possible to attain the business objectives even five, ten and fifteen years hence."

Organisational Structure

'Operating under the marketing concept a large company must have some formal organisational structure. Companies may have the will and the desire to serve the customer, but all too often they are inadequately organised to do so. Proper organisation must result in a total integration and coordination of all factors that can influence the final sale.'[1] In the words of Cundiff and others, "There must be total integration and coordination of all corporate functions (marketing, research and development, manufacturing

1. Cascino, A.E., "Organisational Implications of the Marketing Concept" in Lazer, W. and E.J. Kelly (Ed), *Managerial Marketing Perspectives and Viewpoints*, 1962, p. 371.

and financial, etc.) into single operating system directed toward achieving company goals and at the same time, effectively serving the market and the changing wants and desires."[1] The modern thought is based upon a study of the organisation as an integrated whole. It is a "system" in which neither marketing nor any other organisational unit should dominate. All should be welded into an operating system whose components are important.

In his '*The Practice of Management*' Peter Drucker has said, "Organisation is not an end in itself, but a means to the end of business performance and business results." Organisation structure is an indispensable means for good business performance. It must be put up so as to make it possible to attain the business objectives even five, ten and fifteen years hence.

TYPES OF MARKETING ORGANISATION

In big organisations, there may be divisional type of structure with separate divisions,. Each division may have its own separate executive directors, marketing manager and officials with staff. For example, Tata's have separate division for Tata Iron and Steels, Tata Oils, Tata Timkine, etc. Marketing organisation may be: (*i*) Function-oriented; (*ii*) Product-oriented; (*iii*) Market-oriented; (*iv*) Customer-oriented marketing organisation; and (*v*) The combined type. Following is a description of these types:

1. Function-oriented: This is the most simple and common type of basic organisation structures of marketing tasks. Under this type, the activities are grouped on the basis of function such as production planning, marketing research, advertising and sales. There are four managers for separate functions like marketing, finance, production and personnel. Each of these functions is further subdivided into various sub-functions to be performed to attain the objectives of the main function. The marketing function may be sub-divided into subfunctions like product planning, marketing research, advertising, sales promotion, physical distribution and customer services, etc. The number of sub-functions varies from organisation to organisation taking

1. Cundiff, Edward, W., Richard, R. Still and Norman, A.P. Govani, *Fundamentals of Modern Marketing*, 1980, p. 29.

into account its nature, size and area of operation. Each sub-function, is delegated to a separate manager under the control of marketing manager and such managers are responsible to the marketing manager who reports to the higher executives.

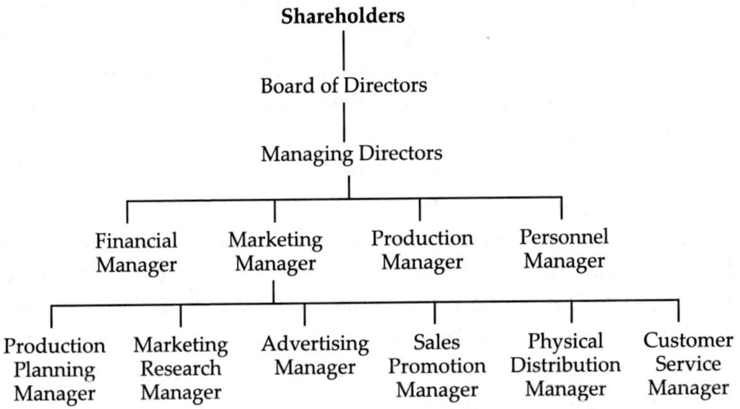

Fig. 3.1: Function-oriented Organisation

Advantages: (*i*) *Efficiency*: As the marketing function is divided into various sub-functions and each sub-function is performed under the supervision of an efficient manager, various activities are carried on efficiently.

(*ii*) *Elasticity*: As the sub-activities may further be divided with the increase in size of the organisation there is elasticity in the organisation.

Disadvantages: (*i*) *Limited Suitability*: This type of organisation is suitable only for small enterprises. As the firm grows in size, this type of structure will lose its importance.

(*ii*) *Difficult Task*: Sub-division of marketing function is a difficult task. Some activities cannot be associated with one type of sub-function or the other. Such activities are performed by more than one department. This duplication of work creates the problem of responsibility.

(*iii*) *Difficulty in Fixing Responsibility*: Marketing is an integrated function as the success of organisation depends very much on successful operation of all the sub-activities. It would be very difficult to fix the responsibility for the inefficiency.

2. Produet-oriented: Big companies as well as smaller concerns exist side by side in the field of production. The smaller companies have another popular form or structure which assigns to product managers or brand managers with the responsibility for marketing decisions of particular products or groups of products. Advertising, sales promotion, marketing research can be a centralised staff activity. As a little marketing manager the product manager takes and executes decisions regarding advertising and sales promotion after taking necessary suggestions from the advertising manager and the sales promotion manager respectively.

As there is a shift from a seller's to buyer's market in India, the importance of product management and the product manager is also growing. This type of structure enables concentration of attention on the performance of a particular brand. The product manager is specifically charged with planning regarding product.

Advantages: (*i*) *Multiple Products*: This type of structure is best suited to industries producing different products or brands.

(*ii*) *Control*: Every department can be controlled efficiently by the department incharge.

(*iii*) *Evaluation*: The performance of different departments may be evaluated and compared.

(*iv*) *Specialisation*: It stresses on specialisation and helps in increasing the efficiency of the personnel.

Disadvantages: (*i*) *Confusion*: The product manager is sometimes confused to be familiar with different jobs. His own background may be too limited to enable him to take the total marketing approach.

(*ii*) *Conflicts*: Conflicts may even develop with other line of activities.

(*iii*) *Limited Suitability:* It is only for medium sized industries producing different products or different brands of a product.

Product-oriented Structure

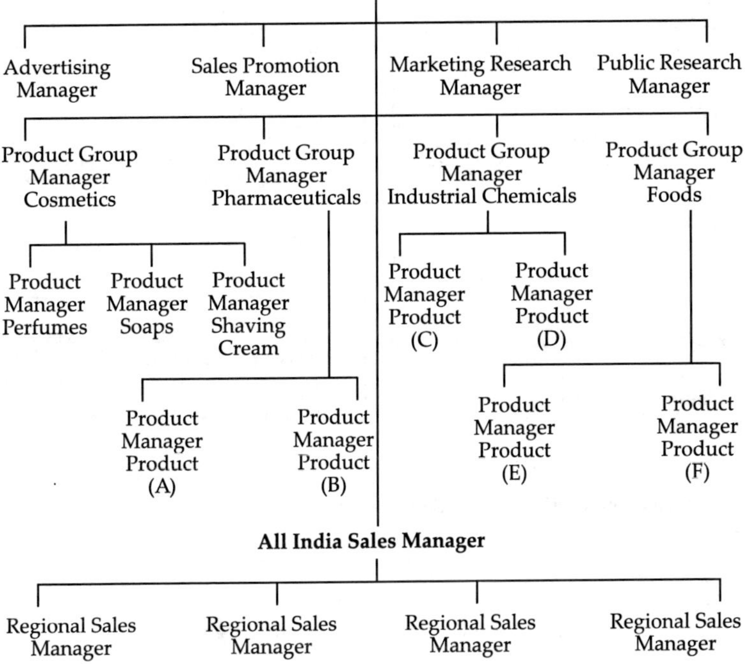

Fig. 3.2: Product-oriented Organisation.

3. Market-oriented: This type of structure is used by big companies who serve a large number of customers spread over very large territory. The structure is based on regional basis and specific areas are assigned to different persons. From the sales point of view the total area may be divided into four or more basic regions.

Each region is sub-divided under the Sales Supervisor. Their numbers depend upon the characteristics and requirements of the particular region. Each supervisor is given a number of salesmen under his direct control. Thus, the market is fragmented into sale territories which may be a district, division or region. This type of structure has the advantage that the regional manager and his staff become experts for the allotted regions about the customers. They are careful about the competitions that mark that area and so they act accordingly.

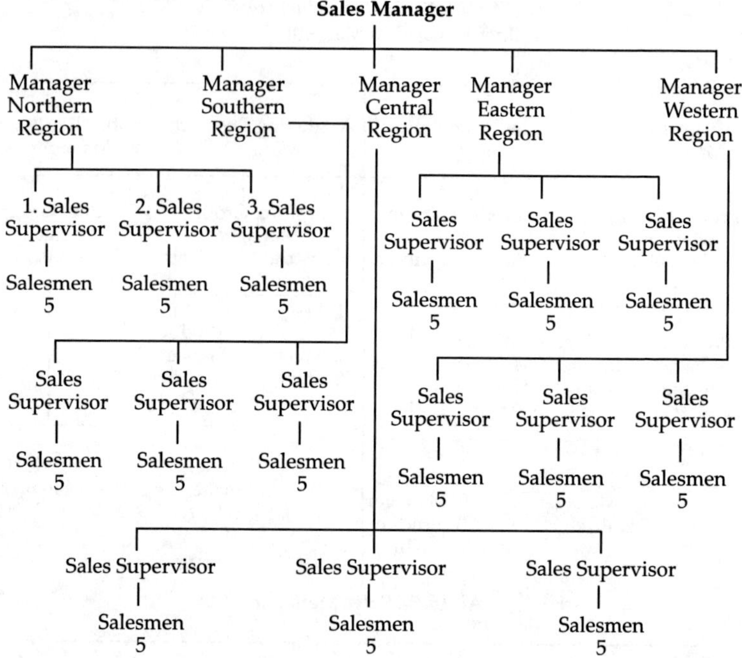

Fig. 3.3: Market-oriented Structural Organisation.

Advantages: (*i*) *Suitability*: This type of structure is suitable for big concerns having their sales-net throughout the country.

(*ii*) *Elasticity*: There is much elasticity under this structure. As the size of business grows, it facilitates better control.

(*iii*) *Functional*: It enjoys all the advantages of functional type organisation.

(*iv*) *Customer Research*: An organisation is in touch with the customers. It comes to know the changing habits, fashion and needs of the customers of every region and therefore can make necessary change in its product within short span of time.

(*v*) *Responsibility*: Responsibility can be fixed easily for any lapse.

Disadvantages: (*i*) *Expensive*: It is not fit for small organisations, as being too expensive.

(*ii*) *No Integrated Policy*: Each territorial division has its separate entity for marketing the product in that area. The organisational policies for each region are different taking into account the nature of customers of the area. Therefore, it is very difficult to formulate or follow an integrated policy for all the regions.

4. Customer-oriented: Under this type of organisation structure, concentration is on the types of customers. Separate groups are designated responsible for marketing programmes for their different classes of customers such as: (*a*) distributors, (*b*) retailers, and (*c*) customers. Sales managers are appointed for different classes of customers.

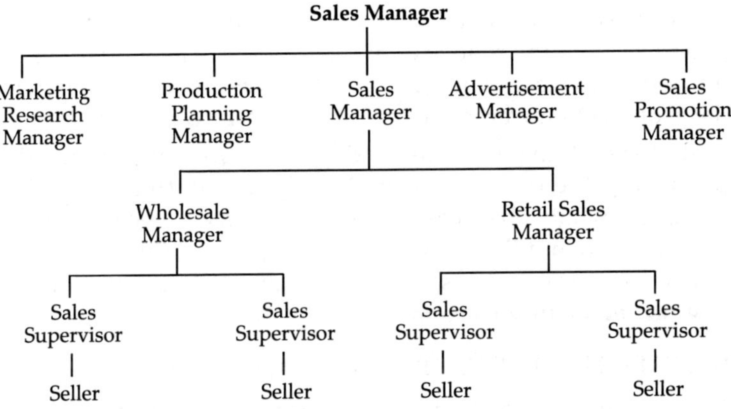

Fig. 3.4: Customer-oriented Organisation Structure.

Advantages: (*i*) *Attention to customers*: Under this type of organisation, full attention can be paid to each class of customers and their problems can be well understood by the organisation.

(*ii*) *Correct Estimates*: As an organisation comes in contact with the customers regularly, it is easier to estimate their demands and satisfy them.

Disadvantages: Although customer satisfaction is the main aim of the structure but, it is suitable in those organisations only where the nature of customers is different.

5. Combined Type: The four types discussed above are basic concepts regarding organisation structures. Any structure in its original form is rarely found in an organisation. In practice, one normally comes across a combination such as; (*i*) Functional structure with territorial structure; or (*ii*) Functional structure with the product-oriented structure; or (*iii*) Market-oriented structure with the product structure.

CHARACTERISTICS OF A GOOD MARKETING ORGANISATION

(*i*) It should be flexible so that we may use any of the organisation structure.

(*ii*) It must give possible future growth and an acceptable philosophy to the whole concern.

(*iii*) Personnel in a marketing department must be willing to take various job assignments.

(*iv*) Connected with the problem of flexibility is the growth potential. With the change of market positions new products are introduced in place of old ones. So, the provisions are required for the growth of new products and segments in concerns in future.

(*v*) In the end, there should be a central philosophy or tradition prevailing in the concern that should be intimated to all. This forms the whole objective of the marketing. Some concerns pay more heed to middle and lower income groups. In this way while policies and programmes change, the central philosophy remains as guide to the future action.

SUITABILITY OF THE ORGANISATION STRUCTURE

1. The Function-oriented Organisation Structure: It is suitable for small enterprises which produces only one type of product.

2. The Product or the Market-oriented Organisation Structure: It is suitable for a big concern having its sales-net throughout the country because due attention is paid under these two structures on each product and in all the territories.

3. The Customer-oriented Organisation Structure: It is suited best to the organisations having different types of customers and where different marketing policies are followed for different class of customers.

QUESTIONS FOR EXERCISE

1. Discuss the bases upon which a marketing organisational structure can be built. Describe the factors which should be taken into account while designing the marketing organisation.
2. "A variety of organisational structure exists for the management of marketing efforts." Explain these structures.

3. Describe the various types of marketing organisation structure. Under what situation each organisation structure would be most suitable?
4. Explain which of the structures you would select for the company? Bring out the relative merits and demerits of the different types of organisational structure from which you have selected the one, you feel best for the company.

4

The Marketing System and Marketing Process

According to Kotler, "A firm's marketing system is the set of significant institutions and flows that connect an organisation to its market,"[1]Stanton points out that "marketing system consists of two interacting elements—the marketing organisation and its target market. These two elements are connected by two sets of flows....one, the distribution of product/service to its customers in exchange for some kind of payment, and the other flow is an information flow from the market to the organisation."[2]

The marketing system of a highly developed country may be a huge, complex network of marketing organisations and facilities engaged in developing, promoting and distributing of goods and services worth millions of dollars. The marketing job is generally performed by a vast army of sales force including a large number of intermediaries and use of different channels of distribution, communication and promotion of the needed goods and services.

ELEMENTS OF MARKETING SYSTEM

1. *Kotler's view*: "(*i*) The core marketing system consisting of a set of suppliers whose heterogeneous inputs are transformed by a company and its competitors into valued outputs that pass through marketing intermediaries to reach the final market.

(*ii*) An environment of several public institutions which individually and collectively affect the performance of the core marketing system. These include the financial community, independent press, government agencies and legislators, interest groups, and the general public.

1. Kotler, Philip, *Marketing Management, Analysis Planning and Control*, 1976, p. 21.
2. Stanton, W.J., *op. cit.*, p. 19.

(*iii*) Forces in macro-environment, such as demography, economic, legal and political conditions, technology and culture, etc. that exercise a profound influence on the core marketing system directly and through the various public institutions."[1]

2. *Stanton's view*: Stanton includes the following "interacting, or interdependent group of items" in marketing systems:[2]

(*i*) Organisation doing the marketing job;

(*ii*) Product, service, idea, or person being marketed;

(*iii*) Target market;

(*iv*) Intermediaries helping in the exchange (the flow) between marketing organisation and its market; and

(*v*) Environment constraints—demographic factors, economic conditions, social and cultural forces, political and legal forces, technology and competition.

He says, "These elements in marketing system are like the components of a stereo system. They do very little separately. But when properly connected, they can fill the air with beautiful music, *i.e.*, synergism."[3]

3. *Views of Berenson and Henry*:[4] 1. The organisation—*i.e.*, any company or firm seeking want satisfaction through exchange—individual producer, large or small scale manufacturer, department store chain or any group set up for achieving a particular objective.

2. All business or marketing institutions engaged in performing marketing activities, *i.e.*, wholesalers, retailers, transport agencies, financial institutions, etc.

3. Marketing channels or channels of distribution.

4. Consumers or customers or target market, whose needs are to be satisfied.

5. Products—Goods and Services, which are produced by the organisation.

6. Marketing Tasks/Functions performed by the marketing system.

7. The marketing environment, *i.e.*, the uncontrollable and controllable forces influencing marketing activities.

8. Non-marketing resources and Marketing Mix, which constitute the core of a company's marketing system.

---

1. Kotler, Philip, *op. cit.*, p. 22.
2. Stanton, W.J., *op. cit.*, p. 19
3. *Ibid.*, p. 20.
4. Berenson, Conrad and Elibert, Henry, *The Social Dynamics of Marketing*, Random House, New York, 1978, p. 4.

APPLICATION OF THE MARKETING SYSTEMS CONCEPT

Marketing systems approach is being applied increasingly in practically every big marketing organisation in its marketing programmes. Symbolic models have been built to describe quantity and evaluate alternative marketing programmes. It was first introduced in the management of physical distribution sub-systems. Later on, the concept began to be applied to such activities as transportation, warehousing and inventory control. By understanding that consumers buy need satisfaction through benefits a product offers, the company can advantageously adopt the systems approach in the product management to develop and market and a related assortment of benefits rather than only some product. The approach is also used in Marketing Information System.

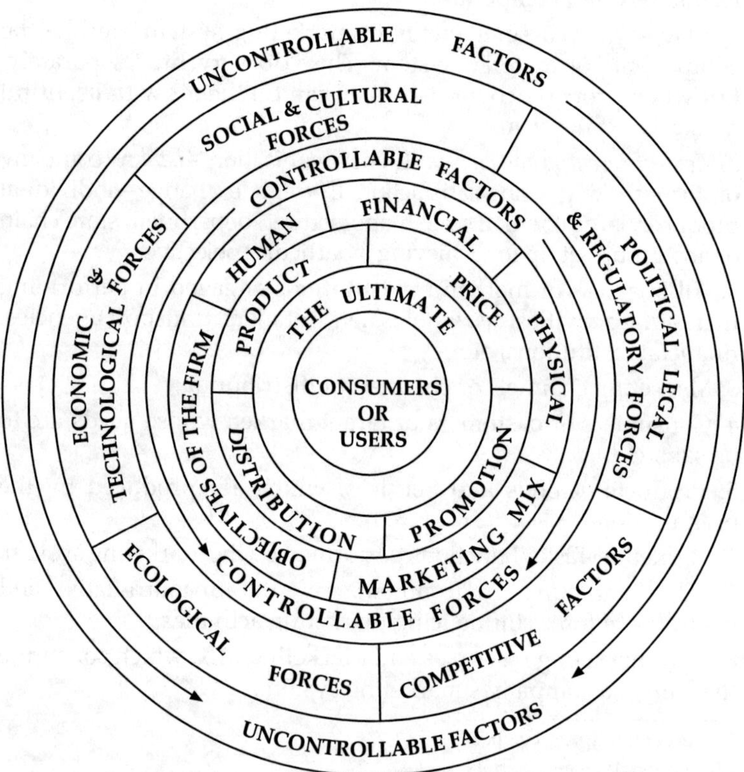

Fig. 4.1: The Total Marketing System

Benefits and Problems of the Systems Approach

About the benefits of systems approach. Lee Adler has observed. "It is a methodical approach to problem solving that considers all aspects of a problem. It coordinates all marketing tools, and it offers greater efficiency and economy in marketing operations. Impending problems can be identified sooner because management can better understand the complex interplay of all the factors and flows. The results can be evaluated quantitatively. Many elements in marketing lend themselves to computer based analysis, so that the complex data, involving many variables, can be processed quickly by the management."

However, Adler is of the view that since the systems approach is still sufficiently new in marketing, it suffers from certain problems such as: (*i*) it can take considerable time, and money to implement; (*ii*) in marketing one must deal with social and psychological considerations that affect the behaviour of people; (*iii*) many marketing people are more like artists than scientists, who prefer to use intuition or hunches. They often resist the fact based research, written plans, and other rigidities that are so much a part of the systems approach.[1]

According to Kotler, "Marketing environment is the totality of forces and entities that surround and potentially affect the marketing of particular product".[2] According to him, this marketing environment is composed of four layers,[3] *i.e.*,

(*a*) *organisational environment,* which includes company department, company division, its organisational structure and company channels.

(*b*) *Market environment,* which consists of all actual and potential consumers or purchasers of the product. This includes the number of buyers, their purchasing power, their needs and wants and their buying habits.

(*c*) *Macro-environment,* which consists of the relevant forces and institutions that affect transactions between the firm and the markets. This includes the economic, political and legal forces, social and ethical influences, technology and culture.

---

1. Adler Lee, "Systems Approach to Marketing, *Harvard Business Review,* May-June 1967, p. 105-118.
2. Kotler, Philip, *op. cit.,* 1972 ed., p. 52.
3. *Ibid.*

(*d*) *Extra-environment,* which forms that part of the environment which the organisation usually does not scan because it seems to be of "negligible or zero relevance to the organisation."

MARKETING PROCESS

According to Clark, "The marketing machinery of today involves three major processes: The concentration, dispersion and equalisation of goods." Thus, marketer is a marketing researcher, inventor, psychologist, sociologist, economist, communicator and lawyer all rolled into one as pleaded by Philip Kotler. Marketing is the managerial process by which products are matched with markets and through which ownership transfers are effected. In the beginning human wants were few and the method of production and marketing was also very simple. There was direct relation between the producer and the consumer. The producer recognised his customers. The consumers also knew the producer from close quarters. The invention of money, improvement in transport facilities, warehousing, specialisation and division of labour, use of new production techniques and the use of power have all brought about a revolution in the fields of exchange in the marketing. Today marketing activities are not direct from the producer to the consumers but products reach the hands of the consumers through various intervening agencies. These marketing proceses are divided into many sub-processes which are more in number and complex in nature than before.

Division of Marketing Process

Clark had divided the modern marketing process into three broad divisions:

(*i*) Concentration,

(*ii*) Dispersion, and

(*iii*) Equalisation.

1. Concentration: In the words of Pyle, "We may think of concentration as that activity in which goods flow from many producers toward a central point of market." In a highly developed and complex economy most of the customers are located thousands of miles away and products must be transported to be accessible to them. In developed countries such as in the United States most manufacturers produce in anticipation of market demand and hold inventories until orders are received and supplied. As countries develop and multinational trade increases both storage and transportation as well as inventory management and the processing and handling of customer's order increase in importance.

Storage is necessary in our complex economic system as products are generally produced in anticipation of market demand. Manufacturers, wholesalers and retailers all hold inventories. When consumers make purchases from retail outlets, retailers inventories are reduced and are replenished from wholesalers. Similarly the consumer's own supply of products is reduced by his own consumption and replenished by his purchases. Stock levels fluctuate all along the line of distribution when a product is purchased at the retail level.

Following are reasons for holding products in storage:

(*i*) *To even out the seasonal factor in production and in sales*: A manufacturer of Christmas ornaments has a market for its products only during the immediate pre-Christmas period, but its costs are lower if production is carried on throughout the year; so he stores its output from one selling season to the next.

(*ii*) *To obtain economies other than business operations*: Manufacturers making products in a large number of sizes such as nuts and bolts use the same machines to produce different sizes. It is often more economical to schedule long production sums of several weeks supply of particular sizes rather than making the total needs of each size weekly.

(*iii*) *To improve their, quality and value*: Products such as cheese, tobacco, rice and wine must be aged or conditioned to improve their flavour and hence to increase their value.

Concentration activity involves purchasing, storage, grading, transportation, financing and risk bearing. In India this activity is now undertaken by the government in case of grains, sugar, rice, coal, etc.

2. Dispersion: The main object of marketing is to take the products to the consumers. Concentration is a step towards that end. Transportation is a necessary and important marketing activity. Markets are separated geographically from production areas. Many things are deliberately located away from populated areas to avoid traffic congestion, health hazards and high costs. Dispersion is meant to carry raw materials to the producers and finished products from the producers to the consumers. It is done by the wholesalers who first store the goods and then sell to the retailers in small quantities. Distribution involves many other supporting activities such as sale, storage, classification and gradation, transportation, financing and risk bearing.

In India the government has also undertaken the distribution activity of certain goods. The State Trading Corporation of India is responsible for the distribution of grains, rice, oil, coal, etc. Some large scale producing companies have also undertaken the work of distribution in their hands.

3. Equalisation: According to Clark and Clark, "Between these processes of concentration and dispersion occurs the activity which we call 'Equalisation'. Equalisation consists of adjustment of supply to demand on the basis of time, quantity and quality." This equalisation is the process of making available the goods in a particular place or market just in accordance to the actual demand so that the chances of loss might be minimised. It is the process of adjustment of supply to the actual demand of a particular place.

After concentration the right kind of goods in right quantity are taken to a particular market according to the demand. If the equilibrium between the supply and demand is diminished, it may cause heavy loss either to the suppliers or to buyers. It may also go against the interests of the consumers who might not get the right type of product in stipulated quantity. Thus, the very objective of marketing is forfeited. It is, therefore, expedient that proper coordination is maintained between concentration and dispersion. Only then equalisation will be ensured.

The above-mentioned three processes of marketing go on simultaneously. The wholesalers procure products from the producers and make available these goods to the retailers on the different markets according to their requirements. In their activity of dispersion they look to the equalisation. Therefore, Clark rightly calls concentration, dispersion and equalisation as the heart of marketing process.

IDENTIFICATION OF MARKETING ACTIVITIES

To identify marketing activities is not so simple as it looks as it is complicated with difficulties met in determining just where marketing commences and where it ends. The marketing process begins and ends with the final buyer, with information flowing back to the producer and products flowing forward to the final buyer. The marketing activities most easily identified are those concerned with bringing products into contact with markets. It is not so easy to identify a marketing activity. The buying of goods for resale is one of the retailer's most important work. To sell goods to the consumers he must buy them according to consumer's needs and wants. His buying decision is influenced by the effect his purchase has on his product's marketability.

Although planning and designing the product may not look like marketing activities, products should possess those characteristics that final buyers want and desire. These wants and desires must be discovered in an early stage of product development otherwise the product is doomed to fail in the market.

Marketers try to move products and services into the hands of final buyers but it does not follow that all marketing stops there. Storage is generally classified as a marketing activity. Potatoes and onions are produced seasonally and stored by marketing concerns till the end of the year. But at times, individual consumers take over part of storage activity—they may purchase sufficient quantity of these things to start in their homes.

ACTIVITIES CLASSIFIED AS MARKETING

Merchandising Activities

It is necessary to determine and meet the various market needs in terms of products and to stimulate market demands.

1. Product Planning and Development: Product adjustment to the buyers needs is essential for successful marketing. In most industries they try to improve the products commencing from the changing technology. Shifts in buyer's expectations create extant product going out of use. Growing recognition of the importance of satisfying buyer's wants and preferences is responsible for making the marketing planning and development-oriented. Non-innovating concerns face gradual elimination from the market. Therefore, product planning and development are being regarded crucial in marketing management.

2. Standardising and Grading: A standard shows what basic quantities or characteristics a product must have to be designated by certain grades. These standards should be based on qualities desired by the buyers or on the use to which the article is to be put. Grading is the act of separating or inspecting the goods according to the established specifications including size, weight or quality.

Standardising and grading are very important for efficient marketing. Both these make it possible for customers to purchase by description instead of by inspection.

3. Buying and Assembling: Assembling means bringing together of: (*i*) different quantities of a wide variety of items for resale by a simple concern, or (*ii*) a large quantity of similar items of resale in a particular region. The first kind of assembling is done by the retailers like departmental stores and superbazaars. The second kind of assembling is done by the wholesalers.

Successful buying needs an ability to estimate customer's needs weeks and even months in advance. When the retailers order goods that will be delivered and placed on sale three or four months later, it is an act of anticipating what consumers will purchase in the future. It is important to know customers' needs and buying habits to predict their buying actions.

4. Selling: Selling is not only transfer of ownership. It has the purpose of identifying prospective customers stimulating demand and providing information and service to buyers. For it the marketer must combine such activities like personal selling, advertising, sales promotion, packaging and customer service. A blend of selling activities coordinated into a sales programme is called a promotional mix. Great skill is needed in planning an optimum promotional mix and coordinating the different selling activities.

(B) Physical Distribution Activities

Under physical distribution activities come the store and transportation. These are necessary to move products from their places of production to their places of consumption. Manufacturers produce in anticipation of market demand.

1. Storage: In the present complex economic system in which products are generally produced before market demand, storage becomes very important. Manufacturers, wholesalers, retailers all hold inventories and manage them. Marketers hold products in storage for seasonal factor, economies in other business operations and improvement of the quality and value.

2. Transportation: Transportation is necessary and important because most of the markets are geographically separated from production areas to avoid population and traffic congestion and high land costs.

(C) Supporting Marketing Activities

Under this head are included Marketing financing; Marketing risk bearing; and Obtaining and analysing marketing information. All these activities support or contribute to the carrying out of other marketing activities.

1. Marketing Financing: Marketers do the work of receivers and sources of credit. As receivers, they utilise short-term financing to tide their operations over seasonal peaks that require additional inventory investments and higher promotional expenses. Most middlemen and many manufacturers finance seasonal variations in expenses through credit. There are two main sources of credit: trade credit, and banks. In short-term financing, trade credit is extended by suppliers. Manufacturers offer their customers credit terms allowing them three to four months to pay. Trade credit tends to be expensive when interest is charged on overdue balance. In recent times instalment credit has become very popular. The system has given more to the development of mass markets.

2. Market Risk Bearing: Some risk is inevitable from both supply and demand variations and natural calamities. The marketers who do the storage activity have to do financing as well as risk bearing. Marketing institutions decide the appropriate size of inventories. There is always risk that an inventory will not be sold if it proves too large, relative to market demand. Risks attached to natural hazards like fire and floods, deterioration of products in storage and damage in transit can often be transferred to insurance companies who are prepared to cover the risks in return for premium payments. But some risks cannot be transferred. Risks of changes in market demand are lessened through accurate sales forecasting and marketing research.

3. Obtaining and Analysing Marketing Information: The success of marketing operations depends largely upon management's knowledge and appraisal of information as the size, location and characteristics of different markets, the nature of present and future customers and their buying habits and preferences, competitors strength; and plan and trends in market supply and demand. Marketing information is gathered in different ways. Marketing Research methods are used in getting information sources outside the company. Economic and business forecasting techniques are used to get important information on future market conditions.

DIFFICULTIES IN CLASSIFICATION OF MARKETING ACTIVITIES

A systematic division of marketing activities helps in studying marketing problems. But no such classification scheme is applicable universally. Packaging and advertising may be of greatest importance for some industries like cosmetic, so much so that they deserve separate classification.

Each company has its own individualised set of concerns. Marketing aims and the list of marketing activities is simply a classification of those needful to secure the aims. That is the significance of classifying activities done under various circumstances, if the numbers and kinds of marketing activities change with the marketers product or distribution method unlike manufacturers. The farmers unlike manufactures cannot alter the design of their products. They have little practical interest in product design. In spite of variances of this kind there are enough goals and activities to justify generalisation about the marketing activities.

PERFORMANCE OF MARKETING ACTIVITIES AND MARKETING EFFICIENCY

Repetition in performance of marketing activities is a sign of efficiency. No doubt, some activities are done at each distribution level. Buying and selling, for example, may be done several times since each middleman interposed between producer and final buyer, customarily both buys and sells. Marketing costs could be reduced through eliminating certain middlemen.

An efficient marketing system would stress direct sales by producers to final users. It is the most efficient marketing system in the case of some industrial products. But under some circumstances it may not prove very efficient and even may not be possible at all. As manufactured products such as soap and toothpaste are produced mainly by a few large companies, their direct sale is impracticable as consumers buy these products in small quantities so that the amount of money got from each transaction would not be enough to cover the costs of reaching the customer. Direct distribution of onions and oranges by many thousands of grocers would not only be prohibitively expensive but greatly inconvenient for consumers most of whom prefer to buy serveral food items in bulk and at a time most convenient to them. Thus, marketing channels for such products are necessarily complex and long. Individual marketing activities must be performed respectively as products move from products and manufacturers to final buyers. At each distribution level, these activities are done in specialised ways. Under these conditions shortening of the marketing channel, often results in increased costs and reduced efficiency.

Marketing efficiency results from finding the optimum division of responsibility among the institutions doing the activities at different distribution levels. The question is, therefore, not which activities have to be done, but rather which combination of marketing institutions can do them most efficiently.

MARKETING FINANCING

Both as receivers and sources of credit, marketers are concerned with financing. As receivers they sometimes use short-term financing to tide their operation over seasonal peaks that require additional inventory investments and higher promotional expenses. For instance many retailers increase their inventories 50 to 60 per cent before Diwali, Holi and also increase their sales forces and advertising outlays accordingly. If permanent capital investments were kept at a level high enough to meet these seasonal needs, much money would lie unproductive in the rest of the year. Therefore, most businessmen finance seasonal variations in marketing expenses through credit.

Trade Credit

Trade credit plays an important role in short-term financing. Manufacturers and middlemen offer their customers credit terms allowing them one to four months to pay. But when interest instalment credit is charged on over due balances, trade credit is more expensive.

Instalment Credit

Instalment credit has now become very popular. T.V. sets, fridges, coolers, furniture, automobiles, etc. are sold on instalment plan. Instalment credit has contributed significantly to the developmental stores and retailers use credit as a means of attracting patronage. At the wholesale level most transactions are on credit basis.

Marketing Risk Bearing

Marketing risks arise from both supply and demand changes and natural hazards. Any institution that carries on inventory takes the risks that supply and demand conditions may change. Thus, marketers who perform the storage activity also perform not only financing but risk bearing. Most marketing institutions have the problem of deciding on the proper size of inventories. There is always risk that an inventory will not be sold if it proves too large relative to market demand. But there is also the risk that if it proves too small, orders will be lost because they cannot be executed.

Risk Transfer

1. Total Transfer: A market may transfer part of its risk burden eliminating some risks and converting others from unpredictable amounts of potential loss to known items of expense. For example, when a seller agrees to reimburse a buyer for any drop in a product's price that may occur within a given period, the buyer succeeds in transferring the entire risk of a price decline during the period to the seller.

2. Hedging: Hedging provides another way to transfer the risks of price changes in a limited number of items traded on organised commodity exchanges. Hedging is a procedure involving simultaneous sales in the future market when purchases are made in the current (spot) market and simultaneous purchase in the future market when sales are made in the current market so that gains or losses or current transactions are approximately balanced off against the opposite experience in the future market.

3. Insurance: Risks attached to such current hazards as fire and floods, deterioration of products in storage and damage in transit can often be transferred to institutions that specialised in assuming such risks. Insurance companies cover all these risks in return for premium payments. When risks are transferred in this way, unpredictable amounts of potential loss become known amounts of expense.

4. Risk Reduction: As many marketing risks cannot be transferred, marketers concentrate on trying to reduce them as far as possible. Risks of changes in market demand are reduced through accurate sales forecasting and marketing research. Available techniques for market measurement are by no means foolproof. A well considered sales forecast can help reduce the margin of error in deciding in inventory size. Risk of a change in market demand is reduced also through aggressive programme of advertising, personal selling and the like. Reasonable accurate sales forecasting also help in reducing the supply risk of being out of stock and unable to fill customer's orders.

5. Product Differentiation: Other risks involved in changing supply conditions such as risk that supply will cause competitors to cut prices may be partially offset by differentiating products so that customers will be reluctant to accept substitutes. A market gains control over the supply to the extent that product differentiation succeeds in building customer loyalty. Its customers will not switch to substitutes supply because of small price differentials. In a limited sense, the marketer gains a degree of monopoly control over the risks of price competition, it does not eliminate it. Few marketers ever succeed in completely differentiating their products.

QUESTIONS FOR EXERCISE

1. "Concentration, Dispersion, and Equalisation are the heart of marketing. It is the need for the performance of these operations that makes marketing necessary"—(Clark). Discuss.
2. "Identification of marketing activities is sometimes a complicated matter." Explain.
3. Explain why no universal general scheme for classifying marketing activities exist? Discuss the relationship of the performance of marketing activities to marketing efficiency.
4. Assess the role of marketing financing.
5. Marketing attempts to reduce marketing risks that cannot be transferred by a variety of means. Explain.

5

Marketing Planning

According to the American Marketing Association, "Marketing planning is the work of setting up objectives for marketing activity and of determining and scheduling the steps necessary to achieve such objectives" Marketing planning is a part of overall managerial planning that decides future actions and plans for marketing functions in the present. Policies and programmes are prepared in advance for carrying out the functions and activities of marketing in order to attain the marketing aims. The marketing planning involves the setting up marketing objectives, marketing activities like purchase-sale, produce planning and development, advertisement, sale-promotion, after sale services, etc. These are determined and scheduled, along with policies and porgrammes to carry out planned activities.

Marketing planning is carried on by the Marketing department. Under the marketing department various sub-divisions or sections submit their proposals while the department prepares the plan for the whole marketing division.

DEFINITION OF PLANNING

1. *William H. Newman*: "Generally speaking, planning is deciding in advance what is to be done."

2. *Philip Kotler*: "Planning is deciding in the present what to do in future. It comprises both the determination of a desired future and the necessary steps to bring about. It is the process whereby companies reconcile their resources with their objectives and opportunities."

3. *ME. Herley*: "Planning is deciding in advance what is to be done. It involves the selection of objectives, policies and procedures and programmes from among alternatives."

4. *Louis A. Allen*: "Management Planning involves the development of forecasts, objectives, policies, programmes, procedures, schedules and budgets."

From the above definitions it follows chat planning is an important activity of management. All firms carry out some planning, such as the preparation of annual budget, the determination of next year's advertising programme, decision of new capital investments and financial borrowings, etc. In all such cases the firm decides now how it will use its resources in the future—men, materials, machinery and money.

VARIATIONS IN PLANNING

Firms vary considerably in their planning. While some firms give little time to planning, other firms pay more attention to planning. Plans are prepared by different departments. These are carefully considered by planning experts and then an overall plan is evolved for the firm. Some firms consider formal planning as the key to corporate survival in the world of rapid social change and keen competition. In the absence of formal planning firms fail to make the best use of their opportunities and resources. However, rigid planning is looked upon with some suspicion. Though "pluck and luck" count for more than careful planning, yet planning does yield positive benefits.

ELEMENTS OF MARKETING PLANNING

Marketing Planning involves the development of forecasts, objective policies, programmes and procedures. Thus, the main elements of marketing planning are: 1. Objectives; 2. Forecasts; 3. Policies; 4. Procedures; 5. Programmes; 6. Schedules; and 7. Budget.

1. Objectives: Setting up of objectives is the first step of planning. It is the responsibility of the marketing executive not only to set the objectives but also to explain them very clearly to the members of his staff and inspire them to achieve those objectives. For example, the marketing executive should fix the objective in respect of the volume of sale and then prepare the programme to achieve that objective. The objectives must be certain and clearly defined to the staff. Long Range Planning involves developing the basic objectives and strategy to guide future company efforts. Planning provides the framework within which the company plans are prepared. It may involve a time horizon of two or more years.

2. Forecasts: Forecasting is an art of drawing conclusions about the future. Modern marketing requires a lot of accurate information, which is the basis of forecasts for future. Marketing planning is based on forecasts for the future. Forecast gives an idea of the possible risks so that the firm gets prepared to meet any eventuality. Promotional strategy depends on the accurate forecasts. On the basis of the forecasts the marketing manager may know the areas where the sale targets are not achieved and where more and fresh efforts are needed. Forecast helps in taking right decisions at the appropriate time so that the chances of loss are minimised. It also helps to take specific action where the sales are declining.

3. Policies: Policies are the guidelines for achieving the set objectives of the firm. They guide the managers, administrators and the subordinates of the company as what is to be done in a particular situation. Policies are the basic principles through which the objectives are attempted to be achieved. Policies set the path to achieve the overall goals of the firm. Policies may be of the following three types:

(*i*) *Basic Policies*: These guide the top management.

(*ii*) *Common Policies*: These guide the middle and lower rank managers.

(*iii*) *Departmental Policies*: These are meant to serve as guidelines to departmental heads,

4. Procedure: Procedures are laid down to serve as guidelines to the actual marketing activity. Once it is laid down, the procedure serves to carry out the programmes of the company. It helps in taking correct decision in keeping with the overall objectives and in proper coordination of departmental relations.

5. Programme: A special kind of planning programme helps the solution of some problems. It is chalked out in keeping with the policies, procedures and objectives of the firm. It may be for long term planning or annual planning. It may be in relation to a particular area or the whole of region. It may be in connection with advertising, promotion of sale, etc. It affects the working of the whole venture and its activities. Therefore, it should be chalked out most carefully.

6. Schedule: Schedule shows the time and period when a particular activity has to be undertaken. It sets the procedure to be followed in carrying out an activity. In the field of marketing when advertising and sales promotion programmes have to be applied, the schedule shows the actual time of starting a particular programme in order to achieve the overall objectives of the firms.

7. Budget: An important part of planning indicates the financial aspect of the marketing operations. Companies use various methods to assign sales goals and budgets to their territories. In allocating marketing budgets to territories company practices are far better in case of large and small porgressive companies.

By comparing the actual progress with the budgeted progress the management can know in which fields the objectives have not been attained and who should be held responsible for it and what have been the causes responsible for the shortcomings. Thus, the budget helps in the control of marketing operations. Different budgets are prepared for each marketing activity.

SCOPE OF MARKETING PLANNING ACTIVITIES

The activities of marketing planning include two divisions according to time—1. Long-term Marketing Planning; and 2. Short-term or annual Marketing Planning.

1. Long-term Planning: It involves developing the basic objectives and strategy to guide future company efforts. It provides the framework within which the other plans of the company are prepared. It may involve a time horizon of two or more years, although it uses even a longer horizon of five to twenty years. It is done by the top management with the help of specialised planning authorities.

Long-term Marketing Planning Process

Philip Kotler had pointed out that the following situations should be considered while preparing long-term marketing plan:

(*i*) *Diagnosis:* The planning process starts with an attempt by the company to size up the present market situation and the factors responsible for it. This is diagnosis which consists of where the company stands and why. It requires developing data on absolute levels of company sales and market shares and their recent trends, by product, territory and other breakdowns. Supplementary data on marketing costs, plant utilisation, profit levels and other variables are also required. Plans must be taken to make a careful analysis of the recent trends instead of relying simply on impressions.

(*ii*) *Prognosis*: In prognosis the company estimates where it is likely to go if present market trend continues, what sales and profits can the company make in the long period. A systematic sales and profit prognosis consists of five steps:

(*a*) Projection of industry sales over the planning period;

(*b*) Forecast of company sales;

(*c*) Forecast of company revenues, costs and profits;

(*d*) Forecast of investment; and

(*e*) Forecast of rate of return on the investment (R.I.O.)

Prognosis shows that if the company's future is bright, its present policies should be continued. On the other hand if the future is dark and doubtful the planning needs modification so that the objectives may be achieved.

(*iii*) *Objectives*: If the prognosis indicates that the company has no future, the company should decide upon fresh objectives about the amount of sales and profits in the changed circumstances.

(*iv*) *Strategy*: It lays down the broad principles by which the company hopes to secure an advantage over competitors, an attractiveness to buyers and a full exploitation of company's resources. Marketing strategy involves the following steps:

(*a*) To develop the highest quality product possible.

(*b*) To charge a premium price.

(*c*) To advertise more heavily than competitors.

(*d*) To use salesmen who feel and exhibit a missionary drive.

The company should carefully study several alternatives of the strategy and choose the best possible alternative strategy under the circumstances.

(*v*) *Tactics*: These suggest how to use the company's strategies to achieve its objectives. Thus, tactics are the methods for carrying out the strategies. Distinguishing objectives, strategies, and tactics Philip Kotler says, "The objectives of a company indicate where it wants to be, the strategy indicates the intended route; the tactics indicate the particular vehicles it will use." Although tactical decisions are not primary, they are nevertheless very important.

(*vi*) *Control*: Long range plan represents the best vision of management at the time of planning of a proper set of objectives, strategies and tactics. It is based on a detailed set of assumptions and expectations whose validity will be revealed in due course of time. New events will occur that challenges some of the basic assumptions in the plan. This means two things. Firstly, the plan must include a control section which specifies the type of monitoring that will go on to check the plan's effectiveness. Secondly, the company might prepare one or more contingency plans to meet new challenges. The control section of a long range plan should contain performance target which should be checked periodically. If at any stage the variations are not favourable the underlying causes are discovered and then changes are introduced to remedy the shortfalls.

2. Short-term or Annual Marketing Planning: Each year companies prepare annual plan. The annual plan is developed in the context of the company's long range plan. Short range plan is not possible where the company has no long range plan. If the short range plans are not to be chaotic series of expedient solution to short run crisis, a long range plan is necessary. Sometimes annual plans only reflect over reactions to previous year's result and next year's problems rather than the progressive implementations of long range plan.

Different Approaches to Annual Planning

(*i*) *External Planning*: In it, the management considers continuing its current strategy and estimates the likely profits and sales it could achieve. If these are satisfactory, they are established as the company goals.

(*ii*) *Goal Planning*: In it, the management sets sales and profit goals for the year that would satisfy the shareholders if achieved. It is left to those for whom the goals are set to find ways of achieving them.

(*iii*) *Optimisation Planning*: In it, the management considers major alternative strategies and their likely impacts on profits, sales, market shares and future investments opportunities. The management selects the strategy with the most attractive consequences. This sort of planning is most logical of the three approaches.

Steps in Annual Marketing Planning

1. Collection of Data: Marketing research manager collects necessary information from the regional sales managers and prepares his report on the basis of the information thus collected to be submitted to the product planning manager.

2. Preliminary Plan: The product planning manager, keeping in view the needs of marketing and the cost of programmes prepares the preliminary plans.

3. Submission to Executive: Product planning manager submits his preliminary plans to the marketing executive.

4. Amendments: The marketing manager considers the report and sees how far proposals set in are practicable, and, if there is a need, he makes necessary changes and amendments in the proposals submitted.

5. **Submission to Top Executives:** The marketing manager sends his report to the top executive.

6. Consent: The chief executive screens the plans carefully and gives his consent to the plan.

IMPORTANCE OF MARKETING PLANNING

About the importance of planning Stanton remarks, "Without planning, a company's operations have no meaning and no direction, there can be no orderly procedure in management's pursuit of its goals." Therefore, planning is very important and necessary in the modern marketing. Research and analysis are required to identify market needs and to clarify company goals as well as to provide relevant information on both aspects for decision-making. The management formulates an overall company operating-integrating marketing, production, financial and other plans into a unified whole. It is only after this extensive planning that the management initiates the actions needed. It puts into effect the various actions required to make the plan work.

1. To Curtail Future Uncertainty: As future is always wrapped in uncertainties, an expert marketing manager makes marketing forecast on the basis of careful analysis of present circumstances and trends and then sets the objectives and goals for the future. He plans to put into effect and achieve the company's objectives and goals. Here marketing planning is necessary to curtail future uncertainty as far as possible.

2. Management by Objectives: Clear-cut objectives of the company help in the management of the various activities, programmes and operations of all the departments which are formulated in keeping the overall objectives of the company in view. This facilitates the work of management.

3. Economy in Operation: Marketing planning is helpful in achieving the objectives of the firm economically. It brings about economy in advertising, sales, purchases and financing.

4. Better Co-ordination: Marketing Planning helps better co-ordination in activities of all the departments. It not only co-ordinates the work of its own department but also helps in the co-ordination of the activities of all other departments to achieve the overall objectives and goals of the company.

5. Better in Control: Planning is an inseparable part of control. It sets performance standards and these are compared with the actual performance of various departments. As unfavourable variation is removed in the next plan. Therefore, planning is useful for better control.

6. Satisfaction of Customer: Under marketing planning, the actual wants of the consumers are studied properly and activities are channelised to provide full satisfaction to customers, the actual users of thc products. This makes the marketing work easier and convenient.

7. **Higher Performance Standards:** Marketing planning helps in evolving higher performance standards. It facilitates easier and quicker decision-making. The various problems are solved quickly. Untoward hurdles are overcome.

DIFFICULTIES IN MARKETING PLANNING

According to Stephen Morse, "Marketing planning is concerned with the identification of resources that are available and their allocation to meet specified objectives." This is not so simple as it appears. Some thinkers consider the whole business of marketing planning a waste of time, energy and money, as planning is concerned with uncertain future and quite uncertain situations.

When future itself is so uncertain how can planning hold cent per cent true. This pessimistic thinking is due to the difficulties which beset the path of marketing planning. The main difficulties are as follows:

1. Diversity of Alternative: One great difficulty in the marketing planning involves many alternatives to deal with a certain problem. For example, there can be many alternatives how to take finished goods to the consumers. Every alternative has its own merit and demerit. This diversity of alternatives presents many difficulties in the way of marketing planning as every alternative present different results.

2. Vacillating Policy of the Government: In India, there is no hard and fast Government Policy. In planning, frequent changes are made by the government from time to time. Sometimes the government encourages exports which at another time restrictions are imposed on exports. Rates of taxation are all the time changing to affect the price level which in its turn influences demand and supply position. This directly affects the marketing planning.

3. Rapid Changes in Costs: As production costs are changing all the time, it necessitates frequent changes in the price of products which in its turn has a direct bearing on the demand in the market. As it exerts its influence on the objective of marketing planning, therefore frequent and rapid changes in costs are also a hurdle in the way of marketing planning.

4. Lack of Time: The top executives always complain about lack of time due to their preoccupations in other affairs. This is a hurdle in the way of preparing a scientific marketing plan which demands time and efforts to analyse and evaluate the available data.

5. Uncertain Marketing Research: The customer's behaviour in India is very uncertain. Correct forecasts are not possible in the face of uncertain behaviour. Marketing planning is a useless effort in the absence of accurate forecasts.

6. Scientific Marketing Planning not Possible: Some experts believe that scientific marketing plan is not possible because the marketing factors are uncertain and changeable and not subject to logical analysis.

7. No Control over Supply: Even if correct estimate of demand is made in the market, there is no control over supply. Supply cannot be controlled in conformity with demand. Therefore, proper marketing planning is not possible. When the production targets cannot be achieved, one cannot succeed in drawing a logical plan. There are certain factors which are beyond the control of the producer. In the absence of adequate control over the forces of supply, marketing planning loses all its importance.

8. An Expensive Procedure: Some experts believe that scientific marketing planning is a very expensive procedure entailing huge expenditure. As most of the companies are not in a position to meet the heavy burden of planning, they do away with the luxury of marketing planning.

The above discussion reveals that though the task of planning involves great difficulties and hurdles yet marketing planning is not a waste and unnecessary. Efforts should be made to overcome the difficulties which in themselves do not prove that marketing planning is useless and unimportant.

Organisation for Marketing Planning

An organisation is the mechanism through which a managerial philosophy is translated into action. The marketing organisation provides the vehicle for making decisions on products, marketing channels, physical distribution, promotion and prices and the machinery through which these decisions are implemented.

The basic goals of a company indicate what the company wants to be, goals tend to override and permeate the rest of the administration. These have important implications for the marketing organisation. Management looks more and more to its target markets for guidance. It seeks to restructure the organisation so that the markets are served effectively and overall organisational goals are reached. Managerial attitudes towards the marketing concept show up the ways in which marketing activities are organised in various kinds of enterprises.

A company which seeks to plan effectively may have any of the following organisations for marketing planning: 1. Marketing planning committee 2. Marketing planning department, and 3. Functional marketing planning organisation.

1. Marketing Planning Committee: A marketing planning committee consists of all the chief executives of the company. It is responsible for drawing guiding principles of the marketing plan. Its meetings are held from time to time but the Vice-President is appointed to look after the day-to-day business planning. He is directly responsible for planning. He works in cooperation with the top management and other executives.

Planning Vice-President looks that: (*i*) necessary research work is carried on, (*ii*) instructions and directions reach each department in time, and there is proper coordination in the departmental plans. He has a planning coordinator and staff to assist him.

Departmental plans are prepared by the heads of different departments in conformity with the guidelines laid down by the Marketing Planning Committee. These departmental plans are sent to the Vice-President for scrutiny and evaluation. The planning staff scrutinises these departmental plans and suggests changes wherever necessary. Sometimes these plans are returned to their respective departmental heads to make the proposed changes. Only in the final form the plan is approved by the Marketing Planning Committee. Following chart shows the organisation for marketing planning of some of the modern companies:

Marketing Planning Committee

Vice-President Marketing Planning

Marketing Planning Coordinator & Staff

Departmental Head

Marketing Planning Committee organisation is suitable only for very big companies. Small and medium sized companies cannot afford such an organisation for marketing planning alone. The top executive draws out the whole plan with the help of the sales, production and other departments.

2. Marketing Planning Department: In some big concerns, a marketing planning department is established headed by marketing planning manager, assigned with the task of collecting the irrelevant information regarding the various aspects of marketing; analysing the information in the light of the marketing objectives; and preparing of various marketing plans. The incharge of the department through the marketing manager sends the plans to the top management, who scrutinises the plans. If he is satisfied, he gives his approval to the plans or he refers back the plans to the planning department which makes the necessary changes in the plans as suggested by the top executive and sends them back to him for approval. The top executive finally approves the plans.

3. Functional Marketing Planning Organisation: In medium sized organisation, the marketing planning is the prime responsibility of the marketing manager, who delegates his authority to managers of various other subdepartments such as sales, sale-promotion and advertisement, marketing research, etc. to plan for their own sub-departments, fixing their authorities and responsibilities. The managers of such departments prepare their plans and submit those plans to the marketing manager. If marketing manager is satisfied with the plans, he prepares an integrated plan and sends it for approval to the top management. The top management finally assigns his approval on the plan.

Among the three organisations for planning a concern one may choose any of them and make certain modifications in the process wherever it desires,

MARKETING PLANNING SYSTEM

An organisation is a mechanism through which a managerial philosophy is translated into action. As this philosophy changes, orgnaisational goals are revised and basic changes made in the organisational itself. While moving toward the marketing concept significant changes occur in the marketing organisation which is a company's main link with the market. It provides the vehicle for making decisions on products, marketing channels, physical distribution, promotion and prices. It is also a vehicle to implement these decisions. Different companies adopt different marketing organisations suited to them. On the whole, marketing planning may be divided under four classes:

1. Product-oriented marketing organisation.
2. Consumer-oriented marketing organisation.
3. Market-oriented marketing organisation.
4. Function-oriented marketing organisation.

1. Product-oriented Marketing Organisation: In it marketing planning is made for each product separately. Targets are determined for each product and detailed scheme programmes are chalked out to achieve these targets and goals. In such planning, amounts to be spent over advertising, sales promotion, product development and marketing research are fixed for each product. Decisions are taken separately for each product in connection with its distribution and marketing, etc.

2. Customer-oriented Marketing Organisation: In it separate marketing planning is prepared for each class of customers. Marketing organisation is centered around the characteristics of different types of customers. The objectives and goals are fixed in keeping with the characteristics of each category of customers. Decisions are taken in regard to advertising, sales promotion, pricing, distribution, etc. accordingly.

3. Market-oriented Marketing Organisation: It refers to an organisation which is regionally based. In this type of marketing orgnisation different targets for different regions are fixed and detailed programme is chalked out to achieve these goals. Decisions are taken in regard to advertising, sales promotion, distribution channels and pricing, etc. keeping in view the nature and intensity of competition in each region. Separate budget is made for each territory or region.

4. Function-oriented Marketing Organisation: Under it marketing planning is prepared on the basis of several small plans such as Product Mix Plan, Sales Force Plan, Advertising and Sales Promotion Plan, Distribution Channels Plan, Pricing Plan, Marketing Research Plan, Physical Distribution Plan and Marketing Organisation Plan, etc.

Development of an effective marketing organisation starts with the identification of overall company goals and determination of its target markets and seeks to structure the organisation accordingly so that the markets are served effectively and overall organisational goals are reached. Managerial attitudes towards the marketing concept show up in the ways in which marketing activities are organised in various kinds of enterprises. Management's approach to total company organisation as well as to marketing organisation should be dynamic. An organisation which is satisfactory today may prove inadequate tomorrow. Markets keep on changing because of changes in income, shifts in population, changes in tasks and lifestyles, etc. Coupled with technological advance, market change result in a flow of new products and the continued modification of old products. Due to developments in mass communications media and in marketing channels more and more such changes are expected. Any change in market factor can reduce the effectiveness of an organisational structure not only in serving the markets needs but as a vehicle for achieving the company's goals.

Continual monitoring and regular reappraisal of organisational effectiveness are imperative as market factors are for ever in a state of change.

QUESTIONS FOR EXERCISE

1. What is meant by Marketing Planning? Describe the elements of marketing planning?
2. List some of the applications of the general managerial concept of planning in the field of marketing,
3. "Management planning involves the development of forecast, objectives, policies, programmes, schedules and budgets." Discuss this statement in the context of Marketing Management.
4. Discuss the scope of Marketing Planning activities.
5. Explain the importance of Marketing Planning. What are the difficulties in Marketing Planning? Discuss the organisation of Marketing Planning.
6. Explain the Marketing Planning system in various Marketing Organisations.
7. Explain in brief the important marketing sub-plans to be prepared in a function-oriented marketing organisation.

6

Marketing Programme, Marketing Mix and Strategies

Definition of Marketing Programme

1. *William J. Stantson*: "Marketing Programme involves determining the level, mix and allocation of marketing resources in pursuit of marketing objectives."

In modern marketing management, all the marketing activities are preplanned. Marketing programme is a part of pre-planning. When a company has finally settled its marketing objectives after a careful appraisal and analysis of all the marketing opportunities, the question arises as to how to achieve the objectives and goals of the company. Marketing programme is made to attain the marketing objective of the company.

2. *Philip Kotler*: "A marketing programme is a set of policy decision on the level, allocation and mix of marketing efforts."

Marketing programme is the programme of marketing efforts in which decisions are taken as to how the marketing objectives can be achieved within a period of time with the use of available resources. Under it, market targets are selected, marketing mix is determined including product mix, distribution mix, communication mix and service mix. All the available resources are mobilised in order to achieve the overall objectives. Most of the enterprises draw marketing programme for a year, though these marketing programmes can also be for longer periods. Annual and six monthly programmes are prepared in a long period programme.

Elements of Marketing Programme

Marketing Programme can be classified into—1. Planning of marketing programme, and 2. Implementation of marketing programme.

1. Planning of Marketing Programme: At the time of planning of marketing programme following factors have to be studied carefully: (*i*) Demand variables; (*ii*) Marketing variables or internal factors; (*iii*) Marketing mix; (*iv*) Marketing strategy, etc. The planning of marketing programme should be prepared only after studying these factors carefully.

2. Implementation of Marketing Programme: Implementation of marketing programme involves: (*i*) Marketing efforts; (*ii*) Marketing allocation; and (*iii*) Market responsiveness, etc.

Justification of Marketing Programme

1. Necessary for Old as well as New: It is necessary for an enterprise to prepare a programme of marketing and to implement it. Marketing programme is necessary for the company whether its product is new or current.

(*i*) *In Case of New Product*: Marketing efforts are needed to familiarise the customer with the qualities and characteristics of the product, to give information about the use of the product, to find out the correct method to use it and to gather information as the main aim of marketing programme.

(*ii*) *In Case the Product is Old and is in a State of Growth*: Here marketing programme is necessary to face the competitors effectively. With the growth of product, the market gets regimented. The rival firms enter the market with their products. Therefore, market programme should mainly include promotional activities and product differentiation. Thus, marketing programme is necessary for old as well as for new products.

2. It Helps in Achieving the Objectives and Goals of the Company: It helps in utilising the available marketing resources in the best possible way. The ultimate object of a company is to earn the maximum possible profit, which can be done by reducing the costs and maintaining the level of production of the optimum favourable point. Marketing programme helps in maintaining the most favourable relation between the sales and costs. It can boost the sales. It increases the profits of the company. Thus, it is perfectly true to say that "An effective marketing programme does not increase the cost of goods sold, it really extends the market, increases the sales and lowers the selling costs finally."

FACTORS AFFECTING THE MARKETING PROGRAMME

Marketing programme is an attempt to coordinate the available marketing resources such as sales promotion, advertising, personal sales and services, etc., in order to achieve the overall objectives of the company by increasing sales and optimum level most favourable to the company at a particular time. The planning of marketing programme is affected by the following factors:

1. Demand variables; 2. Marketing decision variables or internal factors; Marketing Mix; 4. Marketing Efforts; 5. Marketing Allocation; 6. Marketing Strategy; 7. Marketing Responsiveness.

1. Demand Variables: Planning of marketing programme aims at maximising the sales of the company and increasing the profits of the company. Sales are greatly affected by the demand variables such as sales efforts, tastes of the customers, price, conditions of payment, competition pressure, etc. The demand variables can be grouped into two broad categories: (*i*) Controllable, and (*ii*) Uncontrollable.

(i) Controllable Demand Variables: These variables include die decisions regarding the (*a*) Price of product, (*b*) Quality of the product and (*c*) the channels of distribution affect to a great extent the demand of the product.

(*ii*) *Uncontrollable Demand Variables.* Uncontrollable demand affect the demand of the product of the company. As they are beyond the control of the company the company should take proper care of these while planning the marketing programmes. These variables include: *(a) Customer variables*—such as nature of customers, their behaviour, needs, income and numbers, etc.; (*b*) *Competition variables,* i.e., nature of competition and numbers of competitors and strategies adopted by them; and *(c) Environmental variables, viz.*, seasonal, economic, political and social activities, etc.

A company must study both controllable and uncontrollable types of demand variables.

2. Marketing Decision Variables or Internal Factors: Philip Kotler has defined these while saying, "A marketing decision variable for marketing instruments is any factor under the control of firm which to be used to stimulate company sales."

Lazer and Kelley have, divided these variables in following three divisions:

(i) Goods and Services Mix: There include product, its packaging brand labelling, etc.

(ii) Distribution Mix: There include distribution resource such as middlemen and other agencies which help in taking the products to the customers and physical distribution including transport, storage and warehousing.

(iii) Communication Mix: These include all information media, personal selling, advertisement, sale promotion and other sale aids.

(3) Marketing Mix: In the words of Philip Kotler, "Marketing mix refers to the amounts and kinds of marketing variables the firm is using at a particular time." Developing the marketing mix involves following four factors:

(*i*) Product mix; (*ii*) Distribution mix; (*iii*) Communication mix; and *(iv)* Service mix. Marketing mix tries to coordinate all these four types of mix.

(*i*) *The Product Mix*: In it the firm has to see that its products suit the particular market it has selected. The process of marketing the product to confirm a particular market is called product strategy.

(*ii*) *Distribution Mix*: It is the process of taking the products to the real users. It is prepared keeping in view the services of various wholesalers and retailers. It has to be determined how the products reach most conveniently to the customers. It has to be adjusted to the nature of the demand.

(*iii*) *Communication Mix*: It involves giving full information of the company's products to the customers in the absence of which the customer will not know what products are available. Therefore advertising, sales promotion, personal selling, dealer or distribution training campaigns are to be organised.

(*iv*) *Service Mix*: The customers are provided pre-sale service and also after-sale service to capture the markets. The services mix provides satisfaction to the customers.

(4) Marketing Efforts: According to Philip Kotler, Marketing effort is, "The total amount of company input into the marketing process to stimulate sales." Marketing efforts indicate all those marketing activities which are undertaken to increase the sales. These efforts of a company can be studied under two heads: (*i*) Marketing effort level, (*ii*) The amount of money actually used on the marketing effort's effectiveness. It refers to the fact that how far the amount allotted to marketing efforts is effectively and efficiently used. A company's sales are affected by both these factors. Marketing efforts form an essential part of marketing programme.

(5) Marketing Allocation: In the words of Philip Kotler, marketing allocation is, "company's division of its marketing effort among its products, customer segments and sales areas." The total amount of resources to be spent on marketing activities can be known by the marketing effort. Marketing allocation gives an idea that in what way this amount has to be distributed on different products and market segments.

(6) Marketing Strategy: According to Philip Kotler, marketing strategy, is "a set of objectives, policies and sales that guides over time the firm's marketing effort." As the conditions in the market are never stable, marketing strategy refers to the policy which is to be adopted to face the sudden changes in the market situation. In a competitive market the market situation remains fluid. Some new competitors enter the market while some old say good-bye to the market. Some competitors change their strategy in a particular market. Under these circumstances the company has to alter its marketing strategy to suit the new situations and challenges.

(7) Marketing Responsiveness: According to Philip Kotler, market responsiveness is, "the behaviour of sales in response to alternative levels, mixes and allocation of marketing effort." Marketing responsiveness refers to the response and relation in the marketing as result of marketing activities. To be realistic in the company's marketing programme marketing responsiveness has to be kept in view.

A careful appraisal and evaluation of the above factors is essential while preparing a retail marketing programme of the company. Negligence of any of the above factors may jeopardise the attainment of the objectives and goals of the sales.

MARKETING MIX

The idea of the 'mix' of marketing functions was conceived by Prof. Neil H. Borden of the Harvard Business School. According to him, "The Marketing mix refers to the apportionment of efforts, the combination, the designing and the integration of the elements of marketing into a programme or mix which on the basis of an appraisal of the market force will best achieve the objectives of an enterprise at a given time," Elaborating, he says, "Marketing Mix refers to the amounts and kinds of marketing variables, the firm is using at a particular time." Marketing mix includes Product Mix, Communication Mix, and Service Mix, Thus, marketing mix is a plan designed to analyse the marketing problems as follows:

(*i*) By utilising the important forces emanating from the marketing operations of an enterprise.

(*ii*) By adopting procedure and policies for an efficient marketing programme (distribution policies, promotional policies, etc.).

When Neil Borden coined the phrase "Marketing Mix", he wrote, "I liked his idea of calling a marketing executive a "mixer of ingredients", one who is constantly engaged in fashioning creatively a mix of marketing procedures and policies in his efforts'to produce a profitable enterprise."[1]

The marketing mix can be regarded as the "core" of the company's marketing system. Kotler has defined it as "the set of controllabale variables that the firm can use to influence the buyer's responses."[2]

Composition of Marketing Mix

There is no uniformity about the composition of the marketing mix. Albert Frey uses two dimensions: *offering* (product, package, etc.) and *tools* (advertising, personal selling, etc.)[3]. Eugene Kelley and William Lazer use a three-fold classification: the product services mix, the communications mix, and the distribution mix.[4] These authors did not state exactly what variables are available to marketers under each of the classification categories. Jerome McCarthy popularised the concept around a four-fold

---

1. Borden Neil H., "The Concept of the Marketing Mix", *Journal of Advertising Research*, Vol. 4, No. 2, 1964, p. 2.
2. Kotler, Philip, *Marketing Management Analysis, Planning and Control*, 1976. p. 59.
3. Frey, Albert W., *Advertising*, Ronald Press & Co., New York, 1961, p. 30.
4. Lazer William and Eugene, J. Kelley, *Managerial Marketing Prospectives and Viewpoints*, Richard, D. Irwin, Homewood, 1962, p. 413.

classification of product, price, place and promotion.[1] Lipson and Darling have been most explicit in stating the various variables available, from which to blend a marketing mix. They use a four-way classification. Each of the major components is further sub-divided into four dimensions.[2] Each of these is directed at a particular market segment. This is as indicated in the Fig. 6.1.

Thus, the marketing mix denotes a combination of various elements which in their totality constitute a firm's "marketing system". These elements include—Product Place (Distribution), Promotion, and Service mix.

1. Product Mix: It refers to different classes of product in different product lines. The firm has to see that its products suit the particular market, it has selected.

2. Distribution Mix: It refers to the selection of a mix of different types of distribution channels for transmitting the goods from the producer to the final consumer. Goods may reach the consumers through wholesalers and retailers or direct to the customers through chainshops. The company may decide for any one or more channels, taking in view how conveniently, the goods reach to the consumers.

3. Communication Mix or Promotional Mix: It includes the sale promotion techniques like advertising, sales-promotion, personal selling, etc. It gives full information regarding qualities and characteristics of company's products. It gives a comparative study of company's products with similar products of other company to the real consumers so that they can go for the company product.

4. The Service Mix: It refers to the various services to be provided to the customers before and after sale period. Different prices are fixed according to the services rendered to different classes of customers. The company should concentrate on these types of services in order to capture the market and provide satisfaction to the consumers.

---

1. McCarthy, Jerome, E., *Basic Marketing: A Managerial Approach,* Richard D. Irwin, Homewood. 1968, p. 31.
2. Lipson, Harry A. and Darling, John R., *Introduction to Marketing Administration: An Analytical Approach,* University of Albania, 1968.

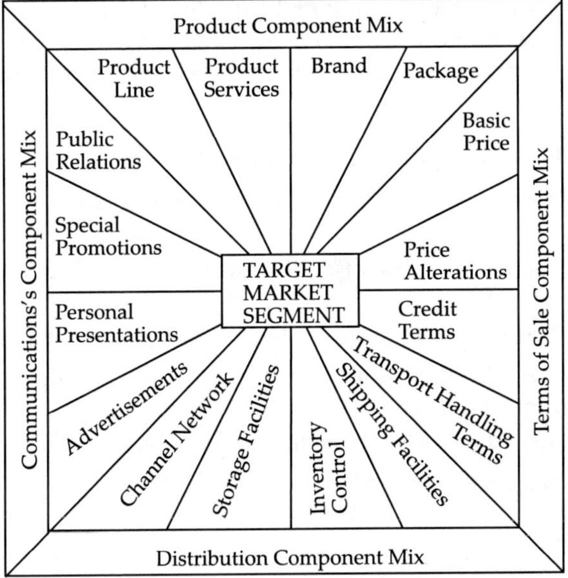

Fig. 6.1: Model of the Customer Market Offering Dimensions of the Marketing Mix

In planning the marketing programme, the company must consider the various marketing decision variables. It should consider what variables are being used by the company and what is the effect of such variable mix. It should evaluate the variable mix from time to time and make the necessary changes wherever necessary in order to make it most suitable to the concern. An ideal marketing mix may give the maximum profits to a firm and the satisfaction to the customers. There are innumerable variables in an ideal marketing mix. An efficient marketing manager should decide upon the ideal marketing mix on the basis of his own experience.

The concept of marketing mix given by Borden has been widely adopted in the marketing field.

Concept of Marketing Mix[1]

The concept of Marketing Mix, according to Borden, consists of (*i*) a list of the important elements or ingredients that make up

1. Borden, Neil H., *op. cit.*, pp. 2-7.

the marketing programmes; and (*ii*) a list of the forces that bear on the marketing operation of a firm and to which the marketing manager must adjust in his search for a mix or programme that can be successful.

Elements of Marketing Mix of Manufacturers

1. *Product Planning*, comprises policies and procedures relating to:
   (*a*) Product line to be offered—qualities and design—and also services.
   (*b*) Markets to sell: whom, where, when and in what quantity.
   (*c*) New Product Policy—research and development programmes.
2. *Pricing*. Policies and procedures relating to:
   (*a*) Price level to adopt.
   (*b*) Sepcific prices to adopt.
   (*c*) Price policy, *e.g.*, one price or varying prices, price maintenance, use of list price, etc.
   (*d*) margins to adopt—for company; for the trade.
3. *Branding*, policies and procedures relating to:
   (*a*) Selection of trade marks.
   (*b*) Brand policy—individualised or family brand.
   (*c*) Sale under private label or unbranded.
4. *Channels of Distribution*, policies and procedures realting to:
   (*a*) Channels to use between plant and consumer.
   (*b*) Degree of selectivity among wholesalers and retailers.
   (*c*) Efforts to gain cooperation of the trade.
5. *Personal Selling*, policies and procedures realting to:
   (*a*) Manufacturer's organisation.
   (*b*) Wholesale segment of the trade.
   (*c*) Retail segment of the trade.
6. *Advertising*: policies and procedures relating to:
   (*a*) The amount to spend.
   (*b*) Copy platform to adopt: (1) product image desired; and (2) Corporate image desired.
   (*c*) Mix of advertising: to the trade; through the trade; to consumers.

7. *Promotions*. Policies and procedures relating to:
   (*a*) Special selling plans or devices directed at or through the trade.
   (*b*) Form of these devices for consumer promotions, for trade promotions.
8. *Packing,* Policies, and Procedures relating to formulation packages and labels.
9. *Display,* Policies and procedures relating to:
   (*a*) Amount to be spent on display to help effect sale.
   (*b*) Methods to adopt to secure display.
10. *Servicing*. Policies and procedures relating to services needed.
11. *Physical handling*. Policies and procedures relating to:
    (*a*) Warehousing
    (*b*) Transportation
    (*c*) Inventories
12. *Fact finding and analysis,* policies and procedures relating to: securing, analysis, and use of facts in marketing operations.

In brief, the four "ingredients" in the Mix are inter-related. These are also known as *marketing decision variables.*

Factors Affecting the Marketing Mix

These factors can be divided into following two categories:

1. Market Factors; and 2. Marketing Factors.

1. Market Factors: These are such factors over which a company has no control while they affect the marketing activities of the company. Such factors are:

(*i*) *Consumer Behaviour*: Consumer behaviour includes wills and preferences of the consumers. It affects the demand of the products. A marketing manager must study the needs, wills and the preferences of the customer. He should analyse their effects on the demand of the product as also the consumer's need. As wills and preferences are affected by the change in income, fashion, social status, etc. the manager should study these factors.

(*ii*) *Competition*: The marketing manager should also study the competitive conditions in the market. He should take into account bases of competition, comeptitors' viewpoint towards the consumers, quality of competitors' products and their marketing strategies.

(*iii*) The *Pattern of Distribution System*: The marketing manager should consider the various forms of distribution system and the nature and behaviour of distributors. As distributors come into direct contact with the customers and their attitude, behaviour, opinion about the product and method of work directly affect the customer. The manager should be very careful about taking the decision in this regard carefully considering the nature and characteristics of the product.

(*iv*) *Government Control*: Government in India and in other countries control the various activities of the marketing. In India the government intervention in the price, quality, distribution system and packing of the products is too much. Hence, a marketing manager should think over the various government controls on the various marketing activities regarding the products of the company in preparing the marketing mix.

2. Marketing Factors: Marketing factors are such factors over which the company has complete control to make them fit according to the requirements of the market. These factors include the following:

(*i*) Product Planning.
(*ii*) Brand Policy.
(*iii*) Packaging Policy.
(*iv*) Distribution Channels.
(*v*) Personal Selling.
(*vi*) Advertisement Policy.
(*vii*) Special Sales Promotion Policy.
(*viii*) Physical Distribution.
(*ix*) Market Research.

(*i*) *Product Planning*: The product of the company must satisfy the needs of the customers. The company should plan and develop its products accordingly. According to A.M.A. Research Study (1963), product planning is the "act of making out and supervising the search, screening, development and commercialisation of new products, modification of existing lines and the discontinuance of marginal or unprofitable items." Therefore, the product quality should be improved to suit the customer's needs.

(*ii*) *Brand Policy*: It includes decisions regarding trade marks and brand name as it influences the sale volume of the product of the company. The marketing manager should go for the alternative policies regarding brands. He may decide one brand name for the different products of the company or different brand names for different qualities of the same product. He may also decide that the product should be without any brand name.

(*iii*) *Packaging Policy*: The marketing manager has to decide whether a product should be sold loose or in packs. If he decides to sell the product in packs, the size and quality and get up of packing should be considered very carefully as sometimes customers perfer the product only because of its attractive packing. Packaging policy serves three main purposes: (1) Protection of merchandise; (2) Enhancement of the product value; and (3) Advertising the product. Thus, it improves the total profits of the company by increasing total demand due to improved product image.

(*iv*) *Distribution Channels*: There are three main channels of distribution:

(*a*) from the manufacturer to the wholesaler, then to the retailers and finally to the customers;

(*b*) from the producer to the retailers and then to the final consumers, thus avoiding the wholesalers; and

(*c*) from the producer to the retailer directly.

The marketing manager should take the decision regarding appropriate channel of distribution for his products taking into account the nature of the product, nature of the distributors, their needs, their attitude towards the product and their morale. The marketing manager may adopt one type of distribution channel for all the products or different channels for different products.

(*v*) *Personal Selling*: Salesmen are the heroes of marketing in many respects. Personal selling is the skill that a salesman matches the customers' needs with the company's product in effecting ownership transfer or marketing sales. Personal selling involves social behaviour. The marketing manager should decide whether to promote the sale through personal selling. This involves decisions regarding recruitment, training and the deployment of salesmen.

(*vi*) *Advertisement Policy*: Advertisement is used not only to stimulate the demand of the product but for many other purposes, such as to maintain the demand of the existing products, to give the information regarding the products, etc. The marketing manager has to formulate the advertising policy taking into account the purposes, area, media of advertisement and advertisement copy, etc. Advertisement policy includes decisions estimating the advertisement expenditure and its control.

(*vii*) *Special Sales Promotion Policy*: Apart from the general advertisement policy, the manager should also provide for the special sales promotion campaigns as a part of sales promotion policy.

(*viii*) *Physical Distribution*: As the above variables create demand but creation of demand is not sufficient, the marketing manager must plan the supply of the product in accordance with the needs of the public of the different markets. He should decide policy of physical distribution of goods including transportation, warehousing and finance management so that the product may be made available at proper time and place with minimum cost of distribution to the customers.

(*ix*) *Market Research*: Market research is the soul of marketing. Necessary information is collected through market research. The marketing manager can use such information in preparing the marketing mix.

Though the study, analysis and evaluation of the above factors help in preparing an ideal marketing mix but in practice the experience, knowledge and forcsightedness of marketing authorities play an important role rather than the above analytical and technical factors. The ratio of different factors and their roles in marketing are generally decided by the marketing authorities on the basis of their experience and foresightedness.

MARKETING STRATEGY

According to Philip Kotler, Marketing Strategy is "A set of objectives, policies and rules that guide over time firm's marketing efforts." It is a policy to maintain the concern's competitive position in the market. Management gives it a shape with strategies for each product, its distribution, promotion and pricing. It tries to balance the controllables with uncontrollables and thus shapes the market needs and wants and fulfils company goals. For this he combines product market distribution, promotion and pricing strategies into a single overall marketing strategy.

Marketing Decision in a Competitive Setting

Skilled in planning and using the controllables on individual the marketer has an opportunity to win the buying preferences of certain market segments on a more or less permanent basis. In monopolistic situation the actions of one marketing manager have no effect upon that of the other while their skill makes major contenders in their industries and those lacking in skill fall back. Every marketer has to consider the moves of competitors and their reactions to his own marketing decisions. Marketing decisions in a competitive setting are influenced by the following factors:

1. The Product: Whether the marketer is an inventor or a follower to market his product successfully, he must be careful about the competitor's timings of actions. By the actions of the competitors many products have slipped below the status and disappeared.

2. Distribution (Marketing Channels): A successful product must reach the central buying places. It must follow the customary channel. The concern should offer a better product, a lower price, a more effective promotional programme or some other combination of other factors.

3. Physical Distribution: Marketers want to have the right resource at the right place and at the right time. They care for reasonable costs. As competitors' actions and operations influence physical distribution decisions, the marketing manager must try to send his goods at the required place at the time when needed.

4. Promotion: The methods applied by the marketer to stimulate market demand are very important. He should spend sufficient amount on advertising giving the knowledge of qualities of his product and a comparison with competitors' products in the market.

5. Price: The price must coincide with the customer's evaluation of the items. Superior quality brands may be marketed to defeat the competitors. Marketers use aggressive marketing strategies when they use the other means of controllables.

Overall Marketing Strategy

In order to achieve careful integration of all dimensions of the marketing efforts, the marketers should determine whether or not the combination of inputs going into the overall marketing strategy is optimal. It involves evaluating of the possible inputs to the overall marketing strategy in terms of the likely outputs. The marketer should make selections from the various inputs in such a way that the combination is the best he can devise for achieving the desired outputs.

Factors Affecting Overall Marketing Strategy

1. Competitors' Counter-moves: These differ with various marketing inputs. Though most competitors can easily and quickly match or otherwise adjust to price changes, they often find it difficult to follow or to retaliate against product innovations. This explains why many marketers seek to gain differential advantage over their competitors by varying product characteristics as altering promotion than prices.

2. Synergistic Potential: Marketing inputs are capable of being mutually reinforcing or having synergistic potential. The marketer should consider this working towards an optimum overall marketing strategy. Displays and advertisements can be made mutually reinforcing since the display repeats the advertising efforts message at a time when the consumer is in an outlet where the product is on sale. Product inputs and marketing channel inputs can be mutually reinforcing, depending upon the effectiveness with which they are integrated.

3. Substitutability: The selection of marketing inputs is also affected by their degree of substitutability. Substitutability is the extent to which one type of input can be substituted for another type inasmuch as the nature of marketing objectives such as that of retaining a certain level of profit presents a decisionmaker from making unlimited use of all inputs. Consideration of substitutability helps in determining which inputs to include and which to emphasise in the overall marketing strategy.

4. Diversity in Productivity Levels of Various Marketing Inputs: The marketers should recognise that all inputs do not have equal productivity. Some inputs need a minimum level of use before they begin to have measurable effects. An advertising message must often be repeated several times before consumers become aware of it. The lower cost per consumer, contact through radio, magazines and billboards often make it possible to present a much stronger impact on consumer with a limited budget.

5. Elasticity of Marketing Inputs: Different marketing inputs are elastic. They influence the demand of the product. The marketing manager must recognise that effect on the product. For example, a manufacturer determines different prices for different customers or for different areas on the basis of varying elasticity of demand. The prices for wholesalers, retailers and consumers are different in almost all markets.

While formulating the overall marketing strategy the marketing manager must consider all the above factors. The strategy must be so elastic as to incorporate all the strategic factors of the competitors as and when required.

Causes of Difference In Strategies

Marketing strategy of a company very much depends upon the nature of the commodity, the company markets, *i.e.*, whether it is a consumer product or industrial product. Consumer product means product which is mainly used by the consumers for the satisfaction of their needs. On the other hand, industrial product is mainly used by manufacturers for further production. The marketing strategy for marketing these two types of product differs widely because the factors affecting the strategy also differ.

1. Strategy of Consumer Product: Because the number of competitors and consumers are innumerable and scattered all over the country, the marketing strategy of consumer products will be quite different from that of the industrial product. The company has to satisfy the needs of innumerable customers who differ widely in nature. The advertisement policy of such products may differ from region to region considering the nature of the customers. Wide publicity is necessary for such products so that it may have permanent effect on the consumers. A wide base is required for other policies such as prices and marketing policies weighing their wide effects on the consumers. The expense on one input may affect the expense on other inputs. The shady of various inputs should be made carefully. A little unawareness may oust the firm from the market.

2. Strategy of Industrial Product: In this case, as the number of competitors are few because of large amount of investment, the number of customers are also few and therefore the demand of such products is low. It results in less expenditure on advertisement and sales promotion. Wide publicity of the product is not necessary. Pamphets or circular, explaining the characteristic of the product may be mailed to such few consumers or they may be contacted personally by the business representatives. The markets can be divided very easily on the basis of nature of customers or area and, therefore, different price policies may be accommodated for different customers or regions. The substitutes of various inputs are also easily available.

It is amply clear from the above study that the marketing authorities should consider the nature and the number of different variables and their productivity and utility while formulating the marketing strategy.

MARKETING AUDIT

According to E.J. Kelley, "A marketing audit is a systematic and comprehensive appraisal of the total marketing operation, a device to use in appraising the extent of integration of the inputs and a way to identify and evaluate the assumptions underlaying marketing operations." Evaluation would follow planning as planning lays down standards of what should be done and evaluation actually indicates what actually was done. A total evaluation programme of marketing activities is described as 'marketing audit'. Horwood F. Merrill defines the marketing audit as a "systematic, critical and impartial revision and appraisal of the total marketing actions." It would include consideration of salesmen's performance, marketing costs involved, the effectiveness of advertising and so on.

Basically the standards of performance used for evaluation of overall marketing operations are: 1. Profits, 2. Sales Volume, 3. Market share, and 4. Cost, 5. Break Even Analysis.

1. Profit: Profit is the ultimate objective of all business. It is essential for marketing. Using it as a standard the company may prescribe a certain return on investment for each of the departments concerned. This, however, poses problems. In case of the manufacturing departments, generally a larger investment is involved than in case of the marketing departments. The nature of the "transfer price" would also determine the ultimate profitability for either of these departments. Though the use of the profit centre concept poses problems, but these can be sovled by (*i*) prescribing a smaller rate of return on investment in case of the manufacturing department than for the marketing department, and (*ii*) fixing the transfer price the market price at which the marketing department could have purchased the same product from outside. The profits concept can be easily and more fruitfully applied in terms of either separate products or groups of products.

2. Sales Volume: Generally sales volume is not a useful standard. As sales may increase, profits may decrease, therefore, it must be supplemented with a cost analysis.

3. Market Share: Market share also suffers from the same defect as a standard as sales volume. However, it helps to measure the position of the company in terms of the industry sales. It also helps in sales forecasting.

4. Cost: Costs must be controlled as they directly affect ultimate profit and constitute valuable standards for evaluation.

5. Break-even Analysis: Generally with an increase in volume unit costs of the produce decrease as the fixed costs are spread over a large number of items. Break-even analysis at different prices can, therefore, considerably help in controlling stage to ascertain whether the present pricing strategy is appropriate or requires a change.

MARKETING TASKS/FUNCTIONS

A marketing function is an act, operation or service by which the original producer and the final consumer are linked together. This functional approach to the study of marketing has made it possible to split economic structure of exchange into smaller parts so that equal weight may be given to its each operation and by studying each function separately the best and most economical method of performing them, may be discovered. Marketing embraces every step "which affects transfer in the ownership of goods and care for their physical distribution." Following are some important views about marketing functions.

1. *Rezvan*: He identifies 120 different kinds of functional elements that are associated with marketing.[1]

2. *Edmund D. McGarry*: He has stated that "the term 'function' should be defined as to meet the purpose for which it is used." To illustrate his point he said, "The function of the heart is not simply to beat, which is its activity, but rather to supply the body with a continuous flow of blood....In like maimer functions of marketing should be used only in connection with activities that must be

1. Duddy and Rezvan, *Marketing: An Institutional Approach*, 1953, pp. 21-22.

performed in order to accomplish the general purpose." He classifies marketing functions into six categories: (*i*) *Contractual,* whereby buyers and sellers are brought together for marketing transactions; (*ii*) *merchandising,* is concerned with making products acceptable to the market; (*iii*) *pricing,* where prices are fixed so low that production may be economical and the consumers may be motivated to make purchases; (*iv*) *propaganda,* under which the buyers are made known of the objectives of the sellers; (*v*) *physical distribution,* consists in transportation and storage services; and (*vi*) *termination, i.e.,* the end of marketing activity.[1]

3. *McInnes.* After saying that "market is the gap which separates producer and consumer," and "marketing is any activity which actualises the potential market relationships between the makers and users of economic goods and services,".[2] *McInnes* gives the functional areas which are of primary relevance enclosing the gaps between markers and users. The particular system through which these functions are combined, integrated, and allocated among various firms comprises a marketing channel, (*i*) Transportation deals with spatial separation and includes all activities directly concerned with moving goods from place of production to the place of sale or such other place as may be designated by the user, (*ii*) Inventory deals with temporal separation and includes those activities directly concerned with holding goods between the time of production and the time of sale, (*iii*) Promotion deals with perceptional segment and includes all activities directly concerned with providing information regarding the nature of goods and services and their relationship to the potential user's perceived needs, (*iv*) Transaction deals with severing of ownership and values. It includes all activities directly concerned with active negotiation and transfer of title.

4. *Richard Lewis*: She gives two functions of marketing to obtain demand and to service demand. All of these activities which are engaged in marketing are means to attain these ends.[3]

---

1. McGarry, E.D., "Some Functions of Marketing Reconsidered." *Theory in Marketing,* Richard D. Irwin, 1960, pp. 269-273.
2. McInnes, William, "A Conceptual Approach to Marketing," in Cox. Reavis, Alderson. Wroe and Shapuro Stanley, J., (Eds.), *Theory in Marketing,* Richard D. Irwin, 1964, pp. 51-67.
3. Lewis, R.J., 'Business Logistics Information and Accounting System for Marketing Analysis'. Michigan University, Michigan, 1964, pp. 62-63.

5. *Maynard and Others*: Marketing function has been defined as "major economic activity which is inherent in the marketing process, pervades it throughout and which through a continuous division of labour tends to become specialised.[1]

6. *Theodore and Others:* These have given eight basic marketing functions, buying, selling, transportation, storage, standardisation and grading of goods, financing of purchasers, assumption of risk, and the transmission of marketing information.[2] All these functions involve interactions between marketing institutions. They also involve flows of goods, money, risk, or information.

Classification of Marketing Functions

1. *Exchange functions*: These are directly related to the exchange of title to or ownership of goods or services. These include buying and selling activities. Incidentally pricing is also included in this function.

2. *Physical distribution functions*: These are concerned with transportation and storage of products.

3. *Auxiliary functions*: These include standardisation and grading, financing, the assumption of risk and the pursuit of marketing information.

4. *Merchandising*: It is concerned with providing the right goods at the right time, in right quantities at the right place and at the right price.

5. *Buying*: It involves scuring goods from producers or manufacturers, after seeking out the source of supply, the making of business contracts, the negotiation of prices and other terms and the transfer of ownership from the producer to the consumer.

6. *Selling*: It includes the many facets of salesmanship, not only personal salesmanship, but non-personal salesmanship such as advertising, display, radio and television commercials, and telephone selling.

7. *Other important activities*: Moving goods from producer to consumer includes, risk management, marketing research,

---

1. Maynard, Harold H. Wilder, Walter and Beckman, T.N., *Principles of Marketing*, 1939, p. 31.
2. Theodore, F. Beckman, William R. Davidson, and W. Wayne Talarzyk, *Marketing*, Ronald Ross, New York, 1973, pp. 19-21.

standardisation and grading, storing, financing, traffic management and accounting.

(*i*) *In Risk management*: In it the business either assumes or shifts through insurance, the risk of loss in order to serve customers immediately.

(*ii*) *Marketing research*: It involves the collection and analysis of information about suppliers, customers and merchandise.

(*iii*) *Standardisation and grading*: It involves establishing uniform specifications for varieties of merchandise and sorting the merchandise according to the standards or grades.

(*iv*) *Storing*: It includes keeping an adequate supply of goods on hand for ready availability to meet needs, and keeping them where the merchandise can be used and processed easily from the warehouse.

(v) Financing: It involves providing needed capital for business operations and for granting credit to customers when they are buying on credit.

(vi) Traffic management: It involves determining the method and route for physical movements of goods throughout the marketing process.

(vii) Accounting: It involves keeping adequate records relating to the merchandise and sales to customers.

Thus, the entire marketing functions can be sub-divided into four classes:

Seeking—Matching—Programming—Consummating.

1. Seeking function: It is the search for an identification of wants that the organisations must satisfy.

2. Matching: It involves assignment of the organisation's ability' to produce a product service for the market or markets identified—in the light of such external factors as competitors'/actions, general economic conditions, laws and government regulations, consumer's tastes and fashions, etc.

3. Programming: It is related to merchandising, pricing, promotion and distribution (known as the four P's—Product, Price, Promotion and Place).

4. Consummating: It involves settling all the details necessary to finalise the exchange.

Thus, marketing involves many different activities and it has a direct influence on the entire economy. Obviously, nothing really happens in business until somebody sells something, and somebody purchases them.

The job of the marketing system includes thousands of different kinds of products and services, serving a widely dispersed and heterogeneous market.

QUESTIONS FOR EXERCISE

1. "A Marketing programme is set of policy decisions on the level, allocation and mix of marketing efforts." Discuss.
2. What is the meaning of Marketing Programme? Explain the main elements of marketing programme. What is the justification of Marketing Programme?
3. "An effective marketing programme does not increase the cost of goods sold, it really extends the market, increases the sales and lowers the selling costs finally". Explain.
4. What factors should be evaluated while planning marketing programme? Explain.
5. Explain briefly the steps involved In planning marketing programme of a company.
6. What do you mean by Marketing Mix? Describe the forces affecting the Marketing Mix?
7. Attempt a short note on "Marketing Mix"?

7

Marketing Management

Marketing management represents pre-planned demand management under customer-oriented marketing philosophy. It looks after the marketing system of the enterprise. It involves planning, implementation and control of marketing programmes. It is directly in-charge of setting the goals/objectives of marketing, developing marketing plans for their accomplishment; organising the marketing activities needed to carry on these objectives, implementing the marketing programmes and controlling them as per needs. It represents an important functional area of business management efforts under which goods and services flow from the producers to consumers.

Definition of Marketing Management

1. *Ben M. Enis*: "Marketing Management is the process of increasing the effectiveness and/or efficiency by which marketing activities are performed by individuals or organisations."

2. *Philip Kotler*: "Marketing management is the analysis, planning, implementation, and control of programmes designed to bring about desired exchanges with target audiences for the purpose of mutual or personal gain. It relies heavily on the adaptation and coordination of product, price, promotion and place of achieving effective response."[1]

To make his definition further clear, he lays down the following facts:[2]

---

1. Kotler, Philip, *Marketing Management, Analysis, Planning and Control,* 1972, p. 13.
2. *Ibid.*, p. 14.

(a) *It is a management process* and includes analysis, planning, implementation, and control activities.
(b) *It is a purposive activity* which aims at bringing about desired exchanges, which may be of goods or services.
(c) *It can be practised by either the seller or the buyer,* whoever seeks to stimulate the exchange process.
(d) *It may be carried on for personal or mutual gain.*
(e) It stresses the adaptation and coordination of several factors, *viz.,* product, price, promotion and place to achieve the effective response.

3. *Still and Cundiff*: "Marketing management is concerned with the direction of purposeful activities towards the attainment of marketing goals.... It directs purposeful activities, consciously planned, organised, coordinated and controlled. Managerial effort in marketing is goal-directed, *i.e.,* knows where it is going."[1]

They say, "The term 'marketing management' is used more often in referring to the marketing operations of manufacturers than to those of the middlemen. The main reason is that marketing managers in manufacturing firms manage and made decision on a wider variety of marketing type activities. These marketing managers are concerned with the marketing organisation, products, brands, marketing channels, physical distribution, pricing, advertising, and personal selling—matters about which marketing managers in all "make and sell" business make decisions...Marketing manager devotes himself primarily to purely marketing-type activities...*Marketing management everywhere is concerned with directing purposeful activities to reach marketing goals.*"[2]

4. *Pride and Ferrel*: "Marketing management is a process of planning, organising, implementing and controlling marketing activities in order to effectively and efficiently facilitate and expedite exchanges. The *effectiveness* and *efficiency* dimensions are two important components."[3]

Thus, Marketing Management is the process of ascertaining consumer needs, working up through product planning,

---

1. Cundiff, E.W., and Still, R.R., *Basic Marketing: Concepts, Decisions and Strategies,* 1972, p. 68.
2. *Ibid.,* p. 69.
3. Pride, William, W. and Ferrel, O.C., *Marketing: Basic Concepts and Decisions,* Houghton Moflin Co., Boston, 1977, p. 32.

organising, directing, controlling and evaluating the efforts of the group of people toward a common goal, with emphasis on profitability with an optimum use of available resources.

ASSUMPTIONS OF MARKETING MANAGEMENT

The major working assumption of marketing management is that desired exchanges do not automatically come about through any process of nature, rather they require an expenditure of time, energy, skill and supervision. Designing, packaging, pricing and distributing require the use of managerial talents. Modern age is the age of cut-throat competition and only those producers survive in this struggle who are able to compete successfully by innovating techniques to reach the consumer. As consumer orientation became the accepted marketing philosophy, marketing management has become most crucial in business planning and decision-making. At present, there is a growing recognition of the role of marketing management. Dynamic changes are taking place every moment and are likely to take place in future with the changes in attitudes and values of society.

IMPORTANCE OF MARKETING MANAGEMENT

Indian Economy

Before Independence no importance was attached to marketing management in India which has always remained an agricultural country. After Independence, steps were taken to industrialise the country rapidly. The government realised that for rapid development of the economy, dependence only on agriculture was not to be both in the private as well as in public sector. The composition of India's export and imports underwent a great change. Capital goods industries were set up under the new industrial policy of the government. The national income and per capita income went up. This brought about a great change in the consumption habits of the common man. The demand for goods in the market registered an upward trend. All these changes in the economy are responsible for the growing importance of marketing management in India.

Importance of Rural Marketing

Though 74 per cent Indian people live in rural areas but most of the producers and sellers concentrate their attention to cater to the needs and wants of the urban population. Hence, the Indian villages present great scope for the development of rural marketing. Recently, the Green Revolution increasing use of chemicals fertilisers, mechanisation of agriculture, use of hybrid seeds and pesticides have helped in the development of rural marketing. The cultivators are economically better off now-a-days. It has brought about a change in their habits of consumption. Their standard of living is rising. They freely use transistors, radios, electronic appliances. T.V. sets and other articles of comfort. Rural marketing has not yet developed in India. It is expedient that more attention should be paid to the study and research of rural marketing so that the maximum number of wants of the rural people be fulfilled so that their standard of living might rise.

Motivation to Export

Much of India's economic development depends on development of her exports. Export promotion can only help in solving the various economic problems facing the country. Marketing Management development programme will go a long way in improving the economy. India commands vast resources both in materials and manpower. Development of marketing techniques will help in finding new markets outside the country also. To increase our exports to foreign markets we need diversification in production, improvement in quality, reduction in cost of production by applying new techniques and methods and adopting new marketing strategies. Our experts have registered a marked increase in promoting exports in the recent years but this increase cannot be said quite satisfactory. The reasons for this slow increase are high costs of production and the lack of use of new marketing techniques. India should search for new markets by using the most advanced scientific methods of marketing management. They should be able to face the challenge of cut-throat competition of the foreign producers by reducing substantially our costs. Marketing management can help us a lot in this direction.

MAJOR PROBLEMS OF MARKETING MANAGEMENT

1. Need of Marketing Personnel: The lack of well trained, efficient and experienced personnel stands in the way of development of marketing management in India. Of late some institutions have started imparting training in this important branch of knowledge. Some universities have also included courses in teaching marketing management. But the need of the country require larger number of well trained and competent personnel to handle the complex problems of marketing management in the fast developing economy of India.

2. Need for Marketing Research: Marketing decisions are a combination of judgement and information on facts. Marketing research helps in collecting the useful information. Modern executive has a difficult task in making decisions and appraisals. Marketing research can help him much to raise the level of their work. It facilitates decision-making. In India very little has been done in the field of marketing research. Both for the development of domestic as well as international trade there is great need of research in marketing management. Special considerations must be borne in mind while preparing the marketing strategy for penetrating markets abroad. Even the sophisticated country like U.S.A. is faced with competition in international markets from other countries like Japan, when selling abroad. In this complex task of finding and winning foreign markets, marketing research is of great importance. Therefore, for good marketing management, there is great need for marketing research.

3. Product Planning: Proper product planning is an act of marketing out and supervising the research, screening, development and commercialisation of new products, the modification of existing lines and the discontinuance of marginal or unprofitable items. Development in marketing management and product planning go hand in hand. In India very little attention is paid toward product planning. The consumers also fail to get the maximum satisfaction by their purchases when the products do not match their likings. Three aspects of product planning which should always be kept in view are developing, modifying or discontinuing products. Few products are developed in some companies as they are afraid of taking risks. Thus, opportunities are lost. Hence, development of product planning must be done properly.

4. Marketing Costs: Marketing research, promotional strategy, advertising effort, packaging, selling expenses are constantly mounting up. Sometimes their costs become forbidding and a great hurdle comes in the way of developing marketing management on scientific lines. For proper development of marketing management, these costs need be kept well within control.

Due to the growth of large scale industries in public sector and private sector after Independence, the need for development of marketing management is being specially felt in India. Efforts should be made to set up more and more institutions to impart training in the specialised fields of marketing research, product planning and marketing management. The industrialists should take more interest in improving quality of their products and reducing costs so that India can have an access to foreign markets and successfully face competition of the foreign producers. This will be possible by developing marketing management techniques.

MARKETING *Vs.* SALES MANAGEMENT

Meaning of Sales Management

According to American Marketing Association, "Sales management is the planning, direction and control of selling activities of a business unit including recruiting, selecting, training, equipping, assigning, routing, supervising, paying and motivating as these tasks apply to the sales force."

The two words 'selling' and 'marketing' are considered to mean the same thing. But selling is normally considered with the plans and ideas of trying to make the consumer exchange what he has (money) for what we have (goods or services). Selling lays stress on sales volume.

Marketing is related to the needs of the buyer. While selling has the seller's need to change his product into cash. Marketing is limited to the idea of satisfying a consumer's requirements by means of product as well as by giving the customer with value satisfaction.

Marketing-oriented concern creates value satisfying product and services that the consumer will like to purchase. It ensures the profitability of activities of the concern. Thus, marketing is a view of the full business with profitability and consumers' satisfaction as the keynote.

Marketing manager is superior to sales manager as he has to deal with supervising the work of the sales managers. Sales manager's functions are limited to planning, directing and controlling the activities of salesmen. But in India marketing management and sales management are regarded synonymous terms. Hence, whether a person is a manager or a sales manager can only be determined by studying the functions he is expected to do. Selling refers to the producer while marketing is related to the needs of the buyer.

Differences

1. Different Scope: The scope of marketing management is wider than of sales management. Marketing management includes all the activities from the beginning of ascertaining the needs and requirements of the consumers to the fulfilment and satisfaction of the wants of the actual users. The scope of the sales management is narrow. It includes the activities connected with transfer of ownership in goods and services from seller to the buyer. It deals with the problems of seller.

2. Different Concepts: Marketing management is a modern concept while sales management is an old concept.

3. Different Objectives: The objective of marketing management is the satisfaction of the wants of the consumers or users to utilise the available resources in the best possible way so as to maximise profitability. The objective of sales management is to maximise sale with emphasis on volume and not on the satisfaction of the consumers.

Thus, sales management is only a part of a wider marketing management. In the opinion of E.F.L. Brech, 'The overall management of sales 'refers to' only a specialised application of the process of management as a whole."

FUNCTIONS OF MARKETING MANAGER

1. Integrated Marketing: The marketing manager has to take decisions in various elements of the marketing mix in an integrated way. The customer does not pay attention only to the price of a product but there are other factors also which affect his decision to purchase a particular product. He is influenced by the firm's advertising and promotional strategy and the convenience of the distribution arranged from the customer's viewpoint. The marketing manager has to keep his company's interests in mind. He should try to reduce the cost of marketing the products while at the some time winning the goodwill of the customers. He should strive to maximise the sales and profits for his company. This task requires constant control and evaluation resulting in improvements in planning of the marketing strategy. The marketing manager should coordinate the activities of all the departments in a productive unit. The production department, finance departments, etc. adjust their policies on the direction and suggestion of the marketing executive. Under integrated marketing some of the important activities of the marketing management are as follows:

(*i*) Collection of necessary information regarding marketing,

(*ii*) Analysing the data and drawing conclusions.

(*iii*) Product development.

(*iv*) Search and development of new marketing techniques.

(*v*) Checking out detailed marketing programme.

(*vi*) Implementing marketing programme.

(*vii*) Coordinating between the wants of the customers and their satisfaction.

2. Determination of Objectives: Based on situational analysis the marketing objectives should be broad enough. Marketing objectives have to be fixed in the light of the overall company objectives. The chief executive must know whether he wants a return on investment of say 12 per cent after taxes or whether his company wants to be a price leader. He must also crystallise the product objectives, pricing objectives distribution strategy objectives and promotional objectives. All these objectives should be integrated and directed towards overall marketing objectives.

3. Product Policy: The marketing executive should be very clear in his mind about the type of customers for whom his products are intended. His product policy objectives must be in terms of customer orientation and in conformity of the overall marketing objectives.

4. Proper Planning: Planning is deciding in the present what to do in the future. All firms carry out some sort of planning. The marketing manager has to plan how the objectives have to be implemented. He has to perform the following tasks for proper planning:

(*i*) Marketing research, forecasting the demand and developing the marketing activities.

(*ii*) Determining product line strategy and planning for product diversification.

(*iii*) Planning sales policies and their implementation.

(*iv*) Planning the long-term marketing programme.

(*v*) Co-ordinating the activities of production, finance and service departments.

5. Selling: In regard to selling the marketing executive performs the following functions:

(*i*) Directing the sales manager to regulate sales.

(*ii*) Organising sales territories and fixing their sales quota.

(*iii*) Selecting and training personnel for the sales department and organise sales.

(*iv*) Organising and developing distribution channels.

(*v*) Advertising and organising sales promotion and public relations.

6. After Sales Service: After sales service is regarded as an essential part of modern marketing management. The maximum satisfaction of the consumers should be the primary concern of marketing. The complaints and the suggestions of the customers should be promptly attended to by the marketing management division.

7. Organising: Organising determines various activities and decides how and who will perform those activities. Various activities and persons assigned those activities are arranged in such a way so as to attain the marketing objectives efficiently. The organisation structure of the marketing department is determined for this purpose. Powers and duties and responsibilities of various authorities and their inter-relations are also determined.

8. Coordinating: The marketing management should coordinate work of an enterprise in such a manner that they present a picture of unified unit and the objectives of the organisation are attained in a better way. The activities of marketing management much as sale forecast, product planning and development, market research, sale, advertising, sales promotion, transport, etc. should be integrated in such a way unitedly to show the best results for the organisation. Coordination among activities of various departments should be maintained.

9. Staffing: Without people objectives and resources will remain unconnected and unutilised. Marketing manager recruits and selects efficient marketing force. He arranges for their training and formulates policies regarding their remuneration. He may seek the expert advice of personnel manager in making the recruitment and selection of the marketing staff.

10. Operating and Directing. Marketing manager is responsible not only for planning and organising the activities but also for guiding and supervising the subordinates. He is the leader of the department and of the subordinates working under his leadership. He should motivate the subordinates through his leadership so that they work sincerely to attain the marketing goals. The function of direction and planning has three essential components:

(*i*) Issuing of orders and instructions;

(*ii*) Guiding and teaching the subordinates in the proper methods of work; and

(*iii*) Supervising the subordinates to ensure that their performance confirms to the plans.

1. Analysing and Evaluating: The marketing manager should collect the data regarding sales and other market activities in an explicit manner. He should analyse and evaluate the performance of various plans and projects so that he may be sure as to how far the marketing goals have been accomplished. For this purpose he may analyse the following:

(*i*) The result of net sales and marketing costs, this should be done area-wise, product-wise, product-line-wise, and customer-wise. A comparative study may be made of various areas, products and product lines and customers and important decisions may be taken in the light of such analysis. Uneconomic product-lines market of customers may be dropped. A new strategy should be developed to conform the marketing and the organisation objectives. Thus, the marketing management will be successful in increasing the profits of the concern by utilising the resources to the maximum extent;

(*ii*) The management should evaluate the performance of individual salesman, their productivity or efficiency;

(*iii*) The manager should evaluate, advertising programmes and their effects on the company's sale;

(*iv*) By analysing the performance of various middlemen, the marketing manager may be aware of the tastes, fashion, behaviour and nature of the customers.

12. Controlling: There are four steps in controlling by marketing manager:

(*i*) Devising proper standards for measuring the process of work;

(*ii*) Measuring the actual performance and work in progress;

(*iii*) Comparing the actual performance with the set standards and noting the deviations, variations and discrepancies, if any;

(*iv*) Identifying the deviations, informing the concerned person and taking corrective actions so that the work may be brought back to the desired course.

Marketing manager performs all these controlling functions. He fixes the sale standards for each of the market and for the individuals. He analyses their actual performance, compares it with the set standards and takes corrective actions wherever necessary. If deviation is positive, he tries to maintain it. If it is negative, he identifies the causes and removes them.

QUALITIES OF MARKETING MANAGER

1. Enthusiasm and Patience: He should be able to enthuse the persons working under him. At times of difficulties he should be able to have sufficient patience.

2. Timing and Judgement: He should be able to take decisions at the appropriate time. He should have a clear understanding of the needs and methods of motivation.

3. Liaison with Other Departments: He should have a close and intimate liaison firstly with his own departments, *e.g., purchase, sales, Research, Production, Advertisement,* etc. Secondly, he should have a liaison with distributors. He should meet his distributors from time to time to understand their difficulties and various problems, their reactions to the products and competition in the market. The sales can be increased by sound marketing policy which should not be rigid but undergo a change from time to time according to the circumstances. The distributors should also familiarise them sales with the actual process of production. Thirdly, he should also have the quality of having liaison with other agencies as to take full advantage, of their experiences.

4. Thinking Objectively: In order to have clear thinking about the objectives of his work, he should be able to carry programmes of training his own staff. Instead of centralisation of duties, authorities should be delegated to others to increase the efficiency of the personnel and the work.

5. Loyalty Towards Company: He should be faithful to the company and its basic policies. Even when he does not agree to any particular policy which has been imposed on him he should carry it on like a disciplined soldier expressing his disagreement and his point of view to his superiors in mild terms.

6. Sympathetic: A good marketing manager has the quality of being very sympathetic towards all persons who serve under him. It does not mean any leniency in executing routine work and not following the directions in day-to- day work.

7. Aiming at Customer Satisfaction: It is on the customer satisfaction that the profitability of the company depends. Customer satisfaction alone can ensure the satisfactory volume of sales. As such we can say, the primary object of marketing is to attract the largest possible number of customers. It is possible by having perfect coordination between the wants of the customers and their satisfaction.

8. Evolving Sound Product Policy: The product policy object must be in terms of customer orientation. It is intimately connected with price policy. If a company desires to improve the quality of its products, it would also seek to increase the price to cover the increased costs involved. The pricing policy should be fixed in such a way that it results in the maximum profit to the company flowing from the total sales volume secured by the business at that price. This objective can be achieved not only by fixing very high price but by widening the scope of market for his product. The overheads of the company can be spread over a larger number of items which may result in consequent lowering of prices making it possible for more and more persons to purchase the product of the company. He may even decide to price his product differently according to different market segments based on incomes or locations.

The marketing executive should be very clear about his distribution strategy. In intensive distribution he will have to provide for intensive sales promotion of advertising. These decisions have to be taken at every stage in order to consider possible innovations and improvement in the marketing strategies.

He will have to keep in mind his company's financial ability and production capabilities while taking such decisions.

Thus, in modern marketing concept, marketing management should make all business decisions in the light of consumer needs and wants. It must insist on the integration and coordination of all marketing and other corporate functions towards the basic objective of producing maximum long range corporate profits.

PRINCIPLES OF MARKETING MANAGEMENT

1. Proper Planning: The success of the company hangs on proper planning. Proper planning is essential to achieve the three underlying objectives of marketing: Increase in sales volume; Increase in net profits; and Growth of the enterprise. Basic reasons for constant attention to proper planning arise from the instability of consumer's preferences and purchasing power on the one hand and the instability of competitive position on the other.

2. Sound Organisation: The marketing manager has to organise its division on the basis of sound modern principles of organisation. He should have a clear-cut understanding of the duties and functions of the personnel engaged in the responsible task. There should not be overlapping of responsibilities and obligations of the persons as it breeds confusion and slackness. Each individual should know the responsibility given to him.

3. Proper Control: Marketing objectives can be achieved if the various marketing activities are properly controlled. Various steps to be taken for this purpose are: (*i*) establishing the standards, (*ii*) evaluating the actual performance, (*iii*) comparing the actual results with the standards fixed and note the deviation if any; and, (*iv*) taking the corrective action for achieving the standards. Control on various activities is necessary to keep the marketing costs within admissible limits.

4. Necessary Directions: The management executive issues necessary directions to his subordinates and coordinates all the activities under marketing divisions. He directs and coordinates the activities of other departments like personnel, finance and production, etc., so far as they are helpful in achieving the marketing goals.

5. Objective Decisions: As the activities of the marketing division are directed towards achieving the overall goals of the management, the marketing expert takes decisions objectively.

6. Sales Promotion: The ultimate objective of all the enterprises is to maximise sales. The marketing executive should make all possible efforts to promote the sales of the company. He should employ all the new techniques and methods for this purpose.

7. Successful Motivation: The success of the management executive can be judged by this ability to motivate the staff under him to maximise its efforts to achieve the targets of the enterprises, *i.e.,* maximum sale and profits with the maximum satisfaction of customer.

8. Research and Development: Change in the habits, tastes, preferences of the consumers take place all the time. The marketing manager should study and carry on research and adopt the product in conformity to the preferences of the final consumers. Slackness in the research and development of the product might cause adverse effect on the total sales of the product or products.

9. Consumer's Satisfaction: Modern marketing stands for fully satisfaction of the consumers. The chief objective of the company is to earn maximum net profit. It depends on the total volume of sales which in turn depends on the consumer's satisfaction.

FACTORS INFLUENCING THE ADOPTION OF THE MARKETING CONCEPT

1. Population Growth: Changes in markets are constantly taking place with the growing population day by day. Larger and growing potential markets exist for the widening stream of new consumer products being introduced to the market. New households are added every year and markets of many consumer durables can look forward to potential markets and grow faster than the consumer markets as a whole.

2. Growth in Disposable Personal Income: Total disposable income after tax payment rose from the past though the real income (purchasing power) has not been so great, yet the increase is striking. In spite of rising prices, the consumer on the whole has enjoyed, continuing increase in the purchasing power at his disposal. The households have now more discretionary income. It is the money left once after the purchase of essential food, clothing and shelter. Incomes of this kind may be spent, saved, used for the purchase of 'nonnecessities' or combination of all these. A rise in discretionary income usually results in more spending on goods of non-necessities nature. It has led to the dramatic expansion of the markets for items like T.V. sets, transistors, coolers, scooters, etc. With the affluence it is imperative to cater effectively to a choice as to what things they would prefer to buy and what things they would accept. The research in the field of consumer's wants and desires has now become an essential feature of marketing. The producers try to adjust their products on the basis of this kind of research.

3. Levelling off Income Distribution Pattern: The modern trend of levelling off income distribution tends to the growth of mass markets for luxury items which were possessed by few till recently. This trend is found in varying degree among the rich, the middle and poor people. More and more products which were once regarded as luxuries have become necessities with the spread of electricity fans, coolers, radios, television, etc. Demonstration effect has also played its role in popularising these products. The middle class people and even the poor always try to imitate the living standards of the rich. The growth of transport and communication facilities have also widened the scope of markets for products which used to have only limited market previously.

4. New Attitude Towards Debt: With the increase of banking and credit facilities people try to purchase new items on credit or on hire purchase and instalment basis with minor payments every month. Many cash buyers take loan from banks, finance companies, insurance companies, chit funds provident funds, etc. So also they even buy on credit but make their payment to lenders or creditors. Buying on credit has, thus become a way of life for millions.

Shrewd marketers of many products have accepted credit plans to accelerate expansion of their market and 'buy now-pay later' plans have even made air passage easy for a common man. The bank credit plans have made credit purchases easy even for those retailers who previously sold their goods for cash only. The changing attitude towards debts and the increasing ability of the consumers money in hand.

5. Technological Changes: Great technological changes are taking place. These technological changes have made the products, whole products-lines and even entire industrial concern obsolete. At the same time these changes have produced vast new markets for other products and industries. Technological changes lead to the shortening of the products life cycle. In this way, technological changes is a key element in the competitive struggle among companies. An ever growing number of new products is being forced to the market each year. The list of the products for the customers choice also grows longer.

6. Changes in Marketing Channels: Marketing channels have greatly changed than the changes in markets or their technologies. Once the manufacturer expected his marketing channels to be stable and proper for a long time, but new types of distributive institution shifts in operating methods of the older institutes and development and change in physical distribution has created new problems and opportunities. Many new types of distributive institutions have come up; the consumer markets have also been invaded for some products by some marketers who did marketing at other places. Grocers in the street now also sell patent medicines like aspirin, besides grocery. Hence, the range of distribution open to the manufactures has broadened.

7. Transport Facilities: Transport facilities have led to the distribution at fast pace, economic and extensive. Technological gains in design, manufacture and utilisation of transport equipment in future will make still further gains so that the manufacture will gain the global market. Manufacturers who are limited to an area will find that they are confronted with the large number of competitions from elsewhere.

8. Growth of Mass Communication Media: Newspapers, magazines, transistors, radios and televisions are the various ways of mass communications. The spread of a new product through advertisement has become easier, faster, wider and more effective than in the past. Mass communication media plays a very big role in marketing these days. It has helped the extension of global markets and large scale production. It has become easier now to reach the potential buyers.

9. Unification of Company's Operations: Sometimes there occur conflicts among department goals. Costs are upper most in importance in the production division. It requires lengthening the interval between model changes and maximising the length of production runs.

The marketing division tends to revive round the sales volume which are pushed by all possible means. Wide variety of products are pressed, models are changed at short intervals.

Finance specialists justify their own positions to maximise short run returns to stockholders overlooking customer's wants and going against research and development projects necessary for the firms standing in competition. They even criticise the efforts of production and marketing division to install innovations that require money in the short run and pay off in the long run and try to minimise costs and maximise revenues at the same time.

Thus, unification of company's operation is essential which can be done by accepting the modern concept of marketing where in all the functions of management are integrated. Modern concept of marketing is based on two basic things:

(*a*) That the company policies and operations should be customer-oriented.

(*b*) That the goal of the firm should be sales on profitable basis. Marketing concept is thus a philosophy of business which believes that the economic and social justification of a company's existence is the satisfaction of the wants of the customers. In the words of P. Felton, "A marketing concept is a corporate state of mind that insists on the integration and coordination of all marketing functions, which in turn are welded with all other corporate functions, for the basic objective or producing maximum long range corporate profits.

QUESTIONS FOR EXERCISE

1. Discuss the major problems of marketing management in India?
2. Is there any difference between "Marketing Management" and "Sales Management." If so, explain how these two functions differ in scope and activities.
3. What is the difference between "Sales Management" and "Marketing Management"?
4. Explain the functions of Marketing Manager.
5. What are the qualities of marketing managers? Discuss its objects and goals.
6. Explain the principles of Marketing Management.
7. Explain the factors influencing adoption of the marketing concept.
8. Discuss briefly how can the marketing executive resolve the conflict among departmental goals.

8

Marketing Decision and Environment

The basic problem of the marketing management is to make adjustments between the forces that are within and outside its control. The forces within control called *controllable forces* comprise organisation, products, brands, prices, marketing channels, physical distribution, advertising and personal selling. These are directly influenced by decisions and actions of the marketing organisation. The forces outside the control, known as *uncontrollable forces* consist mainly of competition, science and technology, economic, social, and psychological forces, political and legal factors and cultural influences. These are influenced by the firm's decision to a very small extent. As Cundiff and Still put it, "The uncontrollables make up the environment in which the firm must operate, while controllables are the means by which it adapts to that environment....Dynamic marketing management is characterised by continual adjustment and readjustment of controllables, in relation to the uncontrollables, which make up the environment."[1] Working within an environment of uncontrollables, marketing management directs the application of controllables, and it does this through planning, organising, coordinating and controlling.

In order to solve the marketing problems, the two essential requisites are:

(*i*) *The availability of the empirical data and quantitative analytical tools*. Quantitative market analysis, transportation, warehousing, establishing channels of distribution, forecasting sales, establishing quotas and territories, and many other

1. Cundiff and Still, *op. cit.*, p. 73.

marketing tasks are performed more easily and decisions are apt to be more sound if analytical tools are used.

(*ii*) *The importance of the contributions made by the behavioural sciences should be recognised.* The contributions made by psychology, sociology, and anthropology can and do help in solving problems related to marketing organisational structures.

Definition of Decision-making

1. *Franklin G. Moore*: "Decision-making is the blend of thinking, deciding and acting."

2. *George R. Terry*: "Decision-making is the selection based on some criteria from two or more possible alternatives.

3. *D.E. McFarland*: "A decision is an act of choice wherein an executive forms a conclusion about what must be done in a given situation. A decision represents behaviour chosen from a number of possible alternatives."

4. *Ernest Dale*: "Marketing decisions are those decisions which are always made in the Course of one of true management activities, planning, organising, staffing, directing, controlling, innovation and representation."

5. *M.H. Jones*: "A decision can be defined as the particular course of action chosen by a decision maker as the most effective mean at his disposal for achieving the goal or goals he is constantly emphasising or for solving the problem that is bothering him."

6. *Philip Kotler*: "A decision may be defined as a conscious choice among alternative courses of action."

The question of decision-making does not arise if there is only one course of action. When more than one alternative courses are open before us the selection of the best alternative is called 'decision-making'.

CHARACTERISTICS OF DECISIONS

1. Selective: Decision-making is a selective process in which are selected only the best alternatives.

2. Evaluation and Analysis: Decision-making involves careful evaluation and analysis of all the alternatives.

3. Responsibility of Management: Decision-making is the responsibility of the management executives at all levels.

4. Continuous Process: Decision-making is a continuous process which goes on throughout the life of an organisation.

5. Mental Process: Decision-making is a mental process, which involves deep thinking and foreseeing things.

6. Positive or Negative: Decision may be positive, that is, to do a certain thing or negative, that is, not to do a certain thing.

7. Based on Time: Decisions are normally taken on the basis of past experiences and present circumstances for a future course of action.

8. Means: Decision-making is not an end in itself but a means to reach the goal.

9. Expert Advice: Experts and specialists should be consulted before making a particular decision, if necessary.

10. Impact: As decisions exert great influence on the success or failure of an organisation, they should not be made in a hurry or without close scrutiny and thinking.

MAIN ELEMENTS OF DECISION-MAKING

1. Best Decision: Rational decisions must conform the basic concept of good decision. Scientific decisions should be made in keeping with this concept. According to Cundiff and Still, "Conceptualisation, information and prediction are three main keys to rational decision-making." Rational decisions help in attaining the goal of an organisation. Hence, the problem should be thoroughly analysed and all the possible alternatives should be fully considered before a rational decision is made. This requires intelligence, insight and experience.

2. Organisational Environment: Formal structure and the organisational environment of the company exert much influence on decision-making. While some organisations believe in rigid centralisation others have faith in decentralisation and leave the routine decision-making function with the departmental heads. The company should retain the policy matter decision with the top management leaving the ordinary day-to-day routine matter decisions to the various departmental heads. External, social, political and economic environment also influence decision-making. Unstable political conditions in the country retard the process of decision-making.

3. Personal Traits: Personal traits like preferences, intellectual maturity, experience, educational standard, social-religious attitudes (optimistic or pessimistic) designation and status, etc. of the person responsible for the decisionmaking exert much influence on decision-making.

4. Timing: A particular decision may be best under prevailing circumstance but with the change in situation and other conditions, it may not be useful in guiding the organisation's activities towards the attainment of marketing aims. Therefore it is very important to make decision at the appropriate time keeping in view the prevailing conditions.

5. Communication: After a particular decision has been taken, it must be communicated to the persons concerned in time. It should be communicated to the subordinate executives in a courteous language. Its language should be very simple and free from any kind of ambiguity.

6. Participation of Employees: The implementation of decision becomes easier if there is participation of the employees in taking a decision. Employee's participation has following advantages: (*i*) It ensures loyalty of the employees towards the organisation, (*ii*) It arouses the feeling of oneness with the company. (*iii*) The decisions are also superior, (*iv*) The chances of opposition from the employees are minimised. Even if there is opposition from their side its intensity is less, (*v*) Issuing directions to the employees becomes easier and simpler, (*vi*) It develops sound human relations between the management and the employees. It helps in enhancing the efficiency of the organisation in attaining the goals.

AIMS OF DECISION-MAKING

1. To recognise problem situations;
2. To determine alternative course of action;
3. To appraise the alternatives;
4. To decide on a particular course of action.

PROBLEMS OF DECISION-MAKING

Management's decisions to resolve marketing problems are made from time to time. These are made after a great deal of deliberations, quickly and through intuition: Sound decisions are information based, They are a combination of judgement and information. Marketing research helps in collecting the useful information.

Information based decision-making solves major problem situations in marketing. Such problems have the following characteristics:

1. As they arise at irregular intervals, decisions on them do not have to be made again and again.

2. They have important consequences while present for a long time as it is very difficult to change management decisions after they are made. This includes cases involving the introduction of new products, opening up new markets; changing the basis structure of sales organisation, choosing marketing channels or determining the type and amounts of personal selling and advertising and other elements in 'promotional mixes'. A decision on such matters is critical to marketing process. Such decisions should be reached only after thorough analysis of relevant information. As their possible consequences are high and far reaching therefore a marketing executive should not risk making decisions intuitively. He should take all steps required to assure the availability of sufficient marketing information to pursue informations based decisions on all major marketing problems. Management and decision cannot be separated. They both go together. Decision-making is the main business, the soul of management.

SCIENTIFIC PROCESS OF DECISION-MAKING

The process of decision-making may be pursued through 1. Traditional method, and 2. Scientific method.

1. Traditional Method: If decisions are taken on the basis of limited knowledge, experience and intuition, there is no scientific analysis involved in such decisions. The decisions are not logical. Some thinkers have called this method of decision-making as method of Symptomatic Diagnosis as the physicians in ancient times diagnosed the ailment on the basis of symptoms.

2. Scientific Method: Nowadays an expert doctor relies not only on external symptoms but makes use of accurate X-ray, ECG reports, etc. In the field of marketing management the old traditional method is being discarded in favour of the scientific method.

The Process of Taking Scientific Decisions

(*i*) *Defining the Problems, Objectives and Constraints*: The first step is to study the nature of problem about which a decision has to be taken. A careful study of the external and internal aspects of the problem should be made carefully. The objectives of resolving the problem and constraints in the way of resolving it must be given due weightages in order to reach the correct decision.

(*ii*) *Analysis of the Problem*: It involves careful appraisal of the various alternatives to decide, as to (*a*) which departmental executive should take the particular decision, (*b*) others who should be taken into confidence, (*c*) whether some specialists are also to be consulted, and (*d*) who should be informed of decisions.

All policies and operating decisions should be taken by the top management. The routine departmental decisions should he left to departmental heads. A thorough analysis of relevant information is needed to make an important decision. If facts and information are not available, they may be taken on the basis of the best of the facts available.

(*iii*) *Finding out Alternative Solution*: After defining the problem it is necessary to find out all alternative solutions. For example, if there is the problem of pushing up sales, there may be various courses open such as spending more on advertisement and publicity, developing the market promotion activities or appointing more salesmen or improving the quality of the product or making packaging more attractive or reducing the price, etc. As it is not possible to pay attention to all the alternatives; only the important ones must be considered. The management should not depend on one solution alone because if that fails under a given situation, the other may be required to be taken up in its pace. It is, therefore, essential to consider all possible alternative courses of action.

(*iv*) *Deciding upon the Best Solution*: The concerns which operate under the marketing concept require a coordinated, systematic and continuous information available from internal and external sources. Following factors have to be taken into consideration while deciding upon the best solution:

(*a*) The ratio of advantages and disadvantages in each solution;

(*b*) Out of the possible solutions which one is such that requires the minimum amount of effort;

(*c*) The financial limitations of the organisation;

(*d*) Solution favourable under the given circumstances.

After considering all these factors, the best possible solution should be decided. Operation research technique may be employed to select the best alternative. Each alternative is quantitatively judged on the basis of experience, knowledge and intelligence.

(*v*) *Converting the Decision into Effective Action*: It is not sufficient to take decision upon the best solution, its effective implementation is equally important. If, not put into practice effectively, a decision cannot serve any purpose. It is necessary that the decision reaches all subordinate officers, staff and all concerned employees for whom it is meant. The language of the decision should be simple and understandable. All the concerned employees and executives should be made to acknowledge it. Their full co-operation for the implementation should be sought in mild and courteous language. They should be made to feel that the management's decision is their own decision. As many as possible subordinates should be involved by their participation at the time of making such decision. This will help a great deal in its implementation and make the matter simple, efficient and effective.

(*vi*) *Follow-up Action*: Follow-up action is a must for a scientific decision. Decision-making by scientific process is no guarantee that it is cent per cent correct. It might be defective and might cause loss to the organisation. In order to minimise the chances of loss, it is necessary that it should be followed up. Any shortcoming in the decision it should be made up by taking suitable steps.

Knowledge is never said to be perfect in the case of business. The marketing conditions are never stable. There is always uncertainty about the future. Therefore, following criteria should be used in taking decisions: (*i*) Criterion of optimism, (*ii*) Criterion of pessimism, (*iii*) Expected monetary value criterion, and (*iv*) Expected utility criterion.

TYPES OF MARKETING DECISIONS

1. Major and Minor Decisions: Decisions which affect the quality of the product or the product line of the organisation are called major decisions. These have to be made very carefully because they have direct impact on the achievements of the company's goals. The decisions which have to be made in the course of implementation of the major decisions are called minor or supplementary decision. If a new product has to be developed, its form, colour, design, packaging, etc. have to be determined only after the major decision regarding the development of a new product has been taken.

2. Routine and Important or Vital Decisions: Decisions which have to be made in routine course repeatedly are called routine decisions. Purchase of day-to-day materials by the purchase department does not require much thinking. Decisions in respect of routine purchase come under the category of routine decisions. On the other hand, vital decisions are those which affect marketing efficiency, profitability, etc. of the organisation. For example, decisions regarding purchase of new plant or developing the capacity of the old plant, etc. come under the category of important or vital decisions.

3. Less Risky and Very Risky Decisions: Decisions involving comparatively no risk or very little risk are less risky decisions such as appointment of a sales representative. Such decisions are made by departmental heads. On the other hand, the decisions which involve comparatively more risk are termed as risky decisions such as appointment of a new-marketing executive. Risky decisions are generally made by top managements.

4. Recurrent or Rare Decisions: Decisions which are made repeatedly about the usual matters of the organisation are called recurrent decision, such as decisions regarding sales quota, advertising, etc. On the other hand, those decisions the necessity for which does not arise daily are called rare decisions such as the change of advertising agency or the re-organisation of the sales organisation, etc.

5. Organisational and Personal Decisions: Decisions which pertain to the organisational activities are called organisational decisions such as decisionmaking by the management regarding the quality of the product. On the other hand, the decision by the authority for himself such as proceeding on leave is an example of personal decision.

CHARACTERISTICS OF MARKETING DECISIONS

1. Complexity: Marketing decisions are comparatively complex because the marketing problems are mainly human problems relating to the human behaviour of the consumers and distributors, etc. As human behaviour is complex, so the marketing problems are complex in nature.

2. Human Behaviour-oriented: Marketing decisions are human behaviour-oriented. Their success depends on the study of human behaviour. If the marketing executive understands human nature as to what the customer buys, where he buys, how he makes purchases, when he likes most to purchase, etc., he can succeed in making sound and scientific decisions. But it is not so simple to understand human behaviour. In the first place the consumers are rational beings. They think differently and, therefore, show their preferences differently. All the consumers are not of the same temperament. Their preferences vary very widely. Human behaviour is also subject to change, therefore, it presents difficulty in its proper appreciation.

3. Organisational Effect: Marketing decisions are affected by the position of the organisation. If the company is strong and well managed, the management is in the habit of making scientific decisions and if those decisions are properly and strictly implemented, then marketing decisions contribute largely in achieving the objectives of the organisation.

4. Extensive and Long-run Effect: Marketing decisions not only affect the marketing department but also the activities of all other departments of the organisation. For example, the decision regarding the production of a new product will affect not only the marketing department but also the other departments such as research and development department, production division, finance department, etc. The marketing decisions exert long run influence. They cannot be altered quickly because they involve great deal of expense and far-reaching effects. Hence, the marketing decisions are very important for the organisation. This enhances the responsibility of the marketing executive. Therefore, marketing decisions should be taken very carefully.

5. New Decisions: Some marketing decisions give birth to new decisions. For example, the decision for a new product will lead to make decisions in respect of the design, quality, colour, brand, packaging, price, distribution, advertising, etc.

6. Rationality: Marketing decisions are made very carefully as the very success of the organisation depends on them. They should be reached only after a great deal of deliberations and thorough analysis of relevant information. Their possible consequences are of high and far-reaching importance.

MARKETING' ENVIRONMENT

Meaning

The marketing environment comprises the "non-controllable" actors and forces that have an impact on the company's markets and marketing. Company's marketing environment consists of the actors and forces that affect the company's ability to develop and maintain successful transactions and relationships with its target customers." The actors and forces in a company's marketing environment are shown in figure 8.1.

Types of Company's Environment

1. The Micro Environment: It consists of the actors in the company's immediate environment that affect its ability to serve its markets; the company, suppliers, market intermediaries, customers, competitors and publics. Every company's primary goal is to profitably serve and satisfy specific needs of chosen target markets. To carry out this task, the company links itself with a set of supplies and a set of marketing intermediaries to reach its target customers. The suppliers, company, marketing intermediaries, customers chain comprises the core marketing system of the company. The co's success will be affected by two additional groups, namely, a set of competitors and a set of publics.

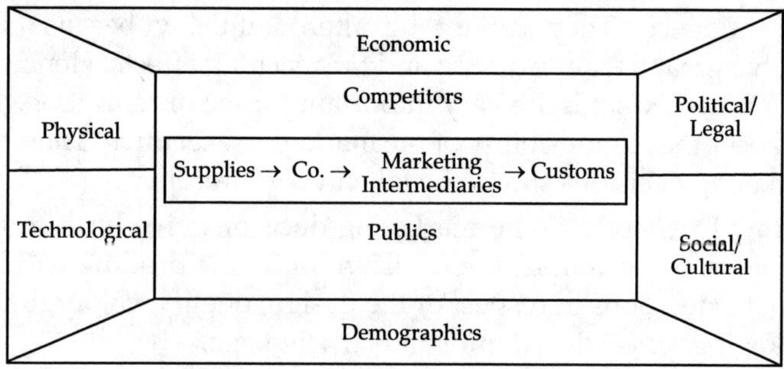

Fig. 8.1: Major Actors and Forces in the Co's Marketing Environment.

2. The Macro Environment: It consists of the larger societal forces that affect all of the actors in the company's micro environment; the demographic, economic, natural, technological, political and cultural forces. These forces represent 'uncontroliables', which the company must monitor and respond to. These macro environment, forces shape opportunities and pose threats to the company. The major components of Marketing Macro Environment are; the company and its suppliers, marketing intermediaries, customers, competitors and public all operate in a larger macro-environment of forces and megatrends that shape opportunities and pose threat to the company. There are six major forces effecting macro-environment, namely, demographic, economic, natural, technological, political and cultural.

(*i*) *Demographic Environment*: Population is the first environment fact of interest to marketers because people make up markets. Marketers are keenly interested in the size of the population, its geographical distribution and density; mobility trends, age distribution; birth, marriage, and death rates and racial, ethnic and religious structure.

(*ii*) *Economic Environment*: It consists of factors that affect consumer purchasing power and spending patterns. Markets require purchasing power as well as people. Economic conditions, economic policies and economic system are the important external factors that constitute the economic environment of a business. For example, the economic conditions of a country, the nature of the economy, the stage of development of the economy, economic resources, the level of income, the distribution of income and assets, etc. are among the very important determinants of business strategies. The economic policy of the government has a very great impact on business. Some types or categories of business are favourably affected by government policy, some are adversely affected, while it is neutral in respect of others. The industrial, monetary and fiscal policies also affect the business in different ways by the incentives and disincentives they offer and by their neutrality.

(*iii*) *Natural Environment*: The deterioration of the natural environment was found to be one of the major issues facing business and public in the 1990s. In many world cities, air and water pollution have reached dangerous levels. There is great concern about industrial chemicals creating a hole in the ozone layer that will produce a "green house effect," namely, a dangerous warming of the earth. Marketers need to be aware of threats and opportunities associated with the following four trends in the natural environment.

(*a*) Shortage of raw materials.

(*b*) Increased cost of energy.

(*c*) Increased levels of pollution.

(*d*) Changing role of government in environmental protection.

(*iv*) *Technological Environment*: Technology is the most dramatic force shaping people's lives. Every new technology is a force for 'creative distraction'. Each technology creates major long-run consequences that are not always foreseeable. Some of the important factors and influences operating in the technological environment are as follows:

(*a*) Sources of technology like company sources, external sources and foreign sources, cost of technology acquisition; collaboration in and transfer of technology.

(*b*) Technological development, stages of development, change and rate of change of technology and research and development.

(*c*) Impact of technology on human beings, the marketing system and the environmental effects of technology.

(*d*) Communication and infrastructural technology and technology in management.

(*v*) *Political Environment*: It is composed of laws, government agencies and pressure groups that influence and limit various organisations and individuals in a society. The main political trends are:

(*a*) Substantial amount of legislation regulating business.

(*b*) Growth of public interest groups.

(*c*) Changing government agency enforcement.

(*vi*) *Cultural Environment*: The basic beliefs, values and norms shape the society of the people. People almost unconsciously absorb a world view that defines their relationship to themselves, to others, to nature, and to the universe. Even when people of different cultures use the same basic products, the modes of consumption, conditions of use, purpose of use or the perceptions of the product attributes may vary so much so that the product attributes, method of promoting the product may have to be varied to suit the characteristics of different markets, even the values and beliefs associated with colour vary significantly between different cultures.

Marketing Environment for a Cigarette Industry

Cigarette industry in India has recorded a growth rate of near about 10 per cent per annum. Essentially meant for middle and upper class urban and rural consumers, this industry offers considerable potential for growth. The business environment in which the cigarette industry exists at present could be explained in terms of the opportunities and threats operating currently. Opportunities are supported by factors like;

1. High demand potential due to rapid increase in population,
2. Rising personal incomes,
3. Increased access to rural markets and increase of purchasing power of rural consumer,
4. Spread of Cable TV as a media for advertisement.

Basing excise duty on cigarette length instead of value enhances opportunities for cigarettes for common masses.

Threats arise due to factors like:

1. Cigarette consumption is considered to be unwholesome and thus attracts organised efforts to discourage their consumption. Prohibition campaigns have been conducted against its consumption.
2. Fear of high taxation on the part of government.
3. Excise duty based on length poses threat for premium brands of cigarette,
4. High taxes, as to curb its consumption and, moreover, cigarettes are considered a luxury item.
5. Advent of societal marketing on the one hand and spread of consumerism on the other.
6. Cigarette consumption lacks social acceptance as belief associated with cigarette smoking people are not healthy.

QUESTIONS FOR EXERCISE

1. Define decision-making? What are its basic elements?
2. Decision-making is the primary task of the manager. Discuss and explain the problem and process of scientific decision-making?

3. Describe the various types of Marketing decisions. What are special characteristics of Marketing decision?
4. What do you understand by Marketing Environment? What are the major components of marketing macro-environment? How do you evaluate the marketing environment for the cigarette industry in India?

9

Responsibilities of the Marketing Manager

Marketing executive is a very responsible authority entrusted with the task of looking after the entire marketing activities of the firms so that the objectives could be effectively fulfilled. *Marketing objectives are the mirror of company objectives.* The statements of objectives that are developed at company level are formulated by the executive in a way that helps marketing achieve company objectives. The manager's influence upon the composite marketing environment varies with the size or the significance of the enterprise which he directs. It measures the social influence that a marketing manager can bring to bear, it is a measure of his social contributions and responsibilities. As Seibert says. "The marketing manager possesses a measure of control that he is obligated to direct toward an outward, social, political, and economic responsibility, as well as toward the inward growth and profitability of his own enterprise."[1] The manager is challenged to achieve "internal accomplishments but at the same time to avoid socially undesirable external consequences that could be self-defeating within the total environment." He must be aware of the interrelationship of the Arm and the system and an appreciation of forces operating in both directions. As Alderson has put it, "The marketing specialist observes how marketing systems work and recommends ways of making them better." He further observes that "marketing practitioners and specialists build a science of human behaviour since decisions relating to products, promotion,

1. Seibert, Joseph, C., *Concepts of Marketing Management,* Harper & Row, New York, 1975, p. 15.

and other marketing activities represent efforts to modify human behaviour."[1]

THE TOTAL MARKETING CONCEPT

The total marketing concept means the integration of various elements of marketing mix into the most probable blend. Under this, corporate objective must be established first.

The Market manager must know all things about market. The business should be so arranged that its main objective is to make and sell what the user wants at the price he is ready to pay and with product characteristic that he wishes to get out of it. The place where he needs them and when he needs them count much for his satisfaction. All aspects of the business must be customer-oriented. It must fulfil all the needs and services of the customer who make the market segments stand. He should be the focus of marketing activities. His importance must become the overall philosophy of the concern.

ROLE OF MARKETING MANAGER

In the light of modern concept (customer-oriented) of marketing, the marketing manager is supposed to be aware of all the aspects and techniques of modern marketing. Marketing manager is mainly responsible for the performance of marketing activities yet his position in the concern is somewhat peculiar. He acts as an administrator; he is a link between the society and the organisation; he serves as a coordinator of different activities of the concern as far as they are related to marketing activities. Following are the different roles of marketing manager in an organisation.

1. Administration: The marketing manager is supposed to be a technically qualified person in the field of marketing. He must be aware of all the aspects and techniques of modern marketing. As administrator who is the chief of the marketing department, he must also possess the traits of a leader or administrator. It is better in the interest of the concern, if he possesses both these qualities though a combination of both the qualities are rarely found in a person.

Being the head of the marketing department, he is an administrator who must apply the principles of general

1. Anderson Wroe, '*A Normative Theory of Marketing Systems*' in Cox, Alderson Shapiro, *Theory in Marketing*, Richard D. Irwin, Homewood, 1964, p. 93.

administration in the marketing function. As an administrator; he is responsible for the planning, coordinating, organising, staffing, directing and controlling the marketing activities by applying the various tools to management. He is at the top of line in the marketing department. He takes all policy decisions for the smooth working of his department.

2. The Staff Function: Marketing Manager advises the top management in matters affecting formulating the overall policy of the business so far as they are concerned with the marketing activities. He advises the other departmental heads in coordinating their activities according to the marketing policies. Therefore, he should be a good leader having the capability to lead the subordinates so that he may direct them in the right direction, that is towards the attainment of overall objectives. He should evaluate the marketing efforts from time to time in order to have a better control over them.

3. Link between the Society and the Organisation: Marketing manager acts as a communication link between the society and the organisation. He puts forth the needs and nature of demand of the society before the organisation. He gets the products and services produced according to their needs and requirements and arranges for their distribution through various channels. For this purpose, he studies and analyses the market reports and informs the organisation about them in time. Without him the organisation will lose a lot and the needs of the society will also remain unfulfilled. Marketing manager should make all necessary arrangement for the distribution of new and existing goods and services to the society and also educate the public regarding them. For this, he should consider the cost factor in marketing the goods and services, otherwise it will effect the standard of living of the society adversely which in turn will also affect the organisation adversely.

4. Coordinator: Marketing, production, finance and other functions of the organisation are closely correlated. The change in one function will bring the change in other functions in the same direction. One cannot spare the other. For example, marketing efforts increase the demand of the product of the organisation and it will require the increased efforts on the production front. But if the required finance could not be arranged the production and the sale targets would also remain unachieved. So, these factors should be coordinated in an ideal form.

As a coordinator the marketing manager establishes coordination between the various activities of the organisation such as personnel or finance and those of the marketing department. He takes decisions within the framework of the objectives of the firm. He should be in close touch with the policies, goals, and the working of other departments such as production or finance, etc. so that he may formulate the policies, set the goals and standards and plan the working of the marketing department accordingly so that all the departments of the organisation may work as a unit to achieve the organisation goals.

In a well organised organisation, the relation of all the factors should be in form. If one factor changes, the other is also bound to change. For example, if the production of the firm is planned to increase, the efforts should be made to sell the product and for this purpose development of marketing activities is necessary. Necessary finance should also be arranged to meet the production and sale targets. But this relation comes to an end as soon as the firm reaches at an optimum point.

It, however will be severed, when the activities could not be taken up because of the higher marketing cost. If the society demands the product while its increased production makes the production process complicated, the firm will not choose to increase the production capacity in spite of its increased demand.

All these problems have to be tackled by the marketing manager as a coordinator.

AREAS OF AUTHORITY

1. Marketing Research Activities: These come under the direct supervision of Marketing Manager as the Marketing Research department collects the necessary facts and figures about the markets of company's product and the most of the marketing decisions depend upon such information.

2. Product Planning and Development Activities: These are also directed by the marketing manager.

3. Personnel Activities: Marketing manager performs the activities of personnel department so far as they are concerned about the sales personnel.

4. Advertising and Sales Promotion Activities: These are also directed by the marketing manager.

5. Credit Facilities: Marketing manager is responsible for taking decisions in respect of credit facilities to be provided to debtors in order to promote the sale of the product.

6. Distribution: Decisions about the choice of channels of distribution are also under the jurisdiction of the marketing manager.

7. After Sales Service: Marketing manager decides the main aim of marketing the products which is to satisfy the customers.

RESPONSIBILITIES OF MARKETING MANAGER

1. Responsibilities in a Seller's Market: If a Company is working in the seller's market, marketing functions are restricted to distribution only. In such cases the position of market manager is quite negligible in the organisational set-up. But it concern will find itself in critical situation if the seller's market changes to buyer's market.

2. Responsibilities in Competitive Market: If the Company is in a competitive market situation, it will stress more on its marketing operation. The position of the chief marketing or sales executive will improve. He will be given exclusive powers and authority with status in the whole structure. He will be endowed with higher authority as he may not be consulting the Board of Directors at every step. Thus, he may be a member of the Board of Directors with the offices of Marketing Directors invested with him. In such a situation he can discuss with the members at the Board meeting on equal footing.

3. Leadership Responsibilities: The marketing manager is like a leader who is connected to the salesmen and sales executives. He must have constant contact with the market requirements. This he should his base on the reports received. These reports supply indications and nature of demand, the changes in the attitudes of the customers and their preferences, the type of services needed by the consumers and the extent and threat from the competitors. The manager must have continuous flow of the information so that he can change his policies if needed. He must plan and organise his activities. He must motivate the personnel under him and incorporate an adequate system for controlling the performance in terms of objectives described by the Company and himself.

FUNCTIONS OF THE MARKETING EXECUTIVE

1. Creation of new market.
2. Supervision of sales.
3. Product planning and development.
4. Distribution.
5. Advertising.
6. Forecasting.

These functions are serially given according to importance. Most managers are known by the name of Sales Manager and not by the name of marketing manager though a sales manager's functions include the marketing management activities.

On the basis of information gathered by situational analysis the marketing activities have to be directed towards the company's overall marketing objectives. In the light of company's overall objectives, the overall marketing objectives have also to be fixed. The chief executive must know whether he wants a return on investment after taxes or whether his company wants to be a price leader. He must also crystallise the product objectives, pricing objectives, distribution strategy objectives and his promotional objectives.

POWERS AMD DUTIES OF MARKETING EXECUTIVE

1. Product Policy: The chief executives must be clear as to the type of customers for whom the product is meant. The company produces a single product or a series of products or goes on to diversities. The product policy should be well grounded on customer orientation and as a result of the overall marketing objectives.

2. Pricing Policy: The pricing and product policy are inter-related. A concern desirous of improving the quality should increase the price to cover the increased cost. If the marketing executive desires to fix the price in a profitable way to the company, he should promote and widen the market for his goods. To widen the market of the goods differently, a different pricing strategy will be useful towards export markets. Thus, pricing decision involves sales forecasting which is a tricky business. However, it has to be done if marketing is to be on a more scientific or systematic footing.

3. Distributing Strategy: The chief marketing executive should be clear as to the nature of distribution that he wants for his product. He has to decide on the policy if he likes limited or widespread distribution of the product whether he wants intensive distribution, *i.e.*, maximum product exposure or selective distribution where he restricts the number of his distribution outlets. His decision in this area is materially affected by decisions in other areas. In case of intensive distribution, he will also have to preside for intensive promotion or advertising that requires a higher amount to be spent on these activities.

4. Advertising and Sales Promotion: Marketing manager's policy towards the price of the products and distribution channels must decide whether the advertising will be done by a separate department in his organisation or to give it to an advertising agency or use both mediums.

5. Integrated Marketing: The marketing executive has to take decisions in various elements of the marketing mix in an integrated way. Decisions about the product affect the decisions regarding pricing. The customer's decision about the purchase of a product does not depend on the price of that product.

The marketing executive must be able to develop an organisation so that he gets the maximum results from his personnel and coordination with the other departments like production, finance and personnel. Responsibilities should be fixed on individuals who must appreciate their relationship to get maximum coordination.

6. Coordinated Marketing Effect: Marketing Executive should see that all departmental heads under him cooperate mutually, despite their different backgrounds and expertise.

7. Coordination with Other Departments: There must be coordination with other departments outside the control of the chief marketing executive like the production department, purchasing department, finance department and the personnel department, etc.

RESPONSIBILITIES TO SOCIETY

1. Marketing Social Needs: The marketing manager studies the actual wants of the people and organises production accordingly. Goods are produced on a large scale at one place. He undertakes the important task of distribution of goods and looks to the total satisfaction of the consumers.

2. Consumer Satisfaction: Consumer satisfaction is the fundamental principle of modern marketing concept. The marketing manager studies the consumers' behaviours, their preferences, tastes and fashions in relation to the products. He endeavours to modify the products according to the needs of the actual users.

3. Providing Employment: A large number of persons are engaged in the marketing activities such as wholesalers, retailers, advertisers, insurance agents, transporters, bankers, clerks, salesmen, etc. Thus, marketing activities provide employment to a large number of people.

4. Reducing Product Costs: Reducing product cost is another obligation of the marketing manager towards the society. He can reduce the costs of the products per unit by making the various marketing activities efficient, economical and effective. It will help the consumers to get goods at reasonable prices. If the company does not transfer the benefits of the reduced cost to the customers, and retains the whole of the profits itself, the society is still benefited as the retained earnings are invested in the development of new products or they are distributed to the shareholders as dividend. In both the cases the society gains.

5. Providing Information: One of the obligations of the marketing manager is to provide information about the qualities of the products of the company in a way the consumers may make up their minds to purchase the company's products. It helps in building the image of the company and selling its products.

Thus, the marketing manager is responsible to the society in many respects which he should execute sincerely.

QUESTIONS FOR EXERCISE

1. Explain Total Marketing Concept. Describe the role of the marketing manager in a modern business organisation.
2. Discuss the position of marketing manager as an administrator. Outline the areas of his authority.
3. What are the responsibilities, functions, powers and duties of the marketing manager?
4. Write a short note on the responsibilities of a modern marketing manager.
5. In what way a marketing manager is responsible to society?

10

Marketing Research

The purpose of research is to observe, to locate source of data and to provide the means of obtaining information from these sources, Research involves editing data for completeness, consistency, uniformity, accuracy and for all other information, which may affect the ultimate usefulness of the data under consideration in one or the other way. Marketing research involves methods of observation and carefully editing of the data collected and extends to tabulation, classification, computation, comparison and correlation.

The term *market research* is loosely used as synonymous with *marketing research.*[1] The term, *market research,* has been more narrowly defined by modern marketing men as the study of those who buy or distribute. On the other hand *marketing research* is a broad and widely used term inclusive of marketing research activities.[2]

Definition of Market Research

1. *P.D. Converse*: Market research is "the constant search for, and analysis of, facts." It is defined as 'diligent, *pro rata* investigation', as 'studious inquiry' or as thorough, honest and impartial study conducted by trained men using scientific methods."[3] Research gets the facts needed to solve a problem.

2. *Charle F. Kettering*: "Research looks forward to see what industry may do when it cart no longer do what it is doing." He further

---

1. Report of the Definitions Committee, in the *Journal of Marketing*, October, 1948, p. 210.
2. Clark and Clark, *Principles of Marketing*, 1942. p. 1.
3. Converse, P.D., *Selling Policies*, p. 51. *Elements of Marketing*, 1935, p. 766.

says that, "research is done in man's minds and not in laboratories although laboratories may be necessary." Market research may be thought of in large measures, as Reid activity whereas physical research is closely related with work in laboratory.

Market Research and Marketing Research

P. Kotler says, "Some companies use the term '*market research*' instead of '*marketing research*'. The former term is accurate for describing research into markets: their size, geographical distribution, incomes, and so forth. However, it fails to cover the idea of research into the effects of marketing efforts on market, for which the term marketing research is more accurate. Marketing research is increasingly coming into favour as the term describing both ideas".[1] He defines marketing research as "a systematic problem analysis, model building and fact finding for purpose of improved decision-making and control in the marketing of goods and services."[2]

The OEEC publication on *Market Research Methods in Europe* makes a clear distinction between 'market research' and 'maketing research.' The term 'marketing' is concerned with the entire sphere of distirbution while the other only deals with the problems of the market in the narrow sense of the term. The essential task of marketing research is that of finding a "quantitative expression" for "mass-phenomena."[3]

Definition of Marketing Research

1. *K. Clodwig*: Marketing research "is the systematic objective, and exhaustive search for and study of the facts relevant to any problem in the field of marketing."[4]

2. *R.D. Crisp*: Marketing research "the *systematic search* for an analysis of facts related to a marketing problem.... It is shifting from fact-finding, information gathering activity to a problem solving and action recommending function."[5]

---

1. Kotler, P , *Marketing Management: Analysis, Planning and Control*, 1972. p. 309.
2. *Ibid*., p. 192.
3. Kapferer Clodwig, *Market Research Methods in Europe*, OEEC', September. 1950, pp. 14 and 19.
4. Crisp, R.D , *Marketing Research*, 1957, p. 3.
5. Stanton, W J., *Fundamentals of Marketing*, 1971, p. 46.

3. *W. J. Stanton*: Marketing research is "the systematic gathering, recording and analysis of data about marketing problems to facilitate decisions-making".[1]

4. *Cundift and Still*: Marketing research is "that part of business research that studies the transfer and sale of goods and service. It may include study of their physical distribution, wholesale and retail merchandising and financial problems. The real function of marketing research is to help the manufacturer or the producer to increase his sale."[2] It is an organised and systematic search embracing all activities involved in the marketing process to draw certain useful inferences such as defining profitable and unprofitable sales territories and channels of distribution, consumers' possible purchasing preferences, marketing costs, guiding sales promotion efforts, discovering production modification to stimulate new demand existing and potential competitors and competitive prices.

5. *Report of the Committee on Definitions (U.S.A.)*: "Marketing research is the inclusive term which embraces all research activities carried on in connection with the management of marketing work. Among other things, marketing research involves the study of the relationship and adjustments between production and consumption, preparation of commodities for sale, their physical distribution, wholesale and retail merchandising, and financial problems concerned. Such research may be undertaken by impartial agencies or by specific concerns or their agents for the solution of their marketing problems...It includes various subsidiary types of research, such as:

(*i*) *Market analysis* which is a study of the size, location, nature and characteristics of markets.

(*ii*) *Sales research* which is largely an analysis of the sales records of a company;

(*iii*) *Consumer research* which is concerned chiefly with the discovery and analysis of consumer attitudes, reactions, and preferences; and

(*iv*) *Advertising research*, which is carried on chiefly as an aid to the management of advertising work."[3]

---

1. Cundiff. F W. and Still. R.L., *Basic Marketing*, 1972. p. 503.
2. Converse, Hugey, and Mitchell *The Elements of Marketing*, p. 663.
3. R.S. Alxender, R.S., in Committee on Definitions, *Marketing Definition: Glossary of Marketing Terms*, 1960, p. 17.

6. *Hasty and Others*: "Marketing research" may be defined as, "the systematic gathering, recording and analysing of data about problems relating to the marketing of goods and services under essentially non-recurring conditions."[1]

7. *J.C. Seibert*: "Marketing research has to do with the gathering, processing, analysis, storage and dissemination of information to facilitate and improve decision-making."[2]

8. *F.F. Webster*: "Marketing research is a part of the marketing information system, and a key to the implementation of the marketing concept. It is usually designed to aid planning and often involves evaluation of previous marketing efforts."[3]

9. *Phelps*, "Marketing research is concerned with getting the best possible answer to certain major questions of business, namely, what to produce or handle, when and how much to produce, where to place the product over the market, where to direct sales effort and what price to charge."

10. *A.H. Delens*: "Marketing research is the systematic and continuing study and evaluation of all factors bearing on any business operation which involves the transfer of goods from production to consumer."

11. *G.B. Giles*: "Market research applies to a study of the market, while investigations into sales methods and terms of trade, advertising reaction, design, packaging acceptability and the effectiveness of sales promotions are perhaps more accurately described as "Marketing research."

12. *Luck and Others*: "Marketing research is the branch of marketing intelligence that conducts specific inquiries into problems in order to guide marketing decisions."[4]

Characteristics of Marketing Research

(1) It involves intensive and systematic study of a marketing problem. This it does by adopting a planned procedure of investigation and analysis.

---

1. Hasty, Ronald, W. and Till R. Ted, *Marketing*, 1975, p. 43.
2. Seibert, Joseph, C., *Concept of Marketing Management*, 1973, p. 128.
3. Webster, Frederick, F. *Marketing for Managers*, 1974, p. 78.
4. Luck, David, J. Wales, Hugh, G. Taylor, Donald, A., *Marketing Research*, 1974, p. 14.

(2) It adopts scientific method and objecitvity in the solution of a marketing problem from a rational outlook based on reason and logic. The purpose of enquiry and the problem under investigation are clearly defined. Accuracy in calculation, in observation and in reporting is strictly ensured, and a standardised process used.

(3) It is an aid or a tool for decision-making and control in the marketing of goods.

(4) It is an integral part of Information System.

On the basis of these elements, we may say that:

Thus, Marketing research is the systematic and objective search for the analysis of information relevant to the identification and solution of any problem in the field of marketing.

Areas of Marketing Research

1. *Business economics research*: It is concerned with economic forecasting and business trends analysis such as the Operations Research, Programme Evaluation and Research Techniques, return of an investment, and inventory analysis.

2. *Product research*: It involves the activities connected with gathering information about customer needs, product concept and prototype testing style, and packaging testing, etc

3. *Sales and market research*: It analyses sales volume and salesman performance data, market penetration rates, new product performance in test markets, and customer-related product data such as opinion or attitude surveys, as well as company's effectiveness of its promotional activities.

4. *Advertising research*: It is concerned with the effectiveness of given advertising media, such as radio, newspapers, films for a given production, advertising, message research, etc.

TYPE OF RESEARCH ACTIVITIES OF 800 COMPANIES IN U.S.A.[1]

(a) Business Economics Research

	Per cent doing
Short-term forecasting	85
Long-term forecasting	82

1. Twedt Dick, Warren (Ed.), 1978, *Survey of Marketing Research*, American Marketing Association, Chicago, 1978, p. 41.

	Per cent doing
Studies of business trends	86
Pricing studies	81
Plant and warehouse location studies	71
(b) Product Research	
New-product acceptance and potential	84
Competitive-product studies	85
Product Testing	75
Packaging Research-design, or Physical characteristics	60
(c) Sales and Market Research	
Development of market potentials	93
Market share analysis	92
Determination of market characteristics	93
Sales Analysis	89
Establishments of sales quotas/territories	75
Distribution channels and cost studies	69
Test markets	54
Consumer-panel operation	50
Sales Compensation studies	60
(d) Advertising Research	
Motivation Research	48
Copy research	49
Media research	61
Studies of advertising effectiveness	67

View of R.D. Crisp

According to R.D. Crisp, the following activities are covered under the scope of marketing research activities.[1]

1. Research on products and services

(*i*) Determining customer acceptance of proposed new products.

(*ii*) Making comparative studies of competitive products.

(*iii*) Evaluating new competitive products.

(*iv*) Determining current or new uses of present products.

1. Crisp, Richard, D., *Marketing Research Organisation and Operation*, American Management Association, New Delhi, 1958, pp. 39-47.

(*v*) Evaluating and market testing of proposed new products or services.
(*vi*) Determining sources of customer dissatisfaction with products.
(*vii*) Simplifying product line.
(*viii*) Making packaging and design studies.
(*ix*) The use, brand preference, etc.

2. Research on markets

(*i*) Analysing size of market for existing products.
(*ii*) Estimating demand for new product.
(*iii*) Sales forecasting and general business forecasting.
(*iv*) Determining characteristics of markets for products.
(*v*) Analysing sales potentials and relative profitability of territories.
(*vi*) Studying trends in market size and composition.

3. Research on sales methods and policies

(*i*) Establishing or revising sales territories.
(*ii*) Evaluating present and proposed sales methods.
(*iii*) Studying competitive pricing.
(*iv*) Analysing salesmen's activities and effectiveness.
(*v*) Setting sales quotas and developing salesmen's standards.
(*vi*) Studying distribution cost.
(*vii*) Establishing salesmen's compensation plans.

4. Research on advertising

(*i*) Evaluating advertising effectiveness.
(*ii*) Analysing competitive advertising and selling practices.
(*iii*) Selecting advertising media.
(*iv*) Making motivational or qualitative studies.

5. Research on miscellaneous activities

(*i*) Analysing opinions of employees, public or stock holders regarding the company, its product and its policies.
(*ii*) Determining location of new sales branches or stores.
(*iii*) Studying current central state and local legislation and its possible imapct on the company.

PROBLEMS OF MARKETING RESEARCH

Reilly groups these problems under three major heads as follows:[1]

1. Those which relate to the product itself;
2. Those which relate to consumer markets; and
3. Those which relate to each phase of the marketing process.

1. The product itself: These studies involve investigations of price at which the product is offered to the public, of present and pontential uses, and of weaknesses and improvements in the physical content or packing of the product. By market investigation of this character the manufacturer is able to adopt his product so that it will meet more nearly the requirements of the consumer for whom it is supposed to have been made.

2. Consumer Market: Consumer research is the careful and systematic investigation of the consumers' attitudes, actions, preferences, and other reactions to the particular problem under survey. For such a research the customers are grouped according to age, sex, race, religion, occupation, class, education, intelligence, income, material possession, and standard of living, of securing data concerning consumers' buying motives and habit, and the finding out of the likes and dislikes of present and prospective customers. Now, information is collected on a number of topics related with the consumers, such as:

(*i*) *Who buys the product*? (By sex, age-group, married, single, occupation, geographical location, social class).

(*ii*) *Where is the product purchased*? (Road side shop, cooperative store, multiple shop, departmental store, chemist, grocer, etc.).

(*iii*) *Where is the product used*? (For breakfast, tea, lunch, dinner, sleeping time, picnics winter/summer/rainy season, festivals or special occasion, like birthdays or marriage).

(*iv*) *How does ike product compare with competitive products*? (For taste, colour, quality, size, shape, price).

(*v*) *In what type of containers is the product desired*? (Design, colour, size and shape of cartons and packages).

(*vi*) *What are the product s factors of appeal*? (Attractive appearance, good quality', easy handling, utility, correct price, etc.).

---

1. Reilly, *Marketing Investigations,* pp. 3-8. White, P., *Advertising Research,* pp. 232-236.

Such a survey helps the manufacutrer in getting from the consumer: (*i*) a critical review of his produce; (*ii*) guidance as to the size of the total market in which he is operating; (*iii*) the sales volume of his competitors, and of his product's potential; and (*iv*) guidance on such problems as selecting a product name, the design and colour of the packet or container, and promotional efforts.

3. The Marketing Process: These studies are concerned with the various marketing functions. However, the marketing manager thinks of them in connection with the actual departments present in his own business organisation. The most common of these departments include advertising, sales and transportation.

(*i*) *Studies on advertising* include investigations of the objectives of advertising, the selection of a particular medium available, finance and money required for the purpose, community influenced, area undertaken, and the general condition of advertising with selling activity.

(*ii*) *The sale research* includes studies of sales volume, turnover for various products, job analysis upon which the selection and training of salesmen might be based, sales talks and procedure, salesmen's routes, salesmen's compensation plans, and channels of distribution.

(*iii*) Investigation of *transportation problems* includes relative cost of different methods of transportation, quantities in which the products might be most economically shipped, and method of shipping and reshipping of goods that permits the lowest possible unit cost.[1]

OBJECTIVES OF MARKETING RESEARCH

According to E.S. Moulton, Marketing research aims at providing the following information to the marketing manager:[2]

(1) To define his present market situation together with the long-range trends which have led up to it.

(2) To discover what major and underlying factors are dominating that situation and how these factors can be influenced or controlled.

---

1. *Ibid.*, p. 5.
2. Moulton, E.S., *Market Research Activities of Manufacturers.* 1930, p. 1; W.J. Donald (Ed.), *Handbook of Business Administrator*, 1931, p. 4.

(3) The set up a plan for keeping in touch with the behaviour of these dominating factors and for measuring the results of any efforts made to influence or control them.

According to P. White, Market research may be used in the following ways:[1]

(1) *Market and their potentialities*: A study of the market, its location and its potentialities.

(2) *Consumers*: Information concerning who they are, where they live, and their buying habits, motives and preferences.

(3) *Dealers*: An investigation of present dealers and their business methods with a view to determining the best type of dealer to choose as official representative.

(4) *Selling policies*: Collection of data concerning the correctness and improvement of present policies and the testing of present policies.

(5) *Sales territories*: An analysis of present territories with a study of the best territorial divisions and routing within them.

(6) *Sales quotas*: The finding of correct facts upon which to base and to develop a sales quota.

(7) *Merchandising policies*: The study of old policies and the finding and testing of new ones.

(8) *Products*: The discovery of desirable new products, their use and improvements, together with a determination of best sizes, prices, and qualities.

(9) *Packages*: The designing and testing of appropriate packages.

(10) *Trade marks and slogans*: The compilation, testing and choosing the best trade marks and slogans.

(11)*Advertising*: The determination of the efficiency of advertising and the testing of window displays, etc.

(12) *Copy appeals*: Finding out why people buy one product rather than another from one firm in preference to another.

(13) *Magazine*: Information with reference to the reading habits of consumers and retailers.

(14) *Competition*: Determination of policies and practices, etc., of competitors and the strength and weakness of each competitor's position.

---

1. White, P., *Marketing Research Technique*, pp. 41-42.

(15) *Persons*: The collection of facts about any particular person's positions.

According to Converse marketing research may:[1]

(1) Supply the data to be used in selling salesman's and territorial quotas and in planning production. (2) Supply the facts for fixing the budget. (3) Determine the advertising methods that should be used and the angle that should be employed in the advertising copy. (4) Supply material for sales talks. (5) Furnish facts to convince dealers of the selling possibilities of given articles and to help them to increase their sales. (6) Predict the trend of business conditions in given industries and furnish a basis for purchasing programmes. (7) Ascertain the consumer's likes and dislikes. (8) Report the methods used by the dealers, display, advertising and selling. (9) Measure the stocks in the dealer's hands. (10) Find the dealer's reactions to given policies. (11) Furnish data for fixing dealer's territories and quota. (12) Find out and tabulate statistics in which the concern is particularly interested. (13) Keep one informed about the developments in other industries which may affect the business of the concern. (14) Measure the purchasing capacity of a given territory. (15) Discover new uses for the product. (16) Analyse the cost data that are available in published form. (17) Study the organisation of the concern involved with a view to suggesting changes or improvements.

CATEGORIES OF MARKETING RESEARCH STUDIES

1. Market measurement studies.
2. Studies of influences of controllables.
3. Studies of the competitive situation.
4. Studies of uncontrollables.
5. Motivation research studies.

1. Market Measurement Studies: These are aimed at getting quantitative data of potential demand which indicate how much of a particular product can be sold to individual market segments over some future period assuming the application of appropriate marketing methods. These data relate to market potential, sales potential or both.

1. Converse, P.D., Selling Policies, pp. 57-58

(*i*) *Measurement of market potential*: It invovles determining for particular market segment, the maximum possible sales opportunities open to all sellers of goods or services during a stated future period.

(*ii*) *Measurement of sales potential*: It involves determining for particular market segments the maximum possible sales opportunities open to a specified company selling goods or services during a stated future period. For example, if the sales opportunities for 19-inch portable colour television sets are calculated during the coming year the market potential for TV set industry is a somewhat higher figure than the sales potential available to a particular manufacturer.

Value of Measurement Data

Market measurement data are helpful in planning overall marketing strategy. In evaluating a proposed new product, the management must estimate its probable marketing success. Analysis of market measurement data gives valuable insights as to whether a potential market exists and if so, its likely size. Market measurement data are again helpful in determining the geographical sequence of market introduction, if the management decides to add new products. In addition, breakdown of potentials by types of customers makes it possible for promotional efforts by differing amounts and in that order. Management makes use of maket measurement data in resolving questions regarding dropping certain products from the line or de-emphasising their promotion to particular market segments.

2. Studies of Influences of Controllables: The widest variety of marketing research studies deal with the influences of controllables, *i.e.,* products distribution, promotion and price management. These studies provide needful decision-making guidance about where the management manipulate the controllables. Management uses studies of controllables to appraise the effectiveness of current product, distribution, promotion and pricing policies. For example, many companies make frequent studies of the effectiveness of advertising and other promotional devices, individual salesman, existing sales methods and sales compensations plans. These formal studies draw management's attention to situations requiring changes in policies and practices. Management can manipulate controllables without such formal studies, but with the added insight gained from special studies manipulation is more effective.

3. Studies of the Competitive Situation: Some companies lay more stress on the studies of the competitive position of their own products more than they do to studies of the nature and impact of their competitor's activities. Specifically measuring the 'share of the market' that a company's product has is a much more common type of study than one appraising the marketing strengths and weaknesses of a competitor's product improvement, measuring the imapct of a competitor's price change, or apprising the effects of a competitor's change in advertising approach. This is so because the market information is often obtainable through outside research organisations generally on a subscription basis. Companies find it easy to estimate share of the market percentages for their own products particularly if industry sales figure are gathered and distributee by trade associations. Most companies could benefit significantly if they would do more 'intelligence' type studies designed to have a view of competitor's marketing practices and policies. Management needs this information to understand how competitor's actions affect the company's marketing situation that it can do a really effective job in plotting marketing strategy and counterstrategy.

4. Studies of Uncontrollables: Few marketing research studies focus directly on the influences of uncontrollables because most executives feel that they can get the needed information in the course of their regular business readings. Published information is readily available on such controllables as the level of consumer credit, business expansion plans, age and income distribution trends and consumer buying intentions. Government commerce department gathers and publishes data on the national economic situation and outlook and the balance of international payment. It also maintains field offices to help businessmen looking for specific types of information. Considerable information on the uncontrollables also appears in such publications. Even though the executives get much information on the uncontrollables from their regular business reading, they seldom have the time required to organise data gathered from many sources and analyse the results in terms of their own company's marketing problems.

5. The Motivation Research Studies: These probe psychological and sociological variables affecting buying behaviour. Many companies fail to do motivation research because it requires trained specialists, psychologists and sociologists. As concerns have now employed such people most of the motivation research is still comparatively new. Many exectives doubt its value and are suspicious of many of its findings.

IMPORTANCE OF CONSUMER ORIENTATION

Marketing studies need a thorough knowledge of the consumer's preference, attitudes and motivations which change over a period of time. Marketing research can help the management in remaining consumer-oriented in its decisions. Companies desiring to sell their product abroad must realise that habits and preferences of people differ in different countries. Export decisions based on inadequate information about the consumers may result in unsuitable products being offered at unsuitable prices with the help of ineffective promotional strategies. For example, many conventional modes of dressing have largely gone out of fashion. These changes require adequate consumer orientation on the part of the management.

In some industries the management decides production on the basis of their own views on the consumers' tastes. This often results in unwanted stock lying in the market and unsold stocks at the mills. The Millowners' Association have therefore come to realise the importance of marketing research.

In Asia, Japan takes keen interest in Marketing Research. During the Swadeshi Movement in pre-Independence era in India most of the so-called Jawahar waistcoats, Gandhi caps and khaddar kurtas were supplied to India by Japan. The paper marks of chief characters of Ramayana sold during Ramlila days, in India are supplied by Japan.

IMPORTANCE OF MARKETING RESEARCH

1. Reduction of Risk: Marketing research reduces the risks involved in marketing decisions. Facts got from research can form the basis of planning, selling, sales promotion, advertising, etc. If the marketing manager has the relevant information about customer preference, the performance of alternative packing materials, prevailing prices of competitor's products and dealer's reaction to different sales promotion, marketing manager's past experience may give a basis for reaching a decision. Sometimes observation and experience are not enough. Many a time the decision-making authority is not able to see customer's reactions directly from the point of sale. Conditions change and policies that work at one time may not be effective at a later stage. It is possible to learn fully erroneous facts as direct observation and experience are insufficient guides to marketing manager's research. Therefore, it is necessary to get the details required for selecting from intelligent alternatives.

Marketing research helps in reducing the risks involved in marketing decisions by providing:

(*i*) Current information required by the marketing manager to take decisions.

(*ii*) Generalised knowledge or theory about the marketing process.

2. Production of New Items: The marketing manager gets valuable information and facts regarding customer's habits and preferences through marketing research. A company may develop new products and make necessary improvement in its existing products in order to satisfy their needs.

3. New Uses of Products: Marketing research provides information regarding various uses of the product. If a company's product is being used by the people, it can widely publicise the alternative uses of the product and create demand of the product in the market.

4. Information about Customers: Various valuable informations about the customers are made available by the marketing research. By collecting such information, marketing manager comes to know the weaknesses in his product and the marketing activities. He can improve the effectiveness of the marketing activities by improving the product.

5. Selection of Channel of Distribution: As the marketing manager comes to know about the need satisfaction of his customers and the marketing strategies of his competitors, he can select the best channel of distribution for his product to meet the needs of the customers effectively.

6. Knowledge about Demand: Marketing research studies the nature of demand of the company's product whether it is elastic or non-elastic or highly elastic or seasonal. By this study the producer can plan his product programme effectively to produce goods when they are in demand and can avoid the cost of production and of marketing.

7. Discovery of Potential Markets: Through marketing research, potential markets are discovered where company's product can be sold. It widens the scope of company's operations and extends its marketing activities to such markets.

8. Coping with Competitive Situations: After a company studies the marketing policies, practices and strategies of its competitors through marketing research, it makes necessary changes in its policies, practices and strategies so as to give them a suitable fight in the market. Thus, the company can survive in competitive situations otherwise it may lose the markets.

9. Planned Production: As Marketing research helps in estimating the demand of the product, it facilitates the production of the product in a planned way which may result in maintaining the equilibrium in demand and supply position in the market.

Thus, marketing research is very useful for the planning and development of the marketing activities in the right direction.

PROCEDURE OF MARKETING RESEARCH

1. Crystallising the Marketing Problem: In it the marketing problem is defined and emphasis is laid on the marketing problem. While solving the complex marketing problem like unexplained decline in sales, efforts are done to define the problem to establish a general framework of major marketing elements like:

(*i*) Industry element; (*ii*) Competitive elements; (*iii*) Market elements; (*iv*) Company elements.

(*i*) *Industry Elements*: These include the question of the size of the industry's volume, its trend and the economic climate affecting such volume.

(*ii*) *Competitive Elements*: These include the ascertainment of the company's major competitors, their market shares, changes in such shares, the emergence of new competitors, comparative product innovation and price changes.

(*iii*) *Market Elements*: These deal with characteristics of the market for products of the industry and the major changes, if any, in such characteristics may be the subjects for research.

(*iv*) *The Company Elements*: These deal with characteristics of company's goods and their comparison with major competitors as regards customer acceptance, pricing practices, quality of the sale organisation and distribution channels.

2. Identifying the Research Problem: A necessary step in research is the situation analysis survey of available data regarding the product and market and its advertising dealer situation that can be gleaned from discussions from executives, available published materials and internal records. The researcher arrives at a hypothesis or a theory or presumption arrived at provisionally which may form the basis or guides as to the reason why certain things have happened, so that further investigation may be proceeded with along those lines. After the situation analysis, the analyst continues to formulate his hypothesis and refine his problem definition by going outside the company and talking informally with informed people like intelligent and efficient retailers, wholesalers, consumers and key men in the industry to get their point of view and in this way get the feel of the problem.

3. Determining Needed Information and Sources: At one time the decisions can be made on the basis of experience and judgment without assembling the facts. At other time it is necessary to collect and analyse information by a formal research.

The objectives of research may be borne in mind before securing the relevant facts from any source—Original or Secondary. The sources of information are company records, consumers, buyers, dealers and government and private sources reports.

4. Securing the Relevant Facts: The next step is to select the method for research, if the available secondary data is quite insufficient. The basic methods are three:

(*i*) *Observational Method*: In it direct observation of the phenomenon is relied and contact of the people is avoided.

(*ii*) *The Experimental Method*: In it small-scale experiments are made.

(*iii*) *The Survey Method*: In it the consumers are contacted directly.

5. Analysis and Interpretation: The tabulated data have to be manipulated into the best form of statistical summarisation in order to help the steps of interpretation. Both for percentages or averages, the form of statistical summarisation must be so selected as to fix the data to give the greatest value in the imperative work which is to follow. Collection and tabulation of data are quite useless unless analysed and interpreted to resolve the problem.

6. The Research Report: Results are extracted from the analysis and interpretation of data in the form of a report presented to the marketer so that he can come to know the details of the problem and its solution. Generally, this report is presented in writing but at times it may be orally explained.

7. Follow-up Action: Although the marketing research procedure comes to an end as soon as the marketing research report is submitted to the maketer yet it is useless unless follow-up action is taken and the measures suggested in the report are implemented in their true spirit.

LIMITATIONS OF MARKETING RESEARCH

1. Limitation of Time: The researcher has to complete the research work within given time. If the time is sufficient enough, he can carry out the research work satisfactorily. If time is short, it is possible that he may not collect the original data and has to depend upon the secondary data whose reliability is doubtful.

2. Limitation of Money: The researcher is provided a limited money within which he has to complete the research work. Owing to limitation of money, small samples are chosen and the secondary data are extensively used. Reliability of both small samples and secondary data is questionable. Therefore, it does not mean that a good research can only be followed with more money but it is true that sufficient funds are necessary to carry out a good research programme.

3. Limitation of Skill: The marketing research work needs a lot of statistical work such as collection and tabulation of data, their interpretation with statistical methods and drawing out the necessary results. It requires an able, efficient and experienced research worker who has to assess the reliability of the secondary data. A man who is proficient in the work should always keep the objectives of the research in mind. If the researcher has all these qualities, the results are reliable. As qualified researchers are not easily found and they ask for the good remuneration, this is another limitation for concerns whose financial resources are not good.

4. Limitation due to Bias: Limitations of money, time and skill also give birth to bias. If the researcher is biased to the problem, the results of such research will be erroneous and the very purpose of marketing research is lost.

5. Limitations in the study of Human Behaviour: Marketing research studies the behaviour of consumers who are rational but that may not express their feelings correctly. In such cases, their habits, practices and preferences cannot be assessed correctly.

In spite of the above limitations of marketing research, one can present correct information about consumer's behaviours if proper care is taken. It can help solve the problem by collecting, interpreting, analysing, and presenting the fact.

METHODS OF MARKETING RESEARCH

1. The Observation Method: In this method, data are collected through direct observation. No talks take place. By observing, a person can make an inventory about product used by him at his home or kept as retailer's stocks. If a retail shop is to be established in a locality and the situation traffic is counted on the road, observation gives more accurate information than could be secured by making calls on members of the family. No questioning work is done in observation. This method simply involves "watching or listening or both" with no attempt of probing the reasons. For example in a departmental store the total number of people passing by a display the number stopping, the number picking up and examining the product and the making purchases may be made by observation.

2. The Experimental Method: It is based on the concept that small-scale experiment is useful to indicate the expectations of large-scale experiment. If two advertisements appear in the same paper on front page and last page the people are more attracted to the front page. This is known as 'Split-on' test. These conclusions are adopted in shops where things having more sales are kept in front position. So also about the advertisement in black and white. This experiment takes more time and is expensive. Nevertheless, a well designed experiment can provide guidance and information for decision-making even though it cannot replicate total market conditions. Test conditions are never the same as parallel conditions in the broader market.

3. The Survey Method: This is also referred to the 'Questionnaire Technique'. In it responses to direct questions are expected. It is a more widely used method. It has three main uses: (*i*) to gather facts from respondents, (*ii*) to report their opinion, (*iii*) to probe the interpretations they give to various matters.

It is most accurate and reliable when used to gather factual data. It is reliable less when used to record opinions and least reliable when used to gain insight into respondent's interpretations. The survey is of three kinds: factual survey, opinion survey and interpretative survey.

(*i*) *Factual surveys*: In it the respondents are asked to report actual facts such as what brand of cigarettes do you smoke? The answer might be wrong as respondents may answer wrongly to please the interviewer.

(*ii*) *Opinion Survey*: It is designed to gather expressions of personal opinion to record evaluation of different things. By forcing immediate answers to the questions from the respondents there is possibility of wrong answers as in the case of factual survey.

(*iii*) *Interpretative Survey*: In it the person not only reports to the questions but acts as interpreter also. Its limitation is that personal feeling and motive and attitude cannot be interpreted. In panel research the same person gives information on many occasions. In panel method the respondent should be cooperative.

SURVEY TECHNIQUES

1. Personal Interview Survey: In it information is gathered by face to face interviewing. The respondent is shown the exhibits and advertisements to know his personal opinion and attitude. This method requires much time and energy. It is difficult to contact a large number of persons as some are unable to be contacted. Moreover, some areas are difficult to be covered.

Merits

(*i*) It is an easy and intensive method.

(*ii*) Reliable information can be gathered.

(*iii*) It serves specific requirements of the survey.

(*iv*) It avoids unnecessary details and thus saves time and money.

Demerits

(*i*) Personal prejudices may destroy authenticity of information.

(*ii*) Extensive use is not possible because time planning is necessary. Moreover, all persons cannot be contacted.

2. The Mail Questionnaire Survey: In it, the covering letter explains the purpose of study. A prepaid post envelope or reply card is sent and sometimes a gift is offered. The method is economic if the response is good. The cost should be calculated on the whole expense. The advantage of this method is that distant areas can easily be covered with limited expenses. Even those persons are available for survey who cannot be contacted through interviews. The data is more accurate as it is free from personal bias.

Merits

(*i*) Cost is relatively less.

(*ii*) Speedier than all other methods.

(*iii*) Widespread use as it can be used extensively.

(*iv*) Convenient to respondents.

(*v*) Establishing contact is simple.

Demerits

(*i*) Sometimes there is very poor response. All persons contacted do not bother to the return of questionnaire,

(*ii*) Only limited amount of information can be collected because some do not answer all the questions,

(*iii*) Information is relatively useless for qualitative studies.

(*iv*) The questionnaire once prepared cannot be altered.

(*v*) Preparation of mailing list is an uphill task.

(*vi*) Answers may not be received in time; hence, it is time consuming process.

(*vii*) Answers may not be proper and correct; hence, the very objective of survey is defeated.

3. The Telephone Survey: Here both the interviewer and questionnaire are on the telephone. It saves time and travelling. More interviews can be held in a short time. Its demerit is that only rich persons who own telephones can be approached. In the absence of observational information, people cannot be classified as to occupation, age and economic condition. The persons who do not have telephones are completely omitted thus rendering the sample imperfect.

Merits

(*i*) It is economical and saves time.

(*ii*) Surveyor finds immediate response to the questions.

(*iii*) Increased speed, as so many persons can be contacted in limited time.

(*iv*) Flexibility.

(*v*) Simplicity.

(*vi*) Orderly, as the questions could be asked in a planned manner.

(*vii*) Personal contact becomes possible.

Demerits

(*i*) Possibility of personal bias.

(*ii*) Sufficient time may not be available for the respondent because he is to answer the question immediately.

(*iii*) The persons not having telephones cannot be contacted rendering the sample imperfect.

(*iv*) Product inspection by the respondent is not possible.

SOURCES OF COLLECTING MARKETING RESEARCH DATA

1. Internal Sources: A business organisation has to maintain records of financial accounting, sales records, reports of salesmen, etc., which provide sufficient information. Proper use can be made of the various informations in possession of the organisation. The sales analysis may help product analysis, territorial analysis and culture analysis.

2. External Sources: When the internal records are insufficient the organisation will have to depend on external sources. The external sources fall into two categories: Primary data and Secondary data.

(i) Primary Sources: It is one from which information is got directly as for instance through questionnaire and interview. It includes consumers and buyers, middlemen, salesmen, trade associations executives and others.

(ii) Secondary Data Sources: These are mostly published materials, such as government census publication and Sales Managers Survey of buying power. Sometimes, company files or marketing research and other reports contain the desired information although this may not be known to the decision-maker needing it. Thus, secondary data sources are repositories of material assumed for other purposes not of items of information gathered specifically to get the objectives of the research project being planned.

The researcher should always look to the secondary sources for if the needed information is already available, the time and expense of gathering it from primary sources is saved. Some information may be gained from secondary sources such as population and income statistics. Daily newspapers, monthly magazines or special annual numbers, the Economic Times, Financial Express, Journals of Marketing, Yogna, Eastern Economist, etc. are important sources of useful information. Following are External Sources of information for marketing Research:

(*i*) **Private Sources:** There are a large number of publications dailies, weeklies, monthly magazines, etc. in different languages. These give a wide coverage of information.

Voluntary organisations such as Chambers of Commerce, Trade Association, etc. also issue bulletins regarding prices and stocks of articles.

(*a*) Magazines and Journals: *Commerce, Eastern Economist, Journal of Marketing, Capital, State Bank of India, Monthly Review, Economic and Political Weekly*, etc.

(*b*) Newspapers: *Economic Times, Financial Express, The Hindu, Survey of Indian Industry*, etc.

(*ii*) **Government Sources:** *Reserve Bank of India Bulletin, Agricultural Situation in India, ISI Bulletin, Publication of ICAR, and NCERT, State and Central Gazettes, etc.*

(*iii*) **International Sources:** *U.N. Statistical Year Book, IMF Balance of Payments Year Book, Year Book of Food and Agricultural Statistics, International Reports on Cotton. Sugar and Tea, etc.*

SAMPLING

What is Sampling?

According to Richard D. Crisp, "If a small number of items or parts called a sample are chosen at random from a large number of items or a whole called universe of population, the sample will tend to have the same characteristics and to have them in, approximately, the same proportion, as the universe." Thus, a sample is only a portion of the universe from which it is drawn.

By studying the characteristics and attitudes of the numbers of a sample, rather than of all numbers of a universe, we can draw the near-correct conclusions in less time and with lower research costs. In sample study, the errors are possible because the sample is the representative of the universe, not the universe itself. But, if proper care is taken in selecting the samples, results may be near correct.

Attributes of a Good Marketing Sample

1. Random: Random, means that everybody in the group has an equal chance to represent the group.

2. Representative: It means that the sample must include the important kinds of units in the total universe.

3. Proportional: The same sample should contain a lot of various segments in the same proportion in which they appear in the whole lot.

4. Adequate: The larger the sample the more nearly correct would be the result.

Types of Sample

1. Probability or Random Samples: Random samples are those which are selected in such a manner that every member of the universe has an equal chance of being included or excluded in it and in which the probable error that may creep in the studies or results is mathematically known in advance. Thus, the word random does not mean 'haphazard', it is predetermined and an arranged method of selection.

Probability or Random Sample may take the following forms:

(*i*) *Systematic Sampling*: The first unit of sample is selected at random. Then the random selection is followed by systematic sampling.

(*ii*) *Stratified Sampling*: These samples are useful in industrial marketing research. This kind of sampling is made when certain factors are known. For example, the manufacturer knows the volume of output. The hetrogeneous population is divided into blocks on the basis of age, sex, etc. each of which is then sampled at random in the same proportion.

(*iii*) *Cluster and Area Sampling*: It is survey conducted on a group simultaneously. This reduces cost and time. Clusters or groups are selected on the basis of predetermined strata.

(*iv*) *Multistage Sampling*: It is just an improvement of the principle of cluster sampling. Sampling is done at various stages or levels. For example, one may start in the first stage with a sample of a nation as a whole then proceed to different states. The process may be narrowed down into smaller and manageable parts.

(*v*) *Sequential Sampling*: Under this method the ultimate size of the sample is not fixed in advance but determined only later and that too according to some mathematical basis.

2. Non-Probability or Purposive Samples: These are made to meet the specific requirements of a special nature. They are more popular in the field of marketing research. The various kinds of such samples are:

(*i*) *Convenience Sampling*: Information is collected from any convenient group whose views may be relevant to the subject of inquiry.

(*ii*) *Judgement Sampling*: A group is selected to be interviewed in advance on the basis of expert judgement. But the method of selection is not very scientific and is haphazard in nature.

(*iii*) *Quota Sampling*: Samples are selected on a convenience basis, but maintaining an overall structure of the sample. These samples are referred to as quotas. Within quotas, a further selection is made to form the ultimate sample.

Merits of Sampling Method

(*i*) *Quick Results*: This is so because the collection and dissemination of data is quicker.

(*ii*) *Better Results*: This is so because the samples are selected carefully.

(*iii*) *Skilled Analysis*: This is because the sampling is based on scientific methods.

(*iv*) *Lower Cost.*

(*v*) *Errors could be Assessed Mathematically.*

(*vi*) *Practical Method.*

Demerits of Sampling Method

(*i*) *Personal Bias*: Errors cannot be completely avoided.

(*ii*) *Faulty*: Irrelevant samples are likely to make the process faulty.

QUESTIONS FOR EXERCISE

1. What do you mean by Marketing Research? Describe its scope and benefits.
2. Discuss the present-day importance of marketing research. What is the contribution of marketing research in decision-making?
3. What is Marketing Research? Outline important areas of research and describe the benefits it is expected to confer.
4. "Marketing Research is vital for evolution of sound marketing strategy?' Critically examine this statement.
5. Marketing Research is the key tool used by management in its problem solving and decision-making in the field of marketing. Examine.
6. Explain the procedure and limitations of Marketing Research.
7. Briefly explain the steps in the marketing research process.
8. What is Market Research? Discuss the need and scope of Market Research in Indian Economy.
9. Distinguish between Market Research and Marketing Research. What is the utility of Marketing Research to a marketing executive?
10. Distinguish clearly between Marketing Research and Market Research.
11. The following are generally the three basic methods of collecting information number:

    (*a*) Personal interview.

(*b*) Telephone enquiry.

(*c*) Postal enquiry.

Which method would you recommend for collecting information on consumer preference of a high price soap? Give reasons for your answer and disucss the relative merits and demerits of each of these methods.

12. Explain in brief what are the various sources of collecting Marketing Research Data?
13. What is Sampling? Compare and contrast the relative merits and limitations of probability and non-probability samples.

11

Market Segmentation

Definition of Market Segmentation

1. *Stanton:* "Market segmentation consists of taking the total heterogeneous market for a product and dividing it into several sub-markets or segments each of which tends to be homogeneous in all significant aspects."[1]

2. *Kotler*: "Market segmentation is the sub-dividing of a market into homogeneous subsets of customers where any subset may conceivably be selected as a market target to be reached within a distinct marketing mix. The power of this concept is that individual sellers may prosper through creatively serving specific market segments whose needs are imperfectly satisfied by the mass-market offerings."[2]

3. *Ronald Hasty and Others*: Segmenting markets simply divide the heterogeneous mass market into groups, each of which has one or more homogeneous characteristics,[3] the number and nature of which depends on the purposes and imagination of the analyst. For example, an industrial market might be segmented as follows:

1. By size of customer large, medium and small accounts, in terms of purchases, number of employees, sales volume, or other measures.
2. By geographic area.
3. By method of distribution.

---

1. Stanton, W.J., *Fundamentals of Marketing*, 1983, p. 66.
2. Kotler, Philip, *Marketing Management: Analysis, Planning and Control*, 1972, p. 166.
3. Hasty, Ronald, W., and Will, R. Ted, *Marketing*, Canfield Press, San Francisco, 1975, p. 65.

4. By Standard Industrial Code.
5. By amount of technical service required.
6. By reasons for buying and benefits derived from use.
7. By nature of buying decision process.

4. *Webster*: "Market segmentation is a method for achieving maximum market response from limited marketing resources by recognising differences in the response characteristics of various parts of the market. It is a strategy of "divide and conquer" that adjusts marketing strategy to inherent differences in buyer behaviour."[1]

Thus, segmentation is the delineation of a customer group or groups with homogeneous wants/needs which the organisation might successfully satisfy. It is the process of grouping individuals whose expected reactions to the producers' marketing efforts will be similar during a specified time period. It involves two closely related areas from the perspective of the marketing manager, (*i*) The total market for any product can be sub-divided or segmented into groups of potential customers who are homogeneous with respect to certain wants or desires, (*ii*) It might be advantageous to the organisation to serve one or more of these market segments.

Degrees of Segmentation

As segmentation of market is generally consistent with the changing needs of the population, any one of the following kind of segmentation may be practised by marketers:

1. Partial market segmentation: In it the entire market is divided along broad, categorical lines. For example, in the automobile market, one consumer may be looking for station wagon, or jeep, another may seek to buy a car run by diesel or a light vechicle like a scooter or Luna cycle. In such situations, some manufacturers market to each group separately.

2. Extreme market segmentation: It occurs when marketers tail their product to the specialised needs of a selected few customers. This particularly occurs in luxury industries, or female garments such as when the tailor prepares the dress according to the measurements of the lady concerned or the hosiery dealer sells 'bras' or 'panties' only or the ladies toilet preparations.

1. Webster, Fredrick, F., *Marketing for Managers*, 1974, p. 46.

3. Market aggregation: It is often practised by a company that is production-oriented. The entire market is treated as a single homogeneous unit, whose parts are all uniform. Marketers develop one product and one marketing design to reach as many customers as possible. It enables a company to maximise its production on a large scale at a low cost, and make its production economical. Examples of such market are markets for blankets, suitings, refrigerators, radios, cycles, etc.

TYPES OF MARKET SEGMENTATION

1. Territorial or Geographic Segmentation: India can be divided into two distinct regions: rural markets and urban markets. Similarly, Indian market can be divided state-wise and each state may represent a segment. This type of segmentation is very commonly used in allocating the territories to the salesmen.

2. Demographic Segmentation: Customers are classified in homogeneous groups under demographic similarities like age, sex, educational level, income, etc. It is believed that persons in the same age groups can be approached by the same type of appeal and publicity media. Income level grouping may be useful as regards ability of the persons to purchase the offered product. Grouping on the sex basis plays an important part in such segmentation.

3. Socio-psychological Segmentation: Different social classes have different spending behaviour patterns. Social classes have different aggressiveness, submissiveness, degrees of cautiousness and venturesomeness with value. These differences determine this type of segmentation.

4. Need-oriented Segmentation: In it segmentation is done on the basis of needs or benefits a group seeks from the goods.

5. Volume Segmentation: It involves segmenting of marketing judging the event, of use such as heavy, medium, light users and those who do not use the product at all. Volume segmentation may further be segmented on the demographic basis.

6. Qualitative Segmentation: In it emphasis is placed on repeat purchases by the buyers. This is just the extension of the volume segmentation. However, socio-economic characteristics cannot be correlated with heavy or light consumption.

7. Product Segmentation: It is directed towards differences among the product that comprise markets. Product segmentation is a less rational approach than market segmentation unless there are great differences among the products involved. Differentiated marketing helps the organisation to market products to satisfy market demands and it is more proper to satisfy its customers needs.

8. Life-style Segmentation: It emphasises segmentation on the basis of the distinctive mode of living, the segments involving questions regarding how they spend their time, the nature of their interests and the basic characteristics like stages in the life cycle, income, education, etc.

TECHNIQUES FOR DEFINING MARKET SEGMENTS

The most popular techniques used for defining market segments are: (1) Forward segmentation—based on demographic, socio-economic and geographic variables; (2) Backward segmentation; (3) Benefit segmentation; (4) Usage segmentation; (5) Physiographic segmentation; and (6) Lifestyle.

(1) Forward Segmentation: In it segmentation the demographic data (such as age, family size, sex, religion, stage in life, etc.) and the socio-economic data (income, occupation, etc,) are used to reflect the purchasing power, expectations, and values of specific segments of population. Different stages of life such as bachelor, married with children and older couple with children living apart, etc. do affect the purchase of consumer goods. For example, while bachelors often purchase personal item as sport shirts, shoes, books, toilet preparations, etc.; young married couples buy durable furniture, home appliances, cosmetics and perfumes, apparels, etc.; those with children need infants' clothing, vitamin and toys for children; while older people or solitary couple purchase medicines, tonics, luxuries, products that aid sleep, health and digestion, vehicles, etc.

(2) Backward Segmentation: It is used to identify groups of consumers with a specific set of needs, dispositions and common experiences. Hence, consumer behaviour is analysed so that customers can be classified according to characteristics. Products having the same market can be displayed and advertised together in retail stores by the same media.

(3) Benefit Segmentation: It assumes that the benefits people seek in consuming a product are the basic reasons for the existence of market segmentation. For example, the market for tooth paste has four segments, the decay-prevention segment, the bright teeth segment, the flavour segment, and the price segment.

(4) Usage Segment: It differentiates between those who are heavy users and those who use it occasionally or those who are light users or non-users. Usually, the behaviour of consumers who are heavy users of a product and have strong brand loyalties is different from the behaviour of light users or non-users who show little or no loyalty to a given brand.

(5) Physiographic Segmentations: These are based on the idea that individual activities, interests and opinions can be measured. Physiographic studies place a heavy emphasis on personality traits. These are reserved/outgoing; dull/bright; humble/assertive; affected by feelings/emotionally stable; sober/ happy-go-lucky; expedient/conscientious; shy/venturesome; tough-minded/ tender-minded; trusting/suspicious; practical imaginative; forth-right/astute; self-assured/ apprehensive; conservative/experimenting; group-dependent/self-sufficient; undisciplied self-conflict/ controlled; and relaxed/tense.[1]

(6) Lifestyle Segmentation: Lifestyle segmentation technique tends to focus on broad, cultural trends or on the needs and values thought to be closely associated with consumer behaviour, measuring attitudes, interests, opinions, and attitudes. Lifestyle segmentation begins with people instead of products and classifies different ways of living reflected in people's activities, interests and opinions. In the following table lifestyle dimensions are shown:[2]

1. Raymond, B. Cartell, Herbert Weber and Maurice, M. Tatsuoks, *Handbook for the Sixteen Personality Factor Questionnaire*, 1970, pp. 16-17.
2. Plumner, Joseph, T., "The Concept and Application of Life Style Segmentation," *Journal of Marketing*, Vol. 38, January 1974, pp. 33-37.

Activities	Interests for	Opinions about
Work	Family	Themselves
Hobbies	Home	Social Issues
Social events	Job	Politics
Vacations	Community	Business
Entertainments	Recreation	Economics
Club merchants	Fashion	Education
Community affairs	Food	Products
Shopping	Media	The future
Sports	Achievements	Culture

IMPORTANCE OF MARKET SEGMENTATION

1. Adjustment of Product and Marketing Appeals: As market segmentation presents an opportunity to understand the nature of the market, the seller can adjust his thrust to attract the maximum number of customers by various publicity media and appeals.

2. Better Position to Spot Marketing Opportunities: As the producer can make a fair estimate of the volume of his sale and the possibilities of furthering his sales in the regions where response of the customers is poor.

3. Allocation of Marketing Budget: It is on the basis of market segmentation that marketing budget is adjusted for a particular region or locality. It is no use allocating a huge budget.

4. Meeting the Competition Effectively: It helps the producer to face the competition of his rivals effectively. The producer can adopt different strategies for different markets taking into account the rival's strategies.

5. Effective Marketing Programme: It helps the producer to adopt an effective marketing programme and serve the consumer better at comparatively lower cost. Different marketing programmes can be attached for different segments.

6. Evaluation of Marketing Activities: Market segmentation helps the manufacturer to find out and compare the marketing potentialities of the products. It helps to adjust production and using his resources in the most profitable manner. As soon as the product becomes obsolete, the product line could be diversified or discontinued.

BASIS OR CRITERIA FOR MARKET SEGMENTATION

Cundiff and Still has mentioned the following criteria for market segmentation:

Basis for Consumer Product	Basis for Industrial Product
1. Income of the consumer.	1. Kind of business.
2. Age of the consumer.	2. Usual Purchasing procedure.
3. Sex of the consumer.	3. Size of user.
4. Degree of urbanisation of the consumer.	4. Geographical market segmentation.
5. Geographical market segmentation.	
6. Educational attainment of the consumer.	
7. Religion of the consumer.	

CRITERIA FOR SEGMENTATION OF CONSUMER PRODUCTS

The various criteria for segmenting the consumer product markets may be grouped in the following four categories:

1. Socio-economic Factors.
2. Geographical Factors.
3. Personality Factors.
4. Consumer Behaviour Factors.

1. Socio-economic Factors: The most common way of segmenting the markets is on the basis of socio-economic characteristics of the consumers dispersed over a geographical segment. Such factors are the following:

(*i*) *Age*: The producer should know for what age group his product would be most suited so that he can plan his pricing policy, advertisement policy, marketing policy and strategy accordingly. For example, some breakfast products are aimed to suit the tastes of children while some others are attractive to consumers within broader range of ages. Similarly, cloth market may be segmented on this basis.

(*ii*) *Sex*: Markets may be divided on the basis of sex, *i.e.*, ladies and gents. Some products are exclusively produced for women while some others are for men. For example, lipstick is meant for women while shaving cream is only for men. As the attitude, needs, mental and physical attributes and motivational factors are different in men and women, therefore, advertisement strategy may differ for both types of products. Manly desires, personality, sense of family security and social prestige are some of the factors which are given top priority in an advertisement for a product meant exclusively for men. On the other hand, beauty and purchasing ability are some factors for advertising a product meant for women.

(*iii*) *Income*: The producer should also bear in mind the income of the prospective buyers of his product. This factor also affects the advertising and distribution policy, *i.e.*, media of advertisement and pricing policy. Consumers' needs, behaviour, habits, preferences, persuasion, etc. differ in different income groups. For example, as people in high income group prefer quality of goods, design, fashion-oriented products, etc. they can be motivated on these factors. Certain items like refrigerators, video cassette recorder (VCR) are produced only for high income group people. People in low income group attract towards low price. Different models of television sets are introduced to meet the needs of buyers of different income groups.

(*iv*) *Educational Level*: The consumers can be divided on the basis of educational levels such as educated, semi-educated and uneducated. The marketing activities and strategies are ascertained accordingly. For example, a book market may be segmented on this basis in Primary, Jounior High School, High School, Intermediate, and Degree books markets. Advertisting policy may be chosen accordingly. Products used by uneducated or low-educated people, may be advertised through Radio, Television and Cinema whereas the advertisement for educated people may be given in newspapers, journals and magazines, etc.

(*v*) *Race and Religion*: In India there is co-existence of many religions, communities, castes and sub-castes and the market may also be segmented on this basis because their feeling, life styles and attitudes differ depending on their origin and communal associations. Brands, designs, language on packing and packing decisions may differ for a product meant for different regions. For example, utensils or book market may be divided on religion basis.

(*vi*) *Size of Family*: Market may also be segmented on the basis of size of family. Refrigerators and cookers are produced in different sizes to suit needs of families of different sizes.

2. Geographical Factors: The markets are divided on the basis of geographical factors, such as area, climate and the density of population. According to area, states may be taken the basis for segmentation. Each state may be recognised as a separate market. The area may further be segmented in rural, town and urban areas or where market is international the division may be national or international market. On the basis of climate, markets may be hill areas and plain areas. Such type of segmentation is best where the customers are stretched over a vast area and the production is done on large scale. The producer may design his marketing strategies taking the characteristics of the individual markets into consideration.

3. Psychographic or Personality Factors: These are not the same in all the consumers. Some customers are crazy for novel design or products of new fashion that may increase their prestige in the society. The motto of some other customers is simple living and high thinking and they never aspire for showy items. For example, Sarvodaya workers wear khadi irrespective of their income- level or social status.

4. Consumer Behaviour Factors: Consumer behaviour divides the markets on three bases:

(*i*) *Usage Habits*: This include non-users, light-users, medium-users and heavey-users, etc. Non-users may also be divided in expected and unexpected users.

(*ii*) *Buyer's motives*: These include factors like economics, quality of goods, reliability and prestige in society, etc. Several groups may be formed on these bases and the market may be segmented accordingly.

(*iii*) *Brand Loyalty*: Customers may also be grouped according to their loyalty to a particular brand. If, suppose, four brand of a commodity are in the market, customers may be grouped in four classes on the basis of their preference of a prticular brand.

CRITERIA FOR INDUSTRIAL PRODUCT

The industrial market is as large as the consumer market. It is also made up of different market segments, appropriate for industrial products. Following criteria are used for segmenting the industrial market:

1. Kind of Business or Activity: This is generally used where an industrial house produces several products or services. For example, insurance company's market may be segmented in fire, marine, general and life insurance businesses. A separate division may be formed for each segment representing a specific kind of activity. This may again be broken down in procurement division and lending division.

2. Usual Purchasing Procedure: Industrial buyers are generally more systematic buyers than are ultimate consumers. But among industrial users there is much variation in the amount of consideration given to buying different items. The decision to buy a major installation requires extensive market and other technical investigations plus the approval of several high executives and technical experts in the industrial users' organisation. But the same firm may purchase some routine articles like stationery or panels, etc. through ordinary suppliers and agents. The industrial marketer must apply different selling tactics and strategies to each of these buying situation.

3. Geographical Location of the User: Factors like variation in geography, climate and historical traditions cause considerable variation in the way industrial marketing is conducted in different areas. The topography of an area affects the transportation cost. Variation in climate affects the needs of the industrial users for building materials, and heating and cooling equipments. Geographical segmentation may also exist, because some kinds of business and service organisations seem to settle in particular areas.

4. The Sizes of User: Sizes of industrial purchases very according to the size of industrial user. According to size the market may be divided in large buyers and small buyers. As it is generally more economical to sell in large lots than small, the industrial markets quote lower rates to buyers of large quantities. This is often the main reason why marketers use different methods for industrial users who vary greatly in size.

ALTERNATIVE STRATEGIES TOWARDS MARKET SEGMENTATION

Market Aggregation or Undifferentiated Marketing

Market aggregation is the opposite of segmentation. Aggregation implies the policy of lumping together all the markets for the products into one. Mass production-oriented firms usually adopt the method of aggregation instead of segmentation. Under this concept, the management having only one product considers the entire buyers as one group. Market aggregation enables an organisation to maximise its economic or scale of production, pricing, physical distribution and promotion. However, the applicability of this concept in consumer-oriented market is doubtful. The total market concept as envisaged by market aggregation may not be realistic in the present-day marketing, when consumers fall under heterogeneous groups. In the total market concept the economies of organisations do not permit the division of market into segments in the case of fully standardised product and where substitutes are not available differentiation need not to be undertaken. Under such circumstances firms may adopt mass advertising and other mass methods in marketing.

2. Market Segmentation or Differentiated Marketing

Market segmentation is "the process of taking the total heterogeneous markets for a product and dividing it into several submarkets or segments each of which tends to be homogeneous in all significants." Under this strategy, the firm groups the buyers on the basis of their common needs and desires. It differentiates one group from the other on the basis of their needs, region, characteristics, personality or behaviour. In other words, the classification of markets based on consumer's characteristics is called market segmentation. For instance, instead of mentioning a single market for shoes, it may be segmented and differentiated into several sub-markets, *e.g.*, shoes for children, ladies and gents and so on. On the very similar lines, Geographical segmentation is also possible for certain other products.

Under this concept, a firm decides to operate in several or all segments of the market. It designs separate product-marketing programmes. This also helps developing intimacy between the producer and the consumer. Most firms now- a-days prefer to have a strategy of differentiated marketing because consumers' demand is diversified. It provides an opportunity to the consumers to select their choice. Each kind of product offers a basis for segmentation. As the differentiated marketing is sales-oriented, it is a costly affair for the organisation.

3. Concentrated Marketing

Both the concepts of undifferentiated marketing and differentiated marketing imply the approach of total market. Another option is to have concentrated efforts in a few markets capable of opportunities. Instead of spreading itself in many parts of the market, it concentrates its forces to gain a good market position in a few areas. This method is adopted when new products are introduced, here the advantage of one segment is never offset by the other because firm's efforts are to concentrate only in one segment of the market.

Philip Kotler has illustrated the three kinds of segmentation as follow:

Fig. 11.1: Three Kinds of Segmentation.

ELEMENTS OF MARKET SEGMENTATION

1. Company Resources: Market segmentation involves heavy expenditure in implementing it. Market segmentation cannot be undertaken at all unless the company has got enough resources.

2. Products' Characteristics: Most products are heterogeneous in character but some other products show homogeneity. In the case of former type, market segmentation is necessary but in the latter case the necessity of segmentation is disputed. Salt, kerosene, etc. come under this group of articles and in their case undifferentiated marketing is enough.

3. Position of the Products in the Product Life Cycle: The various stages of product life cycle, *viz.*, introduction, growth, maturity, saturation and decline have to be taken into consideration. During the introduction stage the necessary data cannot be collected and in the last phase the necessity for segmentation does not arise at all.

4. Homogeneous Nature of Market: Proper segmentation of market is required only when the customer preferences vary from group to group. When the market is of a homogeneous nature there is not much use of segmentation.

5. Competitive Marketing Strategies: Sometimes it is necessary to fall in line with the competitors' activity or market segmentation. Arrangements similar to be undertaken by competitors have to be made to meet the competition effectively.

The above discussion shows the need of studying consumer behaviour to enable a manufacturer to gain from the market. In the past, the manufacturer's selling responsibility virtually ended at the retailer's level It was not the marketer but the retailer who undertook almost the entire job of selling goods to the consumer. With the multiplicity of the products in the market, with the variety of brands, grades and prices within each product category, the manufacturer can no longer afford his delegated selling job to the retailer. He must not only make the product but must be a seller too. To perform this function successfully he must have with him all the tools needed to handle a customer. Market segmentation is one of such tools.

INFLUENCE OF PSYCHOLOGICAL FACTORS

Man is a perpetually a needy animal. When one need is satisfied a new need emerges at a higher level. Various promotional devices are designed to convert needs into wants and then creating potential customers. The needs are essentially psychological and instinctive in nature. It is these psychological factors that create an uncertainty for the manufacturer to predict the market for his product. To overcome this difficulty only markets showing identical characteristics are segmented. This is possible because people live in social groups, membership of which modifies behavioural response to the extent that it would be more correct to identify these factors as psycho-sociological or socio-psychological The study of these influences has created a whole new field of marketing usually referred to as consumer behaviour.

1. Motivation: It is the underlying force of any human activity including buying. Wishes or desires initiate the sequence of events known as behaviour. Motives correspond to needs, a fundamental determinant of demand. Motivation depends on psychological needs, safety needs, love needs and esteem need. Man is a bundle of unlimited needs. He never feels fully satisfied. As soon as one need is fulfilled, he feels the presence of new needs. The so-called cultural progress is just the multiplication of human needs. It is the marketers function to discern the nature of these needs and attempt to satisfy them.

2. Cognition: It is a psychological theory which studies the response of consumers. According to it, stimulation of wants is conditioned by a customer's knowledge, his perception, beliefs and attitudes. Perception is the sum total of physical stimuli and personal factors. Certain stimuli are stronger than others while some are perceived by more people. Beliefs and attitudes also play an important role in the cognitive process. Strong beliefs and attitudes are difficult to be changed and modified. Advertisements stressing special appeals are purposely designed by the manufacturers to overcome this kind of resistance by the customers.

3. Personality: It is the total of so many personal or individual traits. So many theories have been developed to explain the personality and its influence on the behaviour of people. Branding is a personality given to the product to suit the personality of the buyer. For example, different brands of cigarettes attract different categories of smokers in the society.

4. Reference Groups: These indicate the position of a particular group of person in a society. Man is essentially a social being and interacts with other individuals in a variety of social groups. In spite of personal differences people may be forced to accept the decisions of society, for example, in the Group Insurance Scheme individual differences of opinion may not be given much consideration.

The present-day marketing is consumer-oriented. Consumers' psychology, their social and economic causes form the cornerstone for marketing decisions. This recognition as accorded to consumers have given rise to the concept of market segmentation. Any market could be segmented to a considerable extent because buyers' psychological characteristics are never similar. The psychological traits of the rural population in India are quite different from the psychological traits of an urban society. Therefore, the same kinds of products will not appeal to the kinds of people living in villages and towns. As the major motives underlie the purchases of a product, the marketing men are placed in a better position to develop an effective marketing strategy to satisfy such motives. For example, while the use of low prices, cigarette may fulfil the desire for saving money, high priced cigarette may suggest approval and quality. If the marketing programme is to be appropriate, it should be so in terms of products and advertising strategy.

QUESTIONS FOR EXERCISE

1. What bases or criteria are used for segmenting a market?
2. What is market segmentation and what factors influence it? Give examples.
3. Write a short note on a criteria for segmenting a market.
4. 'Explain the alternative strategies towards market segmentation.

12

Marketing Information System

Douglus McGregor has called 'Manager' a 'professional decision-maker', Marketing managers and different marketing executives working at different levels in the organisation have to make certain decisions relating to various problems such as product planning, product line strategy, pricing decisions, marketing strategy, product development, etc. These decisions can be made by the marketing executives either on the basis of intuition or on the basis of certain information. Decisions based on relevant information are always scientific, rational and fruitful. Information provides the means by which problems are recognised, defined, analysed, interpreted and eventually solved. If the information is better, more complete, more reliable and timely, it is easier for the manager to make a sound decision.

MEANING OF INFORMATION

Webster defines 'information' as 'knowledge communicated by others or obtained by study and investigation *(i.e.,* surveys, etc.). Information provides the means by which problems are recognised, defined and eventually solved. If the information is better, correct, complete, reliable and timely, it is easier for managers to take a sound decision.

Concept of Marketing Information

Every company has different systems of information such as financial information system; personnel information, logistics information, marketing information system, etc. Marketing information consists of facts, figures and reports about products, prices, market conditions, consumers' responses, customers' needs and desires, market competition, advertising developments, selling methods, information regarding physical flow of goods, transportation, warehousing inventory position and also regarding other elements of marketing-mix. Thus, marketing information includes all facts, estimates, opinions and other information about providing services. The characteristics of marketing information system differ widely among different companies.

MARKETING INFORMATION SYSTEM

A marketing information system or a marketing intelligence system may be defined as "an interacting, continuing, future-oriented structure of people, equipment and procedure designed to generate and process an information flow which can aid business executives in the management of their marketing programmes."[1]

A marketing information system involves broader and more inclusive activity than marketing research.[2] It includes (*i*) "determining and specifying the data needed; (*ii*) the generation of this information by means of marketing research; distribution cost analysis, or some other tool, and then (*iii*) processing of these data. Marketing intelligence suggests a process, while marketing research is often concerned with techniques. Marketing intelligence is a system concept whereas marketing research usually deals with fragmented, unrelated research projects, done to solve an existing problem identified by some executive. Thus, a marketing information system is conducted on continuing basis serving as a prognosis as well as a diagnosis; it is preventive as well as curative medicine for marketing system.[3]

Information Needs of Different Levels of Marketing Executives

Marketing department has its own hierarchy whose marketing information needs also differ significantly. While lower management is interested in operational information, *e.g.*, detailed reports generally control-oriented for taking operational decision, middle level management is interested in tactical information, *e.g.*,

1. Lee, Adler, "Systems Approaching to Marketing", *Harvard Business Review*, May-June 1967, p. 110.
2. Berenson Cond, "Marketing Systems", *Journal of Marketing*, October, 1969, pp. 16-23.
3. Stanton, W.J., *op. cit.*, pp. 63-64.

comprehensive reports basically planning/control-oriented, for taking tactical marketing decisions. Thus, marketing men need a good marketing information system continuously as an ongoing process to facilitate sound marketing decisions on marketing plans, policies and programmes. Sound marketing decisions cannot be made in a vacuum. They are made with full awareness of market conditions, competition, public policies and above all with adequate knowledge of market demand, *e.g.*, customer's needs and desires. The success of marketing research programme fully depends upon sound marketing information system.

Marketers are called upon to anticipate changes in the marketing environment-involving opportunities, risks and uncertainties. They are required to forecast the direction and intensity of these future changes in the environment and then adjust their plans to meet anticipated changes in the environment and secure favourable relationship with changing environment. Markets can be understood through the study of such information-messages, opinions, responses and communications (reports and letters). The effectiveness of marketing system depends, on having and using the right and adequate information.

IMPORTANCE OF MARKETING INFORMATION

1. Anticipation of Consumer Demand: Mass production and mass distribution in ever-expanding markets are based on anticipation of consumer demand. Under customer-oriented marketing approach, every marketer needs up-to-date knowledge about consumer needs and wants. In dynamic economy, consumer tastes, fashions and liking are constantly changing. Without precise information on the nature, character and size of consumer demand, marketers will be simply groping in the dark. Decisions based upon hunches, guess-work, intuition or tradition cannot give desirable result in the modern economy. They must have support of facts and figures.

2. Systematic Approach: Modern marketing process has become much more complex and elaborate. Ever-expanding markets and multinational marketing activities require adequate market intelligence services. Hence, we have systematic approach to organised information system. Marketing communications provide information cues in non-price competition through advertising and sales promotion.

3. Significance of Economic Indicators: Forces of demand and supply are constantly changing. These determine prices and general market conditions. In a wider and complex economy, fluctuations in demand, supply and prices are tremendous. Marketer must have latest information on the changing trends of supply, demand and prices. For this purpose, he relies on the market reports and other market intelligence services. Economic indicator acts as barometer indicating trend of prices and general economic conditions. Intelligent forecasting of future is based on economic indices, such as national income, population, price, money flow, growth rate, etc.

4. Significance of Competition: Modern markets are competitive. A marketer cannot make decisions in a competitive vacuum. Modern business is a many-sided game in which rivals and opponents continuously try to formulate strategies to gain advantage over one another. Predicting the behaviour of one's competitors and outguessing of the competitor will need the services of marketing intelligence. A marketer cannot survive under keen competition without up-to-date market information particularly regarding the nature, character and size of competition to be met.

5. Development of Science and Technology: An expanding market creates conditions that lead to technical progress. In most cases, the market was the mother of inventions. The energy crisis has given great encouragement to discover other alternative sources of energy, *e.g.*, atomic energy, solar energy and so on. Innovate or perish is the slogan in the existing marketing environment. But innovations are based on information given by research and development. Marketer must have latest information regarding technological development. New products, new markets, new process, new techniques are based on facts and figures.

6. Development of Consumerism: In an ever-widening market we do have a communication gap between consumers/users and marketers. This gap is responsible for unrealistic marketing plans and programmes. Many marketers are isolated from day-to-day marketing realities, which lead to consumer dissatisfaction. Consumerism and increasing consumer grievances indicate that product do not match consumer needs and desires and marketers have no up- to-date knowledge of real and precise consumer demands. Many marketers have discovered that marketing agencies incharge of distribution do not offer expected services to their customers. Up-to-date marketing information system alone can establish proper two-way flow of information and understanding between producers and consumers in a wider market.

7. Marketing Planning: In this age of planning and programming, plans and programmes are based upon information supplied by economic research (economic forecasts) and marketing research (marketing forecasts) which provide the requisite information about the future economic and marketing conditions. For example, sales forecast is the base of production plan, marketing plan, financial plan and budgets. Marketing information can inter-relate and coordinate the product and user/consumer demand so that both supply and demand can travel on the same wavelength.

8. Information Explosion: Management today has literally a flood of information knocking at its door. Computer is the most immediate force behind the information explosion. Computer and electronic data processing equipment act as rescue boats to face successfully the fantastic flow of information. The speed with which the computer can absorb, process, and reproduce large quantities of information is simple staggering. When a computer is effectively programmed, it can certainly add tremendously to the quality of information flow.

NEED OF MARKETING INFORMATION SYSTEM

K. Cox and R. Good define Marketing information, "As a set of procedures and methods for the regular and planned collection, analysis and presentation of information in making marketing decisions." Market research is conducted to reduce the areas of uncertainty surrounding business decisions. In order to achieve this objective, companies should collect information and data regarding the nature of current and future demand of the product, effect of economic changes on the purchasing power of the consumers, possible impact of industrialisation and rural development, impact of substitutes, changes of fashions, habits and tastes on the demand for the commodity, effectiveness of advertisement and salesmanship and so on. Information and data relating to the above variables are significant to business enterprise. They keep the organisations well informed about the need and change of the society and consequently help the concern to device its marketing strategy suitably.

In this connection, it may be noted that no organisation can ran successfully without giving adequate consideration to the above determinants of marketing strategy. Being an entity of this living society, business concerns are supposed to have a clear knowledge of the society they serve, otherwise, any endeavour to devise their marketing strategy is likely to be futile. Marketing information system enables the business enterprise to have a good grasp of such knowledge. It helps the enterprises to appraise the society and be dynamic. It furnishes such important information as (*i*) size, character and composition of the market, (*ii*) characteristics of buyers, (*iii*) position of the product marketed, (*iv*) buyers' attitude and response to the product, (*v*) various uses of the product, (*vi*) nature and extent of competition, (*vii*) nature of substitutes, (*viii*) impact of broader economic forces, (*ix*) degree of consumer satisfaction, and (*x*) effectiveness of advertisement and salesmanship.

Information and data pertaining to the above aspects are vital to any business enterprise. It essentially serves as a guide to thought and action in the area of marketing.

Examples of Uses of Marketing Information System

1. Substitution: Substitutes these days are common and continuous phenomena in any economy due to progressive scientific and technological developments. For instance, paper bags are taking the place of jute bags; rayon is replacing silk and cotton; aluminium is taking the place of copper and so on. In fact, marketing information system keeps the business enterprises alert to the changed situation and thus enables management to devise suitable marketing strategy.

2. Consumer Research: Similarly, study of prospective consumers, choice, taste, habit purchasing power also help the organisation to determine the nature of product that it may introduce in the market and get expected result. Such a study is frequently made by the cigarette manufactures and other consumer goods manufacturing companies.

3. Marketing Effort: The assessment of a company's marketing effort in respect of promotion, advertising and distribution can be made only with the help of necessary marketing feedback which may be collected only through the marketing information system.

4. Marketing Research: It is a valuable tool to optimise the marketing efforts so that we have minimum of waste and maximum of advantage. And marketing research is based solely on marketing information system.

5. Systems Approach: Marketing information system is based on the systems approach to marketing and business planning. Effective planning and control depend on new ways of managing information. A firm's profitability and survival is governed by effective handling of marketing information.

Thus, a good marketing information system can help any commercial organisation a lot. It is marketing information system that makes or unmakes any organisation in the perspective of marketing strategy. Marketing information system has been very aptly called the life-blood of marketing.

DECISIONS IN MARKETING

Key decisions in marketing should be based more or less on factual information rather than on 'intuition' or "gut feel." In other words, marketing problem situation should be resolved, chiefly, through analysis of the facts, even though management must resolve complete bulk of marketing problems, largely, on an intuitive basis.

However, the decision-making relates to the choice of course of action aimed at achieving desired outcomes.

In different problem situations the manager devotes different amounts of attention to the four decision-making steps. Hence, he takes some decisions with minimal forethought, and others, only after a great deal of deliberation.

In general while decisions made quickly, are intuition-based those made after consideration are information-based.

Intuition-based Decision-making

Every problem situation in marketing is not sufficiently important to justify decision based on rigorous and time consuming factual analysis. For example, a super-market manager cannot afford to spend much time in deciding whether to stock one or two dozen crates of tomatoes for his week end trade. Some serious situations need immediate decisions before the situations worsen. Even if a marketing executive could consider all problems before they become serious, their sheer number would force him to make most decisions, intuitively.

While making intuitive decision, generally, an executive draws on more than just his "intuition". Mostly, he draws on his previous experience and his knowledge of similar problem situations adding commonsense and judgement. Only when he has no information does he base intuitive decisions completely on "hunches".

Time and expense consideration also force him to make most decisions intuitively. They should try to confine intuitive decision-making to relatively minor problems, situations which are similar in that their possible consequences, financial and otherwise, are not particularly serious and decisions on them are relatively easy to change, if it becomes necessary.

Information-based Decision-making

Information-based decision-making needs major problem situation in marketing, which have two characteristics:

1. They arise at irregular intervals and hence decisions on them do not have to be made again and again.
2. They have important consequences that must be lived for a long time as it is very difficult and "awkward" to change such decisions, once they are made.

Due to these features, marketing executives should take whatever steps are required to assure the availability of sufficient marketing information to permit information-based decisions on all major marketing problems.

QUESTIONS FOR EXERCISE

1. What do you understand by marketing information system?
2. What part do the marketing information and marketing decisions play in achieving the marketing goals?
3. Define Information and explain the concept of Marketing Information System. Examine the marketing information needs of different levels of executives in the marketing department of a concern.

4. What is the importance of marketing information system? Discuss.
5. Who should be responsible for initiating development of a marketing system? Discuss.
6. What are the characteristics of a good marketing information? Discuss.
7. State the need for an efficient marketing information system? Describe different sources of information.
8. "Marketing information system has been called the lifeblood of marketing." Comment on this statement.
9. "Management makes some decisions with minimal forethought, others only, after a decision." Explain.
10. "Only, when he has no information whatever, does he base wholly on intuitive decisions, on "hunches". Elucidate.
11. Identify the appropriateness of intuition-based decisions and the need for information-based decisions, giving descriptions of different marketing problem situations.

13

Buyer (Consumer) Behaviour and Buying Motives

As marketing success or failure depends on target consumers' individual and group reactions expressed in the form of buying patterns one must understand buyer behaviour. In order to undertake the marketing programme among different segments, the marketing management must find out buying motives. In America, USSR and U.K., decision may be taken by women themselves or in consultation with the male head of the family. In India excepting the sophisticated so-called higher class, decisions and purchses are even now taken by men. It is only in the educated elites that husband and wife may jointly decide what, where and when to buy.

Definition of Buyer (Consumer) Behaviour

1. *Webster*: "Buyer behaviour is all psychological, social and physical behaviour of potential customers as they become aware of, evaluate, purchase, consume and tell other people about products and services."[1]

2. *B.M. Enis*: Buyer behaviour is a process, which through *Inputs* (buying power, intra- and inter-personal influences marketing effort and environmental factors) and their use through *process* (perfection of wants, search, purchase decision, product use, and evaluation) and *actions* leads to *satifaction* of needs and wants.[2]

---

1. Webster, Frederick F., *Marketing for Managers*, 1974, p. 19.
2. Enis, Ben M., *Marketing Principles: The Management Process*, 1974, pp. 228-29.

3. *Walters and Paul*: "Consumer behaviour is the process whereby individuals decide what, when, where, how and from whom to purchase goods and service."[1]

Thus, buyer behaviour may be viewed as an orderly process whereby the individual interacts with his environment for the purpose of making market decisions on products and services.

Chief Characteristics of Buyer Behaviour

1. It consists of the mental and physical activities which consumers undertake to acquire goods and services and obtain satisfaction from them.
2. It includes both observable physical activities, such as walking through the market to examine merchandise, and making a purchase and mental activities—such as forming attitudes, perceiving advertising materials, and learning to prefer particular brands.
3. It is very complex and dynamic, and therefore, constantly changing; managements need to adjust with the change otherwise market may be lost.
4. The individuals' specific behaviour in the market place is affected by internal factors, such as needs, motives, perception, and attitudes, as well as by external or environmental influences such as the family, social groups, culture, economic and business influences.

To achieve a better understanding of the consumer behaviour, study of these disciplines, is required which may provide some explanation as to "why people behave as they do". Such disciplines are economics, sociology, psychology, and anthropology. Economics explain consumer behaviour in relation to economic factors. Sociology and cultural anthropology supply explanations concerning the influences of family and group behaviour upon individual behaviour, the diffusion of new products and ideas (Innovation): among various groups, and the impact of culture on its members. Psychologists explain the motivation that underlines buying behaviour, the perceptions individuals have of themselves and the products they buy. The internal and external forces and influences interact in highly complex ways, affecting the individual's total pattern of behaviour as well as his buying behaviour.

---

1. Walters, C. Glen and Gordon, W. Paul, *Consumer Behaviour, An Integrated Framework*, Richard D.Irwin, Homewood, 1970, p. 7.

DETERMINANTS OF CONSUMER BUYING BEHAVIOUR

At the centre of the buying behaviour process is the 'buyer' who is motivated by certain needs and goals. He gathers information from environment and responds to the information according to his predispositions and the influences of the physical, economic, psychological, social and cultural factors.

EXTERNAL INFLUENCES ON CONSUMER BEHAVIOUR

(1) Society: Practically all buyer behaviour is influenced by other people. The individual is influenced by members of his family, friends and members of the community. They provide information and standard of behaviour against which alternative buying behaviours are measured.

(2) The family: The impact of family is particularly seen on the formulation of values, attitudes, and purchasing patterns. The

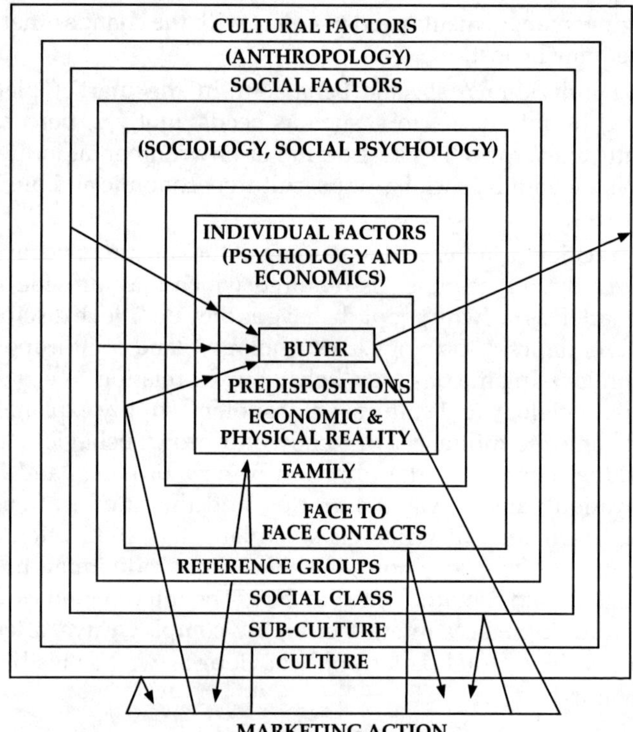

Fig. 13.1 : Determination of Buyer Behaviour.

family defines purchase needs. It puts financial strains within which the buying is to be done. Different members of the family play different roles, *viz.*, *initiator* (who senses the need for purchase), *influencer* (who provides inputs into the purchase decision), *decider* (who finally decides what to purchase), and the *user* (who directly uses the product or Service). Therefore, marketers must know and study the influence of who makes the decision in the family whether the head of the family, or husband and wife or both, or children. The influence of wife predominates on food items and household furnishings, kitchenwares, her toiletries and also on men's garments. Husbands' influence predominates on purchase of durables, drink, car, life insurance. They may take joint decision in the case of enjoying vacations, selection of schools for children, entertainments, housing, living room furniture, etc.

(3) Culture: Culture is the social heritage of the society. It encompasses the social values, attitudes towards work, social intercourse, language, belief, art, morals, law, customs, traditions and any other capabilities and habits acquired by man as a member of the society. Its influences are so pervasive that they are hard to identify and analyse. These can provide an important basis for market segmentation, product development, advertising, etc.[1] For example, the Gujaratis, Maharashtrians, Tamilians and the U.P. Brahmins have diverse culture and need different products for their worship and even the type of utensils used and the clothing worn. Personalisation of life-styles has led to an increased refinement of market segments in the luxury and leisure markets. Branding and packaging have come to reflect the desires of consumers for excitement and seriousness by making use of bold colours and unusual designs. Most products connote values that relate to work, play, the family, morality, etc.[2] These values should be not contradicted by any aspect of the product, its promotion and distribution.

(4) Social Class: The population is generally divided into upper class, middle class and lower class on the basis of income category. In U.S.A., Warner has categorised six classes: Upper-upper class

1. Louden, David, J and Albert J. Della, Bitta, *Consumer Behaviour; Concepts and Applications*, McGraw Hill, New York, 1979, pp. 132-133.
2. Engel, James F., Roger, D. Blackwell, and David, T. Kollat, *Consumer-Behaviour*. Dryden Press, Hindsdale, 1978, p. 90.

and Lower-upper class (3%); Upper middle class (12%), Lower middle class (30%), Upper Lower class (35%) and Lower-lower class (20%).[1] These classes have different lifestyles and therefore, they can be reached through different advertising media, which may range from radio and newspaper to T.V.

(5) Reference Groups: These are collection of individuals providing the individual a sense of identity, accomplishment, and stability. As these groups influence the individuals' opinions, beliefs, and aspirations, they play key roles in marketing. If they try or use a product their followers are prone to do the same. Therefore, marketers, often target their promotional efforts to reach reference groups and through them reach their followers by words of mouth or other subtle influences extended by the group.

(6) Status Symbols: People express their personalities not so much in words as in symbols *e.g.*, mannerisms, dress, ornaments, possessions. Most people are increasingly concerned about their social status. Different products vary in their status symbol value. For some a car may be a status symbol while for others a beautiful well furnished modern bunglow may be a status symbol.

The marketer should understand not only how the product satisfies certain needs but how it fits into culture, because social classes exhibit differences in lifestyle.[2] Hence, in designing marketing strategy, the marketer must carefully consider the nature and extent of social and cultural influences on the potential customers.

INTERNAL INFLUENCES ON CONSUMER BEHAVIOUR

Internal or intra-personal influences are reflected in motivation, perception, learning, attitudes and personality of buyers. These are also known as the *psychological determinants* of consumer behaviour.

Motivation

Motivation is a complex network of psychological and physiological mechanisms. Motives can be *instinctive* or *learned*;

1. Warner, W.L., and P.S. Lunt, *The Status System of a Modern Community*, Yale University Press, New Haven, 1942, pp. 88-91.
2. Robertson, Thomas, S., *Consumer Behaviour*, Foresman and Co., Glenview, 1970, pp. 116-129.

product or *patronage, primary* or *selective*; conscious or unconscious, rational or irrational. They range from *biogenic needs,* such as hunger, sex, food or drink and bodily comforts to the most advanced *psychogenic needs.*

1. Needs: Maslow's Theory: Abraham Maslow developed a Holisti-dynamic theory of motivation which focuses the points of view of different schools of psychological thought, and which conforms to know clinical observational and experimental facts. Identifying a hierarchy of needs, he postulated that "at any given time a person may be faced with a number of motives, but that he probably cannot act on all of them at the same time. Therefore, each person has a hierarchy of motives, with the motives arranged in ascending order according to their importance. The most urgent motive is acted upon first. Motives representing wants and desires, lower in hierarchy, remain unsatisfied at least temporarily." Maslow listed human needs as below:

(*i*) *The psychological needs*: These include needs for satisfying hunger, thirst, sleep, shelter and sex gratification. These are the most basic needs and until they are satisfied, other needs are of little importance.

(*ii*) *The safety needs*: These are related to economic and social security such as economic security, protection and family stability.

(*iii*) *The belongingness and love needs*: These must be satisfied to avoid frustration and maladjustments in life. These relate to affection and belongingness to a group, love, acceptance by some one.

(*iv*) *The esteem needs*: These comprise self esteem, a high evaluation of self-respect, prestige, status and esteem of others in society. Their fulfilment provides a feeling of self-confidence and usefulness to the group, failure to fulfil these needs produces feelings of inferiority and helplessness.

(*v*) *The need for self-actualisation*: It is the desire to achieve the maximum of one's capabilities. Its fulfilment depends upon the prior fulfilment of the more basic needs.

(*vi*) *The desire to know and understand*: It refers to the process of searching for meaning in things around us.

(*vii*) *The aesthetic needs*: These may not appear to be present among many individuals because of their failure to satisfy more basic needs but among others the need for beauty is important.

Implications of Marketing

The marketing management may be successful if products satisfy several needs of an individual. Marketing both encompasses and addresses itself to the full range of human needs. The most basic needs are directly related to the immediate functions of the products and services that marketers provide. As one ascends the ladder of needs, one finds that the input of marketing becomes more and more subtle. Product design and advertising promise love and acceptance; and the need of self-actualisation is encouraged with cultural programmes of various sorts.

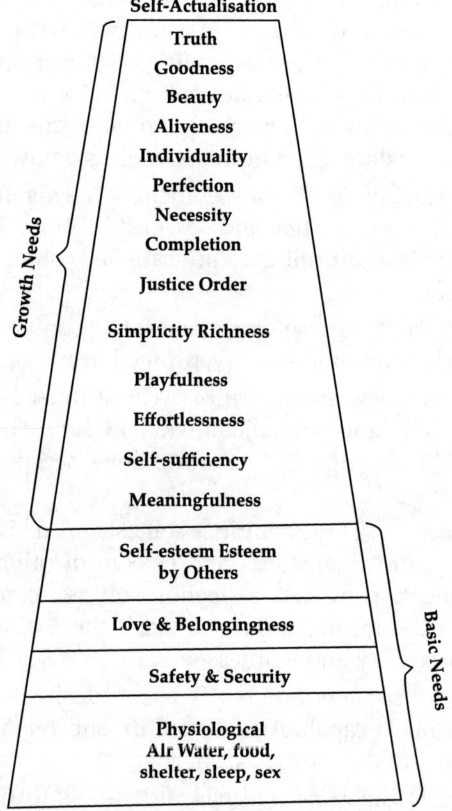

External Environment
Pre-conditions for need satisfaction: Freedom,
Justice, Orderliness, Challenge (Stimulation)
(From Goble, Frank, G's *Third Force*, 1970)

Fig. 13.2: Hierarchy of Needs.

The basic creative, natural or existence wants are the starting point of the economic progress. These are generally recurring. Their satisfaction is necessary to continue the life of the individual and of the group. These wants vary according to age, sex, mode of life, habitat, individual constitution and racial characteristics.

The cultural and social needs add more refined and sophisticated desire to the basic wants. There are neither subject to minimum or maximum set by nature nor are they constant or recurring. Wants related to enjoyment, love, affection, respect, reputation, prestige, esteem, beauty, colour, luster, taste, recreation, etc. all belong to this type.

Though "psychological needs" are more important in terms of psychological development, they began to tapper off as they are fulfilled and attention now turns to "Safety needs". After these are fulfilled, "belongingness and love needs" become potent. Most of the psychological and safety needs are largely fulfilled in industrial societies though few people reach self-actualisation.

2. Perception: Perception is the sensing of stimuli external to the individual organisation. It is the act or process of comprehending the world in which the individual exists. It is a complex process by which men select, organise and interpret sensory stimulation into a meaningful and coherent picture of the world. It determines what is seen, felt, heard, smelt or tasted by the consumers when numerous stimuli are directed to them. As it leads to thought and thought leads to action, marketing is concerned with understanding the process of perception.

The individual perceives things according to many personal factors such as needs, moods, memories, values, etc. Therefore, the marketers must make sure that a given message is correctly perceived by the consumer. Buyers see the products in terms of *images* which are the formalised impressions residing, consciously or unconsciously in the minds of individuals with regard to the "brand" and the "price" of the product, or companies or retail-outlets and themselves *(i.e.,* self-image) or risk. The brand is 'imagined' in terms of benefits that the product would provide. The consumers do not perceive products in isolation from the total context of their desires and aspirations. They have two price limits in mind when purchasing, an upper limit and a lower limit. Anything above the upper limit might be costly and below the lower limit it might be of poor quality. Therefore, advertising and packaging must reflect the same quality as imagined.

3. Learning: It is the process of acquiring knowledge. The basic factors influencing it are: repetition, motivation, conditioning, and relationship and organisation, (*i*) *Repetition* is necessary for the progressive modification of psychological functions. To be effective it must be accompanied by attention, interest and goal, (*ii*) *Motivation,* is an important factor in initiating and governing one's activities, which may bring satisfaction, (*iii*) *Conditioning* is a way of learning in which a new response to a particular stimulus is developed which does influence behaviour pattern, (*iv*) *Relationship* and *organisation* also facilitate learning. This stimulus response approach is useful for marketers. If past experience with a product is satisfying the consumers' response will be favourable if not the consumer may reject the brand. Brand loyalty is beneficial for marketing. The marketer may have to offer some benefits—discount coupons—to the consumer for a new brand placed in the market.

4. Attitude: It includes an individual's consciousness, feelings, beliefs, values and the "mind sets". It develops gradually due to experience and interactions with family, friends and reference groups. There are three main components of attitude:

(*i*) *The cognitive component*: It is that which individual believes about the object—whether it is good or bad, necessary or unnecessary, useful or useless. It is the mental process which is concerned with gathering information, and interpreting it logically.

(*ii*) *The affective component*: It is what the individual feels about the object—whether pleasant or unpleasant, tasty or tasteless. It is concerned with the individual's emotions.

(*iii*) *The conative component*: It is concerned with *how* the individual responds to the object.

After knowing the attitude of the consumers, the marketer may adopt three alternatives in marketing: (*i*) He may confirm the existing attitude, by reminding the consumers of why they like a product and why they should continue to purchase it. (*ii*) The existing attitude may be changed, through improved media of advertisement, (*iii*) A new attitude may be created by placing a new product in the market and making a mass appeal for it.

The following diagram presented by F.E. Webster provides a simple model of individual buying behaviour that identifies three mental processes—motivation, cognition and learning.

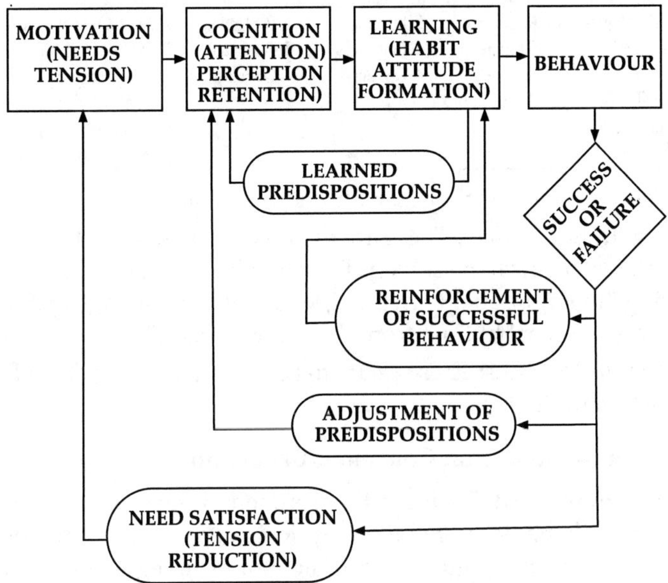

Fig. 13.3: A Simple Model of Individual Behaviour, (after F.E. Webster, *Social Aspects of Marketing*, 1974)

5. Personality: It reflects individual differences in behaviour, An individual responds with a certain amount of consistency to similar stimuli. Personality traits such as degrees of dominance, adventurousness, sociability, responsibility, etc, influence behaviour. However, generalisations about the effects of personality on consumer behaviour may prove oversimplifications.

Determinants of Organisational Buyer Behaviour

According to Webster and Wind, organisational buying is influenced by a variety of environmental forces, organisational structures and factors, organisational participants; psychological factors and organisational decision process.[1] This is clear by the following chart:

1. Webster, Frederick, E. and Yoram Wind, "A General Model for Understanding Organizational Buying Behaviour", *Journal of Marketing*, April 1972, p. 15.

Organisational Buyer Behaviour

Environmental factors	Organisational factors	Organisational participants	Psychological factors	Organisational Decision Process
1. Geographical	1. Goals	1. Users	1. Motivation	1. Problem, recognition
2. Technological	2. Resources	2. Buyers	2. Perception	2. Selection of alternatives
3. Economic	3. Structure	3. Influences	3. Personality	3. Outline of specifications
4. Political		4. Deciders	4. Learning	4. Search for suppliers
5. Legal				5. Analysis of proposals
6. Cultural				6. Selection of Suppliers
				7. Post-purchase evaluation

The above factors satisfy task and non-task motives.

(*i*) *Task-related motives*: These are those concerned with the specific buying problems to he solved. They involve the general criteria of buying "the right quality in the right quantity at the right price for delivery at the right time from the right sources."

(*ii*) *Non-task motives*: These relate to achievement motives and risk reduction motives.

External Influences on Consumer Behaviour

1. Environmental Factors: Environmental factors influencing consumer behaviour include physical (geographic, climatic or ecological), technological, economic, political, legal and cultural factors. These influences are exerted through business firms (suppliers, competitors, and customers), governments, trade unions, political parties, educational and other institutions. Environmental factors influence the buying process: (*a*) by defining the availability of goods and sendees; (*b*) by determining general business conditions; (*c*) by creating the social and cultural norms and values relating to the conduct of negotiations, transactions and other relationships; and (*d*) by providing information to the organisation especially about supplies, product and services.

2. Organisational Factors: Due to these individual decision-makers act differently than they would if they were functioning alone. Four organisational variables affect buying behaviour: (*i*) *Buying Tasks.* These are identification of the need; establishment of specifications; identification of alternatives; evaluation of alternatives; and selection of suppliers, (*ii*) *Organisational Structure.* These include communication, authority, status, reward and work flow, *(iii) Buying Technology.* It includes management and information system involved in the buying decision process, (*iv*) *Buying Centre.* It means all members of the organisation who are involved in buying process.

3. Organisational Participants: These include the organisational factors involved. Those in a buying situation such as: (*i*) *Users.* Those who use the purchased product; (*ii*) *Buyers.* Those who have formal responsibility and authority for contracting with supplies; (*iii*) *Influencers.* Those who influence the decision process by providing information and criteria for evaluating alternative buying action; (*iv*) *Deciders.* Those who have authority to choose among alternative buying actions; and (*v*) *Gatekeepers.* Those who control the flow of information and materials into the buying centre.

4. Individual Influence: The individual is motivated by a complex combination of personal and organisational objectives, constrained by policies and information filtered through the formal organisation and influenced by other members of the buying centre.

An undestanding of organisational buying helps marketers to know when and how to segment the organisational market, how to influence it, and what strategies to use with organisational buyers. The following model presented by Webster and Wind show factors involved in Buying Organisation Behaviour.

CONSUMER AND BUYING MOTIVES

Buying motives induce an ultimate consumer, industrial consumer or user, organisational consumer or merchant buyer to purchase a product. These are controlled by the socio-economic psychological and other factors. Some of these operate from outside and some from within a person. These impel/stimulate him to realise his need or wrant; choose a product or service that will satisfy it; select the place from where to purchase it; and decide upon the price he will be willing to pay; and also decide upon the time when he may actually purchase it.

Buying motives may range from satisfying hunger to seeking protection against clemencies of weather and attack of wild animals, to gratification of sex urge or that for love, curiosity, prestige, social status, personal advancement, and convenience, etc. Some of these motives may be instinctive, while others are acquired from environment, education, social status, age, etc.

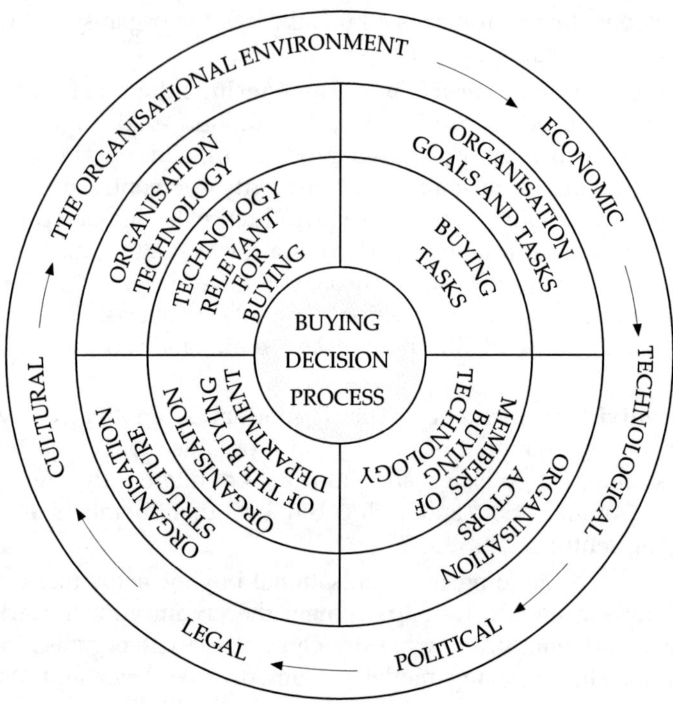

Fig. 13.4: A Model of the Buying Organisation Behaviour.
(After—F.E. Webster & Y. Wind, *Organisational Buying Behaviour*)

An individual consumer buys goods or services to satisfy his personal or household wants. He is the most important class of buyer and among it the principal customer is the family. He is located in villages, towns and cities. He purchases product for three important reasons: (*i*) Desire which needs to be satisfied; (*ii*) Urge which induces him to purchase; and (*iii*) reasoning. He is motivated to buy by external and internal forces: external and internal motive.

1. External motives: These are outside oneself. A consumer is the product of his environment. His attitudes and behaviour influence his culture and various factors like income, occupation, religion, culture, family and social environment act as motives to buying behaviour.

2. Internal motives: These originate in the minds of the people and are both physical and psychological in nature. They are broadly classified into two classes: (*i*) *Rational.* These are based on logical reasoning or thinking, (*ii*) *Emotional.* These are based on personal feelings.

Classification of Buying Motives

The simplest classification is based on primary, selective and patronage motives.

1. Primary buying motives: These relate to the reasons why consumers buy one class of goods rather than another. These result directly from the needs and wants. They include the desire to achieve recognition, physical well-being, preservation of self-image, relaxation, beauty creation, knowledge, money gain, etc. The seller must discover the customer's primary motives and then direct his appeal as effectively as possible.

2. Selective buying motives: These relate to causes that induce a consumer to purchase certain class or quality goods. Selection is based on such selectives as the desire for both economy and convenience. Some of the most common selective buying motives include desire for convenience, versatility, economy, dependability and durability.

3. Patronage buying motives: These cause a customer to buy products from a particular manufacturer or retailer. These are those concerned with fashion, exclusiveness, dependable repairing service, convenience of location, quality, large selections, price, friendship for or reliability of the seller, punctuality in delivery, variety of selection, etc.

David Schwartz View[1]

Prof. David Schwartz classifies motives according to factors that affect consumer behaviour in following categories:

(1) Eco-related motives: These include self-interest; desire for a better self-image, desire for status among one's peers.

(2) Rational motives: These are motives because of the feeling of gaining economy, efficiency, dependability.

(3) Emotional motives: These are motives to attract the opposite sex; to care for the loved one; to excite admiration from others; to win social acceptance and conform to grant more; to be superior;

1. Schwartz, David J. *Marketing Today*, Harcourt Brace Iovanolvich, Inc., New York, 1973, p 142-159.

to overcome fear; to satisfy curiosity; to find rest and relaxation and to follow a leader.

(4) Patronage motives: These emphasise such considerations as the price, location, quality, after-sales service, integrity, variety, etc.

1. Rational Motives

Based on a man's reasoning, logic and ability and a consideration of economic consequences, rational motives include the immediate monetary cost, and long-range cost effecting the buyer such as durability, depreciation, length of usage, degree of labour needed and ultimate benefit achieved. Prof. Copeland enumerates following rational motives: handiness; dependability in quality and use; durability; happiness; healthfulness; efficiency in operation and use; reliability of auxiliary service; economy in purchase and use; enhancement of earnings; and enhancing productivity of property.[1]

(1) The desire for economy: The purchases that buyers make enable them to gain monetary gain or personal benefits or to acquire better product at a comparatively low cost. Some examples of appeals made are:

— "Buy now-only 10 per cent above cost."

— "A bumper sale at 15 per cent discount."

— "Shop at ours, get the choicest product at the cheapest price."

(2) Efficiency for doing a task: It provides motive for use of mechanical devices which reduce the physical or mental tiresomeness in completing a task such as electric can opener, knife sharpeners, blenders, mixers, razors, crushers and grinders in the kitchen and automatic bottlers, sealers, stampers, packaging machines, etc., and in offices, electric typewriters, copiers, pencil sharpeners, and long-distance communication devices. Examples of appeals made are:

— "Fabric that never needs ironing."

— "Fabrics that never shrinks if they have sanforized mark."

— "Push button control".

(3) Dependability motive: It compels an individual to buy to satisfy his desire to obtain "quality" goods of "reliable" and durable nature. Examples of appeals made are:

---

1. Copeland, M.T., *Principles of Merchandising*, 1924, pp. 164-184.

— "The Firestone tyres rolls at least 3000 miles".
— "This mixie is guaranteed for 2 years".
— "It is most dependable for nutrition and purity".

2. Emotional Motives

Based on personal feelings emotional buying motives cover a wide range of irrational motives including impulses, instincts, habits and drives and are varied in nature. According to Prof. Copeland, these include: emulation, pride and ambition, economic emulation, social achievement, happy selection of gifts, maintaining and preserving health, satisfaction of appetite, proficiency, expression of artistic taste, ambition, romantic instinct, securing personal comfort, security from danger, securing comfort and obtaining greater leisure, distinctiveness, desire for recreation and entertainment, cleanliness, pride of personal appearance, satisfaction of physical and emotional appetites, alleviation of laborious task; and pleasing sense of taste.[1]

(1) Attraction for opposite sex: It works in both young and old and involves pleasing or flattering the opposite sex, or appearing attractive before the other. Men dress in their best to appeal to women; and women put attractive hairdos, jewellery, pleasing perfumes and make-up in a modern style to appeal to men. Appeals to this motive are made in marketing of almost everything—perfumery, cosmetics, lipsticks, deodorants, shampoos, shaving lotions, toiletries, corsets, imitation or real jewellery, birthday presents, sexy books, clothing, automobiles, soft drinks and even cigarettes. The appeals are usually indirect, implying that if you buy a particular product you will be more popular with the opposite sex. Some examples of such appeals are:

— "Every women has a right to look younger than she is".
—"Bold, defiant—the male scent".
—"It gives your face a sex appeal".

(2) Love and affection for others: It includes a sense of duty, love for family members and society and a desire to see justice done to oneself and others. Baby food, readymade baby suits, toys, children's books and insurance for children; labour saving kitchen appliances, beautiful birthday or marriage anniversary presents of costly jewellery, beauty preparations, fashion goods,

1. Copeland, *ibid.*

perfumes, romantic and sexy novels, costly furniture and prize bonds for wife are generally purchased to satisfy buyer's affection motive. Examples of its appeals such are:

— "Don't leave your family helpless".

— "Because you love them, protect them".

— "Wise parents give their children good education and breeding".

"Wise mothers give their family a nourishing breakfast".

(3) Social acceptance motives: Every individual wants to have respect and conformation from the group to which he belongs and to escape rejection and loneliness. Taking advantage of this motive the marketers issue appeals such as the following:

— "Your neighbours shop here—you should too".

— "It makes you nice to be near all day".

— "It's the 'in' thing to do".

(4) Recreation and relaxation motive: Vacations, sports and leisure time activities such as indoor games or going to cinema shows, music concerts, musharies and Kavi sammelans are activities of the good life desired by most people. Hence, people purchase sports and games materials, indoor games, tickets for cinema shows or horse racing, boxing; they buy bathing suits, radios, television sets, record players, light books and magazines. Examples of appeals:

— "Quiet heaven for you to spend your holidays—come and stay at Shalimar".

— "Relieves all pains and brings safe and restful sleep".

— "Enjoy the beauty of nature, warm sunshine, cool breezes on the beach—come and visit once and again".

(5) Conquering fear motive: Due to fear, physical or psychological people are induced to buy seat belt, burglar alarms, door locks, lockers in banks; life insurance or general assurance policy; home fire extinguisher, pistol, exercising machines, woollen clothings, medicines and tonics, etc. Example of appeals are:

— "Save now for the rainy day".

— "Drive slowly, some one is waiting for you at home".

— "Safety first, speed next".

(6) Curiosity motive: Adolescent boys and girls and even adults are curious about certain things—such as curios, old paintings, old coins, blue films, cabaret dances, or sex litterateurate. Examples of appeals are:

— "For Adults only".
— "Something new has been added—come and see".
— "Be in the know of the Eighth Wonder of the World".
— "Everything about Sex and Love Life—Read and enjoy".

(7) Satisfaction of pride and vanity motives: People like to feel important in the society, among friends, in associations and clubs, to achieve status symbols which feed their vanity. Hence, ladies purchase costly costumes, jewellery or join expensive clubs; go to theatres and purchase products of arts; have improvements and expensive home decoration objects. Men purchase television, refrigerators, costly furniture, coolers, scooters and cars, fancy ties, after-shave lotions, perfumes, and other variety goods. Appeals are made as the following:

— "Be the first to own one".
— "Designed exclusively with you in mind".
— "It is a limited edition, so buy yours now".

(8) Emulate motive: Some people are motivated to buy what is reported to be used by persons whose opinions matter. Hence, a new company may hire highly respected leaders as Corporate Directors to entrap the investors to buy its shares. Five Star Hotels may say that film artistes patronise them. Popular entertainers, athletes, film actors/actresses may give testimonials about the use of a product which are utilised for creating demand for that product.

(9) Comfort and Convenience motive: It plays an important part in the sale of luxury articles, labour saving devices, gas cylinders and gas oven; stoves, pressure cookers, electric irons, lounge chairs, sofa set, soft bed, good nourishing and tasty food, some type of conveyance, airconditioners, washing machines, etc. Mortimer gives ten kinds of convenience to be reckoned with in marketing:[1]

(*i*) *Form*: Products must be available in a wide variety of form. The drug products, for example, may come in liquid, paste, syrup, powder, pill or inhalent form.

---

1. Mortimer, C.G., *Creative Factors in Marketing*, 1959, pp. 10-16.

(*ii*) *Quantity or units*: Goods must be offered in all sizes, quantities or units desired by the consumer.

(*iii*) *Time*: Products must be available at the time the consumer wants them.

(*iv*) *Place*: Sellers must offer opportunities to consumers for shopping in the most convenient locations possible.

(*v*) *Packaging*: Packages must be easy to find, open, use and store.

(*vi*) *Combination or "packaging" convenience*: It found in service industries.

(*vii*) *Automation*: Many consumers dream of push button home.

(*viii*) *Credit*: Instalment and credit purchases of furniture, appliances, radios, and other time saving devices, where products are purchased now and paid in future.

(*ix*) *Selection*: A seller must offer his products at convenient prices and in an assortment of colours, materials, or flavours.

(*x*) *Readiness*: Everything one purchases must be ready and easy to use.

3. Patronage Motives

Patronage motives explain why a consumer purchase a product only from one seller rather than another. Following are the key patronage motives:

(1) Price: As the budget is limited, an individual would like to purchase cheap or at discount. Hence, following "price appeals" attract him:

"Price slashed by 50%"

"Old price ₹ 135. Today's price ₹ 50 only, Rush and make a choice before the stock runs short".

"Price right for quick sale".

(2) Location: Nearness to one's residence induces people to buy from a particular store which may say:

"Five conveniently located cooperative stores waiting to serve you. Come and be satisfied".

"Location in the heart of the city, accessible from all sides".

(3) Quality Consciousness: It appeal some customers to buy standard quality goods, even if costly. The usual appeals are:

"Our products are priced a bit higher because quality is so much better".

"We guarantee price back, if quality is found inferior".

"The quality goes in before the name goes on".

"We guarantee every product we sell".

(4) Services: Services like credit, home delivery, good gift, attractive wrapping, easy returns, guarantees, and free installations, maintenance and technical assistance help in attracting and holding a clientele. Examples of appeals are:

"All this at no extra cost".

"We service what we sell".

"Free home delivery within the town."

(5) Integrity of the merchant: It attracts buyers, especially of the product is an intangible such as insurance, security or pest control or when post-sale service is likely to be needed as in the case of automobiles.

(6) Variety of goods at one place: It saves time and energy in marketing. Hence, appeals like these attract buyers:

"We have the largest selection in town".

"See our complete line of latest fashions in maxies, bikinies and bras".

(7) Likeable and competent personnel: Sympathetic and helpful salesmen and clerks do attract customers. Marketers stress that services of trained experts are available. They assure the buyers by saying:

"You are never a stranger when you shop with us".

"The friendliest place in town to shop for you—visit once and be convinced".

According to Carter, buying motives include: Money, vanity, acquisitiveness, rivalry, comfort, adornment, cleanliness, companionship, collecting, amusement, sensual gratification, construction, aggrandisement, mental culture, affection, social-achievements, ambition, inhibitiveness, reverence, romance, aesthetic tastes, sex, imitation, curiosity, self-preservation, sympathy, gratitude, patriotism and so on.

Barriers to Recognise Buying Motives

Following barriers may be recognised rational and emotional buying motives in the customers:

1. Unawareness: The customer may be unaware of his own motives which prevents him from communicating to the seller his desires for wanting certain goods and services. Hence, the salesman must play detective, during his talks with the customer, in order to gain necessary knowledge and insight regarding buying motives of the customers.

2. Unwillingness: The customers are sometimes unwilling to disclose their real motive. Hence, it requires a great tact on the part of the marketer to induce them to express their needs.

3. Complexity: The actual motives may be complex or independent that it is very difficult, if not impossible to recognize them.

4. Barriers to Buying: (*i*) Incompatibility of the product with the self-concept. If a product does not coincide with or support a self-concept or how the customer really thinks of himself the customer reacts negatively to sales representation.

(*ii*) Lack of authority to buy or power to make purchase of a particular product.

(*iii*) The risk of moving away from one's ideal self-image.

(*iv*) The feeling of guilt.

Buying Motives of Industrial Consumers or Organisational Market

Industrial consumers are "business or institutional organisations that buy products and services either to use in making other goods and services or to use in their own business. According to Canfield, following are three types of industrial consumers, *viz.*:[1]

1. Manufacturers: These purchase goods for turning them into finished goods such as cotton, pig iron or steel sheets, and all types of raw materials.

2. Manufacturers and service organisations: These buy goods for consumption in the operation of their business, such as lighting equipments and furniture and fixtures fitting in a cinema hall.

3. Industrial distributors: These buy for resale to industrial consumers. According to R.F. Elder, typical industrial buyers are interested in extractive, processing, construction and transportation industries, public utilities, services and distributive industries, governmental institutions, commercial institutions,

1. Canfield, B.R., *op. cit.*

specialised sendee industries (hotels, restaurants, theatres, laundries, dry cleaners, tailoring and barber shops, etc).[1]

Distinction between Organisational and Consumer Market

1. Derived demand: The organisational market has a dervied demand, *i.e.*, the demand does not exist as an independent force but is dependent upon the demand for consumer goods and services.

2. Fewer buyers: It has fewer buyers, as compared to millions of buyers in case of consumer goods.

3. More concentrated: It is more concentrated than the consumer market, which is usually widely dispersed.

4. More valuable: It is more valuable to fluctuating demand.

5. Greater cash flow: It has a greater cash flow than the consumer market.

Comparison between Ultimate and Industrial Consumer Behaviour[2]

Items	Ultimate Consumers	Industrial Consumer
(1)	(2)	(3)
1. *Product Considerations*		
(*i*) Total volume of sales market	Smaller than industrial consumer market	Larger than ultimate
(*ii*) Variety of products offered	Virtually unlimited	Virtually unlimited
(*iii*) Making of products to buyer's specifications.	Uncommon	Very common
(*iv*) Number of product suppliers	For most products comparatively large.	For most products Comparatively small
(*v*) Average size of purchase	Small	Very large
(*vi*) Nature of demand	Sets pace for industrial goods demand	Derived from ultimate consumer demand
2. *Promotional Consideration*		
(*i*) Advertising	Extensive use of mass media	More selective—little use of mass media
(*ii*) Personal selling direct	Very limited	Very extensive
(*iii*) to consumer Use of trade shows and exhibits	Minor	Major

Contd

1. Elder, R.F , *Fundamentals of Industrial Marketing*, 1953, pp. 3-4.
2. Schwartz, David J., *Marketing Today — A Basic Approach*, 1977, p. 203.

Items	Ultimate Consumers	Industrial Consumer
(1)	(2)	(3)
(*iv*) Rationality in purchase decision-making	Limited	Great
(*v*) Purchasing skills	Limited	Sophisticated
(*vi*) Number of people involved in purchasing decision	Usually one, some time two or more.	Usually several.
(*vii*) Visibility of purchasing behaviour	Open, easy to observe	Closed behind the scenes
(*viii*) Reason for purchase	Satisfy personal or house-hold need	Satisfy business, institutional or governmental need
3. *Pricing Considerations*		
(*i*) Price Policy	Usually one price to sell	Often negotiated
(*ii*) Use of discounts	Limited	Very common.

According to Stanton, the industrial buyers have two goals: to improve their position in the firm (personal self-interest) and to further his company's position (in profits, competition, acceptance by society).[1] According to Nystrom, the following motives impel industrial consumers to purchase.[2]

1. *Efficiency*—performance, practicability and increased capacity.
2. *Economy* in money, in use or in time.
3. *Good quality* materials and workmanship.
4. *Simplicity* in construction, operation and application.
5. *Increased saleability* of user's product.
6. *Ease of operation* such as easier handling, greater convenience, handiness or light touch.
7. *Space moving* i.e., compactness, ease of storage and holding.
8. *Obsolescence* which need improvement, replacement or additions.
9. *Safety'* to employees, clients and customers.
10. *Cleanliness* in plant, user's product, of workmen.

1. Stanton, W.J., *op. cit.*, p, 169.
2. Nystorm, P.H., *Marketing Handnbook*, 1948, p. 295.

Schwartz emphasises that "since industrial consumption is impersonal and for an economic/business reason, it is understandable that industrial users are motivated chiefly by rational or economic factors, the principal being: (*i*) production quality; (*ii*) cost; (*iii*) post-sales sendee; (*iv*) efficiency; (*v*) seller reliability; (*vi*) the terms of sale; (*vii*) ease and speed of delivery, and (*viii*) variety. They generally make a conscious and deliberate attempt to "think rational" and "do what is best for the company." However, they are also influenced to some extent by their emotions."[1]

According to Alexander and others, an analysis of the buying motives, practices, and habits in industrial and organisational markets should produce answer to questions such as the following:[2]

1. What functional activities are affected sufficiently by the purchase so that men responsible for these activities have something to say about it?
2. What part in the purchasing procedure does each of these men play?
3. What language do they understand best?
4. What buying appeals are most likely to influence them favourably?
5. What are the most effective and economic ways of transmitting the selling messages to these men?
   (*a*) If through salesmen, what should their qualification be?
   (*b*) If through advertising, what media should be employed?
6. How can buying appeals used in advertising be presented to fit peculiarities of the men and the media?
7. How rapid delivery is required?
8. What are the service needs? In connection with sale? After sale?
9. What are market customs regarding discount structures and credit terms?
10. How important is reciprocal buying?

---

1. Schwartz, David, J., *op. cit*, pp. 193-196.
2. Alexander, S. Cross, James, S. and Cunningham, Ross M., *Industrial Marketing*, Richard D. Irwin, Homewood, 1961, p. 117.

What Industrial Consumers Buy?

According to Vergil Reed, industrial consumers generally purchase following wide variety of goods:[1]

1. Building and Sites: Factories, warehouses, piers, car, casks, store buildings, office buildings, land, mining properties and drilling rights.

2. Installations and/or Major Equipments: Boilers, generators, rolling mills, conveyor systems, seamless tube mills, furnaces, kilns, and other items of a stationery or installed nature constituting the major operating equipment and involving usually a high cost per unit.

3. Accessory or Secondary Equipment: Meters, gauges, hand-drills, time systems, hand trucks, slactiers, jacks, and pinion pullers; office equipment, typewriters, accounting machines, furniture, etc.

4. Supplies: Finished goods comprising: (*i*) *Operating goods,* Lubricating grease and oil, graphite, grinding or polishing compound, wielding wire coal; (*ii*) *Maintenance*: Paint, nails, night bulbs, cleaning supplies, and (*iii*) *Administrative goods*: Typewriters, ink, pencil, clips, etc.

5. Fabricated or Semi-finished Materials: Steel bars, billets, wires, rods, skelp, steel sheets, blank stampings, grey cotton piece goods, wood planks.

6. Process Materials: Dyestuffs, acids, waxes, gums, compositions, alloys and other products of chemical processes or combinations.

7. Parts: Finished, or about to be assembled, needed for grinding, polishing, fitting and other finishing operation.

8. Complementary Equipments: Finished goods of one manufacturer purchased by another to be supplied with his product at the time of sale and for the purpose of increasing its utility or aiding in its operation, *e.g.*, jacks supplied with coal mining machines and dredges, clamshell buckets supplied with dredges and cames, tools supplied with trucks and automobiles, tool supplied with milling and grinding machines.

9. Receptacles and Packages: Bottles, jars, cars, cartons, cases, drums, barrels and bags, wrappers, lables and stickers, etc.

---

1. Reed, Vergil, *Advertising and Selling Goods.*

10. Services: Electric power, telephone and telegraph, insurance, banking, advertising research, legal, medical and dental assistance, employment, credit transportation, warehousing and business consulting.

Some Common Buying Motives

1. Freedom from Fear and Danger: Fear is a negative but very powerful motive. The most basic instinct of a human being is self-preservation. A person can do almost any thing to guarantee his safety. Fear is a very powerful and compelling force in human affair interlinked with the buying motive. The marketing man must ascertain the possible fear of death, fear of loss and fear for the future. Fear can sell anything like hair oil through fear of getting bald.

2. Economy: Persons desire money to satisfy their other desires. A businessman wants money to make more profits or lower costs. Saving money is a universal desire. Customers spend money to get more money. Dealers who purchase goods to sell to the customers get more money and profit. The manufacturers make purchase of high priced heavy machinery to lower down their cost of production and thereby increase profits. A housewife will go round the shops to save money for other purchases. This is a motive to which every body would respond.

3. Vanity: Women spend much time, thought and money on their personal appearance like cosmetics, hairdo and new styles. Both of men and women like to be admired. Hence, vanity is a powerful motivate in the hands of the marketing man.

4. Appreciation: Everybody desires to be appreciated and complimented and recognised as an important person. He wants to be in a position from where he can issue orders to others. Because of this human trait, it may be useful to use indirect method in place of direct method that might prove offensive.

5. Fashion: Everyone desires to imitate what others are doing. This is imitation motive. Closely linked with pride or desire for importance, everyone is motivated by the desire to show oneself superior and to be in fashion with the elite. This motive can be well exploited by the marketer.

6. Possession: The instinct of possession or a desire to call things as 'mine' leads persons to hoard and collect things. A miser takes delight in possessing money. Some persons collect postage stamps and old coins. Here the boarding instinct is at work which can be used in selling even unnecessary things.

7. Sex or Romance: Fancy clothes, cosmetics, perfumes, etc. are in great demand on account of sex instinct or a desire to attract the opposite sex. Without sex little interest will remain in styles for men and women. While women spend more on fancy cloths, hairdo and cosmetics to appeal men, men also do their best to attract women. The sex motive is very powerful, it can sell almost anything. Therefore, this instinct is very often used by marketing men.

8. Love of Others: This motive plays an important part when parents purchase all kinds of things for their children like toys, fancy garments and other presents. They go in for life insurance to make provision for future of the families. The insurance salesmen use this motive to include the prospect to protect his loved ones by purchasing an insurance policy. The young husband purchases all kinds of labour saving devices for his wife. A bachelor going to marry soon will purchase numerous domestic articles. This particular motive is as time described as that of 'home building'. It is also related to comfort and convenience motive.

9. Health or Physical Well Being: Many persons purchase health foods, vitamin tablets and patent medicines to maintain their health and physical well being.

10. Comfort and Convenience: Most people like to be easy going and don't to exert much. This motive may be well exploited in selling luxury items like motor cars, sofasets, furniture, vacuum cleaners, washing machines, television sets, etc.

Using Buying Motives is Marketing

Human instincts make a person behave differently at different times. The motivation research is meant to measure the changes of instincts of people. The marketer should plan to make full use of these motives. Marketing men are in a better position to develop an effective marketing programme to satisfy such motives. The use of low priced cigarettes may supply the desire for saving money while high priced one may suggest approval and quality. If the marketing programme is to be effective and appropriate in terms of product features and advertising strategy, the appropriate motive must be crystallised.

Patronage Motive in Retailing

Many people buy their daily requirements from a certain store out of patronage motive. The choice depends on factors such as location, variety of goods stocked, reputation of the store, attitude adopted by the salesmen, the services offered, the general appearance of the store, etc. Advertisement made by the store is to a large extent responsible for the image of the store. Social status plays an important role in the choice of the store and the type of clientele attracted by the store. Some people prefer shopping at glamorous stores while other select economical stores. Thus, persons prefer to match with their own values and expectations of the store. The industrial buyer is more objective in his decision. He is inclined to profit consideration. He seeks to justify his purchases on the ground of measurable performance. Thus, industrial customers are influenced in their patronage motives by factors like product quality, service and price.

IMPORTANCE OF STUDY OF CONSUMER BEHAVIOUR

An modern marketing is customer-oriented, the study of customer's behaviour is vital in framing production policies, price policies, decisions regarding channles of distribution and above all decisions regarding sales promotion. This is as follows:

1. Production Policies: Consumer behaviour helps in formulating production policies. The consumer behaviour gives an insight into the various factors which prompt him to purchase and like a particular product. As the packing attracts the buyer the producer pays special attention to the packing of his product.

2. Price Policies: The buyers behaviour is equally important in price policies. Some buyers purchase only because particular articles are cheaper than the competitive articles available in the market. Hence, the price of such products cannot be raised. On the other hand, some other articles are purchased because it enhances the prestige and social status of persons. The price of such things can easily be raised. Some articles such as khadi garments are purchased due to particular attitudes and emotions. Prices of articles purchased under emotional motive can also be raised.

3. Decisions Regarding Channels of Distribution: Goods sold and purchased solely on the basis of low price must have cheap and economical distribution channels. Articles which require after sale service such as TV sets must have different channels of distribution. Thus, decisions regarding channels of distribution are taken on the basis of consumer behaviour.

4. Decisions Regarding Sales Promotion: The study of consumer behaviour is also vital in making decisions regarding sales promotion. It enables the producers to know what motive prompts buyers to make purchases. These are utilised in advertising media to awaken desire to purchase. The marketer takes decision regarding brand, packaging, discount, gifts, etc. on the basis of consumer behaviour for promoting sales of his products.

INFLUENCE OF IMAGES

Buyers look at the self and the goods they buy in terms of images which are in the form of consciousness or unconsciousness in the minds. Patterns are influenced by the images consumers have already in their mind. Images affect consumer buying behaviour. Differences among individuals and product brands result in different images and detect the implications for marketing action. A market executive must have a knowledge of all these factors.

1. Self-image: The term self-image means the person's self-picture which differ with every individual. It segments the market on psychological lines. A housewife differs from a social leader. In most buying situations an individual likes to buy such products and brands whose images look consistent with his self-image. He makes different buying decisions at different times.

2. Brand Image: Brand image results from all the impressions the consumer receives about a particular manufacturer's brand from any sources. He is familiar with a particular brand. He knows the brand personality. For competitive brands he forms different images. So also, reatil stores produce distinct images as do corporations. All this has important implications for marketing. When a person knows that a thing is better than the competitive brands, he gives preference to it. The producers change at times the brand while physical attributes remain unchanged or are changed. When consumers believe that there are no differentiating physical attributes, the brand image tends to be associated with the people's personalities who are tempted to buy.

Many brands have got definite images. Before introducing a new brand to the market or an established brand to a different market, etc. management should ascertain the sort of image it desires to build.

FESTINGER'S THEORY OF COGNITIVE DISSONANCE

Festinger has pointed out that when a person makes a decision, dissonance or discomfort will almost always occur. After deciding, the person tends to expose himself to information that the sees as likely to support his choice and to avoid information that may favour he rejected alternatives. Festinger intended his theory to apply only to decisions involving post-decision anxiety, but it equally holds for situations involving pre-decision anxiety. A buyer may be terrified as the decision time comes and either rush into buying as an escape from the problem or delay it because of the difficulty in deciding among alternatives. An important goal both of advertising and personal selling is to reduce cognitive dissonance on the part of buyer. Customers suffering cognitive dissonance may need reassuring that their decisions are wise ones. This can be done by giving information that permits them to rationalise their decisions.

INSIGHTS FROM SOCIOLOGY AND ANTHROPOLOGY

Insights in Sociology and Anthropology establish that marketing involves the activities of groups of persons with group pressure and individual desires. They emphasise the significance of reference groups, the individual's concept of social role, the diffusion process, social class and culture as influences on human behaviour. These studies have shown the importance of social factors in analysing and influencing customer behaviour.

1. References Groups and the Diffusion Process: An individual mixes with people of strong influences to agree with them to gain group acceptance. He is more influenced by the people with whom he has regular contact but others also influence him. These groups, known as reference groups, include family, religious or paternal organisations.

2. Primary Groups: Primary groups involve face to face contact and cooperation. These determine the social nature of the individual. The family is the first that influences him greatly. Peer groups have the individuals of common age spending more of their time together with social background. Among children there are playmate groups. Adults have neighbourhood and community groups. Besides, there are religious, educational and political institutions and work-groups. One individual may owe his membership to many different primary groups. The peer group has the greatest influence on the individuals as a consumer because the group's general interests and mode of life are most like his own.

3. Individual's Social Role in Group: An individual's role in a group of which he is a member, is important to explain his motivation. The group-oriented individual is anxious to fit in the behaviour of the peers. As group norms change he adjusts accordingly. If he is to be motivated to action, he must first be persuaded that the suggested action is accepted by his peers as the proper thing to do.

4. Influential: An influential is that person who is said to be the opinion- leader of group. Influential are not restricted to one social class. They are found at all levels of society. They are of similar incomes, occupations and family backgrounds.

Influential play key roles in marketing. If an influential tries or uses a product, his followers are likely to use the same brand. Therefore, mareketers often target their promotional efforts to reach influentials, and through them, reach their followers by oral words or other subtle influences exerted by the influentials.

5. The Diffusion Process: The social precess of spreading information about new products to persuade customers to accept is known as diffusion. Studies of the diffusion process reveal that most users do not adopt an innovation, it is only a small group, who applies it. Gradually, others also, follow them and thus, it reaches market situation. The diffusion process is witnessed to reach normal distribution. It is also important to identify target market segments at reach stage in diffusions process. In the initial stages, money and energy may be wasted if the marketer tries to cultivate the entire market all at once. The various adopter groups differ markedly. The innovators are youngest but affluent persons to status, who have high-reaching contacts in social circles. The adopter groups have influence in their groups only and enjoy high status in their own local groups.

Those in early majority group are the most deliberate. They do not consider buying a new product if their peers have done so. Those in the late majority have below average income and social prestige and are older than members of earlier groups. Laggards have still lower incomes and social status and by the time they buy a new product, the earlier group is often already trying something newer.

6. Population Composition: Most of the population growth in metropolitan areas is in suburbs rather than in the cities themselves. The trend has marketing significance because the suburbanite, often represent a very different market than the city dweller. The suburb retains much of the character of a small town. In this way, neighbourhood and local social groups strongly influence individual consumption patterns. The population composition of the central core cities has been changing to predominantly low income and poverty-level group of consumers. At the same time, an increasing proportion of central city residents are members of minority groups. Low-income groups are often served by different marketing institutions than those serving others. Recent studies have raised questions whether such groups are being served adequately. One counter-trend deserves mention, the "back to the city movement", a social phenomenon evident in certain large cities, which can be traced to the increased living inconvenience resulting from the extreme sprawling of suburban areas.

MOTIVATION RESEARCH

Meaning

In the words of Lawrence C. Lockley, "Motivation research is the currently popular terms, is used to describe the application of psychiatric and psychological techniques to obtain a better understanding of why people respond as they do to products, advertisement and various other marketing situations." The study of consumer behaviour is very important for a producer, so that he may successfully sell his product in the market. Information regarding consumers may be: *(i)* quantitative, and *(iii)* qualitative. Both types of information are required for marketing decisions. Quantitative facts may be collected through secondary data but qualitative information cannot be collected without much difficulty. The information like—why people respond to particular product or brand or when, where and how they purchase the product, are not easy to collect. Thus, Motivation Research is to get the qualitative aspect of consumer behaviour through psychological methods. The marketer comes to know the inherent and unknown qualities, habits, attitudes of consumers through motivational research. It predicates how people react in a given marketing situation or how they receive a new product design? There are occasions when the people are reluctant to tell why they like or dislike a certain product. The psycho-analysis techniques are increasingly applied to study the consumer behaviour.

Attitude Research

In a product, class groups have different behaviour patterns. A group of consumers purchases only one brand and do not like to have another brand because of the reputation of the manufacturer. They buy high priced articles with the evidence of high quality. This group is probably quality conscious and assume that the products of a well known manufacturer offered at a higher price must be of higher quality.

Another group that purchases the same brand may do so without even being convinced of the superiority of that brand over the other brands. This is because of the ignorance of habits or mere habit. Another batch goes from shop to shop and distinguishes one from the other brand. They are discriminating in their choice. When they come across some new introduction of a brand they try it. Other groups will go from brand to brand without being sensitive to differences existing between brands.

In this way different groups of people have different attitudes towards the products they purchase and how they make their buying decision. What complicates matters sometimes is the fact that an individual consumer's behaviour as well as attitude with regard to one class of product is no indication of his behaviour and attitude with regard to another class of products.

The marketing man decides how his marketing is to be spent in searching different types of groups. If the majority of the consumers for his product class are looking for bargain, he has to maintain his price at a competitive level. Where the consumer group is quality conscious, the advertising should stress the reputation as well as dependability of the manufacturer.

Psychographics: It has its roots and depth in motivation research and permits marketers to think beyond the product and demographics. It enables the marketers to view the consumer as a total person or to perceive his lifestyle and how products and services fit into such a lifestyle. Psychographics tell why a drinker belongs to middle income groups. It may give a new approach to advertising with a lifestyle campaign.

DIFFICULTIES IN THE STUDY OF BUYING MOTIVES

1. Consumers' ignorance: Sometimes the consumers themselves do not understand their inner urges which prompt them to react in a particular way to purchase a product. They cannot explain their motives to the researcher who confronts them with questions.

2. Consumers' hesitation or misstatement: Sometimes, even when they understand their buying motives, they hesitate to explain the same to the interviewers or give misstatement which leads to miscalculation.

3. Difficulty in identifying the buying motives: Sometimes there are more than one motives which prompt a consumer to purchase a particular product. He is not in a position to identify the primary motive which influences his purchases.

4. Existence of contradictory motives: Sometimes there is a conflict in motives due to which it becomes very difficult to tell which particular motive influences the consumer's buying.

5. Dynamic nature of buying motive: Buying motives are constantly changing with the changes in income, fashions, taste, time and circumstances.

The motives which influenced the buying some time before might not hold good to day. The organisation should be always on the look out for changing new motives.

6. Consumer's personality: The personality of the consumer is also not always the same. It undergoes a constant change. The information gathered by sampling method in regard to buying motives sometimes before might altogether change after some time. Decision making on the basis of such information once for all might not be justified.

7. Imperfect techniques: Research techniques have not yet been evolved to provide perfect data to base our conclusions and, therefore, their reliability is doubtful.

STAGES OF BUYING PROCESS

1. Need Arousal: The buying process starts with need arousal. A need can be activated through internal or external stimuli. The basic needs of a common man arise to a threshold level and become a drive. He knows from his previous experience how to satisfy those needs like hunger, thirst, sex, etc. This is a case of internal stimulus. A need can also be aroused by an external stimulus such as sight of a new thing in a shop while purchasing other things.

2. Information Search: After need arousal, the consumer tries to solve it and gathers the sources and information about the product. Depending upon the intensity of need, it produces two states of individual: (*i*) The first state is called heightened attention when the consumer becomes more receptive to the information regarding the item he needs. He becomes alert to information bearing on the need and its gratification, (*ii*) If need is more intense, the individual enters a state of active information search and he tries to collect more information about the product, its key attributes, qualities of various brands and about the outlets where they are available, (*iii*) Having collected the information, the consumers clarify and evaluate the alternatives. There is, no simple and single evaluation process used by all consumer or even by one consumer in all buying situations. The most current process of evaluation is to judge the produce largely on a conscious and rational basis. Various considerations form the parts of judgement such as product attributes, important weights, brand image, utility function for each attribute, and attitude, etc. After evaluation of various alternatives, he takes the decision to buy.

3. Purchase Deicision: Evaluation behaviour leads the consumer to form a ranked set of preferences. Normally a consumer buys the article, he or she likes most but there are three more important considerations for taking the buying decision: (*i*) attitude of others such as of wife, relatives, and friends, but it depends upon the intensity of their negative attitude and the consumer's motivation to comply with the other person's wishes; (*ii*) anticipated situational factors as expected family income, expected total cost of the product and the expected benefits of the product; (*iii*) unanticipated situational factors as looks or manner of the salesmen or the way business is carried on or worry about his income situation.

The marketer must consider these factors and should try ot provoke the feeling of risk in the consumer and attempt to provide information and support that will help him.

4. Post-purchase Feeling: After buying and trying the product, the consumer will feel satisfaction or dissatisfaction. This level of satisfaction depends very much on the expectation and the product's perceived performance. If the product matches up to his expectations, the consumer is satisfied; if it exceeds, he is highly satisfied; and if it falls short of expectations, he is dissatisfied. Consumers form their expectations on the basis of messages and claims send out by the seller and other communication sources. If the seller makes exaggerated claims, the consumer will naturally feel dissatisfaction. So, the smart seller must make claims about the performance of the product that are consistent with its quality so that the consumer would feel satisfied.

PARTICIPANTS IN THE BUYING PROCESS

1. Initiator: The initiator is a person who first suggests or thinks of the idea of buying the particular product.

2. Influencer: Influencer is a person who explicitly or implicitly has some influence on the final buying decision of others.

3. Decider: The decider is a person who ultimately determines any part or whole of the buying decision, *i.e.,* whether to buy, what to buy, how to buy, when to buy or where to buy. Children are the deciders for buying the toys, houselady for kitchen provisions and head of the family for durable or luxury items.

4. Buyer: The buyer is the person who actually makes purchase. Buyer may be the decider or he may be some other person. Children (deciders) are the deciders for purchasing the toys, but purchases are made by the parents.

5. User: User is the person who actually uses or consumes the services or products.

The marketer's task is to study the buying process and its main participants and their role in the buying process. He should initiate all of them to make the purchases of his product at different stages and through different strategies.

TECHNIQUES OF MOTIVATION RESEARCH

1. Experience and Knowledge Technique: In it buyer's behaviour is estimated on the basis of experience and knowledge gained by the marketing executives because of their close association with the consumers. Through experience, they come to know what are the main buying motives for their products and why.

2. Traditional or Questionnaire Technique: A questionnaire is prepared by the marketer with the help of psychologists under this technique. The questionnaires so prepared, are sent to the selected consumers for their return to the company after they are duly filled in. The completed questionnaires received by the company are analysed and results are extracted about the buyers' motives and behaviour. This technique is not much in use because of its limitations.

3. Depth Interview Technique: The depth interview technique is the most widely used and popular technique of psychiatry in motivation research. It is the method of probing the unconscious mind. It is a time consuming technique and requires considerable patience. Under this technique, no direct question is asked by the interviewer but the interviewer talks to the consumer in free atmosphere so that the interviewees may express their views intensively. It is possible for the skilled interviewer to go deep and uncover information buried below the conscious mind.

4. Projective Technique: The projective technique provides the subject with stimulus situation that gives him an opportunity to impose upon it his own private needs and his particular perception and interpretation. The subject projects the inner aspects of his personality while interpreting the circumstances and unconsciously reveals what is below the surface and which could not be revealed through the normal questionnaire survey method. The main projective techniques are as follows:

(*i*) *The Thematic Appreciation Test (T.A.T.)*: It uses a series of pictures of people in some unstructured doubtful form of action. The respondent is presented to these picture one at a time and is required to narrate the story of the picture. The answers are then interpreted by an analyst skilled in the test. Seeing a picture of a lady, he amy say that she is a lazy woman which presented less personnel emotional involvement.

(*ii*) *The Sentence Completion Test (S.C.T.)*: In the motivation aspects of marketing research this test is used to uncover emotional responses to products or marketing situations but the reliability of the conclusion depends much on skill of the interpreter.

(*iii*) *The Word Association Test (W.A.T)*: Here, instead of a phrase of a sentence, a single word is used. The informant is required to say immediately what other word comes into his or her mind. In this way a whole series of individual words can be gone through. The test may be written or oral. It may require words with similar meaning or opposite meaning and so on.

(*iv*) *The Paired Pictures Test (P.P.T.)*: In this, two persons are shown the pictures opening in ratio sets of two different makes. Respondents show the story of their choice on them. For example, one picture shows woman opening a popular brand refrigerator and another picture shows a similarly dressed woman opening a refrigerator of another brand. The respondents are asked to tell any story about these two women opening the refrigerators. The difference in interpretation tells their different attitudes they have about the set of pictures.

QUESTIONS FOR EXERCISE

1. Are psychological and sociological motives within the individual likely to be in conflict at times? If so, would such conflicts affect the marketer? Explain and illustrate.
2. How is buyer's behaviour influenced by the insight from Sociology and Anthropology?
3. What is an 'influential'? How would you go about identifying influential?
4. If "influentials are found at all levels of society" how would those in the upper and middle classes differ, it at all, from those in the lower class?
5. Explain how a marketer contemplating the introduction of a radically new type of product might use Roger's model of the diffusion process in planning his market strategy.
6. Explain the following as influences on human and buying behaviour: reference groups, the individual's concept of social role, the diffusion process, social class and culture.
7. Explain how the concepts of self-image and brand image and Festinger's theory of cognitive dissonance help to explain buyer behaviour.
8. What do you mean by Motivation Research? What kinds of information are sought in Motivational Research?
9. Explain the importance of customer's psychology in marketing strategy emphasising the role that can be played by Motivation Research.
10. Write short note on Consumer Behaviour Research.
11. Explain in brief the main difficulties in the way of study of buying motives.

12. Briefly explain the various stages in the buying process. What is the role of influences, deciders, buyers and users in the buying process? Illustrate with suitable examples.
13. Explain in brief the techniques of Motivation Research.

14

Market Measurement, Sales Forecasting and Sales Budget

Definition of Sales Forecasting

1. *Allen*: "Forecasting is a systematic attempt to probe the future by inference from known facts."

2. *Henry Fayol*: "To foresee in this context means both to assess the future and make a provision for it, that is forecasting is itself action already."

3. *American Marketing Association*: "Sales forecasting is an estimate of sales in dollars or physical units for a specified future period under a proposed marketing plan or programme and under an assumed set of economic and other forces outside the unit for which the forecast is made. The forecast may be for a specified item of merchandise or for an entire line."[1]

4. *Philip Kotler*: "The Company Sales forecast is the expected level of company sales based on a chosen marketing plan and assumed environmental condition."

5. *Cundiff and Still*: "Sales forecast is an estimate of sales during a specified future period, which estimate is tied to a proposed marketing plan and which assumes a particular set of uncontrollable and competitive forces."

6. *Anderson*: "A forecast is nothing more than an estimate of a future condition."

7. C.*E. Sultan*: "Business forecasting is the calculation of probable events to provide against the future. It, therefore, involves a look ahead in business and idea of predetermination of events and then financial implications as in the case of budgeting."

---

1. *Marketing Definitions* (1960), p. 20.

OBJECTIVES OF SALES FORECASTING

1. Short-run Objectives

(*i*) *To Formulate Suitable Production Policy*: The first object of the short-run sales forecasting is to formulate a suitable production policy so that problems of underproduction or overproduction might not arise and production may be made according to the demand forecast.

(*ii*) *To Make Provision for Regular Supply of Raw Material*: The second objective is to make provision for the regular supply of raw material for the production on the basis of estimated sales during a short period.

(*iii*) *To Achieve Best Utilisation of Machines*: One of the important objectives of sales forecasting is to make the best utilisation of the available machines so that in case of increase in demand there should not be any shortage of production and in case of decrease in demand the machines should not remain idle.

(*iv*) *To Determine Appropriate Price Policy*: Sales forecast has an important bearing on production policy which in its turn influences the production-costs which again affect the organisation's price policy. Therefore, to determine an appropriate price policy is an important objective of sales forecasting.

(*v*) *To Arrange Regular Availability of Labour*: One of the objectives of sales forecasting is also to arrange for trained personnel and non-technical workers so that the organisation might not experience any shortage of personnel and at the same time they do not remain idle when the production is curtailed.

(*vi*) *To Forecast Short-term Financial Requirements*: The financial requirements of the organisation depends on the level of sales and production volume. On the basis of sales forecasting of short-term requirements and arrangements can be made accordingly much in advance.

(*vii*) *To Set the Sales Target and Establish Controls and Incentives*: Sales forecasts help in setting the sales target for different market segments on the basis of which control can be exercised on the personnel engaged in the work and necessary incentives can also be provided for implementing the programmes and achieving the targets of sales, etc.

2. Long-run Objectives

(*i*) *To Estimate Cash Inflows*: Cash inflows from sales can be well estimated through sales forecasting by determining the cash and credit sale ratio. It can also help planning for credit policy of the organisation.

(*ii*) *To Determine Dividend Policy*: The profits can also be forecasted on the basis of gross profit ratio on sale and dividend policy can be determined.

(*iii*) *To Plan Plant Capacity*: A long-run objective of sales forecasting is to plan plant capacity in accordance with the demand. If the estimates of the sales forecast reveal that the plant capacity will fall short of meeting the future demand then decision in regard to increase the production capacity of the present plant or setting up of new plant can be made.

(*iv*) *To Achieve Man-power Planning*: Another long-run objective of sales forecasting is planning for man-powers so that production work might not suffer in the long-run.

(*v*) *To Plan Long-run Production*: Long-run production planning also depend upon sales forecasting. In the long-run products has to be adjusted to the market demand and other condition.

(*vi*) *To Forecast Long-run Financial Requirements*: Sales Forecasting also determines the long-run financial requirements of the organisation for working capital as well as for capital expenditure.

(*vii*) *To Achieve Budgetary Control over Expenditures*: In forecasting the sales, all the activities are to be forecasted for which purpose budget is to be prepared for the income and expenditure of the organisation. The budgeting figures for income and expenditure are then compared with the actual performance and any variation is removed. Thus, budgetary control over expenditures is possible.

IMPORTANCE OF SALES FORECASTING

According to John D. Luth, "A good sales forecast is undoubtedly the most important single planning tool. It is the basis of fund budgeting, all budgeting starts with the sales forecast. Financial planning for working capital requirements, plant expansion and other needs are based on anticipated sales. Scheduling of all production resources and facilities such as setting man-power needs, purchasing raw material requirements and determining the rate of production output depends upon the sales forecast. It is essential to review the sales forecasts periodically. Manufacturing concerns give great importance sales forecasting. They base their production on the expectation of future demand. On the basis of correct forecast the producer adjusts his production to the market demand and adjusts the productive capacity of the plant. Thus, production policy and price policy all depend on accurate sales forecasting. It influences all the activities of the organisation such as production and distribution, for the success and achievements of the overall objectives of the organisation. Sales forecasting is equally important in the Field of organising personnel management.

Thus, the importance of sales forecasting may be seen in (*i*) Importance in promotional (*ii*) Basis of planning, (*iii*) Correctness of management decisions; Status of effective control; (*v*) Incentive to cooperation and coordination; (*vi*) It facilitates the estimation of future needs of business; (*vii*) It is the basis of succession business; (viii) Singleness of purpose which help the management in achieving the overall goals of the organisation.

ROLE OF SALES FORECASTING

1. Base for Marketing Planning: No marketing plan can be made dependable and strong unless it is based firmly on sales forecasting. If the marketing manager has no idea about the future expected sales, he cannot decide about correct marketing programme and various production activities. Therefore, sales forecasting is the base for marketing planning.

2. Discovery of Marketing Opportunities: Sales forecasting helps in discovering new marketing opportunities. The possibilities of tending new markets encourage the personnel of the marketing department to take more and more interest in their work.

3. Reduction of Marketing Risks: Sates forecasting throws light on the **future** marketing risks. The marketing manager can guard himself against such risks on the basis of sales forecasting. He can face the challenges of new situations in a better way. He can modify and make necessary changes in the marketing programme and thus reduce the chances of loss.

4. Help in Control: Sales forecast reveals the weak areas where more control and intensive attention is required.

FACTORS AFFECTING SALES FORECASTING

1. General Business Conditions: While making sales forecast the marketer should give due consideration to the general conditions of the economy, growth of population, distribution of income and wealth, general customs, government policy, fashion and seasonal fluctuations, etc. during the future period.

2. Conditions within the Industry: The marketing manager cannot expect to win over the whole potential for his company. He has to be satisfied with a share of this potential. The ratio of the company's sale is only a part of this potential. While making sales forecast the forecaster should keep in view the changes going on in the total demand of the product, the number of other units engaged in the industry and their sales, research potentials and product development, etc.

3. Changed Market Situations: The marketing manager should always be alive to the various factors which bring about changes in the market demand. A change in the total market demand is bound to reflect the demand for the company's product. In making sales forecast, the market behaviour in the past should be analysed and evaluated properly. Future market conditions should also be analysed.

4. Conditions within the Company: Internal changes within the company in the coming future in price structure, distribution channel, sale promotion measures, product or other marketing policies of the company also affect future sales. Therefore, it is necessary to anticipate the extent to which such measures may affect the future sales. As such factors are well within the control of the company, therefore, sales forecast may take them into consideration.

5. Factors Affecting Export Trade: Such factors include export and import controls imposed by the government, export conditions, export-import policy, export finance, new agreements, etc. If the company is engaged in the export trade, the marketing manager must consider the various factors in forecasting the export sale because such factors greatly influence the export trade.

LIMITATIONS OF SALES FORECASTING

1. Changes in Consumer's Needs, Tastes, Fashion, etc.: Introduction of new fashion product is seldom accurate. Future sales depend on the reception by the market. If it becomes popular, sales will be enormous; otherwise it be the reverse, in the face of the ever changing tastes, fashions and styles.

2. Lack of Data Regarding History: There is no past sales history for new products. Guess work proves limitation of the accuracy of forecast.

3. Anticipatory Growth Element: As it is difficult to maintain a rapid rate of growth over an extended period of time, the market manager must estimate the probable rate of growth and consider it while preparing the sales forecast for his company.

4. Psychological Factors: The consumer attitude can change suddenly from confidence to apprehensiveness about the future. A rumour of war for example would create a fantastic demand for motor car tires and tubes.

FORECASTING IN INDIAN CONTEXT

As compared to the advanced countries, forecasting by business enterprises in India is practically unknown. Functioning in an economy insulated from foreign competition and boosted up under the impact of price inflation due to excessive demand and money expansion, the Indian business enterprises have operated for long in a "seller's market" where demand exceeded the supply. However, during the recent years the situation has materially changed, though this cannot be described as a complete transformation. There has been a marked shift towards market mechanism and the market forces can be as much helpful as devastating. Consumer resistance has developed with the result that a large number of consumer goods industries find it difficult to maintain their regular levels of sales. Prize competitions, special discounts, gift coupons, etc. have been employed to push up sales. For example, the recession that originated in the engineering industries spread its tentacles to consumer goods industries. Contrary to the popular belief that the economy was slowly reviving, the recession widened and deepened. At no other time was there a greater need for forecasting. Business enterprises should seriously undertake the exercises in forecasting their sales. Reverting to competitive mechanism is not easy after enjoying buoyant conditions for more than a decade. The transaction period has already posed a number of problems. It is imperative that business enterprises should take to forecasting and evolve their production programmes on its basis.

For example, in recent years, the motor car industry in India has found itself to be priced out of the market. The prices kept shooting up until customer resistance overtook the industry. Instead of waiting list, a car can now be secured from off the shelf. The same thing also happened with the television industry. There was a slump in the sales after an initial boom. Here the government came to the rescue of the industry. An excise cut was offered by the government in its budget whereby the basic price of the set did not exceed ₹ 1800 as the excise duty payable was reduced from 20 per cent to 5 per cent. Accordingly a large number of manufacturers immediately pegged then price at ₹ 1800 and charged extra for glass screen, antenna, etc. Other factors which helped the industry was a cut in the price of picture tube by about ₹ 190. The Electronics Corporation of India the prime supplier of sets to Greater Bombay found its sets selling about 1000 sets per month with bookings around 1400 to 1500 a day, while formerly it was barely selling 500 to 600 sets a month.

Thus, sales forecasting helps in determining what is likely to happen in the future. It can give indicators of direction in which efforts could be made to improve the situation before it hits the industry or unit concerned.

STEPS IN THE PROCESS OF SALES FORECASTING

1. Determination of the Objectives: The objectives of sales forecasting should be determined first of all. Certain points in this regard should be very clear before taking up the forecasting task such as, short-term or long-term period of forecasting; area for sales forecasting (whole country or a specific area for a specific product), unit of sale for forecasting in quantities or value and the time, labour and money to be employed on forecasting. These points are determined taking into account the objectives of sales forecasting.

2. Sub-division of the Task of Forecasting: The second step in making the sales forecast is to sub-divide the forecasting programme into homogeneous groups according to product, area, activities or customers. The total sales forecast of the company is the sum-total of the sales forecast of all the groups.

3. Determination of the Relative Importance of Factors: Having subdivided the task of forecasting, the relative importance should be determined so that due weight may be given to different factors affecting sales forecasts.

4. Selection of Method: The method is to be selected by the appropriate authority taking into account all the relevant situations, purposes of forecasting and the degree of accuracy required.

5. Collection and Analysis of Data: By applying the appropriate method, the necessary data for the forecast are collected, tabulated, analysed and **cross**checked. The data are interpreted by applying statistical techniques to draw necessary deductions. Therefore, it may be called the preliminary sales forecast which forms the basis of final sales forecast.

6. Study of Correlation between Sales Forecast and Sales Promotion Plans: Making the forecast reliable, the sales promotion plans such as advertising policy, personal selling and other policies should be reviewed with reference to the sales forecasts. A study of correlation between sales forecast and sales promotions plans should be made in order to establish their role in promoting the sales in the past.

7. Study of Competitor's Activities: As the volume of sale of a company is largely affected by the activities of competitors, therefore, the efficient marketer must study the competitors' activities, policies, programmes and strategies and their effects on the market. Marketer should guess their behaviour and adjust his own forecasting results accordingly.

8. Preparation of Final Sales Forecasts: Taking the sales promotion plans and competitor's activities into stock, the preliminary sales forecasts results are converted into final sales forecasts results relating to the products and territories involved. The aggregate of sales forecasts of different products, or territories or customers or activities may form the sales forecasts of the company.

9. Evaluation: The figures for final sales forecasts are the basis for the operations of the company in the next period. The actual sales performance in the coming period should be reviewed and evaluated from time to time. The evaluation work may be made monthly, quarterly, half-yearly or yearly. The forecasts figures may be revised in the light of difficulties experienced during the course of actual operations.

10. Adjustment: On the expiry of forecasts period the actual sales and forecasted sales should be compared and causes of variation be found out which would help the marketer improve the next period sales forecasts figures.

METHODS OF SALES FORECASTING

A. **William J. Stanton** has mentioned the following two types of techniques for sales forecasting:

1. Build-up Techniques

(*i*) Past Sales and Trend analysis

(*ii*) Executive Judgement.

(*iii*) Sales Force Composite.

(*iv*) Analysis of Market Factors.

2. Statistical and Quantitative Methods

(*i*) Direct Derivation Method.

(*ii*) Correlation Analysis Technique.

B. **Philip Kotler** has explained the following methods:

1. Methods Based On 'What People Say?'

(*i*) Survey of Buyers' Intentions.

(*ii*) Composites of Sales Force Opinions.

(*iii*) Experts' Opinions.

2. Methods Based On 'What People Do?'

(*i*) Market Test Method.

3. Methods Based On 'What People Have Done?'

(*i*) Classical Time-series Analysis.

(*ii*) Statistical Demand Analysis.

1. JURY OF EXECUTIVE OPINION OR EXECUTIVE JUDGMENT METHOD

It is a process of combining and averaging or evaluating the opinions and views of top executives. Opinions are sought from the executives of marketing, finance and other divisions of the company and forecasts are made:

(*i*) The process is easy and simple. Speedy forecast can be done.

(*ii*) There is no need of collecting elaborate statistics for the forecasts because forecasts are based on the experiences of experts of different departments.

(*iii*) It permits pooling of specialised viewpoint,

(*iv*) It is the only feasible means of forecasting in the absence of adequate data.

(*v*) It is economical also.

Disadvantages

(*i*) It has no factual basis so it is inferior method.

(*ii*) It disperses responsibility for accurate forecasting. Moreover accuracy cannot be claimed.

(*iii*) It utilises costly executive time.

2. SALES FORCE COMPOSITE METHOD

In this method, views of the salesmen and sales executives are utilised for the different market segments. There are many variations. The combined view of the sales force as to future sales expectations may be secured and careful scrutiny may be made at successive executive levels for the future sales estimate submitted by the individual salesmen. An alternative may to rely upon the knowledge of the company's sales executives in preparing the sales forecasts.

Advantages

(*i*) The advantage of specialised knowledge of persons who are close to the market, can be obtained.

(*ii*) It imposes greater confidence in sales force.

(*iii*) It places the responsibility for the forecasts on those who are expected to produce results.

(*iv*) Market segmentation can be developed on the basis of products, territory, customer or salesmen.

(*v*) It provides greater stability through magnitude of sample.

Disadvantages

(*i*) Being unduly optimistic or pessimistic salesmen are poor estimators. So, accuracy of forecasts is always doubtful.

(*ii*) Salesmen are not aware of the broad economic patterns and therefore cannot forecast long-term trends.

(*iii*) The salesmen's time for their primary job of selling is curtailed.

(*iv*) Salesmen can intentionally underestimate the demand if sales quota are to be fixed on the basis of this information.

3. THE USERS' EXPECTATION METHOD

In this method actual users of the product are contacted and asked to submit the estimated quantities of the product they expect to purchase in a given future period. Total sales forecast of the product is estimated by combining such responses. From this an estimate is made for the demand which can be filled by the company preparing the forecast.

Advantages

(*i*) Sales forecast is based on direct information from the actual users whose buying action will really decide the future demand.

(*ii*) It proceeds from a subjective feeling of the market and of the thinking behind the buying intention of the actual users.

(*iii*) This method is more appropriate for sales forecasting in cases where new product is to be introduced without any previous sales record or the number of customers are limited.

(*iv*) It is most suitable for short-run forecasting.

Disadvantages

(*i*) It is not practicable when consumers are numerous.

(*ii*) Users' estimates are mainly based on expectations which may change later on.

(*iii*) It is not fit for long-term forecasting.

4. EXPERTS OPINIONS

In this method the organisation collects opinions from the outsider specialists in the field such as opinions given in the newspapers and journals, wholesalers and distributors, agencies or professional experts. Forecasts can be done by analysis of these opinions and making deductions for the companies sales.

Advantages

(*i*) Forecasts can be made easily and speedily.

(*ii*) Different experts' ideas and opinions are taken into consideration for forecasting and they may be evaluated.

(*iii*) It is suitable where past record of sales is not available or a new product is to be introduced.

(*iv*) It is economical because the expenses for seeking the opinions of experts are much less than that of the actual survey.

Disadvantages

(*i*) Market segmentation on the basis of product, territory or customers is not possible.

(*ii*) The reliability of forecasting is always doubtful because forecasting is based on opinions and suggestions and not on the facts.

5. MARKET TEST METHOD

It is most appropriate when product is quite new in the market or good estimators are not available or buyers do not prepare their purchase plan. Thus, under this method, the seller sells the product in a part of the market for some time and makes the assessment of sales for the full market on the basis of results of test sales.

Advantages

(*i*) It is best for introducing the product in the market.

(*ii*) Any defect in the product may also come in the light and it may be removed immediately to make the product successful in the market.

(*iii*) Sales forecasts are based on actual results. Hence forecasts are more reliable.

Disadvantages

(*i*) It takes a long time to test the market.

(*ii*) The sales forecasts data are projected on the basis of results of a part of the market. As all the parts of the market are not homogeneous forecasts may not be reliable.

6. STATISTICAL AND QUANTITATIVE METHODS

(*i*) *The Trend Method:* The statistical methods commonly used are trend and cycle projection and mathematical approaches including moving average correlation analysis. The relationship is often expressed as a mathematical formula or model. With the help of the formula, trend is projected and the sales forecasts are made assuming that the same trend would continue in the future.

The trend method can be used for both linear and non-linear relationship. The basic assumption in this method is that factors which had been responsible for the past movements will also play an important role in the future. Where steady progress was noticed in the movement of the product over a considerable period of time, it may be felt reasonable to project the past trend into future. Before projecting the trend, one must be aware of causes about the applicability of the assumption.

(*ii*) *The Regression Technique*: Here an attempt is made to estimate a statistical series of dependable variables through fixed relationship by using another variable called the independent variable to which the first is related instead of using regularly spaced time intervals. In this sense, part data is also used by the regression techniques. Under this method, like trend method, a curve is drawn with the help of correlationship between the dependent and independent variables. The methods used are either the least squares or the graphical correlation method. Sales forecast is made on the basis of economic indicators. For example, the demand for paper will increase with the increase in the number of students. Number of students is an indicator for the demand of paper. This method is based on the presumption that the one variable affects the other dependable variables.

Advantages

(*i*) They help to describe in measurable objective terms, the factors and their relationship with the course of sales.

(*ii*) The degree of reliability is indicated.

(*iii*) These methods force the forecaster to quantify assumptions underlying his estimates and thus enable a checking of results by managements.

(*iv*) They force the forecaster to consider the major factors influencing sales.

Disadvantages

(*i*) These methods correlate sales to indicators which are themselves generally estimates.

(*ii*) Such techniques rely largely on statistical methods and do not rely much on personal skill and experience.

(*iii*) They involve complicated statistical methods.

(*iv*) They require considerable technical skill and experience for it to be effective.

WHAT IS SALES BUDGET?

Sales budget is an important part of the general budget of the company. It is the basic budget because it affects the budgets of other departments such as production budget, cash budget, personnel budget, etc. Sales budget shows the estimated amount of sales in a specified future period normally a year. It Must indicate both the quantities expected to be sold as well as the receipts anticipated from such sales.

It is only after preparing the sales budget, that production capacity and inflows and outflows of cash are anticipated, expenses on various heads are estimated and cost data are considered. The accuracy of sales forecasts is the main basis for the accuracy and reliability of other budgets.

Sales budget is prepared by the marketing manager or sales manager on the basis of figures collected through one of the various methods of sales forecasts with the help of market researchers, regional managers, branch managers and salesmen.

Presenting sales forecast is not the sales budget. The necessary adjustment in respect of the following should also be made in the figure of sales forecasts:

(*i*) Opening stock of saleable items of the product.

(*ii*) Sales orders, outstanding at the beginning of the budget period.

(*iii*) Estimated volume of production during the budget period.

(*iv*) Estimate quantity of saleable product at the end of the period.

Thus, sales budget serves as a measuring device to inform management as to how far the company is making the desired progress towards the achievement of the predetermined objectives. It serves as a control device presenting the standard against which actual performance can be measured and a control mechanism for the sales volume and the distribution cost. Sales budget can be prepared area-wise, product-wise, cosumer-wise, and sales representative-wise. It offers a better control on sales.

FACTORS IN PREPARING SALES BUDGET

1. Internal Factors: These refer to those factors which relate to the internal situations of the concern and are in most cases within the control of executives. Such factors include:

(*i*) Sales-volume of the last year and sale-trend.
(*ii*) Long-term sale-trend of different products of the concern.
(*iii*) Profitability of different products.
(*iv*) Production capacity of the concern.
(*v*) Plant development programme.
(*vi*) Possibility of fluctuation in future production.
(*vii*) Seasonal changes in company products.
(*viii*) Advertisement and other sales-promotion measures.
(*ix*) Selling and distribution systems.
(*x*) Market research and product development possibilities.
(*xi*) Price policy—its effects on product demand.
(*xii*) Level of efficiency of salesmen.
(*xiii*) Sales orders outstanding at the beginning of the budget period.

2. External Factors: These are such factors which occur outside the concern and are to a great extent uncontrollable. Such factors are:

(*i*) General trend of industrial activities in the country.
(*ii*) Business, industrial, economic and taxation policies of the government.
(*iii*) Change in population.
(*iv*) National and international trade conditions such as business cycles, monopolistic tendencies, monetary policy, etc.
(*v*) Purchasing power of the general public-income, national production and employment positions are to be studied.
(*vi*) Standard of living of the masses-purchasing habits, fashions, ways of living, etc.

(*vii*) Competition position—in relation to price, product, etc.

(*viii*) Market conditions of the market segment for the product.

QUESTIONS FOR EXERCISE

1. Define Sales Forecasting? Discuss its objects and importance.
2. Discuss the role of sales forecasting in marketing planning.
3. Explain the limitations of sales forecasting.
4. Explain in brief the major steps in the process of Sales Forecasting.
5. It is said that the investigator can build his forecast on the basis of what people say, what people do, and what people have done. Discuss and analyse the various methods of forecasting demand.
6. What is Sales Budget? Discuss the principal factors that should be considered in developing the Sales Budget.

15

The Product, Product Mix and Product Cycle

Marketing involves two essentials:

(*i*) Product (Goods and services); and

(*ii*) Markets (Customers-buyers and sellers).

There can be no marketing without these two essentials. Unless there are both a market and product, transfer of ownership cannot take place. Markets and products are the foundations on which the whole edifice of marketing is based. The demand existing in different markets for a product constitutes the market for that product. It forms the basis for the modern market study known as market segmentation.

IMPORTANCE OF PRODUCT

Someone has well said, "If the first commandment in marketing is known the customer, the second is known the product." Following is the importance of the product:

(*i*) *Central point for all marketing activities*: Product is the pivot around which all the marketing activities revolve, such as, selling, purchasing, advertisement, distribution, sale promotion, etc. Product is a basic tool by which the profitability of the firm is bargained. It is the soul of business and without it nothing may happen.

(*ii*) *Product starting point of planning*: No marketing programme may be prepared in the dozens of products because planning for all marketing activities such as distribution, price, sales promotion, advertising, etc. is made on the basis of the nature, quality and the demand of the product. Product policies decide all other policies.

(*iii*) *Product is an end*: The main objective of all marketing activities is to satisfy the customers. Various policy decisions are techniques to provide the customers benefits, utilities and satisfactions through product. Thus, product is an end for satisfaction of customers. The producer must insist on the quality, size, etc. of the product so that it may satisfy the customers needs. The life of low quality products in the market is very short because they fail to satisfy the customers needs.

(*iv*) *Product is a must*: Thus, the product is a must for marketing activities. All marketing activities are done for the satisfaction of customer. The producers must know their customers and their needs. They should also know their product and its qualities. The product must contain the qualities which can satisfy the customers, should make continuous and sincere efforts to know their product through marketing research and planning and to improve it wherever it is lacking.

CLASSIFICATION OF GOODS

According to the traditional classification the two major categories of goods are: (*i*) consumer goods, and (*ii*) industrial goods. This classification is based on the purpose for which they are primarily used. Typewriters and electric motors are classified as industrial goods whereas soaps and sweets are regarded as consumer goods. This classification does not classify products in watertight compartments, for example, writing paper is industrial goods when used for business purposes, but it is a consumer goods when used for writing by a student. The same article may be an industrial goods under one set of circumstance and under other a consumer goods.

However, classification is necessary for a student of marketing as the buying motives differ from buyer to buyer. Marketing situation and problems vary depending upon the category of a product.

Consumer Goods

According to the American Marketing Association, the consumer goods are "Goods destined for use by the ultimate consumers or households and in such form that they can be used without commercial processing." Meloin T. Copeland classified the consumer goods further into three classes:

1. Convenience Goods: These are the consumer goods which a customer usually purchases frequently and wants immediately and with minimum of efforts. It includes a wide range of household products of low unit value like cigarettes, newspapers, drugs, grocery products. These goods are non-durable in nature. These are consumerd rather rapidly and are also called 'one shot items'. The habits dominate the consumer's behaviour. The convenience in availability and that too with less shopping time is the basis of buying these goods. Therefore, the producer must secure the widest possible availability of his goods if he has to maximise his sales.

2. Shopping Goods: Shopping goods are bought by the customer only after comparing quality, price, suitability and style. In these goods selection thus becomes an ingredient of the buying motive of a customer. Products of this group are more complex than convenience goods. They exhibit a high degree of differentiation. They are purchased less frequently and are of high unit value. The brand name is also of much use here. Wide distribution arrangements are not necessary speciality as the customers are not hasty in deciding what to buy. Examples of shopping goods are readymade garments and shoes.

3. Speciality Goods: In the words of American Marketing Association, goods are those "having unique characteristics and/ or brand identification for which a significant group of buyers are habitually willing to make a special purchasing effort." Comparatively of higher unit value these goods are infrequently purchased. Brand loyalty influences the buying motive of customers to a great extent. In the case of sepciality goods the customers make a special purchasing efforts.

4. Insistence Goods: These are goods which may or may not be generally available but for which the consumer refuses to accept any substitute. For example, if a customer wants to buy a car and insists on buying an Ambassador Car only then Ambassador Car becomes an insistence item for that transaction. This type of goods are sometimes included under speciality goods.

Classification on the Basis of Goods Theory

Leo V. Aspin Wall introduced a classification based on the colour of the products. He termed convenience goods as 'red goods' and shopping goods as 'yellow goods'. These are the extremes and the goods falling in between are termed as 'orange goods'. This classification now known as 'goods theory' is given in the following table devised in L.V.A. Walls.

Table 15.1: Classification of Consumer Goods According to the Characteristics of Goods Theory

Characteristics	Colour Classification		
	Red Goods	Orange Goods	Yellow Goods
Replacement Rate	High	Medium	Low
Gross Margin	Low	Medium	High
Adjustment	Low	Medium	High
Time of Consumption	Low	Medium	High
Searching Time	Low	Medium	High

INDUSTRIAL GOODS

The American Marketing Association has defined the industrial goods as "Goods which are destined to be sold primarily for use in producing other goods or rendering services as contrasted with goods destined to be sold primarily to the ultimate consumers." Industrial goods are meant for use in producing other goods or rendering services. These are the goods meant to be sold to ultimate consumers. Further classification of industrial goods is less difficult because industrial users exhibit more uniform patterns of buying behaviour than the ultimate consumers. The main characteristics of Industrial goods are: Geographical concentration of the market, limited number of buyers, large unit of individual purchase and technical considerations. These goods have a derived demand.

CATEGORIES OF INDUSTRIAL GOODS

1. Raw Materials: Most of the agricultural products or semi-manufactured goods are raw materials which require further processing after which they become consumer goods or industrial goods. Parts of the assembled goods are also to be included in Raw Materials which are as follows for the product TV.

(*i*) Agricultural products : Natural rubber, cotton.

(*ii*) Semi-manufactured goods: Steel, glass.

(*iii*) Parts of Assembly goods : TV or refrigerator or bicycle parts.

2. Equipments. These include industrial goods of three sub-categories. Installations, Minor or Accessory Equipments and

Plants and Buildings. These goods do not become part of the physical product, they only facilitate the production process. Some Examples are:

(*i*) Installations : Boilers, Lathes, Saw mills.

(*ii*) Accessory Equipments : Tools, welding equipment, time clocks, typewriters, calculators.

Equipments are highly technical in nature and require considerable sales efforts. They are generally characterised by 'short distribution channels', *viz* direct from manufacturer to industrial users.

3. Fabricated Materials: These become a part of the finished goods going through complete manufacturing process but which reach the ultimate user only after they are assembled or combined with other products. They do not change their form. For Example, Electric motors, batteries, automobile parts, etc.

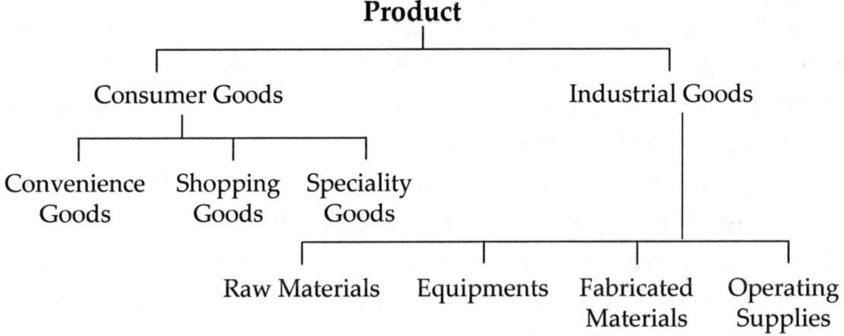

Fig. 15.1: Classification of Goods.

4. Operating Supplies: These products are essential to the business operations of industrial goods but they do not form a part of the finished product, *e.g.*, fuel, coal, cleaning materials, etc.

1. Difference in Nature: Industrial goods and consumer goods are two broad divisions of manufactured goods which show latent differences. According to the American Marketing Association, "Consumer goods are destined for use by ultimate consumers of households and in such forms that they can be used without commercial processing." Against this, industrial goods are defined as "those goods which are destined to be sold primarily for use in producing other goods or rendering services as contrasted with goods destined to be sold primarily to the ultimate consumer." These definitions bring out following two differences:

(*i*) Industrial goods are not meant for consumption, so their buyers are different from the buyers of consumer goods.

(*ii*) Further processing is required in the case of industrial goods before they can be finally consumed.

2. Difference in the Marketing: In the industrial products the customer is well informed and knows the relative merits of a particular product, alternative sources of supply and also the various competitive products available. An industrial product may serve the two markets simultaneously. For example, a typewriter may be used in industrial concern and it may also be used for personal purpose. In the latter case it is pure consumer product.

Following are important differences in marketing the industrial products and marketing consumer products.

(*i*) *Nature of demand*: The demand of consumer goods is 'original' while that of industrial goods is 'derived'. The industry is to supply the goods according to the demands of actual consumers or users. Thus, the demand of industrial goods is derived from the demand of consumer goods in making which the industrial products play an important part.

(*ii*) *The knowledge and sophistication of customers*: The industrial buyer is well informed of the relative merits and demerits of the alternative sources of supply of various competitive products. The number of customers of industrial product is small as compared to the number of consumers of consumer products. Therefore, in marketing industrial products, greater emphasis is placed on personal selling through salesmen. In marketing the consumers' products, on the other hand, emphasis is laid on mass marketing. Hence, most of the selling has to be done through advertising.

MEANING AND DEFINITION OF PRODUCT

The term 'product' has been defined in narrow as well as broad sense. In a narrow sense, it is a set of tangible physical and chemical attributes assembled in an identifiable and readily recognisable form. In a *broader sense,* it recognises each separate brand as a separate product.

Following are some important definition of product:

1. *S.W. Stanton*: "A product is a complex of tangible and intangible attributes, including packaging, colour, price, manufacturer's

prestige, retailer's prestige and manufacturer's and retailer's sendees which buyer may accept as offering satisfaction of wants or needs.'[1]

2. *W. Alderson*: "Product is a bundle of utilities consisting of various product features and accompanying services".[2] It consists of those physical and psychological satisfactions that the buyer receives when he buys the product, which the seller provides by selling a particular combination of product features and associated services.

3. *Rewoldt and Others*: "A product is anything that one receives in an exchange transaction; a complexity of tangible and intangible attributes including functional, social and psychological utilities or benefits may be part of the , product."[3] The production can be an idea, service, goods or any combination of these three. This definition includes goods and supporting services such as installation, guarantees, production information, and promises of a repair or maintenance. Goods assist with mechanical and functional tasks. Ideas provide psychological stimulation. Product images may aid individuals in social integration and personal adjustment.[4]

Characteristics of Product

1. It can be a single commodity or a service; a group of commodities or a group of services; a product service combination, or even a combination of several products and services.

2. Its meaning is determined by the needs and desires of the consumer. The purpose of a product is to satisfy some need of the consumers. The industrial buyers purchase problem-solving and time for creativity, not computer system.

3. It may be durable such as those that are expected to deliver a stream of satisfaction over a period of time, *e.g.*, watch, a radio or a typewriter; or it may be non-durable such as an apple, cream, a sports shirt, etc.

---

1. Stanton. J.W., *Fundamentals of Marketing*, 1983. p. 161.
2. Alderson, W., *Marketing Behaviour and Executive Action*, 1957, p. 214.
3. Rewoldt, S.H., Scott, J.D. and Warshaw, W.R., *Introduction to Marketing Management*, Richard D. Irwin, 1973, p. 231.
4. Pride, William M. and Ferrell, O.C., *Marketing Basic Concepts and Decisions*, Houghton Mifflin Co., Boston, 1977, p. 156.

4. Products may be *luxuries* which might be needed as a symbol of prestige and status such as a television, a well-furnished bungalow in a posh colony or *necessities* which are needed to keep the body and soul together, such as bread.

5. It may be an agricultural, mineral, forest or semi-manufactured or manufactured product.

THE PRODUCT CONCEPT

The term product concept was used by Theodore Levitt, who said, "It refers to the *augmented product*, or the aggregate of satisfactions that a user obtains." "When an industrial marketer sells a major item of machinery, it may augment the product in serveral ways. A diesel engine manufacturer might (*i*) provide long-term financing, (*ii*) assure a constant supply of maintenance and replacement parts, (*iii*) guarantee the performance of engine for a specified period, (*iv*) make technicians available to advise the customer on the installation and use of the product, and (*v*) train the customer's people who actually will operate the engine. The customer does not just buy a diesel engine; the customer purchases an augmented product—a product augmented by financial warranty, service, and training benefits."[1]

Three Dimensions of Product Concept

1. Managerial dimensions: These include the total product that the marketer puts in the market, (*i*) *The core product (or service).* It has certain identifiable characteristics and functions that distinguish it from other products or services; (*ii*) *The related product features.* These are brand name, package type, safety components, etc.; (*iii*) *The related product services.* These include delivery, installation maintenance and repair, and warranty etc. The product plays an important part in marketing operations. The marketing management is involved in formulating product strategy which sets down the objective of offering the product that balances or satisfies the needs of the consumers.

2. Consumer dimensions: A product conveys a message indicating a bundle of expectations to a buyer. If the expectations are fulfilled, its repeat demand is the result. The total benefits received from the products are important to the consumer. These

1. Levitt, Theodore, *Marketing for Business Growth*, McGraw Hill, New York, 1975, p. 9.

may take a tangible form warm or shelter or an intangible form status, glamour, knowledge.

3. Social dimensions: These presume that the society too is offered desirable or salutary product which brings not only an immediate satisfaction but also yields in the long-run consumer welfare, such as tasty, nutritious eatables, readymade products, conservation and best use of scanty resources, safety to users, quality of life, concern for a cleaner and better environment, etc.

PRODUCT MIX STRATEGY

The proliferation of products within the company means that product policy decisions are made at three different levels of product aggregation, *viz.*, product item, product line and product mix.

1. Product Item: It is a specific version of a product that has a separate designation in the seller's list.[1]

2. Product Lines: According to P. Kotler, product line is a group of products that are closely related either because they satisfy a class of need, or used together, are sold to the same customer group, are marketed through the same types of outlets, or fall within given price ranges or that are considered a unit because of marketing, technical, or end-use considerations.[2] Thus, a broad group of products, which are meant for essentially similar uses and possess reasonably similar physical characteristics, constitute *product line.*

3. Product Mix: Product mix is the full list of all products offered for sale by a company. Some examples are Kodak's cameras, photographic supplies, chemicals, plastics and fibres; or Tafas' hair oil, cosmetics, locomotives, textiles, iron and steel goods, mercedes trucks, etc.

Organisational Goals and Product Mix

The fulfilment of the marketer's goal to supply goods and services to consumer for satisfaction of their needs is possible if due attention is given to the product mix—sales growth, sales stability and profits.

1. Kotler, P., *Marketing Management*, 1972, p. 439.
2. *Ibid.*, 1976 Ed., p. 185.

1. Sales growth: It can be achieved either by increasing its share in existing markets or by finding new markets. Product mix can be adjusted to achieve goals in four ways: (*i*) *Market penetration.* In it market share is increased by expanding sales of present products in existing uses; (*ii*) *Market development.* In it markets are expanded by creating new uses of present products; (*iii*) *Product development.* In it market share is increased by developing new products to satisfy existing needs; and (*iv*) *Diversification.* In it market is expanded by developing new products to satisfy new consumer needs.

2. Sales stability: Stable sales allow for more efficient planning in all phases of production maintained and distribution. A proper balance should be maintained in total sales and product mix so that a product losing marketing may be counteracted by another selling high.

3. Profits: These are determined by the components of the product mix. Some items are usually more profitable than others. Low profit items perform a valuable part in helping to sell company's more profitable product. They may also prove as insurance against an unforeseen failure in profitable products.

Structure of Product Mix

1. Width: Width of the product mix means the number of different product lines found within the company. Thus, breadth is measured by the number of product lines carried. For example, Bajaj Electricals produces bulbs, fluorescent lights, mixies and grinders, toasters, scooters, pressure cookers and a host of other electrical appliances.

2. Depth: Depth of the product mix refers to the average number of items offered by the company within each product line. It is measured by assortment of sizes, colours, models, prices and quality offered within each product line.

3. Consistency: The consistency of product mix points out how closely related the various product lines are in terms of consumer behaviour, production requirements, distribution channels or in some other way. For example, the products produced by the General Electric Company have an overall consistency in that most products involve electricity in one way or the other.

According to Kotler, "all three dimensions of product mix have a market rationale. By increasing the width of the product mix the company hopes to capitalise on its good reputation and skills in present markets. By increasing the depth of its product mix, the company hopes to entice the patronage of buyers of widely differing tastes and needs. By increasing the consistency of its product mix, the company hopes to acquire an unparalleled reputation in a particular area of endeavour.

The dimensions of the product mix and their relation to each other are important for marketing management. Changing the product item involves the issues whether to modify, or add or drop product items. Changing the width of the product mix involves altering policy at the product-line level, whether to deepen or shorten an existing product line. Changing the product mix involves the issues as to what markets the marketer should enter or leave; and how to handle communications for the various product lines or items.

Causes of Decision about Change in Product Line

1. Changes in Market Demand: (*i*) *Population.* Changes in market demand may be due to changes in the component of population served. If there is an increase in the number of births the industries would like to increase new lines of baby products, such as baby food, baby shoes, perambulators, toys, etc. with other lines.

(*ii*) *Increase in the purchasing power of the consumers*: It also leads to the improvement in the quality of the product as also the dropping out of the line certain low-price, low quality goods.

(*iii*) *Change in the consumer behaviour*: This may be realised through changes in his motivation, attitudes, preferences and buying habits which may encourage the marketing executive to expand or contract his product mix to satisfy the more varying needs. He may add many new lines, such as the departmental stores do by adding to the general merchandise, the light reading material, health and beauty aids, ready to wear apparels, household requisites, indoor games, sports materials, etc. Sometimes changes in product mix are also made to suit the requirements of the middlemen who would like to have a varied line of products for reasons of competition, cost and promotion.

2. Competitive Action and Reaction: A firm may differentiate its product line to meet price competitions, and save it from unduly low profits.

3. Marketing influences: New product line may be added for two reasons: (*i*) to increase sales by exploiting new market or expanding the present ones; and (*ii*) to use the firm's capacity more efficiently by a better use of its resources of salesmen, warehouses or branch offices.

4. Product Influences: A firm may change its product mix to use its manufacturing capacity more effectively, thus reducing its net production cost. New line may be added when its production has been discontinued by another firm. New lines may be added to make a better use of the by-products or waste products.

5. Financial Influences: A firm may add or drop out product line as per its financial resources. The product mix may be expanded to increase a firm's profitable sales volume; or a product line may be dropped to meet depression in the market.

PRODUCT LINE STRATEGIES

According to W.J. Stanton major product line strategies are:[1]

1. Expansion of product mix;
2. Contraction of product mix;
3. Alteration of existing products;
4. Development of new uses for existing products;
5. Trading-up and trading-down;
6. Product differentiation and market segmentation.

1. Expansion of product mix: Expanding the line may be a valid decision in an area in which consumers traditionally enjoy a wide variety of brands to choose from and are accustomed to switching from one to another; or if the competitors lack a comparable product or if competitors have already expanded into this area themselves. The main limitation in expansion is the availability of sufficient finance, time and equipment. Expansion in the present product mix may be done by increasing the number of lines and/ or the depth within a line. For example, a large provision stores may add drugs, cosmetics and house wares (width) while at the same time increasing their assortments of dry fruits, baby foods, detergents (depth), etc.

2. Contracting or dropping the product: When contraction is decided upon, various alternatives are available to the marketers.

---

1. Stanton, W.J., *op. cit.* pp. 179-182.

The product may be consolidated with several others in line so that fewer styles, sizes or added benefits are offered. Or, the position can be simplified within a line. If even then a product fails, the company may stop it altogether.

3. Alteration of existing products: Sometimes improving an existing product may be more profitable and less risky than developing and launching a new product. Alterations may be made either in the designs, size, colour, texture, or flavour, or packaging, or in the use of raw materials or in the advertising appeal, or a quality may be changed. This strategy is followed regardless of the width and depth of the product mix.

4. Development of new uses for existing products: A company may find out new uses for the existing products as when a soap may be used not only for washing clothes but also for cleansing the floor, utensils and glass products.

5. Trading up and **trading down:** Trading up is the adding of a higher priced prestige product to the existing lines with the intention of increasing sales of the existing low-priced product. The seller continues to depend upon the older, low priced product for the major portion of the sales. Ultimately' he may shift the promotional emphasis to the new product so that larger share of sales may go to the new products.

Trading down means adding of the low priced items to its line of prestige product, so that the people who cannot buy the original product may buy these new ones because of the status of the higher priced goods.

But this type of trading up and trading down is harmful because the consumer may be confused about the new product, and the sale in the new line is also adversely affected as it is done at the expense of-the older product. This may be avoided by using differentiating brands, channels of distribution, promotional programmes, or product design.

6. Product differentiation and market segmentation: Product differentiation means "developing and promoting an awareness of differences between the advertiser's product and the products of the competitors". It enables a company to remove itself from price competition so that it may compete on the non-price basis, *viz.,* that its product is different from and better than, competitive models. This differentiation is done either in quality, design, brand or packaging. This strategy is mostly used where reasonably standardised products are sold, such as soaps, cigarettes, gasoline, etc. to a broad horizontal market which is fairly homogeneous in its wants.

In market segmentation strategy is used where the total market is made of many smaller homogeneous units, each of which of its units has different wants, motivations, etc. To meet these different demands, different products are developed to make tailor-made products to suit these requirements. Whereas the product differentiation seeks breadth in a more generalised market this strategy attempts to penetrate a limited market in depth. As Smith observes "The differentiator seeks to secure a layer of the market cake, whereas one who employs market segmentation strives to secure one or more wedge shaped pieces."[1]

THE PRODUCT LIFE CYCLE (PLC)

Products have a certain length of life, during which they pass through different stages. For some the life cycle may be as short as a month, while for others it may last for a sufficiently long period. A product goes through the various phases of its development from the time the product idea is born during its development, and up to the time it is launched in the market. Its life begins with its market introduction. Next it goes through a period during which its market grows rapidly. Finally, it reaches marketing maturity after which its market declines and the product dies. The duration of each of these stages is different among products. Some takes years to pass through the introductory stage, while others may be accepted in a few weeks. Then all products as not go through all stages, some fail in the initial stages, others reach the maturity stage after a long time. As Stanton puts it, "In virtually all cases decline and possible abandonment are inevitable because (1) the need for the product disappears; (2) a better or less expensive product is developed to fill the same need; or (3) a competitor does a superior marketing job."[2]

Stages of the Product Life Cycle

1. Introductory, pioneering or development stage.
2. Growth or the market acceptance stage.

---

1. Smith, Wendell R., "Production Differentiation and Market-Segmentation. As Alternative Marketing Strategies", *Journal of Marketing*, July, 1956.
2. Stanton, W.J., *op, cit*. 1976 Ed., p. 224.

3. Maturity stage.
4. Saturation stage.
5. Decline stage and Death stage.

1. Introductory Pioneering or Development Stage: During this stage the product is put in the market with full-scale production and marketing programme. The product has gone through the embryonic stages of idea screening, pilot models, and test marketing. The entire product may be new or the basic product may be well known but a new feature or accessory is in the introductory stage. In this stage, there is virtually no competition. The innovating company sets out to inform that target market segment and the intervening middlemen of the product's existence, through personal selling and advertising. The distribution is limited to a small area and sales rise slowly, since the product is usually offered to the higher income people. In the later stages of the life cycle, demand "filters down to lower income groups."[1]

During this stage technical defects often appear in the product due to insufficient prior testing. These defects may be detected and eliminated. The pioneering stage is most risky and expensive as there is a high percentage of product failures during this period. Operations in this stage are characterised by high costs, low sales volume, limited distribution, and heavy promotion. The type of the product rather than the sellers' brand is emphasised.

2. Growth or the Market Acceptance Stage: In this stage, the product is produced in sufficient quantity and immediately put in the market. The demand generally continues to outpace the supply. The sales and profit curves rise, often at a rapid rate. If the profit outlook appears to be very attractive competitors enter in the market in large number. The number of distribution outlets increase, economies of scale are introduced and prices may come down slightly. Sellers shift to "buy my brand" rather than "to buy my product" promotional strategy.

Now the product methods became established. Though products still continue to appeal to the "cream of the market", however, second level market, middie- income bracket consumers also begin to become important.

---

1. Staudt, T.A., and Taylor, D.A., *A Managerial Introduction to Marketing*, 1985, p. 145.

3. Market Maturity State: During this stage, sales continue to increase though at a decreasing rate, while the sales curve levels off, the profits of both the manufacturers and the retailers start to decline because of rising expenditure and lowering prices. Hence, marginal producers are forced to drop out of the market. Price competition becomes increasingly severe. In order to retain his dealers, the producer assumes a greater share of the total promotional efforts. New models are introduced as manufacturers broaden their lines. Supply exceeds demand for the first time, making demand stimulation essential through advertising and salesmen's efforts.

As the third level market (low-income group) is developed, the consumer market becomes very widespread. The consumer accepts the product, knows it, and is prepared to buy it. Product development becomes heavily style-oriented.

4. The Saturation Stage: During this stage, each of the characteristics mentioned under different stages, is intensified. Replacement sales dominate the market. The sales curve reacts to changes in economic conditions. "Owners of durables like automobiles and appliances are bombarded with pleas to trade in their present possessions "for new and improved models," while users of non-durable goods such as cosmetics, and toiletry and constantly reminded to keep on buying favourite brands.

5. The Decline Stage: The decline stage is characterised by either the product's gradual replacement by some new innovation or by an evolving change in consumer buying behaviour. The buyers do not buy as much as they did before, as superior products are being introduced to the market many of which meet the consumer's demand and needs more closely. The sales drop off and many of the competitors withdraw from the market. Cost control becomes increasingly important. Advertising and other promotional expenditures are drastically curtailed as price is more and more used to obtain business. It lays emphasis on efficient distribution at lowest cost. It becomes concentrated in a relatively few large and efficient mass distributors. Most managements shift their attention to other products, gradually phasing out the declining product as its future grows increasingly dark. Some stay with the dying product a little longer and try to review the market, though usually with disappointing results.

Despite the variation in the life-span of products the concept of product life cycle is useful in deciding the marketing strategy. The pioneering state would need heavy advertising, extensive selling and introductory inducements. In the 'growth stage' the sales pick up. Subsequently, a large number of producers enter the market with the gaining of greater acceptance by the consumer of the product. Now, marketing strategy is shifted to emphasise price appeals and product improvements. Finally, when the sales begin to level off, the management may only try to recover costs. In the meantime new product may have been placed in the market through research.

MANAGEMENT OF PRODUCT LIFE CYCLE

The shape of a product's sales and profit curves can be controlled and managed by timely and effective implementation of specific marketing actions such as through new packaging, repricing or product changes. The life cycle of the product may be extended or stretched out. The key to life cycle management is to forecast the profile of the proposed product's cycle even before it is introduced. Then at each stage, the management should anticipate the marketing requirements of the following stage.

The Problem of Declining Sales

The management has the following alternatives to resist the declining sales:

(1) It may improve the product or revitalise it.

(2) It may review the marketing and production programmes to be sure that they are quite efficient.

(3) It may streamline the product assortment by pruning out unprofitable size, styles, colours and models.

(4) It may cut all costs to the bare minimum level which will optimise profitability over the limited remaining life of the product; or

(5) It may abandon the product.

CHARACTERISTICS OF NEW PRODUCTS[1]

(*i*) *Products which are 'really' innovative, truly unique*: Such products are those for which there is a real need but for which there are

1. Wasson, C., "What is 'New, about a New Product", *Journal of Marketing*, July 1960, pp. 52-56.

no existing substitutes generally considered satisfactory such as hair restorers or a cancer cure. But there are others, which have substituted the existing products, such as television which has replaced radio and movies; plastics compete with wood and metals; cement replaces steel; atomic power compete with other energy sources; artificial fabrics have replaced cotton goods.

(*ii*) *Adaptive replacement of existing products involving a 'significant' differentiation in the existing article*: Instant Coffee replaced ground coffee and coffee beans; and annual model changes in cars and new fashions in clothing.

(*iii*) *Imitative products which are new to a company but not new to the market*: The business may want to enter that existing market with essentially a "me—too" product.

According to C. Wasson, buyers do want some elements of newness in a product; such as those that make familiar patterns of life easier, cheaper and otherwise more pleasant. Other product features require new patterns of life, new habits, assimilation of new ideas or viewpoints, acquisition of new tastes and acceptance of things now difficult to believe.[1] Stanton observes, "In any classification of new products the lines between categories are not very sharp. Perhaps the key criterion as to whether a given product is new is how the intended market receives it. If buyers receive that a given item is significantly different (from competitive goods being replaced) in some characteristics (appearance, use, performance, construction, etc.) then it is a new product.[2] Thus, the basic requirements of a new product are:

(*i*) Consumer or Customer acceptance;
(*ii*) Satisfactory performance;
(*iii*) Economical production;
(*iv*) Adequate distribution in depth and breadth;
(*v*) Effective packaging and branding;
(*vi*) Adequate after-sales service; and
(*vii*) Ultimate replacement.

1. Wasson, C., *Ibid*., p. 56.
2. Stanton, W.J., *op. cit*., 1976, Ed., p. 193.

PRODUCT INNOVATION

Peter Drucker has rightly observed, "Because it is its purpose to create a customer, any business enterprise has two and only these two basic functions: marketing and innovation."[1]

Innovation in product planning is the process of doing something that has never been done before. An innovative product is completely differentiated product for a firm.

Product Innovation Factors Causing

1. Market Changes: As the market is dynamic, existing products and product lines prove inadequate for meeting buyer's demand. Sophisticated buyers buy products tailored to their individual needs rather than to the total market's generalised needs. With the development and growth of new media of communication, the ease of reaching this media, and the changes in fashion. Market changes have been rendered possible, Therefore, the manufacturers emphasise on product innovation to avoid their products going out of market.

2. Changes in Technology: Changes in technology have widened the existing markets for the old products. They have also brought entirely new markets in existence, through the creation of entirely new products. Therefore, large amounts of money is being spent on technical research for product innovation.

3. Profitless Price Competition: The competitive forces in the modern system do not permit the continuance of a firm if it does not produce new products or make improvements in the existing products. Markets for mature and 'dying products' are highly competitive. Therefore, manufacturers engage in continuous product innovation not only to escape profitless price competition, but also for satisfying customers' expectations.

4. Diversification of Risk: The existing product may not be liked at all by the buyers, which means that they become obsolete with the passage of time. The greater the variety of products placed by a firm, the smaller is the chance of going that product out of the market. It needs continuous innovation to offset the losses which may result because of the older products going out of market.

---

1. Drucker, Peter, *Practice of Management*, 1954, p. 37.

5. Other Factors: Other reasons for product innovation are:[1]

(*i*) A company may develop new products to utilise the basic materials it is already making or to utilise waste or scrap from present production;

(*ii*) A company may add new products to even out sales fluctuations resulting from seasonal or cyclical factors.

(*iii*) A company may seek new; products to counteract the highly erratic buying behaviour of certain customers, such as government buyers;

(*iv*) A company may add new products to make more efficient use of marketing and production skills and/or to utilise marketing and production abilities more fully.

All these factors are related to management's desire to improve profitability. When the consumer is being increasingly selective, and the market is being flooded by imitation products or products which offer only marginal competitive advantages, it leads to "product indigestion", the cure of which is to develop really new products and to *create* really new markets. A company's product planning efforts should be designed *to innovate* and not just *imitate*; these efforts should place emphasis on leading not just *meeting* competition."[2]

New products, if successful, contribute to economic growth, company growth, and consumer satisfaction. In the words of Seibert, "The record of new products is the record of economic advancement and of social change."[3] Due to this profound influence, the developers of new products ought to be aware of their social as well as their economic responsibilities. If "the members or the business would take on a perspective of moral responsibility, the way in which new products can assist in answering man's quest for a wholesome identity will be enhanced."[4]

Organisation for Product Innovation

(1) Product Planning Committee: A committee may be set up either to assume full responsibility for product innovation or to assist

1. Cundiff, E.W. and Still, R.R., *Basic Marketing*, 1972, p. 206.
2. Stanton. W.J., *op. cit.*, 1971 Ed., p. 191.
3. Seibert, Joseph C., *Concepts of Marketing Management*, 1975, p. 161.
4. Francis, Roy C., "*Moral Responsibilities in New Product Development*", quoted by Seibert, p. 162.

product management executives. This committee may include the firm's president and persons from research and development, production marketing, engineering, and accounting and finance. These committees seem to work best when they serve as adjuncts to definite staff groups that have primary responsibility for the product mix.

(2) Separate Staff Department: A separate and formally organised department may be created to coordinate and guide product innovation activities such as scientific research, process development, market development, pilot plant production, engineering, test marketing and marketing research. It has the advantage of making new product development a full time activity. There is less risk that it will become a step-child in a department which is more concerned with day-to-day short range problems. But there are two operating weaknesses *viz.*, that of failure to plan thoroughly as to how the department will work; and the failure to staff the department with adequate background."

(3) Product Managers: In product management departments the product managers have the responsibility for carrying on, or coordinating product innovations. He is responsible for planning the complete marketing programme for his brand or group of products. He may be concerned with new product development as well as the improvement of existing product. He has the responsibility of setting marketing goals, planning marketing strategies, pricing, developing, advertising and sales promotion plans, preparing budgets, helping field sales managers and salesmen to do more effective selling job, securing dealer cooperation, keeping competitors under surveillance in terms of design, styling, and performance characteristics. However, he has no line authority over the field sales force or sales managers, he can only advise them but cannot order then to do something.

(4) Outside New Product Consultant: Sometimes, the services of a special type of new product department and outside firms/ consultants known as *stylist and industrial designers* are taken to speed up the new product development process and to sell off their unused products. Product consultants are used under following conditions:[1]

(*i*) When a company is very small to support a full time product group.

---

1. Cundiff and Still, *op cit.*, pp. 209-210.

(*ii*) Management wants to investigate an unfamiliar product area.
(*iii*) Detailed information is needed on possible new products, and usual sources cannot provide it.
(*iv*) Technical information is desired on competitors' products.

Criteria for Developing New Product

(*i*) *Adequate market demand*: The size and location of potential market should be well determined.
(*ii*) *Fitness in present marketing structure*: The product should fit into the company's present marketing structure. In this the company's past experience may be a guide.
(*iii*) *Fitness in present production structure*: A new product idea can be more favourably received if the items fit in with existing production facilities, manpower and management.
(*iv*) *Fitness in financial resources*: The product should fit as per the financial resources available, *i.e.*, whether adequate financing is available and feasible.
(*v*) *No legal restrictions*: The patents must be registered or applied for, labelling and packaging must be consistent with the legal requirements.
(*vi*) *Adequate management*: The executives should have sufficient time and ability to handle the proposed new product.
(*vii*) *Consistency*: The product should be in keeping with the company's overall image, self-concept and objectives.

1. Enlarging the Width: This means increasing the product-lines, by which a company can satisfy the needs of different types of customers and may increase its goodwill.

2. Going deep: This means that a company can satisfy the needs of the customers by producing different qualities of products, such as fans of different sizes and qualities keeping in view the range of customers. In this way a company specialises in that product-line and thus increases its goodwill and profitability by reducing the costs of production and distribution considerably. A company can also carry out the research work to improve the quality of its products, it can decide whether to add another product or improve the existing one meeting out the needs of the customers, if it is in demand or to scrap it altogether if it has no following. These days a consumer pays more attention to quality rather than the price to the product. If product-line are consistent or if they relate to the same category of consumer goods, it will reduce the cost of production to a great extent, by using the same channels of distribution and advertisements. For example, an electric company may produce fans, bulbs, radio, transformer, etc. at low cost of production and distribution.

QUESTIONS FOR EXERCISE

1. Define Product and explain its importance.
2. The first commandment in the marketing is, "know the customer", the second is "know the product". Explain.
3. Clarify the product-classification and explain what are the differences in the marketing of goods according to this classification.
4. Explain consumer and industrial goods. What are the differences in the marketing of the both types of goods?
5. The three way sub-division of consumers products into convenience goods, shopping goods and speciality goods is based on consumer buying habits rather than consumer products. Do you agree? Explain.
6. What classifications are adopted for differentiation of consumer goods in India?
7. Define product mix. Explain the influencing factors in the change of product mix.
8. What is meant by 'Product Mix'? Indicate reasons why manufacturers consider it necessary to change their 'Product Mix' time to time.
9. What do you understand by width, depth and consistency of the product mix? Explain.
10. Explain the concept and uses of product life cyles.
11. What do you mean by product life cycle? What are the gradual stages in the product life cycle of a particular product?
12. Examine the concept of product life cycle and discuss how it is related to the different stages of market development.
13. Explain the nature of promotional job in relating to the life cycle of a consumer product.

16

Product Planning and Development

What is Product Planning

1. *W.J. Stanton*: "Product planning embraces all activities which enable producers and middlemen to determine what should constitute a Company's line of products."

2. *Johnson*: "Product planning determines the characteristics of product best meeting the consumer's numerous desires, characteristics that add stability to products and incorporates these characteristics into the finished product."

3. *Karl H. Tietjin*: "Product planning is the act of making out and supervising the search, screening, development and commercialisation of new products; the modification of existing line and discontinuance of marginal or unprofitable items."

Thus, product planning signifies following three considerations:

(*i*) Development and introduction of new products.

(*ii*) Modification of existing lines as may be needed in items of changing consumer needs and preferences.

(*iii*) Discontinuance or elimination of marginal or unprofitable products.

ELEMENTS OF PRODUCT PLANNING

1. Research before Production: Before taking a decision to produce, a new item, market research should be carried out extensively. The company should decide the characteristics of the product that can meet the requirement of the people.

2. Possibility of Production Method: The possibility of production method which would be followed and is practicable to develop a product exactly what the consumer wants should be examined before taking a decision of producing a new product.

3. Modification in Existing Lines: The existing product lines should also be examined whether they can be improved and to what extent to meet the new requirements of the consumer or a new product is to be developed.

4. Elimination of the Product: Product planning also involves the decision regarding the elimination of the unprofitable product lines so that the resources may be used to some other product profitably.

5. Improvement in the product: Product planning includes decision regarding the improvement of the existing product in terms of quality, packing, etc. taking in view of the competitor's strategies in the market.

6. Price determination: One of the main element of the planning is determining the price of the product. The prices may be fixed on the basis of the prices fixed by the competitors for their products or on the basis of its cost of production or on the basis of the forces of its demand and supply in the market. This is an important decision by the management concerning product planning.

7. Commercialisation of product: Products commercialisation and sale of the product can earn a good profit to the company and may satisfy the needs of the consumers. It requires an attractive introduction of the product in the market.

8. Coordination: Product planning attempts to coordinate the various products and their efforts so that the company can maintain or rather improve its competitive position. This can be done by taking timely decisions for marketing conditions from time to time.

Thus, every decision from the start of an idea of producing a product to its elimination from the product line of the company forms a part of the product planning.

IMPORTANCE OF PRODUCT PLANNING

1. Starting point of the marketing programme: Product planning involves decisions regarding the product at different stages of its life cycle from time to time. Any decision regarding the production, modification and elimination of a product may affect the marketing policies, programmes, procedures and strategies.

A decision taken without proper consideration or planning, may ruin the firm because other programmes, policies, etc. are the outcome of the product plans. Thus, product planning is the starting point of all marketing programmes.

2. Influence on marketing activities: Lack of product planning implies managerial bankruptcy in the organisation and amounts to leaving the enterprise to follow its own luck. Marketing activities revolve around the product planning. All elements of marketing programme of a business unit, *i.e.,* price policies, distribution channels, advertising policies and programmes, sales promotion and personal selling, etc. are affected by the decisions concerning product planning.

3. Customer satisfaction: Customer's interest is supreme and it must be protected by all means. Examination of customer needs should be the main consideration in product planning. It should decide how the product must contain those qualities which can satisfy those needs, production is made accordingly. A company can sell only that which is required by the customers otherwise the life-cycle of the product would be very short and the company may even lose its existence. Product planning determines how to satisfy the consumers' needs.

4. Ensures profitability of **the product:** No businessman would be ready to do anything without profit motive. Customers' needs must be satisfied while reasonable and sufficient profits must be earned by the firm. Product planning is one of the way to coordinate the customers' satisfaction and the profitability. The firm should carry out different types of surveys to know the changing habits, needs, latest fashion and the status of the customers and modify its product accordingly. It will ensure at the same time both profitability and consumer satisfaction.

5. Prediction of profit: If the firm knows the life cycle concept of a product, it can very well predict its profits during various stages of life cycle but only through product planning. It can decide what new product should be developed or eliminated to maintain the profits of the firm even in declining or obsolescence stage.

6. Successful production and marketing: Thus, product planning is an important tool in the hands of marketing management to make the product and the marketing programmes successful. If it is lacking, it will affect the marketing activities and ruin the business completely. It is a foundation on which the whole structure of marketing programme stands.

PRODUCT LINE POLICIES AND STRATEGIES

Meaning

Product line policies and strategies is the alteration and modification in the product line. Product line refers to a group of products that are closely related because they satisfy a class of need. They are used together or are sold to the same types of outlets or fall within given price ranges. In order to achieve the long-term objectives, a firm should alter or modify its existing product line. It becomes necessary. The changes in the firm's own long-term objectives or change in the government policies regarding the product or the business and the changes in the political and social environment of the country compel a firm to alter or modify its product line policies and strategies. It becomes imminent to alter or modify the product line in order to survive.

Classification

The following is the classification of product line policies and strategies generally employed by the producer or the wholesaler of the product:

1. Product line contraction: Also known as 'simplification' or contraction of product mix, it is a method by which either the number of product lines or the depth of a product line is thinned out. This decision to reduce the product items may be due to the decision of management to suspend the production of unprofitable products or product line. Marketing problems also compel the manufacturers to withdraw certain items. The product mix will be altered on such occasions.

According to R.S. Alexander, "Many sick or marginal products never die, they are allowed to continue in the company's product mix until they fade away." In course of time these products eat away the profit earned by the other products. The decision to give away a product often results from changes in the market condition. Products may also be abandoned even though it is profitable that the management feels that the same resources could yield a higher profit from other products. The process of avoiding or stopping the production of a particular product altogether is called 'Simplification' or 'Product Line Contraction'.

It is the opposite of diversification. R.S. Alexander remarks, "But putting products to death or letting them to die is a drab business and often engenders much of the sadness of a final parting with old and true friend." This is done partly due to logical and partly sentimental reasons.

2. Product line expansion: It is just the opposite of the product line contraction. A firm may expand in both breadth and depth referred as diversification to utilise fully the marketing opportunities. The expansion of the product line is undertaken by increasing the lines or items of products which may be related or unrelated to the present products. For example, manufacturers of radio sets may start producing television sets and tape recorders. Following are the objectives and uses of product diversification:

(*i*) To eliminate seasonal slumps;

(*ii*) To eliminate cyclical slumps;

(*iii*) To reduce the danger of declining demand;

(*iv*) To acquire social approval;

(*v*) To make use of discoveries accidental in the company laboratories;

(*vi*) To use excess production capacity;

(*vii*) To utilise profitably the by-products of the production process;

(*viii*) To use cash and undisturbed earning during high profit periods.

3. Trading up: Trading up and trading down are the two forms of the strategy of product change. As very few products fully satisfy the needs of more than one market segments, concerns must change product features to match them better with the individualised needs of new target market segments.

Concern trades up when it adds higher priced, better items to gain sales of a present lower priced article. This may bring involvement of new markets with the stress on increasing sales to an old market segment. It may take up old and new segments also: Companies trading up make up the difference of a low priced with the high priced article at the same time. It adds to the goodwill of the firm.

4. Trading down: A company sometimes adds a low priced article for the better marketing of present high priced one so that more people can buy it easily. In trading down new market is looked for where the old product has not reached. This leads to success. The difference in profit is adjusted through the high priced one. Both trading up and trading down are riskful strategies.

5. Changing models or styles of the existing products: Continuous changes in fashion create a problem for the producer by compelling him to assess such changes in advance. The desires and needs of the consumers are also subjected to continuous changes, compelling the management to review this problem with farsightedness.

6. Quality variations: Under certain circumstances a manufacturer is forced to produce differing qualities of a particular product. A single quality may not be enough to retain the market even if the quality of the produce is good. For example, manufacturers of hair oils produce hair oils of different varieties with varying quality at different prices.

The manufacturers of consumer goods often face the problem of changing the quality to suit the market, by either trading up or by trading down.

7. Product identification: The position of a product in the market is determined by contrasting its image with competing products as well as other products marketed by the same company. Image is partly created by brand image while a market is easily identifiable by the buyers in the market place. But as the brand image is not a permanent one, it cannot retain a permanent market. It is only a name and the acceptance of a product finally rests on the real worth of the product. Every manufacturer must find out by market information and product testing whether his product will have a potential market or not.

8. Test marketing: Test marketing is necessary before finding a new product to the market. The product should be first introduced and tried in a small segment of the market and the reaction of the customers studied carefully. The test reveals the shortcomings of the product which may be removed and improved before the product is actually sent to the market. Test marketing also reduces risks. It is a trial and error method to know what is likely to happen when a new product is introduced commercially. Thus, it can remove future difficulties and problems.

PHASES OF PRODUCT PLANNING

1. Creation of new product ideas: The planners evaluate the extent and importance of identified market needs through marketing research and buyer behaviour and appraise the extent to which present products fulfil market needs. Based on scientific and technical knowledge of the concern for new products a company's capabilities are valued as such.

2. Investigation of competitive market situation: Market research is carried on to know the size and type of marketing organisation. Analysts of company resources assess the adequacy of plant capacity, product service facilities, marketing channels, engineering abilities and other human resources. It shows relative profitability, target market segment and opportunity to attain product leadership.

3. Development of product: Thus, the management gets the programme and the project is executed. This includes overall plan for eventual marketing of the products.

BASIC REQUIREMENTS OF A NEW PRODUCT

1. Customer of consumer acceptance;
2. Satisfactory performance;
3. Economical production;
4. Adequate distribution in depth and breadth;
5. Effective packaging and branding;
6. Adequate servicing where required after the product is sold;
7. Ultimate replacement.

STEPS IN THE PROCESS OF NEW PRODUCT DEVELOPMENT

According to Booze, Allen and Halmilton, the process of new product development consists of: (1) Exploration; (2) Screening of ideas; (3) Business Analysis; (4) Product Development; (5) Test marketing; (6) Commercialisation of the product.

1. Exploration: The internal management of the company or the people is directly involved with the creation of new ideas. While the management gives the policy decision to the product launching, technical department makes research. As the marketing of a new product is an important contribution to an industrial growth, failure to do so on a new concept can be disastrous.

2. Screening of Ideas: Development of a commercial possibility is a part of marketing. An unsatisfied customer can also create commercial possibilities. New and better packaging material may be used. A firm may see the imports and judge the product it can produce to be comparable to import. Thus, marketing research and collection of data about the needs of the people are important at the stage of 'searching' for ideas of a new product.

The creation of ideas for new products must accompany the technical knowledge and possibility of markets. Ideas should be analysed and evaluated for sales potential, profitability, existing facilities and availability of other resources like finances. Thus, the main work before planners of the product is to identify specific customer needs and expectations and align company capabilities with the changing demands.

3. Business Analysis: The consideration of market potentials and profitability requires assessment of product facilities, availability of raw materials, possibility of using existing plants and finance allotted for the project. The finance, cost accounting section and marketing department are involved in the project of new product. Marketing department is responsible for sales policies and sales strategies. This whole responsibility goes to sales department in the absence of marketing department. Thus, all departments coordinate in new product project. Departmental heads frequently meet to evolve the new product. The data are examined and tested for its application. Some products can be needful in creation. The next step is to form specification of a product that market needs and its minimum requirements.

4. Product Development: The higher authority must get prepared samples or designs of the product to suit the consumer needs. Decisions regarding brand and packaging should be taken and consumers tastes should be investigated.

5. Test Marketing: The cost of testing will be much less in an industrial product because the users of such product are less and can be approached easily. In a consumer product, it will take more time for testing the product and the cost of testing will be much higher. The result of testing is analysed. If the product proves successful, the decision is taken to produce it on commercial basis. If it proves unsatisfactory, it may be withdrawn. Test marketing is done for test purposes. The product is sold in some selected market segments for a specified period. This reduces the risk of the producer.

6. Commercialisation: The last stage in product development is the introduction or launching or marketing the product on commercial basis. From top to bottom every one is busy in calculating for the vast investments as the product may not prove profitable for three or four years in future. Top management must finally approve the introduction of the new product.

CAUSES OF FAILURE OF NEW PRODUCT

1. Inadequate Market Analysis: This will yield only wrong data. Acting on such data will lead to product failure.

2. Product Defect: This is due to technical flaws in the process of production. Low quality of products, poor design or packing may lead to product failure which can be aided by proper marketing.

3. Higher Costs: Higher costs than anticipated at the time of product planning might be partly due to wrong pricing policies adopted by the firm and because cost estimates often go wrong when the products are finally introduced into the market.

4. Poor Timing: A fundamental principle to be followed in product planning is to find out the exact time at which the product is to be introduced in the market. A close analysis of the market conditions and consumer behaviour and attitudes is essential to find an answer to the two problems: when and how.

5. Competition: Cut-throat competition tends products to struggle hard in the market. There are various methods to overcome severe competitions including price cuts and various kinds of discounts, etc. However, it is not the low prices alone that will help a product to compete and succeed in the market. Offering, high quality products excelling the existing ones is the basic determinant in deciding the success of a product in the market. Ultimately, it is the quality of a product which enables the product to withstand competition.

6. Insufficient Marketing Effort: A manufacturer does not end his efforts after a product is ready for sale. Advertising and proper promotional activities also form a part of his job to make the product known to consumers. Proper selection of the channels of distribution and the methods of physical distribution help in proper and efficient marketing of products.

7. Inadequate Sales Force: Impersonal methods of sale include advertisement and similar promotional activities. Personal methods, on the other hand, are more intimate and more efficient. The promotional activities should be backed by adequate sales forces to introduce the product properly in the market. If salesmen are not trained or do not possess required qualities, the product will not succeed.

8. Weakness in Distribution: The distribution of the product is one of the major marketing quality, which enables the product to reach the proper markets at proper time and at a proper price. Distribution management should know where management decisions require farsightedness and vision.

Blain Cooke opines that "the new products which fail are not in literal marketing sense products at all—they are merely interesting but worthless artifacts of the production process."

TEST MARKETING

Testing involves trial and error method to ascertain what is likely to happen when a product is introduced commercially. Appropriate test area will provide clue about models, their sizes, their types or complete remodeled product required. A knowledge of sale of the product will be required for higher scale. Test marketing gives ability to understand the market for the product and know what the customer wants of the product should one may offer the product to their needs.

Information Requirements for Field Testing

1. Various applications of the product.
2. The environment or the circumstances for the use of the product.
3. Necessary general characteristics to meet the customers' needs and requirements.
4. Nature of general competitive situation.
5. Modification of design if needed.
6. Focusing of marketing efforts in the area.
7. Specific product advantages or benefits for advertisement and sales promotions campaign.
8. Latest demand and new applications.
9. The environment and circumstances of current use.
10. Competitive situation.

The above informations received will help in forming marketing strategy for ultimately launching the new product.

Ways of Marketing Selection

1. Classification of market in terms of the major applications or uses of the product and testing three or four different uses of the product.

2. Testing of the geographical angle and selecting an area which is representative of the habits and psychological characteristics of the whole market where it will be sold.

3. By customer classification.

The method of selection will be based on the nature of market. After defining cross section of the market one should choose:

(*i*) Representative participants for testing.

(*ii*) A suitable number of participants, *i.e.*, sample must be large enough to know significantly and provide necessary information from one or two sources.

(*iii*) Secure written reports from sufficient members on whom these tests are made so that analysis could be done properly to know the interest.

Procedure of Test Marketing

1. Determination of the Number of Cities: Two main factors worth consideration in this respect are: (*i*) representativeness, and (*ii*) cost of testing. Markets should represent all types of customers and their behaviour. The cost of testing should be within limits. The number of market should be an ideal one, representing all types of customers bearing the minimum cost of testing. Thus, the number depends upon several factors like nature and demand of the product, probable area of sales, regional disparities, competitors' efforts and cost of testing, etc.

2. Selection of Cities: In selection of cities, the cities must represent the whole country so that appropriate results may be extracted from the test. Cities to be selected should possess the following characteristics: (*i*) Existence of various types of industries, (*ii*) Average competition, (*iii*) Presence of chain and departmental stores, (*iv*) Critical nature of the population, etc. Metropolitan cities like Delhi, Bombay, Calcutta, Madras, etc. are more often selected for the purpose of test-marketing.

3. Duration of the Test: Duration may be a month or a year. It may depend upon various considerations of which three main factors are the following:

(*i*) *Average Repurchase Period*: Test duration shall be long where repurchase period is long. If repurchase period is short, test duration will also be short.

(*ii*) *Situation of Competition*: Competition will define the duration of test. In a competitive situation, the test duration should not be too short to draw the required results nor too long to give time to the competitors to improve their products and introduce their improved products in the market.

(*iii*) *Cost*: Cost and duration have positive correlation. The longer is the period the higher is the cost.

4. Collection of Necessary information: Necessary information includes nature of product, nature of customers, channels of distribution, buyers' behaviour etc. Unbiased results should be drawn from the information. It should be decided beforehand what information, one has to collect during the test period.

5. Action after the Test: After market testing there are many alternatives. If the sales are excellent plan for commercial introduction may be decided. If sales are fair, new market test may be made to modify the product and take it again to market. If the sales shown by test is poor one may drop any idea or have a retest of the market with modifications in the product or one may redesign the area for test after improving the product.

Thus, before deciding to launch the product, proper marketing strategy is to be done based on the information of market testing about pricing policy, promotional strategy and organisation of physical distribution system.

PRODUCT SIMPLIFICATION

Meaning

Product line contraction, also termed as 'simplification' is the decision to reduce the product items and to suspend the production of the unprofitable products. Marketing problems compel the manufactures to withdraw certain items. The product mix will be altered on such occasions.

Many sick or marginal products never die, they are allowed to continue in the company's product mix until they fade away.

"These products will in course of time eat away the profits earned by the other products." Market salinisation makes a product unprofitable. It may be abandoned even though still profitable, if the management feels that the same resources could yield a higher profit from other products.

Thus, simplification is the process of avoiding or stopping the production of a particular product. It is opposite to diversification. In spite of the advantages, most managements do not like "product pressing programmes".

Most managements are always on the look out for finding the weak products and adopting a gradual elimination of some products.

Advantages of Simplification

1. Reduction in Cost: Cost of production is reduced considerably by the process of simplification because production of unprofitable products is stopped and the resources are made available to other products. Production of some items is made on large scale and large scale economies are secured. Supervision expenses are also reduced.

2. Use of Specialised Plants: Specialised plants standardised for production of one or two items method are used for production of one or two items. It helps specialisation and standardisation.

3. Use of Specialised Personnel: As the firm can make use of the skill of specialised personnel hence better quality of products are produced.

4. Increase in Efficiency: As the number of products are limited, the production is made on the principles of specialisation and division of work. It also increases the efficiency of labour and of the firms.

5. Increase in profits: By increased efficiency reduced wastage and lower cost of production, the profits of the firm increase.

6. Market Control: Market control becomes easy because marketing activities such as market analysis, consumer analysis and competitions analysis can be made extensively.

DIVERSIFICATION

Meaning

Diversification means that something new will be added such as new products, new markets, new technologies or even new company. It means adding a new product to the existing product line or mix. For example, if a sugar manufacturing company starts producing paper, it is a case of diversification. The new product cannot be complementary or an allied product to the existing one. It may be a product which is entirely distinct and different from existing products. Diversification is applicable not only to production but also to selling. For instance, if a wholesaler dealing in electrical goods starts selling simultaneously synthetic textiles, it is a case of diversification.

Product line just opposite to simplification is called diversification. A firm may extend in both breadth and depth to utilise the marketing opportunities. Depth refers to the number of product items offered by the organisation within a particular product line. Width means the extent of different product lines in the product mix offered by an organisation. Consistency describes the relatedness of the various product lines.

Increasing depth of the product mix helps the organisation to attract customers with deficient needs and preferences. It helps the concern to capitalise on its established reputation and marketing skills existing facilities like production and distribution and to establish a high reputation.

Reasons for Diversification

1. There is a technological development in the process of production.
2. New markets are to be created.
3. The advantage of the reputation of company's name and its existing products is to be spread to other products.
4. There is constant threat for the existing product due to abrupt changes in fashion.
5. The spare capacity of the factory is to be fully utilised.

Diversification is profitable only in the case of large companies which have multi-market and multi-product, which are financially available and supported by a well organised management. Diversification of product is capable of preventing recessionary trends entering the industry. Diversification is brought into effect by means of merges like one company acquiring another.

Objectives of Diversification

In his book 'Product Diversification and Public Interest' Prof Kenneth, R. Andrews has enumerated the following objectives and uses of product diversification:

1. Stability in Earnings and Organisation

(*i*) To eliminate seasonal slumps.

(*ii*) To eliminate cyclical slumps.

(*iii*) To reduce the danger of declining demand.

(*iv*) To acquire social approval.

2. Efficiency in Utilisation of Company Resources

(*i*) To make use of the discoveries accidental or purposeful in the company laboratories.

(*ii*) To use excess productive capacity arising from abrupt decline in demand and from imbalance the vertical integration.

(*iii*) To capitalise the foreseen demands for a product developed for company's own use.

(*iv*) To capitalise a unique production process.

(*v*) To make new uses of the basic raw materials.

(*vi*) To utilise profitably the by-products.

(*vii*) To meet the government requests arising out of the knowledge of the company's resources.

(*viii*) To make full use of a developing management and staff.

3. Efficient Marketing

(*i*) To increase in sale of the basic products.

(*ii*) To meet the demands and convenience of the diversified retailer.

(*iii*) To exploit the value of an established trade mark.

(*iv*) To meet the requests of specific customers.

(*v*) To reduce the ratio of sales costs to total sales.

4. Profitable Use of Opportunities

(*i*) To use cash and undistributed earnings during high profit periods.

(*ii*) To take advantage of the large company's access to debt financing at relatively low rates.

(*iii*) To manipulate capital gains versus income and inheritance taxes for the material benefit of the buyers and sellers in prospective mergers.

(*iv*) To capture merger bargains too good to pass up.

(*v*) To avoid the cost of constructing facilities under existing economic conditions.

(*vi*) To make the best of diversification unwillingly or unwillingly acquired with a purchased company.

PRODUCT DIVERSIFICATION

Meaning

Production diversification or Product Differentiation refers to the production or distribution of more than one product-line which may be related or unrelated or each other.

Objectives of Diversification

1. To use more effectively the existing selling and distributing facilities.
2. To meet the customers demand or request especially in industrial products.
3. To take the advantage of its existing reputation as a producer of quality products.
4. To increase the sale of existing products where diversification is suggested in related products.
5. To use the distribution channels fully.
6. To increase the profits by offering different types of products.

Forms of Diversification

1. Diversification into Related Product Line: It is diversification planned in such products which are related to the existing product-lines. Generally, the suggested product may be grouped with the existing product on one and the other basis. The purposes of such types of diversification are: (*i*) to reduce the average selling cost, (*ii*) to recognise its sales organisation, (*iii*) to combat competition, and (*iv*) to increase the profits.

2. Diversification into Unrelated Product Line: This is diversification in such product lines which are quite unrelated to each other and which cannot be grouped together. The decision to diversify in this form is taken with the objectives: (*i*) to capture the market, (*ii*) to take advantage of its goodwill in the market, (*iii*) to have stability in the trade, etc. This type of diversification requires extensive market analysis before taking decision to diversify.

3. Product Replacement: In this form of diversification a new product is added to the product line to replace the other product of the same product line. If a company thinks that its product is to die, it adds the other product of similar nature to the market so that it can maintain its sale-volume and profits. It is a defensive policy against the risk of dieing out of one of the products of the company.

FACTORS MOTIVATING PRODUCT DIVERSIFICATION

1. Utilisation of Unused Capacity: If company resources such as capital, labour, managerial skill, research and marketing facilities, etc. remain unutilised or underutilised, a company can take the decision to diversify its products to make the best use of such unutilised or underutilised resources. Change in product mix reduces the cost of production because the company has not to bear the cost of unutilised resources unnecessarily.

2. Scientific and Technical Development: Diversification may be the result of scientific and technical developments in production methods which make the existing products obsolete and the demand of the new product increases. So, using the modern technological methods the company can replace the old product with the new one. It may take advantage of its goodwill if it is pioneer in the field.

3. Efficient Management: If the management of an organisation is efficient and takes interest in the development of the concern, it may come out with the decision to produce new items related or unrelated to the existing product-line.

4. Industrial and Economic Policies of the Government: If the government's industrial and economic policies motivate the producers to produce new items and does not restrict the monopolistic tendencies on sound basis or amalgamation and absorption, diversification takes place.

5. Social Changes. Social changes such as changes in nature and behaviour of the customer's demand, fashion and style motivate the producer to diversify his product accordingly to meet the demand of the new product.

6. Desire of the Producer: Sometimes, a producer has very strong desire to produce different products either to take the advantage of his goodwill or to control the market or to dominate the will of the buyers. So he goes on to diversify.

7. Consumer Satisfaction: If the faith of consumer is favourable to one company and he likes that the company should produce other products also, the company takes decision to diversify in such areas where it is confident enough of consumer's faith. For example, in India, consumers have faith in the products of Tata or Hindustan Lever and any new product from them will be easily saleable in the market because it is produced by Tata or Hindustan Lever.

PRODUCT ELIMINATION

Meaning

R.S. Alexander has said, "Putting products to death or letting them to die is a drab business and often engenders much of the sadness of a final parting with old and trusted friend." However, most managements are always on the look out for finding weak products and adopting a thin gradual elimination.

There are some products which cannot be improved or modified to suit market. Here the profitable alternative would be to withdraw the product. The process of withdrawal is technically known as 'Product Elimination'. Products are removed from the product-line at times. Continuation of sick product will lead a company to lack of profitability. These products require a disproportionate amount of management's time and may even spoil the company's reputation if they are unsuitable to the customer. Hence, the management introduces a new product and reviews existing products from time to time and at times cancels the production.

According to Lawrence, accurate costing and experimentation helps making right decisions regarding whether a product should be dropped or retained.

Process of Elimination

1. Selection: To select the products which are to be considered for elimination.

2. Collection of Data: Now, information would be collected and analysed about deficiency in product, substitutes, product life cycle, price, profitability, inability of the product to satisfy the needs of the consumers, etc. If it is found that the product can be modified to suit the needs of the consumers and it can be done profitably, the product would be improved or modified. On the other hand, if the analysts find that the product cannot be modified to the aspiration of the customers, a decision is taken to eliminate it.

Reasons or Indicators of Product Elimination

1. **Continuous decrease in the Sale of the Product:** This may be due to the last stage of the product life cycle or incoming of better quality products of the competitors in the market.

2. **Reduction in Product Effectiveness:** Certain products particularly pharmaceutical products and certain drugs lost their effectiveness for providing the benefits for which they were produced originally. These may have to be eliminated or substituted by other drugs.

3. **Emergence of a Superior Improved Product:** If an improved substitute of the existing product emerges in the market, the management must consider its elimination even at the time when the substitute is in its introductory stage otherwise the company will lose the battle.

4. **More Administrative Time:** It is better to decide elimination of the product, if a management devotes disproportionately excessive time on one product in comparison to the other products of the product mix due to the product being sick.

5. **Product Life Cycle:** If the product is in its obsolescence stage, it would be wise to eliminate the product in time to restrict the fall in profits otherwise the product will die itself within short time.

Problems Involved in Product Elimination

1. **Sensitiveness of Executives:** The management always avoid the problem of product elimination and is interested in continuing the present product mix. Executives are sensitive to the elimination.

2. **Undue Optimism:** It is thought that the market will turn favourable to the product and its sales will go up very soon.

3. **Defect elsewhere:** Sometimes, it is realised that the defect does not lie in product, it is somewhere in marketing function and it can be improved.

4. Facility in Sale: Very often a poor sick product is allowed to continue because it facilitates the sale of other products of the concern.

5. Improvement: Where management is of the view that the sale of the product shall have been increased after its proper modification by developing its quality, style, brand and packaging.

6. Liabilities: In order to meet the liability of its fixed overhead charges and to utilise its fixed resources, the management has a hitch in eliminating the product. Until and unless those resources are utilised profitably, the management cannot take a decision of losing its capital.

7. Vested Interests: Vested interests, sentiments of managements and consumers and the sense of responsiveness of the firm are some other factors which help continuing the sick product.

Though the above factors favour the continuance of the sick product in the market for a fairly long time, the management should be cautious enough in taking the decision to eliminate the product. If the management thinks it desirable to eliminate the product, it should do it immediately to avoid the loss.

QUESTIONS FOR EXERCISE

1. "Product planning is the starting point of planning in a firm." Explain.
2. "Lack of product planning implies managerial bankruptcy in the organisation and amounts to leaving the enterprise to trust its own luck." Discuss.
3. "Product planning and development is a top management responsibility that affects the survival and growth of the firm." Comment.
4. "Product planning is also an important means of discharging social responsibilities of the business." In the light of this statement explain the importance of product planning,
5. What do you mean by product-line policies and strategies? Explain the various product-line strategies.
6. Comment on the factors which you would take into account in developing successfully a new product and its commercialisation.

7. Explain the process of developing a new product. What are those reasons that contribute to the failure of a new product?
8. Explain the nature of the three major phases in new product planning.
9. What is test marketing? Discuss the various activities involved in developing a test-marketing plan for a branded consumer product.
10. Describe Simplification and Diversification as a part of product policy.
11. Explain the meaning and benefits of product diversification. Distinguish between diversification in related and unrelated products.
12. What is meant by product elimination? What are the reasons of product elimination?
13. Highlight some of the problems involved in the product elimination decisions.

17

Product Identification
(Branding, Packaging, Labelling and Sampling)

BRAND AND CONNECTED TERMS

1. Brand: "A brand is a name, term, sign, symbol or design or a combination of them which is intended to identify the goods or services of one seller or group of sellers and to differentiate them from those of competitors."[1]

—American Marketing Association

2. Brand Name: "Brand name is a part of a brand consisting of a word, letters comprising a name which is intended to identify the goods or services of a seller or a group of sellers and to differentiate them from those of competitor."

—American Marketing Association.

3. Brand Mark: "A mark is the part of the brand which appears in the form of a symbol, design or distinctive colouring or lettering."

—William J. Stanton.

4. Branding: Branding is the management process by which product is branded. It is a general term covering various activities such as giving a brand name to a product, designing a brand mark and establishing and popularising it.

5. Trade Mark: Trade mark is defined as a "brand or part of a brand that is given legal protection because it is capable of exclusive appropriation" (AMA). Thus, the trade mark is essentially a legal term protecting the manufacturer's right to use the brand name of trade mark. When a brand mark is registered and legalised it

1. Committee on Definitions, American Marketing Association, *Marketing Definitions; A Glossary of Marketing Terms*, Chicago, 1960. pp. 9-10.

becomes a trade mark. Thus, registered brands are Trade Marks. All trade marks are brands but all brands are not trade marks.

BRAND *Vs.* TRADE MARK

1. Meaning: While trade mark is used in the narrow sense, brand is used in broader aspect. Trade Mark is that part of brand which has a legal protection. In this way all trade marks are brands but all brands are not trade marks.

2. Indication: While brand denotes the qualities of a product, the trade mark denotes the producer. So, trade mark can be used with every brand.

3. Practice: While some businessmen use the same symbol or design or mark for their brands and trade marks some others give different brands to their different products with the same trade mark.

CHARACTERISTICS OF A GOOD BRAND NAME

Branding is the management process by which a product is branded. It is a general term covering various activities such as giving a brand name to a product, designing a brand mark and establishing and popularising it. The success of any product is determined primarily by the worth of that product in relation to the competiting products. But names are in one way a necessity for they serve to create identity. Identity is essential in competition because without a means of identification there is no way of making a choice. It is here that brand name enters the scene of marketing.

The following are some of the general considerations in selecting a good brand name.

1. Pronunciation: The name should readily come to the minds of customers. It should be easy to remember.

2. Easy: The name should be easy to read and understand.

3. Appropriate: The name should be appropriate for the product.

4. Descriptive: It should, as far as possible, be most descriptive in nature.

5. Unique: It should be different from other brand names.

6. Registered: It should be got registered so that any other firm might not take advantages of its popularity.

7. Helpful: Brand name should be helpful in advertisement.

8. Short: It should be short and pointed.

9. Not Absent: It should be far from absence.

10. Economic: It should be economic so that it could be easily printed and embossed on packages.

11. Impact: As far as possible it should be heart touching so as to influence the mind of the customer and catch his imagination.

CLASSIFICATION OF BRAND

In his *"Semantics of Branding"* Thomas F. Schutte classified the brands into following two broad categories:

1. Manufacturer's Brands: These stress the identity of manufacturers.

- (*i*) *National Brands*: Brand for a particular region.
- (*ii*) *Advertising Brands*: Brand stressing symbols.
- (*iii*) *Blanket Brands or Single Brands or Family Brands*: One brand name for all the products of a manufacturer, *e.g.*, Godrej products, Bajaj products, etc,
- (*iv*) *Multiple Brands or Individual Brands*: Brand name given for each variety of product, *e.g.*, various brand soaps of Tatas or Hindustan Lever.

2. Distributor's Brands: Distributor's brands stress the identity of the retailer. These are:

- (*i*) Private Brand.
- (*ii*) Store Brand.
- (*iii*) Dealer Brand.
- (*iv*) House Brand.

CONTROVERSY ABOUT THE PURPOSE OF BRANDS

1. Controversy between the manufacturer's and distributor's brands: While some authorities argue that the former is strong and others are of the view that distributive brands is more popular because it is the distributor who ultimately deals with the consumers. In India there are no large distributors like Roebuck of the U.S.A. whose quality excels that of the manufacturers.

Recently most of the manufacturers have developed their own distribution system which has made distributor's brand out of quesiton. In India, the retailers are not very strong to carve their own name in the distribution field. Manufacturers are more powerful in designing a brand name and repeating and stressing it through packages and repeated advertisements.

2. Controversy between the use of family brand and individual brand: It is a management's decision whether to choose single brand name for all its products or to have individual names for each of the product. Each has its own advantages and disadvantages. Where a manufacturer has established a name, he may prefer to introduce the new products under the same brand name used for his own previous product. The new product will also enjoy the reputation created by earlier brands without any additional expenditure. However, it may turn to be disadvantageous in case of failure of product. The effect of failure will spread to the other products also. Use of one brand also reduces the advertisement expenditure.

The use of individual brand name calls for high advertisement expenditure for its establishment. Though in it the products of the same manufacturer will compete with each other. However, it is advantageous for clear identification where different quality and variety products are manufactured. Liberty Shoe Company manufactures a variety of shoes and individual names are essential to identify a particular variety. The decision of a manufacturer to choose a family brand or individual brand depends on the following factors:

(*i*) Name of the product.

(*ii*) Varieties manufactured.

(*iii*) Promotional aspects.

(*iv*) Nature of the market for which the product is intended.

(*v*) Consumer's attitude and sentiments.

IS BRANDING SOCIALLY DESIRABLE?

It is said that branding leads to Brand monopoly, which is created by brand loyalty to the products in the minds of consumers. This criticism is baseless since such a situation is not possible in the case of consumer goods unless they are necessary items. When a monopolistic tendency is found, consumers will react to it by changing the brand.

Brand names do not always assure good quality. Manufacturers sometimes place inferior goods in the market under a glamorous brand name, particularly, when brand name becomes popular.

However, the brands are not socially undesirable. Its advantages are much more though its criticisms are not baseless. If brand name may prove useful to the consumers, certain legislative measures are taken to improve the situation.

FAMILY BRAND *Vs.* INDIVIDUAL BRAND

A company selling more than one product must decide whether to sell each under a separate brand or to use family brand. In other situations greater returns can be realised through making one choice rather than the other. Such decisions require evaluation of three factors:

1. Nature of the product-line;
2. Promotional policy; and
3. Desired market penetration.

1. The Nature of the Product-line: Similar products are naturally related in the consumer's minds such as sheets and towels benefit particularly from family branding. Favourable reaction to one item often leads buyers to buy others in the line. But this 'Helo' effect can also detract from a marketer's reputation, because unfavourable experiences with one item turn consumers against the whole line. Therefore, particular care must be taken, that all items earning the family brand conform to consumers' standard of acceptance.

2. Promotional Policy: Products lacking common marketing attributes are usually best marketed under individual names, since little benefit comes from jointly associating them. There may even be adverse sales reactions from family branding such as food and foodstuffs sold at one association handicaps the food consumers because of the soap's unpleasant taste.

3. Desired Market Penetration: All products do not lend themselves to sale under a family brand. The quality of family brand products should be very nearly similar so that no single item in the line can lower the quality reputation of others. The products should be fairly compatible. The perfumery applies the same scents to the soaps under the same label. The product should be sold to the same market. Family brand does not give gains if an article is sold to industry and the other with the same brand to consumers. Individual brand should be used here.

BRAND TESTING

Purpose

Before launching a brand of product into the market the product should know whether it would succeed or not. For this purpose the manufacturer resorts to brand testing. It purposes are as follows:

1. Memory Testing: Under this, a selected group of persons are asked to remember certain names or symbols. After sometimes, they are asked those names. Most of them forget the names or symbols. By a careful study of this kind, it can be known easily as to which names can be easily remembered. On the basis of such a study the name of the brand of symbol can be selected.

2. Preference Test: Under this test a list of names or symbols is presented before a selected group of persons. Then they are asked to rearrange the name in order of preference. The name which scores the highest preference by most of the persons is chosen for brand name.

3. Learning Test: Under this test a group of persons is given a list of possible brand name. Then they are asked to pronounce and write the name of the different brands. The name which is pronounced most easily and written correctly by most of the persons is generally chosen for the brand name.

4. Association Test: Under this method some names are read out before different persons or they might be shown the names written prominently. Then they are asked to write down the name which comes easily to their memory. The name which scores the first position in the response of the majority of persons is chosen for the brand name.

5. Uniqueness Test: Under this test, a group of persons is first given the proposed brand name of the producer. By this test the producer can easily understand by which other brand names his own brand name could be confused. Keeping in view this point, he can select and modify a unique brand name.

Causes of Brand Use

To present times the continued use of brands in business has been largely due to: (*i*) growth in competition; (*ii*) growth of national and local advertising; (*iii*) growth of packaging; and (*iv*) the development of consumer brand consciousness.

An organisation brands its production for three special reasons: physical identification, legal protection, and as a basis for promotional efforts.

1. The physical identification: It is found in case of individual products and product-lines are important in shipping, sorting, grading, labelling, and managing the inventory of various products. There are three recognised degrees of physical identification: (*i*) *Brand insistence.* The consumers insist on a brand when they perceive it as having few close substitutes. Brand insistence is the ultimate goal of production differentiation and market segmentation, (*ii*) Brand *preferences.* It may stem from habit or experience. Preferences exist among groups of consumers for almost all well-known brands, (*iii*) *Brand recognition.* It results when consumers remember having seen or heard of a brand but make no special attempt to purchase it because they are satisfied with their present brand.

2. Legal protection: It is vested in the trade mark/the brand over which the organisation has an exclusive right. Trade mark details have been given elsewhere.

3. Marketing effort: The purpose of the marketing programme is to convince the consumer that the organisation's product will satisfy his wants and desires. The consumer is first acquainted with the brand and recognise if he would want it. It is through the brand that this recognition is sought. Thus, branding is done: (*i*) to gain recognition for their products, (*ii*) to bring about a certain amount of consumer's preference, and (*iii*) to firmly fix the product in the mind of the buyer that he will believe that it is the only one which will satisfy his wants and as a result will refuse to accept a substitute.

Types of Brand Names

(1) Personal name: Personal brand name can be that of the founder of the company. The name may be that of a deceased historical person; fictional names; mythological names.

(2) Company name: An established and reputed company name may be used as a brand name.

(3) Dictionary word: Any word or words may be chosen from the dictionary.

(4) Coined names: Any name may be coined by the advertiser for his brand.

Brand Image

A brand image may be defined as, "the impression of a particular product that has formed in the consumer's mind".[1] The following exract will provide a clear explanation of the term:[2] "The image of a product associated with the brand may be clear cut or relatively vague; it may be varied or simple; it may be intense or innocuous. Sometimes the notions people have about a brand do not even seem very sensible or relevant to those who know what the product is really like. But they all contribute to the customer deciding whether or not the brand is the one "for me...."

Branding Policy/Strategy

Companies that seek to issue a brand have to decide several policy issue First, whether it will distribute wholly through national or manufacture's brand and private or distributor's brand or through mixed brand. Second, it must decide whether it will employ a multibrand policy and third, whether it will use family brands.

1. The National or Manufacturer's brand: It is a brand used by the producer that enjoys wide geographical distribution. They are able to achieve this because they have high annual sales value, extensive warehousing and physical distribution facilities; the capacity and experience in conducting marketing operations, which includes maintaining a large sales force and conducting cooperative and national advertising programmes; continued consumer and marketing research programmes and maintain extensive warranty and service programmes.[3] Companies using national brands can easily compete with others because of these facilities. National brands once acceptable to the consumer bring large profits to the distributors and the producer. Such brands help merchandise a product, because promotional campaigns can be developed around the brand.

2. Private Dealer's or Distributor's brand: It is one which is sponsored by merchants or agents' firms. By using it, additional sales and profits are achieved, payment is promptly received, and

1. Hardy, L., *Marketing for Profit*, 1962, p. 54.
2. Gardner, B.B., and Levy, S.J., "The Product and the Brand", *Harward Business Review*, March-April, 1955.
3. Cook, Victor J. and Schutte, Thornes F., *Brand Policy Discrimination*, Allyn and Bacon, Boston, 1967, p. 68.

manufacturer's working capital position is also improved. This is so for several reasons: small size with little marketing know-how, distribution system or scarce resources; the belief that their distributors would offer their customers these brands to franchise those customers by offering them better profit margins. Such brands are generally adopted for woollen hosiery, sports goods, etc.

3. Mixed brands: These may be used by a company for the following reasons:

(*i*) as a defensive measure to accommodate major customers;

(*ii*) a means of achieving greater flexibility in pricing.

(*iii*) a means of lower customer service costs through spreading marketing overhead to private label accounts:

(*iv*) a way to reduce product costs through economies of scale.[1]

4. Multibrand policy: It is followed by some companies, when they offer two or more products that are labelled under different brands but that are designed to appeal to basically the same customers. For example, the Chrysler Corporation of U.S.A. provides an example that use multi-brands by offering Plymouth, Dodge, Chrysler and Imperial brands. Each of these brands competes with the other brands.

5. Family brand: It is used by firms that offer all their merchandise under one brand. International Business Machine (IBM) in U.S.A. and the Tatas in India are examples that follow a family brand policy.

Importance of Branding

1. Vehicle of goodwill: It works as a vehicle to the seller by which the goodwill of the public for the article presented for sale may be organised and made effective as a cumulative force in selling. It may prove a valuable asset to the seller.

2. Stability of Sales Volume and Price: The seller achieves greater stability of sales volume and greater stability of price through transforming his product, to the maximum possible degree in a speciality goods.

3. Identification: Consumers used trade marks originally to identify the maker or the source of specific goods: today they are

1. Cook and Schutte, *Ibid.*, pp. 70-71.

almost exclusively interested in the identifications of products rather than the makers of those products.

4. Symbol of Quality: Consumers look upon the brand name as a symbol of product quality of a product's characteristics and features and as a symbol of the satisfaction products supply.

5. Insurance: Branding is an insurance of merchandise comparability when the buyer uses more than one source of supply. Phillip's light bulbs are Phillip's light bulbs, regardless of where purchased.

6. Improvement in Quality: Branded products tend to improve in quality over the years. Competition forces this improvement, for brand owners constantly seek new ways to differentiate their products in order to secure a stronger market position.

7. Demand Stimulation: The brand is often of greater help in demand stimulation than the company name or the technical aspects of the product.

8. Product Mix: If a firm has one or more lines of branded goods, it can add a new item to its product mix much more easily than a company selling unbranded merchandise.

Choosing the Brand Name

Selecting the right brand name is one of the most vital yet a tricky and frustrating element in developing a new product. A good product with a lacklustre name may not sell as well as a mediocre product with an intriguing name. And once it is chosen and the product is out on the market, changing or modifying the name is not only harmful but also rather difficult. Getting it right the first time is essential.[1]

The first hurdle to be overcome is to decide what type of name is appropriate. These are: (*i*) names that sound interesting but have no meaning ("Kodak", "Sony"), (*ii*) name whose meanings bear no connection in the product ("Aravalli Scooters", "Arrow Shirts", "Metex Underwears"); (*iii*) names that suggest a function or quality of the product ("Cool Foam", "Agfa Films"); (*iv*) names that are borrowed from words in other languages ("Lux"), (*v*) names that belong to company founders ("Ford", "Tata");

1. Gensamer, Blair E., "Brand Name Most Vital Element in Developing New Products", *Marketing News*, February 13, 1976, p. 4.

(*vi*) or famous people ("Gandhi", "Pratap"), (*vii*) names that are taken from myths and legends ("Atlas" "Hercules"; or (*viii*) names that are company initials (HMV, GEC), etc. In each of these categories, various innumerable possibilities may be explored. Therefore, the main criterion should be to see whether or not the name selected will help to sell the product.[1]

Undesirable Characteristics in Brand Names

1. Common Place: The names should avoid being commonplace such as dalda, linoleum, kerosene, nylon, Kodak, etc. Such identification is overused, and difficult to protect because it is not distinctive. It fails to be functional, causing confusion in consumer's minds instead of certainty.

2. Vulgar: It should not sound like some vulgar or obscene word. If there is any unpleasant or disagreeable association possible in consumers' minds, then the name or mark is defective.

3. Similar: The names should not be too similar to other brand names already in existence, because limitation shades into infringement.

4. Confused: Trade names are belaboured when they baffle or confuse consumers, when they are meaningless, and of abstract design, and when they place too much emphasis or dependence on colour.

TRADE MARK

Meaning

A trade mark has been defined as: any sign, mark, symbol, word or words, which indicate the origin or ownership of a product as distinguished from its quality, and which others have not the equal rights to employ for the same purpose.[2]

Legal Requirements

(1) It must not be identical with or confusingly similar to marks already being used in the same field.

(2) It should be one which helps the public to recognise the goods.

(3) It must not possess a flag or coat-arms of a foreign nation.

---

1. Littlefield, J.F. and Kirkpatrick, *Advertising: Mass Communication in Marketing*, 1971, pp. 75-78.
2. Copeland, M.T., *Principles of Merchandising*, 1924, pp. 264-275.

(4) The brand or mark must be associated by the public with a definite source of supply and it should not be possible to confuse this significance.

(5) The public gives its own meanings to the words and terms it uses in trade, even as it does to any other word and this use of a word or term cannot be controlled or restricted by the proprietors of a brand or trade mark.

(6) The word, term or slogan selected as a brand or trade mark must be one which can be monopolised and used exclusively for the identification of the owners goods without interfering with the rights of others.

A registrable trade mark must not be deceptive and must not be descriptive of the goods, their use, character or quality.

Characteristics of Good Trade Mark

(*i*) Distinctive and attractive to the eye and pleasant to the ear.

(*ii*) Easy to remember, simple and short.

(*iii*) It should be similar to that which is already in use.

(*iv*) It should be easy to pronounce

(*v*) It should be easy to illustrate strikingly.

(*vi*) It should be easy and economical to reproduce.

Branding and Monopoly

Trade mark is a form of monopoly and that, too, lawful, limited only by the use to which brand or trade mark is registered. The law court will protect such a monopoly. There are very few products which cannot be copied, imitated or duplicated. The monopoly of brand names for the specific use to which they are put is legal. No one else can legally imitate or even simulate these. Dartnell says that "the commercial value of this monopoly depends, of course, on the reputation for desirability is established, the manufacturer has no longer any need to sell to wholesalers and retailers on variable price. The product is lifted from the level of direct price comparison and is sold to these dealers on its ready resaleability on the basis of consumer preference and demand. It enables the manufacturer to stabilise the price to the consumer and dictate the terms of sale."[1]

---

1. Dartnell, *Handbook of Sales Management.*

Inadequate Brand or Trade Mark

1. Imitative or Duplicating: Any word that is an imitation or duplication of any brand or trade mark already in use in connection with goods of the same kind should not be used.

2. Descriptive: Descriptive terms include all words that show the kind or quality or use of the product; also adjectives in praise of the quality of the goods or intended to recommend or advertise their quality.

3. Geographical names: These are also objectionable. They are not registrable except under exceptional circumstances.

4. Family names: These are sometimes unsatisfactory though there are a great many well-known trade marks that are family names: Colgate, Waterman, Kale, Bose, Batliwala, Tata, Birla, Motiwala, Mafatlal, Bajaj, Patanwala, etc. The main objection is that it may become troublesome since others entitled to the same name have the right to use it in connection with their product of the same class.

Generic Brand Names

A brand name becomes generic or descriptive, when the public refers to that type or class of product by the manufacturer's brand name. The generic names result in loss to the owner involving loss of time, loss of money, and effort spent in establishing the name. The following steps may be taken to prevent a brand name from becoming generic:

(1) To use two names, the brand name in conjunction with the company name, or the brand name together with generic name, such as Eastman Kodak.

(2) To give actual notice to the public that the brand has been copyrighted.

(3) To protect any and all misuse of the brand name. The market must be policed vigorously.

(4) To take legal action.

SLOGANS

Useful sales promotion methods also include slogans and sentences used to win sales and increase business when used intelligently. Someone has said, *"If you coin a lucky phrase you coin your future success."* Good slogans never depreciate or wear out, they are as good today as they were yesterday and will remain so far coming hundred years. A writer in discussing such slogans as "we put punch into our service," and "the store of chevy chase," says that these "not only put the necessary punch into advertising but when broadcast, letterheads, bill heads, newspaper and other forms of advertising, circulars, blotters, post cards, handout cards and other advertising material may be fittingly described as the unbreakable links in the chain of business catching for every time a progressive producers drives home his slogan, with a gripping meaning, it hits the prospect and customer alike squarely between the eyes. Such slogans sink with a pleasant feeling and are not readily forgotten. They give people something to think about.[1]

Coined Words as Brands

Majority of businessmen believe that the best trade mark is a coined word. There is no legal objection in their use but they may prove troublesome if not used wisely. It is difficult to invent such a word which is distinctive. It loses monopolistic value especially when the consumer does not deal directly with the owner of the trade mark but with irresponsible sellers of his goods who are generally the initiators of the public's misuse of a trade mark. It cannot be refused that with some class of goods the coined word has been an important factor in the success of the line.

PACKAGING

Meaning

According to Stanton, 'Packaging' is the general group of activities which concentrate in formulating the design of a package, and producing an appropriate and attractive container or wrapper for the product.[2] Packing means *"the wrapping and crating of goods before they are transported or stored."* It is a physical action which provides a handling convenience, *e.g.*, rice, cotton, wheat or any other agricultural produce. It is necessary to prevent flowing out of liquids. It is essential to maintain freshness and quality. It can prevent the danger of adulteration.

'Packaging' is the sub-division of the packing function of marketing. It involves more than simply placing products in containers or covering them with wrappers. 'Packaging' has

1. *Advertising World*, February 1928.
2. Stanton, W., *Fundamental of Marketing*, p. 229.

been defined as "an activity which is concerned with protection, economy, convenience, and promotional considerations.[1] The Indian Institute of Packaging has defined packaging as "the embracing functions of package, selection, manufacture, filling and handling." Packaging obviously is closely related to labelling and branding because the label often appears on the package and the brand is typically on the label. A package defines the space in which a product is contained. The package contents may be pre-measured, pre-weighted, pre-stored, pre-assembled, then placed in a specially designed wrapper, box, carton, can, crate, bottle, jar, tube, barrel, drum or pallet for convenient distribution.[2]

Kinds of Packaging

Packaging may be *'primary'* which refers to the producer's immediate container, such as the can or a box; or *secondary,* which refers to additional layers of protection that are removed once the produce is ready for use, such as the tube of tooth paste, which comes in a card board box.

Functions of Packaging

Basically, packaging fulfils three functions, *viz.,* containment, protection, and identification. But additional functions of packaging are convenience, attractiveness, promotional appeal, and economy.

1. Containment: Packaging provides space in which a product is contained, *e.g.,* vegetables can be boiled in the bags in which they are packaged. Beer cans can be made easy to open. Salt and spices are packed for table use or for convenient use in the kitchen. Hair preparations can be sprayed in. Facial powders and cosmetics are packaged in containers of pleasing designs and in a choice of colours suitable for use in bath or bedroom. Aerosal containers are used to spray or to apply such diverse products as paint, baby powders, room air freshers, shaving lather, hair preparations, bug killers, wax, colognes, deodorants and mosquito repellants.[3]

2. Protection: Packaging protects its contents on its route from the manufacturer to the consumer, and even during its life with the consumers. Products, if kept in open, may be adversely affected

1. Kotler, Phillip, *Marketing Management,* 1976, p. 216.
2. Schwartz, David, J., *Marketing Today — A Basic Approach,* 1977, p. 384.
3. Seibert, Joseph C., *Concepts of Marketing Management,* 1975, p. 187.

by weather, too hot or too cold; temperature; shock, light, water or dampness; passage of time or by insects, pests—as may be the case with sugar, gur, honey, tea, salt, etc. They may spoil, discolour or lose flavour, damage, break or contaminate, or lead to physical deterioration of the product. The idea production is that the product will reach its ultimate consumer in sound condition, and may be kept so till it is used up.

Protection starts at the factory, moves to the point of purchase in retail stores, and then continues in the home. Proper packaging can protect the consumer against: (*i*) such hazards as leaky cartons and cut-fingers; (*ii*) breakage (of glassware), spoilage of food, volatile or gaseous articles like spirit, gases and acids; (*iii*) contamination; (*iv*) pilferage and theft; (*v*) deterioration in the quality of goods because of the effect of light, air, or other weather conditions.

3. Identification: When goods are stored in warehouses or in godowns, till they are transported elsewhere or used, they need to be identified as to type and make, and be clearly distinguished from one brand to another. Most packages, therefore, bear the name of the product, its maker, and its ingredients (in case of medicines and food preparations) instructions for use (as "Glass with care") safety warnings or limitations on use. Product of one manufacturer can be easily identified by the consumer from the rival's as packaging creates individuality and helps quick identification.

4. Convenience: All people—wholesalers, retailers, middlemen, ware-housekeepers, and consumers—demand convenience in package *i.e.*, they should be light enough to be hand carried (such as carton carrying 10 cigarettes or a strip of 10 analgin tabs) easy to open and close, and easy to dispose off or reuse. Formerly, soft drinks were packaged in glass bottles with lift-off caps that required a can or bottle opener (as in case of Coca-Cola or Fanta or Gold Spot, etc.). Later on, these were substituted by aluminium can, which were light-weighted, unbreakable, and non-returnable but opening still required a special tool. Ultimately, now they are packaged in pop-tap can which can be opened even by hand.

5. Attractiveness: Packaging enhances the appearance of the product. The design and the label on the package printed matter, picture, lay-out or get up of the package, colour combination all are special means of attracting consumers. Colours are often used to improve the appearance and appeal of a product. For example, some producers of oranges, package them in transparent plastic bags with an orange tint which gives the appearance of having a fresher, deeper colour. Certain colours are repeated throughout the product-line so that distinctiveness is maintained. For example, cosmetic manufacturers, who may package an entire line in a particular shade of lemon yellow or soft pink, lest the consumer recognise the maker of the various products in the line. They also create impressions of richness, luxury, and exclusiveness by using packages that have certain colours, designs, shapes and textures.

6. Promotional Appeal: Product must sell themselves. This is possible if they are placed in more attractive and eye-appealing packages. Several factors contribute to a package's promotional appeal. The package must be of a suitable size, shape, texture, or a startling colour. It should be large enough to hold the product. It may be taller or shorter. Vertical thin lines make a package appear taller, while horizontal wide strips make a package appear shorter because many people view something that is taller as being bigger. Successful marketers offer men packages with angular shape and wood or burlap textures, while women's packages have rounded, curved shapes, and soft, fuzzy textures.[1]

Colour on packages often attract people, who associate certain feelings and connotations with specific colour. For example, *red* is associated with fire, blood, danger, and anger; *yellow* suggests sunlight, caution, warmth and vitality; *blue* can imply coldness, sky, water and sadness.[2]

7. Economy: Packaging costs range from 3 per cent to 80 per cent of the "total product" selling price. Representative of 80 per cent would be aerosol tooth paste, and that of 3 per cent would be men's hosiery. Other illustrative packaging costs within the range are: lamp shades 6 per cent, cereals 13 per cent, beer 27 per cent, bar soap 50 per cent, and cleaning compounds, 53 per cent.[3] Naturally, the consumers would prefer economical packages.

---

1. Baker, Stephen, *Visual Persuasion*, McGraw-Hill Book Company, New York, 1971, pp. 56-59.
2. McNeal, James U., *An Introduction to Consumer Behaviour*, John-Wiley & Sons, New York, 1973, pp. 98-99.
3. Weiss, E.B., *Merchandising for Tomorrow*, McGraw-Hill Book Co., 1962, p. 174.

Other functions of packaging are:

8. Contribution to Sale: Packaging makes a positive and significant contribution to the sale of the product. In other words, it results in sales appeal because consumers dictate which products are to be stocked by retailers. "Packages which rate well on appeal are eye-catching and provocating, capturing the buyer's attention and arousing his interest. Good packaging promotes both impulse buying and repeat, planned purchases."[1]

9. Help in Marketing: Packaging can be used effectively to help introduce a new product or to help increase or maintain the market for existing products. Sometimes a packaging change can rejuvenate an old product by giving it a new image.

10. Profit Possibilities: Packaging may also lead to increased profit possibilities. A package may be so attractive that customers will pay more just to get the special package.

Attributes of a Good Package

A well designed and attractive package must have informative labelling. The headlines, illustrations, guidelines, and selling points on the package must be clear and prominent so that the matter is readable by every shopper at a glance. Visibility of the product in the package helps to sell the product better. Hence, glass, celophane and plastic packages have become very popular these days.

According to I.B. Steel, packages to be effective must possess the following qualities:[2]

(*i*) It must attract attention.

(*ii*) It must tell the product story—What is it? What size? How much?

(*iii*) It must build confidence.

(*iv*) It must look clean and sanitary.

(*v*) It must be convenient to handle, to carry out of the store and to use.

(*vi*) It must look like good value.

(*vii*) It must look like a fast seller.

1. Littlefield, J.F. and Kirkpatrik, *Advertising: Mass Communication in Marketing*, 1971.
2. Steel, I.B., "Address before the National Packaging Exposition", sponsored by the American Management Association, Packaging series, No. 9.

(*viii*) It must deserve a preferred display.

(*ix*) It must minimise the clerk's time.

(*x*) It must be convenient to stock and display.

(*xi*) It must prevent spoilage during the selling period.

(*xii*) It must resist soiling.

According to Seibert a good package must: (*i*) protect the contents; (*ii*) meet retailer requirements; (*iii*) meet consumer requirement; (*iv*) meet trade characters, and (*v*) be easily identifiable.[1]

Type of Packages

1. Consumer package: It holds the required volume of a product for ultimate consumption and is within the means of a buying household. In other words, the consumer has the option to purchase the pack size which he considers adequate for the consumption of his family over a length of time and which does not involve extra investment during that period.

2. Bulk package: It is the opposite of consumer package. It is either for the industrial consumer's use or for loose dispensing. The consumer package also very often requires an outside package in which it is transported and which is sometimes referred to as a transit package or an outer container.

3. Industrial package: It is a bulk package or the package for durable consumer goods.

4. Dual use package: It has a secondary usefulness after its contents have been consumed. For examples, drinking glasses, boxes of jewellery or cigarettes waste baskets, refrigerator dishes, cloth from flour and feed sacks.

Besides these basic package types many other sub-divisions can be listed, *e.g.*, strip package, multiple package, etc.

Package Forms

Packages are often selected on *prima facie* grounds of cost, international practice, type of the product, quality of product, conditions of display, likely consumer appeal. Packages may be in the form of tin plate cans, cardboard containers, polythene bags, paper or cloth or gunny bags, wooden boxes, teak chests,

---

1. Seibert, Joseph C., *Concept of Marketing Management*, 1975, pp. 188-191.

squeeze bottles, collapsible tubes, aerosal cans, aluminium foils, clear film wrappings, plastic container, etc. Colour may be used to identify sizes, models, flavours and qualities. The true economy of packaging lies in the total packaging operation—tiding, sealing, other packaging, storing handling and distribution.

Package Material

The more common packaging materials are metal, glass, wood, paper, cardboard, plastic, cloth, jute and cellophane. A wide variety of packaging material is used according to the availability, possible shortages, competition, economy, transport worthiness, and shelf life in every conceivable environmental hazard for a stated period.

Packaging involves selection manufacture, filling and handling of packages. Selection is guided by the dictates of the three processes of package, *viz.*, manufacture, filling and handling to which have to be combined the marketing end, *viz.*, knowledge of the consumer or the user; the shelf life desired and the conditions of retail outlet.

Evaluating a Package's Effectiveness

According to a report in the Nelson Researcher, positive answers to the following questions will help to ensure a successful package.[1]

1. Does the package tell consumers what they want and need to know?
2. Does it instantly identify the type of product the package contains, *i.e.* does it reflect quality?
3. Is the package distinctive?
4. Is it compatible with the firm's advertising image?
5. Does its size make it compatible with similar products?
6. Is it adaptable to other products? Does it suit the product?
7. It is acceptable to the trade? Will it stack?
8. Will it last? Is it tamper proof?
9. Does it look well in competition with other packages?
10. Does it attract attention from a reasonable distance?

1. Adapted from "Package Needs Again Stressed by Management," The *Nelson Researcher*, May 1969, p. 12.

11. Does it tell the consumer how to use the product or suggest new ways of using it?
12. Does it what the consumers' appetite for the product?
13. Is it easy to open?
14. Does it protect the product?
15. Is there a prominent spot for the price?
16. Are the brand, symbol, and name easy to see?
17. Does the package have promotable features?

Copy on Packages

The mandatory information as required by the Food and Drugs Act (India) includes following items about the medicine:

1. *Common name of the product.*
2. *Name and address of the manufacturer or distributor on two or more panels.*
3. *Common names of ingredients.*
4. *Capacity in terms of weight, measure or number.*
5. *Warning against the use of the product in an amount or for a length of time that may endanger health.*
6. *Direction for proper use: Dosage.*
7. *Manufacturing Licence No.*

Batch

8. *Retail Price.*

Consumer Problems with Packaging

(1) Blind purchase: Unless the package is transparent, the buyer cannot judge the contents of the package by its mere appearance. If quality information on it is lacking, purchase has to be made almost blindly.

(2) No Checking: The consumer cannot check weight and volume of the contents, unless he opens it. Prepackage shortages have been found to the extent of 25 per cent and above.

(3) Inflated contents: Frequently, the package sizes and designs inflate the contents. Price reduction may often follow with less of the quantity in the packet.

(4) Deception: Deceptive packages accompany many unfair trade practices like hidden declaration of contents, fine attractive printing, glorified illustrations, unexplainable fractions, etc., as a result of which consumers get less than what the package is supposed to contain.

(5) Reduced contents: Although packages are identical in size, contents are reduced and apparently same prices are charged.

(6) Health hazards: Some packages create health hazards for consumers. For example, food articles packaged in plastic materials may cause cancer; Packages stored in godown are susceptible to infection by rodents and insects.

LABELLING

Meaning

Label consists of verbal information that accompanies the product. It identifies: Date of manufacture and expiry; the price to be charged; brand name, net quantity of contents, weight, measure, numerical count, etc. Some labels consist of tags attached to the product or package, as in the case of most clothing or hosiery articles. Others are imprinted on the product itself as part of the printed material on the package. The label is a strong sales tool. It is an integral part of the point of purchase advertising. It is designed to help the promotion of a product. The arrangement of type, the illustrations, and the colour are chosen to attract the consumer's eye, make a package distinctive, and encourage recognition by the consumer who often views it in the midst of many other products.

Kinds of Labels

1. Brand label: It is simply the brand alone applied to the product or to the package, such as some clothes carry the brand label "Sanforised".

2. Grade label: It identifies the quality by a letter, number or word: such as canned mangoes may be graded as A, B, C, or Fancy-Grade 1, 2, 3, etc.

3. Descriptive and informative labels: These are used synonymously to give written or illustrative objective information about the characteristics, use, construction, care, performance, or other features of the product.

MARKING

Meaning

'Marketing' is putting some identification mark on the packages during transportation and warehousing. Goods sent by Railways require the use of a slogan P.L.M., *i.e.*, give a "sound package, proper label and indicate **a** distinct mark on the label" in addition to the name and address of the consigner and the consignee. This secures that the goods may reach its destination easily.

Guarantee

'Guarantee' is the general policy of the producers/manufacturers with regard to defective products. Guarantees expressed or implied are obligations assumed by the seller promising buyers that they will receive certain services or satisfactions. A guarantee is a bundle of satisfaction a buyer receives when he buys a product.

A guarantee may (*i*) protect against the abuses of the service policy and to limit his liability, or (*ii*) provide an additional promotional media in his programme for selling against the competitors.

In the market introduction of a new product, promotional guarantees can help in overcoming buyer resistance, gaining initial, distribution adding new dealers and opening new market areas. Promotional guarantees are most effective in introducing new products and remerchandising established products under the following conditions:[1]

1. High price: The product has a high retail price—the higher the price, the more assurance buyers want that the product will perform as represented.

2. Infrequent purchase: The product is purchased infrequently.

3. Complex product: Buyers visualise the product as complex—complex products frequently are costly to repair and complexity is likely to increase buyer uncertainty.

4. Small market share: The firm's market share is small—a promotional guarantee may overcome consumers uncertainty about little known product.

---

1. Udell, J.G., and E.E. Anderson, The Product Warranty as an Element of Competitive Strategy, *Journal of Marketing*, October 1968, p. 7.

Warranty

Warranty' is an assurance of quality, service and performance given by the producer to the consumer. It is a written guarantee of the intrinsic value of a product. It points out the responsibility of the maker for repairs, service, and maintenance in case of consumer durables. The warranty is the outcome of the rule of law, *viz.*, let the buyer beware. Producers developed warranties to create confidence in buyer's mind and to provide conpensation in case the product is not up to reasonable expectations. The warranty provides the name of the warrantor, which products and parts are covered and which are not, exactly how they are covered, who pays, and how long the warranty applies.

Guidelines for Warranty

(*i*) Ensure the integrity and credibility of the warranty.

(*ii*) Institute a meaningful education programme regarding use of the product.

(*iii*) Strengthen the company programme for quality control in manufacture.

(*iv*) Provide high quality maintenance and repair service.

SAMPLING

Function

The main function of sampling is to make prospective or would-be customers more intimately acquainted with the qualities of the merchandise offered for sale and to induce them to buy from them. In modern marketing sampling gives the prospective customer an opportunity of discovering the qualities of the product for himself. Customers may be given an opportunity to use, try, handle, taste, hear or see the articles offered for sale.

Sampling Channels

Samples may be distributed into two different channels:

(1) From manufacturer or sales agent directly to the homes of consumers either through the post or through a sampling crew.

(2) From the manufacturer to dealers who distribute the sample to their consumers.

Persons to whom the samples are to be given may be selected as follows:

(*i*) *List of Interested Persons*: The names and addresses of such persons may be obtained from dealers or from some directory or selected by members of sampling crew during their itineraries on some predetermined basis such as persons who live in houses whose rents are above ₹ 100,00 a month or persons who own motor cars or radio sets or who have telephones installed in their homes.

(*ii*) *Advertisement*: Selection may be done through advertising in newspaper and magazines and using a coupon to be filled in and posted by the enquirer asking for a sample.

Fundamental Principles of Sampling

1. Free: It is often the quickest way to make them customers because human nature attaches too great value to anything that it gets for nothing. However, though people like to receive samples free of cost they resent it later when the samples are not procurable and they find that they have to pay for what they want.

2. Desire and Attention: Before samples are distributed people should be made to desire the product by advertising that directs their attention to its benefits and advantages.

3. Value: Value should be attached to the sample itself both by the advertising and by making a small charge for it or by otherwise insuring that the recipient does something to deserve it.

4. Acceptance: The product must be made acceptable to the public before samples are offered. When a new product is to be sampled, the suspicion and distrust of the people for all innovation must first be overcome either by educational advertising or by demonstrating the product use or consumption or the results of using it or by combining both advertising and demonstration.

5. Fighting Competition: Competition can often be satisfactorily fought by frequent distribution of samples, say once a year, to select customers. This keeps the product and its advantages in the minds of customers and prevents their being enticed away by competitors or wins them back if they had been indifferent.

6. Modest Claims: When advertising precedes or accompanies the distribution of samples, its claims must be modest because the test made by the recipients of samples will only prove their exaggeration and falsity and all confidence in the manufacturer will be shattered.

7. Standardisation: Samples should be put attractively and their packing and presentation should be similar to the standardised packages offered for sale.

8. Testing: Sampling should be neither condemned nor rushed into without due consideration of its value and purpose and tests on a small scale should be made to obtain some idea of the results which may be expected.

9. Relative Value: The relative value of small sized and standard-sized packages for use as samples should be considered.

10. Reminding Benefits: The need for keeping the value and benefits of the product before the recipients of samples during the time they are testing the product should be remembered.

11. Relative value of channels: The relative value of two channels of distribution for samples should be carefully studied before making a choice.

12. Causal Approach: When results are disappointing one should look for the cause never forgetting the other factors in successful marketing, distribution, advertising and dealer co-operation.

AFTER-SALES SERVICE

After-sales service covers repairs, spare parts and smooth maintenance availability at lower charges after the product has been sold and is being used. Its need arises to prevent dissatisfaction, frustration and ill-will among consumers against the manufacturer's product they are using—so as the quality of its working is concerned. In after-sales service free services for repairs and replacement of defective parts are given during the guarantee period and thereafter at lower charges to hold on the consumers for future. It is generally given for costly and durable goods—such as electrical appliances and equipments, complex machinery; refrigeration and coolers, duplicators, TV sets, radios, tape recorders, stereos; washing and sewing machines and other costly domestic appliances, automobiles—cars and scooters, etc.

The marketers often provide after-sales service in the following ways:

1. By upgrading the efficiency and reliability of dealer-provided service through training programmes.

2. By developing company owned service centres which repair consumer goods.

3. By placing greater emphasis on product design—through more testing, research, and quality control than before.

INDIAN STANDARDS INSTITUTION (I.S.I.)

Establishment

The Indian Standards Institute (I.S.I.) was set up in 1947. It occupies the position of National Standards Organisation of India. Its chief aim is to lay down national standards for commodities, materials, practices and processes. It promotes standardisation, quality control and simplification in industry and technology. It operates an I.S.I. Certification Marks Scheme under the Indian Standards Institution (Certification Marks Act, 1952). It imparts training in standardisation methods and techniques to Indian and foreign company officials and technical personnel. It furthers India's interests in the field of International Organisation for Standardisation (I.S.O.) and International Electrotechnical Commission (I.E.C.). It started standardisation on an organised basis in India.

Aims and Objectives

1. To prepare standards relating to products, commodities, materials and processes.
2. To promote general standards at national and international levels.
3. To certify industrial products.
4. To help the production of quality goods.
5. To circulate information relating to standardisation.

I.S.I. works through a large number of technical committees appointed by the Division Councils. There are at present ten such councils working in the country.

Advantages

1. It protects consumers through assured quality and performance of product.
2. It minimises wastage.
3. It cuts unnecessary varieties.
4. It increases productivity and reduces cost of production.
5. It promotes overall economy and brings about the best utilisation of human material resources.

6. It is highly essential to a nation's industrialisation and modernisation.

Working of I.S.I.

In order to adopt a standard for his product, a producer has to obtain a licence from the I.S.I. under his marketing scheme. The licence prescribes certain procedures to be adopted for quality control and testing. It has to be renewed every year. I.S.I. inspectors keep a constant check on whether the producer is maintaining the specified quality or not. They take samples even from the open market which are tested in I.S.I. laboratories. Manufacturers are liable to punishment, if they use I.S.I. mark fraudulently. There are 17 laboratories for the purpose of testing products: Alleppey, Bangalore, Mumbai, Calcutta, Cochin, Guntur, Jamnagar, Kanpur, Kozikode, Chennai, Mangalore, Patna, Rajkot, Sahibabad (Ghaziabad), Thiruvananthapuram, Tuticorin and Virudnagar. A regional office is working at Chennai to manage the South Indian laboratories and to coordinate the activities.

QUESTIONS FOR EXERCISE

1. What do you understand by Brands? Distinguish them with Trade Marks. What considerations are taken in selecting an effective brand name?
2. What are Brands? Differentiate them from Trade Marks?
3. Write a short note on 'Brand Classification'.
4. What are the advantages of brand names?
5. Explain different kinds of brand names. Distinguish between Family Brand and Individual Brand.
6. Explain Brand Testing, Brand Image and Product Image Constituents.
7. "The main objectives of packaging are protection, brand differentiation and identification, sales promotion and handling convenience." Explain.
8. Discuss the role of Indian Standards Institute (I.S.I.) in maintaining standards for products in India.

18

Pricing Policies and Strategies

PRICE POLICY AND PRICE STRATEGY

According to Converse, "Decisions concerning price to be followed for a period of time may be called price policies." Marketers activate their long range pricing objectives through both price and price strategies. Management utilises price policies to guide itself in making pricing decisions over long periods. Pricing strategies are the pricing decisions management makes to fit the changing competitive situations met by specific products.

Thus, while policies are general and long range, pricing strategies are specific and for shorter periods. In the formulation of pricing strategy, its selling price is a key element. As the competitive situation changes with different states in the product's life cycle, so also changes the relative amount of freedom management has in setting prices.

Pricing Strategy in the Competitive Situation

Pricing strategy changes with competitive situation. It is uncontrollable when management cannot determine prices. At the other extreme pricing is cent per cent controllable in those rare cases where the marketer has a long term monopoly. The monopolist sets his price to maximise profits by "charging what the traffic will bear." In the real world various external pressures prevent him from having a pure monopoly type price, but he keeps the administered price once set by management and held stable over a long period.

Pricing is controllable in moderate cases. It becomes controllable through combination of marketing skill. The marketers differentiate their products hoping to reduce what the buyers have for choosing competitor's offerings on a price basis. Promotion is used to differentiate their products in buyer's minds. They also differentiate total offerings through their individualised choices of physical distribution system, marketing channels and middlemen. Most modern marketers manipulate controllables to increase their ability to make pricing controllable.

Kinds of Competitive Situations

According to Joel Dean, there are the following three kinds of competitive situations for a product:

1. Lasting Distinctiveness: When any product enjoys lasting distinctiveness which is very rare, the marketer enjoys the monopolists' pricing freedom. This distinctiveness of a product is up to the extent that it could he sold above or below the competitors price without changing prices or sales. However, vary few products have lasting distinctiveness except diamond if lasting means more than ten-year and no substitute exists.

2. Perishable Distinctiveness: Most products have perishable distinctiveness in pioneering stage. It slowly diminishes in growth and maturity stages when competitors bring in their products to the innovator's approximation and when their strategies come close to the innovators.

3. Little Distinctiveness: In maturity stage products of perishable distinctiveness become products of little distinctiveness in market and continue in decline.

Pricing Strategies During Market Pioneering

During market pioneering, marketer's proper pricing strategy depends both upon the distinctiveness of his new product and how long he expects this distinctiveness to last. The more distinctiveness a product possesses the more freedom is expected in pricing. If the product is highly distinctive having no substitute, the marketer can choose profitable price. Profitable price is restricted if the product is slightly distinctive with minor changes from existing and substitute products. A wider range of profitable price can be expected if distinctiveness is for longer period.

New products, howsoever distinctive they may be, have only limited period free of competition which depends on innovation, potentiality, the rate of market acceptance and potential competitor's product development capability. During the market pioneering stage, the innovative marketer enjoys enough pricing discretion. This freedom from competitors he cannot hope to enjoy for more than three years for most products. The marketer must formulate pricing strategy during the market pioneering stage on the assumption that as competitors enter the market product distinctiveness will deteriorate in a relatively short time.

TYPES OF PRICING STRATEGIES

The marketer has the following three price strategies in the market pioneering stage:

1. Skim the Cream Pricing.
2. Market-Penetration Pricing.
3. Follow the Leader Pricing.

1. Skim the Cream Pricing Strategies

This strategy uses a very high introductory price to skim the cream of demand at the very outset. Prices continue to be high till the competitors begin to enter the field. As soon as competitors enter the market, the producer reduces the prices of his product. This method helps in recovering the product development cost very soon. A short-range pricing objective is followed when the producer feels that there will be rapid competitive in-roads. By this strategy the marketer takes the cream before keen competition starts.

Cases of Attraction of Price Skimming

(*i*) *Beginning*: In the beginning, there is lack of competition and, therefore, innovative company can fix the monopolistic price of its product.

(*ii*) *Luxury Products*: This policy is suitable for pricing the luxury products because it is an index of social status with lesser price sensitivity.

(*iii*) *Prompt Returns*: It attracts the prompt return of investment.

(*iv*) *Highly Distinctive Price*: This strategy tends to have more price in elastic demand at first, then it will be reduced later on, because advertising and personal selling have more influence on sales than price does during a product's market pioneering stage.

(*v*) *Tapping Insensitive Market*: As high introductory price divides the market into segments differing in their responsiveness to price. The skimming price taps the market segment that is relatively insensitive to price. The company can reach more price conscious market segments through later price reduction.

(*vi*) *Easy to Reduce*: If an Introductory price is too high, it is easy to reduce it but if it is too low it is difficult and awkward to raise.

(*vii*) *Greater Sales and Profits*: A high introductory price often generates greater rupee sales and profits than a low introductory price. Thus, price skimming provides funds which the marketers can use later in expanding sales to other market segments.

(viii) Chance to recoup development expenses: Price skimming gives the innovating marketer a chance to recoup his product development expenses before competitors with lower product development expenses enter the market.

2. Market Penetration Pricing

This is just opposite of the 'Skim the Cream' strategy. It offers a low introductory price to speed up it sales and widen the market base. As low price is used as a major tool for rapid penetration of a mass market the strategy is based on a long-term viewpoint to capture the market. If there is already a competing product, the strategy may aim to capture a share of the market from a company product which the new product is hoped to replace. It will also discourage competitors from entering the market.

CONDITIONS MAKING PENETRATION PRICING APPROPRIATE

(*i*) *Highly price elastic acquired*: When the new product's demand is highly price elastic even early in the pioneering stage.

(*ii*) *Economies:* When the marketer can realise substantial manufacturing and marketing economies if he obtains a large sales volume. Such economies bring down average total costs.

(*iii*) *Expected competition*: When the marketer expects strong competition very soon after introducing the product, *i.e.,* when he expects the product's market pioneering stage not to last long.

(*iv*) *Lack of elite market*: When there is little or no 'elite' market for the product in a market segment made up of buyers who will buy regardless of price.

Likely Reactions of Competitors

In choosing between price skimming and penetration pricing the innovating marketer's most important consideration is the relative ease and speed with which competitors can launch their own version of their own products. Penetration pricing is usually the most appropriate strategy for revolutionary new products which have large potential markets because the existence of a large potential market shall attract many large competitors soon after introduction of the innovation. Penetration pricing, as it is less profitable, helps to discourage prospective competition. A price skimming strategy is appropriate if the marketer expects that competitors will need considerable time and will meet great difficulties in coming up with their own version of the product type. If the marketer's new product is only slightly distinctive than as implied earlier, his best choice is penetration pricing at a price either at or very slightly above those of the competitive substitutes.

3. Follow the Leader Pricing

Some big firms assume the role of a leader in pricing in a competitive market. When a company starts production of such competitive product, it follows the pricing policy of the leader firm. It fixes the prices generally lower than those of the leader. This policy provides no scientific and rational basis for fixing the prices.

CONDITIONS MAKING POLICY ATTRACTIVE

1. Competition: This policy is suitable when competitive situation exists in the market.

2. Small firms: Small firms which cannot afford various market survey techniques generally follow the big firms, on the assumption that big firms in the field have broad marketing research base and their prices are more scientific.

3. Price-Conscious Buyers: Such pricing is successful when buyers are price-conscious.

Follow the Leader Pricing policy has no scientific base. Under this policy the cost of the product and other marketing factors are not considered.

PRICING STRATEGY DURING MARKET GROWTH

Innovating Marketer's Pricing Strategy

In the market growth stage the innovating marketer's pricing strategy for a product of perishable distinctiveness must take direct account of the pricing strategies of his competitors as they enter the market. If he used price skimming during the market pioneering stage, he may switch to penetration pricing when significant competition first appears. Alternatively, he now reduces his price in several successive steps as more competitors enter the broadening market.

If the innovator used penetration pricing during market pioneering he should continue with that strategy during the market growth stage. In either case his main pricing objective during market growth is generally that of retaining a particular market share.

Competitors Pricing Strategies

Competitors new to the market should take note of the innovator's pricing strategy and his price with the objective of gaining and holding some target market share. If the innovator has been using price skimmings, the first few competitors to enter the market may seek to 'under price' him slightly. As he steps down his price they should try to 'keep one jump ahead' by timing their price cuts preceding his steps.

During market growth competitors entering the market late are likely to use penetration pricing from the outset. If the innovator has been using penetration pricing all along, the new competitors have no choice but to do the same though it is not necessary that all use identical penetration prices.

Non-price Competition During Market Growth

During the market growth each marketer's pricing strategy becomes increasingly dependent upon those of host competitors non-price competition which also increases at this stage. Different competitors seek to gain advantages through promotional efforts changing or improving the product and extending its distribution. Firms succeeding to become leading brands also succeed in pricing their entries at a 'price above the market'. Thus they find it possible to use a premium pricing strategy. Those who do not succeed in becoming leading brands, must generally price either at competitive levels or under the market. Hence, in making his own pricing strategy each competitor considers not only the non-price components of his own overall marketing strategy but those of his competitors as well. All competitors find that both their pricing and overall marketing strategies are increasingly interlocked as market growth proceeds.

Pricing Strategy During Market Maturity

A product of perishable distinctiveness loses its distinctiveness at an increasing rate under market maturity stage. Brands become more and more alike. There is increasing substitution among brands. Market shares among brands stabilise and in the contest to maintain market shares, leading brands cannot command as large a price premium as before. As production methods stabilise and individual manufacturers develop excess production capacity, private-label competitors enter and secure important market shares by offering private labels at under the market price.

These developments of pricing strategy affect the case of entry and the number of competitors into the market if market entry is difficult and the number of competitors small. If market entry is easy and the competitors are large in number then monopolistic competition prevails and governs individual marketer's pricing strategies,

BASIC PRICING POLICIES

Consumer situation and cost considerations use the fundamentals which may affect price decisions though many films have no clear pricing policies. The following are the basic policies recognised for pricing:

1. Cost-oriented pricing policy.
2. Demand-oriented pricing policy.
3. Competition-oriented pricing policy.

1. Cost-oriented Pricing Policy: Following are the principal methods of pricing based on cost:

(*i*) *Cost-plus Pricing:* This method assumes that no product is sold at a loss since the price covers the full cost incurred. Costs furnish a good point from which the computation of price could begin. Under this method, fixing a tentative price is easier. But this policy ignores the influences of competition and market demand.

Cost-plus pricing is often used by retail traders and in manufacturing industries where the production is not standardised. This method of pricing is based on simple arithmetic adding a fixed percentage to the unit cost. The retail price of a particular item might be the manufacturer's cost with the addition of his gross margin, the wholesaler's gross margin and the retailer's gross margin. Therefore, this method is also known as the Sum of Margins method.

Advantages of Cost-Plus Pricing

(*a*) *Difficulties in Forecast*: This method is appropriate circumstances where it is difficult to forecast the future demand.

(*b*) *Few Buyers*: If there are few buyers of the products, pricing can be justified.

(*c*) *Public Utility Services*: Public utility services like railway, post offices, electricity, etc. are priced through this method.

(*d*) *Long-Term*: It is a long-term policy.

Disadvantages of Cost-Plus Pricing

(*a*) The two important factors in fixing the prices, the demand and supply forces and competition, are ignored.

(*b*) This method is totally based on cost-concept but while costs do not influence the prices, prices influence the cost.

(*c*) Correct cost cannot be calculated as only the costs of joint products are estimated.

(*ii*) *Target Pricing*: Target Pricing is another common method used under cost-oriented pricing. It is invariably adopted by manufacturers who fix a target return on the total cost. They use Break-Even analysis for deciding cost plus pricing. It helps to calculate in advance the likely relationship between the cost, volume and profit over various time periods. Target pricing has also proved to be a highly useful technique for the broad planning of manufacturing facilities.

(*iii*) *Break-Even Pricing*: Break-Even analysis helps a firm to determine at what level of output the revenues will equal the costs assuming a certain selling price. For this purpose the cost of manufacture is divided into fixed and variable costs. Fixed costs such as rent, rates, insurance, etc. theoretically remain constant overall levels of output. Variable costs such as labour and material vary with changes in output level. When production increases fixed costs per unit naturally decrease. On the other hand variable costs change as production varies, no production no variable cost, more production more variable cost.

The break-even point is a point where there is neither loss nor gain. It is calculated by using the following equation:

$$\text{BEP} = \frac{\text{Total Fixed Costs}}{\text{Margin of contribution}}$$

Margin of contribution = Unit selling price – unit variable costs.

Limitations of BEP

(*a*) Break-even analysis helps to establish prices only when the costs of production remain reasonably constant.

(*b*) Another trouble is found in accurately forecasting demand at various prices.

(*iv*) *Marginal Cost or Incremental Cost Pricing*: In this method, the price is fixed on the basis of additional variable cost associated with an additional unit of output. The cost of producing and selling one more unit, *i.e.*, the last unit is taken as the base for the pricing.

Advantages

(*i*) *Introductory Campaigns*: This method is useful in introductory campaigns for introducing a new product where this new product does not bear its share in fixed cost, while other products bear the full fixed cost.

(*ii*) *Checking Shut-down*: This method is also helpful in order to check the shut-down and keeping the labour force busy in slack seasons.

(*iii*) *Perishable Product and Weak Competitors*: If the product is perishable or where the competitors are weak, this method is useful to sell the perishable product or to oust the competitors.

(*iv*) *BEP*: The method can be used where break-even point has been achieved.

Limitations

(*i*) *Short-term Policy*: This method cannot be followed indefinitely as its share of fixed cost remains to be unabsorbed and if other products are made to absorb all the fixed costs involved in an organisation, the seller is selling a proportion of his output at incremental cost and the customers of other products are paying a higher price.

(*ii*) *Loss of Market*: The producer may lose the market of other products because of the high cost and the competitors may drive away the customers.

2. Demand-oriented Pricing Policy: Under this method of pricing, as the name indicates, the demand is the pivotal factor. Price is fixed by adjusting it to the market condition. A high price is charged when or where the demand is intense. A low price is charged when the demand is low.

3. Competition-oriented Pricing Policy: Most companies set prices after a careful consideration of the competitive price structure. Deliberate policies may be formulated to sell above, below, or generally in line with competition. In this method there cannot be any rigid relation between the price of a product and the firm's own cost or demand. In spite of change in cost or demand the firm maintains its prices. It changes its prices when the competitors change theirs even if its own cost or demand has not altered.

PROBLEMS INVOLVED IN NEW PRODUCT PRICING

Pricing a new product is one of the most important and puzzling marketing problems faced by a firm. It is important in two ways as far as the new product is concerned:

(*i*) It affects the quantity of the product to be sold.

(*ii*) It determines the amount of the revenue of a firm.

New products appeal to many as novel items, though this distinctiveness created by novelty is only temporary. Ignored initially, the price factor would become important when the product becomes an ordinary one due to constant use. Competitors may also appear in the market. Therefore, the new products are hard to be priced rightly. Incorrect pricing leads to product failure. Therefore, following guidelines are adopted for setting a price on a new product.

1. Making the product accepted.
2. Maintaining the market.
3. Retaining the profit.

1. Skimming: If a product is entirely new in the market skimming method could be used. A strategy of high prices coupled with large promotional expenditure in the initial stages proves successful in a number of cases. Skimming pricing is recommended due to the following reasons:

(*i*) It helps to take the cream of the market through high prices.

(*ii*) People may like to own a new product even at a higher cost.

(*iii*) It helps to develop demand as the price is gradually reduced.

(*iv*) High sales volume on account of higher price though initial sales would be less.

However, high initial price may also prevent quick sales.

2. Penetration Pricing: A comparative analysis of two pricing systems reveals that both these methods suffer from errors. When an electric clock was first introduced, consumers were reluctant to buy it because it was relatively low priced when compared to a quality spring wound clock. Consumers apparently felt that a quality clock could not be sold so cheap. The clocks were withdrawn from the market and reintroduced subsequently at a higher price which sounded attractive; after that they sold clock successfully.

In the case of new products, pricing has to be made with little knowledge of demand, cost and competition. The new product has to bear the cost of promotion or creating a market. The cost incurred in constructing a proper channel of distribution may also be accounted for in pricing. Therefore, the initial cost is higher.

LEGAL RESTRICTIONS ON PRICING

The major law's affecting pricing decisions in India are the following:

1. Monopolies and Restrictive Trade Practices Act, 1969 (MRTPA): This Act prohibits the increasing of prices unreasonably. It prevents monopolistic organisation and hence monopoly pricing too.

2. Essential Commodities Act, 1955: This Act imposes price controls on most of the essential commodities.

3. Durga Price Control Act.

RESALE PRICE MAINTENANCE (RPM)

The terms 'resale price' and 'retail price' are often used synonymously. But while resale price maintenance is a policy adopted by a manufacturer whereby he fixes a price for his product to be sold to customers by retailers, retail price is that price at which a retailer sells the product to his customer. Usually, the retailer sells his product on the basis of cost plus expenses, plus his margin of profit. By reducing his own margin, a retailer is free to sell the product at any price he deems fit. But resale price maintenance is an arrangement of a contract entered into between the supplier and the reseller (wholesalers or retailers). This contract normally stipulates a condition that the reseller will have to sell the product at a price fixed by the supplier. If the dealer does not maintain the specified prices, the supplier will even withhold further supplies. Strict enforcement of the suggested price is possible only when a manufacturer uses a selective or exclusive distribution system. The particular brand should have achieved a high degree of customer acceptance and popularity, in order to maintain resale price.

MRTP ACT

In India resale price maintenance is controlled through MRTP Act which elaborates the term 'Resale price maintenance' as follows: 'Resale price in relation to sale of goods of any description means any price notified to the dealer or otherwise published by or on behalf of the supplier of the goods in question (whether lawfully or not) as the price or minimum price which is to be charged on, or is recommended as appropriate for a sale of that description or any prescribed or purporting to be prescribed for that purpose by any contract of agreement between the wholesaler or retailer and any such supplier.

Type of Resale Price

1. A minimum price below which the products cannot be sold.
2. A maximum price above which the products cannot be sold.
3. A stipulated price from which no changes are allowed.

According to MRTP Act, the first and the third are restrictive trade practices. The second one normally allow a flexibility for the retailer to fix the final price. Hence, it is not treated as a restrictive trade practice.

Evaluation of RPM

The original ideas behind the Resale Price Maintenance (RPM) was to avoid unhealthy competition by retailers. Later on, this became a source of additional profit for the manufacturers through exclusive or selective distribution system through which a sort of brand monopoly could be developed and a high price could be charged from the consumers. Such a practice caused hardships to small scale organisations. In certain cases it led them to their extinction.

The Resale Price Maintenance is also injurious to the interest of the consumers, though they get the product at a fixed price. The fixing of such a minimum price control cannot be justified due to following difficulties:

1. The producer adds the remuneration of the middlemen at the highest rate permissible but, actually, all middlemen are not paid with that rate. Their remuneration is fixed through agreement.
2. If prices of a product are reduced, the advantage is not given to the consumers because they cannot sell the product at a lower price.
3. If the last retailer gets his supplies direct from the producer and thus removes the other middlemen, he would be also eligible to other middlemen's remuneration. Consequently, if he desires to reduce the price by passing on the additional remuneration to consumers, he cannot do so.

This policy is against the consumers' interest. In order to safeguard the interest of consumers, Indian government has imposed a restriction to fix the Resale Price Maintenance by section 39 of the Monopolistic and Restrictive Trade Practices Act (MRTP). RPM has been declared an offence. Hence, the producers fix the maximum price of their products while the retailers are free to charge any price below that maximum.

ECONOMIC CONCEPTS RELEVANT TO PRICING

Pricing is a critical decision as it affects sales revenue and the profits. In order to be in a position to determine adequate pricing strategies, the marketing manager must be familiar with the relevant economic concepts which include demand elasticity and economic environment.

1. **Demand Elasticity:** According to the economic concept of demand a fall in the price of product is likely to increase the quantity that would be demanded. Where a change in the price has no effect on the quantity purchases, the demand is described as perfectly elastic if an unlimited quantity would be purchased without a change in price. Different goods have different degrees of elasticity of demand. Necessaries of life have generally inelastic demand, articles of comforts and luxuries have highly elastic demand. The extremes of perfectly elastic and perfectly inelastic demands do not apply in fact. Hence, the marketing manager is more concerned with whether the demand is relatively elastic or inelastic, *i.e.,* whether the demand is materially affected by a change in the price. Where the price is relatively elastic the price should be fixed as low as possible in the interest of total profitability.

2. **Economic Environment:** In India the marketing manager should be aware of the present trend of political and economic thinking against concentration of economic power in the context of the socialistic pattern of society in India. Appointed in 1964 the Monopolies Inquiry Commission indicated that there was a product-wise concentration in a large number of industries in India where a single undertaking was the sole supplier. Such power would enable the organisation to indicate prices to the consumers. The commission also mentioned the following as some of the monopolistic and restrictive practices.

(*i*) Hoarding to create artificial scarcity.

(*ii*) Resale price maintenance.

(*iii*) Fixation of prices by competitive agreement.

The commission felt that the emergence of monopolies will result in the evils of high prices such as the consumer deterioration in quality and keeping out of the small industrialists. In other countries, particularly in Great Britain, European countries and U.S.A. the government tries to protect the consumer through legislation against monopolistic and restrictive trade practices.

Thus, pricing must take into account economic concepts that are relevant as well as the trend of economic and political thinking in a particular country. Besides economic factor, the marketing manager should also take into account legal, social and ethical considerations.

PRICE DISCRIMINATION

Meaning

The monopolist can and does charge different prices from different people provided those people are from 'different markets' or belong to what are called non-competing groups. This is known as price discrimination.

Kinds

Price discrimination may be personal or local, or according to trade or use.

1. **Personal:** When different prices are charged from different persons.
2. **Local:** When the price varies according to locality, *(e.g.,* dumping).
3. **According to Use:** When different prices are charged according to the uses to which the commodity is put, *e.g.,* electric current is usually sold cheaper for industrial purposes than for domestic uses.
4. **By Means of Special Labels:** Hence, the marketer charges discriminating prices for different labels.

Causes

1. Consumers' preference of prejudices.
2. The nature of the commodity.
3. Distance and frontier barriers.

Discrimination is possible because of the variations in the intensities of demand for the same commodity which enable the monopolist to divide the demand into series of markets according to its intensity. He can thus charge higher process from those who can afford to pay higher prices and lower from those who are only able to pay lower prices. This can happen only if the commodity cannot be transferred from the cheaper to the dearer market. Discrimination prices can be also charged when owing to imperfection of the market, the customers cannot readily move from one seller to another.

Conditions for Price Discrimination

1. The Elasticities of Demand: It should be different in different **markets,** so that the monopolist can go on dividing and sub-dividing his market. No two buyers with different elasticity are put in the same group, till in each market the elasticity of demand is the same. The monopolist will find it profitable to charge more in the market where elasticity is low and low price where it is high. To quote Mrs. John Robinson, "The sub-markets will be arranged in ascending order of their elasticities, the highest price being charged in the least elastic market, and the lowest price in the most elastic market."

2. Costs of Division: The costs incurred in dividing that market into sub-markets and keeping them separate should not be so large as to neutralise the difference in demand elasticities.

3. Agreement: There should not be complete agreement among the sellers otherwise independent competitors will gain by selling in the dear market.

4. Discrimination: Discrimination is possible when goods are sold on special orders, because then the purchaser cannot know what is being charged from others.

According to Prof. Pigou, following two conditions are essential for profitable and successful discrimination:

(*i*) *It should not be possible to transfer from one market to another any unit of the commodity sold in one market*: This is the case when services are rendered direct to consumers, *e.g.*, by teachers, lawyers, doctors, etc. or services applied direct to commodities, *e.g.*, transportation by railways. Transference may be obstructed by high transport costs or high tariff charges or by contracts penalising resales.

(*ii*) *It should not be possible to transfer a unit of demand, proper to one market, to another market*: This happens when markets are split upon the basis of wealth. A rich man cannot become poor simply to enjoy fee concession. A silk merchant cannot become a coal merchant to avail of lower freight rates.

Price Discrimination and Output

When the elasticities of demand in the two markets are different, marginal revenue from the sale of a unit of output will be more where the elasticity is high than where it is low. It will be profitable to reduce the output and raise the price where elasticity is low and increase the output and lower the price where the elasticity of demand is high. Thus, the marginal revenue in the two markets will be equalised. But will the output on the whole, increase or decrease or remain the same? Mrs. Robinson gives the answer: "It is possible to establish the fact that total output under discrimination will be greater or less than under simple monopoly accordingly as the more elastic of the demand curves in the separate markets is more or less concave than the less elastic demand curve; and that total output will be the same if the demand curves are straight lines or in any other case in which the concavities are equal." This holds good, however, if marginal cost is the same under simple monopoly and discriminating monopoly. But if marginal cost is rising, then the decrease in the output will be accentuated. On the whole discrimination will increase rather than decrease output. For example, in case of certain books, the first edition is issued at a high price, they purchase it at that price whose marginal utility (intensity of demand) for the book is very high. After the edition is exhausted, a second edition is issued which is priced lower than the first. People of lower marginal utility can now purchase the book. This process may be repeated several times and a very wide sale obtained. People with greater intensity of demand will not wait for cheaper editions. Thus, the monopolist appropriates the major portion of the consumer's surplus and increases his monopoly revenues to such point which are not possible otherwise.

IS PRICE DISCRIMINATION BENEFICIAL TO SOCIETY?

In certain cases, price discrimination may be beneficial to society, for instance, when a particular product or service may be very useful to the community. If the price is fixed low enough for the poorer classes, production costs may not be due to absence of normal profits per unit. If the price is fixed too high, the total receipts again may be low due to meagre sales. The commodity may, therefore, not be produced at all. At least some output may be held up, because average revenue in a discrimination monopoly is greater than under simple monopoly. It may happen, for instance, that a railway would not be built or doctor would not be set up in practice, if discrimination were forbidden. It is clearly desirable that price discrimination should be permitted in such cases. If discriminatory prices are charged the total receipts may be adequate to meet the total cost with profit. Thus, everyone may gain from the production of such a commodity when discriminatory prices are charged.

As discrimination involves raising the price for some people and lowering for some others, price discrimination is beneficial to some and harmful to others. But the net effect on social welfare will depend on which group the society likes to favour. If the price is lowered for the 'masses' and raised for the 'classes' the society has nothing to regret, as such an arrangement is obviously intended to promote economic welfare. But in the case of geographical discrimination it is also possible that the less elastic market may be the home market whereas the market abroad may happen to he more elastic and for them the price will, therefore, be lowered. Such a price discrimination is clearly detrimental to the community concerned. However, if the industry obeys the law of increasing returns (or diminishing marginal costs) even the less elastic market will gain from the larger output (at reduced costs) in discriminating monopoly than under simple monopoly. Thus, dumping abroad is likely to lower the price for the home market too and benefit the country concerned.

To conclude with Mrs. Robinson, "From the point of view of society as a whole it is impossible to say whether price discrimination is desirable or not. From one point of view, therefore, price discrimination must be held to be superior to simple monopoly in all these cases in which it leads to an increase of output, and these cases are likely to be the more common. But against this advantage must be set the fact that price discrimination leads to a maldistribution of resources as between different uses. Before it is possible to say whether discrimination is desirable or not, it is, therefore, necessary to weigh up the benefit from the increase in output against this disadvantage. In those cases in which discrimination will decrease output it is undesirable on both counts."

QUESTIONS FOR EXERCISE

1. How does a pricing strategy differ from a pricing policy? Discuss the effect of the kind of distinctiveness possessed by a product on its pricing.
2. What are the various strategies during market pioneering? Explain.
3. Differentiate between 'Skimming' and 'Penetration'?
4. Would you agree or disagree with following statements? Give reasons:

(*i*) A price skimming strategy is usually directed toward maximising profits.

(*ii*) If the product has an elastic demand, then, usually a penetration is the best choice during its pioneering stage.

(*iii*) One way to discourage new competitors from entering a market is to use a penetration price.

5. Contrast the pricing strategies during market growth of (*i*) The innovating marketer, and (*ii*) His competitors.
6. Explain the following:
   (*i*) Oligopolistic Pricing.
   (*ii*) Pricing under Monopolistic Competition.
   (*iii*) Run out strategy.
7. Describe in brief the basic pricing policies which can be followed to determine the price of a product.
8. Explain the following:
   (*i*) Rate of Return on Investment Pricing (Target Pricing).
   (*ii*) Cost-plus Method.
9. Distinguish between:
   (*a*) Cost-oriented pricing.
   (*b*) Demand-oriented pricing.
   (*c*) Competition-oriented pricing.
10. What problems are involved in pricing a new product? Should the product adopt skimming pricing policy or penetrating pricing policy in case of his new product? What are legal restrictions on pricing?
11. Resale Price Maintenance is to the disadvantage of the consumer? Do you agree? Explain.
12. "Pricing must take into account economic concepts that are relevant as well as the trend of economic and political thinking in a particular country.' Discuss.
13. What do you understand by 'Price Discrimination'? Explain the conditions which make it possible and profitable.

19

Pricing Decisions

Meaning of Pricing Decision

According to Converse, "Decisions concerning price to be followed for a period of time may be called price policies." The determination of price is a very important and crucial decision. It affects all parties involved in the production, distribution and consumption of goods. Price affects volume of production and the amount of profit. It is a source of income to distributors. It is important for consumers because all their buying decisions are influenced by prices. It reflects the purchasing power of the regulator of production and allocator of resources. It is the instrument most generally identified with a market economy. A free-enterprise system cannot flourish without price competition. It is the universal index of value. It is the best measure of demand. It serves to bring the supply of goods and services produced into equilibrium with the quantity demanded. Among various marketing decisions, the decisions relating to pricing of products are the most significant because they are the very basis of survival and growth of the firm.

OBJECTIVES OF PRICE DECISIONS

1. **To Provide Suitable Return on Investment:** A business organisation aims to have minimum return on its investment, *e.g.*, 10 per cent to 20 per cent after-tax. This rate is to be decided by the management and followed in pricing policy.

2. **To Maximise Profit:** Pricing policy directly affects the earnings of the concern and, therefore, its successful functioning. Hence, the first objective of a price policy is the maximum of profit for the firm.

3. To Acquire Market Position: Another objective of price policy is to acquire a position in the market. Hence, a firm prepares its pricing policy keeing in the mind this objective also.

4. To Achieve Price Stabilisation: The price fixed once should be reasonably stabilised as it will give a continuous income to the firm and bring reputation also. It is possible only when all short-term and long-term aspects are taken into account while fixing prices.

5. To Charge According to 'Ability to Pay': The firm fixes its prices in such a manner that 'ability to pay' principle of taxation is followed. It helps in maximisation of earnings.

6. To Face the Competition: The price policy of a firm aims at facing the competition successfully.

7. To Achieve Long-run Welfare of firm: The next objective of price policy of a firm is its long-run welfare.

CONTENTS OF PRICE DECISION

Price decisions involve the following matters:

1. Determining the broad objectives of price policy.
2. Studying the factors affecting price policy.
3. Formulating various price policies for different products.
4. Developing a long-term integrating price policy for the firm.

IMPORTANCE OF PRICE DECISIONS

Henry Ford once stated, "Our policy is to reduce price, extend operations and improve the product." It shows the importance of pricing decisions in a marketing-mix. Price is a matter of vital importance to both the seller and the buyer in the market place. There cannot be marketing in a money economy without prices. Price denotes the volume of a product of service expressed in money. Pricing decisions interconnect marketing actions with the financial objectives of the enterprise. Among the most important marketing variables influenced by pricing decisions are: (*i*) Sales volume, (*ii*) Profit margins, (*iii*) Rate of return or investment, (*iv*) Trade image, (*v*) Advertising and sales promotion, (*vi*) Product image, and (*vii*) New product development programme. Thus, pricing decisions play a very important role determining the firm's position in the market *vis-a-vis* its rivals. Pricing policy affects production. It shows the importance of pricing decisions in the marketing-mix.

FACTORS AFFECTING PRICING DECISION

1. Objectives of Business: The management has to review the objectives of the firm as they are the real deciding factor. A firm may have alternative objectives such as a suitable return on the capital employed, maximisation of sales, capturing market from competitors, etc. Against this background one has to decide while framing a price policy.

2. Cost of Goods: Price charged must be such as will enable the manufacturer to recover unit cost and earn a reasonable profit. If the price of product falls short of the average total unit cost and thus results in a loss no business can continue for long. The cost itself will require appropriate adjustments to be made in price for the different conditions under which sales are to be made.

3. Market Position: The next factor in pricing policies is the study of nature of market. It is the nature of prospective buyers of the product concerned. The management should attempt to find out the composition of their market. They should consider such questions as follows: Is the market of their product composed of industrial users or commercial houses or individual consumers or householders? Does their market consist of individual consumers? Are they rich, middle or poor class? Is the product meant for young men or for grown- ups? Should it be used by males or females? What is the relative utility of the product to the consumers? What is their elasticity of demand? Such questions guide the management in fixing correct prices.

4. Competitor's Price: Next factor is competitor's price for similar merchandise, and the effect of one's own price policy upon the price policies of the competitors, the sales of the merchandise in question and one's reputation in the community. No sales manager can ignore the prices charged by other suppliers of identical products. A price higher than the one charged by others will wean customers away from him. A very much lower price may create a suspicion in their minds about the quality of the product. This may not increase sales. It is not suggested that no margin should be provided for the form's reputation, the products superiority and the sales organisation's efficiency and efforts. A higher price may be charged along with product differentiation even in cases where competition is very keen.

5. The marketing policies pursued by the sales organisation: It is important to consider here the channel for distribution selected to market the products. The longer the chain of distribution the higher is the margin added to cost in fixing the price. Warranties and after-sale service facilities attached to a sale also have a bearing on the pricing of goods. Proper adjustment should be made for regular or irregular rebates, concessions, cuts or other reductions in prices, allowed to customers as an incentive to promote sales.

6. Social and Ethical Considerations

(*i*) *Public Policy*: Sometimes, the government may announce a general policy about pricing of goods. For example, these days in India the government is averse to any rise in prices of necessities of life. The government may specifically fix and control prices of goods as in the case of iron and steel, cement, coal, sugar, etc. Under these circumstances the sales manager has little or no control over the prices and he has to fall in line with the public policy.

(*ii*) *Reasonable Price*: It is a business ethics to charge reasonable and just prices for products. Though the rules of 'what the traffic will bear' and 'what competition will allow' have been popular, the principle of reasonableness has also guided the prices.

(*iii*) *Attitude of Labour Leaders*: Attitude of labour leaders is also a guiding factor in pricing decisions. If prices are fixed high, workers demand more wages and more bonus, etc.

(*iv*) *Consumer's Reactions to Rising Prices*: It should also be taken into account while making pricing decision.

Information Useful for Pricing Decisions

1. Information relating to markets: This includes production costs, excise duty and octroi, price regulation if any, packaging, after-sales service costs (if any).

2. Information relating to markets: It includes the prices of substitutes; sales condition; chief competitors: national production data; consumption pattern; the brand loyalty of the customers; needs for sales promotion; commission payable to middlemen; etc.

3. Information relating to the firm: It includes production capacity of the firms, financial resources of the firms, past records of sales and prices, etc.

PRICE DETERMINATION PROCESS

Pricing of products is a complex problem. It is a twilight zone between business interests and public good. A firm has to reconcile both these objectives. There cannot be a model process for pricing the products of each firm. The following steps can be described as the gradual steps in this process:

1. Estimation of Demand for product.
2. Anticipation of Competition.
3. Establishment of Expected Share of Market.
4. Selection of a Suitable Price Strategy.
5. Consideration of a Company's.
   (*i*) Product Policies.
   (*ii*) Channel of Distribution Policies.
   (*iii*) Promotional Policies.
6. Selection of a Specific Price.

1. Estimation of Demand: The pricing of product requires the estimation of the total demand for the product. It will depend upon the expected price. Experienced wholesalers/retailers may evaluate products. Regular survey of potential buyers may be conducted. One can determine the expected price in a few test markets, by trying different prices in different test markets and comparing the results with a controlled market in which price is not altered. Once he knows the expected prices, one can compute sales volume at special prices.

2. Anticipation of Competition: The second step is anticipation of competition which is a crucial factor in price determination. Sellers do not operate in a vacuum. If the area of operation is easy and entry of new producers into the market is easier, profit prospects are immense. It is quite obvious that the threat of competition is considerable.

3. Determination of Share Market: It is determination of the share of the market one expects at the expected price. Higher initial price may be fixed if one anticipates a smaller share. If one expects a much larger market share, he will have to prefer relatively lower prices. Proper pricing strategy is to be evolved to research the market target through skimming price, penetrating price or working out a compromise.

4. Consideration of Company Policies: Various policies of company relating to product, channel of distribution and promotional activities should be given proper consideration.

5. Selection of a Suitable Price: Selection of a suitable price is the last step in the process of price determination. Its most appropriate method is the cost-plus mark-up method, usually called cost-plus method, very suitable for wholesalers and retailers. According to it:

Price of Product = Cost of Production + Operating Expenses + Profit Margin

Yardsticks Used in Pricing a Product

Following factors affecting the price range of a product are used as yardsticks in pricing a product:

1. Cost of production of distribution.
2. Price of rival producers.
3. Consumer reaction and response.
4. Middlemen's reactions.
5. Prices of substitute products.
6. Government rules and regulations.

Price fixation is not the right of one department or one manager only. It is the prerogative of top governor management to decide it. A foresighted management should try to involve all the important functional executives in the process so that an integrated price policy may be evolved for different products of the firm. Adjustments and revision in the prices are very much essential as there is nothing static in a competitive economy. Such judgement should be based on facts, with a realistic regard for the current position of the firm and an optimistic eye towards the future.

ECONOMIC ANALYSIS OF COST

A marketing executive should have a basic knowledge of the different market structures and the method of price determination in each case. Economic theory of price determination provides a universally acceptable terminology to discuss the concepts of cost and demand. Hence, it is very important to know the different types of costs associated with the production of goods and services in the firm. One should examine their behaviour and impact in the short-term as well as in the long-term periods.

Cost of the firm refers to the total monetary cost paid to all factors of production in producing a given amount of output. It is the sum-total of the wages paid to labour, interests paid to capital, rent paid to land and profit to the entrepreneur. Some people believe that profit paid to the entrepreneur does not form a part of the total cost. Profit, however, means the normal return on invested capital which tempts an entrepreneur to undertake a business activity and forms a part of the total cost.

Average total cost (ATC) is the part unit cost and is obtained by dividing total cost by the number of units produced or sold.

Marginal cost (MC) represents the cost incurred in producing an additional unit of a product of service.

The economists classify costs into fixed and variable categories. They also use short-term and long-term time periods for the purpose of determining the price of a commodity. The short-term is a period of time in which a business unit does not change its inputs of fixed factors of production. The quantity of variable factors be changed in the short-term. Long-term is a period long enough to make all factors of production variable.

In the short-run, certain costs remain fixed irrespective of the level of output implying thereby that average fixed cost will decline with the increasing output. The variable costs, however, change with the changes in the level of output. Because of economies of sale up to a certain level of output and later diseconomies of sale, average variable cost per unit of output declines in the first instance but ultimately starts rising, meaning thereby that the average variable cost curve of the firm is U-shaped. When one adds both the average fixed cost and the average variable cost one gets average total cost per unit of output.

In the long-run, all costs are variable and the cost curve of the firm is U-shaped because of the operation of the laws of returns.

Another useful cost concept is that of marginal cost. Marginal cost is the cost of producing one extra unit. It is also a U-shaped curve and has a definite relationship of the average total cost curve of the firm both in the short-run and long-run.

PECULIAR MARKET CONDITIONS

A business firm has to operate under peculiar market conditions of which the most important may be as follows:

1. Perfect Competition: A perfect competitive industry is one in which every buyer and seller is so small in relation to the entire market, that he cannot affect the market prices by changing his purpose or output. Following are the characteristics of perfect competition:

(*i*) There is a large number of buyers and sellers of which each enjoys so small a share of the market that he has no influence on prices.

(*ii*) The commodities dealt in the market are homogeneous, *i.e.*, identical in every respect.

(*iii*) Entry into and exit from the industry are unrestricted and easy.

(*iv*) Buyers and sellers are fully aware of the terms and conditions of sales.

2. Monopoly: The sole producer of a product is known as monopolist. The industry in which he operates is the monopoly industry. In a monopoly, the seller has complete control over the output of a product. There is only one firm in the industry which has no direct threat of competition. Delhi Electric Supply Undertaking (DESU) is a typical example of monopoly industry in the city.

3. Imperfect Competition: In real life, industries are more or less not totally competitive in nature. The number of firms is either fairly large or fairly small and they produce, more or less, identical products. This leads to two extreme types of markets—monopolistic competition and oligopoly.

(*i*) *Monopolistic Competition*: It is a market situation where there are a large number of firms producing closely related but not identical commodities. Product heterogeneity or product differentiation separates monopolistic competition from perfect competition.

(*ii*) *Oligopoly*: Oligopoly is the market situation in which there are comparatively a small member of firms producing closely related products. The number of firms is so small that the market activities of one seller have an important effect on the other sellers. Firms in the industry are interdependent. The firms take into account the existence of other firms at the time of changing their marketing policies.

PRICING AND OUTPUT DECISIONS OF THE FIRM

As revenue conditions of a firm depend upon the type of market, it is in, the pricing and output decisions will have to be studied independently for each type of market situation. However, since cost curve of a firm varies according to whether one studies in the short-run or the long-run under each market condition, one will have to study pricing both in the short-run and in the long-run.

1. Under Perfect Competition: A perfectly competitive firm is a price taker and not a price setter. It has the only choice of varying the units of output so as to decide on the level of output consistent with the objective of profit maximisation.

(*i*) *Short-run*: The firm will equalise its marginal revenue and marginal cost to arrive at the desired level of output.

(*ii*) *In the Long-run*: A firm makes only normal profits. Therefore, while deciding the level of output, not only Marginal Cost (MC) but also Average Cost (AC) should be equalised.

2. Under Monopoly: Unlike a perfectly competitive firm a monopoly firm is a price maker and not a price taker. A monopolist has to decide the level of output as well as the price at which to sell the product.

(*i*) *Short-run*: In the short-run, the monopolist maximises profit by equalising MC and MR. At this point a monopoly firm is in equilibrium and earns an extra profit which may be termed as monopoly profit.

(*ii*) *Long-run*: The monopoly firm determines its price in the long-run in the same manner as in the short-run. It changes its capacity in accordance with the changes in the long-run demand and determines its long-run equilibrium position. Since entry is prohibited, there is always a tendency on the part of monopoly firm to secure monopoly profits.

Monopolistic Competition

Every monopolistic firm faces a downward sloping demand curve, as in the case of a monopoly firm, and determines its equilibrium position by equalising MC with MR.

3. Under Oligopoly: In oligopoly the number of competitors is so small that the actions of each competitor have a direct effect on every other firm in the industry. As the firms are mutually interdependent, an oligopolist cannot adopt policies without showing any concern for what others do. In such a situation, business-making policy may become a matter of guessing one's competitors' actions which is a difficult task. Hence, there is need for making assumptions about mutual interdependence and competitive reactions. As there can be numerous assumptions it is difficult to give a general theory that will explain all the conceivable situations. Hence, oligopolistic situations cannot be specifically described. In an oligopoly a firm will try to equate marginal cost and marginal revenue in order to maximise profit.

Limitations of the Economic Theory of Pricing

The economic theory of pricing does not describe the real pricing process because it is based on unrealistic assumptions.

1. The assumption that a businessman is a rational economic being is not always true in the real world. Businessmen are not as rational as they are assumed to be. The assumption of a complete knowledge of market situation on the part of buyers and sellers is wrong.
2. Buyers and sellers in actual world do not possess complete information relating to the cost and demand.
3. The assumption that a firm wants to maximise profit is also not always true, firms have objectives other than, and in addition to, profit maximisation.

QUESTIONS FOR EXERCISE

1. What do you mean by pricing decisions? Describe their objectives and contents. Explain the importance of pricing decision.
2. Discuss the fundamental objectives of price policy and explain the various functions involved in pricing decision.
3. Enumerate the factors which affect pricing decisions. What information is useful for pricing decisions in a firm?
4. Enumerate briefly the steps that are followed in pricing a product.
5. Write short note on the economic analysis of costs that is relevant to price determination.
6. Explain the different types of market in which a firm has to operate. How is price determined in each case?

20

Channels of Distribution

Definition of Channel Distribution

1. *Philip Kotler*: "Every produce seeks to link together the set of marketing intermediaries that best fulfil the firm's objectives. This set of marketing intermediaries is called the marketing channel, also trade channel or channel of distribution."

2. *William J. Stanton*: "A channel of distribution (sometimes called a trade channel) for a product is the route taken by the title to the goods as they move from the producer to the ultimate customer or industrial users."

3. *Richard Buskirk*: "Distribution channels are systems of economic institutions through which a producer of goods delivers them into the hands of their users."

4. *McCarthy*: "Any sequence of institutions from the producer to the consumer including one or any number of middlemen is called channel of distribution."

Distribution is the function of getting goods into the hands of the consumer. Channel of distribution denotes the middlemen engaged in moving goods from the place of production to the place of consumption. It is the channel through which goods move as smoothly as possible to the desired places. It is the route by which goods move from the place of production to the place of consumption.

Channels of distribution are the means employed by manufacturers and sellers to get their products to the market and into the hands of users. These management tools used to move goods from place of production to place of consumption. These are the means by which title of goods is transferred from sellers to buyers. The process of transferring in the present-day marketing is characterised by hetrogeneity on both the demand and supply sides. The channel is the vehicle for viewing marketing organisation in its external aspects and for bridging the physical and non-physical gaps.

Definition of Marketing Channels

1. *Philip Kotler*: "Every producer seeks to link together the set of marketing intermediaries that best fulfil the firm's objectives. This set of marketing intermediaries is called the marketing channel or trade channel or channel distribution."

2. *American Marketing Association*: "It is the structure of intra company organisation units and extraordinary company agents and dealers, wholesale and retail, through which a commodity, product, or service is marketed."[1] Channels of distribution is the sequential linkage of institutions and relationships through which a product flows from the producer to the consumer.

3. *Cundiff and Still*: "It is a path traced in the direct or indirect transfer of title to a product, as it moves from a producer to ultimate consumers or industrial users."[2]

4. *Beckman and Others*: "The course taken in the transfer of the title to a commodity constitutes its channel of distribution. It is the route taken by the title to a product in its passage from its first owner, the agricultural producer, or a manufacturer, as the case may be, to the last owner, the ultimate consumer or the business user."[3]

Thus, the distribution channel is *the movement of goods and services between point of production and the point of consumption through organisations that perform a variety of marketing activities. The major participants* in the distribution channel are: producers, intermediaries, and consumers. The producers produce the food and services needed by the consumers or industrial users. The intermediaries direct the products and service to consumers. The consumers are the ultimate link in the channel for whom

---

1. American Management Association, *Marketing Definition: A Glossary of Marketing Terms*, New York, 1960, p. 10.
2. Cundiff, E.W., and Still, R.S., *Basic Marketing: Concepts, Decisions and Strategies*, 1972, pp. 273-274.
3. Beckman, T.N., Maynard, H.M. and Davidson, W.R., *Principles of Marketing*, 1957, p. 7.

goods are produced, and who purchase them. Each of these three participants has a stake in the distribution channel and contributes to its operation.

OBJECTIVES OF CHANNEL OF DISTRIBUTION

In any developing economy there is an increasing emphasis on specialisation and the division of labour. Thus, a gap gets developed between producers and users. The primary purpose of a distributive channel is to bridge this gap by resolving spatial (geographical distance) and temporal (relating to time) discrepancies in supply and demand. It involves following activities:

1. Transfer of title to the goods involved.
2. Physical movement from the point of production to the point of consumption.
3. Storage.
4. Communication of the information concerning the availability characteristics and price of the goods in transit, inventory and on purchase.

The importance of these functions depends upon the nature of goods themselves. Activities of distribution channel involve price fixation, routinisation of decisions, managing finances, promotional activities, aiding communications, minimising total transaction and serving the consumer.

MIDDLEMEN INTERMEDIARIES

A channel of distribution includes the original producer, the final buyer and any middlemen—either wholesaler or retailer. The term middlemen refers to those institutions or individuals which take title to the goods to negotiate or sell in the capacity of an agent or broker. From the marketing point of view the middlemen and intermediaries are divided into merchant middlemen, and agent middlemen. Merchant middlemen take a title and later effect sales on their own accord. Agent middlemen do not take title to goods. They simply get an order from the buyers and pass it on to the producer and seller. The middlemen on the basis of their position also classified into wholesalers and retailers in the channel of distribution. Wholesalers are closer to the manufacturers while retailers have a close touch with customers.

Kinds of Middlemen

1. Agents: These are middlemen who do not take any title to goods but take active part in the marketing mechanism rendering all services required.

2. Brokers: These are agents who have no direct and physical control of the goods in which they deal. They represent either the buyer or the seller in negotiating purchases and sales for their principals.

3. Dealers: These are persons who buy or resell products at either retail or wholesale basis.

4. Distributors: It is a general term used to mean wholesalers.

5. Jobbers: In certain trades and localities these are designated as special types of wholesalers. They are usually found in stock markets.

6. Rack Jobbers: The rack jobber, usually but not always, puts his merchandise in the store of the retailer on consignment. Rack jobbers are most common in the food business. It is a wholesaling business unit that markets specialised lines of merchandise to certain types of retail stores and also provides special services such as arrangements, maintenance and stocking of products in display racks.

7. Resident Buyer: It is an agent or a person who specialises in buying on a fee or commission basis chiefly for retailers

8. Retailers: These merchants are occasional agents whose business is selling directly to the ultimate consumer.

9. Wholesaler: It is business unit which buys and resells merchandise to retailers and other merchants and/or to industrial, institutional and commercial users but which does not sell insignificant amounts to ultimate consumers. Generally, wholesalers render a wide variety of services to their customers.

10. Commission Houses: Also referred as commission merchants or commission agents, these usually exercise physical control over the goods and negotiate the sale of the goods they handle. The commission house usually enjoys more powers over the prices, methods and terms of sales than the brokers though they are bound to obey instructions, issued by the principal. They generally arrange delivery, extend necessary credit, collect the sale price, deduct their fees or commission and remit the balance to the principal.

11. Consumer Cooperative: It is a retail business, owned and operated by ultimated consumers, to purchase and distribute goods and services primarily to the members. Such societies are generally referred to as purchase cooperative and registered under the Cooperative Societies. Act of the land.

12. Industrial Store: It is retail store owned and operated by a company to sell primarily to its employees. Non-governmental establishments are often referred to as "Company Stores'.

FUNCTIONS OF CHANNELS OF DISTRIBUTION

1. Help in Production: The producer can concentrate on the production leaving the marketing problem to middlemen who specialise in the profession. Their services can be best utilised for selling the product. The finance, required for organising marketing could profitably be used in production where the rate of return would be greater.

2. Matching Demand and Supply: The intermediaries assemble the goods from many producers in such a manner that a customer could effect purchases with ease. According to Alderson, 'The goal of marketing is the matching of segments of supply and demand." The matching process is undertaken by performing the following functions:

(*i*) *Contractual Function*: Finding out buyers and sellers.

(*ii*) *Merchandising Function*: Producing goods that will satisfy market requirements.

(*iii*) *Pricing*: Process of attaching value to the product in monetary terms.

(*iv*) *Propaganda Function*: Sales promotion activities.

(*v*) *Physical distribution*: Distribution activities.

(*vi*) *Termination*: Settlement of contract, *i.e.*, paying the value and receiving the goods.

3. Financing the Producer: Middlemen collect huge orders and purchase products in bulk from the manufacturers in cash. It enables the producers to undertake large-scale production and adopting better techniques of production because they have no problem for finance. Sometimes manufacturers and producers appoint stockists and distributors and collect deposits from them as security. In this way, finance problem is solved by the channels of distribution.

4. Aid in Communication: The middlemen are connection link between the producers and the buyers. Middlemen have complete knowledge of consumer's behaviour and the market. They communicate the necessary information to the producer so that they may produce according to the needs of the consumers.

5. Stabilising the Prices: The middlemen help to stabilise the price by stocking goods and assuring constant flow of goods to the market. They make the goods available at a place where they are wanting and at proper time. They create place, time and possession utilities to the products and maintain the prices.

6. Promotional Activities: Middlemen perform various promotional activities like advertising, personal selling and sales promotion. Sometimes a wholesaler does it alone for the producer. Retailer also performs such activities by displaying the product in his window which attract the customers.

7. Routinisation of Decisions: Middlemen rountinise the sale of the producer. Once the route for reaching the goods is fixed, the problem for selling the product is automatically solved. It reduces the cost of distribution as well.

8. Help in Pricing: In pricing a product, the producer invites suggestions from the middlemen who are very close to the ultimate users and know what they can for the product. Pricing may be different for different markets or products depending upon the channel of distribution.

9. Forecasting: They help forecasting the demand.

10. Source of Market Research: They are source for information at the time of market research.

KINDS OF CHANNELS OF DISTRIBUTION

Channels of Distribution for Consumer Goods

1. Distribution through an agency: It stands between the manufacturer and the wholesaler. In this channel there are the export merchants. The manufacturer use this channel when he cannot afford to invest the amount required to develop a sales force of his own.

2. Selling to wholesalers who sell to retailers: Traditionally, the wholesaler buys the large quantities from the producer and sells it to a number of retail buyers. The wholesaler is always a merchant middleman who tries to sell for more than he pays. The difference is called the margin, mark-up or gross profit. The defect of the system is that the manufacturer loses contact with retail dealers. It the wholesaler has various products of different manufacturers to sell he might be unable to push up the sales of a particular producer.

3. Selling direct to retailers or dealers: Here the manufacturer assumes the functions of the brokers and wholesalers. It requires an efficient sales force to eliminate wholesalers from the channel of distribution.

After the creation of super markets and departmental stores, this channel is currently receiving increased attention.

Limitations

(*i*) It is viable only when the manufacturer has resources to take up the marketing functions.

(*ii*) It requires large-scale production.

(*iii*) There should be full line goods.

(*iv*) The product should be generally bought by the customers in large quantities.

(*v*) The demand for goods must be constant.

4. Selling direct to customers: It is most common in industrial marketing where capital goods are marketed. Direct sale is undertaken in the case of agricultural commodities especially in the case of small production. In consumer goods, certain manufacturers sell directly to the consumers through multiplication stores.

A manufacturer must constantly review his channel policies as the conditions are constantly changing and never static. This marketing policy can never be permanent.

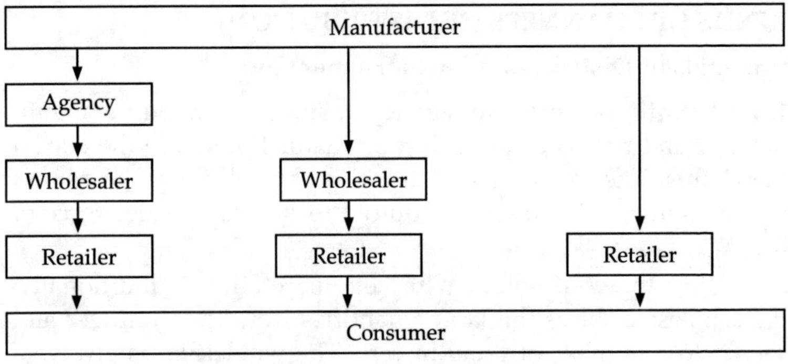

Channels of Distribution of Consumer Goods.

These four channels only suggest possibilities. There are many more possible variations which should not be seen as competitive channels. Each should be considered a separate possible channel to reach particular target market. The channel system must deliver the goods and provide all the functions of marketing.

B. Channels of Distribution for Agricultural Products

A characteristic feature of the distribution of agricultural products is the presence of a large number of brokers and agents who stand at par with the retailers in the consumer goods channel and perform a number of functions of their own. They sometimes act as assemblers and sell to wholesaler instead of selling the products to ultimate consumers. The direct sale is only very meagre. The presence and involvement of the cooperative societies in the channel is peculiar to agricultural products. These channels are not at all permanent. They may vary from product to product and even from one season to another. For example, the channel for paddy has no resemblance to the channel for cotton or jute.

C. Channels of Distribution for Industrial Products

As the industrial goods have more or less fixed pattern, their channels are also less complicated. Major channels recognised in industrial market are the following:

1. Producer-industrial user: It is the most commonly used channel in the distribution of industrial goods. Manufacturers of machinery prefer to adopt this channel to avoid unnecessary expenditure on transport,, insurance, etc.

2. Product-industrial distributor users: It is used in the distribution of accessory equipment which are required by users. The user cannot always approach the manufactures for their requirements. Therefore, industrial distributors arranged on an area-wise basis become available.

3. Producer-agent user: Small sized manufacturers who do not have their own marketing departments find it convenient to have agents at different selling points. This arrangement is suitable for introducing new products.

4. Producer-agent-industrial distributor user: It is a combination of the above two channels adopted to suit varying conditions on the basis of geographical factors.

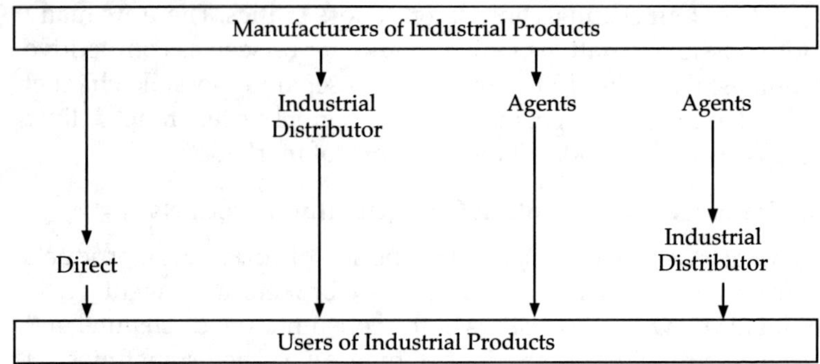

Fig. 20.1: Distribution Channel of Industrial Products

FACTORS AFFECTING THE CHOICE OF CHANNEL OF DISTRIBUTION

Such factors may be classified as factors relating to: (1) Product characteristics, (2) Market factors, (3) Company characteristics, (4) Middlemen considerations, and (5) Environments factors.

1. Product Characteristics

These product characteristics are as follows:

(*i*) *Purchase Frequency*: The more frequently purchases are made, the more feasible it is for a manufacturer to use direct distribution. It requires extensive distribution which involves a financial consideration.

(*ii*) *Perishability*: Perishable and fashionable products such as dairy and bakery products, fruits and vegetables or sea foods must be placed in the hands of the final users after its production. These require more direct marketing due to the dangers associated with repeated handling and delays.

(iii) Weight and Technicality: Products that are bulky, large in size, and technically complicated are usually sold directly by the company to other consumers because of the difficulty of finding middlemen for these lines.

(iv) Selling Price Per Unit: If selling price per unit is low, the channel of distribution may be long as in case of cigarettes and watches, if selling price is more the channel is more direct as in case of television and radio.

(v) Standardised Products or Ordered Products: In standardised product each unit is similar in colour, weight size, quality, etc. These have indirect or lengthy channel of distribution. If products are not standardised and are produced on order, they have direct selling.

The product characteristics conducive to short channels are: (*i*) heterogenous units, (*ii*) heavy weight, (*iii*) large size, (*iv*) perishable, and (*v*) technically complicated. Long channels are indicated in cases where the products are: (*i*) homogeneous, (*ii*) light weight, (*iii*) small size, (*iv*) non-perishable, and (*v*) technically simple.

2. Market Factors or Consumer Factors

(*i*) *Consumer or Industrial Market*: The producer of consumer product may choose a long channel involving wholesalers and retailers depending upon the nature of product. In case of industrial product the channel is comparatively short because retailer's services are not required in such cases.

(ii) Number of Purchasers: If the number of consumers is large, the channel may be indirect and services of wholesalers and retailers become necessary. If customers are few, direct sale can be entertained through representatives.

(*iii*) *Geographical Distribution*: If customers are geographically dispersed, the channel may be long. If they are concentrated, the direct selling may be done.

(iv) Size of Orders: If customers purchase small quantities frequently and regularly, lengthier marketing channels are indicated. If the order from the consumer is large, the channel may be shorter.

(v) Customer's Buying Habits: If customers expect credit facilities, desire to purchase all necessaries at one place or desire for the personal services of the salesmen, the channel may be lengthier or shorter depending upon the capacity of providing those facilities and meeting out the needs of the customers. If producer can afford those facilities, the channel will be shorter otherwise lengthier.

3. Company or Enterprise Factors

The choice of channel is also influenced by company characteristics such as its financial position, size, product mix, morale of its employees, past channel experience and executive prejudices and overall marketing policies.

(*i*) *Financial Resources*: The financial strength of the company determines which marketing tasks it can handle efficiently and which ones are to be delegated to the middlemen. A company having good financial resources may engage itself in direct marketing in profitable manner. A weak financial position may force a company to use financially strong intermediaries even if this is not profitable.

(*ii*) *Size of the Company*: A large company already handling a wide line of products is in a good position to take an additional product of the same line and handle it the same way, usually directly. A smaller firm or one with narrower lines, would find middlemen more practical.

(*iii*) *Product Mix*: A fresh expansion of plant capacity may require more aggressive channels. If the product mix of a company is wider, it can deal with its customers directly. Consistency in the company's product mix ensures homogeneity of its marketing channel.

(*iv*) *Attitude of Company Executives*: The attitude of company executives may also influence the channel selection. Their experience of working with certain type of middlemen may tend to develop channel preferences or prejudices.

(*v*) *Marketing Policies*: The company marketing policies such as speedy delivery, after-sale services, heavy advertising, uniform-retail price also influence the decision of channel. If it believes that the intermediaries can provide the services to customers according to company marketing policies, it can delegate its selling activity to middlemen, otherwise, it may engage itself in direct selling.

4. Middlemen Considerations

(*i*) *Services Provided*: If middlemen can provide the services to the customers which the company requires to provide, the middlemen can be appointed otherwise company will sell the product direct to the consumers.

(*ii*) *Attitude*: If some middlemen desire to fix their own price for the product and if the company agrees to allow them to do so, they can very happily agree to sell the products of the company. On the other hand, if the company likes to follow the Resale Price Maintenance policy, the choice is limited.

(*iii*) *Availability*: If the company is a late entrant in the field and its competitors have already tied up, the middleman is a necessary part of a selective or exclusive distribution policy. Aggressive market oriented middlemen are usually not available. In such cases, the firm manages its own channel.

(*iv*) *Sale Volume Potential*: A channel's sales volume potentials may be estimated through special marketing surveys. Suitable adjustments for the strengths and weaknesses of competition should also be made. However, there may be no single channel capable of releasing the targeted sales potential. Two or more may be required and accordingly estimates will have to be used for the different channel combinations.

(*v*) *Cost of Channel Usage*: These channels should be chosen which ensure efficient distribution at least expenses and which secure the desired volume of sales. However, from the consumer's point of view, the justification for the intermediaries is that they make it easy for him to buy.

5. Environmental Factors

(*i*) *Economic Conditions:* When economic conditions are depressed the producers choose shorter channels to cut costs. If there is multipoint tax on sales, the line should be shorter to avoid the tax burden of the consumers and they prefer to sell directly to the retailers or consumers.

(*ii*) *Legal Restrictions*: If there is any legal restriction on any selling activity, the producer will be restricted to do so. For example, under MRTP Act, any practice which may have the effect of unreasonably preventing or lessening competition in the supply of goods or services is not permissible. So, also is resale price maintenance. In case of controlled items the channel should be strictly according to the government policy.

CRITERIA OF EFFECTIVENESS OF CHANNEL'S DISTRIBUTION

1. Economic Criteria: The economic criteria are the most important for evaluating the effectiveness of channels of distribution since the film pursues the profits. From economic point of view, three factors are to be considered:

(*i*) *Estimate of Sales Volume*: What would be the sale volume under each of the channel alternatives? Would a channel be able to push up the sale of the company? This can be judged by having a market survey of the sale volume of different channels of distribution and the sale can be estimated under each alternative.

(*ii*) *Estimate of the Selling and Distribution Costs of Each Alternatives*: For this purpose it would be considered whether the costs of a particular alternative are reasonable and within the capacity of the company considering its sale volume and the financial resources.

(*iii*) *Comparison of the Sales and the Costs of Different Alternatives*: This is for having a comparative view of cost-effect on the net profit of the firm. Company's own sale force should also be taken in view and should decide whether there should be its own sales force or it should use the sales agency.

In comparing the estimated net profits available from each alternative, cost associated with different sales levels should also be considered. For this purpose, the total costs should be splitted into fixed costs and variable costs. Smaller firms having low sales volume or larger firms marketing in smaller territories would have larger fixed selling and distribution costs if it decides to instal its direct channel so in such circumstances, services of middlemen should be sought. On the other hand, for larger firms or smaller firms when their costs for using their own sales force and using other agency reach at break even point, it would be better to have its own sale force.

2. Control Criteria: How would the marketer be in a position to have a control over a particular channel? The more control, the better is the channel of distribution. For this purpose one should consider the relationship between various channels of distribution, their interests and attitude towards company's product and conflicts among them. Legal aspect should also be considered in appointing a particular channel.

3. Adaptive Criteria: This is to see whether the channel would be suitable to adapt the changing conditions in future. Each channel alternative involving a long commitment must appear to be greatly superior on economic or control grounds in order to be considered but it is not valid on the ground of adaptability.

METHODS OF DETERMINATION OF MARKETING CHANNELS

1. Adjustment to Buyers' Needs and Expectations: Producers determining the market channels adjust to buyer's wants and expectations. In case of the consumer goods marketing, the final buyers are ultimate consumers and they buy from those retailers who best serve their needs.

2. Determining the Best Channel Alternatives: The best channel involves:

(*i*) Recognising what best means.

(*ii*) Comparing various alternatives in terms of this meaning.

Best means most profitable sales volume and cost. The producer must have long-run estimates of market potential. He should be free to choose single channel or a number of channels. The ultimate test of a policy must be the effectiveness and economy of serving the customer.

3. Distribution Intensity: (*i*) *Intensive Distribution:* Under this method the management seeks to use as many channels as possible. It is referred to as maximum expansion. It is adopted in the case of convenience goods such as cigarettes, sweets, etc.

(*ii*) *Selective Distribution*: Under this policy a manufacturer selects a limited number of wholesale or retail distributors and works closely with them to further the sale of his products. It requires considerable planning and thorough knowledge of the market. Selective distribution can be used on any type of product. There are certain distinctive advantages of the policy. The manufacturer can pick the best outlets he wants.

Selective distribution is suitable in the case of shopping goods which carry a higher unit price and which are not purchased as frequently as convenience goods. Goods which require after sales service are often sold through selective distribution outlet such as television.

(*iii*) *Exclusive Distribution*: It refers to the practice of selecting and giving a distributor exclusive area of sale called 'Territory'. The distributor agrees not to handle or deal in any competing product. It gives some sort of prestige to the product as having an exclusive dealer. The exclusive dealer is protected from competitors in the area allotted.

(*iv*) *Consignment Selling*: It is a method of placing goods in the hands of middlemen with the title and control remaining in the hands of the seller. The distributors are neither wholesalers nor retailers but occupy only the position of agents. They usually get a commission on the sales effected together with charges incurred thereon. The manufacturer specifies the manner, time and price of sale. This system distributor runs no risk of buying and being struck with goods. He need not invest any money. The manufacturer can retain all his control over his merchandise even when it lies in the distributor's hands. This kind of distribution is not very commonly found now-a-days.

(*v*) *Franchise Selling*: This method is typically American. In it the manufacturer arranges distribution with some individual outlets providing the usually called cost-plus method required machinery for selling. This method is necessary when the owners of outlets lack capital and knowledge of marketing the products. The parent company provides loans, designs for building, training for both the owner and his staff.

QUESTIONS FOR EXERCISE

1. Discuss the various approaches to the selection of elements of distribution.
2. Explain channels of distribution, which may be made available by the manufacturers of consumer goods in India.
3. What do you mean by channels of distribution? Explain the various kinds of channels of distribution and their functions.
4. Write a brief note on the factors you consider important for selecting suitable channels of distribution for consumer goods.
5. Discuss in detail the various factors influencing the choice of channels of distribution.
6. The producer does not always enjoy complete freedom in selecting marketing channels.
7. Explain different methods for evaluating the effectiveness of channels of distribution.
8. How can you say that a particular channel of distribution is more beneficial among the available alternatives?
9. What are various problems involved in initial determination of marketing channels?

21

Physical Distribution

Physical distribution is the handling and moving of raw materials and finished products from producer to consumer. It has been used synonymously with logistics, the branch of military science concerned with procuring, maintaining and transporting equipment and facilities, etc. Physical distribution creates 'time' and 'place' utility, which maximises the value of products "by delivering them to the right customer at the right time and place." Its objective is to "put the product within an arm's length of desire," by administering its physical flow from the organisation to the customers at the time and place where they want them at a reasonable cost.

Definition of Physical Distribution

1. *D. J. Bowersex and Others*: "A term employed in manufacturing and commerce to describe the broad range of activities concerned with efficient movement of finished products from the end of production line to the consumer."[1] Thus, physical distribution refers to the physical flow of the product from producers to consumers. A related term 'physical distribution management' consists of the design and administration of systems to control the flow of products.[2]
2. *Wendell M. Stewert*: "Physical distribution is the science of business logistics whereby the proper amount of the right kind of product is made available at the place where demand for it exists. Viewed in this light, physical distribution is the key link between manufacturing and demand creation."

1. Bowersex, Donald J., Bernard, J. Lalonde, and Edward, W. Symkay, *Readings in Physical Distribution Management,* Logistics of Marketing, Macmillan Co. New York, 1969, p. x.
2. *Ibid.*

Physical distribution is a two dimensional process. It involves the flow of information from the individual consumer or organiser to the producer and the flow of materials from the producer to the consumer or the user. Retailers and wholesalers are usually involved in both these dimensions which are inter-related, though information flow generally triggers the material flow into motion.

Objectives of Physical Distribution

1. To move products: The principal broad objective of physical distribution is to move products to other channel members and to consumers in an efficient way consistent with the level of service that customers require. Efficiency and satisfactory service are key goals of physical distribution, although there might be some conflict with each other.

2. To provide better customer service: This is done improving the physical distribution system. The firm's promotional efforts are strengthened so that better sales result.

3. To increase sales: This is done by ensuring that basic products in regular demand are always available, and having contingency plans for quick order processing of items, so that the product is not out of supply even in the slack or off season.

4. To reduce cost: This is done by intelligently managing the physical distribution system and determining the optimum number and location of warehouses, improving materials handling, increasing stock turnover, using sealed containers to ship products, correcting inefficient procedures in order processing, and moving offices, plants, retail outlets to low cost locations.

5. To establish differential advantage over rivals: This is done by performing customer sendees more effectively—such as arranging for rapid and reliable delivery, avoiding errors in order processing, and delivering undamaged goods.

6. Developing communication system: It permits salesmen to transmit orders on a daily basis capable of accurately responding to customer inquiries on order status within shortest possible time.

According to W.M. Stewart, the achievement of above levels, needs consideration of certain key variables: (*i*) the *order cycle time, i.e.,* the period between placement of an order and receipt of goods; (*ii*) *inventory control,* the reliability of inventory service in maintaining items in stock and making them available for dispatch; and (*iii*) *order processing practices, i.e.*, the specific privileges of customers in placing orders.[1]

The achievement of service levels requires performance of a number of inter-related organisational activities, as depicted in the diagram 21.1 after Wendell M. Stewart,

CAUSES OF LOSSES FROM INEFFECTIVE PHYSICAL DISTRIBUTION

Schwartz has shown that if physical distribution is not properly managed, following direct and indirect losses result to the firm.[2]

1. Too Long Storage: Goods kept in storage for too long incur unnecessary costs in (*i*) obsolescence and deterioration, (*ii*) taxes, (*iii*) lost use of money tied up in inventory, (*iv*) theft, (*v*) insurance, and (*vi*) costs of space storage facilities unsuited to product and inappropriate location of warehouses are other important potential losses.

2. Improper Materials Handling: It results in damaged merchandise, "losing" products by placing them in "wrong" location in the warehouse, and excessive product damage.

3. Ineffective Inventory Management: It results in: (*i*) inaccurate records of what products in what location, quantity, and condition are available and (*ii*) too much or too little merchandise being available in relation to demand.

4. Ineffective Order Processing: It may resuslt in: (*i*) taking too long to fill, (*ii*) being shipped to the wrong customers, (*iii*) being inaccurately filled, and (*iv*) not being billed properly.

5. Malperformance of Transportation: It results in: (*i*) shipment of products to the wrong location, (*ii*) selection of modes or combination of modes, (*iii*) excessive time used to deliver products, and (*iv*) damage of products in transit.

COMPONENTS OF PHYSICAL DISTRIBUTION

The physical distribution system includes: warehousing, traffic and physical handling, order processing, transportation, inventory

---

1. Stewart, Wendell, "Physical Distribution," in Victor P. Buell (Ed.), *Handbook of Modern Marketing*. McGraw Hill Book Co., New York, 1970, p. 74.
2. Schwartz. J.C., *op. cit.*, p. 410.

control and information monitoring."[1] These elements are inter-related and interact with one another to provide consumers at a reasonable cost, the goods they desire at the time and at the place where they want them.

1. Warehousing: Warehousing is the holding and housing of goods between the time they are produced until their sale. It includes at activities taking place from the time the goods arrive at the warehouse until they are released to the customers. Warehousing is made up of two primary activities: (*i*) storage, and (*ii*) breaking bulk.

(*i*) *Storage*: It gives dimension to the market for a product. While transportation and communication define the length and breadth of the market area, storage and give depth to the market. Storage invests goods with time and place utility as determined by the warehouse locations.[2]

Functions of Storage

Storage of products is necessary due to irregular and untimely production and consumption. Besides acting as a buffer between regular demand and irregular production, it provides following benefits:

(1) Protection of physical characteristics of the goods.

(2) Facility to the consumer for the articles required throughout the year though there is a vast difference between its production and consumption timings:

(3) Storage of the commodities for preserving maturity or to enable the product to ripen.

(4) Storage of goods which improved in quality and fetch better prices with passage of time like wine, liquor, rice, gur, honey, pickle, vinegar, etc.

(5) Storage of grape fruits, mangoes, bananas and sweet potatoes prove better if kept for reasonable length of tune.

(6) Aid to financing the business because necessary loans can be raised on the collateral security of these goods stored.

(7) Adjustment of demand and supply.

---

1. Magee, John F., *Physical Distribution Systems,* Tata McGraw-Hill Publishing Co. Ltd , New Delhi, 1980 Ed., p. 2.
2. Duddy, E.A., and Rezvan. D.A., *Marketing: An Institutional Approch.* 1954, p. 62.

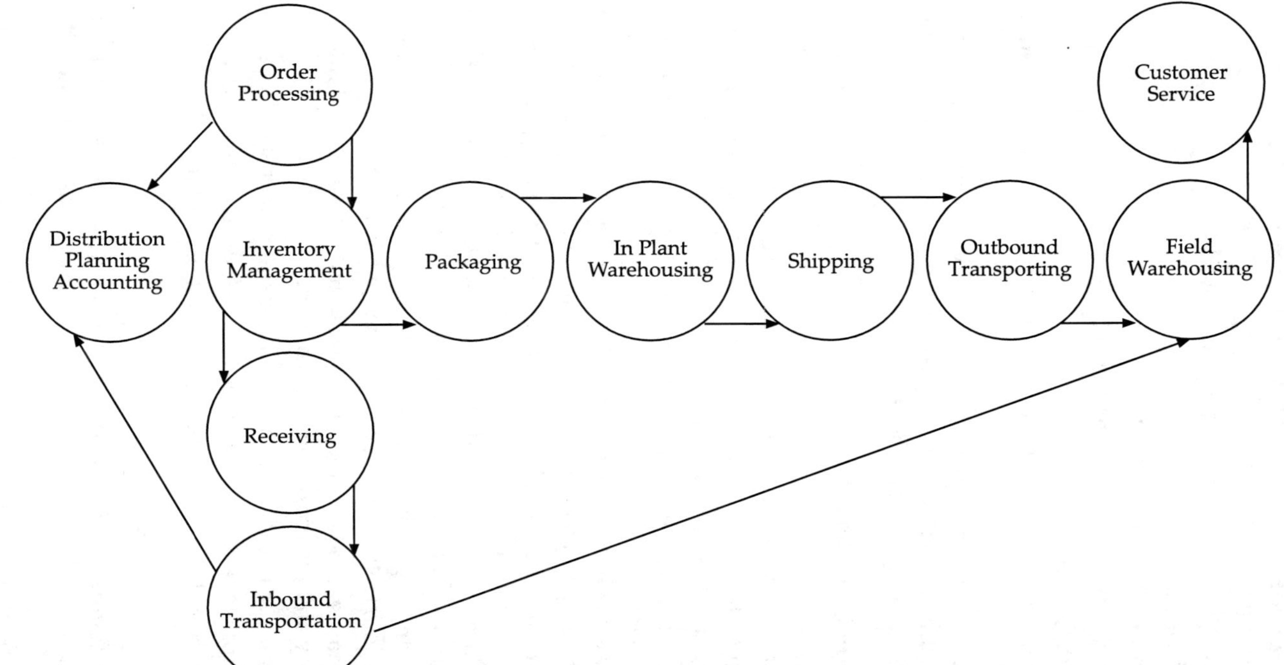

Fig. 21.1: Relationship among Physical Distribution Activities. (After Wendell M. Stewert)
(*"Physical Distribution: A key to Improved Volume and Profit," Journal of Marketing, January 1965, p. 66*)

(8) Smoothing out of irregularities in production.

(9) Creation of new wealth.

(10) Promotion of regular employment of labour.

(11) Stabilisation of prices.

(12) Promotion of orderly marketing.

(13) Lengthening of marketing period.

(14) Shifting of risks.

(15) Furnishing of physical support to speculative and competitive industry.

Thus, the storage provides time utility. It corrects the time maladjustment resulting from goods being produced at one time or season and used at another time.[1]

Necessary Consideration

The marketing management should take following issues into consideration while deciding about storage of product:

1. The inventory should be managed in such a way as to minimise spoilage, damage or obsolescence.
2. The level of inventory should be optimal. If inventory is too low, customers may be unable to get goods when they want them and will buy elsewhere. If inventory is too large, not only is excessive capital tied up but stocks may deteriorate before they are sold.
3. The inventory should be appropriately situated geographically. Should a firm, for example, maintain one large warehouse to serve a large area, or would it be better, all factors considered, to maintain small branch warehouses in strategic market areas?
4. The firm may maintain its own warehousing facilities, or may use public warehouses whichever is more advantageous.
5. The management should know at all times the exact volume of inventory and the condition of each item.
6. The most efficient materials handling equipment should be.
7. The storage facilities should be right for the merchandise.
8. The goods should be moved in and out of storage easily.

Computation of Storage Costs

(1) The Capital invested in the goods: If the goods stored are purchased with borrowed capital, interest cost has to be paid. If it

1. Pyle, *Marketing Principles*, p. 96.

is done with the firm's own fund the cost is in the form of income lost by not using it in some other way.

(2) Warehousing expenses: It includes cost of storage space, handling and transfer costs, administration costs, and other direct and indirect expenses of operating a physical facility.

(3) Taxes.

(4) Insurance, for covering damages or losses.

(5) The risk of product obsolescence or deterioration.

Impact of Storage on Prices, Storage of product helps in the adjustment of supplies and thus exerts an influence in stabilising prices throughout the year. When surplus supplies are kept off, the market prices are maintained during the period of abundance. Consumers pay less when the stored products are sold during the period of scarcity.[1] As perishable goods merchandise cannot be stored for longer periods huge supplies are available at the time of production. This creates a glut in the market resulting in low prices. Prices tend to rise at the time of natural scarcity. Towards the end of the storage season prices rise and fall again when natural or fresh supplies are in abundance. But the extremes of fluctuations are less pronounced due to storage in periods of abundance when prices are low, and sale in the periods of scarcity when prices are high.[2] Risk of preserving goods is based on the assumption of making profit by future sales.

Transmitting large lots to markets—moving goods from the factory to warehouses located near consumers—and breaking these down into individual orders for consumers is known as Breaking Bulk. Transport Carriers such as trucks and railways charge lower per unit rates for larger than for small packets. It permits efficient distribution.

WAREHOUSING

Classification of Warehouses

Warehouses may be classified on the basis of: (A) the commodity stored, and (B) the ownership.

---

1. Schwartz. David J., *Marketing Today: A Basic Approach,* 1977, pp. 412-413.
2. Clark and Clark, *Principle of Marketing,* 1947, p. 471; Daddy and Rezvan *op. cit.* p. 76.

(A) *On the Basis of Commodity Stored*

1. Special commodity warehouses: Cotton warehouses, grain warehouses, potato warehouses, etc. provide storage for owners and perform specialised services essential in the marketing of these commodities.

2. Public warehouses: These provide tanks for storage of hulk liquids as oils, molassess and liquid chemicals, etc.

3. Cold storage warehouses: These provide facilities for commodities that are perishable (fruits, vegetables, fish, meat, eggs and milk) and which needs refrigeration before being sold or used.

4. Public merchandise warehouses: Manufacturers or shippers, receivers and distributors use these the storage of finished goods and raw materials or semi-manufactured goods until they are required by retailers, distributors, industrial consumers or household consumers.

(B) *On the Basis of Ownership.*

1. Private Warehouses: These are the warehouses where the goods of an individual only are stored and operated by himself. They are generally used by retail dealers. They may or may not be separate or an independent building situated near the main market. Manufacturers generally own their private warehouses so as to store raw materials till they are needed for further transmission to factory or mill. Wholesalers have their own warehouses to store the goods ordered and received.

2. Co-operative Warehouses: It is a combined effort of two or more private parties to store goods at a central place. It is not so commonly found. Its difficulties are:[1] (*i*) it requires lumpsum to build, equip and maintain the warehouse; (*ii*) considerable time necessarily elapses from the beginning of the plan until the house is ready for occupying; and (*iii*) sufficient loyalty and cooperation do not exist.

3. Household Warehouses: It is a temporary storage used for the safety of furniture, rugs, furs, paintings, tapestry, etc. which may be spoiled by dust, rust, rats, mice or from other miscellaneous causes. The reasons of its development are "high rentals incidental to growth of cities, separation of families through divorce, breaking up of homes after death, the increase of the habit of

1. Harring, H.A., *Advertising and Selling*, Vol. XIV, No. 7, pp. 17–18.

travel, the man who would rather board than keep house and uncertainty of future plans or various reasons."[1]

4. Bonded Warehouses: These are the licensed warehouses which accept imported goods for storage till payment of duty is made. Their proprietors are bound for the safe keeping of goods. The importer is allowed to a privilege of putting goods under the custody of a Revenue Officer on payment of storage charges and the duty when goods are finally removed for consumption. He may take delivery of the goods without paying the duty, provided he does so for the purpose of re-export. Goods are placed continuously under guard. The owner of goods stored in bonded warehouses may perform such functions as are necessary to maintain the physical characteristics of goods, *e.g.*, bottling and vatting in case of wine and spirits may be done.

5. Public Warehouses: These are the places of storage for the general public where a variety of merchandise are stored, These are held for public utilities. The rates of rent are usually fixed by the states in which they exist. Some of them specialise to store only one commodity. These have been their utmost development in U.S.A., *e.g.*, Baltimore has several warehouses which store only canned goods; Michigan and California warehouses are specially built for beans and seeds; Whichta and Oklahoma cities specialise in storing principally broom corn; Sac and Ida countries of Iowa are dotted with popcorn storages; New York has its kraut houses; everywhere are found warehouses for flour sacked feed while in certain cities 'cellarages' have been constructed, for storing in damp and cool places syrups and molasses in tight cooperage barrels.[2]

Advantages of Public Warehouses

1. Low Cost and Low Facilities: Public warehouses enable many manufacturers to avoid cost of having local sales representatives. They furnish the warehouseman with a credit list of their local and out-of-station customers to be served from stock. The warehouseman accepts orders and reports to the manufacturers for billing. This cuts down on sales expenses and saves time. The warehouseman issues receipts for the goods received. These can be used as collateral for loans. When goods are placed in a

1. *Ibid.*, p. 121.
2. *Ibid.*, p. 132.

warehouse they are available for loans not possible while they are still a part of owner's general assets.[1]

2. Modern Equipments: Public warehouses are generally constructed on modern lines and are fire-resistant and equipped with sprinkler system which together with other facilities, tend to lower risks, reduce accidents by fire or theft.

3. Low Insurance Rates: Insurance rates of merchandise are low in public warehouses because the risk of fire is lessened due to their fire-proof construction, etc.

4. Railroad Sidings: They are invariably provided with their own railroad sidings which is not always possible for private warehouses.

5. No Building Expenses: Users of public warehouses are relieved from the expense and trouble of erecting and maintaining their own warehousing buildings or of leasing buildings owned by others.

6. Limited Expenses: The users of the public warehouse need to pay only for the space actually used and for periods when such space is not needed.

7. Skilled Staff: Public warehouses make available to users the co-operation of skilled accountants, correspondence clerks, freight tariff experts and packers. They are familiar with every physical detail of warehousing and with the effects of local ordinances, insurance laws and tax rulings upon stored property.

Factors Determining

Rates of Public Warehouses. (1) Value, (2) Fragility, (3) Liability, (4) Small volume, (5) Possible damage to other goods, (6) Protection against freezing, (7) Isolation. (8) Attractive to vermin, (9) Hazardous, (10) Malodorous, (11) Dusty, (12) Mussy, (13) Requires access to examination or treatment, (14) Lost space in piling, (15) Illegibility of marks.

Warehouse Receipt: Licensed warehouses issue receipt only when the goods for which it is issued are physically placed in the store and surrendered to the warehouseman before taking delivery from storage. This receipt contains the following information:

(*i*) The licence number of warehousemen.

(*ii*) The name location of the warehouse.

---

1. Frederick, G.H., *Increasing Your Sales*, pp. 12-18.

(*iii*) The name and address of the licensee.

(*iv*) The fact whether the receipt is negotiable or not.

(*v*) Name and addresss of the man from whom goods have been received for storage.

(*vi*) Whether the commodity is issued, if so upto what extent.

(*vii*) Period for which goods are accepted.

(*viii*) Trade mark, weight, quality, measurement (if so) and condition of the goods.

(*ix*) Whether the classification is made by any registered weigher, inspector, or any other man lincensed under law to do so.

(*x*) The amount charged by the warehouseman.

(*xi*) Date on which receipt is issued.

(*xii*) Signature of the warehouseman or his authorised agent.

(*xiii*) Whether the warehouseman is interested in the articles stored and if so the extent of his interest.

Location of Warehouses

Goods must be stored in a warehouse in such a way as to serve the best purpose of producer, manufacturer, distributing agencies and the consumers, (*i*) *Private warehouses* should be located near the factory of the source of supply. In case of the wholesalers and retailers they are generally on their business premises or form a part of their shops, (*ii*) *Public warehouses* are located in the distributing centres of the country or in the port towns, (*iii*) *Custodian warehouses* are found on the premises of the owner and are, therefore, decentralised, (*iv*) *Household warehouses* are in the cities where their services are required, (*v*) *Custom bonded warehouses* are usually situated at custom outposts or near docks and internal revenue bonded warehouses are situated at or near strategic points of production. Location of the store depends on the nature of the goods stored. Storage for fruits and vegetables should be on the terminal markets near consuming centres.

TRAFFIC AND PHYSICAL HANDLING

The term "traffic" refers to those activities which involve the movement of goods between transportation carriers such as trucks, railway wagons, etc. on the one hand and manufacturing facilities and warehouses on the other.

After the goods have arrived at the warehouse, they are identified, assigned appropriate storage areas, and moved to those areas. This process of movement can be either manual by coolies or mechanical by conveyor belts, overhead cranes, forklift equipment, and even tractors, etc. After the goods have been moved, they are brought together into a central point and prepared for despatch wrapped, boxed, or baled or put into special purpose containers, etc.

Material-handling decisions and costs are inter-related with other decisions and costs. Improved material handling cuts the cost of handling goods. It also provides the relative effectiveness of transportation and storage, besides making for more effective utilisation of storage space and a reduction of investment in facilities, as it makes possible, "Ceiling high" stocking of goods: By speeding up the processing of orders through computerisation and movements of shipments, improved material handling also contributes to improved customer service.

Therefore, the marketer should give due consideration to these following issues: (*i*) how can the product change to minimised in warehouses, in distribution centres, and while the goods are in transit? (*ii*) what kinds of equipments are needed to help move goods inside warehouses and to transportation modes in the most efficient manner and with the least damage? (*iii*) How can it be made certain that products are shipped in the most efficient manner? (*iv*) Can containerisation (use of sealed containers for sizing) and palletisation (use of pallets for handling materials) be used more effectively?

ORDER PROCESSING

It is undertaking the processes that are needed to make orders processed quickly, accurately and efficiently. It includes receiving, filling and assembling orders for execution. By placing an order, customers set in motion a flow of products and information that is known as the *order cycle.* The seller receives an order, assembles the goods and despatches them off to the buyer.

The methods used by a marketing organisation for processing customer's orders affect its service to them in terms of re-order time and consistency of delivery time. Variations in these two time variables exert influence upon the buyers' profits by changing their minimum investments in inventory, altering their ordering costs, and changing the probability that they will be out of stock. Due to these considerations, buyers tend to shift their orders to suppliers who provide better order processing service. The marketing manager should remember how best to process the orders so that the customers could be retained and repeat orders received. Rapid order processing may enable the organisation to attain economies in other physical distribution areas, as and when it makes a reduction in inventories possible or the use of a low-priced but relatively slow means of transport.

TRANSPORTATION

An essential element of physical distribution transportation consists of moving products from the plant or warehouse of the seller to the receiving facilities of the buyer. The main parties in transportation are carriers and shippers.

1. Carriers: These are companies whose primary objective is to bring transportation services to others. Thus, the Indian Railway, Indian Airlines, or Indian Shipping Company are all carriers.

2. Shippers: These are those orgnisations and individuals for whom the carriers provide transportation services.

Transportation regulatory bodies in India:

1. *The Civil Aviation Department G.O.I.*—for air carriers.

2. *The Shipping Corporation of India*—for ocean-going and coastal water carriers.

3. *The Oil and Natural Gas Commission*—for transporting crude and refined petroleum through pipelines.

4. *The Road Transport Corporation of the States*—for motor-trucks.

Types of Carriers

1. Common or Public Carriers: These include all railroads, petroleum pipelines, airlines, trucks, and the country boats. These have to obtain a permission from the appropriate authority. They provide service between designated points on a fixed schedule. They are not allowed to change operating routes or schedule without permission of the regulatory authority. They cannot refuse to transport goods of any organisation, unless it violates carriers rules. Rate fixing and rate changes on the part of common carriers subject to the approval of the appropriate regulatory authority.

2. Contract Carriers: These do business on more selective basis. The regulations for them are less vigorous. They must obtain permission certificates to operate. They are not required to maintain fixed routes and schedules. They can refuse the business of any organisation. They make contracts with particular organisation to move goods from one point to another.

3. Exempt Carriers: These transport a wide range of goods that are largely exempt from economic regulation.

4. Private Carriers: These own their own facilities such as a fleet of trucks they get permit to operate throughout the country but have to follow regulations regarding safety.

Modes of Transportation

Major modes of transportation are rail, air, motor-trucks and water carriers. These are generally used for long-distance movement of goods. Motor-tracks are principally used for shorter distances. Most firms use a variety of transportation modes. Raw materials such as wood, minerals, coal, grains, etc. are moved by a combination of railroad or water or transport carriers. Finished goods are transported by trucks or by rail. Small shipments of perishable goods are transported by truck, air or even postal service. The method chosen depends upon distribution patterns as illustrated in the tablc 21.1. Before adopting any general rules of thumb each company considers the nature of its product. For instance, petroleum and natural gas can be transported from the oilfield to the refinery via pipeline; while books, newspapers and magazines are always sent by post, if of small weight, otherwise by rail or truck.

Table 21.1: Transport Needs Suggest Transportation Modes

Need	Pattern	Probable Mode
1. Production Scheduling	Plant to plant	Rail or Truck
2. Replenishing Stock	Plant to warehouse	Rail or Truck
3. Balancing Stock	Warehouse to warehouse	Truck
4. Service	Warehouse to Customer	Truck
5. Emergency	Plant to Customer	Air

Source: Smykay, Edward, W., *Physical Distribution Management*, Macmillan Co., New York, 1973, p. 196.

1. Railroads: The main carriers of goods, these are specially suited for handling heavy bulky items, over long distances at low costs.

Grain, coal, wool, stones, sand, etc. are transported by railroads at a relatively low cost. However, rail transportation is slower than motor-truck or air traffic and goods are sometimes damaged while in transit.

2. Trucks: Being flexible, fast and dependable they are useful for transporting all sorts of packaged goods and general merchandise. They are suitable for moving a large volume of goods at short distances. These trucks can travel on a wide variety of roads to almost all directions. Trucks can pick up goods at the producers godowns and deliver them directly to customers without unnecessary interchanges.

3. Airlines: As air transportation is the most expensive mode of transportation, it is mostly used for (*i*) goods of high unit value, (*ii*) perishable goods, and (*iii*) emergency shipments to fill important orders that could not be filled out of inventory.

4. Water Transporters: Country boats and small steamers ply on inland navigable rivers, while large cargo ships or tankers are used on ocean highways. This mode is very low cost but slow moving and, therefore, usually heavy and bulky items such as coal, cement, petroleum, foodgrains, etc. are carried by water carriers.

5. Pipelines: These are specialised carriers that transport crude and refined petroleum and natural gas, from the wells to the refineries and from there to the distribution centres. This mode is relatively inexpensive as it involves a minimum of handling and labour costs.

Table 21.2 provides a summary of advantages and disadvantages of various modes. The importance of each mode is, by the particular benefits desired by individual users decided.

Table 21.2: Relative Advantages and Disadvantages of the Various Transportation Modes

Mode	Cost	Damage in transit	Speed	Reliable delivery	Specialised facilities	Ability to reach inaccessible areas
1. Railroad	Superior	Inferior	Inferior	Inferior	Average	Inferior
2. Motor-trucks	Average	Average	Average	Average	Average	Superior
3. Air	Inferior	Superior	Superior	Average	Superior	Superior
4. Water	Superior	Inferior	Inferior	Inferior	Average	Inferior
5. Pipeline	Superior	Superior	Average	Superior	Superior	Inferior

Source: Symkay, Donald J. Bowersex, and Brank Mossman, *Physical Distribution Management: Logistic Problems of the Firm*, 1961, pp. 47-49.

(The terms "Superior," "average" and "inferior" indicate the standing of each mode relative to that of other modes).

Coordinated Transport

Due to the rising cost of fuel, different modes of transportation are now being increasingly combined so that transport could be cheap and distribution efficient.

The most commonly used system of coordinated system is the *"piggyback:'* or the *tailor on flat car* (TOFC). It involves picking up the goods by truck, driving them to train, removing the truck's trailer and placing it on a flat-car for a long distance haul by train, and at the destination, re-attaching the trailer to a truck which makes the final delivery. Other systems include *fishy back,* which combines boat and truck services in the same way as piggyback combines train and truck services. Exchange of goods containers between air and truck carriers is referred to as *airtruck* or *birdyback.*

Questions to be Decided by Marketing Manager. The marketing manager has to decide as to (*i*) What mode or combination of modes of transportation (rail, truck, pipeline, waterways or air) should be used to transport products to warehouses and from there to customers?

Should the transport equipment be owned or leased? (iii) How can transportation cost be reduced and the desired levels of customer sendee still maintained?

INVENTORY CONTROL

Inventories are reservoir of goods held in anticipation of sales. Goods available for sale received at irregular intervals is added to this reservoir. Out of this sales are made, which may also fluctuate considerably. Therefore, the quality held does not remain same. In deciding inventory size, one must decide what should be the maximum and minimum quality that may be needed at any time. This requires sales and cost considerations.

In maintaining any inventory the main objective is to meet market demands, *i.e.,* to make sales and fulfil customers' orders. Therefore, inventories are kept in anticipation of market demand based on the sales forecasts. Management keeps two other considerations in mind:

(*i*) How much inventory would be probably needed to fulfil the near demand;

(*ii*) What is the ability of the distribution system to get the needed inventory in time.

Three types of costs are associated with inventory:

(*i*) *Holding costs:* These include warehousing and storage charges, costs of capital tied up in inventory, costs of adverse price movements, obsolescence, spoilage pilferages, and taxes and insurance on inventory.

(*ii*) *Costs of shortages:* These include special clerical administrative, and handling costs; losses of specific sales, of goodwill, and even of some customers.

(*iii*) *Costs of replenishing inventory:* Inventory decisions should seek to balance the above three costs. While holding costs rise as inventory increases, the cost of other two decreases. Holding, shortage and replenishment costs are all related to inventory size. Total costs are a function of amount store. A correct estimate of inventory costs is necessary to hold inventory and cost level down to a minimum. It helps the marketer in terms of its cash flow and also in terms of its ability to maintain production at a consistent level.

INFORMATION MONITORING

Persons handling physical distribution, need to constantly keep themselves alert and up-to-date on inventory, transportation, warehousing, and other aspects of physical distribution. In the flow of information among producers, intermediaries and customers. Tags on inventory; computers, memory systems, display equipment and other communication technology can be of great help.

UTILITY OF PHYSICAL DISTRIBUTION SYSTEM

1. Control on Distribution Cost: A detailed analysis of transportation and storage costs is made in view of controlling or minimising the distribution cost under an efficient system of physical distribution. It aims at reducing the sale price to the consumers. Hence, stress is laid on improvement in packaging, control over channels of distribution, simplification of distribution system and technical improvements.

2. Increase in Sales Volume: Physical distribution seeks to increase sales volume by inventory control. It reduces the quantity of stock held by the consumer as he is assured of regular supply. On the other hand, a concern can produce more with the same amount of finance because of low inventory and reduction in distribution cost.

3. Coordination of Demand and Supply: Physical distribution facilitates the coordination between demand and supply. Two main factors are involved in the process, *i.e.*, time factor and place factor.

The industries producing articles having seasonal demands such as woollens or fans produce throughout the year only because modern storage facilities are available and are supplied in the sufficient quantity in the season. On the other hand, where production is seasonal as in case of sugar or wheat, storage facilities play a dominant role in order to maintain their supply throughout the year.

As quick and modern transportation system makes it possible to transport even the perishable goods to the consumer places in no time, all the commodities are available in all seasons throughout the year. Sea foods are made fresh available even at distant places due to efficient transport system.

Thus, an efficient physical distribution system establishes equilibrium between demand and supply at reasonable rates.

4. Stabilisation of Prices: Control over supply position helps in stabilising the prices in the market. If demand exceeds at any time the supply available in the market, additional supplies can be released from the warehouses. On the other hand, if supply position improves, the production may be kept in storage in order to arrest the fall in prices. Transportation system also helps to maintain the price level. The supply can be transported from the place of abundance to the place of shortage which equalises the prices of two places.

5. Help in Product Planning: Activities of physical distribution affect the product planning. Transportation and storage facilities—their type, nature and place—are considered vigorously while taking a decision regarding size, wieght, packing, price, etc.

6. Help in Deciding Channel of Distribution: Physical distribution system affects the decision on channels of distribution.

If the product requires storage, it should be sold out through wholesalers who own their own godowns or storing facilities. If a company decides to manage its warehouses, it should decide the points where to establish them and what type of transport facility should be arranged to carry the goods to the warehouses of its own or of middlemen. These factors are important while taking the decision on channel of distribution.

7. Help in Deciding Size of Inventory: If transport facilities are good, the size of inventory may be kept at low level because goods can be purchased as and when it is required. Storage and transport facilities are short, heavy stock of raw materials shall be preserved to maintain continuous flow of production.

Thus, the development of physical distribution facilities has made the production possible throughout the year at lower cost of production and distribution.

DECISION AREAS IN THE MANAGEMENT OF PHYSICAL DISTRIBUTION

Decisions in following areas are taken in order to acheive the various objectives and advantages of physical distribution.

1. Size of Inventory: Inventories are reservoirs of goods held in anticipation of sales, *i.e.*, of filling demands along the marketing channels. Incoming quantities of product or completed stock production increase the inventory and outgoing quantities of product or sale reduce it. Thus, the inventory fluctuates with every unit of production or purchase and of sale. The fluctuation in inventory is always on with every change in rates and quantities of input and output. Hence, in deciding on inventory size, the management must determine both maximum and minimum allowable extreme limits. This involves two main considerations: (*i*) Sales considerations, and (*ii*) Cost considerations.

(*i*) *Sales Considerations*: The inventory management aims at meeting the market demand, to make sales and to file the customers' orders. As inventories are kept in anticipation of demand, the upper and lower limits should be set on the basis of sales forecasts. The more accurate the sales forecasts, the greater the opportunity is for gain from economical inventory levels. In this regard the two following additional factors need attention:

(*a*) *Management's concept of acceptable level of customers service*: The proportion of orders of the customers that the ready stock can satisfy without delay has a definite bearing on the upper inventory limit.

(*b*) *Distribution System responsiveness*: Distributors should be able to communicate their needs to the producer and get needed inventory into the field. The amount of management responsiveness determines how quickly the firm can adjust inventory to demand changes. This responsiveness influences the lower limit of the inventory.

(*ii*) *Cost Considerations:* Following three mams types of costs are related to the inventory:

(*a*) *Holding Costs*: These include warehousing and storage charges, cost of capital blocked in inventory, cost of adverse price movement, obsolescence, spoilage, pilferage and taxes and insurance on inventory.

(*b*) *Costs of Shortages*: These include special clerical, administrative and handling costs, losses of specific sales, of goodwill and even of some customers.

(*c*) *Costs of Replenishing Inventory*: These differ in composition depending upon whether a business does its own manufacturing. These include labour and machine set up costs, cost of materials used during set up testing, cost of production, time lost during set up, clerical and administrative costs, transportation and unloading, placement in warehouses and performing necessary related activities, etc.

Inventory decisions should seek to balance all the above mentioned three types of costs. The holding costs bear a direct relation to the size of inventory.

The costs of shortages and replenishment have negative correlation with the size of inventory. Thus, all the three costs are related to inventory size.

2. **Storage and Inventory Locations:** The next area of decision regarding physical distribution is the decision on storage and inventory location. It closely relates to the decision on inventory size. Reduction in the size ot inventory will require less storage space. Marketers use following four important storage decisions:

(*i*) Geographic deployment of inventory.

(*ii*) Comparison of inventory concentration and dispersion.

(*iii*) Ownership of warehouse facilities.

(*iv*) Number and location of warehouses.

(*i*) *Geographical Development of Inventory*: Following are the three decision alternatives on geographical deployment of inventory:

(*a*) Concentration at or near the plant or at some other control location.

(*b*) Dispersion at several distribution points located in or closer on the main markets.

(*c*) Concentration of substantial inventory at a few distribution centres and redistribution to a large number of distribution points dispersed throughout the market.

Among these, while the first two alternatives are opposite extremes the third one is a compromise between them.

(*ii*) *Comparison of Inventory Concentration and Dispersion*: It reveals opposite sets of strengths and weaknesses. The firm which concentrates its inventories can minimise the number of customers' orders unfilled because of stock outs. On the other hand, it may increase the transportation costs and delay customer services. If it decides to disperse its inventories it may reduce its total inventory investment and use sub-inventories to be sold in a particular market. This reduces total transportation charges and speeds up customer services. As dispersion decision needs a larger enough reserve stock maintenance at each branch each marketer should combine these two alternatives.

(*iii*) *Inventory Dispersion and Warehouse Ownership*: If the manufacturer decides for the dispersion of inventories, he may choose between manitaining its warehouses or using public warehouses. The choice depends upon the various factors, such as the amount of sales originating in a particular market, fixed and variable warehousing costs, degree of flexibility, relative warehousing efficiency and the market channels. These factors are inter-related to each other. The manufacturer should prefer owned warehouses if the volume of goods moved is substantial with little seasonal fluctuations.

As the public warehouses charge on the basis of time taken and space occupied, these can be preferred only when less goods are handled or large volume of goods is handled through seasons.

(*iv*) *Number and Location of Warehouses*: The decision about the number and location of warehouses is influenced by several important variables such as customers' buying patterns and delivery expectations, freight rate structure, transport service available, warehousing costs, location of factories, production capacities, product mix, suitable renting of warehousing in different localities, etc.

3. Modes of Transportation: Decision on modes of transportation largely depends upon the size of inventories and the location of the storage both of which are inter-related because economy in transportation charges may increase the storage cost or *vice versa*, the overall cost of physical distribution and not only the cost of one aspect should be borne in mind.

With the increase in transportation services the manufacturer should take a decision about the mode of transportation, such as road, rail, air or sea, taking into account their comparative freights and other related costs. Cost and time factors should be considered well before deciding the mode of transportation.

4. Material Handling: Among the areas of physical distribution material handling decisions have experienced the greatest change and improvement in efficiency. Two major changes which took place in this area are (*i*) elimination of man-handling, and (*ii*) Containerisation.

(*i*) *Elimination of man-handling:* The first improvement was the replacement of man-handling by machine handling though it is still used in retail or final buyer stage. Improved conveyer systems and left equipments has changed to total mechanisation.

(*ii*) *Containerisation:* Containerisation is a method by which a large number of units of a product are combined into a single compact unit for storage and transportation. It reduces material handling cost and time spent. Use of improved handling equipments and containerisation will increase the efficiency and reduce the wastage and costs. It will make possible best utilisation of space in storage.

5. Order-Size: Orders of quantities less than a container will increase the cost of handling because the handling process will be done entirely by hand instead of machines. It will increase costs and consume more time. Less than container size orders increase the costs of storage and inventory control and add to their complexity. They also affect the cost of transportation because transportation charges are lower for bulk quantity. Hence, the management must make order size decisions concerning minimum order sizes, units in increment in order sizes, and preferred order sizes.

6. Order Processing: The methods of processing customers' orders affects a concern's service to them in two ways:

(*i*) Recorder time is affected, and

(*ii*) Consistency of Delivery time is affected.

Variations in these two variables affect the profits of the buyers through changing their required investment in inventory, their ordering costs and the probability that they will be out of stock. Therefore, the buyers tend to shift their orders to other suppliers providing better processing services.

APPLICATION OF OPERATIONS RESEARCH (OR)

Physical distribution decisions involve an attempt to optimise several variables. Business community today uses new approaches like mathematical stimulation; linear programming, heuristic programming and integer programming, etc.

1. Mathematical Stimulation: By mathematical stimulation the whole physical distribution system can be managed through computers. Various schemes of management can be tested for improvement in distribution methods or lowering of distribution costs. The management after comparing such stimulation on the alternatives selects that which fulfils the need. These can be tested on warehouse for shipping arrangements. Though these stimulations can schedule the shipments, it may not prove to be in favour.

2. Linear Programming: Transportation is used in planning shipment from one destination to the other for minimising the total shipping costs through linear programming. These destinations include factory, warehouse, distribution centre, store or customer. It is to decide which warehouse will supply to which customer for minimising costs. Cut and dry method was applied before transportation technique.

The simplest method to find solutions to multidimensional problems includes various time periods, different products and one or more intermediate storage points in the distribution system.

3. Heuristic Programming: It is used to reduce problem solving effort. A particular problem to be solved is a collection or combination of sets of instructions making possible computerised solutions to problems. Heuristic programming finds out a way to solve a complex problem in physical distribution with less computational effort.

4. Integer Programming: The optimal solution giving 'whole numbers' determines the optimum solutions from among considerable large number of alternatives than with linear programming and without excessive time and effort. Recently several companies have used this method.

QUESTIONS FOR EXERCISE

1. What do you understand by Physical Distribution? Disucss its utility in the business world?
2. Explain the decision areas in the management of Physical Distribution.
3. Describe the various applications of operations research to Physical Distribution Problems.

22

The Wholesaler

Definition of Wholesaler

1. *Cundiff and Still*: "Wholesalers buy and resale merchandise to retailers and other merchants and to industrial, institutional and commercial users, but do not sell insignificant amounts to ultimate consumers."

2. *Morris E. Hurley*: "Wholesalers are marketing middlemen who occupy a position midway between retailer and the producer or manufacturer."

3. *William J. Stanton*: "Wholesaling or wholesale trade includes the sale and all activities directly incidental to the sale of products or services to those who are buying for the purpose of resale or business use."

On the basis of above definitions we may conclude that the wholesaler is a person who invariably buys in large quantities and sells them to the retailers for resale or to industrial and commercial consumers with a view to earn profits. However, the wholesaler may be identified on the basis of the purpose of sale or the nature of purchaser and not on the basis of quantities sold. Thus, wholesaling is not necessarily the work of wholesale middlemen alone. The manufacturers who sell directly to retailers or to other manufacturers are also involved in wholesaling. If in a transaction the buyer is buying for purposes of resale, or to further his business operations, the seller in that same transactions is engaged in wholesaling.

CHARACTERISTICS OF WHOLESALERS

1. Direct Large Buying: Wholesalers generally buy merchandise direct from the producers in large quantities mainly in cash.

2. Sale Through Agents: Wholesalers are trading concerns having an army of agents and stock the large quantities of goods, supply or sell goods to the retailers directly or through their agents in small quantities.

3. Good Financial Position: Generally, wholesalers possess good financial health. They purchase goods in cash from the manufacturers and sell to the retailers on credit.

4. Small Profit Margin: Wholesalers' profit margin is very small so that they maximise their sale-volume to earn maximum profit.

5. Limited Product Margin: Wholesalers deal in limited, generally in one or two products or product-line. More often they deal in products of one manufacturer.

6. Warehouses: Wholesalers maintain warehouses and godowns at different places in the country to facilitate the trade at minimum transportation charges.

7. Grading: Wholesalers sometimes make grading of the goods under their own name or brand.

CLASSIFICATION OF WHOLESALERS

According to T.M. Beckman, "Wholesaling includes all marketing transactions in which purchases are intended for resale or are used in marketing other products".[1] The wholesaling functions include assembling of merchandise, breaking bulk, storage, selling, and delivery, etc. These functions are all parts of wholesaling whether they are performed by a manufacturer, a wholesaler or a retailer.

Bases of Classification of Wholesalers

1. On the basis of the area served.
2. On the basis of commodities they deal.
3. On the basis of functions performed.
4. On the basis of breadth of their line product.

1. On the Basis of Area Covered

(*i*) *Local wholesalers*: Those who deliver their purchases to the local retailers and specialise in the distribution of nationally advertised goods and unbranded products.

(*ii*) *Provincial or state wholesalers*: Those who sell to the retailers of a particular district or state.

1. Beckman, T.N., *Wholesaling*, p. 30.

(*iii*) *National wholesalers*: Those who are located at strategic places and from there distribute goods all over the country. National wholesalers often serve as local and state distributors as well. They distribute a general line of merchandise in a narrow territory close to headquarters. They push a wide line of private brands over serveral states. They sell a narrow line of specialities over the entire country.

2. On the Basis of the Commodities They Deal

This is the most common grouping of wholesale concerns. Its examples are tinned provisions, agricultural produce, cloth, automatic spare parts, and radio dealers, etc. According to Haltizclaw, Three distinct grounds can be adopted to classify their jurisdiction on any particular basis: (*i*) the way in which certain goods are distributed; (*ii*) the sources of supply; (*iii*) the utilisation of the commodity by those who purchase it from the wholesale establishment.[1] For example, primarily on the basis of utilisation of the commodity by those who purchase it. Fruits and vegetables are classified under food products.

3. On the Basis of Functions Performed

(*i*) *Full function wholesalers*: They perform many functions for their customers. When they perform a full range of wholesaling functions, they are termed as "service wholesalers" also called a *full-function wholesalers, distributor, industrial distributor* or *rack jobber*, depending upon the usage in his line of business. They may handle consumer and/or industrial projects—manufactured or non-manufactured and imported or exported. They carry complete stock of the firms they represent, handle delivery of goods and offer credit. Some even offer personal sales and assist in their clients merchandising operations.

There are three types of full function wholesalers: (*i*) Merchant wholesalers, (*ii*) Converters, and *(iii)* Industrial distributors.

(*a*) *Merchant Wholesalers*: They are more numerous. They account for greater sales. They normally perform more of the eight marketing functions than do any of the other five general types of wholesalers. The wholesalers in any town include grocery wholesalers, the grain and drug wholesalers, etc. Merchant wholesalers buy and sell goods in their own name, operate warehouses for storage, normally carry rather complete stocks in lines they handle, offer

1. Haltzclaw, *Principles of Marketing*, 1936, pp. 142-143.

credit, solicit business on telephone or through salesmen who call their customers' establishments, delivery orders and sometimes extend marketing or administrative assistance to their customers.

(*b*) *Converters*: They operate both as manufacturers and wholesalers in the textile, paper and other industries. In the textile trade they purchase cloth in the grey, perform such processing functions as bleaching, dyeing, printing, mercerising and preshrinking and sell the finished cloth to large retailers, wholesalers or garment manufacturers. A converter's production operations are relatively simple. His primary service is that of selling. He selects the colours, styles and patterns for the finishing of the cloth. His success depends upon predicting accurately what the market desires. Such wholesalers are more common in America and very few in India.

(*c*) *Industrial Distributors*: These are full function wholesalers who sell wide lines of industrial products to industrial consumers. The many types of industrial distributors include such firms as mill supply houses, beauty shops supply houses, supply and machinery' distributors, hotel and restaurant, supply firms and oil-drilling equipment dealers. Many of the customers of mill supply house are small manufacturing concerns of many kinds which need such products as hand-tools, cleaning materials, abrasures, hardware, semi-processed parts, metal cutting files, portable electric tools, paint products and various maintenance supplies. Like service wholesalers of consumer goods in many respects industrial distributors practise widespread buying operations, maintain large stock of merchandise to which they take title, use salesmen to canvass their territories and offer such services as credit and delivery to their customers. They normally sell not to retailers for resale but to industrial consumers for use in their own operations.

Majority of the goods produced for distribution by manufacturers reaches the consumer through either of the wholesale channels.

(*ii*) *Limited Function Wholesalers*: Limited Function Wholesalers are wholesalers who perform only a few of the functions normally assoicated with wholesaling operations. Their main types are:

(*a*) *Truck wholesalers*: Those who combine selling, delivery, and collection in one operation. They carry a limited range of stock, such as advertised goods, short-term products and items that need special handling like bakery products. They mainly call on retailers, and deal mostly in perishable and semi-perishable goods.

(*b*) *Cash-and-carry wholesalers*: They generally deliver orders, grant credit to retailers, allow them to pay at later dates. They require retailers to come to the wholesale warehouse, "pick" their own orders, pay cash for what they buy, and carry away their own purchases. They provide retailers services who handle food staples and other last moving goods.

(*c*) *Drop-shipment wholesalers*: They do not physically handle the goods they sell but leave the storage and transportation functions to the manufacturer whom they represent. When goods are ordered, the manufacturer despatches them directly to the retailer, but the bills are made in the name of these wholesalers, which they ultimately recover from the retailer. They are much used in industrial marketing and for goods which bear high transportation charges.

(*d*) *Rack jobbers*: They are wholesalers who market specialised lines of products, such as toiletries, and housewares to grocery retailers and super markets and also provide certain special services. Merchandise is generally supplied on consignment basis.

4. On the Basis of Breadth of their Line Product

These are general types of wholesalers on the basis of breadth of line product: (*i*) general merchandise, (*ii*) general line, and (*iii*) speciality wholesalers.

(*i*) *General merchandise wholesalers*: These sell a number of unrelated or loosely related lines of merchandise of such types as hardware, furniture, household appliances, farm goods and even food products. Their customers are general stores. While they are relatively unimportant in the total wholesaling picture, they do enable small retailers to concentrate their buying with one wholesaler.

(*ii*) *General line wholesalers*: They offer complete stocks in one major line and sell such products as groceries, drugs, dry goods, electrical appliances, hardware, or jewellery, soaps, detergents school supplies, etc.

(*iii*) *Speciality wholesalers*: These are those who handle only specialised goods, such as canned foods, coffee, tea, spices, dairy products, soft drinks. They also perform such functions as promotional activities as erecting special displays, handling demonstations and distributing samples.

WHOLESALERS AGENT

Agents are business units which negotiate purchases or sales or both on behalf of their principals who may be buyers or sellers or both but do not take title to the goods in which they deal.

Common Characteristics of Agents

(*i*) They serve more for industrial users.

(*ii*) They are usually compensated by a percentage commission based on the volume of sales or purchase they negotiate.

(*iii*) They either act as substitute for a manufacturer's sales force or serve as an addition to it so that the manufacturer has the advantage of selling in markets even beyond the limits of his salesmen.

(*iv*) Although most of them work for a seller, they often act in the best interests of the buyer.

While wholesalers, agents are active in many lines of trade, individual agents customarily concentrate on such lines as foodgrain, machinery or textiles. The main types. of wholesalers agents are brokers, commission agents, manufacturers' agents, selling agents and resident buyers. Less important types of agent middlemen are auctioneers, import agents, export agents, warehousers and underwriters, etc.

1. Broker: A broker is an agent whose business is to negotiate and make contracts for the sale or purchase of goods, without physically handling the goods involved. He is generally the agent of the owner of goods seeking a buyer than the agent of a buyer seeking for the sources of supply. His main service is to bring buyers and sellers together. He has also no authority to set prices. Within a given field he is expected to have an extensive knowledge of supply, demand and prospective customers. He negotiates a sale and leaves it up to the seller to accept or reject the buyer's offer. He does not have the direct physical control over the goods, but sells by description or sample. Whenever he arranges a sale, the seller despatches the goods directly to the buyer. He receives his commission from the principal for whom he works. He also furnishes his clients with useful market information about prices, prospective buyers, credit conditions, competing products, inventory positions and the general market conditions.

Broker's services are utilised by producers who sell their products at infrequent intervals and find it costly to establish their own sales force. With completion of a particular transaction the services of the broker come to an end but they may be used again when needed by the producers. Broker receives a fee or commission from his principal, but never from both the buyer and seller in the same transaction.

2. Commission Agents: A commission agent also known as commission merchant or commission house is a middleman who usually exercises physical control over and negotiates the sale of the goods he handles. He acts on behalf of the principal to sell or buy goods at the best possible terms and conditions. He enjoys wide powers about prices, methods and terms of sale although he is required to carry out the instructions issued by his principal. The title to goods never passes to him. He sells in his own name, prepares bills, extends necessary credit, makes collections, deducts his fees and intimates the balances to the principal. Thus, he does not take title. He performs functions very similar to those of service merchant wholesalers. His services are generally used in the marketing of agricultural products such as fresh fruits, vegetables and grains.

3. *Del Credere* Agent: He is a particular type of agent employed for the sale of merchandise. He charges an extra remuneration *(del credere),* over and above the usual one, for which he gives an undertaking to his principal that the parties brought by him for contractual relations will faithfully perform their promises.

4. Manufacturer's Agents: A manufacturer's agent is employed by a manufacturer to sell part or all of the producer's products in a given area/territory. He normally: (*i*) uses sales techniques of his own design, (*ii*) selects the accounts he will cultivate within his territory, (*iii*) works when he chooses, (*iv*) maps out his own itinerary, (*v*) may employ sales representatives who work for him and who do not have direct contact with the manufacturer, (*vi*) has an extended contractual relationship with his principal; (*vii*) handles not competing but related lines of products; (*viii*) handles sales for his principal within an exclusive territory; and (*ix*) possesses authority with regard to prices and terms of sales for these are established by the manufacturer. Generally, he arranges for despatches of goods to be sent directly from the factory to the buyer. As his main function is selling, he has to maintain a large sales staff to cover his market. He receives commission for his services, on the basis of the sales made.

According to J.C. Schwartz, manufacturer's agents are used extensively where one or a combination of the following conditions prevail: (*a*) when a small manufacturer has a geographically widespread market; (*b*) when experienced and knowledgeable representation is needed; (*c*) when a product is new and demand is uncertain; (*d*) when the market is too wide to justify a company sales force; and (*e*) when it is convenient for managerial and administrative reasons.[1] Such agents are used extensively in the distribution of many types of consumer and industrial products. In marketing of industrial goods, they employ the services of the technical personnel, while in consumer goods marketing, they themselves call on retailers. As they have intimate contact with the market, they also supply useful information about variety, design, style and price of the goods to the manufacturers.

5. Selling Agents: A selling agent is an independent middleman who operates on an extended contractual basis. He negotiates all sales of a specified line of merchandise or entire output of his principal and usually has full authority and control over prices, terms and conditions of sale.

Selling agent differs from the manufacturer's agent because (*i*) he is ordinarily not confined to operating within a restricted territory; (*ii*) he has much control over authority to set prices and terms of sale, (*iii*) he is the sole selling agent for the line he represents, (*iv*) He frequently supplies financial aid to manufacturers, (*v*) His services are often used in the marketing of textiles, food products and to some extent coal, timber, metal products.

6. Resident buyers: A resident buyer is an independent agent specialising in buying for principals who are mostly retailers. Resident buyer operates mostly in lines of trade such as furniture and readymade garments. He helps the retailers to get the desired products. He receives his remuneration on a fee or commission basis.

---

1. Schwartz, Joseph C, *Marketing Today: A Basic Approach*, 1977, p. 285.

7. Auctioneers or Auction Companies: These are usually appointed by sellers and occasionally by both buyers and sellers. They may sell "with reserve," or "without reserve." In case of "without reserve" they sell the goods to the highest bidder. They are particularly employed by agricultural or livestock producers, used car dealers, and art dealers and wool, cotton, tobacco merchants. They provide services like a location for bidding auctioneers and temporary storage. Their overhead is generally low, as their facilities are quite functional. They charge commission for their services from the sellers.

8. Packing and Forwarding Agents: They are employed to collect, deliver and forward goods on behalf of others. Manufacturers who feel the necessity of relieving themselves from the trouble of collecting, delivering and forwarding goods to proper destinations, utilise the sendees of these people. Their expert nature and promptness is highly appreciated. Compared to other agents their remuneration is very meagre.

9. Warehouses: Warehousers are independent middlemen who receive goods from or on behalf of the principals for the purpose of storing, for which they receive remuneration. They take all possible care and exercise diligence to preserve the goods entrusted to them.

10. Export-Import Agents, Brokers and Commission Agents: They operate in leading port cities. They serve the needs of principals seeking foreign markets or overseas supply. Their greatest economic contribution lies in arranging the financing of purchases.

11. Purchasing Agents: They are independent middlemen who specialise in locating sources of supply for buyers of industrial goods,

12. Factors: A factor is a person who is appointed to sell goods. He is entrusted with the possession of goods which he is to sell. He has an implied authority to act in his own name. He uses his own name on any contract made by him. He allows credit as per the usage or customs of trade. He exercises his intelligence as to when and where to sell and how his principal can be benefitted. He enjoys the authority to receive payment and gives a valid discharge to the buyer for any goods sold by him.

Often the wholesalers have been categorised as: (*i*) *Independent wholesalers* who operate on their own ownership. They include *merchant wholesalers,* who take title to the goods they distribute, and *agent wholesalers* who do not. About these we have discussed above. And (*ii*) the *captive wholesalers,* who are owned by a producer or a retailer.

1. *Producer-owned Wholesalers* are established by the producer in the form of their own sales office and branches, which perform wholesale functions and help distribution of goods directly to retailers and users. They often do business in drugs, medicines, chemicals, metals, books, etc.

Sales offices are often maintained in cities with large population where the producers do not have a central office or plant. When these offices make sale, the products/goods are dispatched from the nearest production plant, company warehouse or a merchant wholesaler.

Sales Branches are opened as various places to sell producer's goods. These carry limited stock. They generally handle installation, maintenance and service work—especially concerning electrical goods industrial machinery, automobiles, and chemical substances.

2. *Retailer-owned Wholesalers* operate in the form of chain-store warehousing operations, retail co-operative stores, purchasing offices and auxiliary offices that usually handle research and development, testing, and receiving and despatching. They do not perform retailing or warehousing functions.

ORGANISATION OF WHOLESALE BUSINESS

The most important thing in the organisation of a wholesale business is the distribution of the work amongst the different members of the staff. One should avoid overlapping and consequent friction between them. Each member is made responsible for the work entrusted to him. A wholesale business has generally two departments, namely, Administrative and Executive. While the *administrative department* deals with finance, accounts, correspondence and general administration, the *executive department* deals with buying, selling, packing, publicity, warehousing and despatch of merchandise.

1. Administrative Department: An administrative department of a wholesale business takes care of finance and capital requirements at the time of starting the business. In a registered company, the legal provisions in this respect have to be followed. Capital

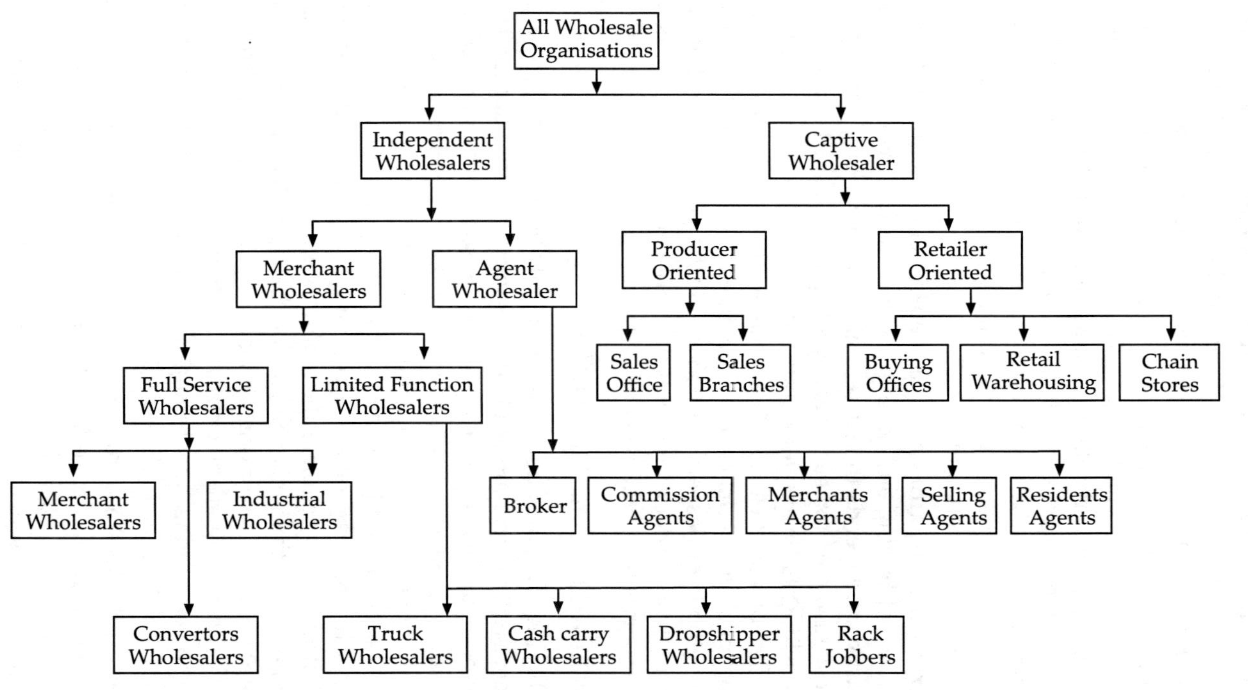

Fig. 22.1: Classification of Wholesaling Types

required in consideration of the nature and size of the business must be secured beforehand. There should be a fair distribution of work amongst the various departments of the business.

Administrative department also looks after the accounts and correspondence of the business. The finance section is in touch with the buying and selling organisation so that the use of the capital of the business may be according to the requirements of the latter. A wholesale business requires huge capital to carry a large stock to give long credits to the retailers or to finance the manufacturers of small means.

2. Executive Department: This department is entrusted with the work of buying and selling. On the efficient working of the department depends the success of the undertaking. Ordinarily there is a buyer for each variety of goods stocked. In smaller establishments one buyer is put incharge of purchase of goods of different varieties. The despatch section is attached to this department. A special officer acquainted with rules of transport and methods of despatch of goods is incharge of this section on whose efficiency depends success of the business. This department also supervises warehousing and advertisement sections.

DISTRIBUTION OF FUNCTIONS

1. Buying Organisation: The General Manager directs and supervises the operations of the buyers who are supposed to be experts in their lines. They select the sources of supplies for the stock. Their decision about these sources depends on the consideration about the quality, price, time of delivery and punctuality in supply of the goods. They remain constantly in touch with the customers to ascertain what goods are in demand so that they may regulate their purchase accordingly. They are responsible to the management for their purchases. They have to report on their working and buying commitments, through which the management exercises a 'budgetary control' which coordinates buying and selling so that the available working capital may be used to its best advantages.

2. Selling Organisation: The profit-earning capacity of a wholesale concern depends on the efficiency with which sales of the goods are affected. The primary object of the wholesale is to find out purchasers either amongst the retailers or amongst the general public. 'This is entrusted to the salesman who draws customers to purchase the goods stocked by the wholesaler, at a price which is sufficiently remunerative. Sometimes the functions of the buyer and the salesman are combined in one person so that there may not be any shifting of responsibility. This is possible when a person incharge of the work is specially qualified for this purpose and when business is not very extensive.

FUNCTIONS OF WHOLESALERS

1. Assembling: The wholesaler collects varieties of a product from different manufacturers and keeps them in stock for sale to the retailers. Some wholesalers collect product only from a single producer.

2. Dispersion: The products assembled and kept in stock to be distributed to the retailers or manufacturers or producers are kept in stock in warehouses pending their sale to the retailers.

3. Warehousing: The goods assembled from manufacturers or producers are kept in stock in warehouses pending their sale to the retailers.

4. Transportation: The wholesalers have to move the goods from the place of production to their godowns or warehouses and from there to the place of retailers. They arrange and maintain their own vans for the movement of goods.

5. Financing: Wholesalers sometimes finance the manufacturers and retailers. They purchase goods from the manufacturers in cash or deposit security to assure the purchase of goods. They also supply goods to the retailers on credit.

6. Grading and packaging: The wholesaler performs the task of sorting out different grades of products purchased either from one producer or from different producers according to quality and other considerations and packing the goods into smaller lots for retailers.

7. Pricing: The retailer determines the price to be charged from customers on the basis of the price fixed by the wholesaler. Wholesalers can say more particularly about the produce and also suggest the price to be fixed by the producer.

8. Risk-assuming: Wholesaler undertakes the risk of manufacturers and retailers. Having purchased the goods from the manufacturers in large quantities, he assumes the risks arising out of changes in demand and spoilage or destruction of goods in his warehouse. He takes the credit-risk by selling the goods to the retailers on credit.

WHOLESALER'S SERVICES

Services to Manufacturers

(*i*) *Help in Concentration on Production*: By taking over the marketing function from the manufacturer, the wholesaler enables him to concentrate on the problems of production.

(*ii*) *Help in Large Scale Production*: The manufacturer gets the benefit of large orders for goods of more or less standard type through the wholesalers. The wholesalers either purchase goods in bulk from the manufacturers for resale or collect orders from the retailers and pass them on to the manufacturers. Thus wholesalers enable the manufacturers to produce goods on large scale.

(*iii*) *Distribution Facilities*: Wholesaler is a vital link between manufacturers and consumers. The manufacturer does not have to take the trouble of collecting small orders and supplying them to a large number of retailers scattered widely.

(*iv*) *Demand Analysis and Forecasting*: The manufacturers can regulate their production and estimate their sale or demand according to the changes in the direction and pattern of demand, indicated well in time by the orders placed by the wholesalers. Wholesalers remain in touch with the consumers through retailers and keep themselves informed about the changes in task, fashion and demand.

(*v*) *Financing*: Wholesalers provide financial assistance to the manufacturers by purchasing the goods in bulk in cash and by depositing security with the manufacturers.

(*vi*) *Warehousing*: The manufacturer is saved from the problem of warehousing large stocks of finished goods as the wholesalers purchase the goods in bulk as soon as they are ready and stock them till they are sold to the retailers in smaller lots.

(*vii*) *Help in Production*: The wholesalers help the manufacturers in maintaining an even pace of production by placing advance orders for periods which are generally characterised by slack demand.

(*viii*) *Help in Sales Organisation*: The wholesaler also helps the manufacturer by having his own sales organisation as the wholesaler generally has a ready sale organisation of his own.

(*ix*) *Help in Price Determination*: Wholesalers who are in constant touch with buyers through retailers know the needs and reactions of the customers and also what the customer can pay. Hence, they can suggest the manufacturer the best price he can fetch in the market for his goods.

(*x*) *Advertisement*: Generally dealing in one or two items, the wholesalers advertise for the goods they deal in. The manufacturers are also benefited by this activity of wholesaler because their product draws more attention of buyers.

(*xi*) *Grading and Standardisation of Goods*: Where the manufacturer produces unstandardised goods, wholesalers purchase them in lots and grade them according to their quality. They sometimes pack then in smaller lots and after standardisation and processing give a brand name to them.

(*xii*) *Widening of Market*: Wholesalers widen the markets for the goods of the producers. They sell their goods in new markets through their own sales organisation. They create demand of the product in foreign markets and thus increase the goodwill of the producers.

2. Services of Wholesalers to Retailers

(*i*) *Purchasing Facilities*: Wholesalers stock the goods from different manufacturers and provide the facility to the retailers to buy their requirements at convenient intervals without much difficulty. A retailer has a large number of customers to deal with. He has, therefore to keep a wide variety of products in store to cater the individual needs. It is not feasible for him to purchase such a variety of products from a number of producers directly.

(*ii*) *Low Inventory*: The retailers generally suffer from the dearth of capital and of storage facilities. It is not possible for them to purchase goods in bulk and store them to maintain the steady supply in the market. The wholesaler himself warehouses the goods and releases them in smaller lots to the retailers who require low inventory.

(*iii*) *Risk Taking*: Wholesalers assume most of the risk of marketing the goods. As the wholesaler warehouses the goods and takes the risks of market fluctuations in prices or spoilage of goods in warehouses due to pesticides and natural calamity, he saves the retailers from such risks.

(*iv*) *Financial Assistance*: Wholesalers finance the bulk of retail trade by supplying goods on credit. Due to small capital, most of the retailers buy goods on credit from wholesalers and pay them only after they collect the money by selling the goods to the ultimate customers. Thus, the wholesalers enable the retailers to trade without much working capital.

(*v*) *Information about New Product*: Through his travellers and salesmen employed for this purpose the wholesaler brings to the notice of the retailers the new types of goods which are being manufactured. Trade circulars, advertisement in papers and showroom also help in this function.

(*vi*) *Benefits of Specialisation*: The wholesalers generally specialise in a few lines of goods and buy from the manufacturers who produce the best and the cheapest goods. The advantage of such specialisation is automatically passed on to retailers who purchase their goods from them.

(*vii*) *Advantage of Advertisement*: The wholesalers advertise their goods very extensively and create the demand in the market which is virtually met by the retailers. Thus, retailers need not advertise. They are directly benefited from the advertisement by wholesalers.

(*viii*) *Consultancy Services*: Wholesalers provide consultation or advice to the retailers on various marketing activities such as displaying of goods on the shop, etc. They also supply the advertisement materials to retailers which explain the qualities of the products.

(*ix*) *Transport Facilities*: Wholesalers generally have their own transport to supply the goods to the retailers according to their requirements. As they more often deliver the goods on the shop of the retailers on the basis of traders collected from them the retailers save the transport charges.

(*x*) *Stability in Prices*: Wholesalers hold the price line by maintaining the demand and supply equilibrium. They release the goods when they are in short supply and stock them when they are not in demand. This saves the retailers from the risk caused by fluctuations in prices.

Thus, the wholesaler is a valuable link between the producer and the consumer in the channels of distribution.

SHOULD WHOLESALER BE REMOVED?

Some critics believe that the institution of wholesaler is a wasteful and avoidable link between the producer and the retailers and it should be eliminated immediately. This opinion is based mainly on the following grounds:

1. Responsible for increasing the cost distribution: If there are more than one wholesealer in the chain of distribution, their commission or their profit margin is included in the price of the commodity before it finally reaches the hands of final consumers. It is additional burden for the consumers. Wholesalers are, therefore, called parasites thriving at the expense of the consumers.

2. Create a long chain between the actual producer and consumers: Thus, they prevent the two classes of people who are mutually interdependent to come into direct touch. Hence, the producer is not in a position to know the actual demand for the grievances of the consumers. The consumers cannot approach the producer to enlighten him about the actual trend of the market.

3. The producers are kept in dark about the actual demand potentials: Wholesalers generally suppress the market trend in favour of their interest. Due to the main relations of these wholesalers, the producers are not able to conform production to demand and it often results in overproduction or underproduction.

4. Encourage black marketing by cornering all the available supply of goods: Wholesalers corner the available supply of commodities and then dictate any price which the consumers have to pay or go without it. This is against all business ethics. The situation becomes more aggravated if the commodity is food, drink and clothing or any other essential commodity.

5. Against the modern trend towards direct marketing of merchandise from producers to consumers: The growth of multiple shops, departmental stores, super bazaars, etc. is one step in the direction of elimination of wholesalers. In India, several producers such as DCM, Bata, Liberty, etc. have started their multiple retail stores which have proved successful. This practice may be extended to other commodities replacing wholesalers.

6. Develop their own brand and earn goodwill for themselves on the cost of producers: Most of the producers have in recent years begun to develop their own trademark and advertise that. It is therefore not necessary to depend on the wholesalers for selling the produce.

7. Do not serve much to the new entrants in the field of manufacturers: As the wholesalers generally prefer dealing in popular products the selling of which is not a problem, they do not make much efforts of selling new products which generally die in their infancy.

8. Generally interested in higher profits: Wholesalers sell the commodities of producers who offer them lucrative commission irrespective of the quality of goods. This tendency is neither beneficial to producers nor to consumers.

From the above arguments, it seems that the wholesalers are useless in the channels of distribution and they should be eliminated as soon as possible. With the development of large scale retailing and cooperative movement their necessity has been minimised. On the other hand, they render some disservices and create many problems to the producers and the consumers. However, their invaluable services to manufacturers and retailers cannot be ignored. Their elimination from the chain of distribution will create hardships. This agency should be properly controlled through proper legislations. The dependence of producers on them for marketing functions should be reduced. The existence of wholesalers does not depend on the manufacturers or customers. They exist due to their services rendered to various parties.

QUESTIONS FOR EXERCISE

1. Outline the services of wholesalers to manufacturers and retailers. Should the wholesalers be abolished?
2. It is said that the wholesaler is a parasite and therefore an unuseful link in the chain of middlemen from the producer to the consumers.
3. Explain with reference to the services rendered by the wholesaler to the manufacturer and to the retailer.

23

Retail Distribution

The word 'Retail' is derived from a French word with the prefix *re* and the verb *tailer* meaning "to cut again". Thus, retail trade is one that cuts off smaller portions from large lumps of goods. It is a process through which goods are transported to final consumers. It consists of the activities involved in selling directly to the ultimate consumer for personal, non-business use. It embraces the direct-to-customer sales activities of the producer, whether through his own stores, or by house-to-house canvassing or by mail order business."[1]

Thus, retailing includes the activities in selling consumer's goods to the ultimate consumer. It focuses on ultimate, rather than industrial consumers. Mandell, etc. have observed that "If we think of production and consumption as the two poles of the distribution process, wholesaling would be nearer to the production pole and retailing would be nearer to the consumption pole."[2]

Difference between Retail and Wholesale

1. Most retailing is conducted in stores, where the customer initiates the transaction. In marketing or the wholesale level, customers are actively pursued by sales personnel, who spend much of their time travelling.

2. Wholesalers place greater reliance on transportation to move goods to consumers than retailers do.

---

1. American Association of Marketing, *Marketing Definitions,* 1960.
2. Larson, Carl M., Robert, E. Weigand and John, S. Wright. *Basic Retailing,* Prentice-Hall, Englewood Cliffs, New York, 1976, pp. 6-7.

3. The typical retail store sale involves a small quantity of goods while the typical wholesale transaction involves a bulk order. Goods are sold in bulk to retailers somewhat at lower rates. It allows retailers to add a mark up and earn a profit. Thus, both the wholesaler and the consumer pay for the convenience of the retail outlet.

DEFINITION OF RETAILING

1. *R.S. Davar*: "Retail outlets are shops from whom the consumer ultimately buys."
2. *Report of the Definition Committee, US.A.*: "Retailing includes all activities incidental to selling to the ultimate consumer."
3. *William J. Stanton*: "A retailer or a retail store is a business enterprise which sells primarily to the ultimate consumers for non-business use."
4. *Cundiff and Still*: "Retailing consists of activities involved in selling directly to ultimate consumers."
5. *McCarthy*: "Retailing is selling final consumer products to householders."

Dictionaries define retailing as "the sale of goods in small quantities to ultimate consumers." From the bulk of products procured by the wholesaler, small lots are cut and distributed through retailers. In the chain of distribution between the manufacturers and the ultimate consumer the retailer is the last link. Retailers make the goods of industry conveniently available to millions of consumers. There could be no mass production without them. Even the Industrial Revolution would not have taken place in the absence of retailers. The retail shops are the oldest and most widely used business establishments in any country of the world.

RETAILER AND RETAILING

A retailer or a retail store also known as a dealer is a business enterprise which sells to ultimate consumers. Retailing, on the other hand, includes all activities directly related to the sale of goods or services to the ultimate consumer, irrespective of who sells. The distinction of retailing is made on the basis of to whom the products are sold. For example, if a manufacturer sells direct to the consumer that also is retailing. Even a wholesaler is said to be engaged in retailing when he sells directly to an ultimate consumer.

Therefore, it is remarked, "If the buyer in the transaction is an ultimate consumer, the seller in the same transaction is engaged in retailing." Thus, regardless of what he calls himself any one selling to the ultimate consumers is performing the functions of a retailer.

Retailers are the buying agents for their customers. They are the marketing or merchandising arm of many manufacturers. Retailing is subjected to constant changes which increase both the risk and opportunities of the participants. It is influenced by many forces such as population growth and the mobility of consumers (social forces), increased personal income, changes in the distribution of income, consumer credit and competitive changes, etc. (economic forces). Technological innovation also affects retailing. It is also influenced by Government policies which prevail over social, economic and scientific influences.

RETAILING FUNCTIONS

1. Assembling: Assembling of goods from various wholesalers.

2. Transport: The physical movement and storage of goods for the supply to the final consumers to meet their needs and requirements.

3. Information: The providing of information concerning the nature and use of goods to the wholesalers and producers. It also informs about the market trend.

4. Standardisation: Grading and Processing. The standardisation, grading and final processing of goods which have been left ungraded or unstandardised by wholesalers.

5. Provision: The provision of ready availability of goods of various qualities and of various manufacturers.

6. Risk Bearing: The assumption of risk concerning the price, nature and extent of demand of goods as long as they remain unsold.

7. Financing: The financing or inventory and the extension of credit to consumers for a short period.

SERVICES RENDERED BY THE RETAILERS

1. Stocking: The retailer keeps stock of different varieties of goods. An average consumer cannot afford to stock goods that he requires for every day use. By holding stocks of these goods the retailers relieve the consumer of performing this function for himself.

2. Variety of Choice: The retailer keeps a good assortment of various varieties of a product manufactured by different firms. In this way, he provides a variety of choice to his customers.

3. Creation of Demand: Most of the demand creation methods are undertaken by retailers for the manufacturers and wholesalers. They arrange for the display of goods, supply necessary information to the customers and provide various similar services.

4. Distribution: The retailer is an expert in the distribution of consumer goods. Out of his experience, training and intimate knowledge of the goods he is in a position to help the customers in the proper selection of goods. His success in his business ultimately rests on the effective rendering of these services.

5. Credit Facilities: The retailer often extends credit facilities to the consumers. These alone account for larger sales volume.

6. Personal Services: The retailer provides many personal services to the customer such as home delivery, after-sales service, liberal exchange of goods, etc.

7. Information: For the manufacturers, a retailer collects information about trends in marketing, change in fashions, tastes, etc. It is through the retailer that a customer meets the manufacturer.

8. Other Services: Besides the above service rendered by the retailers, they make available goods according to season, give advice to their customers, provide facility or return of goods, increase in the knowledge of customers and periodical services.

ESSENTIALS FOR A SUCCESSFUL RETAIL TRADE

1. Selection of Proper Goods: A retailer should be able to select proper goods which can meet the requirements of his customers. He should exercise his foresight, use his past experience and keep in view the changing fashions for proper selection.

2. Perfect Knowledge about Goods: A retailer should have thorough knowledge about the goods he deals in order to be able to satisfy his customers and answer their questions.

3. Proper Sales Policy: A retailer should adopt the policy of buying the bulk and increase his sales by satisfying himself with a lower margin of profit. By this policy he can also face any local competition from other retailers in the market.

4. Adequate Capital: A retailer should command adequate capital at his disposal because he has to allow some credit facilities also to his customers.

5. Suitable Business Location: It is very necessary that a suitable business location easily accessible to the customers should be selected. A suitable location will depend on the nature of goods one deals in. For example, posh colonies should be selected for sophisticated goods.

6. Business Education: The retailer should be well versed with the art of salesmanship. He should underline the habits and temperaments of his customers.

7. Attractive Display and Advertisement: In order to attract more customers the retailer should arrange things in an attractive style. Goods should be prominently displayed and advertised.

8. Credit Facility: In modern times providing credit facilities has also become necessary, for which the retailer should know the financial position of his customers and their habit also.

9. Provisions of Other Facilities: The retailer should also provide free advice, facility of return of goods if possible, home delivery facility and periodical services or repairs, etc. of durable items.

FORMS OF RETAIL TRADE

Retailing has changed very drastically during the last two decades. Some institutions have disappeared whereas newer ones have been added. This process of deletion and addition still continues in newer forms. Large-scale retailing shops are working simultaneously with very small units. These range from hawkers and dealers who have no permanent place to well organised settled shops like chain-stores, departmental stores, super bazaars, etc.

Following is the classification of the important kinds of retailing business units on the basis of their place of business:

1. Itinerant retailers, and
2. Fixed shop retailers.

1. Itinerant Retailers: Itinerant retailers have no fixed business places and move about from place to place as the season changes. They sell low-priced items in very small lots. They invest a very small capital and do not stick to a particular line of business. Some of them are as follows:

(*i*) *Hawkers and Pedlars*: Sale by hawkers and pedlars is of a very old origin. They carry the goods from place to place with the help of a beast of burden or a hand cart and sell them at the very doors of the customers. The same function is done even by pedlars with the difference that they carry their goods on their persons. Both of these retailers do not have any fixed place of business. They keep on moving from locality to locality on the basis of prospects of the business. They generally handle cheap goods with low unit value like pens, handkerchiefs, knives, combs, cheap cosmetics, toys, etc. There is no guarantee about the quality of goods which are of inferior variety. Hence, while buying goods from hawkers and pedlars one must be careful about their quality. These retailers sell goods at very tempting prices considerably lower than the market rate. Hawkers and pedlars are found in streets of busy cities, towns and villages and at places where exhibitions, fairs are held. They are seen outside the temple or bathing ghats where people throng in large numbers.

(*ii*) *Market Traders*: These are retailers who open their shops at different places on fixed days known as market days like Som Bazaar, Mangal haats, etc. Such days are fixed on weekly, fortnightly and monthly basis. Such traders carry on their business in one locality or at different places on different days when the market is open. They open their shops on important festivals and have roaring business on those days.

(*iii*) *Cheap Jacks*: A cheap jack has independent shop in a business locality. His shop is not of permanent nature and he may shift it if he finds that another locality is more profitable.

(*iv*) *Street Traders*: Street traders carry on their business in the busy streets or foot paths of busy town roads. They are often seen near railway stations, bus stops, and similar places where there is huge floating population. They handle only light goods that are largely in demand. They mainly deal in one kind of goods at a time.

2. Fixed Shop Retailers: Fixed shop retailers generally retain permanent places of business. These may be classified on the basis of their size of operations, *i.e.,* small scale and large scale.

(A) Small Scale Retailing

(*i*) *The Street Holders*: These have their stalls in a street where they may find heavy traffic. They exercise much care in selecting the location as the site once selected is more or less permanent. These retailers get their supplies from the wholesalers as well as from local suppliers. They handle goods on a very small scale. They deal in different types of articles like pens, towels, underwears, socks, etc.

(*ii*) *Second-hand Goods Dealers*: These dealers deal in second-hand goods or articles like books, furnitures, clothes, etc. They purchase and sell goods particularly to those customers who cannot afford to buy new goods at higher prices. They mainly get their supplies from public auction. They do not take any responsibility either for durability or quality of the goods.

(*iii*) *Speciality Shops*: These shops sell goods of particular variety. The dealers specialise and deal only in one line of goods. Some examples are shops exclusively meant for books, leather goods, toys, medicines, readymade garments, etc.

(*iv*) *General Shops*: These shops sell the whole list of products required for every day use. Their size is generally decided on the basis of population they have to serve. They claim permanent local customers.

(*v*) *Independent Store*: These are small non-integrated retail establishments having a lesser degree of specialisation in their management. The owner himself manages the business. He maintains intimate personal contact with customers. He gets supplies from the wholesalers. Independent stores may be classified into: (*a*) general stores, (*b*) single line stores, and (*c*) speciality stores.

(*vi*) *Automatic Vending Machines*: Vending machines sell a variety of products through coin operated machines, automatically, without the aid of any sales assistant. The use and importance of such type of retailing is yet to prove its viability in India.

(*vii*) *Discount Houses*: During post-war period the discount houses grew out of the practice of manufacturers giving large discount to retailers on certain types of goods. A discount house is a retailing business unit which features consumer durable items like jewellery, household appliances and wares and similar merchandise. These houses operate on a relatively low make-up and a minimum customer service.

(viii) Syndicate Stores: It is an extension of the chain and mail order house but relatively on a small scale. One of its chief characteristic is that while it offers a variety of merchandise to customers, it seldom sells well-known brands. Most of the merchandise it sells would be of unknown. They buy unbranded merchandise which are sold under their own brands later on.

(B) Large Scale Retailing

These days, several types of large scale retail organisations have sprung up in a bid to eliminate the wholesaler middlemen and to get the economies of large scale operations. Some of the large scale retail organisations are: (1) Departmental Stores, (2) Chain stores or multiple shops, (3) Mail order business, (4) Hire purchase and instalments, (5) Consumers' cooperative stores, (6) Super bazars, and (7) Hyper markets.

DEPARTMENTAL STORES

Meaning

The departmental stores are considered to be of French origin. It is stated that in Boa March'e and the other places departmental stores came into existence and flourished during the period of the Second French Empire (1852-1871).

The departmental store is a large-scale retailing business unit which handles a wide variety of shopping and speciality goods and is organised into separate departments for the purpose of promotion, service and control. It has decentralised selling. Technically it is a horizontally integrated retail institution. It has many departments with each department specialising in one kind of merchandise such as cloth department, drugs department, stationary department, readymade garments, toys department, etc. In it each unit resembles a speciality shop. All these departments are centrally controlled and work under one roof. The main idea behind the departmental stores is to supply all requirements from a single place. It is said that a departmental store is a place where one could get articles ranging from 'pin to plane'.

Characteristics

1. From Pin to Plane: It is a place where a consumer can get all his daily needs from pin to plane except probably some easily perishable items.

2. Departmental: The working of the store is organised on the departmental basis, *i.e.,* departments are established to deal in different items. Each department works under the supervision of a manager.

3. Centralised Management and Control: In spite of the fact that each department is independent in its day-to-day working all the departments are owned, managed and controlled centrally.

4. Large: The departmental store is large in size, centrally located and capable of attractions to a large number of customers.

5. Convenient Services: Services towards customers such as recreational facilities, free home delivery, post and telegraph, etc., are provided conveniently.

6. Central Location: This is the most important element that decides the successful existence of a departmental store. Being a large-scale institution its profit depends upon the large turnover. There would be a flow of customers only if the location is freely accessible. Further, the building must be capable of providing car parking, recreational and other facilities.

Organisation

Departmental stores usually adopt Joint Stock Company form organisation. The management of the departmental store as a whole is vested in the hands of a Managing Director or a General Manager. Each section or department is controlled by a manager under the direct control of the General Manager. The activities of a department store are divided into the following five major sections or divisions to facilitate smooth working of the store:

1. Merchandise section: It looks after buying and selling goods.

2. Store section: It undertakes advertisement and publicity, window display and other demand creational methods.

3. Service section: It is concerned with the maintenance of the properties of the stores.

4. Establishments section: It supervises selection and appointment, etc. of the employees.

5. Accounting and finance section: It takes charges of all financial matters.

Advantages

1. All facilities under one roof: The departmental store provides all facilities under one roof to enable the customer to buy all his requirements.

2. Central location: Its central location attracts a good number of customers which increases the sales turnover.

3. Variety of goods: A large variety of goods in one line are stored. This has a special attraction to the customers (particularly house-wives).

4. Financially strong: The financial strength of a departmental store enables it to have expert in all sections. It, therefore, can achieve a high level of efficiency.

5. Lower cost: Centralised buying helps it to get merchandise at lower cost together advantages in transporting, storing, etc.

6. Standardised goods: The departmental store plays mainly on the services by providing more or less standardised articles and other services, not offered by its other counterparts.

7. Advertising: Being a large scale organisation departmental store can afford to have effective advertising through press and other media of publicity.

Disadvantages

1. High operating cost: It is estimated that the operating costs of these stores works out to be 35 per cent of sales. Therefore, they often ran to loss.

2. Problem in location: There are problems in finding out proper location particularly because of the need to have large premises which bear high rents.

3. Stiff competition: Stiff competition from other forms of retailing organisations stands in the way of its progress.

4. Losses: Certain departments have to be retained in spite of their recurring losses.

5. Impersonality: There is a lack of personal element in departmental stores. A customer may not be attended twice in succession by the same salesman.

6. Hired employees: Departmental stores are generally run by hired employees far from the sense of ownership. It causes losses and leaks.

7. High overhead charges: The exotic and elaborate services provided, high operating cost, leakage, waste, etc., tend to increase the overhead charges which compel them to mark-up high prices on the articles.

Departmental Stores in India

There are a few departmental stores in India like Spencers Ltd. and Army and Navy Stores Ltd. of Madras, Lainlaw Ltd, of Bombay, Kamlalaya Stores Ltd. Calcutta, and K.G. Thakurdas and Co., Kanpur. These departmental stores are in no way comparable to the giant stores of U.K. and U.S.A. Because of the following reasons the departmental stores are not much popular in India.

1. Dearth of capital: Dearth of capital in India hinders the growth of departmental stores.

2. High prices: Prices in such stores are high due to increased operating cost.

3. Building problem: Acquiring big building in the midst of the city is also difficult.

4. Limited needs: There are limited needs of people in India.

5. Ignorance: Indians are quite ignorant of the importance of the departmental stores.

Multiple Shops or Chain Stores

S.E. Thomas has defined the multiple shops as "a system under which there is a large number of retail shops owned by the same proprietor which are scattered over the various places of a particular city of a country and are engaged in the same line of activity." The name 'multiple shops' itself indicates that under this organisation similar shops are established in multiples but the same management. A chain stores system consists of four or more stores which carry the same kind of merchandise. These are centrally owned and managed. Usually goods are supplied to all of them from one or more central warehouses. A chain store is one of the retail units in chain store system. This chain store or multiple shops is a group of retail stores of the same type, centrally owned and with some degree of centralised control. In

Europe, this system is called as multiple shops. The Americans call it 'chain stores'.

The main idea under the multiple or chain shop arrangement is to approach the customers and not to draw the customer to it as is practised in the case of the departmental store. In order to draw a large number of customers, attempts are made to open a large number of shops in the same city at different places.

In India examples of chain stores system are offered by Bata shop, Usha sewing machines, etc. Such multiple shops have "centralised buying with decentralised selling". They specialise in one product or products of one producer but with all its varieties or models. Their success depends upon how the selection of goods is made. The following considerations are important in selecting goods for retail through such stores:

(*i*) The articles are of every day use with popular appeal;

(*ii*) The articles are branded; and

(*iii*) The articles are portable and have a rapid turnover.

This type of retailing is gaining momentum because it is a system through which the manufacturers can easily eliminate the wholesalers and establish a direct contact with consumers. Of late, manufacturers themselves have started opening their own retail shops of this kind. In such cases they are called "manufacturer retailers". They are known as middlemen multiple shops. When controlled by wholesalers, the chain store system can also be categorised as vertically integrated institution as it takes over and performs for itself functions which would otherwise be performed by separate wholesale institutions.

Important Characteristics

1. Similar Product: Each such shop deals in the same type of products.

2. Articles of Daily Use: The products dealt in are generally that of day- to-day use.

3. Central Purchase: All purchases are effected through the central organisation and uniform sale policy is followed by all stores.

4. Uniform Policies: All shops are managed and controlled from the head office, *i.e.*, all policies are decided by the head office and carried out by the shops. Thus, there are uniform policies.

5. Same Style: Each shop is decorated in the same setting and style. A high degree of standardisation and uniformity is attained in the interior layout of stores, window dressing and outward appearance.

Advantages of Chain Stores

1. Lower Selling Prices: This is made possible due to economy in buying operation, etc.

2. Economy in Advertising: Common advertisements covering all the units are feasible which reduces publicity expenditure. Advertisement for one becomes an advertisement for all other shops.

3. Ability to Spread Nest: Unlike the departmental stores the principle here is not "to lay all the eggs in one basket." By trial and error a unit sustaining losses may be shifted from one place to another or be even dropped.

4. Economical Buying: As supplies are made to all the shops through the central office, it is in a position to gain the economic of large scale buying. It can purchase goods direct from the manufacturers.

5. Speedy Turnover: As chain stores are mainly located in different localities therefore they are in direct touch with the actual customers and know current trends in demand. They can have such stock as sell fast. Multiple shops can achieve a rapid turnover target.

6. Economical Operation: Multiple stores generally work with lower operating costs than many of their competitors due to the following factors: (*i*) rapid turnover, (*ii*) elimination of bad debts, (*iii*) no need for maintaining accounts for credit sale, and (*iv*) common advertisement.

7. No Bad Debts: As it works on cash basis bad debts and detailed accounting processes are avoided in chain stores.

Disadvantages

1. Inflexible in Practice: Multiple shops deal only in standardised products. This creates inflexibility in offering wide varieties. Each unit is controlled by the central office which prevents the unit from adjusting to local conditions.

2. Personnel Problems: Being a large scale organisation it is susceptible to problems associated with large scale business. Transfer and promotion, etc. bring inefficiency to the organisation.

3. Pool Public Image: Various consumer services such as credit facility, door delivery, etc. are absent in chain store. In addition to desiring low price the present-day consumers prefer to have more services than quality.

4. Attempt to Eliminate Retailers: Multiple shops represent an attempt on the part of the wholesalers and manufacturers to eliminate retailers.

5. Rise in Operation Costs: As the number of shops in the chain increases, the control and supervision becomes lose and the disadvantages of large scale operations begin to appear. The increase in the size of chain leads to disproportionate size of operations costs, cost of supervision and cost of delivery.

6. No Set **off:** According to W.J. Stanton, "Price compensation is not possible as such stores are handling only limited items."

DEPARTMENTAL STORE *Vs.* MULTIPLE SHOPS

1. Location: Whereas central location is essential in the case of a departmental stores, multiple shops could be located in any place where the consumers are adequate. The former institution attracts customers to its place of business whereas latter moves nearer to consumers.

2. Clientale: Basically departmental stores are meant for rich people whereas multiple shops do not maintain such distinction.

3. Prices: Departmental stores charge high prices on account of various services rendered for customers. As multiple shops do not provide such facilities their prices are comparatively low.

4. Variety: Departmental stores provide a good variety of goods to their customers who are enabled thereby to make all their purchases under one roof. The multiple shops, on the other hand, specialise in a limited range of merchandise only.

5. Source: Departmental stores sell products manufactured by various manufacturers. The multiple shops, on the contrary, sell only one merchandise of one or a very few manufacturers.

6. Risks: While the departmental stores run greater risks of business in as much as they sell goods only at one place, on the multiple shops reduce their risks by selling goods through different branches at different places.

7. Advertisement: While the departmental stores advertise only in restricted local areas because they are interested only in local customers, the multiple shops organise their advertisement campaign on nation-wide or at least regional basis.

MAIL ORDER BUSINESS

According to F.F. Clark, "A mail order house is that type of retail institution which solicits patronage by means of catalogues of merchandise offered for sale."

Mail order trading also referred to as "Non-store impersonal retailing or shopping by post," is done through the post office and personal selling is avoided. The orders are collected and goods are delivered at the very doors of the customers through the medium of post. No help of middlemen is sought. The seller takes all the necessary steps to introduce the product by sending catalogues, circulars or other printed matter to the prospective customers. Publicity through other media is also undertaken. No personal contact is possible between the buyer and the seller.

Types of Mail Order Houses

1. The Manufacturing types: In it products are sold direct to the public by the manufacturer and there is no middlemen.

2. The Departmental types: In addition to selling goods through different departments the departmental store starts selling goods by mail.

3. The Middlemen types: Run by wholesalers this is the proper and true mail order business. As and when orders are received by post the goods are brought from the manufacturer or other wholesalers and despatched to the respective parties.

Selling through mail depends on how effectively the customers are persuaded to buy. As the buyers are unable to inspect the goods personally there is always an inherent resistance to buy these goods.

Common Characteristics

1. Easy Understanding: The nature of the product should be easily understood from its description.

2. Convenient Selection: The product can be selected conveniently from different models.

3. Immediate Use: Goods must be capable of rendering immediate use as soon as they are delivered.

4. Low Postal Charges: Postal charges should be low compared to the price of the product.

5. Not easily spoiled: Goods must be of such nature that are not easily spoiled or damaged in the transit.

6. Perennial supply: The supply of the product is perennial.

Procedure

The retailing institutions find out the addresses of the prospective buyers from telephone directories, list of car owners, voters lists, etc. and send the illustrative catalogues to their addresses. This is supplemented by advertisements. The catalogues invariably contain an order form together with a stamped self-addressed envelope. The buyer has simply to put his signature in the order form mentioning the quantity required. As soon as the orders are received, the goods are packed and handed over to the post office. The goods are generally sent by V.P.P. (value payable post) and the postman collects the required amount before the goods are delivered to the buyer. The money collected is sent back to the seller through post office.

Advantages

1. Even goods not readily available in the market could be purchased through this method.

2. This business could be operated from any place where the postal facility is available.

3. No bad debts are suffered as money is collected before the goods are delivered.

4 It widens market and helps the traders to discover untapped markets.

5. The system could be operated easily even when the demand is low.

6. Only a small amount of capital is required to undertake this business.

7. As the goods are delivered at their very doors, customers are benefited.

8. No central place is required for business.

Disadvantages

1. The buyers are unable to inspect and select goods before they are bought.
2. Even the most illustrated catalogue is incapable of giving exact idea about the product.
3. Articles required for demonstration cannot be sold.
4. After-sales services is out of question.
5. No credit facilities are provided.
6. There could be delays in getting the goods.
7. Catalogues become obsolete very quickly as prices are subject to quick fluctuations.
8. The demand creating activities being costlier.
9. Higher prices are charged.
10. Sometimes the goods are damaged in transit.

Mail Order Business in India

In India, the Mail Order Retailing system has not made any headway. The reasons which prevent the growth of this system of retailing in the India are following:

1. Illiteracy: India's vast population suffers from illiteracy.

2. Seeing Before Buying: The general mentality of the Indian customers is to see the goods before purchasing them. This mentality is obviously the greatest obstacle in the way of this system.

3. Low Standard of Living: The standard of living of the people is very low.

4. No Daily Supplies: Majority of people buy their requirements on daily basis and this is not possible under this system.

5. Non-availability of Credit Facility: This is another reason for the unpopularity of this system.

6. No Business Ethics: Indian traders do not observe any business ethics. Cheating is very common. It loses the faith of the public in such type of business.

Mail Order Retailing

The system is becoming popular in the case of books and periodicals. In U.S.A. Sears Rose Buck is the largest mail order house which actually controls the lion's share in retail business there.

HIRE PURCHASE

In this type of retail selling, the seller agiees to sell the goods on the condition that the buyer shall pay the purchase price in fixed number of instalments. The article is not legally sold out but is only hired by the buyer. He cannot become the owner until the final instalment is paid. Till then, he will only be a mere possessor of the article and in default, the product will be seized by the seller. As the amounts paid so far by the buyer will he treated as mere hire charges, hence the name is hire-purchase.

Instalment Selling

Instalment selling is basically the same as Hire Purchase but with certain legal differences. Unlike the hire purchaser, the instalment buyer gets legal as well as physical possession over the products. The seller cannot repossess the article and can claim for price if instalments are defaulted. This system is also called as "Deffered payment system". The articles are invariably delivered only after a few instalments have been paid. It enables the consumers of average means to own capital goods. The system provides large markets for the products of manufacturers. In the present-day context the luxury articles such as refrigerators, cars, scooters, TV sets, etc. could only be marketed with such credit facilities provided to consumers. However, all goods cannot be traded under this system. The products traded under the system must possess the following characteristics:

1. Durability.
2. Stability.
3. Profitability.
4. Possibility of standardisation.
5. High unit value.
6. Possibility of after-sale service.

Advantages

1. Articles Beyond Capacity: The consumers could get articles of such nature as are normally beyond their capacities.

2. High Standard of Living: It increases the standard of living.

3. Use to Small Investors: Small manufacturers could use the opportunity to get plants and machinery. They could be put to use and payments arranged from the income arising out of their productive use.

4. Double Advantage: Persons of surplus means could also use this system. While they could get the article, the money retained could be profitably invested elsewhere.

Disadvantages

1. High Prices: The prices are high due to the inclusion of interest for the deferred period.

2. Loss in Default: The default not only makes one lose the product but also the payments made.

3. More Default: It attracts customers who cannot possess such article normally so the chances of default are great.

4. Legal problems: It involves disputes and legal problems. This creates delay in effecting sales.

5. Difficult Contact: The manufacturers often find it difficult to call on customers frequently.

In India this system is a widely accepted form of retailing in towns and cities. It is a popular form of retailing in the case of durable and costly articles. Hire Purchase Act has been passed for proper controlling of these trade activities.

CO-OPERATIVE RETAILING

Types of Cooperatives

1. Types of Cooperatives: Severe criticism against wholesalers and various kinds of middlemen let to a new type of retailing. In U.S.A. Retailing Cooperatives have become important distributors of convenience goods. In India however the system is not found. In the case of food items the Government agencies are playing a dominant role and the retailers are virtually absent.

2. Consumers' Cooperatives: It is a retail business owned and operated by ultimate consumers who purchase and distribute goods and services primarily to the members. The earliest known consumers' cooperative was started in Scotland. The modern form is traced the Rochdale Society of Equitable Pioneer and English cooperatives formed in 1844. It is claimed that the potentialities of the organised cooperatives were first revealed by Raiffesen in Germany in the 1840s.

Rochdale Principles

1. Open Membership: The consumers are free to join the cooperative.

2. Democratic Control: Each member has only one vote irrespective of the number of shares he might hold.

3. Cash Sale: All sales are made at existing market rates on cash basis.

4. Dividend: It is assured though maximum is limited.

5. Purchase Bonus: Members are allowed 'purchase bonus' on the basis of their purchases.

6. Ownership: These principles substitute service motive for project motive, encourage sense of thrift and make more people owners.

Advantages of Cooperative Retailing

1. Low Operating Cost: Because of service motive the cost of operating is kept down. Advertisements are eliminated.

2. Better Quality: Better quality goods can be sold.

3. Ornamentation: Elimination of costly equipment and ornamentation of the ship is preferred.

4. Location: It needs not always be located in busy places.

5. Credits: As credits are allowed hence no problem of bad debts arises.

6. Affiliation: Easy affiliation with other societies is possible, which helps in buying in bulk.

7. Check: It is a check on monopoly and wasteful completion.

8. Equitable Distribution: During product scarcity, equitable distribution is possible. Black marketing is checked.

Disadvantages of Cooperative Retailing

1. Lack of Consumers Interest: It is so because personal attention is not paid to them there.

2. Lack of Finance: Only poor members can contribute to the capital of the society.

3. Absence of Experts in Management: The men in managing committee are elected from among the members who are not experts in managements.

4. Attitudes: Employees show impersonal and discourteous attitudes to consumers.

5. No Large Scale Sellings: There is no advantage of large scale selling.

Consumers' Cooperatives in India

Cooperative movement in India has not been very satisfactory. The consumer's cooperatives have become active only when there is a natural or artiflcal scarcity of essential articles due to hoarding, profiteering, black marketing and artificial inflation. They are confined only to important towns, they fail to create confidence among the general public. Before World War II there were about 400 Consumers' Cooperative stores in the states of Madras, Bombay and Mysore. Post-war effects gave an impetus to cooperatives movement into existence. Their number now runs into thousands. These societies however, have failed to maintain equality in distribution as well as stability in prices.

Causes of Failure

1. Lack of business training: It does not provide experience to those who are incharge of stores.

2. No study: Absence of careful and thorough study of members requirements.

3. Methods: Defective methods of stock ordering and stock keeping.

4. Disloyalty: Disloyalty of the members and admission and cancellation of their membership are very frequent.

5. Dependence: It leads to much dependence on honorary services which suffer from incompetency.

6. Politics: Extension of politics into the field of cooperation has ruined the cooperative spirit.

SUPER MARKET

M.M. Zimmermen defines a super market as "a Departmentalised retail establishment having four basic food departments—

self-service, grocery, meat produce and dairy—plus other household departments and doing a maximum business. It may be entirely owner operated or have some of the departments based on a concession basis." But this definition is incomplete as super markets are 'self-services' states. The origin of super markets dates back to 1930 when the great depression took place. They were successful in effecting cheap price and operated on the cash and carry principles. They generally concentrated on food and grocery items.

Characteristic Features

1. Parking Space: They are located at places where consumers are given facilities like parking. Some super markets are successful without providing space....The trend however is to provide more parking space.

2. Advertisement: They use heavy advertisement and mass display of merchandise.

3. Credit: No credit facilities are offered.

4. Self Service: They do not employ salesmen and hence super markets are often described as self-service stores.

Super Markets in India

In India there is no super market as such. The name is used for most of the departmental stores organised under cooperative principle. These super markets have grocery items and all other convenience and speciality articles. They sell goods in labelled packets through the use of salesmen. They provide packed articles labelled with price tags and stored conveniently in shelves. The customer picks up the required products and places them in tray provided for the purpose. Then he takes the selected articles to the cashier where the articles are billed and payment is made. No bargaining is possible and no credits are allowed in super market.

Advantages of Super Markets

1. Freedom: Perfect freedom is enjoyed by the customers. No pressure selling is possible.

2. Low prices: This is on account of various organisational and establishment savings.

3. Higher Profits: This is due to low costs and high turnover.

4. Packing and Protection: Goods are packed safely and kept properly to protect them for a considerable time.

5. Quick Shopping: Shopping time is considerably reduced.

6. Economies: It enjoys economies of large scale operation.

Disadvantages of Super Market

1. Costly Premises: The large and extensive premises for super markets is not available cheaply.

2. No Explanation: The products which require explanation for their proper use cannot be dealt in through the super markets.

3. No Customer Services: Customer services are practically absent.

4. Capital: A huge capital is required to establish a Super Bazar.

ONE PRICE SHOPS

This is a retail shop concentrating on articles largely demanded by masses. Irrespective of their use and quality the articles from these shops are sold at a single price. It gives the buyers the benefit of getting any article at a fixed price. Bargaining on prices is not permitted. This type of organisation is called 'wool worth chain stores' as such stores were organised as wool worth for the first time. Usually these shops constitute a part of the fairs and exhibitions. In recent years, however, one price shops have acquired permanency in location due to wide population.

CONDITIONS OF SUCCESS FOR RETAILERS

(1) Selection of Goods: The fact that the 'dead stocks' the bug-bear of business and that unsold and unsaleable stock has brought ruin to many business men should never be overlooked.

(2) Knowledge of Merchandise: Due to individuality developed amongst the masses a great variety of goods has considerably increased and is still increasing. A retailer should, therefore, be more up-to-date in this respect. He must have a practical knowledge of the merchandise which will satisfy this new demand. Thus, his work is more complicated. He should take care while appointing salesmen, selecting shop assistants, etc., who would be called upon to deal with the customers.

(3) Buying and Selling: The success of a retail business is dependent on the buying of merchandise in the right market, at the right price, and at the right time. Retailers new in the line, sometimes say to their customers that they cannot sell at the price charged by some other shopkeepers on account of their buying the goods at a higher price. However, customers will not consent to pay a higher price for their article merely for its being purchased at a dearer market. Retailers must compete in price and quality. They should charge their customers at a definite rate of profit which ought to be the lowest possible and which should not be more than what is charged by others.

(4) Cash and Credit Purchases: Many retailers at important trade centres buy beyond the capacity of their capital and thus become inextricably entangled in the debt to their creditor wholesalers, who sell for more than normal price because they grant credit. Such a retailer, finds himself in a helpless position when he is called upon to compete with those who purchase for cash. Buying on credit may be allowed to a limited extent but overbuying should always be avoided. Retailers should not trade too much beyond the limits of their available capital. Financial consideration should dictate the maximum stock that can be safely kept. But a well-selected variety of stock should always be held by a retail shop unless it is a multiple shop, as loss is frequently suffered on account of inadequate stock. Customers, being disappointed to have their wants supplied, transfer their purchases elsewhere. Therefore, while avoiding the risk of overbuying, retailers should have ample stock of commodities according to the demand of the market and should add to the range of the articles to the extent allowed by capital resources.

(5) Price, Quality and Cypher System: Haggling and hesitancy should be avoided. A competitive fixed price should always be asked for with uprightness. The price charged shall be such that the customers may not be in a position to purchase the same article in the market at a cheaper price. The competitive price and quality of the goods sold are the keynotes of success in business. It is better to have a quick turnover of stock at a lower margin of profit. They should see that the goods stocked by them are of the right quality.

(6) Display of Goods: Sometimes goods are so disorderly arranged that the goods required, cannot be produced on the requisition by the consumer. Therefore, goods should be properly arranged and properly displayed to draw the attention of the customers. Window-dressing costs little but is very effective in retail trade as its emotional appeal to the shopping public frequently results in solid business. "In the newer window-dressing," suggests Mr. George Edger, "the three cardinal principles are: (*i*) to show reasonable thing, (*ii*) to show it as simply as possible, and (*iii*) to show it so that the eye can determine every detail put into the window. In such window-dressing instead of crowding the window, the trade aims at a display which represents the prevailing note of the season."

(7) Situation: Locality of the shop is a great factor to attract customers. The best locality is the place where there already exist other shops of the same nature, because for shopping purposes customers generally visit the place where a market for their requirements has grown up shop. While opening shops this essential matter of selection of site in a desirable locality should not be overlooked. No particular place can be pointed out for the retailer to reach his goal. Success can be achieved by combining the various qualifications essential for a businessman with other necessary factors. Personal aptitude, knowledge, enthusiasm with apprenticeship, combined with the possession of saleable goods and adequate stock generally make for success.

Chief Requirements of the Retailers

According to R.H. Nystorm, in order to attract customers retailers should have: (*i*) accessibility to consumers; (*ii*) a satisfactory trading place; (*iii*) suitable stocks of merchandise offering an opportunity for consumer choice; (*iv*) service offered and rendered to customers; (*v*) personal relation of store employees towards customers including not only promptness of attention but also courtesy, interest, friendliness and honesty; (*vi*) reasonable price; (*vii*) sales promotion including all methods and devices for giving the public information about the goods and services offered; (*viii*) window display and counter display (which are the most effective forms of advertising); (*ix*) the demand of customers should be aroused by means of suitable advertising so that they may be persuaded to pay a visit to the shop; (*x*) trained salesmen who are the backbone of the success of the retail house; (*xi*) staff employed should be polite, courteous and attentive to customers;

(*xii*) clearance sales, which are usually organised at the end of a season, attract customers in large numbers.[1]

CAUSES OF FAILURES OF RETAIL BUSINESS

The chief causes of failure of retail business are: (*i*) lack of experience in the line, (*ii*) limited financial resources, (*iii*) change in outlook of customers, (*iv*) unwise credit, (*v*) poor location, (*vi*) excessive general expenses, (*vii*) fraud, (*viii*) neglect of business, (*ix*) personal extravagance, (*x*) intemperance, (*xi*) natural calamities like floods, fire and stickness, (*xii*) speculation, (*xiii*) competition, and loss in contracts. However, some failures are of great benefit to the society because of their dishonesty and fraudulent conduct such as the maintenance of incorrect amounts to evade income-tax.

SUGGESTIONS FOR IMPROVING RETAILING

Three forces may bring about a change in retailing: (*i*) the changing consumer markets served by retailers, (*ii*) the retailer's own constant search for more effective and profitable methods, (*iii*) the manufacturer's realisation that they need mass-marketing methods to keep up with mass production of goods. There have to be product diversification and adoption of automated materials handling systems and automatic vending. The "retailer must be ready, willing, and able to innovate, and change with time, for the alternative is to die."

(1) Promptness: Mail order houses should be prompt in supplies. This promptness is necessary because of the growing competition which a mail order business is forced to meet. Many of them even specially mention in their advertisement or catalogue that orders are promptly filled by mentioning "twenty-four hours services' etc. Modern mechanical devices are adopted to handle orders it saving time as well as energy. If deliveries are not made in time a letter of regret explaining the reasons of delay should be despatched so that customer may not be annoyed.

(2) Guarantee: No one likes to purchase goods on description given in a particular advertisement, unless the purchaser is confident about the firm which he deals with. Mail order houses should try to cultivate confidence by means of the guarantee, for example, Sear, Roebuck and Companies guarantee like "to save your money," "to deliver all merchandises safely," and "to satisfy

1. Nystrom, R.H., *Economics of Retailing*, pp. 10–12.

you perfectly." The company further says, "if for any reason whatsoever you are not satisfied with any article purchased from us, we want to return it to us at our expense. We will then exchange it for exactly what you want, or will return your money, including any transportation charges you have paid." Much of the success of these merchandising concerns is due to their liberal guarantee.

3. Suitable Goods: Goods in sufficient quantity and of different variety must be on hand at all times. According to Holtzclaw a large mail order house stocks 48,000 articles in order that it may render prompt and efficient service to its customers.[1] Even then instances occur when orders cannot be supplied until goods are received from the factory. Necessaries are sold best by catalogue houses, but considerable space is devoted annually to a description of clothing with a style appeal.

4. Technique of **Selling:** As the main purpose of any business house is to sell goods, the advertisement should be correct and technical enough to influence customers. While making appeal to the customers on grounds of low prices, comparison in the catalogue may be made for prices of their own goods and the goods of other companies. Appeal other than prices may be so efficiently used as is almost used in personal selling. The same may be visualised by going through any modern up-to-date advertisement. There will be found descriptions appealing to such emotional and rational buying motives as distinctiveness, pride of personal appearance, emulation, economical emulation, social achievement, personal comfort, dependability in use, durability and economy.[2]

AUTOMATIC VENDING

Automatic vending makes use of machines. Coin-operated, self-service machines make a wide assortment of products available, such as cigarettes, hosiery, insurance policies, hot food and beverages. Such machines are installed near offices, service stations, hotels and shopping areas which supply candy, chewing gum, soft drinks, coffee are purchased in areas of heavy traffic. In India such machines are being installed at important railway stations for issuing tickets.

---

1. Holtzclaw, *op. cit.*, p. 102.
2. *Ibid.*, p. 103.

Standardised products can be sold by machines. They eliminate the use of sales personnel while small space is needed for their installation. But frequent servicing and repair is needed to keep vending machines functioning.

FRANCHISING

'Franchising' operation is a legal contractual relationship between a *franchiser* (the company offering the franchise) and the *frenchisee* (the individual who will own the business).[1] A franchise system is one in which a manufacturer grants selected retailers the exclusive right to sell his products or services in certain areas in exchange for a promise to promote and merchandise the product in a specific manner. There is a contractural agreement between the franchiser (supplier) and the independent franchisees (retailers). Though the terms and conditions of the contract vary widely but usually the franchiser offers to maintain a continuing interest in the business of the franchisee in such areas as the site selection, location, management training, financing, marketing, record keeping, and promotion. He also offers the use of a trade name, store motif, standardised operating procedure and a prescribed territory. The franchisee agrees to operate under conditions set forth by the franchiser. For the help and services provided, the franchisee makes a capital investment in business. He also agrees to pay commission on all of the franchisees' sales and/or agrees to buy from the franchiser all of his products needed.

Franchising exists in such products as soft drinks, automobiles and parts, business services, dry cleaning, fund raising, industrial supplies, building products, vending operations, etc.

For the manufacturers, the franchising is beneficial in these directions; (*i*) it allows them to conserve capital; (*ii*) the distribution system is established in the shortest possible time; (*iii*) marketing costs are lowered; and (*iv*) expenses of fixed overhead, such as administrative expenses of the personnel of the company owned units are cut down substantially. The franchisees also gains in so far as they can go into business because they feel secure through the guidance given by the franchiser.

1. Hasty, Ronald. W, and Will, R. Ted, *Marketing*, 1975, p. 218.

Conditions of Success

It is essential that Franchisee should take into account certain considerations for successful conducting of franchising such as:

(*i*) How long the franchiser has been in business?

(*ii*) How strong is his financial position?

(*iii*) How he selects his franchisees?

(*iv*) Is the area well defined, and does it allow for growth?

(*v*) Is it large enough to support expected sales?

(*vi*) Are other of the firms franchise operations distant enough so that they do not compete?

(*vii*) Is the franchise renewable?

(*viii*) Is it possible to sell or transfer the franchise?

(*ix*) Is there a clause for termination?

(*x*) Does the contract require the purchase of company products?

(*xi*) Does it allow the return of unsaleable merchandise?

(*xii*) Can the franchisee have outside business interests?

(*xiii*) Is there a quota set on sales?

(*xiv*) Is the contract beneficial for both parties?

(*xv*) Are all financial arrangements clearly listed, and are these amounts for payment of fees, royalty and promotion fixed?

The franchisee should also:

(*i*) make reference check from the financial institutions;

(*ii*) make inquiries about the product, concerning its quality, seasonal appeal, exclusiveness, competitiveness, and effectiveness in bringing in repeat customers;

(*iii*) have enough capital to buy the franchise;

(*iv*) be capable of taking supervision work;

(*v*) consult the professionals and seek their guidance in legal matters;

(*vi*) take risks and invest sufficient time.

MERCHANDISING CONGLOMERATES

Recently, a new organisation "Conglo-merchant" or "'merchandising conglomerate" has developed in the West. This is a retailing corporation that integrates often unrelated retail business units under centralised distribution and management functions. It may include department stores, discount houses, food stores, restaurants, catering facilities, speciality chains, wholesale divisions, service speciality outlets, etc. All these are managed through centralised corporations which include market information, computerised inventory control, credit processing, and central-buying staff assistance."[1]

TRENDS IN RETAILING

1. The Wheel of Retailing: According to this concept new forms of retail selling begin their operations with low prices and costs. As competitors notice the success of these innovators, they pursue the same customers with similar or improved product or service offerings. Cost then begins to rise as each firm tries to outdo its competitors. In due course of time, the most successful retailers become caught up in an incessant cost-price spiral. Thus, they are now vulnerable to attack from new innovators whose costs and prices are both low.

2. Advances in Technology: Retailers are adopting such advanced technological innovations as automated retailing, computer systems, mechanical means of moving customers within the store, improved methods of inventory control, and taking orders on telephone. They are also now devoting greater attention to low income groups by opening retail shops in slum areas.

QUESTIONS FOR EXERCISE

1. Define retail trade? What are the functions of retailers? Explain the main conditions for the success of retail business.

2. What do you mean by retailer? Mention the functions and services rendered by them.

3. What are the forms of Retail Trade Organisation? Explain.

4. What do you mean by Departmental Stores? What are their characteristics? How are Departmental Stores organised? How far are they popular in India?

5. What do you understand by Multiple Shops or Chain Stores? What are their advantages and disadvantages?

---

1. Mandell Maurice I. and Larry, J. Rosenberg, *Marketing*, 1983, pp. 407-408.

6. Compare and contrast the Multiple Chain Stores with the Departmental Stores.
7. What do you mean by Mail Order Business? Describe its advantages and disadvantages.
8. Explain Hire Purchase, Installment Selling, Co-operative Retailing, Super Market and One Price Shops.

24

Cooperative Marketing

Definition

1. *International Labour Organisation:* "An association of persons, usually of limited means, who have voluntarily joined together to achieve a common economic object and through the formation of a democratically controlled business organisation, making equitable contributions to the capital required and accepting fair share of risks and benefit of undertaking."

2. *Culbert:* "Cooperation is a form of organisation, wherein persons voluntarily associate together as human beings, on a basis of equality for the promotion of the economic interests of themselves."

Rules for Formation

A cooperative society is a voluntary organisation based on the rules: democratic ownership, equal voting right, security of group interest, service objective instead of profit making and mutual cooperation. Under the Indian Cooperative Societies Act any ten adult persons can get a cooperative society registered for a specific economic purpose. A cooperative society can be organised as: (*i*) Primary agricultural purchase and sale societies, (*ii*) Production and sale societies, (*iii*) Non-agricultural products purchase and sale societies, (*iv*) Multipurpose cooperative societies, (*v*) Central marketing unions, (*vi*) Consumers' cooperative stores, etc.

Need for Cooperatives

The competitive nature of retail distribution makes for many varieties and frequent changes in the types of institutions and retailing methods. The new methods have replaced the old ones. The independent stores suffered and changed their ways to improve their position. Chain stores sold the goods at cheaper rates than the independent stores. Therefore, one finds independent deviced means for reducing their costs.

FORMS OF COOPERATIVE SOCIETIES

1. Cooperative Buying Clubs: Independent retailers formed cooperative buying clubs to get lower merchandise costs and enable the members to meet chain store prices. Most cooperative buying clubs failed because they had no experience. Manufacturers refused to deal with them due to a wholesalers' pressure. They deal like chain stores of cash and carry. Most independents provided credit and delivery services, operated full service stores and made little use of advertising so they had to charge higher retail prices to cover their costs and to compensate for smalls sales volumes.

2. Retailer-owned Cooperatives: These are owned and controlled by retailer stock holders who patronise them and share in any savings in proportion to their patronage. The retailer cooperatives have a warehouse, carry inventories in stock and employ a manager. They render advice and assistance on retail merchandising problems like store layout and location, store operation, record systems, advertising methods and layouts and personnel policies, etc.

Most of them place more emphasis on group buying than on group promotional activities. As heavy group promotion is an important key to success, the retailer owned cooperatives emphasise group promotion. Hence, their members become strong competitors of chain store outlets.

3. Consumer's Cooperatives: These are retail business owned and operated by ultimate consumers to purchase and distribute goods and services chiefly to the members. Rochdale Society of Equitable Pioneer were pioneers of such societies. They laid down following principles:

(i) Open membership to all consumers.

(ii) Democratic control, one vote for a member irrespective of their holding.

(iii) All sales are at market rates only.

(iv) Members got patronage dividend proportionate to their purchases.

Consumers' cooperatives flourished in Europe. In America these were comparatively controlled by chains. They supply goods at fair prices. The surplus profit after the reduction of costs were distributed as dividend among the members. They collected order of the members and purchased at wholesale prices, eliminating profit of the middlemen. They also gave suggestions to retailers about premises, equipment, advertising, display, staff and accounting. They also served as bankers.

COOPERATIVES IN INDIA

The system prevailed in India upon the pattern of U.K. where intermediaries were avoided. The consumer was protected from exploitation by traders. As the scheme was favoured by the Indian Government, cooperatives were established at all levels, with the 'National Consumers' Cooperative Federation (N.C.C.F.) at the top. Its shares were held by Central and Provincial Governments. It guided and assisted the member institutions and consumer cooperatives. Numbering fourteen these controlled about 424 wholesale Central Consumers Cooperative Stores and 150 departmental stores. Thus, the Consumers' Cooperative Movement has achieved a large dimension in India.

The position of cooperative marketing in India was not very satisfactory before First Five Year Plan (1951-1956). After 1954 cooperative marketing became an integral part of the multi-purpose societies in India. In the Second Five Year Plan 1800 and in the Third Plan 544 primary cooperative marketing societies were registered. The number of these marketing cooperatives is increasing day by day.

ADVANTAGES OF COOPERATIVE MARKETING

1. Facility of Proper Weighing: According to a rough estimate, by malpractice in weighing a farmer used to be deceived of 1 kg. grains in every quintal grains that he sold. Marketing societies ensure full proper weight of the product.

2. Better Prices: Marketing societies ensure better prices for the product because they sell when higher prices are prevailing with market. They store the grains and other products and advance money to the owner. Thus, the farmer is not compelled to sell his products just at the time of harvest when the prices are comparatively low.

3. Better Storage Facility: The societies provide better storage facility to farmers.

4. Relief from Unauthorised and Illegal Deductions: The poor farmers were deprived of the full payment of their products when they went to unregulated markets to dispose of their products. The unscrupulous grain merchants used to make several deductions in the name of charity, donations and subscriptions. The cooperative societies have given them much relief from such illegal deductions.

5. Elimination of Middlemen: Cooperative marketing societies have done away with the long claw of intermediaries who were parasites on the hard labour of the poor cultivators.

6. Loan Facility: These societies provide facility for loans on the basis of the products of the cultivators.

7. Collective Bargaining: The farmers also reap the benefit of collective bargaining and better prices through the cooperative marketing societies.

8. Provision for Grading: The societies arrange grading facilities so that the price secured is generally high.

CONSUMERS COOPERATIVE SOCIETY

In India the consumers cooperatives are becoming quite popular as the traders adopt anti-social practices and resort to hoarding, black marketing, profiteering and creating artificial scarcities. Today, poor look to cooperative stores for fair price and quality goods.

Consumers' cooperative is a retail business owned and operated by ultimate consumers. It purchases and distributes goods and sendees chiefly to its member. The Government also help the consumers to form cooperatives and purchase the goods directly from the manufacturers. The Fifth Plan also aims at consumers' cooperative movement in India. These are most popular retailing items of food and grocery. However, there is little motivation for consumers to organise cooperatives in non-food fields, Consumers' cooperatives have been most successful in some countries like Holland, Denmark and Belgium.

Characteristics

1. Voluntary Membership: Any person who is willing to abide by the rule of the society can become its member.

2. Purchase in Bulk: The consumers' cooperatives generally purchase goods in bulk which is always economical. Thus, they are able to arrange goods comparatively at low rate.

3. No Credit: The societies sell only on cash basis. Hence, there is no fear of bad debts.

4. Distribution of Profit: The profit made by the cooperatives is distributed among the members in the proportion of their purchases.

5. Democratic Organisation: Each member has one vote irrespective of the fact how many shares he holds. Thus, the aim of the cooperative consumers societies is not making profit but getting quality goods at reasonable prices.

Advantages

1. Quality Goods: The members are able to get quality goods at reasonable price. There is no need of bargaining.

2. Cash Sales: The articles are sold on cash basis. Therefore, there is no need of having complicated accounts and fear of bad debts.

3. No Exploitation: There cannot be any exploitation of consumers by the wholesalers and intermediaries.

4. Social Service: The societies foster feelings of cooperation, mutual help and brotherhood.

5. Location: There is no need for centrally located building for consumers cooperatives.

Disadvantages of Consumers Cooperatives

1. Loose Management: Consumers' cooperative societies are ran by employees who are quite untrained, inexperienced and free from personal interest. Thus, proper functioning is not possible due to loose management.

2. Fraudulent Behaviour: The cooperative societies are managed and controlled by a managing committee consisting of members duly elected by and among the members who generally misappropriate cash and goods in their own interest.

3. Limited Scope: As only members of the consumers' cooperative stores can be the consumers of the store, outsiders are invariably not permitted to purchase from such markets. Thus, these societies have limited scope for dealings.

4. No Cooperative Feeling: In consumers cooperatives the cooperative feeling depreciates with the increase in the number of members. It has now become a general practice to allege the members of managing committee of misappropriating cash and stores by manipulating the accounts. Unfortunately, the allegations are often true.

The above drawbacks have shaken the faith of the public in consumer cooperatives Therefore, their progress in India has remained very unsatisfactory.

QUESTIONS FOR EXERCISE

1. Define Cooperative Society. What are the fundamental reasons behind its establishment?
2. Write a short note on Consumers' Cooperative Society.

25

Sales Policies

Definition of Sales Policy

A policy may be defined as "a line or course of action to be followed over a considerable period of time usually for years together." It is an art of regulating or guiding a business. It is a code by which a course of action is determined. Examples of policies are: the one price policy; policies regarding discounts to be given to middlemen or an agent; a valuable price policy of bargaining with customers to establish prices on individual sales; selling only through exclusive agencies; making a high quality product and selling at the market plus simplification in product and so on. Everyone who sells must have a sales policy, without it sellers are swayed in their decisions by the exigencies of the moment instead of being guided by a predetermined code. A policy holds one's place in the market.

Objectives of Sales Policy

Usually policies have more immediate objectives. For example, the salesman may be motivated by fulfilling his quota and the bonus which he expects to earn than by the long-term objectives of the company. The labourer in the plant may be motivated more by his pay, his pride in the policy of the company to make a superior product. This does not mean that employees are unaffected by the major policies of their companies. However, the major policies of a company should be supplemented with minor policies. The minor objectives must be reached before major objectives can be attained.

Formulation of Sales Policies

Formulation of major policies should be done either the top executives or the owner of the business himself. In a one man's business usually the owner makes of the major decisions. He shall be successful if he has good judgement and can handle men. However, sooner or later he may get into trouble because he may not have a broad vision or due to the inability of grasping quickly the significance of changes in technology, demand, living conditions, public sentiments or the attitude of labour. Therefore, some of the concerns appoint committees to determine policies. Members of these committees can supplement the information of the chairman, criticise and evaluate the proposals coming to it, and consider the different angles of these problems. If committees function properly, they are an improvement on one man decisions because major policies should not be decided quickly. Policies should be based on facts as far as possible. However, since policies have to do with the future, it is impossible to have all the needed facts. Facts may be obtained from the records of the company, from published sources, from the observations and experiences of the executives or from the reports of research men in or out of the company. Research may be to obtain the facts which serve as the basis of policy formulation.

Predetermined policies in marketing avoid differences and ill-will and prevent annoyance and indecision on the part of executives who have to control these activities. Complications may arise due to haphazard, indeterminate or fortuitous manner of doing business. By policies the road to progress is kept clear of these unnecessary pitfalls and hindrances. Once a policy is determined it should always be given the force of a law. The value of sound business is comparable to the value of good laws in guiding the administration of government. The opinion of one man should not be considered as final in marketing policies. The consequences of policies are far too important to permit so arbitrary or careless a formulation without experience and sound principles no opinion should be given consideration.

Sound policies are developed by the application of experience and thought. The best thought and experience available should be given to the formation of the policies to be followed. Then from time to time desired changes should be made in the existing policies.

Principles in Policy Determination

According to P.E. Holden, following principles are essential in policy determination.[1]

(1) The statement of policy should be definite, clear and understandable to everyone in the organisation.

(2) Policies should be translated into practices, terms and peculiarities of every department or division of the enterprise.

(3) Policies, regardless of how fundamental should not be inflexible; they should, however, possess a high degree of permanency.

(4) Stability of policies is essential constantly and changing policies are fatal to business success.

(5) There should be as many policies as necessary to cover conditions that can be anticipated but not too many policies to become confusing or meaningless.

(6) Policies should be predicted on fact and sound judgement and should not constitute mere personal reflection.

(7) Policies should not prescribe detailed procedure except in rare instances.

(8) Policies should recognise economic principles, be in conformity with federal and other laws, and be compatible with public interest.

Coverage of the Sales Policy

Newman opines that a company must have a sound sales policy covering the following points:[2]

1. *Products or Services to be sold:* (*a*) Type of product; (*b*) Number and variety of products; (*c*) Quality of products.

2. *Customers to whom Products will be sold:* (*a*) Channels of distribution, (*b*) Type of customers, (*c*) Size of customers, (*d*) Location of customers.

3. *Prices at which Products will be sold:* (*a*) Relation to prices of competing products; (*b*) Relation of cost of production and distribution; (*c*) Relation to prices of individual items; (*d*) Quantity and trade discounts; (*e*) Frequency of price changes; (*f*) Resale price maintenance.

---

1. Holden, P.E., *Cost and Production Handbook*, 1934, p. 1332.
2. Newman, *Administrative Action*, 1956, pp. 44-45.

4. *Sales Promotion:* (*a*) Sales appeals emphasised: (*b*) Types and media of advertising; (*c*) Use of personal solicitation.

Elements of Sales Policies

1. Discount, prices, and terms of payment.
2. Distribution and relation with distributors.
3. Publicity.
4. Attitude towards customers and consumers.
5. Attitude towards competition and competitors.
6. Attitude towards the employees of the business.

1. Discount and Prices: "Throughout Europe and America in spite of laws to the contrary, there are to be found cut price shops which thrive by selling at little less than a price that is advertised or known. Besides this form of price cutting, there is the practice of allowing special discounts. So widespread and vicious had this habit become in America that at one time several magazines and articles appeared which stated that anyone who paid retail price was a sap. There were discounts for cash, discounts for trade, discounts for teachers, professors, doctors, advertising discounts and quantity discounts. Industrial discounts entitle all the employees of an industrial firm who placed their orders through the purchasing department of that firm to the wholesale price. Thus, since it was unethical to charge different people different price astute businessmen preserved their dignity under a one price policy and slashed one another's profits with the two-edged sword of discount. Eventually the state stepped in and endeavoured to put a stop to price discrimination and the abuse of discounts by the Robinson Pitman Act.[1]

In India it is rather impossible for a concern to control the price at which its products are sold to the consumer. Manufacturers sometimes advertise to the general public that authorised price for a particular article is so much while it will sell at that price but the vast majority will immediately see in such an attempt an opportunity to increase their sales and their profits by taking business away from their rivals through price cutting. This cutting of prices goes on till the dealers in that product are buying and selling it without a margin making their gross profit from the sale of the packing case. Some dealers sell certain products at a loss

1. Asplev, *Handbook of Sales Management*.

as to demonstrate to their customers that their prices are very low but when the customer asks for an article not so well, known the price is loaded sufficient to take care of the loss on the more popular article.

As dealers are very much influenced by the size of discount offered, therefore, it is a common practice of certain manufacturers and sellers in quoting prices that their catalogue or list price is subject to discounts of 30 per cent and 20 per cent, *i.e.,* the prices are first reduced to 30 per cent and the resultant figure is further reduced by 20 per cent. These heavy discounts are nothing but simply fictions. If a manufacturer desires to sell directly to retailers he must have the same one set of prices and discounts, for all dealers whether they are retailers or wholesale merchants. If the manufacturer does not want to serve the retailer directly he must have one set of prices for the wholesalers and a higher set for the retailers and under no circumstances should he sell to retailers at any other price. Thus, the retailers will get the lower discount from the wholesale dealers, who are ready to slash profits, they will not buy from the manufacturers.

2. Distribution and Relation with other Distributors: Before laying down a policy for the distribution of goods it is necessary to consider the nature of the marketing job and suitable channel for their distribution. The distribution policy should be formulated when this is completed. Deviation from the policy thus decided is not desirable. The purpose to be accomplished by distribution should be the determining factor in selecting sales channels. For example, if universal distribution of a product is considered necessary to its successful marketing the product should be available in all kinds of retail shops. The only way to achieve the purpose would be to sell on the same terms to all retailers and on slightly better terms to all wholesalers, regardless of the particular trade in which they may have specialised. Again, if the product requires the seller to use some degree of salesmanship in order to persuade the consumer to purchase it, the product may be sold either directly to the consumer or merchandiser, or through retailers providing them with sufficient inducement to make the necessary special efforts to sell the product.

The exclusive sales agreements are entered mainly for three purposes.

(*i*) The sole agent promises to sell a sufficient and definite volume of goods to justify his appointment.

(*ii*) The sole agent promises to do a good job of marketing in his territory, co-operating with the manufacturer in his plans and policies and where he resells to other dealers maintaining prices that will yield them a fair profit.

(*ii*) The customs or excise or other political barriers make it possible to secure adequate distribution without some such arrangement.

The policy formulated should outline such activities as the amount of help to be given to retail dealers and wholesalers in reselling the stocks of the producer's merchandise, guarantee of quality, replacement of defective or damaged goods and the return of unsold stocks. It is necessary to first inform the dealers of the established policy of the firm and then showing them firmly and sympathetically that any deviation will hinder their own trade as that of the manufacturers.

3. Publicity: Whatever the form of publicity or propaganda used, a definite policy should always be laid down and strictly followed. Better results will be achieved by sticking to a plan that has been well thought out.

If it is desired that goods should be sold cheap, it is a waste to conduct an advertising campaign for it. Crores of rupees worth of cheap Japanese goods have been sold in India without advertising. Cheapness is an argument that does not need a campaign to get it across as the Americans say. An imposing volume can be built up by a little judicious publicity to get the sales started and then by merely exposing the articles and naming their price. It is more a question of distribution than advertising with cheap goods. The buyers tell others about it, and the ridiculously low price brings people into buying their passing satisfaction.

Where it is felt that product of goods quality should be marketed at a reasonable price, the foundations of successful selling are the following:

(*i*) the quality of the product must be consistent and unvarying;

(*ii*) a brand or name by which to distinguish and identify that product;

(*iii*) the right idea on which to base the appeal to the prospective consumer;

(*iv*) faith and consistency in advertising; and

(*v*) Policy may be chalked out with honesty, as the basis of all claims. But some other technical considerations must also be considered with it.

4. Attitude Towards Customers and Consumers: Honesty demands that the manufacturer lives up to the claims he has made. If he does not do so the consumer soon finds it out and the business is adversely affected. He must give the consumer what he pays for. If he feels that it is necessary for him to guarantee the quality or performance of his goods, he should do so in order to meet or overcome competition, or to make the product easier to sell. However, it is usually better not to guarantee. The consumer will come to know the quality of the product, and if that quality is unvaryingly satisfying the manufacturer can be sure that sales will be steady. If a product reaches the consumer in a damaged condition the manufacturer should exchange it for a prefect, it has a goodwill building force that a guarantee entirely lacks.

5. Attitude Towards Competitors: "Competition," says Mr. Harvey, S. Firestone, "rarely puts anyone out of business; a man usually puts himself out of business either by not making a good article or by wrong methods in sales or finance." This may seem to be an unusual viewpoint, but when thoroughly considered it will be found to be correct. Competition makes men keen and efficient, it forces them to improve their products as well as service, it compels the trade to give respect to the consumer, it cuts costs and decentralises distribution. Inefficiency, lack of proper service, high operating and manufacturing costs, and an intolerant, haughty attitude are the natural off-spring of monopolies. Two important points should be borne in mind while formulating a policy to meet competition. The manufacturer or a seller should first understand what competition is and in which sphere it is working and what will be its effect.

6. Attitude Towards Employees of the Business: An attitude towards employees should be adopted that will secure their goodwill and co-operation in making the product as satisfactory as possible and in securing as large a volume of sales as desired. There should be a policy of give and take with employees. Their complaints and suggestions should be listened to sympathetically. A training programme should be included in the policy governing relations with employees.

WINDOW DISPLAYS AND WINDOW DRESSING

Meaning

By the term *"window display"* is to be understood "the display made in the front part of the retail shops for brining to the notice of the passers by goods that can be procured from inside."

Objective

The object of window display or outside display is to attract persons into store by sufficiently arousing their interest. The outdoor displays play an important part in the personality of the store as the public instinctly assess the nature of the business and type of service of the store from the cleanliness, modern style, and attractiveness of the display.

Principles of Window Display

(1) Cleanliness and well-finished appearance.

(2) Adequate lighting.

(3) For variety of display an adequate stock of table, glass, shelves, etc. should be available and arranged properly.

(4) The window should not be filled up with a miscellany of small objects.

(5) High narrow windows can be given a wider appearance by the use of horizontal lining in the decorations. Likewise, lone and low windows can be made to look higher by the use of vertical lining.

(6) Care should be exercised in the selection of the goods for the window, spoiled or damaged goods must never be displayed. It gives bad impression.

(7) The centre panel of the background should be planned first and the display around it should be done next.

(8) At least one show should be used to carry the message to those who are a bit slow on the 'up-take'. The price should also be narrated.

(9) The window display should be made seasonal. Try to be the first to display for the season.

(10) Effective use of the colour should be made.

(11) The widow displays should be changed regularly. The goods should not be allowed to get dirty or faded.

Conditions to Making Window Display Effective

(1) Rooms are hired in business localities and on the sides of main-roads which are frequented most by the people;

(2) Rooms should be in the vicinity of the competitors because people remember market centres well than individual shops situated in a lonely corner.

(3) The name board should be conspicuous by its appearance so as to have the attention value.

QUESTIONS FOR EXERCISE

1. Define sales policy and explain its elements.
2. Write short note on Window Display.

26

Promotion of Marketing Communication

After product market strategy, the promotional strategy is the key element in overall marketing strategy. It focuses upon fitting the product and its features to the target market's needs. It focuses upon making the product flow through the marketing channels to the target market. It is concerned with the marketer's activities in concert both with members of the target market and the middlemen to increase the chances that the planned sequence of sales takes place smoothly and efficiently.

Definition of Promotion

1. *Douglas, W. Mellot*: "Promotion is the chief means that a firm has of influencing buyers' behaviour without cutting prices. It succeeds or fails to the degree that it communicates or fails to communicate product benefits to customers."

2. *Alderson, Wroe and Green*: "Promotion is any marketing effort is to inform or persuade actual or potential consumers about the merits of a (given) product or service for the purpose of introducing a consumer either to continue or to start purchasing the firms product or service at same (given) price."[1]

3. *Brink and Kelly*. "Promotion is the coordination of all seller initiated efforts to set up channel of information and persuasion to facilitate the sale or a product service or the acceptance of an idea."[2]

---

1. Alderson, Wroe, and Paul, E. Green, *Planning and Problem Solving in Marketing*, Richard D. Irwin, Englewood, 1964. p. 270.
2. Brink, Edward L. and Kelley, William T., *The Management of Promotion*, Prentice Hall, Englewood Cliffs, 1963, p. 6.

Thus, promotion includes activities and processes designed to change or reinforce behaviour and ideas of the consumers, through communication, so that they are persuaded to buy what they might not otherwise buy, what they don't really want to buy. Promotion is "telling" and "selling". It is an exercise in information, persuasion and influence, inter-related in the sense that to "inform is to persuade"; and if "a person is persuaded he is informed."

DISTINCTION BETWEEN SELLING AND PROMOTION

Selling has been defined as "the personal or, impersonal process of assisting and/or persuading a prospective customer to buy a commodity or a service or to act favourably upon an idea, that has commercial significance to the seller."[1] On the other hand, "promotion" is an all inclusive term representing the broad field-advertising, personal selling, and sales promotion. "The promotional mix, therefore, deals with coordination of the sales force activities, the advertising programmes, and other promotional efforts, which may include packaging, branding, direct mail solicitation, point of purchase display, premiums, holding trade shows and exhibitions, use of sample or gifts." Thus, Promotion is a very wide term including advertising, personal selling, sales promotion and other promotional tools that can be devised to reach the goals of the sales programme. "Sales promotion" is only a part of it. "Sales promotion" has been defined as "activities, other than personal selling, advertising and publicity, that stimulate consumer purchasing and dealer effectiveness, such as displays, shows and expositions, demonstrations, etc." The important function of sales promotion is to serve as bridge between advertising and personal selling to supplement and co-ordinate efforts in these two areas.

In retailing, sales promotion is interpreted to cover "all methods of stimulating customer purchasing including personal selling, advertising and publicity."

Promotional Activities

The promotional activities are concerned with stimulating demand, which may be achieved by any of the three activities:

---

1. American Association of Marketing, *Committee on Definitions: A Glossary of Marketing Terms*, 1960, p. 21.

(*i*) *Informing* the people about the existing or new products, distinctive wants—satisfying characteristics and its availability.

(*ii*) *Reminding* the present and prospective buyers periodically about the product and its role in consumption.

(*iii*) *Persuading* the prospective buyers that make them to buy.

TYPES OF PROMOTION

1. Informative promotion: It is a necessity for firms bringing out discontinuous innovations such as automatic kitchenware colour television, radios, pocket calculators, and home video machinery. Thus, informative promotion is needed when a firm has distinctly new product for sale.

2. Persuasive promotion: It is needed where continuous and dynamically continuous innovations are brought out, and the consumer needs to be persuaded that an item is better than the substitutes in the market. Thus, persuasive promotion is used when a firm has a product that is very similar to other products.

3. Reminder promotion: It is used after products are well established.

PROMOTION OF NON-BUSINESS ACTIVITY

Promotion is also used by non-business organisations. For example, a university, or a professional institution uses promotion to get students join and enrol. The promotional techniques used by political candidates are: holding of meetings, issuing election manifestoes, radio talks, etc. These aim at winning votes. Charitable institutions solicit donations through advertising in media, door-to-door visits and collection boxes placed at specified centres. Indian government uses promotional technique for popularising family planning programmes.

NEED FOR PROMOTIONAL ACTIVITIES

1. Closing of Physical Separation: The physical separation of the consumers and producers, and an increase in the number of potential customers, have given significance to communication system. The physical gap is closed by good info-management.

2. Encouraging Distribution: As improvements in physical distribution of facilities have expanded the area limits of the markets, establishment of communication system has become a necessity'.

3. Closing Information Gap: Between the producers and the users there are a large number of wholesalers and retailing middlemen who have developed, necessitating that not only the consumers be informed about the benefit of the product, but the middlemen also need be informed about products. These middlemen, should also communicate with the retailers and consumers. The information gap is closed by promotional programmes.

4. Stimulation of Demand: Promotion works as a stimulant to restore the demand for the existing product. When sale begins to decline, either due to preference for a new product brought out by the competitor or a total dislike for it, it is necessary to maintain a high material standard of living and a high level of employment.

OBJECTIVES OF PROMOTION

Hasty and Will have put the objectives of promotion under three heads:[1]

1. The demand objectives: These aim to influence, stimulate maintain and create demand for a product.

2. The communication objectives: These aim at creating awareness, providing information to the customer and retailers about product features where products can be obtained, and what the products are capable of doing or achieving as brand preferences.

3. The specific or performance objectives: These provide specific information about a product and which influence the decision of purchasing by the customer.

Broad Objectives of Promotion

1. Exposure: It means to expose an adequate number of target consumers to the messages. For this purpose, such promotion media is chosen which as will reach adequate numbers of target consumers. Magazines such as *Readers Digest, Femina, Imprint, Industrial Times, Star and Style,* etc. may be selected according to the nature of target consumers for bringing the product to their knowledge.

2. Attention: Attention refers to the state of focusing one's mind upon something.[2] Attending to promotion consumers focus their

1. Hasty, Ronald W. and Will, R. Tead, *Marketing,* 1975, pp. 295-298.
2. Thompson, Joseph W., *Selling : A Behavioural Science Approach,* McGraw-Hill Book Co., New York, 1966, p. 260.

perception upon it. As innumerable media are available to baffle the target consumers, the marketer must see that the attention of the consumer is drawn by designing messages and utilising media that stand out from others. Consumers are likely to attend to those that are in colour, that feature a well-known personality, that are larger than others or louder than others.

3. Comprehension: It means to have the ability to understand or receive communicated knowledge. It is achieved when consumers interpret the message in the manner intended by the marketman. Messages need to be presented in a clear and unambiguous words. Interest can be generated by creating curiosity and promising rewards by asking questions or by showing the consumer something unusual; and by elucidating the way of getting rewarded by use of that message.

4. Attitude Change: Promotion may aim at changing the existing attitude by promising a reward that consumers value, or by urging consumers to try the brand on a sample basis, if they have not done it before.

5. Inducing Behaviour or Action: The promotional programmes may aim at encouraging consumers to take action in any of these forms: (*i*) buy the make/brand for the first time; (*ii*) continue to buy it; (*iii*) buy more of this brand; (*iv*) urge others to buy it; (*v*) visit retail shops; (*vi*) see demonstrations; and (*vii*) try out the product.

To conclude, the role of promotion is to (*a*) awaken consumer demand; (*b*) add value to the products (by giving them a desirable image and differentiating them from other products); (*c*) inform people whose service and products can be purchased; and (*d*) contact new uses for these.

COMMUNICATION AND PROMOTION

The word "communication" is derived from the Latin word "communis," meaning common. Communication requires "commonness" in the words or symbols used by both the sender and the receiver. The message must mean one and the same thing to both. Communication means "sharing of meaning," transmission of information, because sharing necessitates information.[1] Communication is concerned with who says what

1. Schranam, W., *The Process and Effects of Mall Communication*, University of Illinois Press, 1955, p. 3.

to whom, through which channel and with what effect. According to Crane, a communication process requires only three elements or stages: a *message, a source* of this message and a *receiver.*[1] But some more elements have also been added to it so that five distinct stages are-recognised in communication—a source encoding, message, channel, destination and feedback.[2] The objective of communication system is to reproduce, at the destination, the content of the message originating at the source.[3] Its accuracy depends on the integrity with which a message is transmitted and the correspondences between the meaning assigned to the symbols/language used by the source and by the receiver. Any thing that distorts the quality of transmission, reduces the effectiveness of a message.

MARKETING COMMUNICATION PROCESS

To achieve its objectives a marketer's promotional message must be communicated by the manager and received by middlemen and/or the target consumers. A marketing communication process is a five-stage process:

1. Source: The information source originates the communication, *i.e.,* there must be a person with idea to communicate. For instance, the marketing executive may have ideas, information, instructions to communicate to his subordinates sales force and the target markets; or the middlemen about the product/service.

2. Encoding: The idea/the information has to be encoded by means of sales manuals, charts, copy, artwork, news release, sales promotion merchandise, etc. The various promotional methods make use of a variety of promotional channels, mass communication (by advertising), personal contact (by personal selling), mail, telephone, etc.

3. Message: The message carrying the idea is transmitted from the marketer to the receiver either by print media, some signs and symbols (words—written or spoken), gestures and facial expressions and images. These have to be sent through some appropriate channel—may be simply by air waves that carry

1. Crane, E., *Marketing Communication,* John Wiley & Sons, New York, 1965, p. 11.
2. Aaker, David A. and John, G. Myres, *Advertising Management,* Prentice-Hall, Englewood Cliff. N.J., 1975, pp. 249-267.
3. Stern, Mark E., *Market Planning* : A Systems Approach, McGraw Hill Book Co., New York, 1966.

voices in a room; the electricity that carries voices through a telephone connection, the postal service and the like.

4. Decoding: The message is decoded, *i.e.*, interpreted in the light of the experience of the receiver or frames of reference. Whether the message is recognised or not depends upon the individual's threshold of awareness. Attitudes, motives, experience, expectations, perceptional consistency, and perceptional defences all combined to raise or lower a person's sensitivity to the message.

5. Receivers Feedback: If the sender's message has reached the receiver in its intended form, the receiver will respond with feedback of some kind—he may make further communication, or accept and take action on it, feedback gives an idea whether and to what extent the message has been received or grasped by the receiver. Feedback may take any form—a nod, an expression of interest or anger, or a smile or acceptance of the message by conduct.

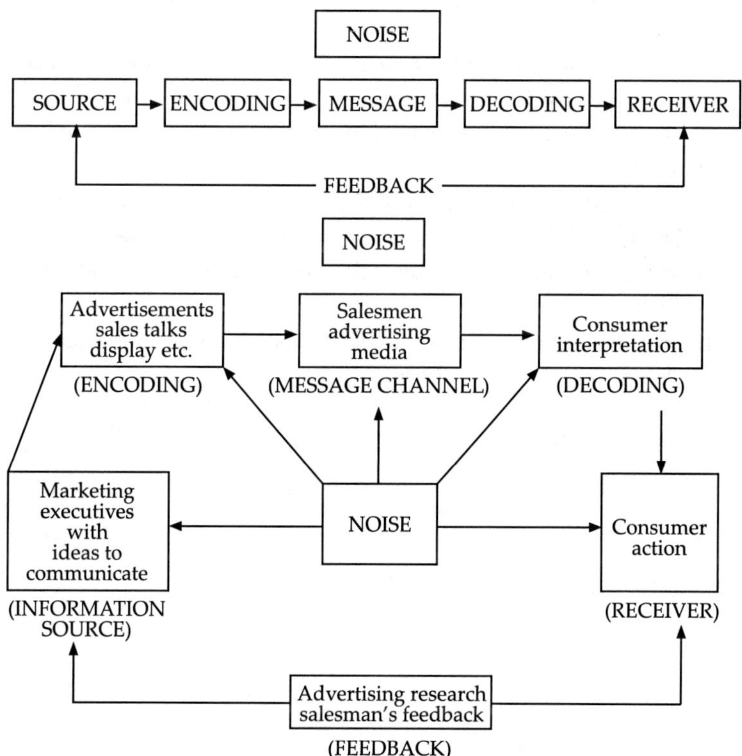

Fig. 26.1: Marketing Communication Process.

STEPS IN PROMOTION DECISIONS

1. Setting of the clear objectives: These objectives may be general or specific. The promotion programmes should reflect a thorough knowledge of the market, the type of the product and the stage in the product cycle.

2. Determining promotion budget: Budget should reflect the finance resources available for undertaking the programme. Allocation of a reasonable account for promotion is necessary to fulfil its role in the marketing strategy. If the budget is too large, funds are wasted that might have been better used elsewhere. Following methods may be used for determining the size of the budget: (*i*) The judgement of the experienced mangeres; (*ii*) imitating competitors, *i.e.*, spending sums that approximate the actual amounts or percentage of sales or profit that rivals spend; (iii) percentage of sales or profits of the firm; and the nature of the programme needed in light of the objectives.

3. Knowing about the target market: Market can be identified by special demographic and geographic characteristics and should accordingly reflect to what particular type of customers goods are to be offered.

4. The appeal—its nature and timing: What type of appeals should be made? When and how often? Depends on what benefits the prospects are likely to enjoy if they use the product sponsored by the firm.

5. The promotion-mix patterns: These should reflect how effective and efficient methods should be applied.

Steps in pormotion decisions have been diagrammatically shown below:

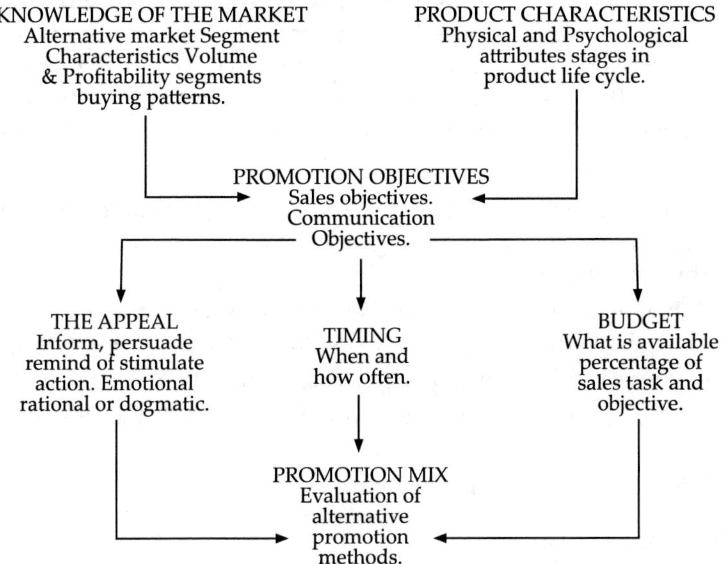

Fig. 26.2: Marketing Promotion Decisions.

PROMOTIONAL MIX

Promotional mix is the combination, types and amounts of different forms of promotion used by a market. These include personal selling, advertisement, sales promotion and publicity.

(1) Personal Selling

The American Marketing Association defines personal selling as: "Oval presentation in a conversation with one or more prospective purchases for the purpose of making sales."[1] Its hallmark is interaction between marketer and customer. It consists of the interpretation of product and service features in terms of benefits and advantages to the buyer and of persuading the buyer to buy the right kind and quantity of the product.[2] Its purpose is "to pair the right products with the right customers." It ranges from basic order taking to creative selling. Its effect is to push the product

1. *Marketing Definitions*, p. 9.
2. Hass, K.B., *Professional Salesmanship*, 1962, p. 3.

through the distribution channel. It involves personal interaction between the source and the destination. It aims at individual, As contrasted to the advertisement, whose approach is "shot gun approach," its approach is "rifle approach". Sales persons tailor their messages according to the unique characteristics of each product. By observing and listening, they receive immediate feedback as to the degree to which these messages are getting across.

1. Advantages: Personal selling is the most efficient and the most costly promotional method. It gives marketers a chance to adopt to fluid selling situation.

2. A personal relationship can develop between a customer and a sales person that gives the sales person a better understanding.

3. It allows products and services to be demonstrated.

4. Allows a customer to get extra details about a product or services.

5. It is a very intensive means of promotion.

Conditions of Utility

According to D. Scott, personal selling is more useful:

(1) when the company is small or has insufficient funds with which to carry on an advertising programme;

(2) when the market is concentrated, or

(3) when the personality of the salesman is needed to establish rapport or create confidence; or

(4) when the product has a higher unit value and requires demonstration; or

(5) where it must be fitted to the individual-customer's needs, as in the case of insurance or securities, or

(6) where consumer goods are to be sold, such as high fashion clothing, or which involves a trade in.[1]

PROMOTION THROUGH ADVERTISING

Tools of Advertising

Advertising is an interpersonal presentation and promotion ideas, goods or services, by an identified sponsor.[2] It is an

1. Scott, D., *Advertising Principles and Problems,* 1953.
2. *Marketing Definitions,* p. 18.

inter-personal method of communicating messages regarding products or services from an identified source to a particular segment of the consumers market or prospective buyers. The means of communication used in advertisement vary from outdoor media, which may be purely *visual* such as newspapers and magazine space; or *aural* media, such as radio; or a combined visual and aural media, such as television. Other tools are direct mail (catalogue, or brochures), motion picture, novelties (calendars, ball point pens, blotters), radio and television (both local and network), billboards, signs and posters, car cards, printed advertisements appearing on buses, taxies and railway compartments; directions and references; programmes and menus, and circulars etc.

Goals of Advertising

The basic goals of advertising are: (1) To sell products and services, (2) To create favourable images of products and firms, (3) To allow firms to compete successfully.

Marketing Advertisement

Advertising is designed to catch the attention of large groups of consumers rather than individuals. Advertising by manufacturers emphasizes *what* to buy rather than *where* to buy. In the retail level, advertising stresses *where* purchase as well as *what* to purchase. It is highly useful for developing initial product awareness or acceptance which makes the final selling job easier. Advertising works best when a large number of prospects are to be contacted, or a special reduction sale done or announce a new credit policy.

Favourable Conditions

Neil Borden has suggested following five conditions under which advertising is profitable:[1]

(1) *A favourable primary demand curve,* because it is easier to sell what is already selling well.

(2) *Significant opportunities for differentiating product,* because advertising is of little value when products are similar. It tends to be more effective when products are more differentiated.

---

1. Borden, Neil H., *Economic Effect of Advertising,* Richard, D. Irwin, Homewood, 1942, pp. 424-428.

(3) *Hidden qualities in the product,* when qualities of a product are hidden and cannot be clearly seen and revaluated, customers are more likely to rely on brands.

(4) *Emotional buying motives,* where they are associated with buying patterns, advertising can be a powerful tool.

(5) *Relatively large sums of money available,* for advertising can be done on a large scale basis only if enough money is available.

The opportunity to make profitable use of advertising generally depends not on any one of the above factors, but rather on a combination of them.

SALES PROMOTION

Definition of Sales Promotion

The term sales promotion has been defined as: "Those marketing activities, other than personal selling, advertising and publicity, that stimulate consumer purchasing and dealer effectiveness, such as displays, shows and demonstrations, expositions, and various non-current selling efforts, not in ordinary routine."[1]

Nature of Sales Promotion

Sales promotion activities are impersonal and usually non-recurring. They are directed to ultimate consumers, industrial users, and middlemen. They serve as a bridge between advertising and personal selling and supplement and coordinate efforts in these two areas. The importance of sales promotion has increased tremendously in modern times millions of rupees are spent on determining the most effective techniques and appeals for arresting the attention of the prospects into the dealer's space of business. Aggressive sales promotion programmes remove consumer's dissatisfaction about particular products of a particular manufacturer while advertising media reach the consumer and may soon be forgotten, sales promotional devices of remind or stimulate the customer to make purchase promptly on the spot.

Objectives of Sales Promotion

(1) To introduce new products: To induce buyers to purchase a new product, free samples may be distributed, or money and merchandise allowance may be offered to business to stock and sell the product.

1. *Marketing Definitions,* p. 20.

(2) To attract new customers: New customers may be attracted by distribution issue of free samples, permiums, contests and similar devices.

(3) To induce present customers to buy more: Present customers may be induced to buy more by knowing more about a product, its ingredients and uses.

(4) To help firm remain competitive: Sales promotions may be undertaken to meet competition from a firm.

(5) To increase sales in off-seasons: Buyers may be encouraged to use the product in off-seasons by showing them the variety of uses of the product.

(6) To increase the inventories of business buyers: Retailers may be induced to keep in stock more units of product, so that more sales can be effected.

Sales Promotion Activities

Sales promotion activities are those done for consumers and those for the dealers.

Consumer's Sale Promotion Programmes

1. Sampling: Free samples may be distributed among the prospective customers for arousing their interest in the product. It is an effective sales promotion device when the product is frequently purchased convenience goods such as detergents, soap, tea or coffee, deodorants of sausages, etc.

Table 26.1: Examples of Sales Promotion Activities[1]

	Consumer Promotion		Channel Promotion
1.	*Sampling* Giving away product to induce trial.	1.	*Bonus* Extra cash payment for sale.
2.	*Coupon* Certificate that reduces prices.	2.	*Push Money or Premium* Bonus on certain brand.
3.	*Cents-off promotion* Reduction in regular price.	3.	*Contests* Prizes to best sales effort in a given period.

Contd...

1. Luick, John F. and William, L. Ziegler, *Sales Promotion and Modern Merchandising,* McGraw Hill Book Co., New York, 1968, and Kotler, Philip, *Marketing Management: Analysis, Planning and Control,* Prentice Hall. Englewood Cliff, 1962, pp. 649-52.

	Consumer Promotion		Channel Promotion
4.	*Premium* Small extra "gift" with product.	4.	*Cooperative advertising* Manufacturer and distributor share advertising costs.
5.	*Competition* Contests, sweep-stakes.	5.	*Dealer-listed promotion* Manufacturer advertisement that lists distributor.
6.	*Demonstrations* Sharing of product in use.	6.	*Consignment* Manufacturer finances distributor inventories.
7.	*Trading stamps.*	7.	*Point-of-Purchase Display* Counter-top, posters, mechanised signs.

However, sampling is not always a good marketing strategy. It is not justified in case of (*a*) well-established product, (*b*) a product that is not superior in some way to competing products or whose points of superiority would not easily be recognised by the consumer, (*c*) a product with a slow turnover, (*d*) a product with a narrow margin of profit, or (*e*) a highly fragile, perishable or bulky product.[1]

2. **Contests:** These may be conducted to attract new customers or to introduce new product by asking the prospects to state in a few words why they prefer a particular product.

3. **Demonstrations:** This devise is generally used when products are complex and of a technical nature, such as rotary duplicators, computers, field machinery, electrical pumping set, chemical fertilisers, cosmetics, or apparel.

4. **Couponing:** Coupons generally supplied along with the product, entitle the holder to either a specified savings on a product or a cash refund. Most coupons are designed to: (*a*) introduce a new product, (*b*) increase sale of an established product, (*c*) sell new and larger sizes of a product, (*d*) induce customers to switch brands, or (*e*) encourage repeat sales.

Dealer's Sales Promotional Activities

1. **Extra cash or trade discount:** This is offered on the basis of orders placed.

2. **Display and advertising allowances:** These are given to compensate the dealers for the space given for the display of manufacturers product.

1. Schwartz, *David J., Marketing Today: A Basic Approach*, 1977, p. 496.

3. Premium: It is a product usually offered free or at less than its usual price to encourage consumer to buy another product. Premiums are used by wholesalers to induce retailers to promote push their products. The objectives of premiums are: (*i*) To induce consumers to switch from a competitor's product to the seller's, (*ii*) To induce consumers to try larger sizes of products, (*iii*) To increase off season sales, (*iv*) To introduce a new product, (*v*) To obtain names of prospects, (*vi*) To off-set price competition.

POINT-OF-PURCHASE (P.O.P.)

Meaning of P.O.P.

Known by several names such as dealer hopes, dealer aids, dealer displays, merchandising and point-of-sale materials. The point-of-purchase display is the silent salesman that calls the attention of the customer to the product in the hope of initiating buying action.[1]

Types of P.O.P.

1. *Exterior items*: These include signs, banners, pendants, and display are utilised by the retail business like service stations.

2. *Interior items*: These are found in store windows, on counters and shelves, and hanging from the ceiling or the walls and on the floor.

Media of P.O.P.

Most of the P.O.P. materials are temporary counter cards, dummy packages, cut-outs, shelf-strips and streamers. But exterior items are permanent-store identification signs, clocks, thermometers, floor cabinets, calendars and racks. The materials of which these are made may be cardboard, metal, plastics, wood, cloths, glass, etc.

The most popular P.O.P. items are magazines and advertisement reprints; window banners and streamers; decals on windows, doors and mirrors; wall posters, racks of wire, metal and wood; plaques; merchandise display on counters and floors; display shopping cartons and exhibition displays.

1. Little, J.E. and Kirpatrick, C.A., *Advertising*, p. 15.

Advantages of P.O.P.

1. Buying stimulus: It arises from the nearness of the consumer to the actual product. Littlefield and Kirkpatrick say, "No other medium enjoys such a combination of time, place and atmosphere; at no other time, are merchandise, money and mood, so co-operative and harmonious."

2. Advantage to the manufacturers: Manufacturers use this medium to help persuade retailers to stock new products; to help increase the size of retail orders; to help introduce special offers, and help the retailer to "trade up" some of his customers.

3. Advantage to Retailers: Retailers use this medium to get the attention of the prospects and then to urge them to buy promptly then and there. "Exterior items and window displays attempt to influence, even to control, sidewalk traffic by converting part of it into floor traffic by keeping passer by from passing-by. Interior display try for a sale by appealing to the impulse of the buyers.

4. Advantage to Consumers: Consumers get useful information about problems, solution and satisfaction.

Criteria of Effective P.O.P.

(*i*) Point-of-purchase promotion must be built around and on a big sales idea, that it should be capable of attracting shoppers.

(*ii*) Copy should be simple, short and direct. It should be legible from a distance of 10 to 15 feet.

(*iii*) The design of display should be bold and distinctive, and suit the decor of the store.

(*iv*) The merchandise displays should be put on store floors, on store counter, and in bins or baskets because consumers like to see, feel, handle and examine products while considering their purchase.

(*v*) It makes the product look valuable and worth at least the price charged.

P.O.P. Advertising

1. Sales promotional activities inside a retail shop: These may consist of:

(*i*) Temporary *price reductions* as in case of clearance sale, or when the product has gone out of fashion, or to increase sales during off season.

(*ii*) *Counter-display cards, wall signs, banners, display bins, baskets* may also be used as in store promotional media.

(*iii*) Demonstrations may also be arranged within the store to convince the prospects of the utility of the product offered.

2. Publicity: It is a means of promoting to the mass market. The most common types of publicity are news releases (also called *press releases*), photography and feature stories about the product or a service.[1]

3. Public Relations: Public relations deal with the relationship of the organisation to its public—the individual consumers, organisational users, the press, the environmentalist, and middlemen. Public relations activities include sponsoring floats in parades, lobbying and using promotion messages to persuade members of the public to take a desired position.

Table 26.2 summarises the characteristics of the various promotional media. Describing the targets, costs to the sponsor, status of the sponsor, feedback status and channel for each media. In chosing the best mix of promotional media, management must select those medias whose characteristics best fulfil the marketing strategy.

Table 26.2: Characteristics of Promotional Media[2]

Promotion Media	Targets	Cost to Company	Status of Sponsor	Feedback Status	Channel
1. Advertising	Groups (mass)	Payment to media	Identified	Neither precise nor fast	Mass media
2. Personal Selling	Individuals	Results in costs to the organisation	Identified	Both precise and fast	Sales persons or channel members
3. Sales Promotion	Groups	Results in cost to the organisation	Identified	Usually less precise and fast than personal selling.	Persons employed by organisation or channel members
4. Publicity	Groups (mass)	Free	No Sponsor nor fast	Neither precise nor fast	Mass media
5. Public Relations	Groups (mass)	Results in costs to the organisation	Identified	Neither precise nor fast	Mass media

1. Hillman, Rollie, and C.A. Kirpatrick, *Promotion: Persuasive Communication in Marketing*. Richard, D. Irwin, Homewood, 1968, pp. 365-366.
2. Peterson, Robin, *Marketing: A Contemporary Introduction*, John Wiley & Sons, New York, 1977, p. 444.

PROMOTIONAL STRATEGIES

Meaning

Promotional strategy consists of design of the four promotion elements personal selling, advertising, sales promotion and publicity/public relations and the development of a strategy to put this design into practice.

Nature

Most promotional strategies use various combinations, types, and amounts of different forms of promotion. Usually a combination of two or more promotional methods may be used; single methods are rarely used. For example, advertising may be supported by personal selling or display. Similarly, personal selling can be more effective if it is supported by some sort of advertisement.

The management sets objectives, determines policies, and formulates strategies for each component of the promotional mix. These individual strategies are blended together into promotional strategy, which in turn is blended with product-market, distribution, and pricing strategies into overall marketing strategy.

Factors Influencing Strategies

Promotional strategy is generally influenced by a host of factors, such as the nature of the product; the nature of the customer; the stage of the product's life cycle; the funds available; brand differentiation; purchase frequency; market penetration, etc.

(*i*) *Nature of the Product*: Different products require different promotional methods. For example, convenience or consumer goods are always sold through manufacturer's advertising with emphasis one dealer displays. Personal selling plays a very significant part. This mix is best for such goods as are widely distributed. Buying decisions are made on the spot. But products of a highly complex and technical nature and speciality goods require great emphasis on personal selling aimed to persuade dealers to display the product where shoppers will see and buy.

(*ii*) *The Nature of the Customer*: Different customers may be best reached through a combination of promotional methods. For example, where markets are small and local and the number of buyers few, personal selling would be adequate while advertising would be preferably used in more widely spread markets and large potential buyers. If the target is the household consumers, advertising would be preferred but if the retailers are to be contacted, personal selling would be used.

(*iii*) *Life cycle of the Product*: The nature of demand varies according to the stage in the product life cycle: (*i*) *The pioneering stage.* In it the seller usually tries to stimulate *primaiy demand* (*i.e.,* demand for a type of product) as contrasted to *selective demand* (*i.e.,* demand for a particular brand). In this stage, necessary information about the product and its benefits are made known to the prospective customers, (*ii*) *Maturity stage.* In it emphasis is placed on advertising as a tool to persuasion, (*iii*) *Decline stage.* In it the promotional activities may be slowed down or entirely stopped. Heavy emphasis is put on personal selling. In the case of promoting a new product or pioneering in a new market.

Table 26.3: Promotional Strategies for Different Types of Customers at Various Stages of Buying Process

Stages in Buying Process	Household product manufacturers (consumer goods)	Automobile dealer (or speciality goods)	Political Candidate
1. Perceived want	mass advertising, coupons, samples	mass advertising	publicity
2. Search	mass advertising, packaging, branding	mass advertising personal selling	mass advertising, direct mail, bill-boards, publicity
3. Purchase decision	mass advertising, price promotion.	personal selling, price promotion	personal selling, mass advertising,
4. Use	mass advertising,	personal selling service	publicity
5. Evaluation	mass advertising,	publicity	publicity, direct mail

(*iv*) *Funds Available or Promotion Budget*: The various methods of promotion vary considerably in the cost per message delivered. If the funds available are small, a combination of relatively low-cost promotional inputs is used even though a more costly combination might prove more productive.

(*v*) *Brand Differentiation:* Individual brands of products have little to differentiate them from those of the competitors brand. Therefore, their promotion emphasises personal selling to get the product stocked by as many retailers as possible, and to secure maximum shelf space display. Advertising is given preference when products are clearly distinguishable.

(*vi*) *Purchase Frequency:* When final buyers buy a product frequently such as consumers buy bathing soap or industrial buyers buy machinery, the marketer invests a large amount of money in advertising than when a product is purchased infrequently.

(*vii*) *Market Penetration*: A sustaining promotional strategy is most widely used when a brand is already known to the final consumer and middleman has a substantial market share. But, a developmental promotional strategy is adopted when the brand is new or has not penetrated is generally done in two ways: (*a*) *push strategy*. It is adopted for a brand with insignificant market penetration, whereby the dealers are persuaded to stock and push the brand; and (*b*) *pull strategy*. It is used where the final buyers ask their dealers to handle the brand or to convince them to go out and buy.

(*viii*) *Coordination with other demands of marketing mix*: Finally, the promotion programme must also be coordinated with other elements of marketing mix—price quoted in promotional campaign must be accurate and promotion must be coordinated with distribution.

To conclude, the promotion strategy formulation requires consideration of all the factors that affect the entire marketing programme and the interpretation of promotion decisions with these factors in mind at three levels: (a) among promotion elements—personal selling, advertising, sales promotion publicity, etc.; with (b) with other organisational objectives and functions.

QUESTIONS FOR EXERCISE

1. Define promotion and discuss its nature and objectives.
2. Explain the various stages in marketing communication process.
3. Explain various steps in promotion decisions.
4. Write short notes on
   (*i*) Promotional Mix
   (*ii*) Promotion Through Advertising
   (*iii*) Sales Promotion
   (*iv*) P.O.P.
5. What factors influence promotional strategies in marketing?

27

Advertising

Publicity and Advertisement

Advertisement in common parlance, the terms 'publicity' and 'advertising' are used synonymously. Publicity has been defined as: "the non-personal stimulation of demand for a product, service or business unit by planting commerically significant news about it in a published medium or obtaining favourable presentation of it upon radio, television, or stage that is not paid for by the sponsor."[1]

On the other hand, advertising denotes a specific attempt to popularise a specific product or service at a certain cost. It is a method of publicity. According to Peter Drucker, "Advertising not only plays a vital role in promoting our economic growth but is a colourful and diverting aspect of life....Many advertising people do a straightforward job. They fill an important and constructive role in our society." It is intentional, openly sponsored by the sponsor and involving certain cost and is paid for. It is a common form of non-personal communication about an organisation and/or its products, idea, services, etc. that is transmitted to a target audience through a mass medium.

Definition of Advertising

1. *Literal Meaning*: The word advertising is derived from the Latin word, *viz.*, "advertero" "ad" meaning towards and "verto" meaning "I turn." Literally it means "to turn people's attention to a specific thing."

---

1. American Marketing Association, *Marketing Definitions, A Glossary of Marketing Terms*, Chicago, 1960, p. 19.

2. *G.R. Green*: "Advertising is a general term for any and all forms of publicity, from the cry of the street boy selling newspapers to the most elaborate attention attracting device. The object always is to bring to public notice some article or service; to create a demand to stimulate buying; and in general to bring together the man with something to sell and the man who has means for desire to buy."[1]

3. *American Marketing Association*: "Advertising is any paid form of non-personal presentation and promotion of ideas, goods, or services by an identified sponsor. The medium used are print, broadcast, and direct."[2]

4. *W.J. Stanton*: "Advertising consists of all the activities involved in presenting to a group a non-personal, oral or visual, openly sponsored message regarding a product, service, or idea. This message, called an advertisement is disseminated through one or more media and is paid for by the identified sponsor."[3]

5. *Neil H. Borden*: "Advertising includes those activities by which, visual or oral messages are addressed to the people for the purpose of informing them and influencing them either to buy merchandise or to act or be inclined favouarbly towards ideas, institutions, for persons featured....Advertising messages are identified with the advertiser either by signature or by oral statement. ...Advertising is a commercial transaction involving payments to publishers or broadcasters, and others whose media are employed."[4]

6. *Harry J. Hausen*: "Advertising includes those activities by which visual or oral messages are addressed to the public for the purpose of informing them and inducing them either to buy merchandise or service or to act or be inclined favourably towards ideas institutions or, persons featured. In contrast with publicity and other forms of propaganda advertising messages are identified with advertiser either by signature or by oral statement. In further contrast to publicity, advertising is a commercial transaction involving pay to publishers or broadcasters and other whose media are employed."[5]

---

1. Green G.R., *Advertising and its Mechanical Production*, p. 425.
2. *Ibid*, p. 9.
3. Stanton, W.J., *Fundamentals of Marketing*, 1983, p. 414.
4. Borden, Neil H., *Economic Effects of Advertising*.
5. Hausen, Harry J., *Marketing Text: Techniques and Cases*, p. 636.

6. *Littlefield and Kirk Patrick*: "Advertising is any paid form of non-personal presentation of ideas, goods or services by an identified sponsor."[1]

Irving J. Shipario: Advertising is a non-personal paid message of commercial significance about a product, service or company made to a market by an identified sponsor."[2]

CHARACTERISTICS OF ADVERTISING

1. **Mass non-personal communication:** Advertisement reaches large groups of buyers. It is not delivered by an actual person, nor is it addressed to a specified person. The communication is speedy, permitting an advertiser to speak to the millions of buyers in a very short time.

2. **Matter of record:** Advertisement giving information for the benefit of buyers. It guides them to a more satisfactory expenditure of their hard earned money. The contents of an advertisement are what the advertiser wants.

3. **Persuades buyers to purchase the goods advertised:** Advertising devoid of persuasion is ineffective. To persuade the buyers the advertiser makes his products buyer-satisfying.

4. **Mass paid communication:** The ultimate purpose of advertising is to impart information, develop attitudes and induce action beneficial to the advertiser *(i.e.,* the sale of a product or sendee).

5. **Diverse Communication Media:** In advertisement the communication media is diverse such as print (newspapers and magazines), broadcast (radio and television), and direct (mail, billboards, motion pictures).

6. **Printed Salesmanship:** Advertising is called *printed salesmanship,* because information is spread by means of the written and printed word and pictures so that people may be induced to act upon it.

Thus, advertising is an art of influencing human action. It is awakening of the desire to possess; and possess one's product. It is a mass persuasion: It is any form of publicity given to products

---

1. Littlefield, Jr. and Kirpatrick C.A., *Advertising: Mass Communication in Marketing, 1971,* p. 160.
2. Shipario, Irving J., *Marketing Terms: Definitions Explanations, and or Aspects,* S.M.C. Publishing Co., New York, 1973, p. 3.

or services at the expense of the person who wants such publicity for bringing his products and services to the notice of the general public. It has grown up parallel to mass production. Marketers use it as a means of communicating with target consumers. It provides a useful means of transmitting message to consumers at a low cost per contact.

WHAT ADVERTISING IS NOT

Littlefied and Kirkpatrick observe that:[1]

1. *Advertising is not a game,* for here when advertising is done properly and profitably, both buyer and seller benefit.
2. *Advertising is not a toy,* for advertising funds come from sales volume and, therefore, efforts are made to increase sales.
3. *Advertising is not a racket,* only few advertisements are designed to deceive, majority are based on honesty.
4. *Advertising is not an exact science,* for the sales are affected by a number of factors such as competitor's decisions, manufacturer's promotional activities, changes in price, products, personnel or policies and these factors cannot be controlled as a physical scientist may control his experiments.

ADVERTISING IN PAST AND PRESENT

Traditionally, advertising has been considered primarily a business function but many non-business organisations, such as hospitals, charitable societies, educational institutions, and ecological groups, etc., use it as a tool to accomplish their communication goals.

In the past "advertising was at the beginning of things a bold statement that some one had desirable commodities for sale, very soon exaggeration and flowry language crept into the simple announcement. Advertisement in early 19th century had become synonymous with clap-trap and misrepresentation."[2] But now advertising is no longer confmed to providing of information, it rather aims at persuading people to take some action on it which will be of benefit to the advertiser. "They are now used for not only informing the public but also influencing them either to buy merchandising or to act or be inclined favourably towards

---

1. Littlefield and Kirpatrick, *op. cit.*, pp. 103-104.
2. Russel, T., *Commercial Advertising,* pp. 2-3

ideas, institutions or persons featured. Advertising messages are identified with the adviser either by signature or by oral statement. It is a commercial transaction involving payment to publishers or broadcasters and others whose media are employed."[1]

"How vast and all pervasive the business of persuasion has become is plain to the most careless eye. A man may deny himself a wireless set, refuse to read a newspaper, and avoid the conversation of his friends; but he cannot get away from the influence of advertising. If a town-dweller, he will see advertisement everywhere on hoardings and shop-windows. If he flees to the country, advertisement will travel with him in the railway carriage, aero-planes and bus; they will flash past him at every wayside station; creep into the pocket where he puts his ticket; confront him as he consults the menu in the dinning car. The calendar on the wall, the sack containing the flour, the grocer's receipt, the tooth paste, and the shaving stick are all in one way or another pressed into the service of advertisement."[2]

EVOLUTION OF ADVERTISING

1. The Beginning: Romans practised advertising. The potentiality of advertising multiplied when the hand press was invented at the end of the 15th century. By Shakespeare's time the posters had made their appearance. Thus, gradually advertising assumed the function of fostering demand for existing products.

2. Mass Advertising: It was in the latter half of the 19th century that mass advertising came into being. As mass production became a reality channels of distribution had to be developed to cope with the physical movement of goods creating a need for mass communication to inform customers of the choice available to them. This development was accelerated by increasing literacy.

3. Advertising in India: In India advertising was accepted as a potent recognised means of sales promotion only two decades ago. This delay is attributable to late industrialisation in India. But as India has become an industrial country, advertisements appear regularly in local as well as national papers.

---

1. *Borden, Neil,* The Economic Effect of Advertising, p. 37.
2. Bishop. F.P , *The Economics of Advertising*. 1946, pp. 19-20.

OBJECTIVES OF ADVERTISING

1. To Prepare Ground for New Product: Advertisement is used for introducing a new product in the market. New product needs introduction as potential customers have never used such product earlier. The advertisement prepares a ground for the new product, Most of the advertisement in cinema halls or at radio and television serve this purpose.

2. To Create Demand: The main objective of the advertisement is to create a favourable climate for maintaining or improving sales. Customers are reminded about the product and the brand. Advertisement may induce new customers to buy the product by informing them about its qualities since it is possible that some of the customers may change their brands. Thus, advertisement may bring new areas and customers to the company's product thereby increasing the company's share in the total market.

3. To Face the Competition: In modern days advertising is undertaken not only to inform the people about a product, but also to maintain and increase the demand of the product by weaning people away from rival products in the market. Under competitive conditions, advertisement helps to build up brand image and brand loyalty. When customers have developed brand loyalty, it becomes difficult for the middlemen to change.

4. To Create or Enhance Goodwill: Large scale advertising is often undertaken with the objective of creating or enhancing the goodwill of the advertising company. This increases the market receiptiveness of the company's product. It helps the salesmen to win customers easily.

5. To Inform the Changes to the Customers: The advertisement is made with the purpose of informing about the change to the consuming public. Whenever changes are made in the prices, channels of distribution or in the product by way of any improvement in quality, size, weight, brand packing, etc., these must be informed to the public by the producer through advertisement. Such advertisements may also be used to maintain or improve sales.

6. To Neutralise Competitor's Advertising: Advertising is also used to compete with or neutralise comeptitor's advertising. When competitors are adopting intensive advertising as their promotional strategy, it is reasonable to follow similar practices to neutralise their effects. It is essential for the manufacturer to create a different image of his product. Advertising helps to create product differentiation by the particular message it sends and the image it creates.

7. To Bar New Entrants: Through long advertising a strongly built image helps to keep new entrants away. The advertisement builds up a certian monopoly for the product. The entrants find it difficult to enter. Whenever a new entrant plans for an investment in that field, he considers the existing market conditions. If he knows that the existing market is dominated by a few producers due to long standing advertisement effects, he may hesitate to make his investment.

8. Link between Producer and Consumer: To conclude, advertising aims at benefiting the producer, educating the consumer and supplementing the salesmen. Above all it is a link between the products and the consumer.

FUNCTIONS OF ADVERTISING

(A) Primary Functions

1. Increase in Sales: Advertisement increases sales of the product by securing greater consumption, attracting new buyers or introducing new uses for a commodity.

2. Boost Stocking: Persuasion of dealers to stock the goods is one of the functions of advertisement.

3. Help in Sales: Advertisement helps the dealers (wholesalers and retailers) to sell the advertised product.

4. More Per Capita Use: Advertising is effectively used to increase the per capita use of the commodity by its constant repetition.

5. Receptibility: By advertisement the receptiveness of a new product or new model increases if producer has earned a name as a producer of good quality products.

6. Insurance: Advertisement creates insurance for the manufacturers' business.

7. Buyer's Dependability: The buyer's dependability on well advertised goods is increased because he knows its quality.

8. Diminishing Fluctuations: Advertisement helps to eliminate or lessen seasonal fluctuations.

9. Brand Image and Brand Loyalty: Advertisement creates brand image and brand loyalty.

10. Raising Standard of Living: Advertisement raises the standard of living of the public by instigating the desire to purchase better and qualitative things.

(B) Secondary Functions

1. Encouraging Salesmen: Advertisement encourages the salesmen and lends them moral support in facing a difficult customer.

2. Information: Necessary informations are furnished to salesmen, dealers and customers about the product. The printed word is manufacturer's guarantee.

3. Public Applaus: Advertisement creates a feeling among executives and administrative staff that they are working in a company having public response.

4. Sense of Security: The workers of a company of well advertised goods feel themselves secure. It means steady work and consequent prosperity. Their jobs are permanent and are likely to be promoted.

5. Better Employees: Advertisement helps the company to secure better employees—executives, salesmen and workers.

6. Help to all: The above functions of advertisement help the producer, salesman, dealer and consumer.

CLASSIFICATION OF ADVERTISEMENT

1. Primary Demand Advertising: Such advertising creates a demand for the product. It is necessary in the case of a newly-developed product or the products which are costly in nature such as cars, refrigerators, washing machines, watches, etc. As such advertising is directed towards a class of customers, it is also described as selective demand advertising.

2. Product or Institutional Advertising: Advertising of this kind is of 'window display of satisfaction' which is purely psychological in nature. To achieve the desired effects and results, the advertising must carry the 'brand' of the product or of the manufacturer. Most of the companies were successful in making an image on the minds of the people by using their names. Such as D.C.M., Bata, Dunlop, Bombay Dyeing, Tata, Bajaj, etc.

The product 'Brand' is also used to achieve the same result such as Horlicks, Dalda, Vespa, etc. Thus, advertising stressing the product or the manufactures is termed respectively as product or institutional advertising. When a company tries to sell its product or services through advertising it is called product advertising. Where the objective of advertising is to project the image of the company, it is called institutional advertising.

3. Cooperative Advertising: In cooperative advertising the manufacturers, wholesalers or retailers jointly sponsor and share the expenditure on advertising. Such advertising carries the names of all the parties involved. From the point of view of the customers this is more beneficial as they may get the articles directly from the authorised outlets. The manufacturers of cars, fans, TV sets, etc. undertake this type of advertising.

4. Commercial Advertising. Also termed as "Business Advertising", it is solely meant for effecting increase in sales. The usual forms of this advertising are the following:

(*i*) *Industrial Advertising*: It is exclusively used for selling industrial products.

(*ii*) *Trade Advertising*: This advertising is relating to a trade.

(*iii*) *Professional Advertising*: It is undertaken by doctors, engineers, C.A., etc.

(*iv*) *Farm Advertising*: For selling farm products such as fertilisers, etc. Some kind of specialisation is found in all the above forms of advertising. All these forms could be collectively called selective advertising.

5. Non-commercial Advertising: These are usually published by charitable institutions to solicit general and financial help, *e.g.*, collection of funds.

6. Direct or Indirect Action Advertising: Advertising that stresses and persuades immediate buying of the product is known as direct action advertisement such as advertising for consumer goods.

As against this an indirect action advertising is done as higher priced item, which is not purchased frequently such as motor car, TV, etc. This advertisement seeks to create a favourable attitude towards the manufacturer's product.

7. Advertising Classified Intended Audience: Advertising can be classified on the basis of intended audience towards whom the advertising is directed. This is as follows:

(i) Consumer Advertising: It is advertising directed at the ultimate household customers or actual consumers or users.

(ii) Industrial Advertising: It aims at industrial customers.

(iii) Trade Advertising: It is directed at channels of distribution such as wholesalers or retailers.

8. Advertising Classified by Nature of Appeal: Sometimes, advertising is classified by the nature or type of appeal used or motives towards which advertising is aimed. This may be (*i*) rational, and (*ii*) emotional.

(i) Rational Advertising: It explains the medicinal quality or the characteristics of the product.

(ii) Emotional Advertising: It tries to create an image of the product by investigating the emotional feelings such as, for example, advertisement of lux soap explaining how the housewife would look like a glamorous movie star.

BENEFITS OF ADVERTISEMENT

A. Benefits to Manufacturers

1. **Sales:** It increases sales volume by creating attraction towards the product.
2. **Introduction:** It helps easy introduction of new products into the markets by the same manufacturer.
3. **Help Brand Image:** It helps to create an image and reputation not only of the products but also of the advertiser. In this way, it creates goodwill for the manufacturer.
4. **Retail Price Maintenance:** Retail price maintenance is also possible by advertising where appeal is the promotional strategy.
5. **Better Contact:** It helps to establish a direct contact between manufacturers and consumers.
6. **Higher Demands:** It leads to smoothen the dmands of the product. It saves the product from seasonal fluctuations by discovering new and new usage of the product.
7. **More Response:** It creates a high responsive market and thereby quickens the turnover that results in lower inventory.

8. Less Overheads: Selling cost per unit is reduced because of increased sale volume. Consequently, product overheads are also reduced due to mass production and sale.

9. Sense of Pride: Advertising gives the employees a feeling of pride in their jobs and to be in the service of such a concern of repute. It inspires the executives and workers to improve their efficiency.

B. Benefits to Wholesalers and Retailers

1. Easy Sale: Easy sale of the product is possible since consumers are aware of the product and its quality.

2. More Turn-over: Advertisement increases the rate of the turn-over of the stock because demand is already created by advertisement.

3. Supplements Sale: Advertisement supplements the selling activities.

4. Reputation: The reputation created is shared by the wholesalers and retailers alike because they need not spend anything for the advertising of already well advertised product.

5. Economy: Advertisement ensures more economical selling because selling overheads are reduced.

6. Information: Advertisement enables them to have product information.

C. Benefits to Consumers

1. Guarantee of Price and Quality: Advertising stresses quality and very often which forms an indirect guarantee to the consumers of the quality and price. Furthermore, large scale production assumed by advertising enables the sellers to sell the product at a lower cost.

2. Elimination of Middlemen: Advertising helps in eliminating the middlemen by establishing direct contacts between producers and consumers. It results in cheaper goods.

3. Availability: Advertisement helps to know where and when the products are available. This reduces their shopping time.

4. Comparison: Advertisement provides an opportunity to the customers to compare the merits and demerits of various substitute products.

5. Knowledge of Uses: Advertisement is perhaps the only

medium through which consumers could know the varied and new uses of the product.

6. **Information:** Modern advertisements are highly informative.

D. Benefit to Salesmen

1. **Easy Introduction:** Introducing the product becomes quite easy and convenient because the manufacturer has already advertised the goods informing the consumers about the product of its quality.

2. **Reduced Sales Efforts:** Advertising prepares necessary ground for a salesman to begin his work effectively. Hence, sales efforts are reduced.

3. **Better Contact:** The contact established with the customer by a salesman is made permanent through effective advertising because a customer is assured of the quality and price of the product.

4. **Effectiveness:** The salesman can weigh the effectiveness of advertising when he makes direct contact with the consumers.

E. Benefits to Society

1. **Education:** Advertising in general is educative in nature. In the words of the late President Roosevelt of the U.S.A., "Advertising brings to the greatest number of people actual knowledge concerning useful things; it is essentially a form of education and the progress of civilisation depends on education."

2. **More Employment:** Advertising leads to a large-scale production creating more employment opportunities to the public in various jobs directly or indirectly.

3. **Popularity:** Advertisement initiates a process of creating more wants and their satisfaction and higher standard of living. For example, advertising has made more popular and universal the uses of such inventions as the automobiles, radios, and various household appliances. In the words of Sir Winston Churchill, "Advertising nourishes the consuming power of men. It creates wants for a better standard of living....It spurts individual exertion and greater production."

4. **Sustenance of Press:** Newspapers would not have become so popular and so cheap if there had been no advertisements. The cheap production of newspapers has been possible only through

the publication of advertisements. Thus, it is the advertising revenue that makes the newspapers live. It sustains the press.

5. Professional Employment: Advertisement assures employment opportunities for the professional men and artists.

6. Indicator of Present and Future: Advertising provides a glimpse of a country's way of life. It is, in fact, a running commentary on the way of living and the behaviour of the people and is also an indicator of some of the future trends.

IS ADVERTISEMENT A WASTE?

Economic Objections

1. Unproductive: The advertising does not produce any tangible goods. But all productive work does not necessarily result in tangible goods. On the other hand advertisement renders very valuable and intangible services. These services are necessary, especially when one has to choose from among the thousands of products which are similar in most respects. Advertising facilitates selection which in turn leads to satisfaction.

2. Cheap Trap: Advertising forces people to desire and buy those things which are not within their means. Advertising arouses interest for buying. But there is no physical force exerted on customers to buy things. Moreover, cautious people do not fall into "cheap trap" a term very often used to condemn advertising.

3. Multiplication of Needs: Advertising simply multiplies the needs. It just takes business from one concern and gives it to another. For example, when a new kind of Telcum powder is introduced, advertising will only help to shift the demand from one product in favour of another. But advertising also helps in the extension of demand and in comparing the two substitutes.

4. Increase in Cost: Advertising increases the cost of goods. In a sense it is true because expenses on it form a part of total cost. But advertising effects saving on the side of distribution costs and production costs.

5. The Monopoly Argument: Advertising usually lays emphasis on brands which makes the consumer to become a slave of a particular brand. The best answer to this argument is that it is the age of survival of the fittest. As all could advertise, so on monopoly effects.

6. Encouragement to Waste: People are forced to use the product as fast as possible as new products are introduced with improvements. The production of any product requires the use of exhausting natural resources which may be preserved by planned use. This is not considered in competitive advertising.

Social Objections

1. Misrepresentation of facts: Most of the advertisements contain tall claims and the benefits advertised are not enjoyed in full. Such products are short-lived.

2. Wastage of national resources: A more serious objection against advertising is that it destroys the utility of goods before it becomes useless due to change in fashion, improved technology, etc. It results in wastage of national wealth.

3. Impact on the Press: The press is influenced by advertisements because they provide the major source of revenue to the existence of newspapers and journals. But this is also not true because pressmen are not slaves of the advertisers. Moreover, they advertise only what the advertiser says and not at their own.

Ethical Objections

1. Harmful Consumption: Advertising appeals make people to use even such articles as might adversely affect their health, for example, liquors and cigarettes.

2. Consumer deficit: Though the advertisement creates a strong desire to purchase the product, people with less purchasing power cannot afford to buy articles. This leaves this section of the society discontented and frustrated.

CODE OF ADVERTISEMENT

The BBB and the AAF (American Advertising Federation)

1. *Truth*....Advertising shall tell the truth, and shall reveal significant facts, the concealment of which would mislead the public.

2. *Responsibility*....Advertising agencies and advertisers shall be willing to provide substantiation of claims made.

3. *Haste and Decency....Advertising* shall be free of statements, illustrations on implications which are offensive to public good or public decency.

4. *Disparagement*....Advertising shall offer merchandise or service on its merits, and refrain from attacking competitors unfairly or disparaging their products, services or methods of doing business.

5. *Bait Advertising*....Advertising shall offer only merchandising or services which are readily available for purchase at the advertised price.

6. *Guarantees and Warranties*....Advertising of guarantees and warranties shall be explicit. Advertising of any guarantee or warranty shall clearly and conspicuously disclose its nature and extent, the manner in which guarantor or warrantor will perform and the identity of the guarantor or warrantor.

7. *Price Claims*....Advertising shall avoid price or savings claims which are false or misleading or which do not offer provable bargains or savings.

8. *Improvable Claims*....Advertising shall avoid the use of exaggerated or unprovable claims.

9. *Testimonials*....Advertising containing testimonials shall be limited to those of competent witnesses who are reflecting a real and honest choice.

B. American Association of Advertising Agencies and Other Organisations

1. The public is entitled to expect that advertising will be reliable in content and honest in presentation;

2. The advertiser is entitled to regard advertising as a dynamic means of building his business and his profits;

3. The advertising people recognise their obligation to operate within the traditional (American) limitations, to serve the interests of the majority and to respect the rights of the minority.

4. It further says that "in addition to supporting and obeying the laws and legal regulations pertaining to advertising, the members undertake to extend and broaden the application of high ethical standards. Specifically they will not knowingly produce advertising which contains:

(*i*) false or misleading statements or exaggerations, visual or verbal,

(*ii*) testimonials which do not reflect the real choice of a competent witness, (*iii*) price claims which are misleading,

(*iv*) comparisons which unfairly disparage a competitive product or service,

(*v*) claims insufficiently supported, or which distort the true meaning or practicable application of statements made by professional or scientific authority.

(*vi*) statements, suggestions or pictures offensive to public decency.

"We agree not to recommend to an advertiser and to discourage the use of advertising which is in poor or questionable taste or which is deliberately irritating through content, presentation or excessive repetition."

C. Mr. Rai Basford, Canadian Minister of Department of Consumer and Corporate Affairs

1. *Refuse to buy shoddy merchandise*: If your purchase turns out to be unsatisfactory, complain to the manufacturer or retailer.
2. *Don't buy on impulse*: Shop around compare price, styles and models of any major purchase.
3. *Entertainment is no substitute for information*: Read or listen to advertisements carefully to find out what they really say.
4. *Get it in writing*: Don't rely on verbal promises.
5. *Credit buying doesn't create money, it costs money*: Do not buy on the instalment plan, or with a credit card, unless you can afford it.
6. *Don't be fooled into parting with your money* because you've "won a contest" or "been specially selected."
7. *Read labels carefully* to be sure you know what you're really getting, what it costs, and how to use it.
8. *Keep hazardous products* (such as household cleansers) *out of reach of children.* Teach them to know and respect the hazardous products' symbols.
9. *Make a list before you do your grocery shopping and stick to it.*

D. Indian and Eastern Newspapers Society (1939)

"No advertisement will be accepted which contains any matter:

(*a*) Claiming to procure miscarriage of women, birth control or regulation of menses;

(*b*) Dealing with the treatment of habits associated with sexual indulgence or any ailment associated with such habits;

(*c*) Using any of these expressions: sexual disability, impotence, rejuvenation....etc.;

(*d*) Recommending the treatment of any ailment by amulets, talismans, or other means of similar nature......"

E. The Advertising Agencies Association of India

"Members shall neither prepare nor place any advertisement, in any medium, which:

(*i*) is knowingly a copy of or a plagiarism of any other advertisement of any kind whatsoever;

(*ii*) makes attack on personal character or makes uncalled for reflections on competitors or competitive goods;

(*iii*) an indecent, vulgar, suggestive, repulsive, or offensive either in theme or treatment;

(*iv*) an objectionable medical advertising and an offer of free medical treatment, advertising that makes remedial, relief, or curative claims, either directly or by inference not justified by facts of common experience.

(*v*) concerns a product, known to the member, to certain habit forming or dangerous drugs or any advertisement which may cause monetary loss to the reader, injury in health or morals, or loss of confidence in reputable advertising and honourable business;

(*vi*) which is regarded by the Executive Council of the A.A.A. of India as unworthy."

ADVERTISING POLICIES

Advertising policies are management general guidelines to provide direction in making advertising decisions. They derive directly from the advertising objectives and assist management in formulating advertising strategies. The most important decision is to decide whether advertising is to be done at all. After a firm decides to advertise, it must take the following decisions:

1. Where should advertising effort and authority be positioned in the firm? Under the marketing manager? In a separate depeartment with direct access to the top executive?
2. Should the firm retain an advertising agency or attempt to perform the entire function itself? If the decision is taken to use an agency, what criteria should be followed in making the selection?

3. How much should be spent on advertising as a percentage of anticipated sales? Should more or less be spent than the competitors? How should the budget be allotted among different products and product lines?
4. When the advertising budget should be spent? Evenly over the year or proportionately more when sales are normally lowest? Or more at the time of festivals than in normal times?
5. What should be the components (basic strategies, theme lines, approaches) of the advertising campaign? How similar should it be to the main competitors? What specific objectives should be achieved.
6. What media should be used to reach the target customers? How should be advertising budget be allotted to the various media selected?
7. How can the flexibility be built into the advertising campaign to adapt to changes in competition or other elements of environment?
8. How can advertising be evaluated to determine whether or not it is, in fact, helping the firm attain its sales objective?

Types of Advertising Policy

1. Mere Publicity: Under mere publicity a few words describing the character of the commodity are given to let the public know it well. It is very simple but not very successful and influencive.

2. Educational: A comparative study of two arrangements is made under this system of advertisement.

3. Indirect Appeal: An indirect request is rather made to the buying public with an intention to attract them to consume the merchandise in question, e.g., coupons in tins of cigarettes, Poison's butter, Lipton's tea, etc.

4. Creating an Imaginary Alarm: This system of advertisement is only adopted by the manufacturers or by such dealers whose goods are very costly and/or periodical market, for instance, guns, cartridge, and insurance policies.

5. Inciting People's Curiosity: In this policy the entire matter of advertisement is not published at a time, but it is broken into several pieces which are generally released in proper order of sequence in a series of advertisements.

RESTRICTIONS ON ADVERTISING IN INDIA

Advertising and sales promotion have become well established modes of modern business techniques. However, these techniques are often used to deceive the customers. In India we do not have any legislation preventing deceptive advertisements or fraudulent sales promotional methods. The MRTP Act is also silent on these matters on the assumption that consumers will get a fair deal if dealers and manufacturers of producers can be prevented from distorting competition. This indirect restriction is not enough to prevent the sellers from making misleading advertisements or adopting unfair methods of sales promotion.

False Advertisements

Advertisements become misleading when things are intentionally omitted or false claims are made. For example, it is just untrue to claim that any TV set would guarantee life-long trouble-free service or any washing soap will wash 50 per cent more clothes whitest and safest. If a consumer is falsely induced to buy goods that do not possess the quality advertised it can be formed as a false representation. Efforts should be made to eradicate this kind of fraud against the consumers. The Federal Trade Commission Act 1914 (USA) bans this kind of selling methods to prevent the public from being made victims of false claims of products blatantly advertised.

In India a growing concern is being felt against this kind of deceptive advertisements. Appointed to revise the Companies Act and MRTP Act Sachar Committee pointed out, "The objection taken is not to the advertisement of the product which it may be necessary to do in order to acquaint the public with the articles. What is, however, insisted on is that there is an obligation on the part of the seller that if he advertises, he must speak the truth." Sachar Commission has stated in its report the various devices used for sales promotion method also as deceptive. Prices may be advertised as greatly reduced and cut when in reality the goods are being sold at seller's regular prices.

Unfair Trade Practices

The Sachar Committee has declared the following acts of the sellers as Unfair Trade Practices:

(1) Misleading advertisements and false representation.

(2) Delcaring the goods of a particular standard, quality, grade, composition, style or model, though in fact they are not possessing these qualifications.

(3) Representing second hand goods as new goods.

(4) Offering of gifts or prizes with the intention of not providing them and conducting contests.

All the aforesaid unfair trade practices should be punishable as an offence. Any person or undertaking indulging in any of these should be liable to be prosecuted before the commission.

ADVERTISING MEDIA

An advertising medium is any object or device that carries the advertising message. It should be capable of accomplishing following three objectives:

(*i*) To reach the largest number of people possible.

(*ii*) To gain their attention.

(*iii*) To be less expensive.

The character of the medium is largely determined on the objective and factual basis such as whether the coverage of the medium should be national, regional or only local.

Means of Media of Advertising

(*a*) Press Advertising	(*b*) Outdoor or Mural Advertising	(*c*) Direct Mail Advertising	(*d*) Miscellaneous Advertising
1. Newspapers 2. Magazines and Journals	1. Posters 2. Boards 3. Electric Display 4. Sandwitch Board advertising 5. Bus, trams and train advertising 6. Sky advertising 7. Others	1. Circular 2. Business reply 3. Price lists 4. Catalogue 5. Leaflets and 6. Booklets 7. Novelty 8. Personal letters 9. Others	1. Radio and Television 2. Cinema and cinema slides 3. Fairs and exhibitions 4. Loudspeakers 5. Demonstration 6. Posts and Telegraphs Dept.

Types of Media

1. Direct Media: Direct method of advertising refers to such methods used by the advertiser with which he could establish a direct contact with the prospective consumers. Direct mail is an example of this.

2. Indirect Media: Indirect method involves the use of a hired agency for spreading the information. Most of the media, *e.g.*, press publicity, cinema, etc. are indirect in nature.

COMMONLY USED MEDIA PRESS PUBLICITY

This is the most popular method of publicity today. Newspapers and magazines have become a part of the cultural and political life of the people. Press publicity takes two forms: Newspapers and magazines.

(*a*) *Newspapers*: Newspapers are read largely for their news value because they are most appropriate for announcing new products and new development of existing products. Because of their frequency of publication, they are well suited to 'opportunity markets'.

Advantages of Press

(*i*) *High Coverage*: As they reach each and every nook and corner, so their coverage is high.

(*ii*) *High Frequency*: It enables speedy preparation and publication of advertisement.

(*iii*) *Flexibility*: Newspapers offer a lot of flexibility. According to the convenience and necessity of the advertiser, the shape and size of advertisements could be changed.

(*iv*) *Cheap*: Advertising in newspapers is a cheap method of advertising from cost point of view.

(*v*) *Effective*: By inserting local advertisements (in local papers) the effectiveness of advertising copy could be tested.

(*vi*) *Appealing*: Visual appeals could be created.

(*vii*) *Goodwill*: The reputation and the choice of the newspapers is available to the advertiser and their products.

Limitations of Press

(i) No visual effect: Visual effects may not be created in practice as the papers are usually printed on cheap newsprint.

(ii) Short life: As the life of newspaper is extremely short so frequent advertising is required.

(iii) Waste: There is a lot of waste of circulation. The advertisement is carried to places where there is no market existing nor the possibility of creating a new market. This can be avoided by

advertising in local paper as they have a concentrated coverage of a limited area.

Kinds of Press Advertisements

(*i*) *Classified Advertisement*: These are advertisements having common themes such as matrimonial, situation wanted, to let, for sale, etc. These are given under group headings. They are quite cheap.

(*ii*) *General Advertisement*: These are usual advertisements which are published in different places creating some kind of identity.

(*iii*) *Teaser Advertisement*: This is comparatively a new form of advertising. A series of advertisements without any sales message are published over a number of days in the same place in a newspaper. This creates an interest among readers to follow the series until the last advertisement appears. Teaser method is found highly effective.

(*iv*) *News Type Advertisement*: From the outward appearance this would simply look like a news item. The word 'advertisement' is added at the end of the news to denote the purpose. Most of the speeches of the chairmen of companies are given on this basis. For example, Hamdard's Roohafza and Charminar cigarettes.

2. MAGAZINES

Magazines and journals also offer good facility because magazines are read leisurely when the reader is mentally prepared to receive advertisements.

Kinds of Magazines

(*i*) *General Magazines*: In these the content is meant for general appeal, *e.g., Illustrated Weekly, Blitz.*

(*ii*) *Specialised Magazines*: These cater to a readership with clearly defined specific interest. For example, *Capital* for business people, *Femina* for women.

(*iii*) *Special Issues Such as Annuals*: Directories are special types of publications which may or may not have wide coverage of varied interests, *e.g.,* telephone directories.

Merits of Magazines

(*i*) Better reproduction of advertisements than newspapers.

(*ii*) Larger duration of interest.
(*iii*) Magazines are highly selective in nature.
(*iv*) Waste of circulation is avoided.
(*v*) Trade magazines reach specialised groups.
(*vi*) Magazine advertising creates prestige, reputation and an image of quality.
(*vii*) In magazine there is no crowded atmosphere of advertisements as in as the case of newspapers.

Limitations of Magazines

(i) Low Flexibility

(ii) High Cost: Preparation of the magazine is high and hence advertising cost also would be high.

(iii) Inelasticity: The coverage of the magazine and the coverage of the distribution of goods may synchronise.

(iv) Not Timely: The advertisement cannot be brought out as needed by the advertiser. Usually, the preparation of magazine takes time and urgent advertising cannot be undertaken.

(*c*) *New Forms of Printing Publicity*: Along with the increased use of certain articles the printed publicity has come to occupy new horizons, *e.g.*, postal articles such as covers, inland letters offer good place for advertisements. The match box provides another example.

2. Direct Mail: It is direct in its approach and hence referred to as 'direct advertising'. It retains some of the characteristics of press advertising. For instance, here also printed materials are used to spread information. Direct mail may take forms of Leaflets, Folders, Booklets, Catalogue, etc.

Characteristics of Direct Mail

(i) Direct: The message is directly addressed to the prospective customers.

(ii) Flexible: The message could be changed to suit different conditions.

(iii) Economical: Advertising could be termed according to the wishes of the advertiser. It is economical.

(iv) Personal Contact: The greatest advantage of this method is its capacity to create and maintain personal contact.

3. MAILING LIST

The foremost job in such a kind of advertising is the preparation of a mailing list, which should include only those who are able and likely to respond to the advertisement.

Sources of Mailing List

(*i*) Present and past customers.
(*ii*) Salesmen.
(*iii*) Directories such as telephone directory, voters list, etc.
(*iv*) Government records such as income tax list, birth registration.
(*v*) Records of membership kept by civil and social organisations.

The final step in this method of advertisement is the distribution of the printed message. This can be done by mailing inside packages through retail stores.

Merits of Mailing

(*i*) *Selective*: The advertiser could reach any part of the country and have his message conveyed.
(*ii*) *Personal contact*: Press advertising is meant for large masses whereas direct mail is intended for the addressees only.
(*iii*) *Messages*: The messages that cannot be given through advertisements could be managed by direct mail.

Limitations of Mailing

(*i*) It is not cheap.
(*ii*) The preparation of a proper mailing list is not an easy job.
(*iii*) Even the list prepared with utmost care would become obsolete in a short time.
(*iv*) It has not provided its supremacy in all fields.
(*v*) It is ineffective in case of products which need personal examination.

However, mailing is the most suitable method in the field of publication of books. *Readers Digest* and other popular publishing companies adopt this method most effectively.

OUTDOOR ADVERTISING OR MURAL ADVERTSING

The oldest form of advertising, it remains the most common medium even today. Press publicity is basically indoor advertising as papers are generally read indoor. Outdoor advertisements are meant for the moving public and provide the advantage of reminding the people frequently of the product. It has the advantage of repetition found in good advertisements. It projects the message to a large number of people of heterogeneous interests. The products that need a wide appeal use this method.

Merits of Outdoor Advertising

(*i*) *Attention*: It is capable of gaining more attention.

(*ii*) *Selective*: It offers great selectivity. It could be used locally, regionally or even nationally.

(*iii*) *Flexibility*: It is flexible.

(*iv*) *Semi-permanent*: Once the Board is exhibited it could be kept there for quite a long time.

(*v*) For Brand Names: It is a very good medium to stress brand names and package identity.

(*vi*) *More Coverage*: Every moving person comes in its contact.

(*vii*) *Low Cost.*

Limitations of Outdoor Advertising

(*i*) *Brief*: Detailed explanation is not possible.

(*ii*) *Dubious Value*: The exact effect created on prospects is very difficult to measure.

(*iii*) *Supplementary*: It could be used only as a supplementary form to other kinds of advertising.

Kinds of Outdoor Publicity

(*i*) *Mural Advertising*: It refers to posters which are often pasted on walls. Advertising for a movie is done in this way.

(*ii*) *Advertising Boards*: These are also posters but are kept at certain fixed places especially at joints where people frequently assemble. Bus stops, railway stations, etc. offer good places for this kind of advertising.

(*iii*) *Vehicular Advertising*: It refers to moving advertisements or advertisements on moving vehicles such as buses and railway trains. This type of advertising has very large circulation. It is considered to be very' effective.

(*iv*) *Electric Displays, Neon signs*: It is the newest and most attractive form of outdoor display. It attracts attention easily and acts as memoriser when it is dark all around.

(*v*) *Sky Advertising (sky writing)*: Notices and advertisements such as printed balloons, etc. are found usually near the circus tents. A huge balloon is floated from which a board hangs down depicting the name of the circus.

(*vi*) *Sandwichmen*: These are hired persons who move in a procession with boards and notices and also playing musical instruments to attract the attention of the public. The cinema theatres usually arrange this kind of advertising when a new picture is released.

5. AUDIOVISUAL ADVERTISING

Types

These include: (*i*) Film advertising, (*ii*) Documentary film, (*iii*) Straight advertising films, and (*iv*) Sponsored Advertising films. All these have their own merits. Their coverage is very wide. They appeal to all sections of the people. They are able to explain and demonstrate the use of product which makes the product more appealing and acceptable.

Limitations of Audio-Visual Methods

(*i*) *High Cost*: The production cost of a film is very high.

(*ii*) *Restrictions*: Sometimes there are restrictions against screening of films, *e.g.*, there is censoring.

(*iii*) *Limited*: A film can be shown only to the people who come to the theatre. Thus, a large section of people are left outside the scope of such advertising. Besides, cooperation of theatres is inevitable for screening film.

(*iv*) *Boring*: Crowding of such film advertisements, which is very common now, makes the audience feel bored.

(b) Screen slides: Slides covering advertisements are usual today. They are shown in almost all the picture houses during the show. Radio advertising, television, exhibition also offer good media of advertising.

(c) Point of Purchase Advertising: It is a direct method of advertising because the process is either undertaken by the manufacturer direct or through the dealer. These are commonly known as 'store display'. It is observed that the point of purchase is the exact point where the prospective buyers are reminded finally about

the product. The various means adopted for this purpose are the following:

(*i*) *Window Display*: The articles are displayed inside a glass window decorated attractively. The price of the product is shown through price tags. 'Come and have if is the maxim behind this method of advertising.

(*ii*) *Counter-Display*: In this device products are displayed inside the shop. The attention of the real buyers who step into the shop is directed towards the articles displayed.

(*iii*) *Special Displays and Shows*: Putting special displays of several products in selected stores is a good promotional device.

(*iv*) *Show Rooms.* Personal inspection is an important prerequisite in case of certain products. Articles such as mixers, washing machines, cars, scooters, etc. are purchased only after a close look at the product. Therefore, the manufacturers maintain show rooms at a huge expenditure. The location of the show room should be easily accessible.

(*v*) *Exhibitions and fairs.*

(*vi*) *Speciality Advertising*: In it the manufacturers provide various articles of low value to the existing and prospective customers free of cost such as diaries, calendars, ball pens, cigarette cases, paper weights, etc. These bear brief advertisement.

QUESTIONS FOR EXERCISE

1. Discuss the Aims and Functions of advertisement with special reference to India.
2. What do you mean by Advertisement? Discuss the objects and functions of advertisement.
3. Give a suitable classification of advertisement.
4. "The money spent on advertising is an investment and is not wasteful." Do you agree? Give reasons for support of your answer.
5. Explain the benefits of advertisement.
6. "Money spent on advertising is wasteful." Do you agree? Give reasons for your answer.
7. "Advertisement is a wasteful luxury in India where we suffer from shortage of everything." Do you agree with this statement? Explain fully.

8. "All advertisement is a social waste." Discuss.
9. Describe the types of advertising media. Discuss their merits and demerits.
10. What can be the possible media of business advertisement?
11. Briefly describe the forms of business publicity.

28

Advertising Agency

An advertising agency is an organisation whose business consists in the acquisition of the right to use space of time in advertising media and the administration on behalf of the advertisers of advertising appropriations made by them. It renders advice and creative services for its clients. It does not sell any tangible products, but sells creative talents and past experience. Thus, it is an organisation specially created for rendering services in advertising.

NEED OF ADVERTISING AGENCY

Manufacturers cannot look after all the promotional activities especially under the principle of specialisation. Organisations with adequate financial resources set up a separate department for this purpose. Such an arrangement would be beyond the reach of medium or small scale producers. They would hire some specialised people. Advertising is one such field where manufacturers have two options which are either to conduct their advertising for themselves or to hand over the job to a specialist. Advertising Agency undertakes the specialised job of advertising for and on behalf of others. lf has specialised skills and experience that a manufacturer cannot duplicate except at a considerable expense. Even large firms have started depending on advertising agencies, because they are in the market. Advertising is a complicated affair and its success primarily depends upon constant advertisement research and media research, etc.

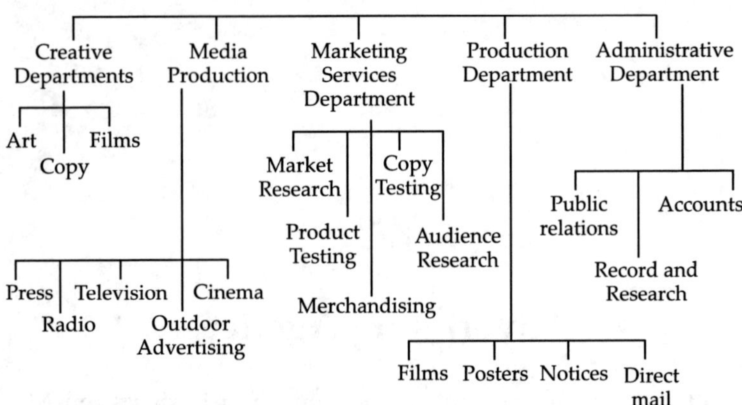

Fig. 28.1: Advertising Agency Services.

In the beginning advertisement agents were mere agents whose main job was to sell space in a medium. But today they have a pivotal position in the marketing process and sometimes called 'marketing agents'. With ever increasing competition, they have extended the range of services they could render. This is evident from the Fig. 28.1 of the multifarious activities undertaken by such agents.

SELECTION OF ADVERTISING AGENCY

The selection of an advertising agency is not an easy task. The advertiser decides to use an agency to sensor additional talent to help him plan and carry out an advertising programme. The problem of selection is one of evaluating the skills and capacities of an agency. There is no standard yardstick to measure the efficiency of such an agency. The following points should be considered while choosing an advertising agency:

(*i*) Financial soundness.

(*ii*) General reputation.

(*iii*) Facilities and abilities available.

(*iv*) Size and adequacy of the staff.

(*v*) Basis of remuneration.

(*vi*) Relationship they maintain with advertiser.

(*vii*) Products advertised.

(*viii*) Availability.

(*ix*) Relation with media-owners.

Whatever be the basis of selection, the relationship between the advertiser and the agency should be cordial after an agency is selected. The success of an advertising programme depends much on the mutual trust, confidence and understanding between the two. The advertising agency should not be mere 'yes man' of the advertiser. It should be capable of giving him objective advice.

ADVANTAGES OF ADVERTISING AGENCY

1. **For small Advertisers:** It is more profitable to use services of an agency than to keep a separate publicity department.
2. **Expert Advice:** Being a specialised agency it could offer expert advice.
3. **Obtaining space on easy terms:** Because of the close association with media owners it can obtain space at competitive rates.
4. **Employment:** An advertising agency provides employment opportunities to artists and similar skilled people.
5. **Other Help:** Besides, advertising agency offers help in other marketing activities such as marketing research, test marketing, etc. Members belonging to a profession such as Solicitors, Advocates, Physicians, Auditors and the like are not allowed to advertise due to custom and professional etiquette and strict adherence to the rules and regulations.

SCIENTIFIC ADVERTISING

Meaning

In the modern business world a business without advertisement will end up in disaster. The advertisement aims at creating and maintaining the demand for the goods of the company. Hence, an advertising programme should be prepared very carefully to fulfil its purposes fully. Efforts should be made to make the advertisement effective and attractive. Scientific method should be used in the formulation and execution of advertising programmes.

Scientific advertising is properly planned advertising based upon a serious deliberation of all factors that have a bearing upon its success. It involves the use of the logical method or reasoning method. Scientific advertising implies the development and use of a fact finding approach to the formulation and execution of an advertising programme.

Before an advertising programme starts, data about the consumers desires, their location and purchasing power and the ability of given commodities to satisfy their wants should be collected. It should be followed by financial planning for advertising and the selection of the media of advertising. Its execution should follow the pattern set out in the advertising plan. Its performance should be evaluated.

Phases of Scientific Advertising

1. Ascertaining Advertisibility of Products: In the first phase advertisibility of products should be established. For this purpose the preliminary demand should be studied, buying motives of the customers, inherent qualities of the product, nature of the product, cost of advertisement and the bearing capacity of the advertising cost by -the product, etc.

2. Preliminary Investigations: Preliminary investigations collect the necessary data vital to an understanding of the markets to which the advertising campaign is directed. It involves the following steps:

(*i*) *Market Identification*: Market identification means that the advertiser knows definitely whom it shall be directed to. The market is usually defined as a group of actual or prospective buyers for a product or service. While some markets are well defined, in some other cases, a considerable amount of research is required to define the market. The market so identified will influence the choice of advertising media and type of copy. The market analyst should know the customs of the market, demand of the product, nature of the product (whether it is meant for grown ups or children, students women or men), traditions and climatic conditions of the market, etc.

(*ii*) *Product Analysis*: Sanadage defines product analysis as "the process of subjecting goods to careful scrutiny to determine the degree to which they have been or might be moulded to fit the mind of the buyer." Such analysis should consider the class into which the commodity falls such as necessary or luxury, producer's or consumer's good, all possible uses of the product. construction and quality, character of package, the common unit of sale, and price, etc. An advertisement may be proved successful in the market only when the characteristics of the product can satisfy the needs and requirements of the customers for whom it is meant.

(*iii*) *Consumer Research of Motivation Research*: Consumer is the king in modern marketing. There is a wide gulf between him and the products who seek to serve him. This gulf can be bridged through consumer research and the other two steps stated above. It will study the facts, needs and desires of the consumers. According to Hepner, "Motivation research tries to discover the relation between behaviour and underlying inner mental processes such as drives, desires, emotions, impulses, attitudes; avoidance and preferences." Instead of making wild guesses about the consumer instincts, the producer should confidently proceed on the firm ground provided by the information collected through motivation research.

3. Preparation of Advertising Budgets: The preparation of advertising budget meaning to appropriate the amount for advertisement taking into consideration: (*i*) Size and financial position of the advertiser, (*ii*) degree of competition in the market, (*iii*) scope of area of the expected market, (*iii*) rivals' appropriations for the purpose, (*v*) clearly defined objectives of the firm, etc.

4. Media Planning: The media of advertisement should be selected after a careful considerations of: (*i*) the effectiveness of the various alternatives in approaching the customers, (*ii*) its cost, and (*iii*) the length of the sales message, advice from experts, etc.

5. Execution: The execution of the advertising programme should be in conformity with the plan formulated for the purpose on the basis of research and investigation. The success of any advertising programme depends upon the copy, appeal, illustration, size, colour, etc. These must be entrusted to advertising agencies for they requires skilful handling.

6. Evaluation of Results: An advertisement will be deemed to be successful if: (*i*) prospective customers have been effected; (*ii*) there is a considerable increase in the sale volume; and (*iii*) it succeeds in changing the habits and behaviours of the customers to the extent desired.

CHARACTERISTICS OF GOOD ADVERTISEMENT

The success of advertisement depends very much upon the copy of advertisement. The main aim of the advertisement is to attract the customer and create an urge to possess that product. If the advertisement does not fulfil this objective, the expensive advertisements are useless. Hence, the advertisement copy should be drafted very carefully.

The person who drafts the advertisement copy must be thoroughly acquainted with the mental process. He should be imaginative enough to think of words and patterns which would produce the desired effect on the prospective customer.

An effective copy of advertisement should possess the following characteristics, qualities or values:

1. Attention Value,
2. Suggestive Value,
3. Memorising Value,
4. Conviction Value,
5. Sentimental appeal Value,
6. Educational Value,
7. Instinctive Value.

1. Attention Value: An advertisement copy must attract the attention of the potential consumers. If it fails in this mission, the money and efforts go waste, for everything else follows this. The copy should be drafted, planned and displayed so ingeniously that it may compel even the most casual reader to notice it and read it with interest. It should be designed in such an attractive manner that it catches the eye. Following devices can be used to make the copy attractive:

(*i*) Use of pictures, photographs or sketches to reveal a great deal about the product;

(*ii*) Use of display types, *i.e.*, appropriate heading in attractive types;

(*in*) Attractive borders, etc. can also be used to separate an advertisement copy from the rest of the setting and to compel the reader to focus his attention on it;

(*iv*) Price quotation being advertised is quite low, the display should be at an appropriate place in the copy.

(*v*) Reply coupons may be inserted in an advertisement to attract the attention of the readers.

2. Suggestive Value: The next quality of an advertisement should be to offer suggestions about the use and the utility of the product.

This can be done if crisp and pointed but simple slogans and suggestions are devised to bring home to the reader the utility of the product in everyday situation. The repeated use of suggestion, a command or slogan can do the trick.

3. Memorising Value: The copy of advertisement should be so drafted and laid out that the product sticks to the memory of the individual reader. Repetition of advertisement is an effective method of creating memorising value for the copy. Use of trade mark brand name should be repeated very often. Lux, Dalda, Aspro, Ponds, Vim, Surf, etc. have become household words through repeated advertisements of memorising value.

4. Conviction Value: An advertisement copy can prove effective when the suggestion contained in it is backed by convincing arguments. In it the advertiser must avoid the two extremes: it should neither be a plain notice nor should it use high flown language. By emphasising the outstanding features of the product; an ideal copy should make an appeal to reason so that the consumer acting on the advertisements may go in for it with confidence, and in its utility and superiority over competitive products. Examples of copies emphasising conviction value may be found in advertisement of Colgate dental cream saying "Stop bad breath with Colgate while you fight tooth decay all day."

5. Sentimental Value: Sentiments reflecting the personal feelings and attitudes of individuals towards various things, indicate reactions of a person in favour or against a particular product. The advertiser should make a sincere attempt to make an appeal to the sentiments of as many buyers as possible. It is more important where advertisement is directed towards the educated and cultured sections of the community.

6. Educational Value: A good copy of advertisement educates the general public about the uses of the new products or the new uses of the same product. It increases the demand of the product. It creates new' habits among people by offering new tempting products to them. It helps creating new' markets. Thus, a good copy of advertisement possesses educative value.

7. Instinctive Appeal Value: Instincts are the mainsprings of human thoughts and actions. Instincts are the underlying forces which compel the men to act in certain ways. A good copy advertisement must induce, persuade and motivate the people to think well of a product and to take to its use. Generally speaking, the following are the basic instincts of the consumers:

(*i*) *Self-preservation Instinct*: The sale of product like medicine, clothes, etc. may be promoted by appeal to our anxiety to preserve our person, our wealth, our family and our belongings. For example, insurance is advertised by appeal to this instinct.

(*ii*) *Hoarding Instinct*: Banking institutions, insurance companies or the Government Savings Organisation make an appeal to the hoarding instinct Slogans like 'Up and Up, Go your Savings' are used for this purpose.

(*iii*) *Parental Instinct*: The parental instinct takes the form of love and affection for the children. Those who deal in children's requirement like toys, baby foods, etc. play upon the motherly feelings of women or the parental sentiment of men through their advertisement copies.

(*iv*) *Instinct for Self-display*: An advertisement copy drafted for dresses, readymade clothing, etc. must be directed towards the aesthetic sense of the people by showing happy and likeable people in dresses that are being advertised.

(*v*) *Something for Nothing Instinct*: Everybody has an instinct to get something without paying for it. An advertisement copy that contains the offer of a prize or a gift is likely to tempt many of the customers. For example, this instinct is widely used by lottery ticket sellers.

The above qualities should be incorporated in an advertisement copy to make it an idea advertisement.

ADVERTISING BUDGET

Meaning

An advertisement budget or appropriation is an organised plan made out for expenditure of money on advertisement. The advertiser has to consider several factors before deciding the amount to be spent on advertisement such as population or income trend analysis, the economic situation and competitive behaviour, product improvement, sales force, etc. These must realise that advertising is really mass psychology. He should have basic information and available statistical data to reduce the guess work involved in the art of getting the product accepted in the minds of the people. He should determine the right proportion of media, the proper sequence of contact and the right type of copy message. The cost factor should be the deciding factor. A planned cost analysis of different media of advertisement and its effectiveness is necessary for preparing advertisement budget.

Budgeting Methods

1. Availability of funds or Affordable approach.
2. Percentage of Sales methods.
3. Return on Investment method.
4. Competitive Parity methods.
5. Objective and Task method.

1. Availability of funds or Affordable Approach: In this method, the company considers what funds are available or what it can afford for advertising. A small business concern cannot spend much on advertisement because its capacity to spend is limited.

This method is not a very scientific method. It totally ignores the need, importance and nature of advertisement. This approach bears good marketing opportunities because of shortage of funds. It cannot plan a long-term advertising programme.

2. Percentage of Sales Methods: Under this method, the amount to be appropriated is arrived at as a fixed percentage of the sales based on preceding year's sale figure or estimated sale figure of the current year. The total amount may be calculated for different products and may be aggregated.

Favourable Arguments

(*i*) The advertisement expenditure does not remain fixed. It fluctuates direct with the sales.

(*ii*) The advertising cost, sale, price and profit per unit are closely correlated and considered by the management in preparing the budget.

Though this method is very common in India, it is not scientific.

Limitations

(*i*) Sale under this method is the cause of advertisement and not the result of advertisement.

(*ii*) In the case when sales are declining the amount on advertisement at a fixed percentage would be declined when in fact advertising appropriation should be increased to arrest the decline in sales.

(*iii*) Introducing a new product requires a heavy initial advertising expenditure although the sales in the initial period may be small.

(*iv*) No long-term advertising programme can be prepared because expenditure fluctuates with the sales.

(*v*) There is no scientific method for determining the fixed percentage.

3. Return on Investment Method: In this method, advertising expenditure is considered as an investment which is correct as the return one gets from advertising is generally spread over a period of time. The advertising budget is prepared by taking into consideration the increased profits generated by an increase in sales and goodwill through the advertising.

Thus, return on investment method is a scientific way of approaching the problem. However, as the return is very often spread over a period of time, it may be difficult to arrive at an appropriate figure on the basis of this method.

4. Competitive Parity Method: This method considers the amount spent by the competitive firms on the advertisement appropriating the amount for advertising.

This method is based on the assumption that competitors are on the right track and the marketing problems and strategies of competitors are similar to that of the company. But, it is never true because the objectives of the firm, objectives of the advertisement, resources and opportunities are never similar to each other.

5. Objective and Task Method: This is the best approach. It fixes the advertising appropriation on the basis of what the advertising compaign is required to achieve. Keeping in view the sale of the products for each area the amount of advertisement is fixed for each segment of the markets and then it is aggregated for the firm. This method carefully considers the advertising objectives and then determines what is necessary in terms of the type of media, frequency of advertising, etc. in order to accomplish these objectives effectively.

This method is suitable when a new product is introduced in the market. However, the cost factor is not considered under this approach.

Thus, no one method is perfectly scientific. Fixing the amount for advertisement requires a mixture of knowledge, assumptions, experience and hopes. Cooperation of all the managers must be sought in preparing the advertising budget so that advertisement objectives may be achieved effectively.

QUESTIONS FOR EXERCISE

1. What is advertising agency? Discuss its role.
2. What is the meaning of Scientific Advertising? Discuss its various phases.
3. How can you increase the effectiveness of an advertisement?
4. What qualities should be possessed by a good advertisement copy?
5. What points would you consider while preparing a good copy of advertisement?
6. What are the more common procedures in use for determining the size of an advertising budget?
7. Compare and contrast the different approaches to determine the size of the advertising budget.

29

Personal Selling (Salesmanship)

Definition of Salesmanship

1. *The American Marketing Association*: "Selling as the personal or impersonal process of assisting and/or persuading a prospective customer to buy a commodity or a service or to act favourably upon an idea that has commercial significance to the seller."[1] Salesmanship is the process of persuading a person to buy goods or services. The act of salesmanship consists of "one human mind influencing another human mind."

2. *A.L. Reid*: "Salesmanship is learning the customers' viewpoint and making him see yours by getting him to think or act."[2]

3. *H.H. Houghton*: "Salesmanship is a personal service rendered to the community in connection with the marketing of goods."[3]

4. *F.A. Russel*: "Personal selling is the ability to persuade people to want what they already need; is the mutual profitable service of exchange between the producer and consumer; is the art of persuading people to purchase goods which will give off lasting satisfaction by using methods which consume the least time and effort; is the art of selling and nothing more or less than making the other fellow feel as you about the thing you have to sell; is the art of satisfying the need of a customer with goods and service."[4]

5. *T.S. Knox*: "Salesmanship is the power or ability to influence people to buy at a mutual profit that which we have to sell but which they may not have thought of buying until we call their

---

1. American Marketing Association, *Marketing Definitions*, 1960, p. 21.
2. Reid, A.L., *Modern Applied Salesmanship*, 1971, pp. 36-37,
3. Houghton, H.H., *Salesmanship and Advertising*, p. 15.
4. Russel, F.A., *Textbook of Salesmanship*, pp. 1-6.

attention to it. Salesmanship is the ability to persuade people to want what they already need."[1]

6. *H.F. Holtzclaw*: "Salesmanship is the power to persuade plenty of people to pleasurably and permanently purchase your product at a profit."[2]

7. *C.B. Strand*: "It is an ability to induce other people to accept you, your enthusiasm and your products with willing, sympathetic or even enthusiastic approval."[3]

8. *B.R. Canfield*: "Salesmanship is the process of analysing a buyer's need for a product or sendee; recommending the product or service that best satisfies the need and persuading the buyer that the price is fair, the source of supply is satisfactory, and now is the time to buy."[4]

9. *R.S. Torda*: "It is' the art exercised by the seller in bringing about directly or indirectly mutually beneficial transfers of goods or sendees, or more briefly, salesmanship is the art exercised by the seller of effecting exchanges."[5]

10. *Peterson and Wright*: "Salesmanship is the process whereby the seller ascertains and activates the needs or wants of the buyer, and satisfies these needs or wants to the mutual, continuous advantage of both the buyer and the seller."[6]

11. *A. Gross*: "Salesmanship is the art of increasing satisfaction by persuading those people who should do so to buy specific goods or services."[7]

12. *C. Hudson*: "Salesmanship basically is the art of persuading somebody either to accept or to follow our ideas, and thus lead them to the action we desire."[8]

From the above definitions it appears that salesmanship is persuasion applied to the sale of merchandise or services. It is persuasive communication between a seller and a buyer. The ideal of offering a real service to the buyer is the modern

1. Knox, T.S., *Salesmanship and Business Efficiency*, p. 179.
2. Holtzclaw, H.F., *Principles of Marketing*, p. 3.
3. Strand, C.B., *Salesmanship*, p. 3.
4. Canfield, B.R., *Salesmanship, Practices and Problems*, 1958, p. 6.
5. Tordal, R.S., *Principles of Personal Selling*, p. 41.
6. Peterson, C.A. and Wright, M.D., *Salesmanship: Principles and Methods*, p. 27.
7. Gross A., Salesmanship: *Principles and Practices of Professional Sellings*, p. 4.
8. Hudson, C., *Professional Salesmanship*, 1967, p. 15.

spirit of salesmanship. Persuasion is the core of selling and salesmanship.

Characteristics of Salesmanship

1. It is the ability to persuade people to buy goods or services at a profit *(i.e.,* a fair price) to seller and with benefit to the buyer *(i.e.,* the service rendered).
2. It is persuading people to buy what you have for sale, in making them want it in helping to make up their minds.
3. It is an attempt to induce people to buy goods.
4. It is an art of so presenting an offering that the prospective customer appreciates the need for it and that a mutually satisfactory sale follows.
5. It is winning the buyer's confidence for the seller's house and goods, thereby winning a regular and permanent customer.

In fact, "modern salesmanship is based upon the principle of customer's satisfaction....for along with the product, a customer buys the services of the salesman and the company which he represents....Salesmanship is a profession established on the basis of service."[1]

Classification of Salesmanship

Canfield classifies salesmanship into three categories:

1. Demand Filling Salesmanship or Order Taking Salesmanship: It is one in which the buyer initiates the sale. He knows his needs, decides about the product that will best satisfy his needs, and also knows about the sources of its supply. In such purchases, no help is taken from the salesman. Cheap articles and service, are thus purchased by the buyers.

2. Creative Salesmanship: It is one in which the initiative is taken by the salesman. Here the salesman does not sell but creates the urge to buy. This type of selling is most frequent in the sale of industrial goods, consumer specialities, and intangible services like life insurance, entertainment, investment, transportation and information services for which the need and desire are created by the salesman.

1. Wilson. J.M., *Open the Mind and Close the Sale.*

3. Professional Salesmanship: It is most highly developed and evinces an established and accepted code of ethics, a set of standards for admission and disqualification and recognises that service to others comes before self-interests. It establishes a link between the buyer and seller through which benefits in the form of comfort, convenience, safety, protection, profit or satisfaction are given to them. This type of salesmanship is practised for the sale and industrial as well as specialities and intangible services.

Role of Salesmen in Selling

Personal selling has been defined by American Marketing Association as: "Oral presentation in a conversation with one or more prospective purchase for the purpose of making sales."[1] The hallmark of personal selling is interaction between marketer and customer.

N. Painter has very specifically said:

"He who works with his hands is a *labourer*, he who works with his hands and his head is a *craftsman*.

He who works with his hands, head and heart is an *artist*.

He who works with his hands, and his head, and his heart and his feet is a *salesman*"[2]

According to Miller, "A salesman is a representative of a business or social enterprise whose principal activity is to disseminate knowledge concerning its products and/or its services for the purpose of persuading individuals to accept certain ideas that result in mutual benefit and that normally result in the exchange of merchandise or the performance of services."[3] The modern salesman helps his customers to understand already existing needs and to realise the value of his product as the best possible means of fulfilling them.

According to L. Hardy, the salesman is the key figure in an economy which relies upon individual initiative and the competitive forces of the market place to stimulate full employment and acheive an orderly and efficient distribution of

1. American Marketing Association, *Marketing Definitions* 1960, p. 9.
2. Painter, C.N., Address "Selling as a Career" delivered before the alumini of the School of Business and Public Administration, University of Missouri, on the 50th Anniversary celebration.
3. Miller, A.L., *Essentials of Selling*.

goods and services. He is the key-man in the marketing team.[1] Salesman, being the bread-winner, is a pet earning son of the family of trade and industry. Profitability and prosperity of a company depends upon its salesman and, as, such, he is the pivot around whom planning, performance and results revolve.[2]

Difference from Other Promotion Methods

1. Personal selling involves inter-personal communication between individuals. Salesmen are in a position to tailor their efforts to the characteristics and desires of individual prospects. They are not forced to satisfy large groups of persons with varying wants as in the case of mass selling.
2. Salesmen can alter their message in accordance with feedback received from prospects. If no interest is shown by the prospect to a particular appeal or in a product, they can switch their focus on others. This interpersonal and flexible nature of personal selling differentiates it from mass selling.
3. Personal selling is not restricted to business alone. It is also used to sell information, messages, appeals by non-profit making organisations.
4. As compared to mass selling personal selling is a widespread activity.

Objectives of Personal Selling

According to E.W. Cundiff and others, the objectives of personal selling are as follows:[3]

1. To do the selling job.
2. To "service" existing accounts *i.e.*, present customers.
3. To search and obtain new customers.
4. To secure and maintain customers' cooperation in stocking and promoting the product line.
5. To keep customers informed of changes in the product time and other aspects of marketing strategy.
6. To assist customers in selling the product line.
7. To provide technical advice and assistance to customers.

---

1. Hardy, L., *Marketing*, p. 36.
2. *Industrial Times*, Vol. (viii). No. 4., December 15. 1966, p. 30.
3. Cundiff, E.W., R.R. Still and N.A. Govoni, *Fundamentals of Modern Marketing*, 1980, pp. 351-353.

8. To assist with or handle the training of middlemen.

9. To provide advice and assistance to middlemen or various management problems.

10. To collect and report market information of interest and use to company management.

11. To obtain sales volume in ways that contribute to profit objectives, *e.g.*, by selling the proper mix of products.

12. To secure and retain a specified share of the market.

Importance of Personal Selling

According to Robin Peterson, "Salesmen can accomplish difficult things through advertising, sales promotion publicity and public relations. They can tailor their messages to the characteristics and desires of particular prospects; modify on going presentations in accordance with the feedback from prospects; they are in a position to ask for an order at a strategic time and if turned down, they can communicate further, in an effort to recoup and obtain an order. It is much easier to ignore or say no to an advertisement or a display than to a sales man."[1] Thus, personal selling is improtant as follows:

(*i*) *Finding prospects*: Sales personnel must possess a thorough understanding of the people's needs for the product so that prospects could be located and identified who are interested in the company products.

(*ii*) *Convincing the prospects to buy*: Personal selling transforms prospects into buyers. To achieve this purpose, sales personal must be well trained regarding their products and the selling process in general.

(*iii*) *Satisfaction of customers*: Personal selling provides repeat purchases to the company. Sales efforts are often directed towards providing buyers with information and service after sale.

(*iv*) *Useful to all Phases of business world*: Personal selling is directly or indirectly useful to all phases of business world. Volume of sales and goodwill largely depend upon the character of salesmanship offered. As Hayward commented the "advertising policy may be excellent, and the price and quality of the merchandise beyond criticism but if the manner of effecting the direct contact between the store and consumer is poor, the store

---

1. Peterson, Robin. *Marketing: A Contemporary Introduction*, 1977, p. 507

will never attain the measure of success to which other factors may entitle it."[1] The act of salesmanship is necessary for the smooth working of industries. Without it mass production cannot take place in anticipation of sale. In its absence manufacturing activities would be adversely affected. Factory production may be hindered and many of the requirements of modern families may not be satisfied. According to R.S. Tosdal, it is essentially for the accomplishment of the selling function which is at once the most difficult and the most important of the marketing functions and the smooth working of the economic order depends upon a continuous flow of commodities from producer to consumer, a flow which could not and would not be maintained under modern industrial conditions without the exercise of selling efforts.[2] While those possessing general monopoly in certain types may continue to produce but the typical or general manufacturing enterprises would be forced to close down immediately without personal selling. Personal selling has created not only national but international markets has increased production of goods.

Different Designations of Salesmen

Account Executive	Sales consultant
Professional Representative	Agent
Communication Consultants	Industrial Representative
Territory Manager	Professional Sales Representative
Key-Account Supervisor	Key-Account Sales Manager
Territory Sales Consultant	Area Manager
Territory Sales Representative	Special Representative
Sales Engineer	Industrial Account Manager
Sales Representative Engineer	Customer Service Representative
Regional Sales Manager	General Agent
Medical Sales Representative	District Sales Representative
Field Representative	Marketing Representative

Duties of Salesman

1. To ensure that the trader is holding adequate stocks of the manufacturer's products and that he is making an effort to re-sell them.

---

1. Hayward, W.S., *The Retail Handbook*. p. 277.
2. Tosdal, R.S., Principles of Personal Selling, p. 41.

2. To obtain product display and display of product promotional material.

3. To maintain goods relations with the customers.

4. To collect outstanding accounts.

5. To determine the product desired by the customer, ascertains its make, type, pattern or design, quality desired and the price the customer is willing to pay.

6. To display the products and assists the customer to make a selection by suggestions or explanations, emphasises the chief selling points of the product and encourages the sale of the costly products.

7. To write out sale slips mentioning the name of the product, its price and the name and address of the buyer, if the sale is on credit or sent as cash on delivery.

8. To receive payments or secures credit authorisation and delivers, or arranges the delivery' of the product at the consumer's residence.

9. To care for stock on sales floor, places new products on shelves and arranges them in an attractive style,

10. To write out accommodation slips in cases where product is returned bucy the customer for the purpose of altering, repairing or for some other reasons.

11. To take periodic inventories of the stocks.

12. To act as a vital member of a customer-oriented, marketing management team that starts its planning with customer's need in mind.

13. To help plan forecast, establish procedures and programmes, fix schedules, and coordinate all thess activities to achieve customer's satisfaction.

Responsibilities of the Salesman

(1) To know his customer's needs and problems thoroughly. This involves a sophisticated understanding of economics and psychological and social behaviour.

(2) To have an ability to speak the customer's language, *i.e.*, things can be sold only by technically trained salesmen.

(3) To have a thorough understanding of his customers' operations and facilities. This will need an intelligent understanding of

finance, credits and collections, inventory control, purchasing, automation, advertising, government regulations, and tax and legal matters.

(4) To be able to meet and advise the management on matters relating to the marketing and customer's problems.

The Salesman's Creed

According to The Sheldon School and the Human Engineering Institute, following is the salesman's creed:

1. To respect my profession, my company, and myself. To be honest and fair with my company, as I expect my company to be honest and fair with me; to think of it with loyalty, speak of it with praise, and act always as a trustworthy custodian of its good name. To be a man whose word carries weight at my home office; to be a booster, not a knocker; a pusher, not a kicker; a motor, not a clog.

2. To base my expectations of reward on a sound foundation of service rendered; to be willing to pay the price of success in honest effort. To look upon my work as opportunity to be seized with joy and made the most of, and not as painful drudgery to be reluctantly endured.

3. To remember that success lies within myself, in my own brain, my own ambition, my own courage and determination. To expect difficulties and force my way through them; to turn hard experience into capital for future struggles.

4. To believe in my proposition heart and soul; to carry an air of optimismin to the presence of possible customers; to dispel ill-temper with cheerfulness, kill doubts with strong convictions and reduce active fiction with an agreeable personality.

5. To make a study of my business, or line; to know my profession in every detail from the ground up; to mix brains with my efforts and use system and method in my work. To find time to do everything needful by never letting time find me doing nothing. To hoard days as a miser hoards dollars; to make every hour bring me dividends in commissions, increased knowledge or healthful recreation.

6. To keep my future mortgaged with debt; to save money as well as earn it; to cut out expensive amusements until I can afford them; to steer clear of dissipation and guard my health of body and peace of mind as my most precious stock in trade.

7. To take a good grip on the joy of life; to play the game like a gentleman; to fight against nothing so hard as my own weaknesses, and to endeavour to grow as a salesman and as a man with the passage of every day of life.

This is my Creed.

Traits of a Good Salesman

1. Capacity to establish good relationship with a variety of people.
2. Learning quickly and adapting smoothly.
3. Planning ahead and efficiently managing his time and efforts.
4. Working hard to achieve goals.
5. Dedicating oneself to providing long-term service rather than having a get-rich-quick attitude.
6. Communicating clearly both in speech and in writing.
7. Thinking analytically by learning to break problems you down to their basic components.
8. Producing constantly both in quality and quantity rather than performing erractically.
9. Persisting steadily one's goals and not giving up easily.
10. Possessing and living up to high moral standards that enable people to admire, respect and trust one.

Types of Salesmen

1. Direct Salesman: He is one who visits or calls on the prospective buyers either in their homes or offices and creates a need for the product by convincing them of its utility and persuading them to purchase it. Such salesman may be:

(*i*) *The Route Direct Salesman*: He is one who follows a regular route and serves an established trade (such as bakeries or dairy product sellers).

(*ii*) *Independent Direct Salesman*: He is one who works as an independent operator, finances himself and buys from the suppliers and sells the product of others, such salesman sells household requisites, cutlery, books, utensils, cosmetics and dresses direct to the consumers.

(*iii*) *The Controlled Direct Salesman*: He is one who is under the direct control and supervision of manuacturer, retailer on an insurance company. He sells specialities and tangible services which require selling skill and technical knowledge. He is also known as *Speciality Salesman.* He sells radios, typewriters, sewing machines, automobiles, refrigerators, engineering goods and such like things. He finds out the buyer's needs and get orders for the same; prepares daily reports and summary of the sales and daily call schedules; mails advertising materials to buyers; secures new prospects; keeps informed about the company's work, product, buyers' motives and competitive products and attends sales meetings.

2. Industrial Salesman: He is one who usually sells to a small number of buyers who purchase in large quantities goods of high value including finished goods of all types, installation equipment, accessories and operating supplies. He represents manufacturers, wholesalers, manufacturers' agents, brokers, and machinery dealers. His secures, interviews and conduct survey of the buyers' need; presents sales proposal and conducts demonstrations by showing applications and explaining principles and create desire for the prorduct, advises the customers about the use of the product; prepares call reports, schedules work, maintains a list of buyers, etc.

3. The Merchant Salesman: He is one who sells for the wholesalers or distributors to independent general or speciality stores. His business is restricted to a limited number of wholesale and retail customers. His duties are two-fold, i.e., to secure new dealers and retain established dealers. His activities are calling on dealer customer regularly; discussing new products; explaining the manufacturers' advertising and promotion plans; checking the dealers' stock, shelf arrangement and prices; selling the manufacturer's merchandising plan and sales aid; discussing management problems; aiding merchants in improving store location, layout arrangement; personnel and stock control; settling claims; making adjustments; helping merchants in carrying out advertising plans.

The most prevalent classification of the salesmen.

1. Manufacturer's salesmen.
2. Wholesaler's salesmen.
3. Retail salesmen.
4. Speciality salesmen.

1. Manufacturer's Salesmen

(*i*) *Missionary Salesmen*: These are those who build up goodwill of the firm. They either expand, strengthen or create goodwill. They work through wholesalers, jobbers, or distributors, whose own salesmen will sell to the ultimate consumers. They are employed by the manufacturer to call on customers of his distributors, usually to develop goodwill and stimulate demand, to help or induce them to promote the sale of his employer's goods, to help them train their salesmen to do so, and often, to take orders for delivery by such distributors. Medical supplies and pharmaceutical products require missionary salesmen to promote to retail druggists, physicians and hospitals.

(*ii*) *Merchandising Salesmen*: They assist dealers in increasing their sales by giving them advice on displays, advertising, store layout, credit policies and service facilities. They arrange wide publicity, hold product demonstrations for distributor's salesmen and even work with them in field. They are also largely invovled in cosmetics drugs, medicines, and grocery business.

(*iii*) *Dealer-Servicing Salesmen*: They call regularly on retailers in their territory, getting large orders on every visit. For example, representative for electrical accessories brings new samples, checks, writes new orders, and even sets up window displays.

(*iv*) *Sales Promotion Salesmen*. Also known as detail salesmen they specialise in sales promotion than rather than on spot order. Representatives of medical firms or publishers belong to this category.

(*v*) *Technical Salesmen*: They are usually highly trained technical personnel. They direct their efforts toward the company's current customers by providing technical assistance regarding numerous dimensions such as applications of the products, system designs, product characteristics, and installation procedures. They usually sell technical products such as computers, heavy equipment, steel and chemicals.

(*vi*) *Trade Salesmen*: They ususally perform the order-taking function. They help customers promote the products, especially within retail stores. They help in re-stocking sales, obtaining more shelf space, setting up displays, providing in-store demonstrations, and distributing samples to the store customers.

(*vii*) *The Order Getter Salesmen*: They increase the company's sales by selling to new customers and by increasing sales to present. Known as "creative selling", their job requires sales people to recognise potential buyers' need and then to provide them with necessary information.

(*viii*) *The Order-taker Salesmen*: They perform repeat sales, and maintain long-lasting and satisfying relationships with customers, (a) The *inside order- takers* are located in sales offices and receive orders by mail and telephone; (b) *field order-takers* travel to customers and secure orders.

2. Wholesaler's Salesmen

They represent the wholesaler who carries stock of many items from several different manufacturers. They serve many retailers or other customers who place one consolidated order for different kinds of products in small quantities. He calls on the retailers at regular intervals and gets orders from them.

3. Retail Salesmen

Retail Salesmen work behind the counters in retail shops or may work outdoor, when they are termed as *'travelling salesmen'*. They have many opportunities to sell items related to the item which the customer comes in to buy. They exercise insight, imagination, and ingenuity in an effort to unearth additional customer needs and to persuade the customer to buy the right product to meet them. They require knowledge of stock, prices, and materials. The travelling salesmen usually covers a large territory or may be confined to a city or a part of it. He goes out in search of business and creates a demand for his goods.

4. Speciality Salesmen

They usually represent a single product or line which they sell by going directly to the consumers. They sell expensive durable goods, furniture, books, home furnishings, vacuum cleaners, washing machines, automobiles, refrigerators, etc. The following are the important types of speciality salesmen:

(*a*) *Product or service salesmen*: They specialise in selling products or services used in office or the factory, such as computers, office machine, training courses, accounting, insurance and other services.

(*b*) *Door-to-door salesmen*: They directly call on the prospects in their homes and induce them to purchase such products as Encyclopaedias, cosmetics, detergents, soaps, etc.

SELLING TACTICS AND PERSONAL SELLING PROCESS

1. Prospecting: It consists of developing a list of potential customers. Its purpose is to identify individually who really needs the offerings and who have the ability to buy (purchasing power) and the willingness to buy (motivation). The names of the prospects can be discovered from various sources, such as the company's sales records, consumer's information requests from advertisements, other customer's newspaper announcements, public records, telephone and trade directories, 'who's who', yearbooks, and Trade Associations Lists, etc. By prospecting, the salesman is able to concentrate upon those prospects that are target customers and avoid those who appear to be unprofitable prospects.

2. Preparation—It includes Pre-approach and Approach to the Customer: Its object is to find out about the consumers' wants and desire so that the product can be tailored to those specific requirements. It is often termed as "qualifying the prospect". It involves knowledge of what products or brands are being currently used by the prospect, his reaction to them; the amount of product that the customer might use; some knowledge about his personal likes and dislikes, a thorough knowledge of product features, performance, capabilities and limitation; knowledge about competitor's products, environmental conditions, and the knolwedge of policies and procedures of his own organisation concerning availability, allowances, services and warranties, etc. This information is used in selecting an approach and in creating a sales representation. By this information a salesman can develop an approach and presentation that successfully communicates with the prospect.

3. Approaching the Customer: It consists of the initial contact with prospect. It is the most critical step because the prospect's first impression of the salesman may be a lasting impression having long-run consequences.

(*i*) *Approach is based on referrals*: The salesman approaches the prospects and explains that an acquaintance, an associate, or a relative has suggested the call.

(*ii*) *The 'cold canvass' approach*: In it the salesman calls on potential customers without their poor consent.

(*iii*) *Repeat contact approach.* In it the salesman mentions a prior meeting when making the contact. A suitable, what type of approach depends upon the salesman's preferences, the product being sold, the firm's resources, and the characteristics of the prospect. Many salesmen find AIDA *i.e,* (Attention, Interest, Desire, Action) technique to be useful in approach.

While approaching the customer the salesman's goals are to capture the prospect's attention and interest. The prospect is convinced that it will be rewarding to spend time with him.

4. Presentation: It is closely rleated to the consumer's buying process. Its purpose is to secure desire and action. Most commonly used technique is AIDA (Attention, Interest, Desire, Action). According to J.W. Thompson, the first step in the sales presentation is to focus the prospect's attention on the product as a means of satisfying a want or desire. Attention may be drawn by (*a*) mentioning the name of the mutual friend, (*b*) placing the product sample or a visual aid before the prospect; (*c*) allowing the prospect to touch, hold, or actually use the product; (*d*) complementing the prospect on the appearance of the store, office, or plant or his residence; and (*e*) ask for a favour, such as advice or where to obtain other prospects' names; (*f*) demonstration about the use of the product.[1]

According to Alfred Grass, the most successful method of securing attention is to use any one or more of the following:

"Paying an honest compliment to the customer; referring to familiar names; referring to specific problems; offering survey or interesting data about the products; showing an interesting exhibit; offering help or service offering a free gift; exciting curiosity by showmanship; citing an instance or telling a story."[2] Other tactics used are to name some one who derived immense benefits by the use of these goods.

After the prospect's interest has been obtained the salesman's next step is to arouse the interest in his product. As the prospect is not searching a way of satisfying his want or desire, the key for

1. Thompson, Joseph, W., *Selling*: *A Behavioural Science Approach*, McGraw-Hill Book Co., New York, 1966, pp. 262-269.
2. Grass Alfred, *Practical Salesmaship*, The Ronald Press Co., New York.

the salesman is to focus upon those product attributes that are meaningful for the particular prospect he is addressing.

Through tact the prospect can be convinced about the merits of the product. The salesman should gain the confidence of the prospect and understand his psychology so that the prospect takes pride in possession of a product sample. Models, photographs, catalogues and other related material like charts, diagrams and statistics are used to convince the prospect.

Overcoming the Objections

1. Direct denial methods: It is also called the *"head-on or contradiction"* method, the salesmen should never contradict the buyers' observation. He should not be offensive, rather he should smile. The retail sales clerk should not attempt this method because he is seldom in a position to keep the customers. The type of customer must be kept in mind, so that his feelings may not be hurt. It should not be used if the objection has any 'ego' involvement in it.

2. Indirect-denial method: It is also known as *"yes but method"* or *"sidestepping the question method"*. It is a method of compromise as both salesman and prospect "bend" a little and admit to each other that though both are right, there is the other side of the problem also.

3. The Boomerang method: It is also called the *translation method* because the objection raised by the prospect often comes back at him as a valid reason for buying the product. It is useful in meeting excuses that are not strongly backed by facts. It is effective only when the salesman is skilled in applying this technique.

4. Compensation method: It acknowledges the validity of an objection, but points out some advantage that is supposed to compensate for the objection, such as lower price, or special care of the product.

5. The question method: The salesman asks questions regarding objections, so that fur.ther analysis be made. The "reason objections" are answered with the word why because why reopens the discussion and the possibility of making a sale.

6. The pass-up method: It is one where the salesman smiles and tries to pass over the objection especially when the objection is of trival nature that it does not deserve a careful or thoughtful answer.

While using any of these methods the salesman must be sure that he is applying the right method in each particular situation.

Sales Strategies for Specific Situations

(1) One may ignore the distraction or interruption and go ahead with his presentation. This course is adopted when people are not serious about what they are saying or whose statements have little or no relevance to the salesman's representation.

(2) One can completely agree with the prospect, and can promise to do same about the situation.

(3) One can challenge the statement. Sometimes it is best not to let a prospect make untrue or irresponsible statement.

(4) One can encounter with his own information.

(5) One may strategically withdraw if the situation looks explosive and if the things might be said that are better left unsaid.

(6) One can ask for more details and encourage the prospect to express his doubts and misgivings. It helps the salesman in focusing attention on the discussion on the actual facts and it lets the prospect unwind and often forces him to re-examine the situation.

(7) One may change the subject.

(8) One can act directly on the statement itself.

Guidelines for Handling Objections

1. Understand the question have an opportunity to think it through, and answer relevant to the sales situation.
2. Use the prospect's language so that his answers are understood by the prospect.
3. Be specific and try to make answers affirm why the prospects should buy. This can turn objections into effective sales points.
4. Answer the objections as early as possible, otherwise doubts and distrust might be created in the minds of the prospect.
5. Make objectionable features look like desirable features, persuade the prospect to think in positive terms and to believe that the product does meet his needs.
6. Do not argue with the prospect while handling objections even though the prospect disagrees violently and persistently.

7. Keep a 'cool head', and do not let yourself become rattled or distracted, even in 'thorny' situations.
8. Do not allow the prospect to give his views, show courtesy towards him, and keep the interview on a friendly basis and avoid creating tension.
9. Be deliberate and unhurried in answering objections.

6. Closing the Sale

Some of the effective ways of closing the sale are: (*i*) to take it for granted; (*ii*) offer some inducements—a price deal, free merchandise, trading stamps or some other incentives; (*iii*) telling business stories how others have benefited by the purchase of the products; (*iv*) fear of loss; (*v*) stressing minor but interesting details; (*vi*) making a straight request for an order, or informing the prospect to "order now to be able to obtain the special sale terms" or "order before we are out of stock." The salesman may employ a *"trial close"* by asking questions that assume the prospect will buy the product, *e.g.*, he might ask the potential customer questions about financial terms, desired colours, or sizes, delivery arrangements, or the quantity to be purchased. A trial close lets prospects indirectly respond that they will buy the product without having to state those sometimes difficult words "I'll like it". As salesman should try to close at several points during the presentation, because the prospect may be ready to buy.

7. Following up

After a sale is closed, it is properly followed. The salesman ensures that the delivery instructions given by the customer are properly followed. He visits the customer often to leam what problems or questions have arisen regarding the prodct. *"After-sales services"* should be punctual, quick and satisfactory. In some industries like the computer sector, he helps in the installation of the product and in ensuring that the customer's employees are operating it effectively. Periodic visits are often made. Besides, salesmen call upon customers to explain newly discovered feature of the product, the problems that others are having with it, or just to maintain friendly relations and show that the salesman is interested in the customers.

Why do Salesman fail?

The Sales and Marketing Executive International U.S.A. gives the following reasons for the failure of the salesmen:[1]

Primary Factors

(1) Lack of planning ability, time utilisation, poor work habits.

(2) Lack of industriousness, drive.

(3) Lack of resourcefulness, aggressiveness.

(4) Lack of observation, an eye for sales possibilities, vision.

(5) Lack of self-evaluation and self-development.

(6) Lack of self-confidence, enthusiasm, too easily discouraged.

(7) Lack of ambition or desire to succeed.

(8) Ineffective calls could not develop interest getting sales presentation.

(9) Inability to answer objections, slow, uncreative thinker.

(10) Inability to develop successful closing techniques.

Secondary Reasons

(1) He could not work.

(2) He was unstable.

(3) He could not assimilate training.

(4) He was immature.

(5) He needed more money now.

(6) He lacked good human relations.

(7) He felt that the new job offered more security.

(8) He did not like to sell.

(9) He had outside interests.

(10) He felt the need for the security of a salary.

P.H. Whiting thus summarised the result of his survey (of 3,000 members of the New York Sales Executive Club) regarding the greatest problems of the salesmen:[2]

(1) Salesmen fail to organise their selling.

(2) Salesmen do not think creatively.

1. Reid, A.L., *Modern Applied Salesmanship*, pp. 80-81.
2. Whiting, P.H., *The Five Great Problems of Salesman and How to Solve Them*, 1964.

(3) Many salesmen do not know how to answer objections effectively.

(4) Salesmen do not know how to motivate themselves to do their best work.

(5) Salesmen rarely communicate effectively.

How to Overcome Salesman's Problems?

Reid offers the following suggestions to overcome these problems:

(*i*) *When you face a task or problem,* get started at once on it. Writing down the words *who, what, when, where, why* and *how* is often all that is required to trigger positive mental thoughts which lead to prompt action.

(*ii*) *When you do not think you have time, set a deadline for yourself and establish priorities,* so that you take care of important things first.

(*iii*) *Concentrate your attention, time, and energy on important things first,* and through concentration complete those tasks first. Ruthlessly eliminate less important or non-essential thoughts or tasks.

(*iv*) *Organise a natural work flow,* and conserve your energy with breaks for rest and relaxation.

(*v*) *Strive to complete task once you have started them.* When that task is complete you can move on confidently to the next, not beset with worries of having to complete countless unfinished tasks.

Practical rules for success as salesman

1. Be tactful.
2. Be courteous.
3. Be sympathetic.
4. Have good manners.
5. Do not criticise.
6. Apologise by saying "I am sorry", "whenever you feel you are wrong.
7. Make up vour mind to be big and learn to keep your temper.
8. If you do a mistake, admit it quickly and sincerely.
9. Do not gossip nor agree with a gossiper because you want to be friendly.
10. Always make the other person feel important.
11. Appreciate other people's interest.

12. Do not pretend, just be yourself.

13. Avoid all forms of boasting.

14. Always look for the good qualities in others and find something to like about each of them.

15. Cultivate good manners at all times in your home, in public, wherever you are—be well mannered.

16. Never say anything, never make a promise, unless you could put the words down in writing and add your signature.

17. Admit honestly that you do not know something than to bluff it out.

18. Be sincere. Have absolute faith in what you are saying.

19. Give praise where praise is due. Do not save your praise for tomorrow. Do not decide to give it next week. Give praise lavishly.

20. Give honest appreciation. Make up your mind right now that whenever any one does anything for you, you will show your appreciation for what has been done.

21. Talk often, but never long. Adapt your conversation to the people with whom you are conversing.

22. Never ridicule anyone. Do not make fun of religion or of people's nationality when in mixed company.

23. Avoid mannerisms such as sniffing, holding a handkerchief after finishing the blowing of nose; dropping of the lips at the side; standing too close to people when talking to them; holding the coat of anyone with whom you are speaking; playing with the tie; drumming on the desk or table with a pencil or finger tips; leaning while standing, putting hands in the pocket while standing; slapping people on the back; such phrases as 'old boy', 'old chap', etc,

24. Be punctual in replying letters or sending reports; making complaints; in giving the maximum amount of inconvenience to the office people; at being disagreeable with anything; and grumbling every time for increases in salary.

25. Do not slough and do not show off while walking. Walk straight towards the customer. Do not shake hands unless the customer offers to shake hands with you; if you shake hands do it politely.

26. Do not be a 'go getter' but be a 'go giver', i.e., if you give a lot to the customers, they are sure to give you a lot in return.
27. Never appear to be cleverer than the buyer.
28. Never criticise the buyer's policy, nor slander competitors or their merchandise before customers.
29. Ask for your seniors' assistance or advice in a difficult case.
30. Make best use of the opportunity.
31. Be steady at all times because such a person can be more successful than the up and down salesman.
32. Never be satisfied with your turnover.
33. Combine all your experience, all the advantages you have of knowing your customers so well, with the enthusiasm of a new salesman who wants to move ahead with the times, and achieve even greater success.
34. Never magnify your troubles.
35. Avoid anger, excitement and resentment while meeting the customers or the boss.
36. Put everything into the job you are doing. Do not think of the next job or the job after that. Do your very best with task you are dealing with at that time.
37. Be Honest.
38. Be enthusiastic.
39. Fit your products into the prospect's business.
40. Never lie; it does not matter even if business is lost.

SELLING STRATEGY

1. The Formula Approach: In it a salesman assumes that customers pass through several stages—Attention, Interest, Desire to buy and Action to buy—before making an actual purchase. He attempts to guide them through these stages using a *canned* talk. Such talks are more accurate and more authoritative than less structured presentations but are less persuasive.

2. The Stimulus-Response Approach: It has four essential elements, viz., drives, cues, response and reinforcement. *Drives* are strong stimuli that impel the buyer's response. *Cues* are weak stimuli. They determine *when* the buyer will respond. *Response is what* the buyer actually does. *Reinforcement* is any event that strengthens the tendency for a buyer to make a particular response—*i.e.,* it may result in repeat orders. This approach consists of repeated appeals to potential customers. The salesman tries to produce positive reactions to a product or service by using a routine series of stimuli. This is particularly effective in selling convenience goods or highly technological goods.

3. The Need Satisfaction Approach. This approach is used mainly in higher-level creative selling situations. It consists of discovering the customer's needs, making customers aware of these needs and demonstrating how a product or service can meet them. Once the need is fully defined and has been discussed by the salesman and the customer, the salesman can concentrate on showing how particular products or services can be useful. Both the customer and the salesman are involved in the purchase decision.

1. The Sales Personality

C.B. Strand rightly said that a "Salesman is a member of the *Great Triumvirate of progress"*—the scientists who conceive the items; the producer who fashions it; and the salesman who makes society aware of its usefulness and promotes its distribution."[1] He is a representative of business or social enterprise whose principal activity is to disseminate knolwedge concerning its products and/ or its services for the purpose of persuading individuals to accept certain ideas that result in mutual benefit and that normally result in the exchange of merchandise or the performance of services."[2] He acts as a link between the producer and the consumer.

The salesman plays many roles—persuader, information gatherer, serviceman, customer ego-builder, expeditor, co-ordinator, problem definer, traveller, display arranger, etc. He represents his organisation to the customer, and the customer to his organisation. He should be capable of performing successfully in different situations. He should have basic qualities of head and heart. He must possess a good personality as personality is the impression one makes on other people by his physical being and by all his reaction towards life.[3]

It is the extent to which the individual has learned to covert his energies into habits or actions which successfully influence other

1. Strand, C.B., *Salesmanship*, p. 33.
2. *Ibid.*, p. 44.
3. *Ibid*

people.[1] Personality is not static but dynamic and is not much innate quality but mostly acquired. It need not be outstanding, vivid, overpowering and domineering; in fact, it should be quiet, silent and unobtrusive, but nevertheless penetrating.[2]

Traits of a Successful Salesman

1. Physical traits: These include appearance (including facial expression, height, dress, posture); health, voice and conversation; and likeable disposition.

2. Mental Traits: These include accuracy, altertness, imagination and resourcefulness initiative; self-confidence; cheerfulness; good memory, etc.

3. Social Traits: These include ability to meet people; dominance; submission; tact, courtesy; appreciation; tolerance; patience, co-operation; helpfulness; manners and mannerisms.

4. Character: It includes honesty, reliability, loyalty, gratitude, industry and persistence.

The selling points differ from article to article. According to Satyanarayan the following are important selling points for certain classes of goods:[3]

1. Fruits and Vegetables: Freshness, weight, vitamin content and its food value, price, taste, small, difficulty or easiness of assimilation, cooling or heating effect in the system, period for which they can be preserved.

2. Mechanical goods: Size, price, shape, portability, durability, freedom from rusting, noiseless operation, quick repairability, weight, quality, absence of danger while working, economy of space, simplicity of mechanism, and appearance, etc.

3. Textiles: Colour, matching quality, seasonal utility, niercerisation, texture, durability, washability, cost of washing charges, stiffness, maintaining neatness and form, price, softness, coarseness, thinness and comfort, etc.

Necessary information may be gathered from a large number of sources, such as personal experience, use of libraries and trade journals and professional magazines; advertisements

---

1. ***Osborne, D.R.,*** *Salesmanship of Today for Sales Managers of Tomorrow,* p. 89.
2. Pradhan. N.S., Jakate, M.N. arid Mail, M.V., *Elements of Salesmanship and Publicity,* 1970, p. 143.
3. Satyanarayan, M., *Salesmanship and Publicity,* pp. 93-94.

of competing firms and other manufacturers; sales bulletins, government sources; sales portfolio, visit to factories; meetings and conferences; motion pictures and audio-visual aids, personal training programmes; correspondence courses, travelling demonstrations; and friendly consultations with the superiors.

Know the Customers and their Buying Motives

Customers have been divided into many categories such as the friendly customer, the timid customer, the impulsive customer, the undecided customer, the deliberate customer, the silent customer, the snobbish customer, the price- minded customer, the argumentative customer, the suspicious customer, the rude and sarcastic customer, the grouse and sorehead, the procrastinator, the determined customer, the conceited customer, the overcautious customer, the clever customer, and the slow thinking customer.[1] To these have been added: talkative customer, handicapped customer, impatient customer, the middle aged and the elderly customer; women customer, the expert buyer; the industrial pruchaser and the group shopper.[2]

In his *Salesmanship,* Professor Alfred Gross has said that, "appearance of an individual or his place of business, his attitude and expressions as the salesman speaks to him, and the actions of people around him help to build up a picture of the prospect". Therefore, it is essential that a salesman should, while sizing up the prospect, observe their carriage, facial expression, clothes, tone of voice, and actions.

By the *carriage* or the manner in which the prospect enters the shop, a salesman should know whether he knows what he wants or if he is one in a hurry. "If he carries himself erect, straight, and to his full height, with his head high and chest thrown out, he is a neat, tidy, positive, determined self-assured and thoughtful customer. If the carriage is poor and careless, he must be timid and nervous. Wild and unsteady looks suggest an impulsive nature".[3]

Face is the index of the customer's attitude as well as his thought,[4] Facial expression may also indicate whether the prospect

1. Pradhan, Jakate and Mali, *op. cit.*, p. 168-173.
2. Dawar, R.S., *Salesmanship and Publicity*, pp. 169-184.
3. Pradhan, Jakate and Mali, p. 166.
4. *Ibid.*, p. 167.

is pompous, a snob, cheerful, frank disbelieving, suspicious or guileful. "Clothes give an idea of the customer's status and taste, while gestures and manners provide a clue to judge whether he is timid, self-assured, quick-tempered or excitable, easy going or aggressive. It is equally important to note the tone of voice, whether soft and pleasant, well-modulated or grating, loud and harsh for it is at time as excellent index to the character and disposition of the customer".[1]

QUESTIONS FOR EXERCISE

1. Define personal selling and discuss the role of salesman in selling.
2. Explain the process, tactics and strategy of personal selling.

1. *Ibid*

30

Sales Management

Definition of Sales Management

Sales management is the administration of the personal selling activities of the organisations.

1. *Dunn and Others*: "The planning implementation, and control of the selling efforts."[1]

2. *Brech*: "The overall management of sales and it refers to only a specialised application of the process of management as a whole."[2]

3. *The American Marketing Association*: "Sales management is the planning, direction, and control of the personal selling activities of a busincs; unit, including recruiting, selecting, training, equipping, assigning, rating supervision, paying motivating as these tasks apply to the personal sales force.'[3]

Difference from other fields of management

1. The imaginative conception of the selling idea is a necessary part of tlv operation before the more function of management in organising a team sales personnel to put the idea into operation.

2. In sales management there is a wider variety of cost incurred and the greater potential of waste than is normal in other fields.[4]

---

1. Dunn, Albert H., Eugene, M. Johnson, and David & Kurtz, *Sales Management Concepts*, Practices and Cases, General Learning Press, Morristown, N.J., 1974, p. 8.
2. Brech, E.F.L., *The Principles and Practice of Management*.
3. *Marketing Definitions: A Glossary of Marketing Terms*, p. 20.
4. *op. cit.*

According to V.L. Srivastava, the tendency towards price competition scientifically planned advertising, more marketing research and analysis, product planning, integrating consumer's wants and psychologies as well as production schedules and other factors have all made selling complex and thereby making the responsibility of the modern sales manager of **dynamic** importance.[1]

1. Establishing Sales Force Objectives: A sales manager must develop sales objectives in precise, measurable terms and should be specific regarding the time period and the geographic areas involved. Sales objectives have to be established both for the total sales force and for each salesman and stated in terms of volume, market share or profit for the total sales force. For the individual salesman, they are to be stated in terms of rupees of unit sales volume; order size, average number of calls per time period; and the number of orders relative to the number of calls.

2. Human Resource Planning: It is the determination of the number and characteristics of sales persons that the organisation needs over a specific period of time (say a year). The size of the sales force depends on the compensation methods used, salesmen's morale, sales forecasts, and the overall management of the sales force. It must be adjusted periodically with the variation in the company's marketing plans and changes in markets and forces in the marketing environment.

Two methods may be employed for human resource planning:

(i) The equalised workload method: In it the sales force size is based on the condition that each salesman is assigned a set of accounts that in total require about the same amount of sales time and effort. This method requires certain conditions to be fulfilled as: (*a*) It must be possible to divide customers into groups based on size of purchases, (*b*) The user must be able to determine the number of sales calls required to serve various account size adequately, (*c*) The average annual number of calls per salesman must be ascertained.

(ii) The incremental productivity method: In it the manager should continue to increase the sales force as long as the additional sales increases are greater than the additional increases in selling costs that arise from employing a greater number of salesmen.

1. Srivastava, V.L., Industrial Management and Business Administration, 1965, p. 245.

The sales managers determine the desired characteristics of recruits. They prepare *job description,* which outlines the duties and responsibilities of the salesmen. Effectiveness in sales force management depends importantly on the completeness and accuracy of the sale job description. Through analysis of the duties and responsibilities, management derives the set of qualifications in the form of *job specificaitons*—which salesmen should possess. Job specification derives from the hierarchy of objectives: corporate marketing, promotion, and down to selling.

3. Recruiting and Selecting Salesmen: The salesman may be chosen from inside the organisation or outside, through advertisement, introductions, educational institutions, small customers, etc. or the sales forces of other firms in the trade. The sales manager should judge the ability of the persons concerned before actually selecting them as salesmen.

Russell enumerates qualities of as: Adaptability, courage, the desire to study, discipline, forcefulness, health, honesty, persistence, resourcefulness and act.[1] Holtzclaw quotes the qualification of a salesman as needed by L.E. Vaterman Co., which should be eight as depicted in the diagram given below:[2]

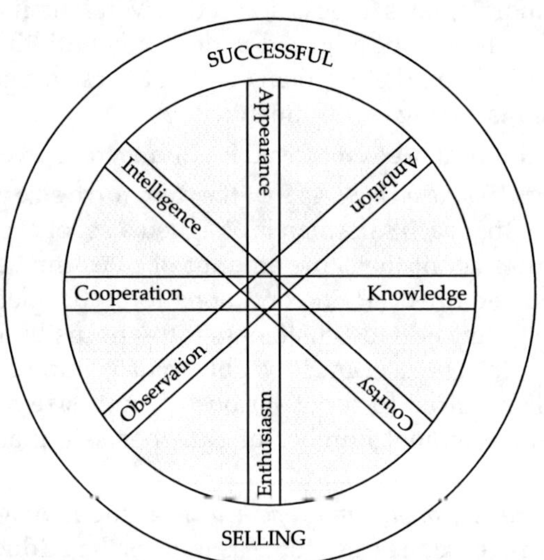

Fig. 30.1: Qualifications needed for a salesman

1. Russell, *op. cit.,* pp. 11-13
2. Holtzclaw, H.P., *Principles of Marketing,* 1936, p. 338.

Another authority sets forth qualification in accordance with the following:[1]

(*i*) *Good character*	Reputation, habits, integrity, self-control, reliability, truthfulness, honesty, fairness, loyalty, sincerity, sobriety, and decency.
(*ii*) *Personality*	Individuality, address, appearance, cleanliness, manners, and voice.
(*iii*) *Health*	Vitality, correct habits of life.
(*iv*) *Mentality or Mental ability*	Understanding, native intelligence and native ability.
(*v*) *Concentration*	Application, tenacity, patience, perservance, study, and self-analysis.
(*vi*) *Industry*	Energy, capactiy for work, enthusiasm, optimism, and ambition.
(*vii*) *Self-confidence*	Courage, preparedness, and conviction of competency.
(*viii*) *Punctuality*	Promptness in all dealings with customer and the household readiness of decision of action, brevity, and directness.
(*ix*). Tact and Diplomacy	Institution and sympathetic comprehension.
(*x*) Initiative	Power of organisation and visualization.
(*xi*) Resourcefulness	Alertness, observation, and imagisation.
(*xii*) Knowledge of goods	To include knowledge of business methods and policy of house, as well as of competitors.

Knox visualised qualities essential for a salesman are as below:

Positive Qualities

Ability	**Reliability**	**Will**
1. Observation	1. Honesty	1. Courage
2. Concentration	2. Loyalty	2. Decision
3. Comparison	3. Sincerity	3. Initiative
4. Memory	4. Enthusiasm	4. Punctuality
5. Imagination	5. Faith	5. Energy
6. Reason	6. Optimism	6. Carefulness
7. Judgement	7. Ambition	7. Discipline

1. Quoted by Todsal, H.S., *Principles of Personnel Selling*, p. 488.

4. Training Sales Personnel: Many people believe that salesmanship is born in a man and if he has not the inherent ability he cannot acquire it. But this is partly true. There are born salesmen, as there are corn lawyers, actors, doctors, engineers or teachers. But all these people require training before they are accepted as qualified. So is the case with the salesman.

Necessity for Training

Salesmen are *not made or born but they are made and born.* Modern management recognises that it is extremely costly not to train salesmen because:

(*i*) the added length of time which the untrained man requires to become self-supporitng, during which time salary and expenses must be paid;

(*ii*) sales opportunities are wholly lost or lost to competitors, because of the untrained salesman's inability to handle difficult situations; and

(*iii*) increased cost of failed supervision during the fumbling period.

Enlightened employers, therefore, believe in educating the sales personnel, on the following grounds.[1]

(1) Businessmen want their sales people to be prepared to interpret the business or the product rather than to accept friendship, personality or popularity to make the sale for them.

(2) Competition is keen and the successful salesman must not only know his product but he must understand sales tactics in order that he may meet the scientific attitude of many buyers and the demand of the alert and competent purchasing agent.

(3) Unity of efforts is necessary when a definite policy is to be carried out.

Training of the proper character aids greatly in making it possible for large organisations to proceed along a predetermined course.

(4) Knowledge of the various departments of a business is essential so that the men of the sales department understand the operations and requirements of the business as a whole and can work smoothly with all executives or department heads

1. Hall, S.R., *The Handbook of Sales Management*, pp. 307-308.

(5) Centralised training makes possible sales research and the assembling of information concerning sales methods and sales policies. Salesmen may draw from this central reservoir as their needs and inclinations prompt them.

(6) Systematised training makes it possible for the employer to observe the new employee and to form fairly accurate opinions concerning his ability to do the work required.

(7) A period of training develops character, schools the candidate in practical psychology; aids him in the analysis of facts and in the delivery of ideas, lessens labour turnover, and though expensive to operate, saves money for the firm later on and finally results in greater net profit to the employer.

FORMAL TRAINING *Vs.* SELF-TRAINING

The gradual steps in the training programme may be divided into three major stages: (*i*) The policies and traditions of the company, (*ii*) The knowledge about product, (*iii*) Sales procedure and selling techniques. The importance of the training function varies substantially between companies, depending upon the complexity of the product, the nature of the market and the variety of training. The prejudices of sales executives also influence training programme. The field salesmen can be trained either by the sales executives of the company, or by the special instructors or by special agencies through instruction method, group discussion method, audio-visual method and practical experience, etc. The training problem of the salesmen is mainly concerned with the formation of sales habit which is not a matter of knowledge as such, but one of procedure. So the problem of training is to inculcate such habits in them before they develop other less effective habits through the trial and error methods. The habit formation is done with the help of psychological techniques.

A formal training of salesmen is more useful than the trial and error method of experience. As the entire production and marketing process depends to a large extent on the sales, hence, the sales management's prime responsibility is to train the salesmen. Good salesmen are not only born but also made. Effective sales training does not only help sales management in discharging its social responsibility of reducing marketing cost but also the sales performance of salesmen. In the long run the company's standing position in the market is determined by the performance of its sales people. Intelligently designed and well executed sales training programme can contribute a lot in this direction. It economises in time, cost and efforts and also increases the efficiency and productivity of the whole organisation a lot. Though experience is always considered better than formal training but they are both complementary to each other.

TECHNIQUES OF CONTROL OVER SALESMEN

Effective supervision and control of the activities of salesmen are essential for the optimum sales performance. It is a continuous process which involves a number of functions to be performed. The basic process of managerial control and its four basic elements are the following:

1. Establishing standards of performance.
2. Recording actual performance.
3. Making comparison or evaluation against the standards.
4. Taking corrective steps.

The same process is repeated in controlling the activities of salesmen. The management guides and directs salesmen in various ways which include:

1. Allocating personal selling effort, *i.e.,* assignment of sales territories, sales quotas, and routing and scheduling salesmen's call.
2. The recording of actual sales performance, *i.e.,* asking for sales report from them.
3. Making comparison.
4. Taking corrective actions.

1. Allocating Personal Selling Efforts: After committing itself to a certain size of sales force and setting the personal sales targets, the management faces the problem of personal selling efforts determination. It involves the following three decisions:

(*i*) *Deciding upon Sales Territory*: Philip Kotler has defined it as the geographical area assigned to a salesman for his operation or selling activity. Each territory represents some potential volume of sales which is helpful in maximisation of sales. The assignment of sales territory makes the maximum use of the ability of salesmen and opportunities.

(*ii*) *Fixation of Sales Quotas*: The most common yardsticks used to measure salesmen's performance, Sales Quotas are quantitative objectives assigned to a specific marketing unit as individual salesman. A salesman might be expected to produce a predetermined volume of sales on the basis of his past performance. Sales quota may be fixed in terms of ₹ or unit sales volume, gross margin, net profit, number of calls, number of new customers and so on. Thus, sales quota is a subjective standard of the measurement of salesmen performance.

(*iii*) *Routing and Scheduling Plans*: An important technique that sales management used for controlling salesmen's activities is routing and scheduling. Its specific purpose is to maintain the lines of communication, to improve the coverage of territories and to minimise the amount of salesmen's wastage of time. Proper routing and scheduling of the activities of the salesmen makes it possible to use the available selling time to maximum advantage. Planning a salesman route eliminates much backtracking, travel time and waiting time. Providing a salesman with a schedule of calls makes it possible to adjust the frequency of call to fit the needs of customers. Routing and scheduling helps sales management in obtaining closer control over salesmen's movements.

2. Recording the Actual Sales Performance: Once sales management has decided the performance standards for use in controlling salesmen it must determine and measure actual performance. It involves the gathering of information on salesmen's performance. Sales management must define its information needs, determine the sources from which to obtain the information and set methods in operation for actually obtaining the needed data. A number of reports are required to be submitted by field sales personnel which provide necessary information about the sales performance, need of sales control and reporting for the needed action.

3. Making Comparison: It is a process of evaluating a salesman's performance which individually and collectively, directly affects the success of the sales efforts. Hence, the management must measure the performance of salesmen, through a good system of performance appraisal which distinguishes between good and poor performance. Standards or norms, against which the actual performance is to be evaluated, must be determined very carefully. The quantitative tools of performance appraisal should be extensively used for decision-making and control purpose. However, in certain cases, qualitative criterion of performance appraisal is also useful.

4. Taking Corrective Action: The performance evaluation of salesmen points out the areas where corrective action is required. No action will be needed if actual performance and predetermined sales standards are in full agreement. On the other hand, if they do not agree, the sales executive has three alternatives open to him: (*i*) To revise the standards in the light of the experiences of salesmen: (*ii*) To lower or raise the sales goal if under assessed. The nature and effectiveness of the corrective actions are affected by the quality of the executive's judgements, his background and experience in the field of performance appraisal, his assessment of the real situations in which the salesmen have to work and his skill in personnel administration techniques.

NEED FOR EVALUATING THE SALESMEN'S PERFORMANCE

1. Determining the Proper Comparison of Salesmen: It is a basic principle that salesmen should be paid according to their productivity and their sales performance. Hence, to determine their fair recommendation it becomes necessary to develop a specific and uniform standard for judging their performance.

2. Proper Sales Planning: A periodic evaluation of the performance of salesmen discloses their relative performance which is needed by the management to make suitable changes in their different assignments as to different territories, products or buyers. Such performance evaluation has a constructive and positive effect on the performance of salesmen.

3. Promotional Decisions: A sound and merit-based promotion policy can be followed on the basis of the performance evaluation of salesmen. It also helps in proper selection and training of the future salesmen.

4. Motivation and Morale: Periodic appraisal of the performance of salesmen motivates them in their efforts and tones up their morale particularly if the salesmen know on what basis their work is being judged.

5. Other Advantages: A periodical review of the salesmen's performance enables the management to draw all its information and impressions about individual salesmen, to discover their weaknesses and the shortcomings of their marketing policies. Such appraisal also reveals the need for changes in procedure or even policy at many points in the selection, training and development process of the sales-force.

METHODS OF PERFORMANCE EVALUATION

1. The Job Description and Norms of Sales Performance: The management should develop the standards for good sales performance which must be established of individual salesmen under the given circumstances. Often these standards are of a quantitative nature. The preparation of the job description defines as clearly as possible what performance is expected for each of the listed duties and responsibilities.

2. Sales Quotas: Sales quotas are the most common yardsticks used to measure salesmen's performance. A quota is a quantitative goal assigned to a salesman in respect of which a salesman might be expected to produce a predetermined volume of sales or a predetermined level of sale. These quotas may be fixed in terms of rupees or unit sales volume or net profit or new number of customers or any other measurable unit. These quotas must be fixed in consultation with the salesmen, and special characteristics of the market and capability of the individual salesman must also be taken into account. It is not justified to fix a uniform sales quota for all salesmen and all sales territories.

3. Reporting and Personal Observation: It is a subjective method of evaluation. Under this system the salesmen are rated by the supervisions of district or branch sales managers and so on. Such rating can be made on the basis of efficiency of the salesman in handling affairs of the territory, diligence and accuracy in reporting, customer relationship and personal qualities like appearance, speech and interest in the work, etc.

Difficulties in Evaluating Performance

1. Complexity of Salesmen's Activity: The duties of salesmen are numerous and varied. Besides actual selling, they may make collections, introduce new products, adjust complaints, advise customers, instal displays, handle service work, check stocks, secure market information, develop good customer relations and engage in yet other activities. Performance of each must be appraised and their relative performance determined.

2. Results are not often measurable: Measurement is difficult, if not impossible for performance on many task customarily assigned. For instance, every salesman is expected to promote good relations with customers and to find new customers for his company's products. Where selling is concentrated and supervision is close, management can determine, whether these tasks are being performed and how well. However, no precise measurement is usually attempted nor would it be feasible. In other situations, close supervision, other than initially in training, is not practised. For instance, it is very difficult to determine whether dealer relations are improving or deteriorating in a particular territory.

3. Joint Efforts are Involved in Sales: In many situations, salesmen actually do not work alone but are aided by supervisors, branch managers, or product specialists. It is most difficult here to determine how much the salesman has contributed to the sale.

4. Variation in Territories and Competitive Positions: The sales territory differs in nature, local condition and extent of competition, etc. Hence, a common standard to evaluate their performance cannot be applied on a uniform basis. Thus, the difference in quantitative evidence is in the territories. Their conditions should be recognised and proper allowance should be made for performance evaluation. Only then the performance of an individual salesman should be compared with that of another salesman.

Role of Performance Evaluation

The performance evaluation of salesmen plays an important role in the formulation of different incentive schemes for them. The basic objective of any incentive scheme is to encourage the salesmen and to create a desire of improving their performance among them. The incentive can be of two types—financial and non-fmancial. In financial incentive schemes the salesmen are given the additional bonus (or premium) for the additional sale they have obtained over and above the standard fixed for their sales territories. Evaluation of the actual performance becomes important in this context. In non-financial incentives too, the role of performance evaluation is quite significant. For example, when a sales quota is assigned to an individual salesman, it is a challenge for him. If this quota is achieved by him, he feels motivated and satisfied. Thus, the performance evaluation exercises a positive impact on the performance of salesmen as well as on their morale and motivation level.

MOTIVATING SALESMAN

Importance of Motivating Salesmen

1. Success in Sale: Sale is the most important activity of business where success determines the success in production and other functions. If the concern does not have motivated salesmen, all fixed assets, modern production set-up and up-to-date orgnisation system are useless.

2. High: The morale of a motivated salesman is always high.

3. Acceptance of Challenges: A motivated salesman always accepts the challenge of changes in products, styles and markets.

4. Job Satisfaction: A motivated salesman derives more job satisfaction from his work and the rate of salesmen-tumover is considerably reduced.

5. Industrial Peace: Industrial peace and non-financial incentives introduced by management to motivate salesmen, bring industrial peace, more harmony between employer and employees and many other intangible advantages.

But a number of studies have proved that man is basically not an economic individual. The economic rewards satisfy only a part of an employee's total needs on the job. In one study salesmen were asked if they would like to quit the work or to continue after receiving a large amount of money. Over 90 per cent salesmen answered they would like to continue the present work even though their economic needs could be fulfilled without a job. Salesmen require additional stimulation both as individuals and as members of a group. Various non-financial incentives provided by sales management improve not only their performance level but also their efficiency and morale. Hence, the sales managers are giving increasing recognition to the problem of salesmen motivation.

Motivation Problems of Field Salesmen

The problem of motivation to the field sales-force is three-fold:

(*i*) The recognition of their needs.

(*ii*) Providing them various financial and non-financial incentives to give better sales performance.

(*iii*) To make an appraisal of motivation schemes.

1. Recognition of Needs: The theory of human needs developed by Maslow is applicable to sales-force also. This theory states that needs are organised into a hierarchy. This means that some categories of needs take priority over others. Maslow gave the following hierarchy of human needs:

(*i*) Physical needs, (*ii*) safety needs, (*iii*) Belongingness and love needs, (*iv*) Esteem needs, (*v*) Self-actnalisation needs. The needs should be recognised and satisfied by the sales manager. The remuneration offered to a salesman must correspond to his position in the hierarchy of unfulfilled needs. Physical needs and safety needs may be satisfied sufficiently by providing an adequate and continuous amount of compensation. Additional pay may not, however, stimulate a salesman if his unsatisfied needs relate to esteem needs or self-actualisation needs. On the other hand, a new salesman often has a strong desire for security. Hence, satisfaction of advance needs will not be sufficient for him.

2. Provision of Non-financial Incentives to the Individual Salesmen.

Some of the non-financial motivational measures are as follows:

(*i*) Communication System.

(*ii*) Inter-Personal Contacts.

(*iii*) Motivational Interviews.

(*iv*) Organising formal sales meeting.

(*v*) Organising sales contests.

(*vi*) Recognition of the group behaviour.

(*vii*) Providing awards.

(*viii*) Recognition of the human behaviour and giving them titles.

All the methods of motivating the sales-force have their own value. Which method will do the best to stimulate the average salesmen to give a better sales performance is a point of question. Most sales managers agree that compensation plan is by far the best method of motivation. They have developed a number of schemes, such as bonus payments, vacations with pay, profit sharing and fringe benefits. Next in order of performance in actual use are sales contests.

3. Appraisal of Motivation Schemes: The sales manager should make a continuous effort to identify not only salesmen needs and goals out evaluation of the schemes also. No single plan or motivation procedure is available to motivate them successfully. Good maintenance of sales force requires that all aspects of sales management must be carried out in a manner which reflects a full understanding of the principles of human relations. The management should not consider motivation as a substitute for sound compensation plans but rather a complement to it.

Techniques of Motivation

The main techniques which can be employed by sales management to motivate their salesmen may be classified into the following:

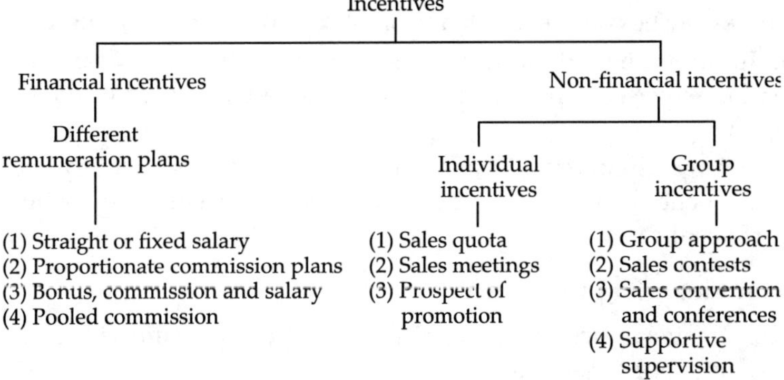

Financial Incentives

A man is basically an economic creature. The proper remuneration of his services is the most important technique of motivation. The sales management follows different methods for remunerating salesmen such as straight salary, commission on sales or profits, bonus, a combined scheme of salary, commission and bonus, share in the profit, leave with pay, reimbursement of expenses and provision of fringe benefits. Except salary and payment of expense, all the other payments to the salesmen are known as a financial incentive. In India the financial incentives are considered the best of the incentives. Hence, a combined scheme of salary, bonus and commission is followed.

The following are the main methods of compensations:

1. Straight or fixed salary.
2. Commission.

3. Combined payment of salary, bonus and commission.
4. Reimbursement of expenses.
5. Fringe benefits.

1. Straight or Fixed Salary: As the payment of a fixed salary gives a definite payment to the salesmen it has not proved to be a strong incentive for continuing increasing performance level. It only provides security in terms of regularity and stability of earnings.

2. Commission: In contrast to salary the amount of commission varies in proportion to some specific measure of the salesmen's performance as gross sales or net profit, etc. Hence, its nature is more motivating.

3. Combined Payment: A bonus is a lumpsum payment for exceptional performance. It may be used as a group incentive. There may be combined scheme of salary, bonus and commission.

4. Reimbursement of Expenses: The payment for salesmen's actual expenses is not acutally an incentive plan but it provides safety.

5. Fringe benefits: Fringe benefits are supplementary to wage benefit and they provide additional incentive to better performance.

Non-Financial Incentives

Non-financial incentives can also be of two types: individual as well as group incentives.

(A) Individual Incentives

1. Sales Quotas: Financial rewards for making or supposing quotas are given by many concerns through additional commission or a bonus. A quota is basically a sales goal set for a specific period in advance, in term of ₹ or physical units. It implies a breakdown of a total sum into parts.

2. Sales Meetings: Sales meetings are motivational in character. The interchange of experiences and emphasis on successful selling have a favourable effect, particularly on younger salesmen. These meetings strengthen the morale and develop a group consciousness among the salesmen.

3. Prospects of Promotion: The promotion chances motivate the individual performance of a salesman. It is very effective in the case of very old and experienced salesmen because in the long run they do not want more money only but also a chance of promotion which increases their status and authority.

(A) Group Incentives

1. Group Approach: It is an effort to promote loyalty, group identity, and recognition of personal dignity and worth. It attempts to reduce the pressure and to induce participation and co-operation.

2. Sales Contests: The word 'contest' denotes rivalry or competition among the salesmen. The sales contests motivate the salesmen as they are given an incentive to improve their performance by competing with others. The sales contests enable the management to focus the attention of the sales-force on certain specific objectives. They also increase the morale of sales-force and unite them.

3. Sales Conventions and Conferences: Convening sales conferences and conventions involves the speeches, physical arrangements, instructions by outside specialists, questions and answers and evaluation of the techniques in actual use.

Essential Features of a Good Remuneration Plan

(*i*) **Regular and Steady Income:** It must provide a regular and steady income to salesmen regardless of the sales level achieved by them.

(*ii*) **Adequate Incentives:** It must provide adequte incentives to salesmen to increase their productivity.

(*iii*) **Adequate Control:** It should give management adequate control over salesmen's activities to make them comply with the policies, procedures and directives of the company.

(*iv*) **Simple and Easy:** It should be simple to understand, easy to follow and should keep operating expenses within the resources of the company. In other words, its operating cost should not be too much.

(*v*) **Developing Sales force:** It should be able to attract, retain and develop a competent sales-force.

Types of Remuneration Plans

1. Straight Salary or Fixed Salary: Under this plan, a fixed amount is paid to salesmen on a periodical basis. It gives salesmen a regular periodical (say monthly) income. In addition to a fixed salary, the salesmen are paid travelling allowances and daily allowances also. There is correlation between the payment and the business done by a salesman in this method.

This plan is simple to understand and easy to follow. It gives a sense of security to the salesmen. They do not have to suffer due to adverse market conditions. However, this method does not provide any incentive to increase productivity. There is no relation between the amount of work and financial rewards received by salesmen. These result in increased cost supervision.

2. Proportionate Commission Plan: Under this plan, the salesmen can be paid commission on a sliding scale on the volume of sales generated by them. The percentage of commission may vary from territory to territory, product to product or for types of sales such as cash sales or credit sales, etc.

This scheme provides sufficient incentives to salesmen to develop in themselves their fullest potential. The need of close supervision of their activities is reduced but the drawback of determination of fair rates of commission is difficult in the plan. Salesmen feel a sense of insecurity as they earn nothing during off season. Applying high pressure tactics to increase the sales volume damage the reputation and goodwill of the company in the long run.

3. Combined Plan: As the name suggests, this scheme is a combination of the above mentioned two schemes, *i.e.*, straight salary and straight commission. These plans may be of various types such as:

(*i*) Salary and commission.

(*ii*) Salary and bonus.

(*iii*) Salary, commission and bonus.

(*iv*) Pooled commission method.

This plan incorporates the positive features of both the schemes and avoids their disadvantages. Besides fixed salary for a specified period of time salesmen are paid commission on total sales volume or on sales above a certain level. An additional amount in the form of bonus may be paid for such activities which cannot be covered by fixed salary and commission. Salesmen are also reimbursed the expenses incurred by them in the proper discharge of their duties and so they put in their healthy sales drive and dash.

From the viewpoint of incentives and creating loyalty among salesmen, the combined plans are certainly better. Large sized firms generally use these remuneration plans for remunerating their salesmen.

QUESTIONS FOR EXERCISE

1. Explain the techniques which are usually employed by the business organisation for exercising control over their salesmen.
2. What is the need for evaluation of salesmen's performance? Describe the methods for evaluating the salesmen's performance and show how it helps the management in deciding proper incentive schemes for the salesmen.
3. Discuss the importance of motivating salesmen. In this connection, indicate some of the special problems associated with the motivation of field sales personnel.
4. What techniques can be used to motivate the salesmen? Explain how a compensation plan be developed in order to motive order salesmen who are well-established together with newly trained salesmen who are not too well-established in the field?
5. What are the various plans of a remunerating salesmen? Which of these plans would provide for adequate incentive as well as loyalty of the salesmen?
6. What are the essential features of a good remuneration plan?
7. What is sales training? Discuss its objectives.
8. "Both training and experience increase the performance of salesmen but training is more important than experience."
9. What are the basic objectives of training the salesmen? Why is formal training likely to be more effective than self-training?

31

Sales Territory, Sales Quotas and Sales Analysis

SALES TERRITORY

Meaning

1. *Philip Kotler*: By sales territory is meant the geographical area assigned to a salesman for his operations or selling activities.
2. *Cundiff and Still*: A sales territory is a particular grouping of customers and prospects assigned to an individual salesman.

Sales territories may be planned either on geographical basis or on the basis of number or nature of customers. Once the territories are defined, personal—selling resources—as well as other marketing resources, can more easily be allocated, monitored and controlled. The nature of the firm, the product and the market will determine the relevant basis for the deviation of territories and the subsequent allocation of personal selling resources.

Objectives of Planning the Sales Territories

According to Cundiff and Still, the following are the main objectives of dividing the whole market into various territories:

1. To cover the whole market effectively.
2. To reduce the sales-overheads.
3. To provide immediate and better customer services.
4. To motivate the salesmen.
5. To bring more clarity and co-ordination in various marketing activities and efforts.
6. To provide a basis for performance evaluation of various salesmen.

Advantages of Sales Territories

1. Proper attention can be paid to all market-segments.
2. It brings economy and efficiency in sales performance.
3. Duplication of salesmen's efforts is avoided.
4. More exploitation of sales opportunities become possible.
5. Sales control becomes easy.
6. Better and prompt customer services can be provided.

SALES QUOTA

Meaning

Sales Quota has been defined by Philip Kotler as follows: "By sales quota is meant a part of the sales goals which has been assigned to a particular salesmen or a territory." Thus a quota is a sales goal set for a specified period in advance, in terms of ₹ or physical units. It requires a breakdown of a total sum into parts. It is the most important and the most commonly used standard for appraising selling effectiveness for specially desired performance level. Having a time dimension it qualifies what management expects from salesmen within a given period.

Reasons for Setting and Using Sales Quotas

1. To Provide Quantitative Performance Standards: If quotas are intelligently set and represent realistic level of desired performance, they can provide quantitative standards of performance appraisal. Comparison of quotas with sales performance identifies weak or strong points of the selling efforts.

2. To Motivate Salesmen: Quotas can be used to motivate salesmen to achieve higher performance level. Some managements use quotas system for this purpose only. If quotas are used as incentives the performance under them is used for compensation, promotions and other decisions. But the management must be very cautious in fixing sales quotas because too high quotas will discourage the salesmen.

3. To Obtain an Effective Budgetary Control Over Sales: Budget quotas serve as a control device for selling expenses. The management assures reimbursement of sales level. The salesmen's performance can be measured in terms of reduction of selling expenses.

4. To Use in Connection with Sales Contest: As the main basis of making awards, the quota fulfilment is a popular technique. If quotas are set accurately and adjusted for differences among territories, they may serve comparison purpose very well.

Problems in Using Sales Quotas

1. Selecting the Proper Types of Quota: Quotas can be grouped into sales volume, activity and financial category. A sales manager should not necessarily use all types of quotas, since some may be more appropriate than others for given products and market situation. Hence, he should make the selection of the right type of quota first. The following are the important quotas:

(*i*) *Sales Volume Quotas*: These are the most widely used types of sales quota. These establish a sales volume for a geographical area, a product line, a customer, a time period or for any combination of these bases. It is useful for smaller market units. It is especially important where sales territory is growing or where a territory's potential has not yet been fully exploited.

(*ii*) *Activity Quotas*: In these the management selects the different types of activities as the basis of salesmen's performance, such as: new calls, new accounts, new customers, interviews; demonstration, display, arranged service calls, collection of partly due accounts, surveys for reports, etc. An activity quota can do much toward increasing fully balanced sales job. It is particularly valuable for new salesmen. But the main problem in using an activity quota is to determine whether the activity was performance worthy and to find out how effectively it was done.

(*iii*) *Financial Quotas*: These are aimed at making the salesmen conscious of cost or profits. These may be fixed for expenses or gross margin or net profit. These are especially useful when maximum market share in a territory has been achieved or when quality of the sales effort is to be measured. But there are difficulties in using financial quota, in case of the determination of the profit or expenses, complication of the accounting procedure, etc.

The decisions about the types of quotas should depend on the following considerations: Marketing goals, calibre of salesmen types of customers, nature of products, nature of the services offered to customers, difficulties in setting the quotas and possible difficulties in the quota plan, etc.

2. Setting the Specific Quotas: The management must follow a scientific approach in setting the quotas. Adequate information about past performance should be collected and their future potentiality must be discussed. The management must determine the profitability' of each effort comprising the salesman's job. It must also consider whether different types of quotas should be used in different territories. As all territories are not of the same nature, some variations in the quotas are useful. The variations on the basis of territories may be either due to the human factor or psychological factors. In setting quotas for the individual salesmen the management should use executive judgement.

3. Administration of Quotas: The administration of quotas involves three aspects—(*i*) determine the relative importance of various quotas, (*ii*) To incorporate the selected quotas into an overall plan which will produce a properly balanced goal for the sales-force. *(iii)* The third problem is concerned with the review or appraisal of the sales performance of individual salesmen. Usually the sales department is responsible for determining and using the sales quotas and also making review. This work can be assigned to any of the several executives depending on the size of the company, the degree of the centralisation in sales-force management and the method used to determine the quotas. The fixed quotas should be adjusted off and on. One of the important tasks necessary for the administration of a quota plan is concerned with the determination of the quota period. Participation of the salesmen in quota setting and administration is also important.

Thus, quotas can provide incentives for salesmen. If properly set and administered they help the sales manager in controlling and evaluating salesmen's performance. Their success depends on three factors:

(*i*) The reliability of sales forecast and budget, etc.

(*ii*) How well the quotas have been set.

(*iii*) How well the sales force accepts its quotas and maintains its enthusiasm in trying to reach them.

SALES ANALYSIS

Meaning

Sales analysis is the first step in a new marketing research programme. It is the analysis of an organisation's own records, past sales and so on.

Importance of Sales Analysis

1. **Marketing Research:** The importance of sales analysis lies in the current operating problems in the marketing foundation of research activities.

2. **Information:** Sales analysis provides a major share of the facts used in research on marketing problems of that type. In many organisations, especially smaller ones, it is the only source of such information.

3. **Raw Material for Analysis:** An organisation's own sales figures are the raw materials of analysis. Those figures exist in readily available form or can be rather easily converted into such form in most organisations. This is true of large or small organisations, whether manufacturers, wholesalers, retailers or service organisations.

4. **Least Expensive:** As internal facts are usually already available, sales analysis is typically the least expensive element of a marketing research programme. This does not mean that sales analysis is widely used merely because it is cheap.

5. **Marketing Effectiveness:** Despite its relatively low cost, creative sales analysis can make many important and productive contributions to marketing effectiveness. The profit contribution made by increased marketing efficiency resulting from applied sales analysis often outweighs the cost of the entire marketing research programme including external research.

6. **No Need of Technical Skill:** Such analytical work does not usually require the high level of technical skill and experience which is needed, for example, in planning and executing a large-scale consumer or dealer survey.

7. **Easy Delegation:** A large share of sales analysis can be delegated to clerical personnel who execute it with the minimum amount of supervision.

8. **Easy Interpretation:** The interpretation of sales analysis requires marketing research skill, but the ability to make such interpretations, particularly when confined to a single industry or company can be acquired rather easily and quickly.

9. Reduction in Research Cost: A careful sales analysis often helps to reduce cost of the external research that requires to be undertaken,

Approaches to Sales Analysis

1. Product Analysis: It is concerned with the variations between different products sold by the same organisation.

2. Territorial or Geographical Analysis: It emphasises the variations which exist between different geographical or territorial units. It is applicable in different varieties of situations, over an extremely wide range of geographical scale.

3. Customer Analysis: It is concerned with variations which occur between customers of different types or individual customers.

4. Time Analysis: It concentrates on the timing of sales. Major sub-types include seasonal and trend analysis,

5. Type of Purchase Analysis: Although it is generally less important than the other mentioned above, this approach is an important element in many sales analysis problems. It is concerned with variations in the manner in which either a sale is made or physical delivery offered.

Difficulties in Sales Analysis

1. Territorial Changes: A sudden decline in volume in a territory is likely to signal the existence of a major sales problem.

2. Extraordinary Transactions: Occasionally a single transaction of unusually large size and non-recurring nature may produce a marked distortion.

3. Untypical Base Period: When a major source of distortion is present, comparison of sales in only one of the periods is often meaningless.

4. Geographical Influences: This leads to distortion which occurs, when geographical marketing units are divided,

5. New Product Information: When a company is introducing a new product, or expanding its operating area by moving into additional territory it checks up sales volume which is partly of a non-recurring nature. Volume in existing territories or products may be declining with the loss offset by the additional volume in the new territories or products. A usually effective "deal" or "promotion" may similarly exert a distorting influence.

6. Change in Consumer List or Operating Method: Loss of a single large customer often produces a marked change in the sales volume of a territory. A knowledge change in customers which are important enough to influence total sales in individual territories is desirable to ensure that such shifts are considered.

7. Combining sales of Different Products: In making sales allocations to geographic units, it is desirable to plan carefully how much details to maintain the questions which arise at this point are:

(*i*) Whether sales of different sizes of a given product should be carried as individual totals or combined into a single figure for that product;

(*ii*) Whether products of the same general type should he carried individually or combined into a product type total; and (*iii*) Whether products which are not alike should be combined into a heterogeneous total.

8. Built-in Inaccuracy: All sales records inescapably contain certain elements of "built-in inaccuracy." A frank recognition of the existence of such limitations is helpful in approaching the sales analysis in a realistic frame of mind. Hence, this limitation should also be kept in mind.

QUESTIONS FOR EXERCISE

1. What do you understand by sales territories? Explain the objectives and advantages of allocation of territories.
2. What is Sales Quota? What are the reasons for setting and using sales quotas? What problems are encountered in using sales quotas as yardsticks of salesmen's performance? How can they be minimised?
3. What are the problems faced by a manager in determining and using sales quotas for appraising performance of salesmen? How much useful is this technique?
4. What is Sales Analysis? What are the major approaches in sales analysis?

32

Evaluating Marketing Performance

NEED OF EVALUATION

The ultimate goal of a business firm is to earn optimum profit which depends on the success of marketing efforts. Hence, evaluation of marketing efforts and their outcome in the crux of marketing control programme. As firms become larger, the need for better controls increases because top management can no longer personally monitor all aspects of the operations. The trend towards diversification and mergers, resulting in loosely controlled, decentralised operations, makes crucial the timely feedback on marketing performance.

Evaluating marketing performance off and on provides the management proper feedback without which problems may go undetected, until they become serious, and corrective actions may be so late that a firm's competitive position and its very existence and financial viability may be jeopardised. Therefore, marketing evaluation should be a continuous function. Its various tools should be used on a current and continuing basis if they are to provide the feedback on how an enterprise is really doing and if they are to give early warning of a worsening situation. A one-time analysis, perhaps of sales and of market- share coverage in various territories, may do almost more harm than good. Without comparative figures for determining whether performance is better or worse than past periods, problem areas may go undiscovered. While sales and market-share analysis may be done every month, marketing cost analysis may be done only once a year. The complete marketing audit also lends itself to periodic use, although many firms view it more as a "crisis" analysis than one that can be used to tap new potentials or prevent crises from occurring.

TYPES OF MARKETING PERFORMANCE APPRAISALS

1. Measurement of Specific Performance, that is, measures of specific individuals or specific marketing function; such as —

(*i*) Measuring Performance of sales people.

(*ii*) Measuring of advertising effectiveness.

(*iii*) Measuring the effectiveness of sales promotion efforts.

2. Measures of Overall Marketing results; such as—

(*i*) Total sales and profits.

(*ii*) Market-share analysis.

(*iii*) Sales analysis.

(*iv*) Marketing or distribution cost analysis.

(*v*) Measures of customer satisfaction.

(*vi*) Marketing audit.

MARKET-SHARE ANALYSIS

Meaning

As long as a firm is making a profit as much or more than the preceding year, everything is assumed to be satisfactory. In some cases net profit results tend to be subordinated to steadily increasing gross sales. As firms become larger, concern for measuring the effectiveness of the various marketing efforts becomes centered on market-share performance. The true measure of success is perceived to be not absolute but relative sales performance, that is, sales compared with those of competitors. This is commonly known as Market-Share Analysis.

Measuring performance relative to competitors can be a highly motivating device for management and subordinates alike. It is of particular value in spotting emerging problems. Data on market share usually avoid the contaminating effects of non-controllable exogenous factors. For example, if sales decline over the preceding year, but market share remains constant or even improves, this suggests that the firm is doing a good job, but that the whole industry is being adversely affected for that particular period.

Computing Market Share

The mathematics involved in calculating market share is not complicated. For example, if industry sales of Asian Alloys Ltd. for a particular period are ₹ 50,00,00,000 and the company, has sales of ₹ 10,00,00,000 then the market share will be:

$$= \frac{\text{Rs.}10,00,00,000}{\text{Rs.}50,00,00,000} = 20\%$$

Sometimes, rising sales can disguise problems. If the next period Asian Alloys Ltd. experiences sales of ₹ 14,00,00,000 supposedly a nice increase of 40 per cent but industry sales rise to ₹ 100 crore, the market share would indicate a worsening situation.

$$= \frac{\text{Rs.}14,00,00,000}{\text{Rs.}10,00,000,000} \times 100 = 14.9\%$$

Industry sales must be obtained or accurately estimated. In most industries this information is not particularly difficult to obtain. There are certain documentary sources of market-share information about different industries. They can be picked up from there and can be used for calculation.

Interpretation of Market-share Performance

Changes in market-share from preceding periods, especially when these changes show a worsening competitive position, should induce strenuous efforts to ascertain the cause and take corrective action. To disregard or treat such events lightly may even jeopardise the viability of the firm. Difference in market share among various geographical areas deserves follow-up efforts to determine the causes of the disparity in performance.

Sources of Market-share Data

Sales of competing brands, products and firms in the various markets must be invariably obtained in order to make a market-share analysis. This is not difficult to get in most industries, although some costs may be involved. Trade associations, syndicates, pools, chambers and trade publications provide reasonably accurate sales figures for many industries. Though such information may not include brand breakdowns, marketers can determine their own share of this total market, as well as the trends. Government agencies also provide data for some industries, such as automobiles, liquor, sugar, tea and insurance, from mandatory reports, such as new car registrations and excise and other tax data.

In U.S.A., several syndicated services provide various measures of competitive brand position to **consumer** goods manufacturers. The two major services are:

1. The A.C. Nielsen Company, It conducts store audit in grocery, drug, and certain other fields, and which is now buying compute tapes from supermarkets equipped with electronic scanning cash registers.

2. The Market Research Corporation of America (MRCA). It gathers information on expenditures through a panel of consumers who maintain a record of their purchases in diaries. These services are expensive, frequently costing a minimum of more than ₹ 35,000 a year, but some manufacturers subscribe to several because they furnish some what different information, as following. Table 32.1 shows in comparison the information provided by Nielsen and MRCA.

Being based on sampling outlets and consumers of questionable representativeness these services can be faulty. They are limited to consumer goods that move through grocery and drug stores. However, their use for several decades reflects their value in providing badly needed information. Another major reason for using these services is the time lag between sale by the manufacturer and purchase by the consumer. As the manufacturer does not sell directly to consumers, but rather through distributors and dealers, its current sales invoices may not reveal the latest information on consumer purchases; sales to wholesalers and retailers may merely indicate building up or replacing inventories as a result of past sales. With rapidly changing conditions, past sales may not typify the present situation. Hence, certain precautions should be undertaken while using this readymade marketing information.

Table 32.1: Data Supplied by Nielsen and MRCA Services

OFFERED BY NIELSEN Dealer mark up	OFFERED BY MRCA Characteristics of families
Average order size by dealers	Buying products and specific brands
Local advertising	
Shelf rice	Repeat buying
Stock condition and inventory	Rate of addition of new customers
Store displays	Source of new customers
	Lost customers
	Frequency of purchase
	Volume moving at various price levels
	Volume accounted for by coupon
Redemptions	
Offered by Both	
Total U.S. consumer sales by brand	
Consumer sales by regions or districts	
Sales by type of grocery and drug outlet	
Sales by size of package	

COMMON BREAKDOWNS IN ANALYSING SALES

Some of the more common breakdowns for analysing sales are;

1. **Geographic Areas:** States, cities, or sales territories.
2. **Sales People and Methods of Sale:** Such as, Mail order, telephone, or direct sale.
3. **Customers by Size:** Type or class of trade, and perhaps by key or major customers.
4. **Products:** By Rupees and/or physical units for various sizes, colours, styles or categories of goods.

Gathering such data is no problem with today's electronic data processing equipment. But special provision must be made for processing this information from sales invoice and other sources; otherwise, it tends to be buried in files after the normal accounting and billing has been performed.

Analysis by Geographic Area

How a sales analysis can be used to uncover and track down a major problem is made clear from the sales performance of a home furnishings manufacturer for the last 6 months of 1988, as shown in the following exhibit. The total performance for the Eastern region was close to expectation. However, breaking total regional sales down into the five areas one finds that performance in Tripura is considerably off the mark. While the entire Eastern region has missed quota expectations only by ₹ 80,000, the Tripura region has missed by ₹ 190,000, achieving only 90 per cent of quota. This unusual situation illustrates the iceberg principle and shows how more serious problems may not be evident from total figures,

Table 32.2: Comparative Sales Performance, Eastern Region, (July-December 1996)

(In Thousands of Rupees)

	Quota	Actual	Difference	Actual as a percentage of quota, %
		₹	₹	₹
Total Eastern Region	15,300	15,220	- 80	99.5
(a) West Bengal	3,400	3,472	+ 72	102.1
(b) Assam	3,200	3,238	+ 38	101.2
(c) Meghalay	3,600	3,640	+ 40	101.1
(d) Arunachal	3,100	3,060	- 40	98.7
(e) Tripura	2,000	1,810	- 190	90.5

At this point is necessitated a more in-depth analysis of the Tripura district. The exhibit shows the breakdown of the four eastern territories. Again, one sees a divergent pattern, with fairly good performance in territories A and B, partially covering up serious problems in C and especially in D, where only 77 per cent of the quota was reached. The more detailed analysis of sales does not provide the answer to why sales results are under plan, but it does flag the problem area, one which needs further investigation to ascertain causes and improve the marketing efforts.

Analysis by Customers

Following Table 32.3 shows the breakdown of sales by customer categories. It can be seen that department stores and smaller independent retailers are contributing mightily to the poor showing, while the discount retailers are showing sales gains over expectations. At this point one does not know the reasons behind the deviations from expected performance, but one does know where the problems lie. At this point it should not be difficult to determine the why. Contacting the affected customers should pinpoint the problems, the cause, and what, if anything, can be done to improve the situation. It does seem obvious, however, that discount stores are taking business away from more conventional retailers in this market area. A change in distribution strategy may be the solution if the situation is not a temporary aberration.

QUESTIONS FOR EXERCISE

1. What is the need of evaluation of marketing performance? Discuss different types of marketing performance analysis.
2. Define Market Share Analysis. How is the Market Share computed? And how is it interpreted?
3. Explain some more common breakdowns for analysing sales.

33

Marketing Control and Marketing Audit

Marketing control is the natural sequel to marketing planning. Modern Organisations need to exercise marketing control concerned with the following aspects.

1. The execution of a sales plan.
2. The utilisation of marketing opportunities with respect to markets, products, distribution channels and the effectiveness of marketing expenditure.
3. The real profitability of marketing action in context with product territory, market segments, trade channel, order size, etc,

SCOPE OF MARKETING CONTROL

1. Annual Plan Control: It refers to the steps taken during the year to cheek on-going performance against marketing plan and to apply corrective measures when necessary. Its essence is the establishment of a system of management by objective (MBO), which consists of four elements: (*i*) The annual plan must establish a clear set of marketing goals for each responsibility centre in the firm. (*ii*) Provision must be made for periodic performance measurement against the goals to spot any serious performance gap. (*iii*) Performance gaps should be subject to casual analysis to determine why they have occurred, i.e., whether the environment has changed, the goals were set too high, or the implements of the plan are not doing their job. (*iv*) Management must take corrective measures to close the gap between goals and performance. The model of control is applied to every level of the organisation. Managers use five performance tools to check the progress in reaching the goals in the annual plan, viz., sales analysis, market share analysis, marketing expenses to sales ratio, financial analysis and corrective measures.

2. Profitability Control: Companies carry on periodic research to determine the actual profitability of their different products, territories, customer groups, trade channels and other marketing variables. This requires an ability to assign marketing and other costs'to specific marketing entities and activities.

Marketing profitability analysis is a tool for helping the marketing executive to determine whether any current marketing activities should be eliminated, added, or altered in scale. Its starting point is the company's profit and loss statement. The marketing executive' s interest would he developing analogous profit statements by functional marketing breakdowns, such as products, customers, or territories. The "natural" expense designation such as salaries, rent, supplies would have to be reclassified into "functional" expense designations.

3. Efficiency Control: It is the task of increasing the efficiency of such marketing activities as personal selling, advertising, sales promotion and distribution, Marketing managers regularly watch certain key ratios that indicate how efficiently these functions are being performed. They also implement studies to find ways to improve performance.

4. Strategic Control: It is the task of making sure that the company is marketing objectives, strategies, and systems are optimally adapted to the current and forecasted marketing environment. In this connection, the use of two tools is worth mentioning, i.e., marketing effectiveness, rating review and marketing audit. Their brief description is as follows:

(*i*) *Marketing Effectiveness Rating Review*: Assessment of marketing effectiveness is not so simple. Good results may be due to a division's being in the right place at the right time, rather than the consequence of effective marketing management. Improvements in that division's marketing might boost results from good to excellent. At the same time; another division might have poor result in spite of the best strategic marketing planning.

The marketing effectiveness of a company or its is reflected in the degree to which it exhibits five major attributes of a marketing orientation, *i.e.,* customer philosophy, integrated marketing information equate marketing information, strategic orientation, and operational emergency. The marketing effectiveness rating instalment can be used to measure the said five dimensions.

(*ii*) *Marketing Audit.* Overall marketing strategy is a composite built up, or put together, by blending various inputs: products, channels and physical distribution, promotion and price in different combinations to achieve given objectives such as targeted return on investment, market share, brand image, etc. Marketing experts advocate the use of marketing audit for evaluating overall marketing strategy. A marketing audit is defined as "a systematic, critical, unbiased review and appraisal of the basic objectives and policies of the marketing function and of the organisation, methods, procedures and personnel employed to implement those policies and achieve those objectives." Thus, marketing audit is an important tool in the hands of marketing executives to assess the effectiveness of different components of marketing-mix.

MARKETING AUDIT

According to Robert F. Hartley, "The marketing audit is an objective total evaluation of marketing efforts including policies, objectives and even personnel." Marketing audit is an important function of modern marketing executives. It has been defined as "a systematic, critical, unbiased review and appraisal of the basic objectives and policies of the marketing function and of the organisation, methods, procedures and personnel employed to implement those policies and to achieve those objectives." Thus, marketing audit is a reviewing function primarily concerned with the evaluation of overall marketing strategy. Its main purpose is to identify opportunities for improving the effectiveness of the total marketing efforts. While carrying out a marketing audit, the management should aim at identifying the strength and weakness of its marketing system.

Characteristics of Marketing Audit

1. **Comprehensiveness:** The term 'marketing audit' is a very wide and comprehensive term. It covers the audit of the company's total marketing environment, its objectives, marketing strategies, organisation and total marketing system. A comprehensive marketing audit is usually more effective in locating the real source of the company's marketing problems.

2. Systematic: The usefulness of a marketing audit increases to the extent that it follows an orderly sequence of diagnostic steps covering the organisation's marketing environment, internal marketing system and specific marketing activities. It is followed by a corrective action plan involving both short-run and long-run action to improve the organisation's overall marketing effectiveness.

3. Independent: A marketing audit may be conducted in six ways: (*i*) self-audit, (*ii*) audit from across, (*iii*) audit from above, (*iv*) company auditing office, (*v*) company task force audit, and (vi) outsider audit. The best audits are likely to come from experienced outside consultants, who have the necessary objectivity and independence, broad experience in a number of industries, some familiarity with the industry and the undivided time and attention to give to the audit.

4. Periodic: Marketing audits are initiated only after sale have turned down sharply, sales-force morale has fallen, or any other marketing problem has arisen at the company. A periodic marketing audit promises benefits for the companies that are in good health as well as companies that are in trouble.

Types of Marketing Audit

Marketing audit consists of examining six major components of the company's marketing situation. Each component has a semi-autonomous status. The scope of marketing audit may be explained as follows:

1. Marketing Environment Audit: It calls for analysing the major macro- environment forces that might have an impact on the company and major trends in the key components of the company's task environment, *i.e.*, markets, customers, competitors, distributors, dealers, suppliers, etc.

2. Marketing Strategy Audit: It calls for reviewing the company's marketing objectives and marketing strategy to see how well these are adapted to the current and forecasted marketing environment.

3. Marketing Organisation Audit: It calls for evaluating the marketingorganisation's capability for developing and carrying out the necessary strategy for the forecasted environment.

4. Marketing System Audit: It involves examining the adequacy of the company's systems for analysis, planning and control in the marketing area as for innovation.

5. **Marketing Productivity Audit:** It calls for examining data on the profitability of different marketing entities and on the cost-effectiveness of different types of marketing expenditure.

6. **Marketing Function Audit:** It involves carrying out an in-depth, evaluation of major marketing-mix components namely products, price distribution, sales-force, advertising, promotion, and publicity.

QUESTIONS FOR EXERCISE

1. Define Marketing Control and discuss its scope.
2. Define Marketing Audit. Explain its major types.

34

Agricultural Marketing in India

AGRICULTURAL PRODUCTS

Characteristic Features

1. **Small-Scale Production:** Indian farmers own very small plots of land. Very often the production is just sufficient to cover the family needs. The production also tends to be small. On account of small holdings therefore the marketable surplus with an average agriculturist is meagre. Commercialisation of agriculture is still a new concept to Indian agriculturist.

2. **Perishable Nature of Products:** The agricultural goods are perishable in nature. They demand speedy marketing activities which are very often prevented by inadequate transport facilities. The primitive and crude storing facilities in villages are not capable of preserving the goods over a long period.

3. **No Concerted Conscious Marketing Activities:** Agriculturists in India do not fully appreciate the value of a joint or combined action for the purpose of bargaining on equal terms with the buyers of agricultural goods. The cultivators concentrate on production ignoring the marketing aspects.

4. **Inelasticity of Demand:** As most products are necessaries, price changes do not bring about any great changes in demand. During the harvest season the abundant supply creates a glut in the market causing a fall in price. Because of this the Food Corporation of India has recently started procuring excess supply or marketable surplus and keeping a buffer stock.

5. **Unorganised Markets:** The markets for agricultural products are generally unorganised and full of numerous middlemen who

have upper hand in the buying process. According to the Central Agricultural Marketing Department, "Wheat cultivator gets only Re. 0.23 out of each rupee paid by the consumer."

6. Malpractices in the Market: Ungraded products are marketed because of the lack of standardisation, the absence of accepted grades makes it possible to indulge in malpractices. Prices are decided not by the producer but by intermediaries.

MARKETING OF AGRICULTURAL PRODUCTS *Vs.* MANUFACTURED GOODS

1. Production: The agriculturist is purely a producer and nothing else. The manufacturer, on the other hand, has to be engaged in continuous production and to utilise his production capacity to the fullest extent possible. He is cost conscious. He concentrates equally on production and marketing activities.

2. Sale Control: A manufacturer seeks an unfettered control over the sale of his products to the middlemen. In the case of the agricultural produce intermediaries like arhtiyas, village shopkeepers (Mahajans), Beoparis and Dalals have entrenched themselves firmly in the marketing scene. These middlemen are notorious for many malpractices including the use of incorrect weights.

3. Quantity: Agricultural produce is collected in small quantities which ultimately swell the mighty stream of marketing. Manufactured goods are on the other hand mostly produced on a large scale and then broken up into smaller lots of each successive stage in marketing.

4. Quality Control: Manufactured goods can be easily controlled both qualitatively and quantitatively and can also be fixed in advance in almost inaccurate terms. Both these aspects are beyond the control of an agriculturist whose entire production is based on natural conditions such as climate, rainfall, soil, etc.

5. Demand Presence: Manufactured goods are subject to effective demand for correlational activities which are completely absent in the case of agricultural marketing.

6. Products Identity: Manufacturers, can identify themselves completely with their products. Many manufactured products are bought not only on the real quality of the product but also on the basis of reputation of the producers. This is impossible in the case of agricultural produce. Once they are assembled the dealers identity alone could be examined by the buyers.

KINDS OF AGRICULTURAL MARKETS

1. Local Markets: These are also called "assembling markets" as their main function is to assemble products from various individual sources. Mostly located within the area of production they are sometimes referred to as village markets or primary markets. The produce from individual farmers is collected and trade into economical lots. Grading and packaging are undertaken in primary markets, having the following large number of intermediaries:

(*i*) *Arhatiya*: Commission agents, assemblers, brokers and financiers.

(*ii*) *Beoparis*: Assemblers.

(*iii*) *Mahajans*: Financiers, large-scale assemblers.

(*iv*) *Palledars*: They undertake transporting and receive *palledari* (freight).

(*v*) *Dallas*: Brokers.

(*vi*) *Tolas*: Weight men.

(*vii*) *Paikars*: Village merchants.

(*viii*) *Gobbers*: They buy in huge quantities and like wholesalers bear marketing risks. For all purposes they are wholesalers.

(*ix*) *Retailers*: They buy products in comparatively smaller quantities exclusively meant for dispersion to ultimate consumers through terminal markets.

(*x*) *Other Dealers*: In regional markets where future and forward transactions are permitted, some other dealers are also found such as speculators, hedgers and floor traders.

The government controls the organisation of cooperatives. The introduction of regulated markets have imposed some kinds of control over the methods and practices followed in these markets.

3. Terminal Markets: These markets represent the final stage in the concentration of the supply of the commodity. They are places from where dispersion to industrial users or to ultimate consumers takes place. In these markets various marketing functions such as grading, financing, warehousing, etc. are undertaken at full length.

MARKETING INTELLIGENCE

An effective system of marketing means a regular supply of accurate information to the producer regarding the prices ruling in a market from time to time. It enables producer to sell in the market taking into consideration the varying costs of transportation to different markets accessible to them.

Marketing Intelligence in India

In India, at present there is no reliable channel of communication of prices to producers who remain in isolation in remote rural parts. In villages, cultivators normally get the information about prices from the local trader who is not at all interested in supplying them correct information. In most cases he gives a wrong information. Lack of dissemination of daily market information has been responsible for the disparities in prices of the same commodity in different markets.

As The Agricultural Price Commission recommended that step should be taken for a better dissemination of marketing news, the Government of India set up a Marketing Department to disseminate reliable and up-to-date information and market intelligence. Besides arranging for broadcasts through All India Radio the directorate issues a bulletin "Agricultural situation in India". Newspapers and journals also provide such information to agriculturist regularly. But while information is available for terminal markets it is hardly available at the assembling and distributing centres. Illiteracy of the rural population is a great stumbling block in the way. The number of markets covered is also not adequate. There must be a well organised market information service. The measures taken by the State and Central Government should be coordinated.

In 1958 a full-fledged department was set up attached to the Ministry of Food and Agriculture. It publishes reports regarding surveys on various commodities. It also undertakes various marketing activities such as standardisation, provision of warehouses, etc. International assistance is extended to Indian agriculturists through Food and Agricultural Organisation (FAO), an associate of UNO.

Steps to Improve the Marketing System in India

As Indian Government had been aware of the problem of marketing, a number of steps were taken during the last few years. As a result of these steps, the situation has considerably improved. Following are the more important of these steps:

1. Regulated Markets: In such markets joint committees representing the interest of the cultivators and the traders have been formed. These committees take various decisions as to the efficient working of the marketing system.

2. Cooperative Marketing Societies.

3. Go downs and Warehousing Facilities: All India Warehousing Corporation of India and the cooperative marketing societies are doing good work in this direction.

4. Gradation: Arrangements have been made for the proper gradation of the agriculture products which helps in the identification of the standardised products. AGMARK is granted to the standardised agricultural products.

5. Price Stabilisation Board: It has been set up to keep a watch on the movement of agriculture prices.

6. Agriculture Price Commission: It was set up in 1965 to advise the Government about the fixation of prices of agriculture products.

7. Media: Market information is spread to the farmers through different media like radio, television, films, etc. Krishi Darshan produced by Delhi Doordarshan is a very popular programme on television. The recently concluded Agri-Expo 77 proved a useful media for the spread of agriculture information.

8. Transportation: Easy availability of cheap and fast means of transportation has been sought to be assured to the cultivator.

9. Purchase Centres: The Food Corporation of India has set up its purchase centres at different villages while the farmers can sell their produce to the corporation at the prices fixed by the Government The Government has also adopted the policy of support prices.

10. Support Price: It means that the Government takes upon itself the obligation to purchase the agricultural produce at a certain fixed minimum price although the price ruling in the market may be low. The system of support prices is proving a significant tool helping the agriculturist.

Basic Facilities Required

1. Waiting Time: The farmer should be able to wait for the time when he could get better price for his produce and not sell away his stocks immediately after the harvest when the prices are usually very low.

2. Storing: He should have proper godown facilities for storing his produce.

3. Roads: There should be good all weather roads. This would enable the farmer to take his produce to the market rather than dispose it off in the village to the village trader at a lower price.

4. Market Information: The farmer should get information regarding the market conditions.

5. Market Regulation: Market should be regulated, the dalal and arhatiyas should all be licensed and controlled so that they may not cheat the poor farmers.

Defects of Agricultural Marketing in India

1. No Facilities: The Indian farmers do not have proper facilities for storing their produce in the village. The storage facilities available in the village at present are so bad that between 10 and 20 per cent of the produce is eaten away by rats, white ants, etc. This much loss of agricultural produce is loss for the farmers and for the country as a whole.

2. No Staying Power: The average of Indian farmer being poor and indebted has no staying power. He requires money badly and urgently to pay taxes and to clear his debts, etc. He is forced to sell his output to the moneylender or to the trader as soon as he harvests the produce, whether the price is good or bad. If he can wait, he can decidedly get better price of his produce.

3. No Good Roads: As most roads are kuchcha and unusable in rainy season, farmers are forced to sell their surplus produce in the village itself. Inadequate and defective transport conditions constitute a serious defect of agricultural marketing.

4. No Proper Warehousing: The farmers are afraid of going to the mandis because of the prevailing conditions there. As proper warehousing facilities do not exist, he is obliged to keep his produce in the open exposed to sun and rain. The dalals and arhatiyas are often in league with each other. The price settled is generally to the disadvantage of the cultivator. The farmers lose much in the form of samples to the arhatiays, use of false weights and measures, unnecessary deductions on the plea that the produce is inferior quality, etc. As they feel cheated in the mandis farmers are generally reluctant to go there.

5. No Price Information: The farmers are completely in the dark about the ruling prices in big mandis. They accept whatever price is quoted to them. They have to believe whatever the traders tell them.

COOPERATIVE MARKETING SOCIETY

To overcome the inherent weaknesses of the farmers, it was suggested that the cooperative marketing societies should be established. Before 1954 separate cooperative marketing societies were set up apart from the cooperative credit societies. Since 1954, however, multipurpose societies have been started giving credit to the farmers and helping them to market their surplus produce.

A group of farmers may join together to form a cooperative marketing society as they form a cooperative credit society. The cooperative marketing society is managed by experienced and paid staff. To be effective it may cover a number of villages. Its members agree to sell their surplus to the society. The society collects the produce of all the members and those of non-members of the village who are willing to sell their produce to the society. The sellers get an advance immediately to carry on with their agricultural operation. By taking the produce to the mandi and selling it to the arhatiyas, the farmer does away with many of the middlemen. If the current prices are not favourable and prices are expected to rise in the future, the society may decide to stock the commodity. The society pays the farmer the balance of the amount due to him as soon as the produce is sold. Sometimes the society itself stocks the produce and then sells it to the wholesalers.

Merits of Cooperative Marketing

1. Collective Bargaining: The average farmer is weak because he has very little to offer in the market and is financially poor. As cooperative marketing society has large supplies at its disposal and is, therefore, strong, it can bargain for better prices. It substitutes collective bargaining in place of individual bargaining.

2. Loans: The cooperative marketing society enables the farmers to wait for better prices by advancing loans to the farmers for their immediate requirements.

3. Storage: The storage removes the damage to agricultural product through rats, ants, dampness, etc. by providing proper storage and warehousing facilities.

4. Transport: It arranges to have quick and cheap transport of agricultural produce to the mandis.

5. Standardised: It helps the farmers produce standardised products so that they can secure good prices for their produce.

6. Elimination of Middlemen: It eliminates the middlemen and, therefore, gets more profit for the members.

7. Agricultural Inputs: It procures agricultural inputs as seeds, fertilisers, implements, etc.

8. Answer to Problem of Marketing: Thus, cooperative marketing societies may be the real answer to the problem of agricultural marketing.

Marketing of Agricultural Goods in India

Directorate of Marketing and Inspection (DMI) under the Department of Rural Development advise Central and state government on agricultural marketing problems. It enforces compulsory quality control on 41 agricultural commodities before their export, Besides a number of important commodities are graded under Agmark for internal consumption. These include cotton, vegetable oils, *ghee,* cream, butter, eggs, rice, wheat, flour, *besan*, jaggery, bura, curry powder, honey, ground spices, potatoes, fruits, etc. In all, grade specifications under Agmark have been formulated for 142 commodities.

Twenty two regional laboratories have been set up to ensure purity and quality of Agmark products. Central Agmark Laboratory at Nagpur functions as the apex body. Laboratories at Nagpur, Bombay, Calcutta and Madras are equipped with biological testing units. A large number of producer level grading centres have also been established in various states to help farmers in getting prices commensurate with quality. Agricultural commodities worth ₹ 3,893.23 crore were graded at 1,051 producer-level grading centres during 1990-91. Regulation of markets is yet another important function of agricultural marketing. It is done by the state government while DMI tenders advice in framing market legislation and its enforcement. There were 6,640 regulated markets in the country by March 1991.

Regulation of Markets

The Directorate of Marketing and Inspection (DMI) is implementing a scheme for providing financial assistance to primary and secondary rural markets to develop infrastructural facilities. The scheme has acted as a catalyst to induce state government in taking up market development programme.

The scheme of marketing research and surveys has two programmes, namely, market research and planning and (*ii*) market planning and design. DMI carries out countryside market surveys on important agricultural, horticultural and livestock commodities to identify and study problems of agricultural marketing. It also suggests remedial measures. Surveys of a number of wholesale markets for fresh fruits and vegetables have been carried out by the Market Planning and Design Centre (MPDC) to make suggestions for their development and improvement. MPDC also gives technical assistance in preparation of state master plans for development of agricultural produce market.

Cotton Classing Scheme

A cotton classing centre was established at Surat in 1969-70 as a pilot project to provide facilities for grading of cotton lint to growers, cooperatives and others. With the success of this pioneer scheme, five more such centres have been established—one each in Maharashtra (Nagpur), Karnataka (Raichur), Tamilnadu (Tirupur), Madhya Pradesh (Khandwa) and Punjab (Abohar).

Cold Storage and Meat Products

The Cold Storage Order 1980, enforced by the Directorate, aims at developing cold storage industry in a planned manner, ensuring hygienic conditions and proper refrigeration and rendering technical guidance for scientific preservation of food-stuffs. There were 1,296 storages with capacity of about 13 lakh tonnes licensed under the order by the end of March 1991, Besides, a large number of cold storages have been licensed by Haryana, Punjab, Uttar Pradesh and West Bengal under their own Acts/Orders. It implements the Meat Food Products Order, 1973 to ensure quality control of meat products for human consumption. Under the Order, 250 licences were granted up to June 1991. It also conducted seven regular training courses for the benefit of employees of state government regulated market committees, cooperative societies and various commodity boards/corporations. As a part of routine activity, the Directorate has organised three national seminars during 1991-92. These are: (*i*) National Seminar on Marketing of Onion, (*ii*) National Seminar on Rural Primary Markets as Growth Centres and Creation of Storage Facilities, and (*iii*) National Seminar on Modern Techniques in the Analysis of Food and Agricultural Products. Producers and consumers are constantly exposed to the advantages of products marked Agmark through various media, trade fairs and seminars. The Directorate also brings out a quarterly journal, *Agricultural Marketing.*

Department of Rural Development is also implementing a scheme to set up mral godowns with a view to creating a network, such godowns in states/UTs primarily to take care of storage-requirements of agricultural producers, particularly small and marginal farmers.

Monitoring

Monitoring is an important tool for ensuring proper implementation of any project/programme. It helps in ascertaining that the project is progressing according to plan and all physical and financial inputs and other requisite supportive activities are available according to schedule. Considering this, the Ministry of Rural Development developed comprehensive system of monitoring in respect of major programmes like JRY, IRDP, UWSP, DPAP and DDP. Physical and financial achievements under each programme are being obtained from various state/districts and implementing agencies at regular intervals on prescribed formats. Performance of various programmes is reviewed on the basis of these reports and corrective as well as supportive measures are taken to improve their implementation.

Concurrent Evaluation

Besides monitoring, perfomiance of various rural development programmes is assessed through periodical returns and visits by senior officers to the field. The Ministry also conducts concurrent evaluation studies (CES) in respect of major rural development programmes. This is done with the help of independent reputed research institutions to ascertain areas of concern and streamline and improve the pace of implementation. First round of CES of

IRDP was taken up from October 1985 to September 1986; second round from January 1987 to December 1987 and third round from January 1989 to December 1989 with the help of reputed research institutions. Findings of these surveys were found very useful which helped planners/implementors to restructure the programme for more effective implementation. Fourth round is likely to be undertaken in the near future. CES of Rural Water Supply programme was undertaken from October 1986 to September 1987 to assess the status of drinking water sources in rural areas and CES to NREP from November 1987 to October 1988. CES of JRY has been conducted by 33 independent research institutions/organisations during the period from January 1992 to December 1992 and a preliminary Report on concurrent Evaluation of JRY has been brought out.

Computerised Rural Information System

For timely flow and proper management of immense data generated under major rural development programmes and thereby improving their monitoring system, the Ministry of Rural Development had started in 1985 a scheme of Computerised Rural Information System (CRISP) on a pilot basis in 10 districts with NIC as nodal agency. The experience showed that it was possible to develop quickly a computerised data base on rural development at DRJDA level. It was decided to set up mini computer centre on all the DRDAs using fund available under administrative infrastructure. Necessary training was given to DRDA staff by NIC with the technical guidance and support of NIC, the software for CRISP has also been developed on DRDA and in about 300 districts the system is operational now. In a recent meeting held in May 1992, the progress of computer activities in DRDAs was reviewed. Based on the feedback received from NIC, linking up activity between NIC district system and DRDA computer has been taken up, subject to availability of telephone line. Six DRDAs in Orissa have been connected to NIC district system and using NICNET facility.

CHARACTERISTICS OF AGRICULTURAL MARKETING IN INDIA

1. Marketing of Farm Products: Marketing of farm products in the country is, by and large, operated under the normal forces of supply and demand. Private trade is the centerpiece of the country's market mechanism. The Government intervention is limited mainly to protect the interest of both producers and consumers through promotion of organised agricultural commodities. To achieve this, most State Governments have enacted the necessary legislation for regulation of produce markets.

2. Regulated Markets: The number of regulated markets in the country as on March 31, 1994 was 6809. The Central Government has provided assistance for the creation of infrastructural facilities in the markets and also for setting up of rural godowns. Grading standards have been laid down for 150 agricultural and allied commodities under the Agricultural Produce (Grading and Marketing) Act, 1937. There are 3124 licensed cold storage with an installed capacity of 8.174 million tonnes as on March 31, 1994. To promote setting up of cold storage under the cooperative sector, the National Cooperative Development Corporation has provided ₹ 74.9 crore for installation of 243 cold storage with an installed capacity of 7.16 lakh tonnes till the end of March 1994.

3. Origination: A number of organisations and institutions function currently to deal with product and area specific problems that have a bearing on production, pricing and marketing of agricultural products. The most important are the Commission for Agricultural Costs and Prices, the Food Corporation of India, the Cotton Corporation of India, the Jute Corporation of India and the Commodity Boards.

4. Cooperatives: Agricultural Marketing is also closely linked to a network of cooperatives at primary level, state level. Marketing cooperatives are operating almost in all "mandies". Cooperative societies are functioning in the area of processing of fruits and vegetables, sugarcane crushing, cotton ginning and pressing, etc.

5. National Level: At the National level, the National Cooperative Development Corporation plans and promotes programmes for the production processing, marketing, storage, export and import of agricultural produce through cooperatives. The National Agricultural Cooperative Marketing Federation of India Ltd. (NAFED) is an apex cooperative organisation dealing in procurement, distribution, export and import of selected agricultural commodities. A few other organisations in the cooperative sector are the National Cooperative Tobacco Growers' Federation Ltd., the National Consumers' Cooperative Federation and the Tribal Cooperative Marketing Development Federation of India Ltd. (TRIFED) which attends specifically to the marketing problems of the tribal areas. However, the share of cooperatives in the total marketing of agricultural commodities is rather small.

6. Specialised Commodity Boards: Specialised Commodity Boards continue to operate for rubber, coffee, tea, tobacco, spices, coconut, oilseed and vegetable oils, horticulture etc. The National Dairy Development Board is also engaged in the marketing of agricultural commodities. Separate Directorates have been created to manage development of agro raw materials like sugarcane, jute, tobacco, oilseeds, rice, millets, cotton, pulses, cashew nuts, cocoa, areca nut, spices etc. Besides, a number of Development Councils have been set up for special commodities like rice, pulses, jute, millets, cotton, tobacco, oilseeds, sugarcane, areca nut, cocoa, etc. In the field of export, besides, the State Trading Corporation, some related bodies are the Cashewnuts Export Promotion Council, the Shellac Export Promotion Council and the Agricultural and Processed Food Export Development Authority. The role of cooperatives in the marketing of agricultural produce has been progressively expending.

7. Farm Export: Farm export provides tremendous resilience to the overall export earnings of the country. Since the import content of the agricultural sector is insignificant as compared to the non-agricultural sector, the country's gain is much more per unit of foreign exchange earned through agro exports.

8. Export-import Policy: It has been progressively rationalised to provide impetus to agricultural exports. Trade policy changes aimed at reducing tariff and non-tariff barriers are expected to open up new vistas for agricultural exports.

9. Commodities for Export: Rice is emerging as a major export product. Minimum export price in respect of all varieties of rice has been abolished. Fruits, vegetables and flowers are non-traditional export products with high potential. Export of these products has witnessed growth during the last three years and has begun to attract the attention of corporate investors. A number of export-oriented units in the floriculture sector are under various stages of completion.

10. Competitiveness: The successful conclusion of the Uruguay Round of Negotiations will improve the competitiveness of India's agricultural products.

Developed countries are required to scale down their prevailing levels of domestic and export subsidies in their respective countries. This is hoped to open up new markets for primary product exporting countries.

11. Agricultural Exports: Agricultural export (other than raw cotton, including wastes) have registered remarkable growth during the last 2 years, from ₹ 7430 crore in 1992-93 to Rs, 10062 crore during 1993-94. The current year should see a further consolidation of the export performance.

Evaluation

1. Pivotal Role: In overall economic development the agricultural sector will continue to play a pivotal role, since this sector still accounts for about 30 per cent of the GDP and almost two-thirds of the population still depend on this sector for livelihood. To accelerate GDP growth rate, a long term trend growth rate of 3 per cent in Indian agriculture should be the desirable goal. To achieve it, a number of key problems in the agricultural sector will need to be resolved.

2. Declining Role of Investment: The declining trend in the rate of investment in agriculture in the recent years needs to be reversed. Specific provisions are required for operation and maintenance of public capital assets. Public investment in irrigation, rural communication and schemes for prevention and control of land water degradation will need to be increased. The resources for this purpose can be augmented only by scaling down the massive subsidies provided for water, electricity and fertiliser. To encourage private investment in agriculture, the thrust of reform policies should continue to improve relative incentives in favour of agriculture.

3. Use of Local Varieties: For raising rainfed/dryland crop yields, more emphasis is required for the use of location specific varieties suited to such agro-climatic conditions. Progress of integrated watershed development projects for promotion of water conservation and diversified production systems need to be closely monitored. Arable land is shrinking due to continuous soil erosion, land degradation and diversion of good cultivable land for urban/industrial use. Therefore, various soil and water conservation technologies need to be vigorously pursued to raise productivity in marginal and rainfed land holdings.

4. Seed Revolution: The seed revolution, which appears to have tapered off after encompassing only the cereal segment, has to be widened to cover other vital segments such as pulses, oilseeds, vegetables and fruits. This is especially important in view of the rise in average income levels having pushed up demand for non-cereal food items. The marked seasonality in these commodities (fruits, vegetables and oils) needs to be moderated to ensure improved year-round supply and dampen inflationary pressures. A pre-requisite for successful development of this sector is provision of adequate and more modern storage and warehousing facilities. Furthermore, investment and induction of new technology in the agro processing sector requires to be accelerated.

5. Need of Improvement: The present system of agricultural credit needs to be substantially improved. To ensure adequate availability of funds to small and poor farmers, the high cost of intermediation will need to be moderated.

6. Need of Incentives: Emerging new post-harvest technologies for agricultural products will require an improved data base for important tree crops, especially in view of their enhanced export potential. While tariff, trade and exchange rate reforms have strengthened incentives for agricultural export, there are still many regulations inhibiting exports of agricultural products, which needs to be phased out. Appropriate policy incentives for investment in technological upgradation for food processing merits a high priority.

QUESTIONS FOR EXERCISE

1. Describe characteristic features of agricultural production. Explain the difference in the marketing of manufactured and agricultural products.
2. Explain different kinds of agricultural markets.
3. How is marketing intelligence useful in agricultural marketing?
4. Explain the defects of agricultural marketing in India. How far can these be removed through cooperative marketing?
5. Describe marketing of agricultural goods in India.

35

Commodity/Produce Exchanges

DEFINITIONS OF COMMODITY/PRODUCE EXCHANGE

1. *Converse, Hugey and Mitchell*: "A produce or commodity exchange is an organisation of dealers in certain commodities, which provides a market place where the members meet at definite times and transact business under the rule laid down by the organisation."

As per this definition, a produce exchange provides a place to its members for coming together and trading in commodities under certain rules and regulations."

2. *Pyle*: "Commodity exchanges are specialised organised markets which provide a place where their members buy and sell commodities of contracts for future delivery under established rules and regulations."

Commodity exchanges specialise in different commodities and members not only buy and sell goods but also contract for future purchases and sales. Both spot and future trading is done at produce exchanges.

3. *Philips and Duncan*: 'It is an organisation or association of individuals which provides a place for trading in a commodity or commodities to be carried on under uniform rules, with facilities for adjustment of disputes among members and for the collection and dissemination of market information and which promotes the interests of those dealing in a particular commodity."

This definition is more exhaustive. According to it commodity exchange is not only a place for purchase or sale of goods by members but there is also an exchange of information about markets which helps the promotion of trade. Product exchanges act as centres of trade and market information. This helps in the growth of trade and the dealers are also benefited in the process.

CHARACTERISTICS OF PRODUCE EXCHANGE

1. Organised Market: A produce exchange is an organised market for trading in agricultural and other goods.

2. Rules and Regulations: The exchange has its own rules and regulations and members have to transact strictly according to the guidelines provided therein.

3. Transaction by Members only: Only members of an exchange can transact. Others can transact only through members.

4. Procedure: The exchange has its own procedure for settling various disputes among members.

5. Centre of Information: An exchange acts as a centre of trade information and this helps in the growth of trade activities.

CHARACTERISTICS OF COMMODITIES

Hundreds of commodities change hands daily in different markets which cannot be listed for trading at produce exchanges. Produce exchanges or commodity markets specialise in few goods only. Different produce exchanges deal in specified goods only. A particular commodity can be traded at an exchange or not due to the reason that trading in these markets is done on certain presumptions about goods. Only those goods can be traded at these markets which confirm to those assumptions or standards. Hence, the goods to be traded at these markets must have following characteristics:

1. Homogeneous Goods: Every unit of the commodity should be the same or identical in different hands and at different places. The transactions in these markets are done on the assumption that the goods will be the same as may be seen in a sample. Non-liomogeneous goods cannot be transacted at these markets because the whole commodity cannot be shown to the buyers.

2. Grading: There may be a difference among various goods. For example, in cotton there may be a difference of staple, length, cleanliness or colour. All these qualities are given different grades. The transactions are made on the basis of different grades. When a spécific grade is mentioned in the contract the buyer and seller know as to which type of goods they mention. Grading also helps in future trading.

3. Stability and Durability: The goods should be stable and durable. If the goods perish in the course of time their delivery will not be possible. The traders store the goods to supply them later on as per the contract. These goods should not change shape and quality otherwise the goods supplied later on will not be the same as **they** were contracted earlier.

4. Large Volume of Trading: The expenses of running exchanges are very high. If the trading is only for a limited quantity then the existence of such centres will not be justified and it will be costly to trade there. If large quantities are traded then expenses on exchanges are spread over and the costs are less proportionately.

5. Large Supply and Demand: The goods should be such that their demand and supply are large. For example, the demand for cotton, tea. wheat and rice are so large that these goods will always be required. The supply of .the commodity traded should be large. This will influence price fluctuations as well.

6. Price-fluctuations: Only those goods or commodities are traded in produce exchanges whose price fluctuations are frequent. Future trading is based on the assumption of rise or fall in prices in future. A buyer in future supposes the prices to rise while a seller feels that prices will go down and he will supply goods by purchasing them cheap. Thus, future trading depends upon price fluctuations. If the prices of products remain stable there will be no speculation in their prices and these goods will not be traded at these markets.

7. Portable: The goods should be such that they can be sent from one place to another at cheap transportation costs. If the goods cannot be sent to other places or their transportation is very difficult they will not be fit to be traded in commodity markets.

8. Suitable for Sale by Sample: The goods should be saleable on the basis of samples. The seller will show a sample and the transaction will be done. All the goods should correspond to the sample shown. If any goods require inspection before contract then such goods cannot be listed on commodity markets. So the goods should be sold on the basis ot sample.

FUNCTIONS OF A PRODUCE EXCHANGE

H.E. Eradman has assigned important functions to a commodity exchange. The exchange, in his view, is not only a meeting place but a centre for crystallising market values. Eradman has given the following functions of a commodity exchange:

1. Provide a convenient place for the members to meet for the purpose of trading and of exchanging views.
2. Collect and disseminate market information.
3. Establish and maintain grades.
4. Provide machinery for arbitration of trade disputes.
5. Help in crystallising market values.

Functions of Produce Exchange

1. Finance Function: The commodities traded in exchanges are standardised, graded and durable. As the exchanges provide ready market for the goods so the liquidity of goods is ensured. On the basis of negotiable warehouse receipts the goods can be easily transferred. The dealers can easily raise loans against these goods. Financial institutions not hesitate in extending credit facilities against these stocks which help traders to transact more business. Thus, produce exchange are helpful in arranging finances for the trading parties.

2. Price Registration Function: The important trading centres receive regular latest information about the prices quoted for various goods at the exchanges and then traders are able to register the prices for their dealers. The producers, speculators and dealers interpret the prices in their own ways and undertake future transactions. The prices prevailing in different exchanges in India and at important centres in the world also reach the exchanges and members make use of this information.

3. Publicity and Information Function: The goods traded for spot delivery and for future contracts are daily quoted in the press. The opening rates, prevailing rates during the day and closing rates at the end of the day are given proper publicity for the benefit of producers, speculators and dealers. The quantities traded at present and for future deliveries are also given in the press. This ensures manufacturers of the prospective demand for products and they plan their production accordingly. The information collected at exchanges is also made available to various users. The price trends at various other exchanges also influence price trends at exchange. The traders can form an idea about price trends in the future and their effect on future production. Thus, exchanges provide not only information but also give publicity to the transactions undertaken.

4. Regulatory Function: The exchanges are run as per guidelines decided earlier. All trading is done according to rules. There is a compulsory arbitration if some dispute is not settled by members themselves. The regulatory function of an exchange is in the interest of general public because in the absence of regulation speculators try to exploit the situation. The success of an exchange depends on how rigorously the rules are enforced and errant members are punished.

5. Insurance Function: The produce exchanges enjoy a wide market of continuous nature. Large amounts are attracted for speculation transactions which otherwise would not have been available. The risk of future price changes can be off-set by 'hedging' which is the process of neutralising the loss or gain that may arise in future on account of changes in prices. It involves two transactions—current buying and future selling or *vice-versa.* Thus, produce exchange also help in covering likely future losses.

COMMODITIES TRADED AT EXCHANGES

1. **Agricultural Produce:** Cotton, Tea, Jute, Coffee, Wheat, Oilseeds, etc.
2. **Mineral Produce:** Copper, lead and other non-ferrous metals.
3. **Manufactured or Semi-manufactured Goods:** Cotton, Textiles, Sugar, Leather goods, Hides and Skin. etc.

ORGANISATION AND MEMBERSHIP OF COMMODITY EXCHANGES

Commodity Exchanges in India are generally governed by the rules and regulations of the Forward Contracts (Regulation) Act. 1952. Most of them are companies registered under Companies Act. 1956, These may be companies limited by guarantee with or without share capital or they may be companies limited by share capital. The exchange is managed by Board of Directors and other officials elected every year. The Board manages the exchange through some Committees like Survey Committee, Rates Committee, Floor Committee, Clearing House Committee, etc.

Membership

A person with good financial standing and reputation can become the member of exchange. The members may be classified as: (1) trading members, and (2) non-trading members must hold at least one share of the association. He is expected to trade according to the rules and regulations of the exchange. Only the members are allowed to trade in the exchange either on their own behalf or on behalf of others. When they trade on their own account, they are called jobbers. Where they trade for others they are known as brokers who may transact on behalf of producers, wholesalers, importers, exporters, etc.

PROCEDURE FOR RECOGNITION OF COMMODITY EXCHANGE

1. Application: An association desirous of being recognised for handling forward contracts will have to seek permission from Central Government by applying in the prescribed form. There are bye-laws for the control and conduct of business of the exchange. There should also be a governing body, office bearers, etc. The provisions for administration of exchange should also be submitted along with the application. The procedure prescribed for admission of members should also be given. After these formalities are completed the government decides about the recognition of a commodity exchange.

2. Granting Recognition: After scrutinising the application and Riles and regulations, the Central Government may grant recognition to an exchange if it feels that recognising the association as an exchange is in the interest of trade and public. After recognition the exchange cannot amend its rules, regulations, bye-laws. etc. without the permission of Central Government. The notification for recognising the exchange is issued both by the Central Government and the State Government where its-main office is situated. The Central Government may withdraw recognition if it feels that such act is in the interest of trade and public. Before taking such step, the association is given sufficient opportunity to explain its position.

3. Powers of the Central Government: The Central Government has wide powers for regulating the working of exchanges. It may ask for the change or amendment of present rules or framing of new rules of the exchange within a prescribed time limit. Every exchange must furnish a copy of annual report to the Central Government which may also call for periodical returns from recognised exchanges. The Government has the power to appoint one or more persons to enquire into the affairs of any commodity exchange or the affairs of their members.

The Central Government can also order the suspension of working of any exchange for a period not exceeding seven days if the government deems it fit to do so. The suspension can be extended from time to time.

4. Powers of Recognised Association: A recognised association can make rules for the conduct of business by the members. These rules are subject to the approval of the Central Government. It can also frame bye-laws for the control of forward transactions which may provide for: (*i*) Working hours of the exchange, (*ii*) Clearing house for settlement of conducts, (*iii*) Deciding about the commodities to be traded, (*iv*) Procedure for settling of claims or disputes, etc.

ADVANTAGES OF PRODUCE EXCHANGES

1. Helpful to Everyone: The organised markets for various goods have been helpful both to the producers and consumers. A place is provided where all types of persons, dealing in goods, come together and purchase and sell according to their needs. The exchanges are also helpful to the public at large.

2. Providing Liquidity to Commodities: The produce exchanges help the purchase and sale of goods throughout the years. The sellers can offer the goods whenever they want to sell, the buyers are readily available at all times. The sale of goods makes them liquid. This liquidity encourages bankers to extend loans against goods.

3. Standardisation and Grading: The produce exchanges help in grading and standardisation of products. Only properly graded goods are allowed to be traded. The purchase and sale is done by giving the grades of goods. Indirectly the exchanges encourage the standardisation and gradation of goods in order to be listed for trade.

4. Shifting of Risk to Speculators: There is always a possibility of price changes in the market. The risk of price fluctuations is transferred to specialised persons called speculators. The speculators transact for future deliveries and producers are ensured of future market. The prices are also decided in advance. As the manufacturers and producers are sure of the possible prices in future the risk which producers have to bear will be shifted to speculators.

5. Controlling Price Fluctuations: The drastic price fluctuations are bad both for buyers and sellers. The exchanges provide hedging facilities where future price fluctuations are offset by counter-contracts. This type of transactions reduce likely price fluctuations.

6. Regular Supply of Goods: At the produce exchanges, the stockists ensure a regular supply of goods at all times. When there is glut of goods or produce in the market the traders are released in the market. The exchanges provide a ready market for goods which stabilises then supplies.

7. Helpful to Producers: The producers are ensured of proper demand and prices for goods in the future. They can estimate the demand for products from the forward contracts among traders. They are somewhat relieved of future uncertainties of demand and prices. They are ensured about reasonable prices when the products come in the market. The stockists purchase the goods and avoid price reductions. Thus, produce exchanges are very helpful to producers.

8. Transmitting Information to Members: While the produce exchanges provide a place for transactions they also collect useful information about possible demand and expectant supplies at various other places along with the information about price fluctuations. All this information is supplied to members who are able to make their own estimates for future. The produce exchanges collect and transmit valuable trade information to the members.

KINDS OF TRANSACTIONS AT PRODUCE EXCHANGE

1. Cash Contracts: These are those contracts where cash payment is made at the time of delivery of goods. These transactions are also known as 'cash market' and 'physical market'. The word 'physical market' is used because the physical delivery of goods is given at the time of transaction.

Cash contracts can be divided into spot contracts and forward contracts. If the goods are to be delivered immediately, then the contract is called spot contract. On the other hand, a transaction will be a 'forward contract' when delivery of goods and payment of price is to be done on an appointed future date. Generally, if the delivery of goods is within eight days it will be a spot transaction and if delivery is after eight days then it will be a forward transaction.

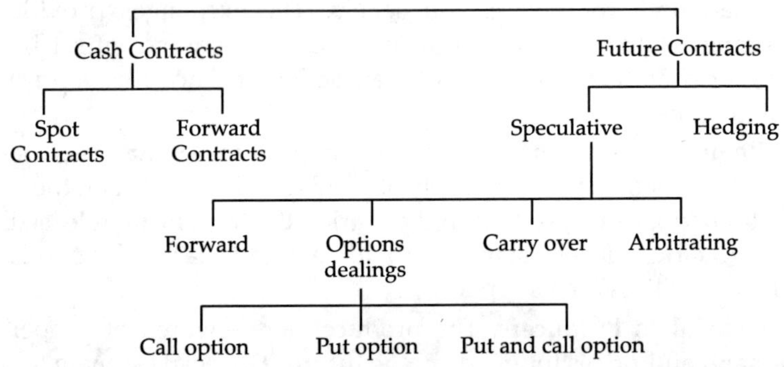

Fig 34.1: Kinds of Transactions at a Produce Exchange

2. Future Contracts: It is a contract to be performed on a future date. The transaction is undertaken by mentioning the quantity, quality and price of the commodities to be traded and a future date is fixed when actual delivery is to be taken and price is to be paid. The future time may be a fortnight, a month, two months, etc. and the contract is completed on that date.

Definition

1. *G.W. Hoffman*: A future contract is "an agreement to buy or sell, in accordance with laws and rules of the exchange, a definite quantity of a commodity at an agreed price at a future date being entered into for the purpose of speculating on or hedging against price changes, and being usually closed out by another offsetting future trade."

2. *J.G. Smith*: "A future contract is a contract in an organised market drawn up in a form standardised by the controlling authority of the market, referring to specific lots of produce, but prescribing the unit of amount and quality while leaving to the contracting parties the determination of total amount, price and time of delivery, it being understood that the choice in the latter case has reference only to definite period of time stated in the contract, and that these periods are prescribed by custom or

the market authority, and not arbitrarily selected by either of the parties to the bargain."

Characteristics

1. Definition: It is a contract for the sale of a particular commodity of a specific grade at a fixed price at a future date.

2. Transaction: The different provisions of the produce exchange determine the transaction.

3. Contract: The contracts can take place only among members and at the exchange.

4. Price: The commodity may be of a specific or near grade. Its price may be adjusted as per the practices of the produce exchange which differ at different exchanges.

5. Date: The delivery can be made at any date between the specified period known as delivery period.

6. Margin Money: The parties to the contract are required to deposit some money known as 'Margin Money' with a third party. This is an insurance against the refusal of a party not to complete the transaction. The future price fluctuations may prompt a party to go back from its commitment but the margin money acts as security against that event.

7. Delivery: The delivery of goods can be given even by handing over the receipt of a warehouse. The commodity must be stored in an approved warehouse situated in the city where office of the exchange is situated. Giving and taking delivery under future contracts is not obligatory. Both the parties can cancel the contract at any time before the end of stipulated delivery period, by settling the margin of profit or loss, as the case may be.

SPECULATION

Definition

The Latin derivative the word 'speculation' means 'to look at from a distance'. Speculation means assuming of risk of loss with a view to marketing profit. It is an activity where purchasing and selling is undertaken to earn profits out of future price changes. The speculation try to anticipate the future trends of markets and purchase or sell goods or shares with a view to earn profits. In the words of H.G. Emery, "Speculators consists in buying and selling commodities in the hope of a profit from anticipated changes of value." Profit is the reward of a speculator. A businessman earns profits by rendering various services to the consumer. He creates form, time, place utilities in goods so that he is able to earn more profits. On the other hand, a speculator is not interested in any type of service. He only wants to benefit from the future changes in prices. The rise or fall in prices in future will bring him profit or loss.

Features

1. Risk of Loss: A speculator takes voluntary risk of loss. He tries to anticipate future price trend of commodities or shares and trade accordingly.

2. Capital Appreciation and Capital Gain: The main aim of speculator is capital appreciation and capital gain out of price changes in future. If price changes are favourable then he will gain, if they are adverse then he will lose.

3. Forward Trading: A speculator always operates in forward market. He buys and sells for forward contracts for future delivery.

4. No Actual Delivery: A speculator is not interested in taking or giving actual delivery of goods. He wants to take or give only the difference in prices. If prices change favourably to him then he gets the difference in prices. On the other hand, if prices are unfavourable then he has to pay the difference.

Significance

1. Stabilises Prices: Speculation helps in stabilising prices in various markets and at different times. When prices are higher at one place and lower at another, the speculator makes buying at the later and sells at the former. It helps in reducing price fluctuations between two periods. When the supply of commodities is large the prices will fall. When goods are in short supply the prices will rise. The speculator will buy at lower prices with an expectation that they may go up in future. On the other hand, when prices start rising then speculator will sell the commodities for future trading. This helps in reducing price differences and thus stabilising them.

2. Increase in Turnover: The speculators indulge in large scale buying and selling with a hope to make money in the future. As the cash transactions in organised markets are very few thus making their existence unnecessary, the speculation keeps the markets active throughout the year.

3. Directs the Flow of Savings: Speculation helps in diverting the flow of savings towards markets. It provides wide scope for trading in different commodities. The investors gel channel to divert their sources. Speculation is based on intelligent judgement of markets. It tends to influence the trends in business.

4. Provides Continuity and Stability of Market: Speculation helps in buying and selling of goods or securities throughout the year. The existence of large number of speculators, bulls and bears, keeps the market open. A person can buy or sell any type of commodity securely as the speculators are always present to offer a market. The abrupt changes in prices are also absorbed by speculators. As a matter of fact, speculators bring stability to the market.

5. Facilitates Hedging Transactions: Hedging is a means by which producers or manufacturers can ensure themselves against future fluctuations in prices. The presence of large number of speculators on commodity exchanges helps in hedging transactions. Effective hedging operations need a large future market. If future markets are restricted to hedgers only there will a larger number of sellers than buyers in one season and *vice-versa* in another season.

6. Encourages Grading and Standardisation of Commodities: Speculation is possible only in those commodities which are properly graded and standardised. In the absence of grading the buyers and sellers may have different type of goods in mind while making contracts. This creates disputes at the time of settlement. When there are proper grades of goods the trading is done by mentioning the grades of goods, etc. If any commodity is to be traded at a commodity exchange, it should first be graded and standardised otherwise trading in these commodities will not be possible.

Evils of Speculation

1. Recklessness: Every speculator does not possess the requisite skill required for scientific speculation. Many persons indulge in reckless speculation which is detrimental both for them and for trade.

2. Manipulation: Manipulation means increasing or decreasing prices which are favourable to speculators. Sometimes, more than one speculator trade in such a way that they try to create wrong impression about the trade trends. They may start buying or selling commodities at high or low prices and create an impression in the mind of others that prices are really going up or down. In reality the speculators want to manipulate the market to their advantage.

3. Fictitious Sales: The speculators may indulge in fictitious or pretended sales. They show to others that the sales are made at high rates. Other persons may take the impression that prices have gone up in reality. This is done to mislead others so that the purpose of speculators is served.

4. Matched Order: This is done to stir up the market artificially. A speculator may indulge in some contracts of buying and selling just to create activity in the market. This artificial activity may prompt brokers to indulge in buying and selling commodities or shares. These prices appear in the official list as well. Thus, the market is artificially stirred up.

5. Corner: When a number of bulls who are optimistic about price rise and bears who feel that prices will go down start purchasing and selling goods so that the prices become favourable to them and they are able to perform there future contracts the bulls may start purchasing the whole supply of goods in order to raise their prices. At the time of performing the contract they demand the goods instead of settling the difference. The bears will be squeezed to the maximum and will have to surrender to the conditions of bulls. This situation mean cornering the bears.

Forms of Speculative Transactions

1. Forward Transactions: Under forward transactions, commodities are traded at a given rate and the transactions are squared up by purchasing or selling respectively at a future date. The speculators purchase the goods at current prices and hope to sell them at higher rates in future. If prices increase speculators earn profits.

2. Option Dealings: Option is a special right given to a party making the contract to execute it in accordance with the terms and conditions agreed upon while granting such option. The person who grants option is entitled to get the premium in case the option is not exercised by the buyer of the option as a result of unfavourable prices.

(*i*) *Call Option*: When the option is exercised by the person towards buying a certain commodity at a fixed price, it is called call option.

(*ii*) *Put option*: When this call is used to sell the commodity then it is called put option.

(iii) Put and Call option: When the option is given both to buy and sell a certain commodity at a fixed price, the premium charged is the double and such a right is called put and call option.

3. Carry Over or Badla Transactions: Carry over means postponement of current settlement period to the next period. Some charges known as 'Badla' are paid for postponing this date. It is carrying over of the risk when prices are not favourable to the speculator and he hopes that in future the prices will be going in his favour.

The practice of carrying over the risk can be undertaken by the operator any number of times till he decides to close the transaction. While doing so the first transaction is to be squared up and a fresh transaction is entered into for next period.

4. Arbitrating: When a speculator makes contracts for buying and selling in two different markets, it is known as arbitrating or spreading. The speculator carefully studies different markets and tries to buy at a lower rate and sell at a higher rate and earn the profit out of the difference.

HEDGING

Meaning

According to J.G. Smith, "The essence of hedging is the making of two contracts at about the same time of an opposite though of corresponding nature. Both are genuine trade contracts, one with a view to obtaining a dealer's ordinary trade profit, the other an insurance or protective contract which counteracts speculative loss or profit on the first transaction." Hedging'is used to reduce risk arising from changes in prices in future. It is the practice of entering simultaneously into two contracts of an opposite though corresponding nature, one in the spot (cash) market and the other in the future market. The contracts are opposite in nature. If one contract is for sale, the other will be for purchase and *vice-versa.* The purpose of undertaking such contracts is to insure against adverse price changes in future. Both the transactions are made in opposite direction. If the trader loses in one transaction, he makes it up in the second/transaction. For example, suppose, a trader contracts to sell 1000 bales cotton at ₹ 650 per bale after a period of three months. He hopes that the price of cotton may be ₹ 625 per bale after three months. If the price goes down as per his expectations he will gain ₹ 25 per bale. In case the prices do not go down or they go up in fact, the trader stands to lose. Since he is not a speculator, he will try to make a counter-contract which will save him from future loss. He makes a contract to purchase 1000 bales of cotton in future at a price of ₹ 625. The change in price in one transaction will offset its effect in the second transaction. If he loses by selling in future in one transaction, he will gain in another transaction by purchasing the goods. The loss in one transaction is offset by the gain in another.

Types

1. Hedge Purchase: If a trader sells some goods in cash market, he may try to protect himself against rise in price by making a transaction to purchase in future. This is known as hedge purchase.

2. Hedge Sale: It is just the reverse of hedge purchase. A person making a purchase of goods in cash market may like to insure himself by making a sale in the future. The quantity transacted in both the cases is the same.

Need

Hedging is done to remove credit and price risks or to minimise them. Its main purpose is to protect the trader from losses due to adverse movement of prices. The traders have to buy goods and keep them in stock for some time By hedging they can protect themselves against fluctuations in prices. Manufacturers can protect themselves against fluctuations in the prices of their raw materials. Exporters can protect themselves against future fluctuations in prices. Besides insuring itself against price changes, a businessman can receive better credit facilities from a bank if he hedges its goods.

Limitations

1. No Protection: The practice of hedging will provide full protection only if prices in cash and futures markets move together in perfect harmony with each other. Cash and future prices do not always move together. If prices in the two markets move in the opposite directions hedging cannot prevent loss.

2. Difficult: The prices of different grades of commodities may not move in a similar fashion. The prices of grades contracted may rise but the prices of other grades of commodities may fall. This will create difficulties in hedging.

3. Useless: The transactions in commodity exchanges are allowed only for a given quantity. An exchange may allow the purchase or sale of 50 bales of cotton or 150 tons of gram, etc. This quantity is known as a trading unit. A trader or a manufacturer may like to trade in different quantities than the trading units. Under such situations hedging will not be of much use.

4. Limited to Raw Materials Only: There may be a rise in prices of products not due to increase in prices of raw materials but because of increase in other expenses like wages and overheads. The manufacturer will not benefit from hedging under these conditions. He can only be protected for changes in prices of raw materials only. So hedging is helpful only in case of raw materials and not for other expenses.

5. Expensive: Hedging involves expenses which a person will have to bear. He will have to pay commission to brokers. He will have to spend time and efforts for estimating future trends in prices also. These expenses and effects increase the costs of goods.

QUESTIONS FOR EXERCISE

1. Define Commodity/Produce Exchange and discuss its characteristics.
2. What are the characteristics of commodities to be traded at Produce Exchanges? Describe the functions of a Produce Exchange.
3. What commodities are traded at Produce Exchange? Describe the organisation and membership of commodity exchanges in India. What is the procedure for their recognition?
4. What are the advantages of Produce Exchanges? Describe the kinds of transaction at a produce exchange?
5. What is speculation? Explain its features and significance.
6. What are the evils of speculation? Describe various forms of operative transaction.
7. Explain Hedging. Show its types, need and limitations.

36

Stock Exchanges

WHAT IS STOCK EXCHANGE?

1. *Pyle*: "Stock exchange is market place where securities that have been listed thereon may be thought and sold for either investment or speculation". Stock exchanges allow trading in securities both to the genuine investors and speculators.

2. *Securities Contract (Regulation) Act*, 1956: "Stock exchange means any body of individuals, whether incorporated or not, constituted for the purpose of assisting, regulating or controlling the business of buying, selling in securities."

3. *Hartley Withers*: "A Stock Exchange is something like a vast warehouse where securities are taken away from the shelves and sold across the countries at a fixed price in a catalogue which is called the official list."

Hartley calls stock exchange a warehouse where all securities are kept and traded on specified prices. It may not always be that every type of security is purchased for sale, there may be investors who do not bring their securities to the market but keep them only as investments.

4. *Husband and Dockeray*: "Securities or stock exchange are privately organised markets which are used to facilitate trading in securities. As per this definition the stock exchanges are the organised places where securities are purchase and sold."

CHARACTERISTICS OF STOCK EXCHANGE

1. It is a place where securities are purchased and sold.
2. A stock exchange is an association of persons whether incorporated or not.

3. The trading in an exchange is strictly regulated and rules and regulations prescribed for various transactions.
4. Both genuine investors and speculators buy and sell shares.
5. The securities of corporations, trusts, governments, municipal corporations, etc. are allowed to be dealt at stock exchanges.

FUNCTIONS OF STOCK EXCHANGE

1. Ensures Liquidity of Capital: The stock exchanges provide a place where shares and stocks are converted into cash. It is a ready market where buyers and sellers are always available and those who are in need of hard cash can sell their holdings. Because of exchanges many persons invest in securities and they can again convert them into cash.

2. Continuous Market for Securities: The stock exchanges provide a regular and ready market for securities. The securities once listed continue to be traded at the exchanges irrespective of the fact that their owners go on changing.

3. Evaluation of Securities: Stock exchanges are helpful in evaluating any type of security listed there. The investors can evaluate the worth of their holdings from the prices quoted at different exchanges for those securities. The securities are quoted under the free atmosphere of demand and supply and the prices are set on the basis of free market.

4. Mobilising Surplus Savings: The stock exchanges provide a ready market for various securities. The investors do not have any difficulty in investing their savings by purchasing shares, bonds, etc. from the exchanges. In their absence many persons who want to invest their savings will not find avenues to do so. Thus stock exchanges play an important role in mopping up surplus finds of investors.

5. Helpful in Raising Capital: The new and existing concerns need capital for their activities. Both the new and existing concerns raise capital while for the first time existing units increase their capital for expansion and diversification purposes. The shares of new concerns are registered at stock exchanges. Existing companies also sell their shares through brokers, etc. at exchanges. The exchanges are helpful in raising capital both by new and old concerns. The intending buyers remain in touch with the exchanges for investing money in securities.

6. Safety in Dealings: The dealings at stock exchanges are governed by well-defined rules and regulations of Securities Contract (Regulation) Act, 1956. There is no scope for manipulating transactions. The safety in dealings brings confidence in the minds of all concerned parties and helps in increasing various dealings.

7. Listing of Securities: Every company desirous of listing its securities will apply to the exchange authorities. The listing is allowed only after a critical examination of capital structure, management and prospects of the company. The listing of securities gives privilege to the company. Only listed securities can be purchased and sold at stock exchanges. The investors can form their own views about the securities because listing a security does not guarantee the financial stability of the company.

8. Platform for Public Debt: The increasing government's role in economic development has necessitated the raising of huge amounts for this purpose. The stock exchanges provide a platform for raising public debt. They act as markets of government securities. However, there is no provision for a separate counter for government securities. These are traded through brokers dealing in these securities.

9. Clearing House of Business Information: The companies listing securities with exchanges have to provide financial statements, annual reports and other reports to ensure maximum publicity of corporation operations and working. The economic and other informations provided at stock exchanges help companies to decide their policies.

LISTING OF SECURITIES

Meaning

Listing of securities means permission to quote shares and debentures officially on the trading floor of the stock exchange. Every security issued by companies cannot be traded at a stock exchange. It fixes certain standards which the company must fulfil before getting the securities listed.

Requirements for Listing

1. Memorandum and Articles of Association.
2. Copies of all prospectuses or statements in lieu of prospectuses.
3. Copies of Balance Sheets, audited accounts; Agreements with promoters, underwriters, brokers, etc.

4. Letters of Consent from Controllers of Capital Issues.
5. Details of shares and debentures issued and shares forfeited.
6. Details of issues of bonuses and dividend declared.
7. History of the company in brief.
8. Agreement with managing director, etc.
9. An Undertaking regarding compliance with the provisions of the Company Act, 1956 and Securities Contracts (Regulation) Act, 1956 as well as rules made, therein.
10. A list of the highest ten holders of each class or kind of securities of the company.

Classification of Securities

The securities are classified into (a) cleared securities and (*b*) non-cleared securities. Cleared securities enjoy forward trading facilities while non-cleared securities have only cash trading and are on the cash list. If the shares are fully paid and have listing privilege for three years the exchange may grant them the status of cleared securities. The securities must be widely distributed and have public interest only then they can become cleared securities.

Procedure for Dealings at Stock Exchanges

1. Selection of a Broker: The intending investor or seller may approach his bank for his purchase. The banks appoint their own brokers at exchanges who contact for dealings on behalf of their customers. On a recommendation from the bank the client's account is opened by the broker. The bank assures about the financial condition of the client. Today, registered brokers work independently to buy and sell securities. Brokers are registered at exchanges.

2. Placing an Order: After selecting the brokers the client places an order for purchase or sale of securities. The broker also guides the client about the type of securities to be purchased and the proper time for it. If a client is to sell the securities the broker tells him about the favourable time for sale. The broker is told to purchase shares, their number and price to be paid. Sometimes a definite price, sometimes the tentative price, sometimes the minimum price is given on which the purchase is to be made. The broker will try to make purchases as far as possible to the nearest price offered by the client. He is given some choice for bargaining. The same type of choice is given to him for selling the securities.

3. Making the Contract: The trading floor of the stock exchange is divided into different parts known as trading posts. Different posts deal in different types of securities. The authorised clerk of the broker goes to the concerned post and expresses his intention to buy and sell the securities. A deal is struck when the other party also agrees. The bargain is struck by an outcry mentioning the price, and number of securities contracted by both the clerks. The bargain is noted by both the parties in their note books. The slip giving brief details of the bargain is put in a box for making announcement in the official price list for publicity. These days computer is being used instead of vocal crying about rates.

4. Contract Note: Next day the buying and selling brokers prepare notes after mutual consent. The seller is sent a selling note and the buyer is sent a buying note. The details of securities traded are given mentioning their number, price, etc.

5. Settlement: The spot dealings are settled then and there in full. The selling broker hands over the transfer form and share certificates to the buying broker after receiving the price. The settlement for ready delivery and forward contacts is done with a different procedure.

(*i*) *Settlement of Ready Delivery Contracts*: The settlement in different stock exchanges is done between 3 and 7 days of the transaction. If the settlement is done by giving actual delivery of securities on receiving the price it is called liquidation in full. Otherwise the dealings are squared by adjusting price differences only.

(*ii*) *Settlement of Forward Delivery Contracts*: The forward delivery contracts are made for speculative purpose. Only the active and broad market securities are traded in forward contracts. The settlement of forward contracts can be done in any of the three ways:

(*a*) *Liquidation in full*: The securities are delivered, and payment is received or *vice-versa* after crossing all intermediate purchases and sales.

(*b*) *Liquidation by payment of differences*: The purchase and sale are offset at the ruling price by paying or receiving the difference among them. The securities are not delivered but only the difference of prices contracted and current prices are received or paid as the case may be.

(*c*) *Carry over to the next settlement*: When the buyer does not want to settle the contract but seeks to carry it to a future date then it is called carry over. The buyer will have to pay certain amount to the seller for this concession and the amount paid is known as surcharge.

QUESTIONS FOR EXERCISE

1. Define stock exchange and discuss its characteristics and functions?
2. Explain listing of securities. What is the procedure for dealing at stock exchange?

37

Market Risks and Insurance

Meaning of Business Risks

There are always risks in business. A businessman makes some premises or assumptions for the future and bases all his decisions on those predictions. If everything goes well and presumptions come true as anticipated, risk may be avoided. As the future circumstances are influenced by so many factors, a change in any situation brings the risk element into play such as change in demand for a product, increased prices of raw materials, labour rates, government restrictions on the business, natural calamity like earthquake, floods, etc. In the factory, a breakdown in machinery, strike by workers, pilferage or theft of goods, misappropriation of cash, etc., become the causes of business risks. A businessman tries to control of minimise the risks though they cannot be altogether avoided. Hence, an effort is made to insure various risks so that some compensation is received when something adverse happens.

CAUSES OF BUSINESS RISKS

Business risks may be divided into two categories: (1) Internal risks, and (2) External risks. These have following causes:

1. Causes of Internal Risks

Internal risks are caused by the circumstances or situations in the factory such as mishandling of situation or lack of precautions and happening of adverse things.

(*i*) *Loss by fire, etc:* These may be due to fire accident in the business by which property is destroyed. If the products traded or produced are fire prone, lack of precaution may cause an accident as in case of coal mines, oil refiners, cooking gas dealers, etc. Fire due to negligence on the part of employees or failure of equipment may also cause loss to the property.

(*ii*) *Business Environment*: The environment in business may be such that there is a possibility of loss because the things are not properly managed. Lack of effective control on cash transactions may cause misappropriation of cash or lack of stock control system may encourage theft of goods, etc.

(*iii*) *Liability of the Businessman*: A businessman is held responsible for the loss caused to employees or a public by the business. If there is an accident on a machine and a worker injured, the businessman will have to pay compensation to the worker. Similarly, a loss caused to the public by way of pollution or wastes of the concern may bring a liability to the businessman.

(*iv*) *Mismanagement of Business*: Risk may arise due to mismanagement of business, such as lack of proper control over labour or production, resulting in increased costs. Lack of demand for products may compel the businessman to slash down prices causing loss. Other factors bringing risks to the business may be a lack of planning, inadequate capital, lack of coordination among different departments, inefficient management, etc.

2. Causes of External Risks

Following factors outside the business or causes generally beyond the control of the management are causes of external risks:

(*i*) *Natural Calamities*: Natural calamities like earthquake, storm, floods, etc., cannot be precisely predicted and a business is always exposed to such risks.

(*ii*) *Competition*: A business may suffer due to competition from other business undertakings. Some concerns might have introduced better methods of production and able to reduce costs of production. The business suffers if prices are reduced due to competition. In case the prices are kept the same, the goods will not be sold in the market because the customer will prefer to buy cheap goods.

(*iii*) *Price Fluctuations*: The price fluctuations may adversely affect costs of materials, costs of other inputs, budget forecasts, etc. These are generally influenced by the factors which are not in the hands of the businessman but he has to bear the risks arising out of them.

(*iv*) *Change in Demand*: There may be a change in demand for the products. Consumer tastes fashions likings or dislikings for certain goods may cause a change in demand. A sudden change in demand may create a problem for disposing of the stocks. New methods of production may be required to cope with the changing situation which will cause unnecessary financial burden on the business.

(*v*) *Government Policy*: Risks may arise due to change in government policies much as increase in the rates of taxes, changes in imports and exports, regulations and restrictions on stocking of certain items, taking up the production of certainly goods government itself, etc. The changes in policies not only cause losses but compel the business to close down its production.

METHODS OF MINIMISING RISKS

The business risks can be minimised in the following ways:

(1) Preventive Measures.

(2) Shifting of Risks.

1. Preventive Measures: These are the measures which reduce the element of risk. When there is a possibility of risk and some steps are taken which can prevent those possibilities, risk can be controlled or eliminated, for example, scientific methods may be used to prevent fire accidents. The market research techniques may be employed to estimate future demands for goods to reduce the possibilities of over- or under-production. Businessmen may try to avoid price cutting by forming trade associations, etc. In preventive measures one tries to find out the possible causes of future risks and then tries to control them by taking the steps reducing risk element.

2. Shifting of the Risks: If the risk cannot entirely be ruled out, one tries to shift the risk to those agencies which specialise in bearing that risk. Insurance is the best way of shifting business risks. Insurance companies offer a variety of policies to the public and undertake to compensate in case of loss. There are policies relating to fire, industrial accidents, consequential losses, marine insurances, etc. A predetermined premium is paid to the insurance company. If some loss occurs due to the reasons mentioned in the policy, the insurance company compensates the loss.

THE INSURANCE SYSTEM

Some future risks can be transferred to specialised institutions known as Insurance Companies. Insurance is a contract between two parties whereby one party agrees to indemnify the loss suffered by the other party for a consideration of some money called 'Premium'. The party which promises to indemnify the loss is called 'Insured' (Insurance Company) and the persons or property subject to risks is called 'Insurer'. The agreement providing for insurance is called an 'Insurance Policy'.

Pooling System

Insurance system is based on an important technique called 'Pooling System'. A large number of persons combine together to reduce or to compensate the future loss of any one of them. They contribute small amounts of money and pay it to the affected party. Pooling System helps in spreading the risk over a large number of units. It is based on the theory of large numbers, or more technically, the science of probability. Insurance companies act as a channel for collecting premium and indemnifying the loss.

Definition of Insurance

1. *Mehr and Cammack*: A social device for reducing risk by combining a sufficient number of exposure units to make their individual losses collectively predictable. The predictable loss is then shared proportionately by all those in the combination."

2. *Schultz and Bradwill*:"Insurance in its technical sense is a social device which employs the use of pooling technique to eliminate uncertainty."

Both the definitions are similar in their approach. 'Pooling System' is the principal device in both the definitions,

3. *Justice Tindal*: "Insurance is a contract in which a sum of money is paid by the assured in consideration of insurers incurring the risk of paying a large sum upon a given contingency."

The insured pays some amount in the shape of premium as a consideration for being compensated in case of loss.

Requisites of an Insurable Risk

An Insurable risk must have the following essentials to be insured against:

1. Homogeneous Exposure Units: There should be a large number of similar units exposed to the same danger. It is necessary for predicting the loss through the law of large numbers that the units must be relatively similar. If the units are heterogeneous, it will not be possible to predict the loss.

2. Definite Loss: The loss suffered should be definite and mathematically measurable. In case of life insurance, the death of a person is definite. In case of fire and marine insurance the amount of loss should be measurable for calculating claims.

3. Accident Loss: If the loss is expected, then it cannot be insured. The loss from depreciation of asset is not insurable because it is certain to occur. The loss must be accidental. It should not be in the hands of the insured. The death of a person is certain, so the loss from death itself is not insurable but as the time of death is uncertain, insurance may be a cover against untimely death.

4. Large Loss: The loss should be so large that the insured cannot bear it himself without economic distress. If the loss suffered is small, it is not worthwhile to insure it.

5. Unlikely to produce losses to majority: There should not be a likelihood that the loss should occur to many units at the same time. If it happens, then it is not possible for the insurance company to bear such a loss. The probability of loss should be spread over a longer period.

Principles of Insurance

1. Principle of Insurable Interest: The person getting an insurance policy must have an insurable interest in the property or life insured, *i.e.,* if he is benefited by its existence and is prejudiced by its destruction. Without insurable interest the insurance contact is void. The ownership of a property is not necessary for establishing insurable interest. A banker has an insurable interest in the property mortgaged to it against a loan. An employer can insure the lives of his employees because of his pecuniary interest in them. A creditor can insure the life of his debtor. A person cannot insure the property of a third party, because he does not have an insurable interest in it.

(*i*) *Fire Insurance*: In case of fire insurance, insurable interest must exist both at the time of contract and at the time of loss.

(*ii*) *Marine Insurance*: In marine insurance, however, insurable interest must exist at the time of loss though it may or may not exist at the time of contract.

(*iii*) *Life Insurance*: In case of life insurance, the person taking up a policy should have insurable interest in the life of insured person at the time of taking up the policy. It is not necessary that lie should have insurable interest at the time of maturity also. For example, a person gets an insurance policy on the life of his wife who is divorced later on. Here, the policy will not become void because the husband ceases to have an insurable interest.

2. Principle of Utmost Good Faith: The insurance contract is founded on the basis of utmost good faith on the part of both the parties. It is obligatory on the part of the proposer (one who wants to get an insurance policy) to disclose all material facts about the subject to be insured. If some material fact comes to light later on, then the contract can be avoided at the discretion of the insurer. The amount of premium is fixed on the basis of all the facts supplied to the insurance company. If some facts are withheld, then the amount of premium will not be properly settled. The insurer should also disclose the facts of the policy to the proposer.

3. Principle of Indemnity: It is applicable to all types of insurance policy except life insurance. Indemnity means a promise to compensate in case of a loss. The insurer promises to help the insured in restoring the position before loss. Whenever there is a loss of property, the loss is compensated. The compensation payable and the loss suffered should be measurable in terms of money The insured will be compensated only up to the amount of loss suffered by him. The maximum amount of compensation will be up to the value of the policy. The value of the policy undertaken is fixed at the time of contract. The actual amount of loss suffered is compensated and the value of policy is only the maximum limit.

The principle of indemnity is not applicable in case of life insurance contracts, because it is not based on the principle of compensation. The loss of life cannot be compensated by any amount of money.

1. Principle of Contribution: If a property' is insured with more than one company, the insured cannot claim more than total loss from all the companies put together. He cannot claim the same loss from different companies. He will be benefited by the insurance which runs counter to the principle of indemnity'. He cannot be restored to a better position than before the loss occurred. The total loss suffered by the insured will be contributed by different companies in the ratio of the value of policies issued by them. The companies make a contribution to restore the previous position of the insured. For example, A has a property of one lakh rupees. He gets an insurance policy for ₹ 50,000 from R & Co. and for ₹ 50,000 from S & Co. Because of fire property is destroyed to the extent of ₹ 40,000. A cannot claim ₹ 40.000 from R & Co. and ₹ 40,000 from S & Co. He can claim a total sum of ₹ 40,000 from either of the companies or from both companies to the extent of ₹ 20,000 from each. In case he claims ₹ 40,000 from R & Co. then S & Co. will pay ₹ 20,000 to R & Co. This is known as the principle of contribution.

5. Principle of Subrogation, it is applicable to all insurances other than the life insurance. If the insured party gets a compensation for the loss suffered by him, he cannot claim the same amount of loss from any other party. The rights of claiming the loss are shifted to the insurer (Insurances Company). For example, A gets his house insured for ₹ 50,000 with an insurance company. The house is intentionally destroyed by B. A claims the loss from the insurance company. A cannot sue B for getting the compensation because lie has already been compensated by the insurance company. Now, insurance company can sue B on behalf of A because by making good the loss suffered by A, the insurance company steps into the shoes of A. If the insured claims compensation from both the sides, he will be put in a better position than earlier which is against the principle of indemnity. The insurance company can also claim only up to the amount it has paid to the insured and not more.

Insurance and Assurance

The word assurance is used for life assurance policies. The contract of *assurance* means that the assured will have to be paid sooner or later. The word *insurance* is used for fire and marine insurance. Under the contract of insurance the risk is uncertain and the liability may or may not occur. Under life assurance the payment is made either on maturity or on the death of the insured, whichever is earlier. So the company will have to make the payment of the policy, it is only a question of time. In case of insurance contracts, the sum insured will be payable only if a there is a loss. Suppose a factory godown is insured against fire. In case the godown is destroyed by fire, then a liability under insurance contract will arise. If there is no fire, then the liability will not arise. So the liability under insurance may or may not arise.

Re-Insurance

An insurance company generally undertakes the risks according to its capacity. Sometimes a company undertakes more risks than its capacity. It tries to share the risk with some company in case of its occurrence. When an insurance company insures the risk with some other insurance company it is called Re-insurance. It may be for the foil amount of the policy or for a. part of It. It case of loss the first company will get compensation from the second company. The insured will be concerned only with the company from which is purchased insurance policy. Re-insurance is between insurance companies only.

Double Insurance

Double insurance means purchasing more than one policy for the same subject. A person may get two or more policies on his life. He can claim the amount on all these policies. The implications of double insurance are different in fire and marine insurance. When a person purchases two or more policies for his property, he cannot claim the same amount as that of loss from different companies. He will be able to claim only total loss from one or more companies. The loss will be contributed by the insurance companies in proportion to the policies issued by them.

Advantages of Insurance

1. Providing Security: There may be a fire in the factory, storm in the sea or loss of a life. In all these cases it becomes difficult to bear the loss. Insurance provides a cover against any sudden loss. In case of marine and fire insurance the loss suffered by the insured is fully compensated and he is restored to his earlier position. In the same way if a bread winning member of the family dies prematurely, the family is provided with money to continue with its livelihood. This insurance gives security to both individuals and businessmen. These days insurance covers various social welfare schemes also. There are schemes providing for unemployment, sickness accident, health and old age insurances. These schemes are helpful for poor people and establish social justice.

2. Spreading of Risk: The basic principle of insurance is to spread risk among a large number of people who get insurance policies and pay premium to the insurer. Whenever a loss occurs, it is compensated out of funds of the insurer. The loss is spread among a large number of policy-holders.

Insurance covers the loss of an individual but the social loss cannot be eliminated. If the property of a person is lost by fire, he will be compensated by the insurance company. The loss of goods will remain a social loss. Insurance cannot eliminate loss but it can reduce the risk to the individual.

3. Source for Funds Collection: The insured pays premium to the insurer in lieu of an insurance cover, the premium is received regularly in instalments. Large funds are collected by way of premium which can be gainfully employed in industrial development from all walks of life. They help in collecting saving from a large number of persons. In India, Life Insurance Corporation of India provides large funds to the industries for long-term investments. These funds are productively used in exploiting natural resources which accelerated industrial growth of a country. The employment opportunities are also increased by big investments made by insurance companies. Thus, insurance has become an important source of capital formation.

4. Encouraging Savings: Insurance does not only protect risks but it provides an investment channel too. Life insurance provides a mode of investment. The insurance develops a habit of saving money by paying premium. The amount of policy is paid to the insured or to his nominees. In case of fixed time policies the insured gets a lump-sum amount after the maturity of the policy.

5. Encouraging International Trade: International trade involves many risks in transporting goods from one country to another. In the absence of insurance the traders will always be worried for the safe arrival of goods. The quantum of trade will be limited because of uncertainties and risk involved during transit. Insurance provides protection against all types of sea-risks. It has helped the development of international trade on a large scale.

6. Insurance Contract: A contract is an agreement between two or more persons by which one or more of the parties acquire legal rights to have the other parties do certain acts. An insurance contract is also a contract in the same way. In this contract insurance company promises to provide a certain sum of money to compensate for the loss suffered by the insured for a consideration of premium.

Requirements of an Insurance Contract

1. Offer and its Acceptance: The offer is given by the person *who* wants to get an insurance policy. When this offer is accepted by the insurance company it becomes a contract.

2. Legal Competence: The parties to the contract *should* be legally competent to enter into a contract.

3. Legal Consideration. The contract should be supported by a legal consideration. The consideration in this case is premium for compensating the *loss* suffered by the insured

4. Insurable Interest: The insured should have an insurable interest in the subject to be insured. The existence of the subject should be in his interest.

5. Good Faith: An insurance contract is based on good faith on the part of both the parties. Neither party should conceal any fact about the contract.

QUESTIONS FOR EXERCISE

1. What are Business risks? What are their causes? Explain the methods of minimising business risks?
2. Define Insurance and explain the requisites of an insurable risk. What are the principles of insurance?
3. Distinguish between Insurance and Assurance, Re-insurance and Double Insurance?
4. What are the advantages of Insurance? Describe the requirements of an Insurance Contract.

38

Transportation

Modern trade and industry depend largely on transport. Improved means of transportation help in marketing functions by creating place utility. It helps in effecting utility to goods and contributes to manufacturing process. As production is regarded as the creation of utilities, transportation is a productive activity

Importance of Transport

1. Marketing: Transportation is a necessary function of marketing because geographically markets are located far from the areas of production. All goods manufactured in the factories or grown in the field are not consumed at the place of their origin. Transport is the physical means by which goods are moved from the point of production to the place of their consumption. Holtz Claw vividly puts this importance in the following words. "Minerals or other raw materials are to be transported from the place of extraction or production to the factory, crops are to be accessed from the farm to the local market or primary market and from there to the places of consumption. Finished products are to be transported from the warehouse to the wholesale warehouse, from warehouse to the dealer, and from the dealer to the ultimate consumer."

2. Distribution: Transport thus plays a prominent part in the distribution of goods. It has shaped and influenced the entire structure of distribution. It has extended the area within which-goods can find purchasers. It has effected competitive costs and the retail prices. With the 'place utility' which transport creates, the distance factor in consumption and the location factor in production, transport is the life blood of distribution system.

FUNCTIONS OF TRANSPORT

1. Growth of industries whose products require quick marketing: Perishable articles like fish and green vegetables are carried to various consumers quickly even in distant markets through transport.

2. Increase in the demand for goods: Through transport newer customers in newer places can be easily contacted and products can be introduced to them. Today markets have become national or international only because of transport.

3. Creation of place utility: Geographical and climatic factors force industries to be located in particular places far away from the markets and places where there may not be any demand for the products. Transport bridges the gap between production and consumption centres.

4. Creation of time utility: Of late transport has started creating the time utility also. It has been made possible by virtue of the improvements in the speed of transport It helps the product to be distributed in the minimum possible time.

5. Stabilisation of prices: Transport exerts considerable influence upon the stabilisation of the prices of several commodities by moving commodities from surplus to deficit areas. This equalises the supply and demand factors and makes the price of commodities stable as well as equal.

6. Flow of commodities transport: It ensures even flow of commodities into the hands of the consumers throughout the period of consumption.

7. Enables the consumers to enjoy the benefits of goods not produced locally: This increases the standard of living, an essential factor for further development of marketing and the economy.

8. Intensification of competition: Transport intensifies competition which, in turn, reduces prices. Prices are also reduced because of the facilities offered by transport for large scale production. Advantages of large scale production are possible only due to transportation.

9. Increase in mobility of labour and capital: Transport increases the mobility of labour and capital. It makes people of one place migrate to other places in search of jobs. Even capital, machineries and equipments are imported from foreign countries through transport alone.

MEANS OR ELEMENTS OF TRANSPORT

The elements of transport may be classified into four: the way, the vehicle, the motive power used and terminals. The way may be natural or artificial. Ocean provides a natural waterway while road is a man-made trade. Waterways are cheaper than landways and airways. Landway vehicles, waterway vehicles and airway vehicles are separate for different routes or ways.

1. Road Transport: All the methods of transport have their own merits and demerits. For example, though road transport is cheap, safe and flexible it has limited load carrying capacity with slow speed.

2. Rail Transport: Rail transport is a comparatively cheap means of transport. Its greatest demerit is its inflexibility. Railways cannot offer door-to- door delivery sendees. They are not suitable for local transport.

3. Water Transport: Water transport is perhaps the cheapest means of transport which is the creator of international trade. But it suffers from seasonal difficulties.

4. Air Transport: With the advent of air transport, distance nowadays is measured not in miles but in hours. No other form of transport can compete with the airways. It is a boon to perishable commodities. As the freight rates are comparatively very high, this mode of transport is opted only for valuable commodities which could fetch high rates. It cannot become a mass transport system.

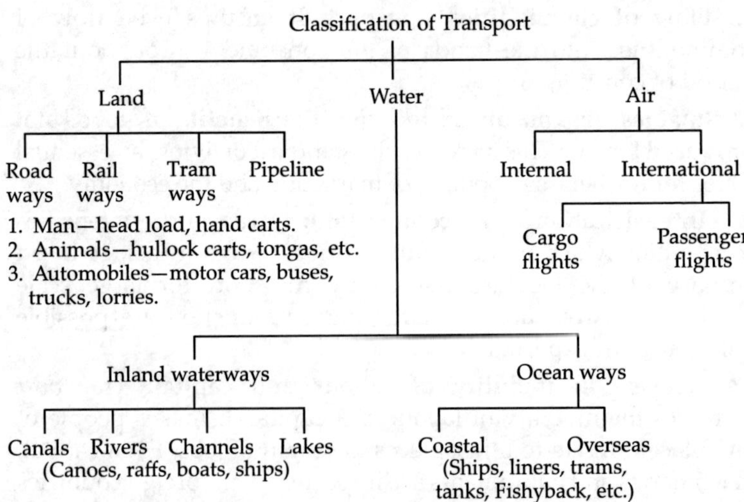

Fig. 38.1: Means of Transport.

Management Aspects of Transportation

The terms transportation means handling, hauling, warehousing, inventory control, physical transportation and delivery. Its management is an important managerial activity because it has become one of the most costly elements of distribution. Its costs represent about twenty per cent of the total cost of manufactured goods. With the vastly expanded markets and with cost conscious customers demanding more value in goods and faster services, the transportation problem has become more dominant. It is a prime target for cost cutting and management economies. In the modern marketing language management of transportation is called "Traffic management". The main considerations about deciding a particular mode of transport are: cost, speed, handling, damages, regularity, flexibility, etc. It is not an easy task to weigh all these elements and coordinate them into a most reconciled form. Thus physical distribution is not merely a matter of getting faster delivery. It also means making sure that the sendee requirements of customers are being met. It is, therefore, of vital concern to the marketing manager.

QUESTION FOR EXERCISE

1. Discuss the importance and functions of Transport for trade and industry.

39

Storage and Warehousing

WAREHOUSING AND STORING

What is Warehousing?

Warehousing is a process whereby the owner of goods keeps and provides protection to the goods lodged in the warehouses on payment of rent with a facility to take out as and when required and with expectations that whatever and whenever service to these goods will be required will gladly be rendered by the warehouses, of course, on due payment.

Characteristics of Warehousing

1. A place where goods are lodged by the owner on payment of hire (rent) prescribed for the purpose;
2. Goods can be taken out as and when required by the owner or his agent;
3. It provides all ancillary service, *e.g.*, packing, packaging, financing, sometimes selling on behalf of the owner; and
4. It is open to all who need its services; though, it does not provide personalized service as storehouses of the organisations do.

What is Storing

Storing is a process whereby the owner of goods receives, inspects, preserves, issues and manages the goods purchased by maintaining the storehouse or stores himself and provides himself all the management activities for having a personalised service to the materials.

Characteristics of Storing?

1. A place within the organisation where goods are managed by the owner himself by having own establishment for the purpose;

2. The goods are received and issued as and when procured or requisitioned by different departments of the organisation;

3. Facilities are fully provided by the materials management department to storing. These are extended to those goods which are procured for the departments of the organisation and preserved for use by the departments for when they have been provided on their requisition; and

It is open only to the materials procured by the organisation and materials produced by the organisation and not for any other one.

The Purpose of the Warehousing

1. To provide storing facilities for those who don't maintain their own storehouses;

2. To provide all facilities in regard to keep, protect and preserve the goods till they are lodged with them;

3. To provide such other ancillary facilities to the owner of the goods which the owner desires so far as trek lodged goods are concerned and so far as the economic requirements pertaining to the goods lodged are concerned, such as packaging, facilities of loan. etc. including that of assistance in international trade matters; and

4. To free the owners from the burden of establishing and managing their own storehouse for the purpose.

The Purpose of Storing

1. To receive raw material components, tools, equipments and other items.

2. To provide adequate, efficient and effective storage and preservation to the items received.

3. To meet the demands of consuming departments on their requisition.

4. To ensure good housekeeping so that materials handling, materials preservation, storing, receipts and issues can be deductively handled.

5. To assist in verification of materials.

6. To provide sufficient information and data foi goods purchasing including replenishment.

7. To take steps to minimise the obsolescence, scraps, etc.

8. To assist in codification, standardisation, preservation and handling of materials.

9. To highlight in particular the stock accumulation, discrepancies and abnormal consumption.

10. To maintain accounts of all store operations with sincerity and effectively.

11. To have effective control measures in all store operations so that nothing is lost during storage and preservation process.

Comparison

While the purpose of warehousing is to keep and protect the goods warehoused, the purpose of storing is to receive, preserve, issue and meet the requirements of the whole organisation with operate efficiency and thoughtful handling.

In India storing is more important than warehousing since 4 to 6 months inventory is common in most of the industries when the materials are indigenously available. If it is to be procured from foreign countries the inventory of 24 months is kept in the store-house. Thus, storing in India assumes greater significance than warehousing. Warehousing is common only among those persons, industrialists, commercial ventures who are to import or export for the purposes for which Indian warehousemen are supposed to be experts. Warehousing is quite uncommon in India for storing and other ancillary functions.

LOCATION AND LAYOUT

Location of a -Storehouse

While thinking of locating a storehouse there is no tradition in India of consulting the materials management department. This situation is prevalent throughout the length and breadth in store management generally.

The store is located near the consuming department or at a central place in the premises. This minimises the handling. It ensures timely issue and dispatch of materials, satisfying the using departments to a larger extent. Receipts and inspection of materials are also facilitated. The storehouse should be located where everyone's accessibility is easy and effective. This ensures better co-ordination, effective service, operative efficiency and least possible consumption of time, energy and also money.

Layout of a Storehouse

Layout of a store means internal arrangement of stores and handling equipment. It has assumed significance due to the need of effective utilisation of available space for every movement of store within the storehouse. Following are the characteristics of a good layout: (*i*) easy movement of materials, (*ii*) good storekeeping, (*iii*) sufficient space for men and material handling equipments, (*iv*) optimum utilisation of storage space, (*v*) judicious use of storage equipments, (*vi*) proper protection from rain, light and air and other natural hazards, (*vii*) effective and meaningful preservation; and (*viii*) easy accessibility on bins, etc.

In large organisations stores are usually attached to each consuming department. Receiving is arranged centrally. While items in common use are stocked in the central stores other items are stocked in the store attached to using departments.

Location of Warehouses

Warehouse stocks finished goods. It is hired for lending assistance in international trade as well as for functioning as an ancillary service provider. Its location depends on the following factors which are quite different than those winch govern the location of a storehouse:

1. It is located in proximity to ports; railway lines, junction of roads, availability of power and proximity to the industrial cities and commercial functionary centres.

2. It is located at central location from four comers of the business activity.

Layout of a Warehouse

Layout of a warehouse depends on the easy accessibility' of men and materials in general and effective and suitable protection and preservation in particular.

Important Factors in Construction

As both the store-house and warehouse protect and preserve the material lodged there, it is necessary that care should be taken about the following while constructing them:

1. Futuristic orientation;
2. Sufficient flexibility for expansion;
3. A construction where swift and economic movement of men and materials is rendered possible and better handling, receiving, issuing and stocking activities are possible;
4. A planning (in advance) for cold storage, heating equipments and air- conditioning such other type of facilities so that in future, if these are needed, construction may be capable of offering such facilities without much of disturbance and alterations.
5. A construction which helps in creating a healthy and congenial working conditions; and
6. A construction which makes a provision for operational effectiveness and efficiency.

Important Factors in the Design

1. Ventilation: Adequate ventilation is required in any construction for creating a proper working condition. Light arrangements should be such which can be accentuated through a judicious choice of colours for the walls. A pleasing environment created by a congenial working condition in the storehouse goes a long way in: (*i*) reducing the monotony of routine stores work, e.g., receiving, checking, stocking, handling and issuing goods, (*ii*) economising the efforts and reducing the operational cost through to a limited extent, and (*iii*) reducing the cost of operation in storehouse.

2. Safety: Safety is a very important aspect for a storehouse and warehouse. As a large volume of items are handled by these houses, accidents considerably reduce the morale of the personnels and the effectiveness of the system. Following measures should be taken to ascertain safety while constructing a building, shed or anything worthwhile for these houses and while training personnels:

(*i*) *Safety Consciousness*: Safety consciousness should be instilled in the minds of the personnels through sufficient training, visual aids, etc.

(*ii*) *Safety Appliances*: Safety appliances must be provided and their use must be encouraged. Gadgets like goggles, hand gloves, forks, etc. should be quite useful and convenient.

(*iii*) *Provision for Gang Ways*: Provision for adequate and wide gang ways should be made so that storage equipments, *e.g.*, forklifts, trolleys, industrial tractors, etc. can be easily moved about and used properly.

(*iv*) *Slocking Facilities*: Provision for adequate and appropriate stocking facilities should be made so as to minimise the handling of materials.

(*v*) *Smooth and Orderly Working*: Provision for smooth and orderly working of the storage equipments must be made in order to avoid halt in the operation and provide gentle good working atmosphere.

(*vi*) *Mechanics*: The storage equipment mechanics should be asked to visit the storehouse periodically so as to maintain them in proper and satisfactory working order.

(*vii*) *Personnels*: The personnels using these equipments should be properly trained for the sake of safety, precaution and proper use.

(*viii*) *Healthy Competition*: Healthy competition should be stimulated by installing safety awards including cash prizes so as to accord recognition to safety conscious personnel in the storehouse. This will naturally motivate others to follow the example.

(*ix*) *Fire Fighting*: Provision should be made for fire fighting facilities and it must be seen that here there is no slackness.

(*x*) *Segregating the Inflammable*: *Provision* must be made for segregating the inflammable materials from other materials and special fire extinguishers are required to be provided.

(*xi*) *Fire Extinguisher, Fire Escapes. Alarms and Sprinklers*: Adequate provision of fire extinguisher, fire escapes, alarms and sprinklers must be made available and must be fitted at a point from where it can be effectively used. The personnel should be appropriately trained in the use of these appliances.

(*xii*) *Toilets*: Provision of toilets and other amenities for personnel.

(*xiii*) *Routine Maintenance Equipment*: Provision would be made for routine maintenance equipments.

(*xiv*) *Safe Electrical Wirings*: Provision should be made for safe electrical wirings.

STORING PROBLEMS AND DEVELOPMENTS

In India stores management is not taken in a sophisticated manner. Till recently it was regarded as a function of clerical or at the most administrative nature. Without any glamour, it usually does not attract talent. But the stores department and its head is the custodian of the single largest group of current assets locking valuable working capital. The stores department plays very vital role, in smooth running of the organisation including that of production and other related activities. This vital role poses the major problem and challenge that Materials Manager has to face and for which he needs total output of all and sundry in the organisation. Decisions in the stores management concerning selection of racks, bins, handling equipments, safety practices, codification, receipt and issue procedure, inspection, accounting and training. The stores personnel are so important that it requires a lot of experience and wisdom to handle the situation, These aspects must be appreciated so as to give due importance to stores functions. Stores functions should be recognised as vital one. Qualified personnel should be recruited for manning the top, middle and supervisory positions in the store organisation.

Dry Storing

Recently a dry-storing practice has developed and gained due recognition in India. Dry-storing is a fairly new concept in scale/bulk stores. It lias resulted in an extremely versatile and economical method of dry storage. Available initially in four sizes, that is, 250, 500, 750 and 1,000 tons; the stores are suitable for storing any type of bagged material, as well as grain and all other types of dry foodstuffs and materials. Made from thick rot proof, butyl rubber laminate and to be either temporary or permanent, they can be moved from one site to another in a matter of hours. An outstanding advantage is simplicity in operation. No mechanical loading aids are used unless desired.

Tools Stores

Tools items are very costly and their usage points are scattered all over that plant/which may even be at a quite distant place (s). Tools have long life and they can be used for a very long period to come. All these factors make it essential to develop tools stores management concept.

The general practice is that tools procured from the suppliers are received, inspected, entered into the records of the central stores and usually stored in a tool room of the central stores. Thereafter the tools are sent to user's departments, attached tools stores or sub-stores at decentralised locations known as tool cribs located near the usage points. For milling cutters, arbours are related tools the ideal place of store is to keep them near the gang milling line. The incharge of this line may be made responsible for their safe custody. The issue should be controlled on imprecated system. The best way of exercising control over tools is that scrap tools should be returned against fresh tools. If tool stores are equipped with regrinding facilities, the tool life will be maximised, quick availability will be ensured and cost of fresh procurement will be saved assuring better utilisation of available funds elsewhere.

THE RECEIPT SYSTEM

Process

1. Receipts may be from outside suppliers and from internal sources such as returns from various departments and finished goods from the production department. The receipt system does not start at the time of actual receipt of the goods, it starts at the time of initiation of purchasing process. When a purchase order is placed, a copy is received by the stores section informing the quantity, delivery date and items ordered. Stores start making preparation for their receipts in the storehouse, In order to assess the volume of receipt at a given time, the copies of the receipt orders are arranged in a chronological order.

2. Now the stores section waits for the receipt of the compliance or advice letter, which is normally sent by the supplier after the despatch of the goods. It provides all details regarding goods despatched such as the date of despatch, carrier's note including all its details, description of the consignment and the scale. This enables the Materials Manager to take action for quick and easy clearance.

3. The third step is the preparation of transport carriers by the transporter. Suppliers employ different transport organisation for

transportation of their materials. Consignment notes are sent by these transport agencies with the help of which the stores office compares the goods received in the storehouse. The purchase order, supplier's advice document and consignment note help the materials management to organise and plan for expeditious clearance of materials and minimise costly demurrages, etc. If suppliers have sent package slip, the packages are compared with the packages received in the storehouse.

4. The above documents are put to use when the goods ordered actually arrive at the storehouse receipt section. The consignment received is identified with the help of these documents. Therefore, they are physically verified by the help of the columns of receipts. This process of identifying and verifying may prove to be very cumbersome. Therefore, fare-weight system may be used with more success and better results so far as the receipts are concerned. If goods arrived tallies with the three documents it is okayed but when there is shortage claims may be prepared and submitted to concerned persons within the time limit prescribed for the purpose in the agreement.

5. If there is excess supply it calls for additional procedure. The supplier in this case is either informed or excess supplied goods are required to be made.

Procedure After Clearance

1. A provisional goods inward note is prepared as soon as the goods are cleared from receipt section.

2. With this provisional goods inward note the goods are sent to the inspection section for inspection and clearance. This document details: (*i*) materials code, (*ii*) quantity received, (*iii*) rate, (*iv*) date of receipt, (*v*) carrier details, (*vi*) supplier details, (*vii*) location code, and (*viii*) description of materials.

3. Now the inspection department endorses this provisional goods inward note indicating that the Inspection is complete, accepted goods are clearly indicated in the note itself.

4. The inspection section prepares the inspection note or report and indicates the goods accepted and those rejected separately in the form of accepted note and rejected note or Acceptance and Rejection Note in one form.

5. Then a final goods inward note is prepared by the store section after the inspection report is received.

6. This note along with invoice, etc. is sent to accounts section for final payment. These documents should follow by a copy of the inspection report as well.

7. Shortage and excess report is also prepared, if there is any.

8. Goods are also received from within the departments returned to stores while transfer notes are exchanged. When scraps are returned 'scrap, card is' exchanged. When finished goods are sent the 'Finished Goods Note' is exchanged. Thereafter the goods are binned and appropriate action is taken.

Advantages of Integration of Inspection Department Under M.M. Dept

1. Reduction of the paper work;
2. Lesser materials movements and consequent less disadvantages;
3. Swift clearances of documents along with materials, etc;
4. The invoices, etc. are cleared paying the way for prompt payment.

Some of the organisations keep the inspection department under respective user departments. Generally, this is good arrangement and ensures quality production. But if production target is ambitious it may result into a trade off in quality building a bad image for the organisation.

Some organisations organise the inspection department independent of all. In such a case the manager incharge of quality control is asked to head inspection department also. He is made responsible to the General Manager. Following are the advantages of this arrangement:

1. Protection of quality standards of organisation ensured thereby maintaining the already built image of the product as well as the organisation;
2. Better co-ordination between suppliers, buyers and end users; and
3. The work is done smoothly and effectively.

If independent inspection department may adopt a rigid attitude so far as the quality is concerned. However, this may lead to delay, bad taste in relations and draining of resources.

Therefore, a midway is the best way in order to ensure better inspection and harmonious working environment in the organisation.

NORMS OF STOCKING

Stocking follows the receipts and inspection. In a bigger organisation the volume and variety of materials are towards the higher side. Therefore, it is necessary to demarcate the stores for which one should follow certain norms. The following should be earmarked for storing:

1. The area for stocking the materials for inspection. Such an area should be near the testing laboratories or inspection outfits or near both.

2. The area for stocking the materials coming out of inspection outfits and testing laboratories should be divided into distinct areas—one for accepted materials and another for rejected materials since both have to be distinctly dealt with.

3. The gangway for moving the accepted materials to the storehouse and rejected materials for preparing a consignment and making arrangement for their despatch to the suppliers.

Advantages of Stocking

1. Easy location;
2. Proper and correct identification;
3. Speedy binning;
4. Proper and correct recording from all points of view;
5. Speedy issuing to the consuming department; and
6. Efficient and smooth sailing and accomplishment of organisation's objective.

CONTROLS OF ISSUES FROM STORES SECTION

This is a sensitive issue which should be treated with all courtesy, thorough application of mind and better vision. It is a final stage in any storing activity.

Issues are broadly divided into two broader activities: (*i*) issues to consuming department, (*ii*) issues to outside suppliers for processing, conversion or for giving finishing touches. In both the cases the following are the issue system requirements:

(*i*) On production programmes and schedules.
(*ii*) On bill of materials.
(*iii*) On work orders received and urged to comply.
(*iv*) On listing of each material.

(*v*) On quantity against each component requiring that particular material.

(*vi*) On requisitions submitted by consuming department.

The above bases are good.to exercise control over the issues automatically. Consumption is required to be controlled. Quantity to be issued should correspond to quality of components to be manufactured. It is better to have a limit of issue authorised to issue only up to certain limit. Thereafter it would be the job of higher ups in the stores department. Top management's attention will form the basis of in-built control over the issues. If issues are being made on loan basis, proper register and proper authorised signatures of recipients and issuing personnel must be strictly followed in order to exercise fuller control.

THE DELEGATION OF AUTHORITY IN MATTERS OF ISSUES

Direct materials for which consumption norms are well established or can be easily established are controlled by work orders and corresponding requirements of the components. However, there are also certain items which are direct in nature but for which norms cannot be easily established such as fuel oil, electrodes, oxygen and tools. The control over these direct items can be exercised only through past experiences and proper delegation of authority in terms of value of unit depending upon the policy as well as nature of the organisation. If delegation is proper, unbiased and effective, responsibility in controlling the consumption can easily be established. Another controlling device is to have periodical consumption statement, review and report with advice and suggestions. Serial number controls can be maintained and issues and receipts are promptly recorded. Index are prepared, the records are updated and interests issues are properly recorded. Replenishment issues are properly guarded against any pilferage and theft.

Good stores system lessens the burden of the Stores Incharge. His time and energy is utilised for improving and better understanding. Significant advantages of a good stores system are stock position reports, expediting of bills for payment, timely detection of discrepancies, prompt clearance of claims, etc. and better understanding corroborated with good all-round relationship.

QUESTIONS FOR EXERCISE

1. "Purpose of warehousing is to keep and protect the goods warehoused but the purpose of storing is to receive, preserve, issue and meet the requirements of the whole organisation with operative efficiency and thoughtful handling." Explain and bring out the difference between warehousing and storing.
2. Compare and contrast location and layout of storehouse and warehouse. Elaborate important points to remember in their counteraction.
3. What are the problems of and developments in storing in India?
4. Explain the receipt system in the stores. Show the advantages of integrating inspection department under M.M. Department.
5. What are the norms of stocking? What are its advantages? Explain control of issues from store section.

40

State Trading and Marketing

In recent years, a growing tendency has been witnessed toward the conducting of international trade by the state. State trading refers to the socialisation of economic policy pertaining to foreign trade. In state trading, the government arranges all the details regarding the bulk purchases and sales of goods, fixing their prices, making payments, negotiating credit, etc. State trading, therefore, implies a partial or full monopoly of state in the sphere of international trade. In pure state trading the private trade is completely taken over by the state. The extent of state trading considerably differs among different countries. In socialist countries like the former Soviet Union and its satellites the foreign trade is an exclusive state monopoly. In the free economies like the United States of America only a small fraction of foreign trade is directly handled by the government. In between are countries like the United Kingdom, which import all or most of certain types of products through a state agency with the largest part of foreign trade being conducted by private traders.

Forms of State Trading

State trading can take the form of a government agency or monopoly which works according to the same principle as a private firm or it can be a government department or organisation which completely controls the country's foreign trade. State trading is an old-fashioned subject of international trade. In central Europe before World War I there used to be state monopolies of such commodities as tobacco and alcohol. However, the significant participation of state in foreign trade was seen at the time of World War I when states regulated and controlled foreign trade for defence and security purposes. After World War I, started the restoration period of free trade whose process of restoration had hardly been completed when the Great Depression of the 1930s gave a severe blow to the free trade policy. The Second World War gave the final blow to the free trade movement.

In the post-war period the need for speedy economic reconstruction of the war-shattered economies and the emergence of welfare states brought the entire filed of economic activities within the orbit of government intervention Today state trading is a world-wide phenomenon. Tire state trading both export and import are complete monopoly in the centrally planned economies of communist countries like the former U.S.S.R., China and other east and central European countries, 50 per cent of country's imports are in the hands of government, in England, the birth place of free trade. Some part of the foreign trade is conducted through the agency of state trading in the U.S.A., Canada, Australia and Sweden. State trading is quite important in many underdeveloped countries where the government have established control over imports and exports in order to control country' s foreign trade and improve the terms of trade. According to the United Nations Commission for Asia and the Far East, in the early 1960s about 80 per cent of export and 40 per cent of Burmese imports were controlled by state agencies. In India too state is playing a significant role and about 50 per cent of imports are conducted by the State Trading Corporation of India.

OBJECTIVES OF STATE TRADING

1. To preserve Foreign Exchange: State trading agencies are considered to be rational tools and potentially powerful weapons for preserving foreign exchange equilibrium and safeguarding the balance of payments position of a country.

2. To strengthen Bargaining Power: By monopolising foreign trade, state trading strengthens the bargaining power of the state.

3. To augment Government revenue: During the process of development of economic planning, state trading in commodities can be resorted to for augmenting the government revenues.

4. To Stabilise Prices: State may participate in international trade for stabilising the prices of essential raw materials and for diversifying the country's foreign trade.

5. To Provide Protection: State may also establish monopoly over foreign trade for providing protection to the domestic industries against foreign competition.

6. To Explore New Export Outlets: State trading explores greater and new export outlets and earns profit for financing the development projects in the country.

7. To Eliminate Malpractices: State trading is a powerful tool for the elimination of malpractices adopted by the private traders in the sphere of foreign trade.

ADVANTAGES OF STATE TRADING

1. Safeguard of National Interests: The development of a proper vision of international trade and a continuous watch for safeguarding the national interests are possible only through a state-owned trading agency.

2. Adjustment of Supply and Demand Prices: State trading can bridge the gap between the demand prices and the cost prices because the state is usually aware of the demand and supply situations. It can suitably adjust the prices of products in which it trades so as to minimise the gap between the demand for and supply of the goods handled by the state trading agency. Thus, state trading can serve as an effective; concomitant of a comprehensive development planning programme in a backward economy. In an inflationary situation, the technique of state trading can be utilised for adjusting the supply price to the demand price and the profit so obtained may be spent for financing the various development projects in the economy.

3. Industrial Coordination: State trading coordinates the whole country's trading machinery and assumes added responsibility for rationalisation and institutionalisation of trade policies.

4. Elimination of Evils: It eliminates several evils like tax evasion, unauthorised dealings in foreign exchange, speculation, black marketing and other such malpractices indulged in by private traders.

5. Supply and Sale: State trading encourages export promotion by supplying essential raw materials at reasonable prices and at assured time, and selling the country's export goods at better prices through enhanced monopolistic bargaining power.

6. Trade with Socialist Countries: State trading in the capitalist and mixed economies is intended to overcome the difficulties encountered while trading with the socialist countries where foreign trade is a complete monopoly of state.

7. Inculcation of Financial Discipline: Among the benefits of state trading the inculcation of a sense.of financial discipline is more important.

8. Minimisation of Inputs and Maximisation of Outputs: By making its management more efficient and careful, state trading minimises the cost of inputs and maximises output.

DISADVANTAGES OF STATE TRADING

1. Defects of Monopoly: State trading is a monopoly in internal trade. Monopoly is always injurious because monopolist is always interested in maximising his net monopoly gain which is not possible without the exploitation of consumers. A public monopoly is worse than its private counterpart because it is far more easier for the omnipotent state to bypass public criticism than it is for a private monopolist who is always afraid of the powerful grip of the state on his malpractices.

2. Inefficiency and Idleness: By eradicating competitors, state trading invites inefficiency and idleness. The talented private entrepreneurs are not given opportunity to enter the foreign trade sector.

3. Against the Principle of Comparative Cost Advantage: State trading functions against the principle of comparative cost advantage. Relative price differences are no longer the guiding principles for the allocation of productive resources.

4. Lack of Quick Decision: Due to its centralised bureaucratic administration state trading lacks in quick business decisions which are essential requirements in a dynamic international trade.

5. Unemployment: State trading hurts private traders and generates unemployment.

6. Non-economic Considerations: These become more important than economic considerations in the conduct of foreign trade when trade is in the hands of state than when it is in private hands. This is more so when the state has a complete monopoly of import and export trade and the state may arbitrarily shift its sources of supply of imports or its export markets. The foreign trade of

Eastern Europe in the post-war period had been deliberately directed towards the Soviet Union for political reasons.

7. Bargaining Spree: Political considerations apart, state trading on a large scale introduces public monopoly elements in the sphere of international trade. From a national point of view, a country may succeed in obtaining a larger share of gains from trade by pursuing monopolistic police is in her international economic relations through state trading reflected in the charging of higher prices for her exports and paying lower prices for her imports. But when other countries also engage in identical state trading activities bargaining replaces price comparisons as the guiding force of trade. In an atmosphere surcharged by bargaining spree, the ability of any one country to obtain the lion's share of the gains from trade becomes uncertain and dependent upon its relative bargaining strength.

8. No Relative Cost Comparisons: Apart from depending upon the extent of monopoly or monopsony in exporting or importing the effects of state trading on the volume and efficiency of international trade also depend upon the internal marketing policies. If the goods imported through state trading are sold in the country at prices that are either above or below the international market prices, the relative cost comparisons lose their important function of guiding international specialisation.

STATE TRADING IN INDIA

1. Deshmukh Committee: Since independence, the Government of India has attached great importance to the question of trading in commodities. The first Committee for its examination was appointed in 1949 under the chairmanship of Dr. P.S. Deshmukh. It recommended that the government might entrust its trading activities in foodgrains and fertilisers to statutory organisation which should be called the State Corporation. It also suggested that the S.T.C. might take over all the import and export operations of a commercial nature which were then handled by different departments of the Central Government. The Committee pointed out that in the case of certain luxury articles whose prices generally remain high state trading could be resorted to for the purpose of raising additional revenue.

2. The Rao Committee: The second committee, with Shri S.V. Krishnamurthy Rao as its Chairman, examined the question of state trading in the country during the second phase of the First Five Year Plan. It was of the opinion that in view of the changed world market conditions, it was not necessary to undertake imports of foodgrains, cotton and fertilisers through state-sponsored trading agency. The committee favoured the setting up of such an agency for dealing with the exports of handloom cloth and products of certain selected small-scale and cottage industries. Thus, both the Deshmukh and Rao Committees were in favour of prescribing a limited sphere for state trading in the country.

3. The Taxation Enquiry Commission: The Taxation Enquiry Commission (1953-54) also probed into the question of state trading. It did not oppose state trading but it pointed out that there was dearth of "personnel with specialised experience of business".

4. Second Five Year Plan: With the launching of ambitious development planning in India under the auspices of the Second Five Year Plan, the government was compelled to make a frantic effort to find additional sources of revenue for the public exchequer. Positive steps were taken by the government in the direction of state trading for this purpose. Almost simultaneously with the commencement of the Second Five Year Plan, the State Trading Corporation of India Ltd., was established with the blessing of the government.

STATE TRADING CORPORATION OF INDIA

1. Establishment: The State Trading Corporation of India Ltd., otherwise known as the STC, was registered in May 1956 under the Indian Companies Act. Not being a statutory corporation it has to comply with all the obligations and requirements of the Companies Act like any other limited company.

2. Activities: The main objective of STC is the broadening and enlarging of the scope of country's exports and the arranging of essential imports. The activities of the Corporation are directed toward diversification of country's exports, expansion of existing markets, development and promotion of exports of certain bulk commodities on a long-term basis and handling canalised imports of bulk commodities. The corporation undertakes price support and buffer stock operation in certain commodities on the directions from Government of India. It works in close association with trade and industry in the country.

3. STC Group: The STC group now comprises the STC, the Cashew Corporation of India (CCI), the Handicrafts and Handloom Export Corporation (HHEC), the Project and Equipment Corporation of India (PEC), the State Chemicals and Pharmaceuticals Corporation (CPC) and the Central Cottage Industrial Export Corporation.

4. Rapid Growth: STC has made a rapid growth since its inception in 1956. This growth is well reflected in the increase of its turnover from ₹ 9.2 crore during 1956-57 to over ₹ 3,500 crore during 1992-93. The STC has emerged as an important exporter accounting for more than 30 per cent of the total exports from the country on account of the unique export performance of the Corporation.

5. Export Programme: The export programme of the STC is divided into five main groups comprising the consumer goods, leatherware, industrial products, development of exports and producers' exports. The Engineering and Railway Equipment Divisions of the holding company the STC were taken over by its subsidiary PEC in April 1971. The exports of the STC comprise canalised and non-canalised items. To develop exports of the products of small and medium scale industries, the STC has organised assistance to small-scale industry through a separate State Marketing Division which liaises with the Small Industries Development Corporation both at the state and apex levels. The STC has been arranging imports of some capital goods and industrial raw materials and also of certain scarce commodities required for the country's economic and industrial development. Large quantities of soyabean oil, hops, chemicals, raw wool, art silk yam, newsprint, alkalies, tractors, printing and textile machinery, copra, palm oil and many other essential goods have been imported by the STC. In pursuance of government's policy to ensure fair prices to growers of agricultural commodities and to maintain internal production at reasonable level, the STC has from time to time undertaken price support and bufferstock operations in respect of jute, rubber, and tobacco. To keep in constant touch with the changing trends of trade in international markets, the STC has a network of offices located at Sydney, Hongkong, Bangkok, Singapore, Colombo, Beimt, Tehran, Nairobi, Lagos, Moscow, Belgrade, Budapest, Prague, East Berlin, London, Paris, Frankfurt, New York, Dar-es-Salaam, Buneos Aires and Dacca. The share of the STC in India's exports has increased from 4.6 per cent in 1970-71 to more than 35 per cent in 1992-93.

The paid-up capital of the STC which was ₹ 1 crore in 1956-57 at the time of establishment was doubled to ₹ 2 crore in 1958-59 and was again raised to ₹ 10 crore in 1973-74 through the issue of bonus shares. During more than three decades up to 1991-92 the Corporation has contributed more than ₹ 350 crore to the public exchequer.

Evaluation of STC's Working

1. Exploration: The STC devoted the first year of its existence to the exploration of markets, formulation of policies, experimentation with business methods and techniques and development of contacts with buyers and sellers both in India and abroad. It has been trying to negotiate link arrangements with foreign firms so that essential items may be imported against the exports of Indian manufactures. A large number of such arrangements were concluded with countries like West Germany, Vietnam and Hungry.

2. Promotion: Within a short period of four decades of its establishment, the STC has succeeded in concluding large and valuable business contracts. On the exports side, vigorous efforts have been made to consolidate and organise the trade in mineral ores which have so far constituted the bulk of the export business of the STC. It has been successfully developing new markets for Indian shoes, woollen fabrics and handicrafts. It takes part in international fairs to promote India's exports. It has also offices in many foreign countries. Economical arrangements have been made for the import of cement, raw silk, skimmed milk powder, caustic soda, soda ash and fertilisers, etc.

3. Restraint: Apart from promoting trade, the STC has exercised a healthy restraint on sharp fluctuations in prices especially in the field of fats and oils. It has also built up business ties with important trading bodies in the foreign countries like Japan and the U.S.A.

In short, the State Trading Corporation of India has distinctly made its mark in the field of foreign trade. Faced with the grave foreign exchange crisis, India requires an effective integration of her export promotion and import substitution policies. The STC can play an important role in this sphere. Apart from reshaping the country's foreign trade policies, the STC can also help in achieving the country's planned economic growth with social justice.

QUESTIONS FOR EXERCISE

1. What is state trading? What are its forms? Explain its objectives?
2. What are the advantages and disadvantages of state trading?
3. Write short note on state trading in India.

41

Regulated Markets

The exchange and marketing of goods are important in equalising the supply and demand in a planned economic development. Agricultural production poses great problem and difficulties in exchange functions. A regulated market is needed to ensure fairness in agricultural marketing and transactions, free competition, regulation of unfair malpractices, fair price to the producer (farmers) etc.

THE AGRICULTURAL PRODUCE MARKETING ACT

Various legislations have failed to maintain uniform rules and procedures throughout India. Thus, the Act lacks uniformity. There is absence of uniformity in the methods and procedures of the Act, which vary from state to state and from region to region within the same state. There is variation in area and enforcement of law, definition of agricultural produce, the byelaws of the constitution, composition of market committees, licence fees, market rates, trade practices, method of sale price quotation. For example, in Tamilnadu the cess is payable by the buyers while in Karnataka, Andhra and Maharashtra the producers bear them.

ORGANISATION OF REGULATED MARKETS

The object of regulated markets is to safeguard the interest of the producers-sellers and raise the standard of the local markets. The first exchange of goods takes place in the local markets. Committees are established in each regulated market.

MARKET COMMITTEE

Regulated market is a wholesale market, where dealings of buying and selling are regulated or controlled by the state government through a 'Market Committee' which consists of representatives of growers, traders, local bodies, marketing co-operative and the government. The Agricultural Produce Marketing Act governs the establishment and working of regulated markets in the prescribed area. The committee is responsible to ensure fair marketing practices.

Constitution

The seminar on regulated markets organised by the Ministry of Food and Agriculture in January 1959 was of the view that:

1. The Market Committee should not be too small or too wide. The strength of the committee must accommodate the various interests in proper proportion.
2. The number of committee members should be between 12 and 18 depending on the size of the market and other considerations.
3. 50 per cent of the seats go to growers, as their interest must be predominant in the committee.
4. For traders the seat shall be 25 per cent at the maximum.
5. The remaining seats shall go to the co-operative marketing societies, the local bodies and government nominees. One seat is reserved for warehousing corporations.

Indirect election is conducted to elect growers representatives through the grower-members of the panchayats and other registered growers associations and agricultural co-operatives.

Finance

The marketing committee receives its finance from the borrowed funds (government loans), government subsidies and grants and other sources including fines, market fees and licence fees, etc. Property incomes are rent on godowns, stalls, canteens, interests on government securities, etc., sale of grass grown on the yards, sale of manures, fees like registration fee, licence transfer fee, copying fee, certification fee, dispute fee, water and weighment charges, etc.

The fund is used for:

1. Maintenance and improvement of the market and its building.
2. Maintenance of standard weights and measures.
3. Salary and pension of the staff.
4. Payment of interest on loans.

5. Collection of market information
6. Propaganda for agricultural improvement.

The Market Committee frames and administers the rules and laws about business transactions conducted within the market area. It fixes the charges, allowances and deductions that can be levied. It looks after the weights and measures. Licensed weighmen do all weighing. Dealers fix the price and submit their accounts periodically to the Market Committee. The dispute sub-committee looks after the disputes, if any, arising between the sellers and traders. Following are the main functions of the committee:

1. Maintaining and management of market.
2. Enforcing the rules and bye-laws of the Act in the market area.
3. Granting licence on the purchase and sale of agricultural produce regulated by it.
4. Granting, renewing, suspending and cancelling a general or special finance for purchase and sale of regulated agricultural produce.
5. Providing all facilities in the market.
6. Fee on the produce which is purchased and sold in the market and it is collected by agents.
7. Managing the income, incurs expenditure and invests the surplus funds.
8. Preparing the budget.
9. Maintaining a register of licensed traders and general commission agents and records the fees collected.
10. Prescribing the market charges, for different market functions.
11. Preventing adulteration of agricultural produce in the market area.
12. Promoting grades and standardising the agricultural produce.
13. Collecting and maintaining the price list of regulated agricultural produce and supplying it to the government when required.
14. Appointing the secretary of the committee.
15. Directing and guiding the persons who use the market.
16. Settling disputes, if any, in the course of transactions.
17. Acting as clearing house to market information-collection and distribution of essential data on markets.

18. Facilitating smooth transfer of good; and orderly transactions.
19. Facilitating the producers to get the best possible price for their produce.
20. Providing proper storage facility.
21. Preventing adulteration in the produces.

ADVANTAGES OF REGULATED MARKETS

1. Reduction in Market Charges: Paid by the producer-seller the reduction is between 28 per cent and 69 per cent in various markets. There is reduction in charges of commission, weighing fee, hamali brokerage, charity, etc. The net saving of producer-seller is about 3 per cent or 5 per cent of the selling produce.

2. Increase in the Number of Sellers: More sellers bring their produce to these markets. The producers assembling markets for rice and wheat are about 73 per cent in the Punjab, 80 per cent in Karnataka, 74 per cent in Madhya Pradesh and 90 per cent in Andhra,

3. Changes in the Social Behaviour: There is a change in the social behaviour of the influential, powerful and economically well off trading section towards the illiterate, ignorant, indebted and economically backward cultivators. They divert their attention to fair trading. Responsibilities are vested with the licensed traders and commission agents of the Market Committee.

4. Clearly Defined and Specified Market Charges: There is reduction in excessive charges and prohibition in unwarranted charges.

5. Assurances of Fair Dealings: There are regulated market charges, and market functions are controlled in order to reduce the marketing cost.

6. Correct Weighing: Periodical verification and inspection of scales and weights assure correct weighing of their produce. Standard weights and measures are used in the regulated markets, *i.e.,* the metric system.

7. Settlement of Disputes: A machinery is set up for the settlement of disputes between traders and sellers. It creates good relation between the sellers and buyers by arranging settlement of disputes regarding quality, weighing and deduction, preventing litigation, etc.

8. Market News Service: Current market news are available to the sellers. Price conditions in various markets are exhibited on the notice board. Newspapers and radio announce the market price. The ruling prices are announced through loudspeakers in many markets.

9. Fair Prices to the Farmers: As there is perfect competition agricultural produces are sold by open methods, benefiting the farmers.

10. Grading and Storing Facilities: These are provided in many regulated markets. Agmark standards, grade specification are framed by an expert committee.

Advantages of Market Committees

1. Amenities: Market committees have provided following amenities in the market yards:

(*i*) Shed for the Sale off produce.

(*ii*) Car parking places.

(*iii*) Drinking water facilities for human beings and cattle.

(*iv*) Rest houses and canteens for farmers.

2. Advertisement for Agricultural Inputs: Proper advertisement is made for agricultural improvements such as use of good seed, fertilisers, pesticides, etc. Regulated markets undertake improved methods of cultivation, use of machinery in farming, etc.

3. Prompt Payment: The producer can receive prompt payment of a fair price from the buyer.

4. Marketing Information: Producers, usually unorganised, are few, scattered and ill-informed about the market condition. Regulated market helps them in these matters. Their interest is protected and they get a fair deal in marketing their produce. Reliable statistics regarding the arrivals, stocks price, etc. is available.

5. Elimination of Middlemen: Elimination of unwanted middlemen is possible only by regulated markets.

DEVELOPMENT OF REGULATED MARKETS

1. Royal Agricultural Commission: In India Regulated Markets were developed as per the recommendations of Royal Commission on Agriculture. In 1928 the Royal Commission on Agriculture observed that various defects of rural and agricultural marketing could be removed only by the establishment of regulated markets. Regulated markets were developed to improve the markets, to increase fair competitive conditions and strong bargaining powers of farmers. Its main object was to regulate sale and purchase of the agricultural products and create conditions for a fair competition.

2. Cotton and Grain Markets Law: In 1897 the Cotton and Grains Markets Law enacted in Berar was passed, "to make available supplies of pure cotton at reasonable price to the textile mills at Manchester." It provided a representative committee which controlled the markets and bazaars.

3. Indian Cotton Committee: In 1917, the Indian Cotton Committee was set up which recommended the regulation of cotton market on the lines of Berar markets.

4. Bombay Cotton Markets Act: In 1927, the Bombay Cotton Markets Act was passed. So far the produces of the farmers were sold to the trader-lender in the village, at a price which was lower than the market rate. In other cases, the produces passed through many middlemen who grabed the major portion of price paid by purchasers. The balance, an inadequate price, went to the cultivator. Hence, the Government notified cotton markets and appointed committees to manage the markets.

5. Bombay Provincial Banking Enquiry Committee: In 1929-1930, the Bombay Provincial Banking Enquiry Committee was appointed to point out the defects in the working of the traditional markets.

6. Other Acts: The Hyderabad Agricultural Markets Act was passed in 1930. In 1935 the Central Provinces Agricultural Produce Act was passed. The Berar Act was modified in 1932-35 by the Central Provinces Cotton Markets Act. The Bombay Agricultural Produce Market Act of 1939 replaced the Bombay Act. In 1933, the Madras Commercial Crops Marketing Act was passed and it applied to cotton, groundnuts and tobacco. In 1948 it was extended to other crops. Bombay, Madras, Hyderabad, Gwalior and Baroda also passed similar Acts.

7. Number of Regulated Markets: The total number of regulated markets increased after the passing of these Acts. In 1939 it was 122; in 1950-51 it was 283; in 1955-56 it was 450; in 1960-61 it was 700 and in 1965-66 it was 1012. At the end of the third five-year plan it was 1600. In 1988 there were 10,512 regulated markets in the country.

8. Market Regulation: Market regulation is enacted by the State Governments and assisted by the Central Directorate of Marketing and Inspection. The Central Directorate gives financial assistance for developing regulated markets in the following areas:

(*i*) command areas;

(*ii*) economically backward areas;

(*iii*) areas producing commercial crops like jute, cotton and tobacco.

Foodgrains are regulated in all the states except Andhra and Kerala. Only a few markets cover agricultural products like fruits and vegetables, livestock and their products.

When legislation is applied to a particular cash market, it is called a regulated market which works under standard rules and regulations. It has an organised character in all respect. A market committee is in charge of management and operations of regulated market.

In his book *'Agricultural Marketing: Theme of the Seventies'*, P.R. Dubhashi says, "The regulated market is not only a place where certain legal conditions are enforced, it is also a centre which provides a package of facilities to agricultural marketing and an economic centre where adequate demand is built up for the sale of agricultural produce. It would be possible to develop the regulated markets not only for marketing agricultural commodities, but also for providing numerous facilities to meet the needs of agricultural machinery." In India, state and central Government are taking concerted action to bring about all round development in the field of marketing.

ORGANISED MARKET

An organised market is public market mechanism or organisation consisting of buyers, sellers, producers, processors, dealers, etc., dealing in one or more commodities or securities which constitute the articles of trade in the market. It is a private voluntary association, consisting of dealers, and professional traders of one or more commodities or securities. In it members meet and conduct buying and selling operations on the trading floor on behalf of their clients. The workings of the organised market are governed by the bye-laws of the market.

Regulated market is an organised wholesale or central market regulated and controlled by the State Government through a marketing committee; whereas the transactions in an organised market are governed by some standard procedure. The rules are framed by voluntary association.

Characteristics

1. **Meeting Place:** It is a convenient central meeting place for buyers and sellers.

2. **Demand and Supply:** It facilitates establishing a close and continuous interaction between demand and supply.

3. **Authority:** An authority governs all business by the established rules and regulations. It is a self-discipline, self-administered and self-regulated autonomous body.

4. **Legislation:** There is legislation to control these organised markets.

5. **Freedom:** In organised markets there is free competition and perfect freedom between buyers and sellers.

6. **Price Registering Device:** A sensitive price registering device is used here.

7. **Clearing House:** Each forward market has a clearing house organisation which clears all dealings and their settlement. It guarantees payment of dues and takes and gives the commodity or securities during the settlement period.

8. **Margin system:** Margin system is common in forward dealings.

9. **Information.** Organised market provides market information.

10. **Price Barometer:** It acts as a price barometer. Perfect market requirements are fulfilled by it.

11. **Speculation:** Speculative trading is necessary in an organised market.

12. **Two Types of Markets:** These organised markets are of two types, *viz.*, organised commodity markets and organised stock markets, popularly known as Commodity Exchanges and Stock Exchanges respectively.

QUESTIONS FOR EXERCISE

1. What is a Regulated Market? Explain the constitution and functions of the Market Committee in this context.

2. Write a short note on the advantages of Regulated Markets with particular reference to India.
3. Trace the development of Regulated Markets in India.
4. What is an Organised Market? What are its characteristics and types?

42

Money Market Trends and Development in India

NON-BANKING FINANCIAL COMPANIES

Non-banking financial companies (NBFCs) have grown in number and volume of business by entering areas which banks were not allowed to enter due to regulatory restrictions. They are mobilising public savings and investing them in the market. The attention of monetary authorities has been drawn to the need for regulation of these companies. RBI constituted a working group on financial companies, whose recommendations are being implemented in phased manner. Non-Banking financial companies with net owned funds of ₹ 50 lakh and over are now required to register with RBI. On June 13, 1994, RBI issued guidelines for these companies covering prudential and income recognition norms, accounting standards, provisioning for bad and doubtful debts, capital adequacy ratio and concentration of credit/investments. They will have to achieve a minimum capital adequacy norm of six per cent, on their risk weighted assets and off-balance sheet exposures, by March 31, 1995 and a ratio of 8 per cent will have to be attained by March 31, 1996. Inter-corporate deposits have also been brought within the discipline of the regulatory framework.

The registered non-banking finance companies will have to obtain rating by one of the credit rating agencies, at least once a year. This will provide objective information to depositors and creditors and help in protecting their interests. Companies with net owned funds of ₹ 2 crore and above have to get their first rating by the end of 1994-95, while companies with net owned funds, of ₹ 50 lakh to ₹ 2 crore must obtain the first rating by March 31, 1996. The existing RBI directions will continue to apply till the new norms are implemented. Their half yearly returns will be used for monitoring compliance with the prudential norms. The deposit limits for registered Loan and Investment companies have, however, been raised from 40 per cent of net owned funds to 100 per cent. Deposits are defined inclusive of non-convertible debenture/bond issues. With the new regulations, the assets side of the operations of financial companies will come under regulatory framework and due attention will also be given to the quality of assets. This is expected to strengthen, the companies and help ensure orderly development of the financial sector.

MONEY MARKET DEVELOPMENTS AND TRENDS

Money markets play an important role in the deployment of short-term funds, and in signalling trends in liquidity and interest rates. These markets, therefore, provide information for monetary policy formulation and management. During the current financial year so far, money markets reflected a fairly steady trend, but for some turbulence witnessed in the months of September and December 1994 and February 1995 during which there were very sudden and large increases in call money rates. This highlighted the urgent need for better monitoring as well as broad basing, deepening and integrating money markets.

Inter-bank Call Money Market

The strong growth in primary liquidity arising from the growth in Reserve Money was the underlying factor responsible for the low level of inter-bank daily average call money rate (2.5-6 per cent) during the calendar year 1994 till August. Average daily inter-bank call money rates shot up to 53 per cent towards the end of September 1994. The call money rates subsequently came down to 2 per cent by the end of September 1994. Spurts in rates was, witnessed in both December 1994 and February 1995.

The stringent conditions in the call money market in September and December 1994 were partly attributable to flotation of six State Government loans and advance tax payments. Since the coupon rate of 12.5 per cent offered on State Government loans was attractive, the aggregate subscriptions received for these loans were as high as ₹ 3,991.43 crore as against the notified amount of ₹ 613.43 crore. Banks did not correctly anticipate the volume of refunds of oversubscription on State Government loans and the cash needed for meeting the statutory CRR. This led to shooting up of call money rates in September 1994. In December, call money rate rose sharply because during the fortnight December 10-23, 1994, the Government also siphoned off about ₹ 4,200 crore of liquidity through the PSU equity sale, advance tax payments and the second instalment on the partially paid Government security. Yet during this fortnight, there was a very mild tightening of liquidity in the market and the money market rates rose moderately, possibly because of RBI injecting additional liquidity through Discount and Finance House of India (DFHI) and Securities Trading Corporation of India (STCI). Another factor leading to fluctuations in call money rates was that some banks had been chronic large borrowers in the call/notice money market for maintaining their Cash Reserve Ratio. These banks had invested in medium and long-term assets by borrowing in the call money market, hoping to be able to roll over their requirements in the future. Ostensibly such borrowing was profitable because of low call money rates. Some banks had run down their cash balances with the Reserve Bank to as low a level as 10 per cent of required cash reserves. This asset-liability mismatch, magnified the volatility in the Call/Notice Money market in September and December 1994. To ensure more orderly conditions in the Call/Notice Money market and also to reduce volatility, banks have been directed by RBI to ensure that their cash balances with RBI does not fall below 85 per cent of the prescribed CRR on each of the first 13 days of the fortnight beginning January 7, 1995, and is expected to greatly attenuate the fortnightly swings in call rates.

Certificates of Deposit (CDS)

There has been a lack of interest among banks in issuing fresh CDs since 1993-94. Secondary market activity in CDs also was non-existent, because every holder sought to keep CDs till maturity. The stock of outstanding CDs declined sharply from ₹ 9803 ciore on March 19, 1993 to ₹ 5571 crore on March 18, 1994. The number of issuing banks also declined from 51 to 48 over the same period. Interest rates which had ranged from 12.5 to 16.5 per cent, were down to the 7 to 12.2 per cent range. There is no bank-wise limit for issue of CDs and banks are free to issue CDs depending upon their requirements. This is tantamount to freeing of CD rates at the wholesale end of the deposit market. The activity has marginally picked up, with outstandings rising to ₹ 5385 crore (by 44 banks at 7.5 to 12.5 per cent interest rate) as on January 8, 1995. The easy conditions in the CD market were, therefore, largely due to the comfortable liquidity position of banks.

Commercial Paper

Rate offered on Commercial papers (CPs) showed a gradual decline in 1993-94. They were in the range 9.35 to 9,50 per cent during November- December 1993. The Indian Banks' Association advised banks in 1993-94 not to suscribe to CPs with a yield below 12.5 per cent per annum. This advice was not effective, as CPs were being taken up at lower rates of 10.5-11.5 per cent. Outstanding stocks of CPs were ₹ 3.264 crore at the end of March 1994 and expanded to ₹ 4511.05 crore at the end of August 1994. The level of outstanding CP came down significantly to ₹ 1393.25 crore as on February 15, 1995. Banks are the principal holders of such paper, and to some extent, lending to well rated companies through CPs was a substitute for direct bank credit in 1993-94.

Issuance of CPs used to result in a reduction of the cash credit limit and *vice versa.* This assured repayment of CPs on maturity, since the issuer company could automatically draw on the cash credit limits, in case of non-roll-over. Companies could also obtain a high credit rating because of this arrangement. RBI has recently stopped this system by abolishing the standby arrangement. When a CP is issued, banks will have to effect a pro-tanto reduction in the cash credit limit. Subsequently, if the issuer wants a higher cash credit limit, he will have to approach the bank afresh and the bank will then take a decision, based on market conditions at that time. This will make Commercial paper a more independent money market instrument, with its rating reflecting the intrinsic strength of the company.

91 Day Treasury Bills

In the weekly auctions for 91 day Treasury Bills conducted since January 1993, a gross amount of ₹ 15,850 crore was raised in 1993-94 and ₹ 11,650 crore (up to December 24, 1994) in 1994-95. The implicit yield at cut off prices ranged between 7.15 per cent and 11.40 per cent in 1994-95 (up to February 1995), compared to 7.08 per cent to 11.10 per cent in 1993-94. The stock of auctioned Treasury Bills outside the Reserve Bank has increased progressively to ₹ 5,245 crore on March 31, 1994 from ₹ 1,646 crore as on December 24, 1994. The outstanding stock of Treasury Bills is affected not just by the issue of new bills and by their maturity, but also by the somewhat unique Indian practice of conversion of Treasury Bills into dated securities 91 day auction Treasury Bills of face value of Rs, 4,088. ₹ 31 crore were converted on October 15, 1993 into 2 year Government stock, carrying a coupon rate of 12 per cent. Again, on April 7, 1994, 91 day auctioned Treasury Bills were converted into 5 year Government stock at the same coupon rate of 12 per cent. Regular weekly auctions have been held in these bills, in which there has been very encouraging participation. The number of bids received for 91 day auction Treasury Bills varied in the range of 4 and 65 during 1993-94 and between 6 and 82 during 1994-95 (up to December 23, 1994). The amount of bids received varied in the range of ₹ 20 crore to ₹ 2,350 crop during 1993-94 and from ₹ 28 crore to ₹ 1,838 crore during 1994-95 (up to February 25, 1995). While RBI subscription was practically nill between May 1993 to January 1994, RBI subscribed in many auctions during the subsequent period up to February 15, 1995, for amounts ranging from ₹ 16 crore to ₹ 477 crore.

Demand for these bills is no longer solely governed by SLR considerations and the secondary market transactions in them are being increasingly driven by the felt need for effective management of short-term liquidity by the participants. The value of secondary market transactions as given in SGL Account was ₹ 17,987 crore during September to November 1994.

364 Day Treasury Bills

In the fortnightly auctions for 364 day Treasury Bills, a gross amount of ₹ 20,323 crore was raised during 1993-94 and an amount (gross) of ₹ 16,469 crore (up to December 23, 1994) during 1994-95. This has not only become an important instrument of Government borrowing, but also a leading money market instrument in the sense that its yield is most reflective of market conditions. It has been recognised as an anchor rate by the financial institutions for floating interest rate instruments. The fortnightly offerings of these bills are not perannounced and the RBI does not subscribe to these bills, which are entirely held by the market. The yield on 364 day Treasury Bills is, therefore, sensitive to market liquidity trends. The implicit cut off yield of 364 day Treasury Bills gradually declined from a peak of 11.36 per cent in June 1994 to 9.41 per cent in September 1994 and thereafter moved upwards again to 11.48 per cent in February 1995. 364 day Treasury Bills have also been funded twice, in 1993-94 and once in 1994-95. The outstanding balance amount has risen from ₹ 8,385.97 crore (after funding) as on March 31, 1994 to ₹ 9749.15 crore (after another funding) on February 17, 1995.

The number of bids received for 364 day Treasury Bills varied in the range of 15 to 162 in 1993-94 and 9 to 165 in 1994-95 (up to February 17, 1995). The amount of bids received range from ₹ 77 crore to ₹ 5,147 crore during 1993-94 and from ₹ 11 crore to ₹ 4028 crore up to February 17, 1995 during 1994-95. Conversion of 364 day Treasury Bills was undertaken thrice, amounting to ₹ 6,946 crore at 12.75 per cent for a three year government stock, ₹ 11,226 crore at 12.5 per cent for a ten year government stock and ₹ 8,078 crore at 11.75 per cent for a six year government stock on April 19, 1993, March 23, 1994 and August 25, 1994 respectively.

Discount and Finance House of India

The success rate of the Discount and Finance House of India (DFHI) in the Treasury Bills auctions (accepted to total bids) has improved from 40 per cent in 1993-94 to 50 per cent in the current year and its Treasury Bills' turnover has increased by 45.5 per cent, compared to turnover in the corresponding period of the last financial year. The total turnover in Government dated securities has however come down in the current financial year. The maturity structure of lending his shifted from long to short term (call and notice money markets). The shrinking trend in lendings started in 1993-94 and has continued in 1994-95.

Credit Rating

Reforms in the financial sector have greatly enhanced the role of credit rating agencies. Credit Rating Information Services of India Ltd. (CRISIL), which is a pioneer in credit rating not only rates debt instruments of banks, financial institutions and companies (non-banking financial and non-financial), but also makes credit assessment of companies and provides various information products like CRISIL VIEW and CRISIL RATING SCAN. Its Credit Assessment is used by State Bank of India and other banks as an input in their decision making process on advances. During the current financial year up to December 31, 1994, CRISIL rated 278 debt instruments with a total volume of ₹ 13742 crore. This means a cumulative total of 1284 debt instruments with a debt volume of over ₹ 61,049 crore rated since its inceptions. During the current financial year, CRISIL developed a methodology for rating development projects, fixed income mutual funds and chit funds.

The other important credit rating institutions, namely, Investment Information and Credit Rating Agency of India (ICRA) which rates bonds, debentures, preference shares, CDs and CPs, rated a cumulative total of 420 instruments for ₹ 14,713 crore, as on December 31, 1994. In the current financial year, up to December 31, 1994, it rated a total number of 147 debt instruments for ₹ 2,419 crore.

GOVERNMENT SECURITIES MARKET

Market Borrowing

As noted earlier, the Central Government has shifted much of its borrowing to the market. The main instruments used for this purpose are dated securities, 364 day and 91 day Treasury Bills. There is also a small proportion of conventional market borrowing. Total market borrowing at market rates of interest, excluding 91 day Treasury Bills, during the First nine months of this financial year has been of the order of about ₹ 17,000 crore. This is 12 per cent higher than the market borrowing of about ₹ 15000, crore in the first nine months of last financial year. The structure of net borrowing has also undergone a transformation. Last year, 89 per cent of net market borrowing was in the form of medium- and long-term loans, while amount raised through 364 day Treasury Bills actually declined. In the current year, medium- and long-term loans constitute only 66 per cent of net market borrowing. The proportion of 364 day Bills has increased to almost 16 per cent.

Institutional Development

With the setting up of the National Stock Exchange, the institutional market for trading in debt instruments has now become available. The NSE started operations in June 1994 by first activation trading in debt instruments. The volume of trading in debt instruments though currently very low has reached ₹ 244.22 crore in the week ended January 21, 1925. The type of instruments traded have included Units of Unit 64 Scheme, Government Securities, Treasury Bills, PSU bonds, Commercial Paper and Certificates of Deposit. The recording of transactions has improved with computerisation of Subsidiary General Ledger (SGL) accounts at RBI's six public debt offices. It has also started releasing on a daily basis, particulars of transactions in Government securities and Treasury Bills put through the SGL accounts. This will provide useful market information, dissemination of which is expected to foster improvement in market efficiency by providing reference rates/prices to all market participants. The Securities Trading Corporation of India was set up in 1993-94 to develop the secondary market in Government securities. It received the certificate of incorporation in May 1994. It has a fully issued paid up capital of ₹ 100 crore and started operations in June 1994.

Primary Dealers

To strengthen the market for Government securities, RBI is launching a system of primary dealers. These dealers are to function as underwriters for the auction of Government securities market. They are expected to act as market makers and RBI will provide credit facilities to them to impart liquidity to their operations. They will also have certain obligations in terms of their presence in auctions, and offer of two way quotes for these securities, besides being subject to prudential norms. The system of primary dealers is necessary for deepening and expanding the market for strengthening the effectiveness of monetary operations.

Partly Paid Government Stock

The Government recently introduced a new dated security called "partly paid Government stock", with standard auction procedures. It has an innovative feature, if the payment can be made in four equal installments. ₹ 2000 crore of securities of eight year maturity were auctioned and then allotted on partly paid basis to successful bidders on November 15, 1994. One-fourth of the face value plus premium, if any, was payable on the allotment date and the balance would be payable in three equal installment on December 15, 1994, January 16, 1995 and February 15, 1995.

Inter-bank Security Transactions

Reserve Bank of India reviewed inter-bank transactions in securities against Bank receipt (BRs) after the report of the Joint Parliamentary Committee (JPC) and has introduced a number of restrictions on the use of BRs in them. The validity period of BRs has been reduced from 30 days (as stipulated earlier in June 1992) to 15 days. It has further advised banks that BRs should be redeemed only by actual delivery of scrips and not by cancellation of transactions/set-off against another transaction within the stipulated period. Otherwise, they should be deemed as dishonoured. In case of default, the bank issuing BR has to refer the case to RBI, explaining the reasons for non-delivery of scrips and the proposed manner of settlement of the transaction. Banks have been warned that any violation of the instruction relating to BRs will invite penal action. This includes raising of reserve requirements, withdrawal of refinance from RBI and denial of access to the money market, or such other penalty as the RBI may deem fit.

On December 21, 1992, banks had been advised, *inter alia*, to ensure that transactions in securities entered into through individual brokers during a year should not exceed five per cent of total transactions (both purchases and sales) entered into by a bank during that year. If for any reason it had become necessary to exceed this limit for any broker, the specific reason thereof should be recorded in writing by the authority empowered and the Board should be informed of this *post-facto*.

Following the Joint Parliamentary Committee report, the need for continuance of the services of brokers was examined by RBI. It has been decided that securities transactions should henceforth be undertaken directly between banks and no bank should engage the services of any broker in these transactions. Banks may, however, undertake securities transactions among themselves or with non-bank clients through members of the National Stock Exchange (NSE), wherein transactions are transparent.

Transactions by banks in securities with non-bank clients, can be done either through the NSE or directly without the use of brokers. Any violation or circumvention of these instructions will also invite penal action, similar to that stipulated for violation of instructions regarding the use of BRs.

DEVELOPMENTS IN THE CAPITAL- MARKET

Capital markets play a key role in the economy as the source of investible funds for the corporate sector. The primary market, which was subdued in the first quarter of 1994-95, regained its buoyancy in the second quarter. The secondary market also exhibited considerable activity, with foreign institutional investors and domestic mutual funds, strengthening the process of institutionalisation of the market. The process of capital market reform continued and coupled with an effective regulatory framework, aimed at improving market efficiency, making stock market transactions more transparent, curbing unfair trade practices, and bringing the capital market upto international standards. The National Stock Exchange of India, which started functioning this year with its screen-based and scripless trading system, can be regarded as a milestone in the development of the Indian capital market. Besides, Bombay and other stock exchanges speeded up the pace of automation in their trading systems. These steps taken together will help facilitate the emergence of a strong and vibrant domestic capital market.

Strengthening of SEBI

The Government has, on January 25, 1995, promulgated an Ordinace to amend the Securities and Exchange Board of India Act, 1992 so as to arm the Securities and Exchange Board of India (SEBI) with additional powers for ensuring the orderly development of the capital market and to enhance its ability to protect the interests of the investors.

To enable SEBI to respond speedily to market conditions and to reinforce its autonomy, SEBI has also been empowered to file complaints in courts without the prior approval of the Central Government, and to notify its Regulations without the prior approval of the Central Government.

The amendments provide SEBI with regulatory powers over corporates in the issuance of capital, the transfer of securities and other related matters. It has also been empowered to impose monetary penalties on capital market in termediaries and other participants for a listed range of violations. Hitherto, the SEBI Act provided for the suspension and cancellation of registration and for the prosecution of intermediaries. As suspension and cancellation lead to the stoppage of business, often adversely affecting others who have had business with the affected intermediary, monetary penalties constitute an alternative mechanism for dealing with capital market violations. It is proposed to create an adjudicating mechanism within SEBI for levying penalties and it is also proposed to constitute a separate Tribunal to deal with cases of appeal against orders of the adjudicating authority. The appellate authority against orders of the Tribunal will be High Courts.

The amendments also provide for deletion of the existing provisions relating to disqualification of a member of the Board of SEBI on his being appointed as Director of a company. This amendment will enable the Government to appoint Directors with expertise and experience of the capital market.

SEBI has also been empowered to summon the attendance of, and call for documents from, all categories of market intermediaries, including persons in the securities market, in order to enable SEBI to investigate irregularities. SEBI will now also have powers to issue directions to all intermediaries and persons associated with the securities market with a view to protecting investors or securing the orderly development of the securities market.

Options Trading

An Ordinace was promulgated on January 25, 1995 for amending the Securities Contract (Regulation) (SCR) Act, 1956 which deletes Section 20 of the SCR Act. This includes the reference to 'prohibition of option' and consequently paves the way for trading in options, which will enhance liquidity in the market. The amendments also reduce the time limit from six months to two months for Stock Exchanges to amend their bye-laws, if so directed by SEBI, and provide for a Stock Exchanges to establish additional trading floors with the prior approval of SEBI. It is also specifically provided that any corporate seeking listing on a Stock Exchange would have to comply with the provisions of the listing agreements of the Stock Exchange, with violations of the listing agreements being punishable under the Act.

Primary Market Reforms

The SEBI has introduced various guidelines and regulatory measures for capital issues for healthy and efficient functioning of the market. Firms are required to make material disclosure about the risk factors in their offer prospectus and get debt instruments rated. Efforts have been made to reduce the cost of raising capital. Merchant bankers now have a greater degree of accountability in the offer document and issue process. Steps have been taken to ensure that continuous disclosures are made by firms which will enable shareholders to make comparisons between promises and performance. The minimum application size had been increased, and the number of mandatory collection centres reduced. The proportion of each issue allowed for firm allotment to institutions such as mutual funds, has been raised; besides, underwriting which was hitherto mandatory, has been made optional subject to several conditions.

Secondary Market Reforms

Since 1992, decade old trading systems in Indian Stock Exchanges have been under constant review. The main deficiencies have been identified in two broad areas: (*i*) the clearing and settlement system in stock exchanges, whereby delivery of shares by the seller and payment by the purchaser is made, and (*ii*) procedures for transfer of shares in the name of the purchaser by the company. Current procedures result in excessive paper work, delays in settling transactions and non-transparency in costs and prices at which customer's order are executed. Measures have been initiated by the Government and SEBI for the setting up of depositories. By immobilisation of securities, this will help eliminate paper work and add impetus to the growth of markets.

DEVELOPMENT OF BADLA SYSTEM

1. The prevalence of "badla" in the stock market had often been identified as a factor encouraging speculative activity. As part of the process of establishing transparent rules for trading, the "badla" system was discontinued by SEBI in December 1993, The SEBI directed the Stock Exchanges at Bombay, Calcutta, Delhi and

Ahmedabad on December 13, 1993 to enforce that all transactions in securities are concluded by delivery and payment and not to allow any carry forward of transactions. Besides, they were also asked to direct members to liquidate their carry-forward positions in a phased manner. This was done in order to ensure the safety of the market in the context of the building up of excessive speculative positions.

2. On March 11, 1994, SEBI decided to permit carry forward facility in specified shares in these exchanges under a framework of transparency and effective regulation. The new trading system proposed by SEBI envisaged that all stock brokers would be required to pay and settle their net position at the end of a settlement period. The Stock Exchanges were however supposed to introduce the new system of trading with carry-forward facility only after they satisfied SEBI that they were in a position to implement the system as proposed.

3. As the major Stock Exchanges could not set up the necessary mechanism for implementing the new trading system in specified shares as formulated by SEBI, trading in specified shares has been taking place without carry-forward of transactions. Accordingly, transactions in securities in the major stock exchanges moved to a system of settlement characterised by delivery and payments. Such a shift in the pattern of trading has strengthened the cash market in securities. The settlement periods have been shortened and settlement on delivery basis attempted. The renewal (postponement of settlement or delivery of scrips) of transactions in 'B' group securities have been prohibited. The various stock exchanges have however indicated their inability to reduce the accounting period from 14 to 7 days. Among the reasons given are procedural requirements, and the delay in receipt of shares/ payment from outstation clients.

4. SEBI's decision to ban the traditional system of "badla" has, however, been criticised in some quarters on the ground that it has adversely affected liquidity and the volume of trading in the market. Both SEBI and the Government are aware of this argument and hold that trading in stock exchanges should largely be guided by principles of safety of the market, transparency and investor protection.

Depositors' Legislation

The settlement of transactions in securities in stock exchanges of the country involves physical delivery of scrips along with duly filled in transfer deeds. The substantial growth in the volume of business in stock exchanges during recent years has rendered the traditional system of settlement of transactions obsolete and made it necessary to replace it by a new and modern Depositories system. The new system will eliminate paper work, facilitate electronic book entry of the transfer of securities, permit automatic and transparent screen-based trading in securities, shorten settlement periods and improve liquidity in investment in securities. Work on bringing forward the necessary legislation for the establishment of depositors is currently at an advanced stage.

NATIONAL STOCK EXCHANGE OF INDIA (NSEI)

Many secondary market problems can only be completely solved by introducing scripless trading and de-materialisation of scrips in depositories. A beginning has been made with the establishment of National Stock Exchange of India (NSEI). Though formally inaugurated in July 1994, NSEI commenced operations in the Wholesale Debt Market (WDM) in June 1994, and trading in equities had been started in the Capital Market (CM) segment in November 1994. A large number of members are successfully trading from their respective offices through NSE's Very Small Aperture Terminal (VSAT) based satellite network. The exchange has opened membership to 13 cities, including Bombay, and operations from other cities are expected to commence shortly using the satellite network.

As a national exchange, it has set fairly stringent criteria for membership in terms of net worth, education and experience, to ensure that trading members are well capitalised and can provide other professional services to investors. The main participants in the Wholesale Debt Market (WDM) segment (Government Securities, Treasury Bills, PSU bonds, CDs, CPs and corporate debentures) are banks, financial institutions and large corporates. RBI has recently directed banks to use only the NSE for all transactions in debt securities done earlier through brokers to ensure transparency and facilitate regulation (in place of the unregulated telephone market). This has raised the volume on NSE's debt trade substantially.

In the capital market segment, the number of securities admitted to trading expanded from 200 to start with to 525 by December 1994. Trading volumes have been gradually increasing since then. An NSE 100 Interim Index was launched on the basis of their market capitalisation and trade volumes. In the absence of a depository and accounting period and settlement cycle-running from Wednesday to Tuesday is operated by NSE. In order to streamline settlement, intra and inter-custodian settlement are maximised. Strict penalties imposed for delayed settlement have resulted in timely settlement and delivery of cash or securities with a low proportion of bad/short delivery. The Over the Counter Exchange of India (OTCEI) (1992) has also introduced an electronic trading system for stocks of relatively smaller firms and it had reached a monthly turnover of ₹ 45 crore in December 1994.

Stock Exchanges

The functioning of the NSE needs to be viewed as an important step in providing efficient and transparent services to investing public, and not as an attempt to weaken the Bombay Stock Exchange or other exchanges in the country. In fact, the operations of NSE is expected to act as a spur for the modernisation of the Bombay Stock Exchange Online Trading (BOLT) system for introducing screen based trading. The Bombay Stock Exchange has also taken the initiative for the establishment of National Stock Market System (NSMS) for providing improved sendees to investors all over the country. Eventually, the NSE and other Stock Exchanges should compete in minimising transaction costs and in providing fair services to investors.

The shift from individual to institutional investors added another dimension to the secondary market, while creating some problems. Given the volume of trade and antiquated systems custodians of the FIIs were unable to cope with post-contract paper work in the Stock Exchanges. The Bombay Stock Exchanges, therefore, proposed a new system of high denomination share certificates and a modification of the software used in the settlement process to reduce the interface between institutions and the retail market.

SEBI continuously monitors the market including the BSE. During 1993- 94, the interests of participants were safeguarded through a series of measures. These included, (*i*) imposition of daily margins on both purchases and sales, (*ii*) limit on jobbing in specified shares, (*iii*) prohibition of speculative deals with transactions being restricted to delivery basis, (*iv*) regulation of purchase and sales, even on delivery basis, (*v*) contraction of outstanding business carried forward from one settlement to another, (*vi*) ban on floor (over the counter) trades outside trading hours, and (vii) application of circuit breakers.

International Comparison

The number of companies listed on the Bombay Stock Exchange at the end of December 1993 was 3585. This was more than the aggregate total of companies listed in nine emerging markets (Malaysia, S. Africa, Mexico, Taiwan, Korea, Thailand, Brazil, Chile, and Argentina). The number of listed companies was also larger than in the developed country markets of Japan, UK, Germany, France, Hong Kong, Canada, Australia and Switzerland. The turnover ratio of the Bombay Stock Market (23 per cent) was also greater than that of Chile (6.3 per cent) and South Africa (6 per cent). It was however less than that of seven other emerging markets such as Thailand (66.6 per cent), Malaysia (69.7 per cent), Taiwan (177.5 per cent) and Korea (151.9 per cent).

FOREIGN INSTITUTIONAL INVESTORS

The interest of Foreign Institutional Investors in the Indian equity market evidenced in 1993, continued in 1994. The number of registered FIIs rose from 10 in January 1993 with cumulative net investments of US $ 0.2 million to 136 in January 1994, with cumulative investments of US $ 1231.3 million. The increase continued during 1994 with the number of registered FIIs rising to 281, with cumulative investments of US $ 3 billion as at the end of December 1994. During April-December 1994, 123 new FIIs were registered and additional investments of US $ 1201.9 million brought in by them. The dedicated funds launched by the FIIs for investment in India constitute 36 per cent of FII investments till December 1994. A total of US $ 1.05 billion has been invested through this route. The quantum jump in FII inflows, though driven by the policy reforms and low interest rates abroad, has been facilitated by procedural simplifications, as well as institutional changes. These include simplification of application forms and operational procedures for custodians. New institutions have been encouraged to set up custodial services. The FIIs were allowed to open multiple cash accounts and custodians accounts for each of their subaccounts. Through an amendment to the Securities Contracts (Regulation) Rules, 1957, the Government permitted joint venture stock broking companies to have non-Indian citizens on their Board of Directors.

GLOBAL DEPOSITORY RECEIPTS (GDRs)

Since 1992, Indian Companies have been allowed to access international capital markets. Up to January 1995, Indian companies had issued US $ 3,616 billion through launching GDR issues and US $ 1.098 billion through launching Euro Convertible Bonds (FCCBs) during the past three years.

Policy Guidelines

On the basis of the experience after May 1994, when the guidelines for Euro issues were issued, further modifications were made in these guidelines in October 1994. The provision that the Euro issue proceeds should be utilised for approved end uses within a period of one year from the date of issue, stands deleted. Instead, the issuing companies will be required mandatorily to retain the Euro issue, proceeds abroad to be repatriated as and when expenditure for the approved end uses (including up to 15 per cent earmarked for general corporate restructuring) are incurred. Among the factors motivating this change was the continued accumulation of foreign exchange reserves with RBI and the long gestation period of new investment.

JOINT PARLIAMENTARY COMMITTEE REPORT

The report of The Joint Parliamentary Committee (JPC) to enquire into irregularities in securities and banking transactions was examined and an Action Taken Report on the Observations/Conclusions/Recommendations was submitted in the Parliament on July 26, 1994. Subsequently in the light of comments and suggestions received from various Opposition parties in Parliament, revised paragraphs of the Action Taken Report in respect of 147 of the 273 items covered in the ATR were also submitted in the Parliament on December 28, 1994.

INSURANCE SECTOR

In Economic Survey 1993-94, a mention was made of the report of the Committee on reforms in the Insurance Sector set up in April 1993, to study the working of Life Insurance Corporation of India (LIC), General Insurance Corporation of India (GIC) and its four subsidiaries and make recommendations of the Committee, including the need for privatisation of the insurance industry (both LIC and GIC) were discussed in a series of consultative meetings taken by the Finance Secretary with the Chief Executives of the insurance industry, major unions of LIC/GIC and subsidiaries and the consumers/academicians/ press. This facilitated the evolution of a broad consensus on the parameters and direction of reform. The matter has also been discussed by the Finance Minister in the Consultative Committee of the Ministry of Finance, at length, in an exclusive meeting on the subject. Based on the above discussions, the views of the Government on the recommandations of the Committee have been crystallised and a decision on major policy changes, including allowing entry of private insurance companies into the industry, is at an advanced stage of formulation.

EVALUATION OF MONEY MARKET IN INDIA

1. Fiscal Deficit and Monetary Growth: Given the decisions taken during the year, the link between the fiscal deficit and monetary growth through the budget deficit will be completely broken in the next few years. This will make monetary policy independent of the Government, and thus devolve much greater responsibility on the RBI. The interaction between the Finance Ministry and the Central Bank will therefore focus on the target growth of money supply, with a view to balancing the twin objectives of inflation control and output growth, as is the practice in developed countries.

2. Market Borrowing Programme: Another dimension of the changing relationship between the Finance Ministry and the Central Bank is the Market Borrowing Programme. In earlier years, the SLR was an instrument of forced borrowing by the Centre from the banks. In this context, the market borrowing programme was the credit counterpart of the budget deficit. With a virtually complete switch over by the Central Government to market rates of interest, the Central Government becomes just like any other borrower in the Financial market (though a riskless one). The

Public Debt Office (PDO) of the RBI is merely the debt/financial manager of the Central Government, a function performed by the Treasury Departments of finance ministries in many countries. In this changed context, only state government debt, which is still issued at below market rates, has a substantive relationship to the SLR. The SLR will become completely redundant when State loans are also raised at market rates. These changes require a reappraisal and reform of the whole system of the Market Borrowing Programme and Central Government debt issue and management.

3. Foreign Exchange Reserves: The build-up of foreign exchange reserves with RBI has slackened somewhat. In November-December 1994. If this slackening continues, RBI's job of controlling the growth in reserves money will become much easier. If reserve growth reverts to earlier levels, however, open market operations to sterilise the inflow will come into their own and become a prominent feature of monetary policy action.

QUESTIONS FOR EXERCISE

1. Write short note on Non-Banking Financial Companies in India?
2. Review the money market developments and Trends in India?
3. Assess Government Securities Market in India?
4. Trace the recent developments in the capital market in India?

43

International Marketing

Geographically speaking, marketing has two dimensions—domestic marketing and international marketing. The basic principles and techniques of both these dimensions of marketing are the same and they have universal applications. The same principles apply to international markets and domestic markets. The same techniques are applied whether marketing the products in domestic markets or abroad. But international marketing has certain peculiar problems. Therefore, special considerations should be borne in mind while preparing the marketing strategy for penetrating markets abroad. Sheltered for so many years by a seller's market, Indian marketers faced a tougher task when selling abroad. Even the sophisticated country like U.S.A. is faced with greater competition in international markets from other countries like Japan.

SPECIAL CONSIDERATIONS IN INTERNATIONAL MARKETING

As U.S.A. and the European countries possess a major sophisticated population, greater expertise is needed, Indian exporters must be armed with the latest marketing techniques. They should be in a position to offer products suitable for a particular market. In International marketing India is faced with competition from more sophisticated countries like Japan, China and Korea. Adoption of the marketing concept and the consumer-oriented philosophy in terms of each of the 4-Ps in marketing is needed to get success in international marketing. Continuous marketing research is necessary here. A number of Indian companies in the same industry can pool their resources to this purpose. Greater attention should be given by Indian exporters to design and packaging to make the product more suitable for display, in super markets and departmental stores abroad. It may be more practicable to engage the services of an agent abroad rather than try to sell through one's own efforts.

ESSENTIALS OF INTERNATIONAL MARKETING

1. Defining the export strategy clearly.
2. Securing a suitable market through distinctive products and well coordinated sales organisation.
3. Setting up the head office functionally so that it may support the overseas' activities.

Use of Marketing Research

Marketing research may be utilised to identify the few who purchase the most. This market segmentation would help in using the limited resources most productively. The exporter must offer a product which is right in terms of consumer preferences with regard to size, colour and price. Marketing research may highlight the appropriate distribution and promotional strategies.

Importance of Distribution System

The distribution system differs ranging from small sole trading shops to large departmental stores. As one moves up the economic scale, retailing is conducted more and more through larger units. Thus, it is necessary to ascertain the appropriate distribution channels in terms of a particular country to which an exporter wishes to market his products.

Importance of Credit

In case of export, the supplier is often required to arrange for credit, therefore the exporter must be in a position to allow credit without—which he will not succeed in the highly competitive world markets. In India, commercial banks are helped by the Reserve Bank of India and the Industrial Development Bank of India through refinance schemes to enable the commercial banks lend the exporters. The Export Credit Guarantee Corporation helps to render the export transactions more creditworthy in the banker's eyes. Bank guarantees are required to be furnished in connection with export transactions. The Export Credit Guarantee

Corporation helps here through its 'Export Performance Guarantee' which is in the nature of a counter-guarantee to the bank.

Criteria of Exportability of the Products

1. Product suitability.
2. Competitive characteristics to competitors and their products.
3. Legal and environmental implications.
4. Selling abroad.
5. Foreign advertising.
6. Foreign sales promotion.
7. Export administration.

Table 43.1: Domestic *Vs.* International Markets

Domestic Market	International Market
1. One language, one nation, one culture.	1. Many languages, many nations, many cultures.
2. Much more homogeneous market.	2. Diverse and Fragmented Markets.
3. Data in marketing research available easily collected and accurate.	3. Marketing research very difficult, costly and without desired accuracy.
4. Political factors are of minor importance.	4. Political factors may play a major role.
5. Minimum Government interference in business decision.	5. Government influence usual in business decision.
6. Single currency.	6. Multiple currencies differing in stability and real value.
7. Uniform financial climate.	7. Variety of financial climates,
8. Standardised and matured Business rules.	8. Diverse, changing and unclear Business rules.
9. Patriotism helps.	9. Patriotism hinders.
10. Democratic management with effective financial controls.	10. Autonomous management unfamiliar with budgets and controls.
11. No problem of exchange controls tariffs.	11. Exchange controls and tariffs normal obstacles.
12. Minimum payment and credit risks.	12. Considerable payment and credit risks.
13. Relatively stable business environment.	13. Multiple and unstable business environments.

MAJOR INTERNATIONAL MARKETING DECISIONS

1. The International Marketing Decision: This initial decision regarding entry or expansion in international marketing must be based on the opportunities open to the firm abroad greater than those present in the home country. The firm must have resources in men, money and materials to capitalise, even if opportunities appear very favourable.

2. The Market Selection Decision: A marketer has three alternatives to enter the market-undifferentiated marketing, differentiated marketing and concentrated marketing, concentrating one or a few market segments. Internationally, most companies prefer a strategy called concentration on a limited number of key market segments. Though this approach is feasible they can operate only in narrow fields in the beginning. International marketing research can help a firm to select a few key markets which offer highest profitability.

3. The Market Entry Decision: The various methods of market entry open to a firm in a given country are exporting, licensing, manufacture abroad (through a foreign subsidiary or a joint venture) or entering into turnkey projects in foreign countries.

4. Marketing Mix Decision: After the decision on market entry is taken, the firm will have to plan and implement a marketing mix perfectly in tune with the typical demands of the marketing environment of the foreign target markets.

FOREIGN TRADE

Trade between two or more nations is called foreign or international trade. As no country can produce all its multifarious requirements and be absolutely self-sufficient, even the matured and affluent countries like the U.S.A, cannot maintain a prosperous economic life without foreign trade.

Further most international trade is the result of national specialisation of productions. Thus, trade between nations takes place due to two main reasons: Due to climatic and other reasons no country is able to have all the natural resources it needs. 2. International Specialisation of labour and production gives a number of economic advantages. Every country avoids the production of some goods for which it relies upon other countries. The principle of territorial division of labour successfully operates in the working of international commerce due to industrial and transport revolutions. The countries all over the world have become mutually interdependent for the goods in which they were deficient. Each country tries to specialise in the production of certain goods in which it enjoys special comparative advantages. It sells its goods to the rest of world in exchange of other goods in which it is deficient.

Two-way Affair

Foreign trade is a two-way affair. No country can expect to sell its own goods abroad unless it is prepared and willing to buy goods or services in return, to achieve a balance to trade. This is essential to ensure adequate foreign exchange reserve in international commerce. Export promotion devices enable a country to boost her exports and solve the problem of balance of payments. Hence, the motto, export or perish.

CASE FOR INTERNATIONAL MARKETING

Following are strong arguments in favour as well as against international marketing.

Arguments in Favour

1. Expectations of higher profit margins in foreign markets or increasing total sales and total profits.
2. Reduction in unit cost of production and distribution due to higher sales.
3. Extension of the product life cycle when a product is introduced into new markets.
4. Minimising seasonal demand fluctuations.
5. Reduction in business risks, *e.g.,* due to change in taxes in the home market.
6. Brighter image due to global business.
7. Serving of national interest of export promotion.
8. Faster growth after fully serving domestic demand.
9. Foreign competition is the best measuring rod of efficiency.
10. Obsolete product can be sold off in overseas market.
11. Expenditure on Research and Development may be amortised over a larger turnover.

Arguments Against

1. Profits are uncertain due to exchange rate fluctuations or political changes in overseas markets.

2. Essential product modifications may prevent advantages of mass production.

3. Resources used for exporting obsolete produces prevent new product planning.

4. Internationalism involves danger of expropriation.

5. International image may be bright but it may not yield higher profits.

6. Danger of anti dumping duties in foreign country may wipe off even marginal profits.

7. Markets offering seasonal pattern of demand may not be attractive in other respects.

8. National need for exports may not be in the company's interest to export. Exporting at a loss is not in the interest of any one.

9. It is very difficult to formulate marketing mix can match precisely with social, economic and political factors in each country.

ARGUMENTS AGAINST DIFFICULTIES IN FOREIGN TRADE

1. Difficulty of Distances: Sometimes international trade involves very long distances covering thousands of kilometers.

2. High Cost of Transport: Proper and quick transport and communications over long distances involve considerable delay as well as cost which is as important factor in foreign trade.

3. Diverse Languages, Customs, Traditions and National Laws: These special problems in foreign trade are due to differences in civilisation.

4. Currencies, Weights and Measures, Marketing Methods: Every nation has its own currency, weights and measures and marketing methods which create difficulties in the settlement of account or dues in international trade.

5. Risks and Uncertainties: Long distances of sea transport, changing exchange rates create a number of risks and uncertainties leading to heavy losses or damages. Thus, compared with home trade, international trade is more risky and cumbersome. Therefore, export-import trade requires specialists.

6. Customs Formalities, Exchange Control, etc.: Every country has its own customs duties and rules and regulations relating to demand and supply of foreign exchange. Exporters and importers have to fulfil all the custom formalities as well as rules controlling exports and imports. As all those are absent in home trade, there is much greater freedom in the movement of goods and in the settlement of dues.

7. Payment of Dues: Due to a variety of currencies and different rates of exchange, one faces a number of difficulties in the settlement of account in foreign trade. Home trade involves no such obstacles.

8. Shipping and Insurance: Shipping and Insurance formalities in foreign trade distinguish it from home trade activities,

9. Foreign Trade Quotations: Due to a number of typical quotations such as C.L.F, & FOB., F.A.S., etc. Foreign invoices are very comprehensive and give a lot of additional information.

10. Multiple Chain of Middlemen: In foreign trade, there are innumberable intermediaries between the primary producer or seller and the ultimate consumer or buyer. These middlemen sell their specialised services at very reasonable rates.

QUESTION'S FOR EXERCISE

1. Explain the essential difference between domestic marketing and international marketing.
2. "Basically, marketing abroad is the same as marketing within the country requiring the same methods and approaches." Give your reactions to this statement.
3. What is International or Foreign Trade? What are the arguments in favour and against international marketing? List special difficulties in Foreign Trade.